Educational Research

Fundamental Principles and Methods

EIGHTH EDITION

James H. McMillan
Virginia Commonwealth University

To Jan, Jon, Tisha, Ryann, Ryan, Dylan and Liam

Content Development: Curtis Vickers
Content Management: Rebecca Fox-Gieg
Content Production: Janelle Rogers
Product Management: Drew Bennett
Rights and Permissions: Jenell Forschler

Please contact https://support.pearson.com/getsupport/s/ with any queries on this content

Cover Image by © Fanatic Studio/Getty Images

Library of Congress Cataloging-in-Publication Data

Names: McMillan, James H, author.
Title: Educational research : fundamental principles and methods / James H. McMillan, Virginia Commonwealth University.
Description: Eighth Edition. | Hoboken : Pearson, [2022] | Includes bibliographical references and index.
Identifiers: LCCN 2020048381 | ISBN 9780135770092 (Paperback) | ISBN 9780135770016 (ePub)
Subjects: LCSH: Education—Research.
Classification: LCC LB1028 .M365 2021 | DDC 370.72—dc23
LC record available at https://lccn.loc.gov/2020048381

ScoutAutomatedPrintCode

Rental Offer:
ISBN-10: 0-13-577009-2
ISBN-13: 978-0-13-577009-2

Print Offer:
ISBN-10: 0-13-577010-6
ISBN-13: 978-0-13-577010-8

About the Author

Jean-Philippe Cypres

Dr. James H. McMillan is Professor Emeritus in the School of Education at Virginia Commonwealth University (Department of Foundations of Education). He obtained his doctorate from Northwestern University and master's degree from Michigan State University. Dr. McMillan has also published *Research in Education: Evidence-Based Inquiry*; *Understanding and Evaluating Educational Research*; the *Sage Handbook of Research on Classroom Assessment*; *Assessment Essentials for Standards-Based Education*; *Classroom Assessment: Principles and Practice That Enhance Student Learning and Motivation*; *Classroom Assessment and Educational Measurement*; and *Better Being Wrong (Sometimes): Using Student Assessment Mistakes and Errors to Enhance Learning*, in addition to more than 80 journal articles and book chapters. His current research interest is focused on student perceptions of classroom assessment and classroom assessment literacy.

Chapter co-authors (Chapters 2, 13, 14, and 15) are colleagues at Virginia Commonwealth University. **Dr. Lisa Abrams** is Associate Professor in the Department of Foundations of Education, **Dr. David Naff** is Assistant Director of Research and Evaluation in the Metropolitan Educational Research Consortium, **Dr. Sharon Zumbrunn** is Associate Professor in the Department of Foundations of Education, and **Dr. Jesse Senechal** is Director of the Metropolitan Educational Research Consortium.

To the Instructor

*E*ducational Research: Fundamental Principles and Methods is for both consumers of empirical investigations and beginning researchers. Consumers locate, read, understand, critique, and then use the results of research to become more effective professionally and to make sound educational decisions. Beginning researchers need to know the fundamental process of conducting good research, a foundation for learning how to conduct research and report results. The book is designed to enable students to become *intelligent* consumers and proficient investigators of educational research. It is intended for a one-semester or one-term course in educational research and is best suited for advanced undergraduate and beginning graduate students in all areas of education. The examples from studies bring sometimes obtuse and dull research principles to life by showing excerpts from published articles. Students will find them interesting and informative. There are over 160 excerpts from recently published studies from 70 different journals, representing various levels of rigor and myriad subject areas. Although the excerpts focus on the field of education and educational publications, this book is also appropriate for students in related social sciences who need to learn how to read and understand research and begin the process of becoming investigators.

The primary goal of this book is to educate students to be intelligent consumers and researchers. This is accomplished by promoting student understanding of a researcher's intent, the procedures, and the results. Students are then shown how to conduct, analyze, and evaluate research, judging the usefulness of the findings for educational practice, and provided guidance in writing research proposals and reports. More specifically, the book will help students develop the following skills:

- Apply the principles of disciplined inquiry to everyday problem solving and decision making.

- Develop a healthy skepticism about "studies" that purport to advance our knowledge.

Understand strengths and weaknesses of different methodologies used in research (quantitative, qualitative, mixed methods, and action research).

- Read, understand, critique, and use published reports of research.

- Understand the uncertain nature of knowledge about educational practice generated through research.

- Keep a balanced perspective about the relative contributions of research and professional judgment.

- Understand how to conduct research.

- Write research proposals and reports using appropriate academic/scholarly voice and style.

These goals are reached with a concise, engaging presentation of principles for conducting research and criteria for evaluating its overall credibility. The style of the book is informal, the language is nontechnical, and no prerequisite courses in measurement or statistics are needed. Numerous illustrations and excerpts from actual studies, as well as complete published articles, are used as examples to familiarize students with the style and format of published articles, to introduce students to the language of research, and to point out key features and parts of published studies.

The book covers fundamental principles in the sequence found in the research process, beginning with the identification of researchable problems and ending with conclusions. The emphasis is on teaching students that all aspects of conducting and reporting research are important in judging the overall credibility of the findings, and how different parts of the research process are interrelated and need to be clearly aligned. The format of research articles is included in the first chapter to help students read and comprehend published studies as early as possible in the course. My experience is that students need as much practice as possible reading and critiquing articles. The first chapter also introduces different research methodologies. I have found this introduction helpful in providing an initial understanding of different approaches, including quantitative, qualitative, and mixed methods designs that are covered in greater depth in later chapters. From the beginning, students are able to identify different types of studies.

The book is now divided into five parts. **Part 1** includes chapters that introduce students to the nature of research, ethical guidelines, research problems and questions, and literature reviews. The purpose of these chapters is to provide students with sufficient knowledge and understanding to begin to design their own empirical investigation and to critically evaluate published articles. Chapter 1 introduces students to the concept of the signal and the noise, a metaphor that is used throughout the text, and provides an overview of the nature of disciplined inquiry and types of research. Chapter 2, on ethics, ethical principles, and ethical practices, is included early in the book to emphasize the importance of these principles in both the conduct and reporting of research, consistent with the new 2018 Common Rule revisions. The following chapter, which focuses on research problems and questions, shows students how to conceptualize and word research questions that align with methodology.

Because good consumers and investigators need to know how to find helpful research, the chapter on reviewing literature includes skills in locating primary and secondary sources, in evaluating a review of literature section of an article, and writing a review of literature. This edition has a much greater emphasis on reviewing literature than most introductory research books. There is extensive discussion on how to write the review, something many students need to accomplish relatively early in research courses if they need to prepare a proposal. The chapter provides hints, sites, and procedures that will make it easy for students to use ERIC as well as other electronic avenues that are now available and widely used, such as Google Scholar.

Part 2 is focused on quantitative design and analyses. Chapter 5 covers participant selection and sampling for quantitative investigations. The next two chapters are devoted to measurement because of the critical role it plays in quantitative and mixed methods educational research. Basic descriptive statistical principles are presented first to enhance understanding of measurement. For example, I have found that students must know about correlation to understand reliability and validity. Nonexperimental designs are presented in Chapter 8, followed by the chapter on experimental designs. Chapter 9 also includes the most comprehensive list of threats to internal validity in the field. The last chapter in Part 2 is focused on a conceptual understanding of inferential statistics and effect size.

Part 3 includes three chapters that cover qualitative research. Chapter 11 presents major qualitative research designs (including a unique explanation of threats to the validity/trustworthiness of results); Chapter 12 has expanded coverage of qualitative data collection; and Chapter 13 is devoted to qualitative data analysis and reporting. Overall, the chapters increase coverage of qualitative research from previous editions.

Part 4 includes both mixed methods and action research, and **Part 5** contains an entirely new chapter on writing research proposals, reports, and manuscripts to be submitted for publication.

As in the previous editions, the chapters include numerous pedagogical aids to facilitate learning essential skills and knowledge:

- **Learning Outcomes** are presented at the beginning of each chapter to help students focus on key concepts and principles.
- **Chapter Concept Maps** are used as an advanced organizer.
- **Key Research Terms** are highlighted in the text and at the end of each chapter.
- A **Glossary** is now included to facilitate understanding of key terms.
- **Check for Understanding Questions**, aligned with **Learning Outcomes** and answered at the end of each chapter, provide students with practice demonstrating knowledge.
- **Discussion Questions** facilitate discourse of important topics.
- **Application Exercises** encourage students to extend their learning.
- **Author Reflections** bring insights and perspective.
- **Excerpts** from published research articles illustrate how research principles are reported.
- **Full annotated published articles.**
- **Consumer (and Researcher) Tips** emphasize the skills needed to judge studies critically.

New to the Eighth Edition

There are many significant changes and additions to the eighth edition, **including two new chapters (Chapter 13: Qualitative Data Analysis, Validity/Trustworthiness, and Reporting** and **Chapter 16: Writing Research Proposals, Reports, and Articles).** The sequence of topics has remained unchanged from the seventh edition, but there have been some important modifications in many chapters. Some of the more significant changes, in addition to updating each chapter, include the following:

- A **new chapter** (Chapter 13) on **qualitative data analysis, validity/trustworthiness, and reporting.** This chapter provides more extensive coverage of qualitative data analysis, with new material on how to report results from qualitative studies. This additional chapter better balances qualitative with quantitative research design and analyses.

- A **new chapter** (Chapter 16) on **writing research proposals, reports, and articles**, with guidelines for scholarly writing, academic voice and tone, elements of style, formatting, and **new APA style recommendations for using inclusive language.** Separate sections emphasize quantitative, qualitative, and mixed methods documents.

- **Greater emphasis on how to conduct research.**

- **Expansion of the** *Signal and the Noise* **metaphor,** incorporating the metaphor throughout the text.

- **A new** *Hedgehog and Fox* **metaphor,** illustrated in each chapter to show the difference between simplistic and more sophisticated, nuanced thinking.

- **New Chapter Concept Maps.**

- **New Learning Outcomes** listed at the beginning of each chapter, keyed to **new Check for Understanding Questions** throughout each chapter (**with answers at the end of each chapter**).

- **Increased number of Author Reflections** (Students have found my author reflections engaging, drawing upon my years of experience teaching, conducting, and publishing research).

- **New coverage of major research paradigms.**

- **New emphasis on implications of Big Data for research.**

- **Inclusion of the 2018 Common Rule revisions for ethical research.**

- **New Listings of Key Terms for all chapters.**

- **New Glossary of definitions of key terms.**

- **Mostly new excerpts from published research articles to illustrate concepts and research writing styles.**

- **More diagrams and figures to aid student understanding.**

- **More references.**

- **Greater emphasis on:**

  - use of Google Scholar for literature searches
  - the importance of replication in research
  - alignment of research questions to methodology
  - sensitivity in selecting samples
  - sample description
  - electronic data gathering

  - inclusion of dosage as a threat to internal validity
  - qualitative data collection
  - writing qualitative research questions and subquestions
  - validity and trustworthiness in qualitative research
  - recursive analysis, reflective procedures, and pattern-seeking in qualitative research
  - reporting qualitative research
  - practical significance

Supplements

A full complement of supplements further enhances and strengthens the eighth edition.

Pearson eText, Learning Management System (LMS)-Compatible Assessment Bank

With this new edition, all assessment types—quizzes, application exercises, and chapter tests—are included in LMS-compatible banks for the following learning management systems: Blackboard (9780137355297), Canvas (9780137355334), D2L (9780137355341), and Moodle (9780137355303). These packaged files allow maximum flexibility to instructors when it comes to importing, assigning, and grading. Assessment types include:

Learning Outcome Quizzes Each chapter learning outcome is the focus of a Learning Outcome Quiz that is available for instructors to assign through their Learning Management System. Learning outcomes identify chapter content that is most important for learners and serve as the organizational framework for each chapter. The higher-order, multiple choice questions in each quiz will measure your understanding of chapter content, guide the expectations for your learning, and inform the accountability and the applications of your new knowledge. When used in the LMS environment, these multiple-choice questions are automatically graded and include feedback for the correct answer and for each distractor to help guide students' learning.

Application Exercises Each chapter provides opportunities to apply what you have learned through Application Exercises. These exercises are usually short-answer format and when used in the LMS environment, a model response written by experts is provided after you submit the exercise. This feedback helps guide your learning and can assist your instructor in grading.

Chapter Tests Suggested test items are provided for each chapter. When used in the LMS environment, true/false and multiple-choice questions are automatically graded.

Instructor's Manual

The **Instructor's Manual (0135769876/9780135769874)** is provided as a Word document and includes resources to assist professors in planning their course. In addition, this manual includes test items for each chapter.

PowerPoint Slides

PowerPoint® **Slides (0135769795/9780135769799)** are provided for each chapter and highlight key concepts and summarize the content of the text to make it more meaningful for students.

Note: All instructor resources—LMS-compatible assessment bank, instructor's manual, and PowerPoint slides are available for download at www.pearsonhighered.com. Use one of the following methods:

From the main page, use the search function to look up the lead author or title. Select the desired search result, then access the "Resources" tab to view and download all available resources.

From the main page, use the search function to look up the ISBN (provided above) of the specific instructor resource you would like to download. When the product page loads, access the "Downloadable Resources" tab.

Acknowledgments

Numerous individuals have contributed much to this book. I am most grateful to my editor of the first two editions, Chris Jennison, for his support, encouragement, and needed recommendations; to my editor for the third edition, Art Pomponio; Arnis Burvikovs for the fourth and fifth editions; Paul Smith for the sixth edition; Kevin Davis for the seventh edition; and Rebecca Fox-Gieg for this edition. I am also indebted to many students and instructors who provided feedback to me on my organization, writing, examples, approach, and materials, as well as to the chapter co-authors, who have provided much-needed expertise.

The following reviewers of previous editions contributed constructive suggestions: Jean Swenk, National University; Anthony Truog, University of Wisconsin-Whitewater; Judith Kennison, Ithaca College; Beatrice Baldwin, Southeastern Louisiana University; Kaia Skaggs, Eastern Michigan University; Ayers D'Costa, Ohio State University; Tamera Murdock, University of Missouri at Kansas City; Andy Katayama, West Virginia University; John W. Sanders, Middle Tennessee State University; Anastasia Elder, Mississippi State University; Lisa Kirtman, California State University, Fullerton; William J. Murphy, Framingham State University; Steven W. Neill, Emporia State University; Keonya Booker, University of North Carolina at Charlotte; Patrick Dilley, Southern Illinois University, Carbondale; Catherine McCartney, Bemidji State University; Nancy Mansberger, Western Michigan University; Pamela Murphy, Virginia Tech; and for the current edition, Rebekah Cole, Old Dominion University; Nicole Hampton, Northern Arizona University; Rebecca D. Hunt, Northern Illinois University; and Xyanthe Neider, Washington State University.

I am grateful to the staff at Pearson, especially Curtis Vickers and Leza Young, who have been exemplary in their editing and production of the book.

As this is being written, further ideas are germinating for possible changes in organization and content for the ninth edition. Please write with any suggestions. Your comments will be most helpful.

James H. McMillan
jmcmillan@vcu.edu

To the Student

It was some time ago that I sat, somewhat nervously, in a university auditorium waiting for my first class in educational research (perhaps you have had or will have similar feelings). It was taught by Irv Lehman at Michigan State University. I remember this initial class session vividly. I distinctly recall thinking, given what I had heard about "research," that I needed to learn only enough to pass the course and would not have to worry about it again! It was another hurdle that I was forced to jump to graduate. I was not bad in mathematics, but my interest was in working with people, not numbers. I certainly never thought that I would someday teach and write about educational research. But something happened to me as I sometimes struggled through the course. What I discovered was that research is a way of thinking, a tool that I could use to improve the work I do with other people, and to enhance student learning and motivation. My hope is that this book can instill similar dispositions for you, providing knowledge, skills, and attitudes to improve your life and the welfare of others.

Although learning the content and skills needed to become an intelligent consumer or producer of research is not easy, my experience in teaching hundreds of students is that you will improve yourself, professionally and otherwise, through your efforts. In the beginning, especially as you read published research articles, not everything will make sense. No worries, that is part of the learning process. As your experience in being an informed consumer and researcher increases, so will your understanding. Many of my students have commented on how "things came together" as the course progressed.

Good luck and best wishes, and please write to me or e-mail me if you have any questions about the content or suggestions for improving the book.

James H. McMillan
jmcmillan@vcu.edu

Brief Contents

Contents

Part I
Getting Ready for Research

We begin our journey with an introduction to what research is all about and how to frame good research questions. This involves an understanding of the nature of disciplined inquiry, types of research, and how empirical studies are located and evaluated.

Chapter 1 introduces two metaphors that will be used throughout the text: The *Signal and the Noise*, and the *Fox and the Hedgehog*. As you will see, the Signal and the Noise represents what we want to know (the signal) and what gets in the way of finding it (noise). Keeping this metaphor in mind helps focus on the varied difficulties of conducting research in applied, complex contexts like schools and classrooms. The Fox and the Hedgehog represent different dispositions about how we think about research. *The Fox and the Hedgehog* is used throughout the chapters to illustrate primitive thinking (hedgehog-like) from sophisticated thinking (fox-like).

Ethical principles are covered in Chapter 2 as foundational to conducting research that is responsible and in the best interests of participants.

Chapters 3 and 4 focus on two steps in the research process—forming research questions and reviewing related literature—that set the foundation for designing appropriate procedures for collecting and analyzing data. These are fundamental initial phases in the research process. You will find that access to research literature is relatively easy. The challenge is to separate what is good research from studies that lack credibility, and synthesize a number of studies into a coherent argument that supports a particular research design.

Chapter 1
Introduction to Research in Education

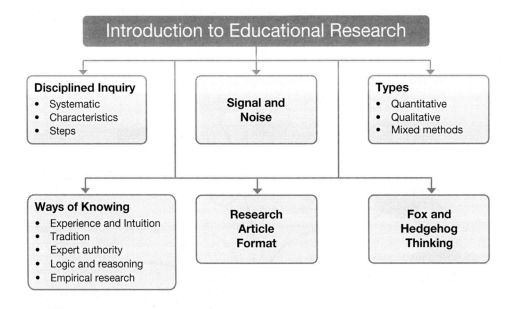

Learning Outcomes

1.1 Know how the purpose of research, finding the signal, is influenced by noise that distorts what is reported.

1.2 Explain why empirical research is important as an approach to generating and applying knowledge.

1.3 Know the characteristics of major research paradigms.

1.4 Understand how the principles of disciplined inquiry ("fox-like" thinking) are important for conducting educational research.

1.5 Distinguish among key characteristics of quantitative, qualitative, and mixed methods types of research.

Chapter Road Map

We begin our journey with a metaphor—The Signal and the Noise—to introduce what educational research is all about. After a discussion of why research is important, different ways knowledge can be identified and constructed are elucidated. This is followed by a focus on how and why characteristics of systematic inquiry, based on principles for conducting research, compose the foundation for obtaining high-quality studies. We then turn to overviews of qualitative, quantitative, and mixed methods approaches to educational research and designs, with an example of a published article.

The Signal and the Noise

Learning Outcome 1.1   Know how the purpose of research, finding the signal, is influenced by noise that distorts what is reported.

You may well be familiar with this metaphor: *The Signal and the Noise*. In science and engineering the signal-to-noise ratio compares the desired meaningful information (the "signal") to the amount of background "noise" that makes the signal less clear. In his delightful book, *The Signal and the Noise: Why So Many Predictions Fail but Some Don't*, Nate Silver (2012) shows how the metaphor applies to many if not most fields, including sports, politics, weather, even wars, and other domains where we often have a great amount of data but still regularly miss the mark. When applied to education, as we will see throughout the book, the sources of noise are even more plentiful than in other fields! For me, this metaphor makes perfect sense as a way to conceptualize the research process, as well as what makes educational research challenging.

The *signal* is what is correct, actual, and true, what we can be certain of when making conclusions about what we understand, what we claim to know, and our predictions and insights. The *noise* is composed of factors that drown out, distort or dilute the signal, such as a poor connection in making a video transmission that clouds the image. In educational research, examples of noise include confirmation bias, random error, and poor methodology. That is, noise manifests itself in flawed, incomplete thinking so that the conclusions that result from research are unlikely to represent the actual signals.

I've illustrated the signal/noise metaphor in Figure 1.1. The idea is that while there is a true or correct signal, what you see as a result from doing research, the *observed finding*, is a combination of the true signal and noise that is always part of the process of conducting research. If represented by a conceptual equation, it would look like this:

$$\text{Observed Finding} = \text{Signal} + \text{Noise}$$

As a researcher you only see the observed finding, which results from the signal *plus* noise. The greater the noise, then, the less likely that the observed finding is the same as the signal. As the noise is reduced, the observed finding is closer to the signal, which, of course, is what you want. Good research is able to identify and mitigate sources of noise so that the observed finding is close to the signal. Noise, then, is distinguished from the signal as separate determinants of the observed finding. For example, if a survey is used to describe reasons students give for why they are not fully engaged in college, the signal would be the true or real reasons; the noise could be the unreliability of the survey and/or sampling bias.

A major emphasis in this book is to know about, identify, and control sources of noise, depending on the nature of the research design. This includes sources of "error" in making qualitative judgments as well as limitations due to sampling, measurement, and statistical analyses in quantitative studies. My point is that educational research, by its nature, is noisy (more so than in the sciences or psychology). To get to the signal as a researcher you must control that noise as much as possible. As a consumer, you need to know about how noise impacts what is found and appropriately temper conclusions.

Figure 1.1 The Signal and the Noise

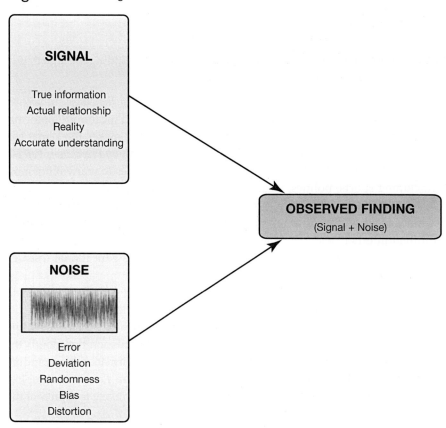

With this metaphor in mind (hopefully soon deeply entrenched), let's look at why educational research is important and how it can improve your life and the lives of those around you.

Check for Understanding 1

1a.   How do the signal and noise affect a researcher's *observed finding*?

Why Research?

This book is about helping you and others lead a richer, more satisfying life. That may seem like a strange beginning for a textbook like this, but I want to stress that there are good reasons for increasing your knowledge of research and the process of systematic inquiry. It is clear that research in education has made, and will continue to make, important contributions to our understanding of teaching and learning at all levels.

Like other professionals, you need to be able to read and interpret research to keep abreast of contributions to the field to make better decisions. Because the quality of educational research varies greatly, it is essential that you are able to make informed judgments about the credibility and usefulness of the studies. Since education is a complex, situation-specific endeavor, we must each make these judgments in our own context. A proper, balanced perspective on research will strengthen the judgments we make constantly in educational settings, and, in that way, touch the lives of many.

Figure 1.2 Use of Data in Decision Making?

Data Driven ⟹ Data Deluged ⟹ Data Doped? ⟹ Deleterious Decisions?

Furthermore, teachers and administrators are increasingly involved in conducting research in their own classrooms, schools, and districts. They have found that even informal, small-scale studies can provide new knowledge and insights to help improve student learning.

Finally, there is a renewed interest at the national level to use "evidence-based" findings to evaluate programs and policy, and the ubiquitous admonition for "data-driven" decision making. The trend is to use research and evidence based on data (both quantitative and qualitative), whenever possible, to make decisions about effectiveness and to determine "what works" in schools. In fact, the need for educators to understand and use results from assessments and other measures has intensified. Just think about the difficult issue of using students' academic progress to evaluate teachers. It is common now to use students' test scores as indicators of learning and judge teachers on how much students improve or how they compare with the progress of other teachers' students. A clear understanding of whether the data are reasonable, and the validity of conclusions about effective teaching, depends on knowing what constitutes good data and good data analyses for this purpose. In other areas, there is so much emphasis on "using data" that I am afraid that the sequence illustrated in Figure 1.2, moving from one end to the other, can sometimes result in disastrous conclusions (e.g., firing teachers on the basis of inaccurate low student test scores, or denying graduation on the basis of low scores from a flawed test).

At the same time, there is a surging interest in conducting research that is based on assumptions about knowledge that are very different from what we think of as "hard data" (e.g., objective results from quantitative measures and analyses). This has introduced new ways of thinking about research and expanded the types of "data" that are examined systematically to reach conclusions. So, in my view, it is best to think about "data" broadly.

I am confident that after reading, understanding, and conducting research in an informed, intelligent manner, you will enhance your professional and personal life, and the lives of others, with the following benefits:

- Developing critical thinking and evaluation skills to examine arguments and claims made by others

Author Reflection *Many of my students begin their study of research with hesitation and anxiety about the content (especially dreaded "statistics"). I tell them that's fine, that my job is to alleviate the anxiety and instill a positive attitude about research. Like most of my students (I hope), you may find that you actually like research! I tell my students that if this happens it puts them in a rather unique group. I hope you will join this special group as well!*

- Enabling a more complete, more accurate understanding of and evaluation of claims based on data
- Improving understanding of educational research reports in the media, especially flawed claims
- Keeping up with recently reported knowledge of best practice
- Improving decision making about best practice
- Informing educational policy
- Fostering the ability to ask the right questions
- Understanding how to design and conduct research

Sources of Knowledge

Learning Outcome 1.2   Explain why empirical research is important as an approach to generating and applying knowledge.

Professional decision making is all about making judgments, and judgments are based on knowing. We "know" something when it is accepted as true or valid (the signal), when we can be fairly certain of its consequences. For example, good teachers seem to "know" when they are losing their students' interest and need to change their method of instruction, when students need a strong rebuke or a soft reprimand, and how to phrase questions to elicit engagement from students. How do these teachers obtain or generate such knowledge? How do we come to "know" things?

In the field of research, we use the term **epistemology** to refer to the origin, nature, and limitations of different ways of accumulating knowledge. Each epistemology includes criteria that are used to justify what constitutes "knowing something" and beliefs. The different sources of knowledge described in this section are compared to empirical research. In the next section, epistemology is applied more specifically to research paradigms.

Experience and Intuition

It has been said that there is no substitute for experience, whether it is your own or someone else's. In education, we rightfully depend a great deal on direct experience to know what works. Professionals become effective through practice, and teaching, counseling, and administering are no exceptions to this rule. However, imagine if experience were the *only* way to obtain knowledge, or if you were confined only to your own experiences and those of friends and acquaintances for coming up with reasonable signals. Not only would it be difficult to know where to begin practice, but it would also be difficult to know how to improve and how to handle new demands and situations.

There are other limitations to using our personal experiences as sources of knowledge. Much of our knowledge from experience depends on what we have observed and how we have interpreted it. As humans, though, we can—and do—make mistakes in our observations. Sometimes, because we bring our own biases to a situation, we fail to see things that are clearly evident, and we make inaccurate observations and interpretations. Finally, because we are personally involved with our own interpretations, we have a natural inclination to protect our self-esteem and ego, and consequently our recollections may be distorted. When other types of knowing can be used to stimulate, inform, reinforce, challenge, and question our own experiences, the intuitive professional judgment that is absolutely essential for effective teaching and leadership is enhanced.

Tradition

Many things seem to be done "right" simply because they have always been done that way. Advice, rules, approaches to handling problems, and "right" and "wrong" answers are passed from year to year, from one group to another, as accepted truths. By accepting what has always been done as the best or right way, tradition mitigates the need to search for new knowledge and understanding. However, reliance on tradition makes accepting new knowledge difficult and may temper your desire to question existing practices. Traditions are also often based on myths or prejudices.

Experts' Authority

People we consider experts or authorities in a particular field are major sources of knowledge. An authority has experience or unique expertise in something and is able to provide insights and understanding that we are unable to see. We depend on such authorities, whether they are doctors, lawyers, professors, teachers, or plumbers. However, as with personal experience and tradition, authority can also mitigate the accumulation of knowledge. Authorities can be wrong and/or biased, and the public has a tendency to accept as fact what are actually opinions.

In fields such as education, in which practice is heavily influenced by complex interactions among students, environments, and teachers, there is room for experts to disagree about what is known. Perhaps you have read one author who suggests one approach and another who suggests the opposite approach for the same situation or question. A good example is the evidence on the effectiveness of charter schools. In 2020, the year this book was revised, the effect of charter schools on student achievement was much debated. Some studies suggested that charter schools are more effective than traditional schools, but there was also research that showed little differential impact on achievement. Both sides of the argument were made by so-called experts and conducted by high-status centers, universities, and organizations. Furthermore, the sheer number of authorities in education can be confusing.

Logic and Reason

Sometimes we can be convinced that something is true because a logical argument is made and defended, and sound reasoning is used to reach a conclusion. Logic and reason (rationalism) rely on accurate premises and foundational facts. However, logic and reason are only as good as the facts and premises that are used. There is a well-known saying that applies here to databases and computer programs that analyze data and generate results: "garbage in, garbage out." Logic and reason are essential in conducting and reporting research, but these operations must be done before and after a careful gathering of facts.

Empirical Research

In contrast to experience, intuition, tradition, experts' authority, and logic and reason, **empirical research** involves a systematic process of gathering, interpreting, and reporting information. Empirical research is characterized by *disciplined inquiry*, by accepted principles to verify that a knowledge claim is reasonable. Defined in this way, research is not simply going to the library, gathering information on a topic, and doing a research paper. Rather, information (data) is gathered directly from individuals, groups, documents, and other sources and used to come up with conclusions that contribute to knowledge. **Educational research**, then, is empirical, a *systematic, disciplined inquiry applied to gathering, analyzing, and reporting information that addresses educational problems and questions. Systematic* means that there are accepted conventions, rules, and procedures for the way studies are conducted and standards for judging quality.

Here are some of the characteristics of this kind of inquiry:

- *Skepticism* about claims—having a healthy, productive distrust of findings
- *Control of personal bias* so a researcher's personal prejudices, beliefs, desires, and attitudes do not result in distorted conclusions
- *Precision* to provide detailed, clear definitions, descriptions, understandings, and explanations
- *Parsimony* to provide the least complicated explanations
- *Tentative conclusions* that are open to change
- *Verification* of findings through replication, when possible
- *Openness to scrutiny* by others (the public)
- *Logic*, inductive and/or deductive, to provide meaning

Why is it important to know about knowing? It turns out that each approach to knowing constitutes a researcher's philosophical orientation, which has consequences for what questions are asked, methodology, how results are interpreted, and conclusions. An awareness of these underlying philosophies will help you plan your own research and understand others' research. For example, if you believe that your own experience is your best source of knowing how to teach, there would great reliance on being aware of how your methods impact students, with self-reflection and an emphasis on an accumulation of experience over time. This way of knowing would be very different from an empirical research approach that seeks to gather data systematically and take a skeptical, questioning perspective about what the data mean.

In characterizing research, it is useful for you to think about two major fields of study that have contributed important knowledge and insights: social science and humanities. The traditions of social science empirical research are grounded in years of studies in disciplines such as psychology, sociology, economics, political science, and anthropology, all of which conduct empirical research to study society, individuals, and groups. Another tradition of research is humanities oriented. This kind of research, which could also be called *analytical*, is based on scholarship in disciplines such as linguistics, history, jurisprudence, philosophy, and religion, as well as some subdisciplines, such as cultural anthropology, and critical arts-based and narrative forms of research—all of which are important in making contributions to knowledge, and all of which contain the essential feature of systematic inquiry. In this book, the focus is on social science methods of empirical research, as distinguished from humanities-oriented research.

Check for Understanding 2

2a. How is empirical research different from other ways of knowing?

2b. What are three characteristics of systematic inquiry?

Now on to a discussion of research paradigms. These elegantly labeled approaches are important because they undergird different methods of empirical research as well as how results are interpreted.

Research Paradigms

Learning Outcome 1.3   Know the characteristics of major research paradigms.

A **research paradigm** is a "world view," a way of thinking about the world, a belief system. It includes philosophical assumptions, shared beliefs, and a theoretical framework about the world and knowledge that guide thinking and methods employed in empirical research. As such, each paradigm is a lens through which research is conducted and interpreted. They influence the motivation for research, what should be studied, criteria for judging research, conceptual framework, methods, and intended use of results. Because most educational research conducted and reported in the 20th century was based on research methods in psychology, which in turn was based on the natural sciences, for a long time a single paradigm, positivism, was what was taught and used. Beginning in the 1970s that changed. There are now four major paradigms used in educational research.

Author Reflection   *If you Google "research paradigms" you'll actually find that there are various terms used, and that different authors disagree about how to label and define different paradigms, in part because they are philosophies. This is frustrating, to say the least! What I've summarized here is my judgment about the best way to approach it for educational research.*

Postpositivism

You can think of **positivism** as being synonymous with the scientific method. The main assumption of positivism, for education, is that phenomena can be studied like the natural sciences, using observation, measurement, quantification, and objectivity to establish cause-and-outcome relationships. The successor to positivism, which occurred after World War II, was postpositivism. **Postpositivism** reflects the reality that human behavior doesn't lend itself as much as the hard sciences to pure empiricism, objectivity, and laws of nature. Postpositivists believe more in probability than certainty, using objective methods in concert with other, more intuitive judgments about the nature of causation. It basically takes a more holistic, less reductionist view of research, but it is still very much wedded to the value of objectivity, measurement, quantification, law-generation, and other characteristics of the scientific method. As such, postpositivism today is sometimes described as synonymous with quantitative research. My view is that the term *quantitative* reflects the methodology inherent in postpositivist research.

Interpretive/Constructivist

A further emphasis on the vicissitudes of human behavior, the importance of context, and the limitations of positivism and postpositivism has led to a major, very influential paradigm I prefer to label **interpretive/constructivist** (some use just one of these terms). The main assumption of this paradigm is that knowledge is socially constructed, contextual, and personalized. As such, knowledge is mainly subjective, focused on the meaning ascribed by each individual. This suggests that research needs to account for these lived experiences and understand meaning from the point of view of who is studied. Much as we do with anthropology, the methods emphasize prolonged engagement, in-depth understanding of others' interpretations, perspectives, values, and beliefs, and situating information within social contexts. This paradigm emphasizes qualitative methods that are focused on meaning and process, as well as recognizing researcher subjectivity in framing and interpreting data.

Postpositivist and interpretive/constructivist paradigms are the two that are most prominent in educational research and most closely tied to different methods of data collection and analysis. Two additional paradigms, transformative and pragmatic, introduce additional approaches for conducting research.

Pragmatic

Pragmatism is a very recently established paradigm in which the focus is on adapting methods to provide the best information based on real-world situations and conditions. The goal is to better understand problems and how they can be ameliorated. As such, the **pragmatic** paradigm shifts from what is emphasized in the first two paradigms to an applied orientation that solves "real" problems. Pragmatic researchers use whatever methods are best suited to improving practice, whether quantitative, qualitative, or mixed methods, depending on the context. Likewise, they embrace other worldviews as appropriate to achieve the goal of improving targeted outcomes (e.g., student learning, teacher and counselor effectiveness, administrative leadership).

Transformative

In the past three decades there have been a number of approaches to research that fall into the umbrella of the **transformative** paradigm. The major characteristic of this paradigm is that the purpose of the research is to improve the lives of marginalized, disenfranchised peoples. With a social justice, oppression, power, and equity bent, transformative studies eschew postpositivist and interpretive/constructivist approaches for mixed methods studies that will provide the best avenue to advocate change in individuals' lives, as well as the broader culture. Thus, this paradigm focuses on how research can be used to promote greater equality, equity, justice, and fairness. This emphasis on the nature of the use of the results is different from the goal of postpositivist and interpretive/constructivist paradigms that seek to contribute to knowledge with some implications for practice.

There are many types of research that are based on the transformative paradigm, including feminist, neo-Marxist, critical race theory, LGBTQ theory, disability, globalization, and race-specific studies. A good example of transformative research would be the study of disproportionate disciplinary actions by race. The intent

Table 1.1 Major Research Paradigm Worldviews

Paradigm	Description	Key Assumptions	Key Methods	Outcomes
Postpositivist	A deterministic view in which the goal is to establish cause-and-effect relationships	Careful observation, measurement, theories, and data are needed to objectively evaluate tentative claims about what governs behavior	Quantitative, with an emphasis on experiments, quasi-experiments, and correlational relationships	Verification and revision of theories, data-based decision making, generalized conclusions
Interpretive/ Constructivist	A discovery of underlying meaning as reflected in personal experience, perspectives, and contextual factors	Close engagement with individuals and contexts is used to acquire in-depth understanding of socially constructed meanings	Qualitative, with an emphasis on participant perspectives, observation, open-ended questioning, and social interaction in specific contexts	A greater understanding of participant perspectives and phenomena, especially the why and how of behavior
Pragmatic	Applied research that improves understanding of practice	The nature of research is dependent on consequences that impact real-world problems	Emphasis on mixed methods and action research, though pluralistic and varied in methodology	Improved outcomes based on solving problems of practice in specific contexts
Transformative	Research that results in positive change for marginalized groups and individuals in society	Focus on uncovering oppression, inequities, and injustices to enable reform of targeted groups	Mixture of quantitative, qualitative, and mixed methods, with an emphasis on qualitative	Improved lives of marginalized individuals and groups

would be to not simply document and understand why, for instance, higher percentages of Black students than White students are suspended, but also study reasons for the discrepancy with an intent to promote more equitable actions. Transformative research, then, goes beyond knowledge accumulation—it is designed to promote social justice.

The major tenets of these four research paradigms are summarized in Table 1.1. Keep in mind that in practice they are not mutually exclusive. Rather, each suggests a major orientation to research. In specific studies there could easily be elements of more than one paradigm. It will be of interest to you to see whether you tend to relate more to one paradigm or the other. Often we do, based on our experiences, values, and outlook for how research can be helpful. In the end, good research aligns the right paradigms with methods to provide the best information to find the signal and reduce the noise.

Check for Understanding 3

3a. What is the primary difference between the postpositivist and interpretive/ constructivist research paradigms?

3b. What distinguishes the transformative research paradigm from other research paradigms?

The Nature of Disciplined Inquiry

Learning Outcome 1.4   Understand how the principles of disciplined inquiry ("fox-like" thinking) are important for conducting educational research.

All research paradigms depend on the use of systematic approaches to generating, interpreting, and using new information. Much like we expect scientists to use the **scientific** approach, researchers in the social sciences, including education, use **disciplined inquiry**. It is easy to understand the usefulness of the scientific approach in fields such as agriculture, medicine, engineering, biology, and the like, but education is far from a science field. I emphasize disciplined inquiry for educational research to encompass all research paradigms and epistemologies. However data are gathered, the approach needs to be *systematic* according to professional standards appropriate to that type of inquiry. The scientific approach is a logical method of inquiry, not a body of knowledge. We can study education and conduct research in education in a *disciplined inquiry manner*, using many different methods and designs (some of which are akin to science).

Purpose

The primary purpose of disciplined inquiry is to understand and explain natural phenomena, identify underlying relationships, and then, using this information, predict and influence practices, behavior, policy, and institutions. For example, we can use disciplined inquiry to explain why some teachers appear to be more effective than others. The explanation leads to a knowledge base that novice teachers can use to become more effective.

Description provides fundamental knowledge about a phenomenon and is usually necessary before pursuing deep understanding, explanation, and prediction. Accurate descriptions, often based on data from observations and interviews, are essential to understanding explanations of events or people. For example, accurate descriptions of various teaching styles and student achievement are needed before the relationship between these two phenomena can be studied. Once these phenomena are adequately described, one may be predicted by knowledge of the other. This predictive power is very important because educators must constantly make predictive-type decisions (e.g., put Jose in group A because he will do better with the children in that group; admit a select group of students for a special program because they will benefit most; use cooperative teaching techniques because they will keep the students interested longer; advise a student against a particular occupation because the student will have difficulty passing the certification examination). Sometimes, after describing phenomena, postpositivist researchers control one factor to study its effect on the other. By controlling factors in experiments (discussed in detail in Chapter 9), researchers can determine whether one factor influences another. (Experiments are not the only way, though, to study the influence of one factor on another.)

The idea that education can be studied "scientifically" (i.e., postpositivist) has been strongly influenced by federal policy. Three significant developments include (1) formation of the Institute of Education Sciences (IES) to provide leadership in expanding scientific knowledge and understanding of education, (2) formation of the What Works Clearinghouse to review studies for scientific rigor, and (3) publication of *Scientific Research in Education* (Shavelson & Towne, 2002). These influences have created unprecedented emphasis on the need for educational research to be "scientific" and policy and practice to be "evidence based." This emphasis has focused educational researchers on what is meant by "scientific," though there has been an emphasis in these developments on postpositivist perspectives and paradigms. So "scientific," in my mind, actually is better conceptualized as disciplined inquiry so that all research paradigms are considered. Thus, the principles of disciplined inquiry provide the foundation for conducting studies, regardless of the specific type of research or methodology used to collect and analyze data.

Principles of Disciplined Inquiry

Disciplined inquiry is guided by six principles (Shavelson & Towne, 2002). These principles provide a set of guidelines that can be used to judge the quality and contribution of research. In concert with some additional characteristics, these principles essentially constitute a set of norms that both researchers and consumers of research can use to judge the overall quality and credibility of studies. (I should note that I've taken some liberty with Shavelson & Towne in substituting "disciplined inquiry" for "scientific," though the report emphasizes the principles for all types of educational research and this change doesn't affect the substance of their recommendations.)

DISCIPLINED INQUIRY PRINCIPLE 1: POSE SIGNIFICANT QUESTIONS THAT CAN BE INVESTIGATED EMPIRICALLY   This principle emphasizes two elements: (1) the need to identify important research questions that will have significant benefits for practice and/or the knowledge base once answered; and (2) the need for an "empirical" approach. As I have emphasized, an empirical study is one that gathers information (data) that is based on observation, measurement, or experience. It is based on concrete evidence—what is seen, heard, or touched, using direct contact with what is being studied. Traditionally, within a positivist or postpositivist perspective, the goal is to minimize the influence of subjectivity and bias so there is little impact of a researcher's personal viewpoint, desires, or speculations. (As we will see, this is not best for some types of educational research.)

DISCIPLINED INQUIRY PRINCIPLE 2: LINK RESEARCH TO RELEVANT THEORY   Some disciplined inquiry, particularly postpositivist inquiry, is focused on the generation and testing of theories that are important for establishing a body of knowledge that will generalize widely. Interpretive/constructivist paradigms use theory in planning studies and understanding results. A **theory** can be defined as a set of propositions that explain the relationships among observed phenomena. For postpositivist studies, such general explanations of behavior can be used in many contexts and have more utility for a large number of people. For example, research on effective teaching has identified general teaching behaviors—such as providing close supervision, giving meaningful and timely feedback to students on their performance, and asking appropriate questions that keep students engaged—that are positively related to student achievement for most, if not all, teachers. It doesn't matter whether the teacher has a fourth-grade class or a high school class, teaches French or science, or has honors or remedial students. The power of a theory to establish principles is what will advance our knowledge of effective teaching and educational interventions.

DISCIPLINED INQUIRY PRINCIPLE 3: USE METHODS THAT PERMIT DIRECT INVESTIGATION OF THE QUESTION   An important principle in conducting empirical educational research is that the method used in the study should be the best one for the research question. No single method always provides the best answers. Rather, start with the question and then match the method to the question. Conclusions are strengthened when multiple methods are used. Method is also influenced by the situation in which the research is conducted and by access to information. For example, experiments are often thought to be the best method for determining whether an educational intervention is successful, but they are difficult to design and carry out in schools.

DISCIPLINED INQUIRY PRINCIPLE 4: PROVIDE A COHERENT, EXPLICIT, AND EVIDENCE-BASED CHAIN OF REASONING   Making disciplined inquiry inferences, explanations, and conclusions requires a logical chain of reasoning that is coherent and persuasive. This occurs when there is a clear alignment between all aspects of the research, from the research paradigm to research question and pertinent literature, to methods, findings, and conclusions. Reasoning is strengthened when researchers identify limitations, uncertainty, possible bias, and errors.

DISCIPLINED INQUIRY PRINCIPLE 5: REPLICATE AND GENERALIZE ACROSS STUDIES   For postpositivist research the findings from a study must be checked and validated through both direct and conceptual replication, and subsequent studies must determine whether results generalize to a broader population and to other contexts. (As we will see, though, some types of research do not "generalize" in the traditional sense.) Unfortunately, our current system of publication of research devalues replications, in my view a factor that prevents establishing accurate signals.

DISCIPLINED INQUIRY PRINCIPLE 6: DISCLOSE RESEARCH TO ENCOURAGE PROFESSIONAL SCRUTINY, CRITIQUE, AND PEER REVIEW   A hallmark of scientific inquiry is that studies are widely disseminated and subjected to review by peers. This public, professional critique is needed to validate the overall credibility of the findings. I like to use the word *skeptical* to describe an attitude and way of thinking as a researcher that is essential for doing good studies and evaluating studies. Findings from "research" are just the starting point for making contributions; the evidence informs subsequent interpretation and judgment.

Skepticism is critical for rooting out and mitigating noise in observed findings. Because in educational research there are multiple sources of noise for any study, an informed critique that identifies noise is needed. This scrutiny-oriented disposition can be illustrated with a second metaphor that, in my mind, has relevance for researchers as well as consumers of research: *The Fox and the Hedgehog*. The parable of the fox and hedgehog, popularized by philosopher Isaiah Berlin, is about the fox, using curious and cunning thinking, that constantly tries new ways to attack and eat the hedgehog. Despite being nimble and inquisitive, the fox always fails. The hedgehog has the same, singular response each time, with a focus that never waivers—to roll up into a ball and expose sharp spikes in all directions.

The Fox and the Hedgehog parable illustrates two ways of thinking. For the fox, thinking is cautious, taking into account complexity and nuance; the goal is to know many things to be adaptable. For the hedgehog, there is one right way to think about things. By knowing one big thing (always rolling into a ball), a myriad of threats is contained. For our purposes the parable makes sense in describing different approaches to predictive thinking. People in all walks of life who make predictions about signals (e.g., sports, weather, politics, stocks, student achievement), as well as those who draw conclusions about understanding phenomena (e.g., why some children are more resilient than others), have different styles of thinking and decision making, different "mind sets," if you will. The ones who tend to make accurate predictions and come up with insightful understandings display habits of thinking and attitudes that are fox-like, quite different from hedgehogs who tend to make inaccurate predictions and draw improper conclusions (refer to Table 1.2). The contrasting fox and hedgehog characteristics correspond to these different ways of thinking (Silver, 2012; Tetlock & Gardner, 2015):

Fox and Hedgehog Thinking

Hedgehogs are overly confident and fail to recognize flaws in thinking. They are intolerant of others' perspectives and tend to be dogmatic rather than open-minded. They keep coming back to a single "big" principle or model that must be correct (e.g., Freud and the unconscious; Karl Marx and class struggle). The goal is to verify a favored signal.

Foxes, on the other hand, are guarded and tolerant of nuance, uncertainty, complexity, and dissenting opinions. They tend to be nimble and "scrappy," comfortable using different approaches and perspectives. Foxes are more self-critical and skeptical. The goal is to find the signal.

You won't be surprised to know that I think good researchers think like a fox, not a hedgehog. In fact, I think it's so important the metaphor is used throughout the rest of the book. As I've already stressed, there are many sources of noise in research that make for flawed results, interpretations, and subsequent predictions, and if you think more like a hedgehog than a fox, your predictions will not be very accurate.

Table 1.2 Characteristics of Fox and Hedgehog Researcher Thinking

How *Foxes* Think	How *Hedgehogs* Think
Multidisciplinary: Incorporate ideas from different disciplines and viewpoints, regardless of origin on the political, social, or philosophical spectrum.	**Specialized:** Single discipline, point of view, or problem holds sway; know one big thing. Tend to view the opinions of "outsiders" skeptically.
Adaptable: Open to new approaches or pursuing multiple approaches at the same time when the original one is not working.	**Stalwart:** Stick to the same "all-in" approach—new data are used to refine the original model.
Self-critical: Willing to acknowledge mistakes in their predictions and will accept blame for them.	**Stubborn:** Keep coming back to the same singular focus. Blames mistakes on bad luck or on idiosyncratic circumstances. Unlikely to admit errors.
Tolerant of complexity: See research as complicated, perhaps to the point of many fundamental problems being irresolvable or inherently unpredictable.	**Order-seeking:** Expect that the findings will abide by relatively simple governing ideas and relationships. Reduce complexity to a simple idea.
Cautious: Express predictions in probabilistic terms and qualify conclusions. Tend to say "however," "although," and "on the other hand."	**Overconfident:** Rarely hedge their predictions and are reluctant to change them. Like to say "without question," "absolutely," and "definitely."
Empirical: Rely more on observation than theory. More pragmatic.	**Ideological:** Expect that solutions to many day-to-day problems are manifestations of some grander theory or struggle—one big idea or philosophy.
Inductive: Tend to aggregate, integrate, and synthesize information from many different sources.	**Deductive:** Use a single big idea, perspective, or theory to explain everything else.

[1]Based on: Silver (2012) and Tetlock & Gardner (2015).

It is useful to add a few more principles to these six. The American Educational Research Association (AERA), the leading educational research organization in the world, for all areas of educational inquiry, describes education research as "the scientific field of study that examines education and learning processes and the human attributes, interactions, organizations, and institutions that shape educational outcomes." In 2008,

AERA convened an "expert working group" to formulate a definition of "scientifically based research." This definition was written to clarify, from the perspective of AERA, fundamental principles of empirical research in the field of education. The principles included the following (retrieved October 14, 2019, from aera.net/):

> The term *principles of scientific research* means the use of rigorous, systematic, and objective methodologies to obtain reliable and valid knowledge. Specifically, such research requires:
>
> A. development of a logical, evidence-based chain of reasoning;
> B. methods appropriate to the questions posed;
> C. observational or experimental designs and instruments that provide reliable and generalizable findings;
> D. data and analysis adequate to support findings;
> E. explication of procedures and results clearly and in detail, including specification of the population to which the findings can be generalized;
> F. adherence to professional norms of peer review;
> G. dissemination of findings to contribute to scientific knowledge; and
> H. access to data for reanalysis, replication, and the opportunity to build on findings.
>
> (From The Definition of Scientifically Based Research, American Educational Research Association. Copyright © American Educational Research Association. Reprinted by permission.)

You can see that the AERA statement breaks out some of the more general principles from the National Research Council, and adds dissemination of findings and access to data. Also note, though, that there is an emphasis on a positivist/postpositivist worldview. In practice, AERA is open to research from all paradigms.

Applying Disciplined Inquiry to Educational Research

The purpose of research is to provide sound understanding and explanations that can become knowledge and promote better practice. The primary mode of inquiry employs a systematic series of steps to conduct the investigation. These steps are associated with questions that help us judge the quality of the research. As a researcher, your goal is to obtain credible answers to research questions by designing, conducting, and reporting data that others will view as credible—that is, as reasonable results and conclusions that make sense.

In its most simple form, empirical research involves four steps:

$$\text{Question} \rightarrow \text{Method} \rightarrow \text{Results} \rightarrow \text{Conclusions}$$

At the start is a question that needs to be answered; then there is some method of gathering and analyzing information. Based on the analysis and results, conclusions are drawn. For example, suppose you are interested in whether grading practices affect student motivation. The study could involve the four steps in the following manner:

Question →	Method →	Results →	Conclusions
What is the effect of grading practices on student motivation?	Teacher and student surveys.	More frequent grades, greater student motivation.	Training teachers to grade more frequently may increase student motivation.

Once the question is established, a method is selected. This involves identifying who will provide data, the nature of the data that are collected, and procedures for gathering data and/or administering interventions. Results are determined by some kind of data analysis. Based on these results, the method, and previous studies, conclusions are drawn from interpretations of the results. This forms an expanded version of the four steps to show that choice of method and data analyses can affect the conclusions (refer to Figure 1.3). That is, depending on the nature of the individuals who are studied, how data are collected, and the procedures, different conclusions can be reached for the same question. Thus, in the preceding example, how motivation is measured could make a big difference (e.g., Is motivation based on student self-efficacy or level of interest, or both?). The conclusion is also limited to the nature of the sample (e.g., fourth- and fifth-graders).

The expanded number of steps in Figure 1.3 shows how researchers actually go about planning and then conducting research. Each step in the process is important and contributes to the overall credibility and usefulness of the research. This book is organized around these steps and questions to provide you with the knowledge and skills you will need to make sound overall judgments about the credibility and usefulness of various studies. I will elaborate on the steps and questions introduced here in later chapters, but it is helpful for you to understand the nature of the entire process from the beginning.

Figure 1.3 Steps in the Process of Conducting Empirical Research

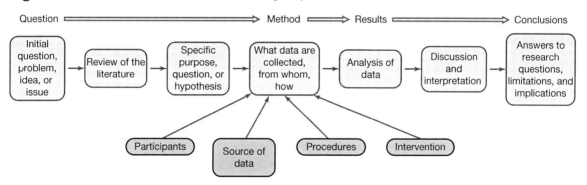

In the first step, the investigator faces an obstacle to effective decision making or understanding, or identifies a general idea or question that warrants further thought. This establishes the purpose of the study. The subsequent step, reviewing previous research on the topic, involves finding relevant research and literature, analyzing it, and relating it to the purpose.

Next, the researcher may formulate a specific research question or even a hypothesis (an informed guess about the answer to the research question). The nature of the question depends on the type of research. As we will see, some research has very specific research questions, whereas other types have more general questions.

The design of the study is based on what will provide an adequate answer to the question. It includes participants, data collection, procedures, and, in experiments, interventions. A carefully designed study is structured so that the explanation provided is the most credible one. The credibility of the results builds on previous aspects of the study, focusing on the reasonableness of the results in light of previous research and the extent to which alternative explanations are eliminated. The evaluation of the conclusions, in turn, also builds on previous credible judgments. Finally, judgments are made on the *generalizability* or *transferability* of the research—that is, whether the findings and explanations are useful in other situations and with other people, times, procedures, and measures. In other words, can the conclusions be generalized to other people in other contexts?

Both the National Research Council and AERA emphasize the importance of a *chain of reasoning* as essential to disciplined inquiry. This principle is illustrated in Figure 1.4, which shows that each step of disciplined inquiry is connected to others. A "chain" with "links" is established, with a weakness in any link sufficient to break the soundness of the study. Keep this illustration in mind—all steps in research are important, and when a strong, aligned, and reasonable chain is established, the credibility and usefulness of the conclusions are enhanced.

Check for Understanding 4

4a. Why is disciplined inquiry important for conducting educational research?

4b. Why does "fox-like" thinking, rather than "hedgehog-like" thinking, result in stronger research?

Figure 1.4 Chain of Reasoning in Disciplined Inquiry

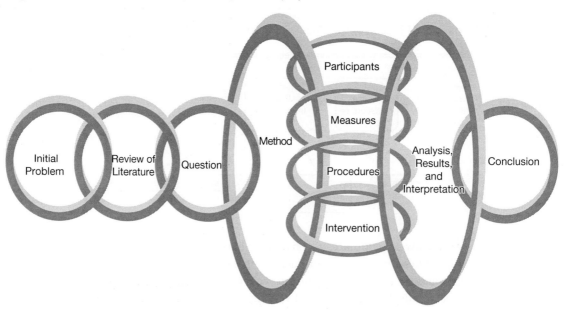

Types of Educational Research

Learning Outcome 1.5 Distinguish among key characteristics of quantitative, qualitative, and mixed methods types of research.

Although all empirical educational research is characterized by systematic, disciplined inquiry, three different approaches of educational research, distinguished most by design features, are typically used: quantitative, qualitative, and mixed methods. There are important distinctions along a number of dimensions for each type, with corresponding purposes, terminology, methods, assumptions, values, and techniques (as detailed in later chapters; summarized here). As illustrated by the chain of reasoning in Figure 1.5, methodology follows from, and needs to be aligned with, the research question(s).

For many decades, most educational research was based on the **quantitative** tradition. This approach, based on a positivist/postpositivist paradigm, assumes that phenomena should be studied objectively with the goal of obtaining a single truth, or at least reality within known probabilities, with an emphasis on measurement, numerical data, and experiments. **Qualitative** research stresses multiple realities that are rooted in participants' views and perceptions. A focus on understanding and meaning is based on social interactions, verbal narratives, and observations, rather than numbers. Qualitative research often takes place in naturally occurring situations. It is usually based on an interpretive/constructivist or transformative paradigm.

More recently, researchers have combined quantitative and qualitative approaches, resulting in a third major type of research called **mixed methods**. These studies contain elements from both quantitative and qualitative traditions in an effort to better match research questions with appropriate methodology, and to use different methods to confirm and better understand more limited information that is gathered solely by either of the two major approaches (refer to Figure 1.5). This approach is based primarily on a pragmatic paradigm, in which what is most appropriate for research is what works best and provides the best answers and intended consequences, using some degree of both qualitative and quantitative methods.

Figure 1.5 Relationship of Quantitative and Qualitative Types of Research to Mixed Methods Research

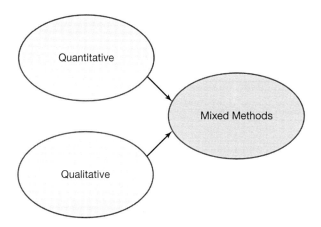

Table 1.3 summarizes the major features of quantitative, qualitative, and mixed methods traditions. Note the different terms that are used to refer to qualitative research. In the next section I introduce different types of quantitative, qualitative, and mixed methods *research designs*. **Research design** refers to the plan for carrying out a study. These designs are summarized here and then covered in greater detail in later chapters.

Quantitative Research Designs

For quantitative research, a major distinction is made between *nonexperimental* and *experimental* designs. In **nonexperimental research**, the investigator has no direct influence on changing what antecedent factor has been selected to be studied, either because it has already occurred or because it cannot be influenced. In other words, the investigator is unable to "manipulate" or control any factors or phenomena, such as an

Table 1.3 Characteristics of Quantitative, Qualitative, and Mixed Methods Types of Research

	Quantitative	Qualitative	Mixed Methods
Other Terms or Phrases Associated with the Approach	Postpositivist Experimental Hard data Statistical	Naturalistic Field research Ethnographic Phenomenological Anthropological Ecological Case study Interpretive Constructivist Transformative Critical	Mixed Multimethodology Multiple methods Multitrait Mixed approach Combined Blended Integrative
Key Concepts	Variables Operationalized Controlled Statistically significant Replicated Hypothesized	Shared meaning Understanding Social construction Context Participant perspectives	Both shared meaning and controlled measurement Collection of both quantitative and qualitative data Both statistical and narrative analyses
Academic Affiliation	Agriculture Psychology Natural sciences Economics	Anthropology History Sociology	All fields as appropriate
Goals	Test theory Statistically describe Show relationships Predict Establish causation	Develop understanding Describe multiple realities Capture naturally occurring behavior Discover	Use various methods, as appropriate, to both document and understand relationships and phenomena
Role of Researcher	Distant Short-term Detached Uninvolved	Close Involved Trusting Evolving	Flexible Both involved and detached
Design	Structured Predetermined Specific Contrived Experimental	Emergent Evolving Flexible Natural Holistic	Varied, could be either predetermined or emergent Both structured and flexible
Sample	Large Randomized	Small Purposeful	Varied, could be both randomized and purposeful
Data	One or few sources Measures/instruments Numbers Statistics Surveys Structured interviews and observations	Multiple sources Narrative descriptions Field notes Documents and artifacts Photographs Semi-structured or unstructured interviews and observations	Both numbers/statistics and narrative descriptions from field notes, interviews, and/or observations
Data Analysis	Deductive Statistical	Inductive Interpretive Text analysis Search for themes	Both inductive and deductive Statistical and narrative

intervention or "treatment," that may influence the participant's (subject's) behavior or performance. This characteristic has important implications for the conclusions that are drawn. It usually means that the study can only describe something or uncover relationships between two or more factors; causal conclusions are possible but more limited than what can be found with experimental studies.

Author Reflection *Coming up with the best way to categorize different types of research designs has kept me up at night. Some in the research community use the term descriptive research to mean any quantitative study that isn't an experiment. My take is that while rare, simple descriptive studies can be differentiated from other types of nonexperimental designs. In all quantitative studies there is some level of descriptive data analysis.*

Nonexperimental quantitative studies can be classified, according to the nature of the design, as descriptive, comparative, correlational, causal–comparative, or ex post facto. *Descriptive* nonexperimental research includes studies that provide simple information about the frequency or amount of something (e.g., How do high school counselors spend their time during the school day?). *Comparative* studies examine the differences between groups on a variable of interest (e.g., What is the difference between male and female attitudes toward taking accountability tests? Do mathematics teachers have the same or different definitions of critical thinking as English teachers?). *Correlational* studies investigate relationships among two or more variables (e.g., What is the relationship between physical conditioning and academic achievement? Is there a correlation between creativity and aptitude?).

Causal–comparative research examines whether a *naturally occurring* "intervention" (one that is not controlled by the experimenter) affects an outcome of interest, such as student performance (e.g., Do students attending a charter school achieve better math performance than students in public school?). *Ex post facto* studies identify interventions that occurred in the past and subsequent responses in such a way that it may be possible to draw causal relationships between them (e.g., Do students who took keyboard typing in seventh grade have more positive attitudes toward using technology in high school than students who did not take keyboard typing?).

In **experimental research**, the investigators have control over one or more interventions in the study that may influence the participants' behavior. That is, they can manipulate an intervention, such as a program or instructional technique, and then see what happens to the participants' responses as a result. The purpose of controlling a condition is to investigate its causal relationship with another factor. For example, investigators may be interested in studying the causal relationship between the amount of time devoted to teaching a given subject, such as math, and student achievement. They control time by having one group of children spend 20 minutes studying the subject and a second group spend an hour studying. If the children who spend more time studying math show higher achievement than the other children, then time devoted to studying *may* be causally related to achievement. As we will see, the determination of what actually or probably causes an observed difference depends on many factors.

There are several types of experimental research, depending on specific design characteristics. A *true experimental* design is one in which participants have been *randomly assigned* to different groups. A *quasi-experimental* design does not have random assignment. *Single-subject* designs use the ideas of an experiment with a single person or a few individuals.

Qualitative Research Designs

Unlike quantitative research, different types of qualitative research are not as clearly distinguished by design characteristics. However, different purposes are identified with specific questions, data collection procedures, and analyses that align with the purpose. The goal in a *phenomenological* study is to fully understand the essence of some phenomenon (e.g., What is essential for students to view teachers as caring?). This is usually accomplished with long, intensive individual interviews. An *ethnography* is a description and interpretation of a cultural or social group system (e.g., What is the effect of high-stakes testing on the climate of the school? How has high-stakes testing influenced teacher–principal interaction?). Ethnographers spend extensive time in the setting being studied and use observations, interviews, and other analyses to understand the nature of the culture. *Grounded theory* studies are conducted to generate or discover a theory or schema, "grounded" in participants' views, that relates to a particular environment (e.g., How do students with learning disabilities adapt to being in regular classrooms?). As in an ethnographic study, many different modes of gathering information are used. *Case studies* concern in-depth study of a single or a few programs, events, activities, groups, or other entities defined in terms of time and place (e.g., examining the culture of a particular magnet school). Again, multiple methods of data collection are used, including observations, interviews, and analyses of documents and reports. In *critical studies* the research is based on the transformative paradigm, with a focus on marginalized people, with investigations of injustice and inequity. There are many types of critical studies (e.g., feminist, race theory, emancipatory, queer theory). *Narrative inquiries* use "lived stories" of individuals and groups to provide a deep understanding of a phenomenon.

Mixed Methods Research Designs

The third major type of research design, mixed methods, is increasingly popular. As illustrated in Table 1.3, mixed methods studies use design characteristics from both qualitative and quantitative approaches in a single study or series of studies. There are many advantages of mixed methods designs, which are detailed in Chapter 14. Briefly, mixed methods designs allow one approach to strengthen the other, address weaknesses that exist in each approach if used by itself, and allow convergence to show how two approaches address the same question. There are three major mixed methods designs—*explanatory sequential*, *exploratory sequential*, and *convergent*—and the relative emphasis given to any particular method (quantitative or qualitative) can vary within each of these designs. The *sequential* designs start with either a quantitative or qualitative phase and then employ the other approach. If quantitative methods are used first, qualitative methods are then employed to explain the quantitative results that were obtained (this is called an *explanatory sequential* design). An *exploratory sequential* study begins with qualitative methods that are used to gather information that is then used for the subsequent quantitative phase. *Convergent* designs use both quantitative and qualitative approaches about equally, gather data from each at about the same time, and merge results from both to address the research question.

Keeping these categories and examples in mind will help you understand important design characteristics of research. Use the decision tree in Figure 1.6 to identify different types of educational research and related research designs. As you read studies and learn more about each one in later chapters, you will be able to identify them quickly, which is very important in understanding and analyzing what is presented.

Figure 1.6 A Decision Tree of Types of Educational Research and Research Designs

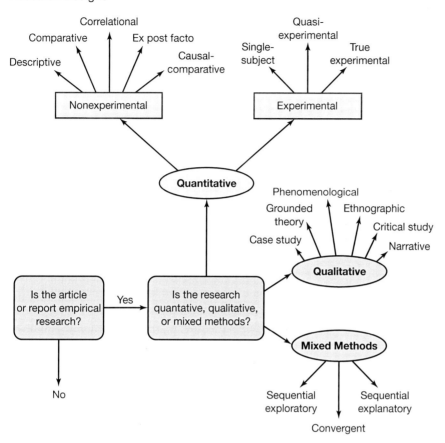

Check for Understanding 5

5a. What are three ways quantitative research differs from qualitative research?

5b. What is the difference between experimental and nonexperimental research?

Author Reflection   *Over the past three decades I have conducted many quantitative and qualitative studies (and a few mixed methods). What have I learned about the two methods as a result of these experiences? First, it is critical to match the reason for the research with the appropriate method. Method should always be determined by the purpose and the research question(s). Second, using each method well is a challenge. Either can easily be used without appropriate rigor, which diminishes the usefulness of findings. Third, on balance, it seems that my qualitative studies have had greater significance. I think this shows the importance of depth of understanding, regardless of the design. It is really important to engage in your topic with sufficient detail and thoroughness. Depth is more important than breadth when it comes to most research.*

Basic, Applied, Action, and Evaluation Research

Another way to think about different types of research is based solely on the overall purpose for which the results will be used, rather than the specific design employed. I have identified four traditional major types of use for research that can be targeted: basic, applied, evaluation, or action. These terms, as with the ones already discussed, are used frequently to describe studies (e.g., "I'm going to do an action research study."). Each of these uses whatever designs are most appropriate. That is, a basic study could use quantitative, qualitative, or mixed methods.

The primary purpose of **basic research** (also called *pure* or *fundamental* research) is to use results for the development of theories. The goal of basic research is to understand and explain—to refute or modify theory that provides broad generalizations about how phenomena are related. It is not concerned with immediate application of the results to real-life situations. Examples include studies of the workings of the memory system, language development, and social development. Not many educational studies would be classified as basic, although those that are can provide very important contributions because the findings, compared with applied, evaluation, or action types, lead to more enduring principles. Basic research in allied fields of study, such as psychology, are used extensively in education.

The purpose of **applied research** is to use results to test theories and other ideas in the context of naturally occurring educational settings. It is usually focused on a problem that needs to be solved to improve the practice of education. The results are immediately and directly relevant to educational decision making. To the extent that general theories are tested in real-life contexts, the results may be generalized to many different educational settings. For example, based on theories of human memory developed through basic research, a new curriculum may be tested for improved retention of science concepts. Other examples of applied research in education are studies that compare different teaching styles, identify characteristics of effective schools, or examine the effect of lengthening the school day on student achievement. As you have probably already surmised, applied research is aligned with a pragmatic research paradigm.

The goal of **action research** is to solve a specific classroom or school problem or issue, improve practice, or help make a decision at a single local site. Also based on the pragmatic paradigm, the intent is to improve practice immediately within one or a few specific classrooms or schools. Teachers may act as researchers in action studies they have designed and carried out to improve practice in their classrooms. Administrators have used action research strategies for school renewal and other improvement efforts. Those engaged in action research find both the process and results very helpful—so helpful, in fact, that I have included an entire chapter (Chapter 14) to explain in more detail how to do it, report it, and use it.

Evaluation research is directed toward making decisions about the effectiveness or desirability of a program. Also based primarily on the pragmatic paradigm, the goal is to make judgments about alternatives in decision-making situations. In most cases, evaluation research is focused on a specific location or type of program and involves judgments about such questions as: Which reading curriculum should be implemented? Did the new program work? Should the district build two small schools or one large school? What is the impact of increased technology on student and teacher knowledge and attitudes? Often, such questions require research methods that are unique to each situation.

A summary of the major types of educational research, with additional examples, is provided in Table 1.4.

Table 1.4 Types of Educational Research*

Type	Purpose	Example
Quantitative	To describe phenomena numerically to answer specific questions or hypotheses	Examine the relationship between amount of homework and student achievement
Nonexperimental	To describe, compare, and predict phenomena without actively manipulating factors that influence the phenomena	Determine the relationship between socioeconomic status and student attitudes
Experimental	To determine the causal relationship between two or more phenomena by direct manipulation of factors that influence the phenomena	Determine which of two approaches to teaching science results in the highest student achievement
Qualitative	To provide rich narrative descriptions of phenomena that enhance understanding	Observe school renewal teams to understand the role of parents
Mixed Methods	To study phenomena using both quantitative and qualitative methods	From a randomly selected sample of at-risk students, use surveys and then interviews to know about and understand their attitudes
Basic	To develop theories	Test the influence of digital compared to paper note taking on memory
Applied	To solve practical educational problems	Determine the best approach to develop students' self-assessment skills
Action	To improve practice in a school or classroom	Determine which grouping procedure results in the highest achievement
Evaluation	To make a decision about a program or activity	Decide whether to keep or phase out a prekindergarten program

*Note that some traits overlap among different types of research. For example, qualitative studies may contain numerical summaries of information.

Research Article Organization

Every year, millions of dollars are spent on educational research and millions more on related research in psychology, sociology, and other social sciences, and hundreds of articles and reports are published annually. One of the primary objectives of this book is to help you become an informed, critical reader of these articles and reports. A research article or report sets forth the research problem, what the researcher has done to collect data, how the data are analyzed and interpreted, and the conclusions. In other words, the article or report is a summary of what was done, how it was done, why it was done, and what was discovered. Most published articles, as well as research reports that are not articles, follow a standard organizational structure, as summarized in Figure 1.7. The figure shows differences in how quantitative and qualitative articles are organized (mixed methods use variations of these). The separate parts are described briefly and then identified in a published article, but please note that these parts, and what they are called in the headings used in articles and reports, can and do vary for different associations, centers, and journals.

Title and Author(s)

The empirical research article or report typically begins with the title and name(s) of the author(s), usually with an indication of the professional affiliation of the author(s). This is each author's affiliation when the research was conducted, not necessarily his

Figure 1.7 Organizational Quantitative and Qualitative Research Articles (Based on Creswell & Guetterman, 2019)

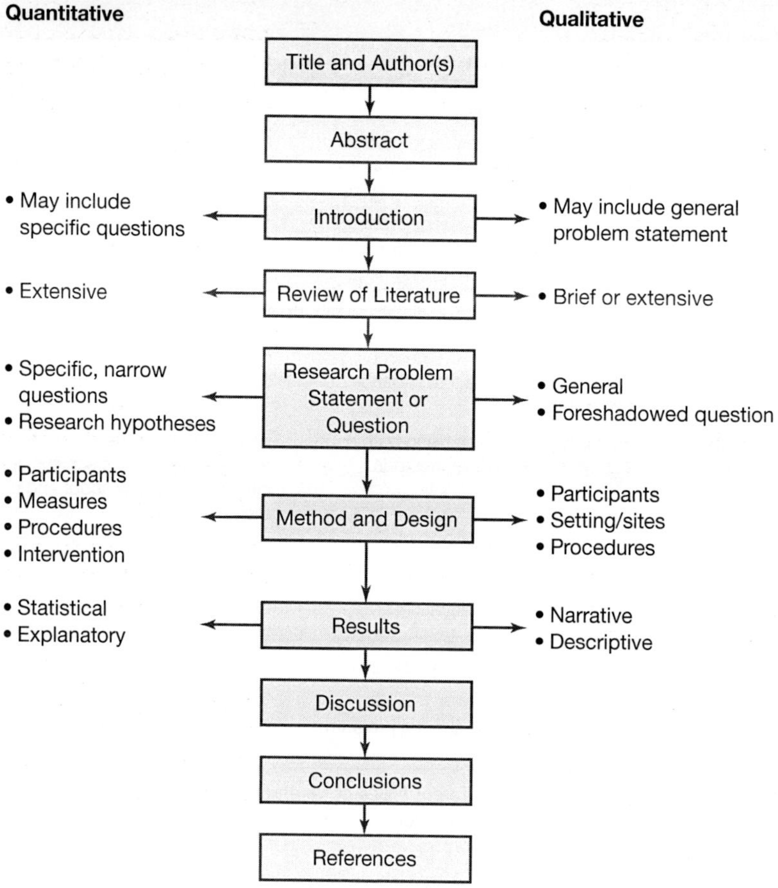

Quantitative   **Qualitative**

	Title and Author(s)	
	↓	
	Abstract	
	↓	
• May include specific questions ←	Introduction	→ • May include general problem statement
	↓	
• Extensive ←	Review of Literature	→ • Brief or extensive
	↓	
• Specific, narrow questions • Research hypotheses ←	Research Problem Statement or Question	→ • General • Foreshadowed question
	↓	
• Participants • Measures • Procedures • Intervention ←	Method and Design	→ • Participants • Setting/sites • Procedures
	↓	
• Statistical • Explanatory ←	Results	→ • Narrative • Descriptive
	↓	
	Discussion	
	↓	
	Conclusions	
	↓	
	References	

or her present affiliation. Good research article or report titles tell the reader, in less than 15 words, something about the major variables and type of participants that are studied.

Abstract

In many reports, especially journal articles, the title and author are followed by an abstract. The abstract in journal articles is typically 50 to 150 words long and is often set in smaller type than or a different font from the rest of the article. The abstract is a brief summary of the entire study, including the problem, methods used, and major findings. The abstract will usually provide enough details to allow you to decide whether to read the entire report.

Introduction

The introductory section is usually one to several paragraphs in length, including a statement of the context for the research, the significance of the research, and the general or specific research problem investigated. The context provides background information relating the study to broader areas. It may also indicate, briefly, the development of the research problem. The significance of the research is contained in a statement about how the results will be useful. It can be thought of as a justification for conducting the research, indicating a contribution to knowledge in a discipline and/or professional practice. Almost all introductions include a statement that indicates the general research problem or purpose of the study. (Sometimes both a broad and a more specific problem are included.) The general problem indicates the focus of the study as concisely and clearly as possible. Most general problems are stated near the beginning of the report, and more specific research questions, if any, just before the review of literature, but the level of specificity or location across articles and reports is inconsistent. In qualitative and some mixed methods articles, you will find a foreshadowed problem rather than specific questions.

Review of Literature

Although the introductory section may include some references to other research or literature, a more formal review of literature begins after the general research problem is introduced (or sometimes research questions). The review, typically several paragraphs long, summarizes and analyzes previous research on the same problem. A good review critiques the studies and shows how the findings relate to the problem being investigated. The length and complexity of the review can vary considerably, from very detailed in quantitative studies to relatively brief in some qualitative and mixed methods studies.

Specific Research Question or Hypothesis

Often (but not always) in quantitative and mixed methods studies, specific research questions and/or hypotheses are stated just before the methodology. The hypothesis, if there is one, follows the review of literature because it is based on what theories and previously completed related studies have found.

Method and Design

In this section, the researchers indicate who or what was studied, how the information was obtained, and, in the case of an experiment, interventions. The first part of the section usually describes the source of data, typically with a heading *participants* or *sample* (although sometimes the older term "subjects" is used in quantitative studies), and how these individuals were selected. Participants are individuals from whom the researcher obtains information to address the research problem. The characteristics of the participants or sample are described. The second part focuses on the methods used to gather information from the participants, including descriptions of measures or instruments and, for quantitative studies, an evaluation of their reliability and validity. In some reports, this section also describes how an instrument was administered; in others, this information is provided in the third part of the section, procedures. The procedures section includes a summary of how the data were collected and, in experimental studies, indicates how the interventions were carried out. The researchers may also discuss the design of the study and materials used, and they may indicate what precautions were taken to reduce bias or otherwise improve objectivity and/or credibility.

Results (Findings)

In this section, the researchers describe how they analyzed the data, and they present the results. Tables, graphs, figures, and models may be used to succinctly summarize large amounts of data. This section should, in my opinion, be restricted to a reporting of what was found, without interpretation or discussion.

Discussion

This is the section in which the investigators explain their results. The data and information that are reported in the results are interpreted in light of other research and possible methodological limitations of the study.

Conclusions

Conclusions are summary statements that reflect overall answers to the research questions or, for some quantitative studies, whether or not the research hypotheses were supported. Conclusions are inferences derived from the results, limitations in the study, and the relationship of the results to previous studies. Conclusions should be restricted to what is directly supported by the findings and what is reasonable, given other research. Implications and recommendations are often included in this section.

References

This is a listing of the sources cited in the report. The style of listing references will vary. The most common style is what is recommended by American Psychological Association (APA). A *bibliography* includes sources that are not cited in the report but are used by the authors.

Author Reflection   *If it seems like learning about all the research terms in this chapter is a bit much at this point, rest assured that this is essentially an introduction to further usage in subsequent chapters. Sometimes my students begin to feel overwhelmed at the beginning, but with repeated exposure become pretty confident about the material.*

Anatomy of a Research Article

The best way to become familiar with empirical educational research, and to become a skilled researcher, is to read published articles. Becoming comfortable with the format and language will allow you to critique and evaluate research and help you design good studies. Don't be too concerned about understanding *everything* you read. You are not expected to be an expert researcher or statistician.

Figure 1.8 is an example of a quantitative research article. It illustrates the format you will find and points out other features of an empirical research article.

Figure 1.8 Format and Features of a Research Article

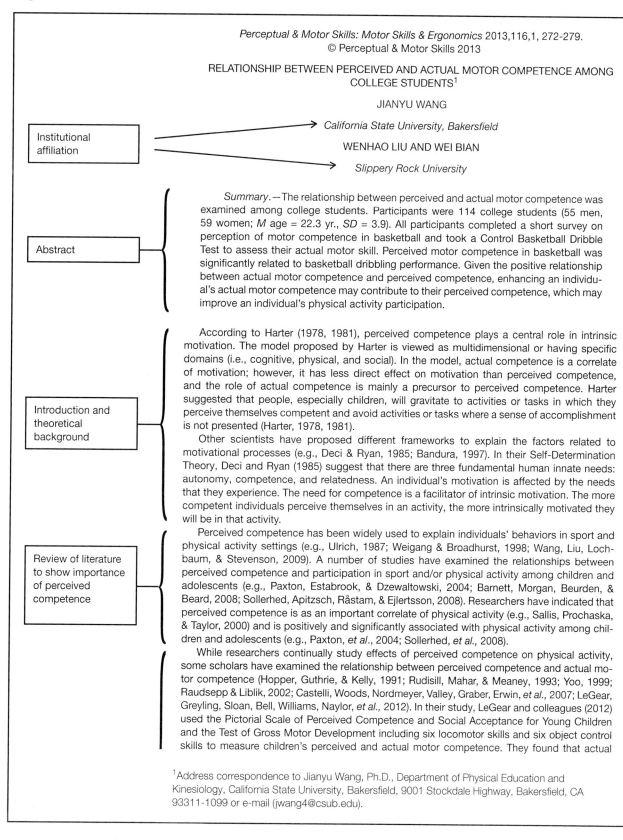

Perceptual & Motor Skills: Motor Skills & Ergonomics 2013,116,1, 272-279.
© Perceptual & Motor Skills 2013

RELATIONSHIP BETWEEN PERCEIVED AND ACTUAL MOTOR COMPETENCE AMONG COLLEGE STUDENTS[1]

JIANYU WANG

California State University, Bakersfield

WENHAO LIU AND WEI BIAN

Slippery Rock University

Institutional affiliation

Summary.—The relationship between perceived and actual motor competence was examined among college students. Participants were 114 college students (55 men, 59 women; *M* age = 22.3 yr., *SD* = 3.9). All participants completed a short survey on perception of motor competence in basketball and took a Control Basketball Dribble Test to assess their actual motor skill. Perceived motor competence in basketball was significantly related to basketball dribbling performance. Given the positive relationship between actual motor competence and perceived competence, enhancing an individual's actual motor competence may contribute to their perceived competence, which may improve an individual's physical activity participation.

Abstract

According to Harter (1978, 1981), perceived competence plays a central role in intrinsic motivation. The model proposed by Harter is viewed as multidimensional or having specific domains (i.e., cognitive, physical, and social). In the model, actual competence is a correlate of motivation; however, it has less direct effect on motivation than perceived competence, and the role of actual competence is mainly a precursor to perceived competence. Harter suggested that people, especially children, will gravitate to activities or tasks in which they perceive themselves competent and avoid activities or tasks where a sense of accomplishment is not presented (Harter, 1978, 1981).

Other scientists have proposed different frameworks to explain the factors related to motivational processes (e.g., Deci & Ryan, 1985; Bandura, 1997). In their Self-Determination Theory, Deci and Ryan (1985) suggest that there are three fundamental human innate needs: autonomy, competence, and relatedness. An individual's motivation is affected by the needs that they experience. The need for competence is a facilitator of intrinsic motivation. The more competent individuals perceive themselves in an activity, the more intrinsically motivated they will be in that activity.

Introduction and theoretical background

Perceived competence has been widely used to explain individuals' behaviors in sport and physical activity settings (e.g., Ulrich, 1987; Weigang & Broadhurst, 1998; Wang, Liu, Lochbaum, & Stevenson, 2009). A number of studies have examined the relationships between perceived competence and participation in sport and/or physical activity among children and adolescents (e.g., Paxton, Estabrook, & Dzewaltowski, 2004; Barnett, Morgan, Beurden, & Beard, 2008; Sollerhed, Apitzsch, Råstam, & Ejlertsson, 2008). Researchers have indicated that perceived competence is as an important correlate of physical activity (e.g., Sallis, Prochaska, & Taylor, 2000) and is positively and significantly associated with physical activity among children and adolescents (e.g., Paxton, *et al.*, 2004; Sollerhed, *et al.*, 2008).

Review of literature to show importance of perceived competence

While researchers continually study effects of perceived competence on physical activity, some scholars have examined the relationship between perceived competence and actual motor competence (Hopper, Guthrie, & Kelly, 1991; Rudisill, Mahar, & Meaney, 1993; Yoo, 1999; Raudsepp & Liblik, 2002; Castelli, Woods, Nordmeyer, Valley, Graber, Erwin, *et al.*, 2007; LeGear, Greyling, Sloan, Bell, Williams, Naylor, *et al.*, 2012). In their study, LeGear and colleagues (2012) used the Pictorial Scale of Perceived Competence and Social Acceptance for Young Children and the Test of Gross Motor Development including six locomotor skills and six object control skills to measure children's perceived and actual motor competence. They found that actual

[1]Address correspondence to Jianyu Wang, Ph.D., Department of Physical Education and Kinesiology, California State University, Bakersfield, 9001 Stockdale Highway, Bakersfield, CA 93311-1099 or e-mail (jwang4@csub.edu).

Figure 1.8 Continued

motor competence was significantly associated with perceived motor competence (r = .26). Raudsepp and Liblik (2002) used the Children's Physical Self-Perception Profile as a measure of perceived competence and the EUROFIT test battery, which includes a 20-meter endurance shuttle run, 30-seconds of sit-ups, and five-area skinfold measure to assess actual motor competence. They found that perceived and actual motor competence were moderately correlated in children (r = .25–.56). Additionally, Castelli, *et al.* (2007) examined the relationship between perceived and actual motor competence in children using the Perceived Competence Scales and three motor performances in basketball, throwing, and paddle activity. They reported that perceived motor competence was significantly related to throwing (r = .57) and paddle activity (r = .8), but not to basketball (r = .24). Moreover, research evidence has indicated significant correlations between perceived competence in soccer and soccer skill test scores (e.g., dribbling and juggling) among youth soccer players (Hopper, *et al.,* 1991).

> Correlation coefficient

> Review of other studies investigating similar variables

In a longitudinal study Barnett, *et al.* (2008) investigated the interrelationships among motor proficiency in childhood and perceived sports competence and physical activity in adolescence. The researchers found that object control skill proficiency (i.e., catch, overhand throw, forehand strike) in childhood was positively associated with perceived sports competence (r = .34) and physical activity (r = .36) in adolescence, whereas locomotor skill proficiency (i.e., hop, skip, gallop) in childhood was not associated with perceived sports competence (r = .12) or physical activity (r = -.08) in adolescence. They also concluded that perceived sports competence mediated the relationship between childhood object control skills (effect size = .14) and adolescent physical activity (effect size = .16).

> Measure of practical importance

Previous studies have shown that there are differences in actual motor skills and perceived motor competence between boys and girls. According to Rudisill, *et al.*, (1993), boys scored higher in both actual motor competence and perceived motor competence than girls. In another study, Barnett and colleagues (2008) also found that boys had higher perceived motor competence than girls. In addition, as for sex difference in actual motor competence, they found that the boys had a higher score in object control skill than girls, while girls had a higher score in locomotor skill than boys.

> Review of studies to show importance of gender

It appears that children's perceived competence on physical ability and motor skills may not be accurate. Researchers have indicated that children tended to overestimate their motor competence (e.g., Rudisill, *et al.*, 1993; Harter, 1999). As children's age increases, their perceptions on motor skills and physical ability are closer to their actual physical ability and motor skills (Harter, 1999).

While most studies on actual motor skill and perceived competence have targeted children and adolescents (e.g., Raudsepp & Liblik, 2002; Castelli, *et al.*, 2007), little research has been done among adults. Recently, Moran (2011) examined young adults' perception in swimming and their real swimming ability and found that there was significant association between actual and perceived competence in swimming among young adults. More research investigating the relationship between adults' perceived motor competence and their actual motor competence is needed. Thus, the purpose of this study was to examine the relationship between perceived and actual motor skill competence in basketball among college students.

> Establishes significance

> Quantitative research problem statement

Hypothesis 1. Perceived basketball competence will be higher among men than women.

Hypothesis 2. Actual basketball skill will be higher (a) among men than women and (b) among physical education majors than liberal arts students.

Hypothesis 3. Perceived basketball competence will be moderately correlated with actual basketball competence.

> Research hypotheses indicating expected findings for all variables

METHOD

Participants

Participants in the study were 114 college students (55 men, 59 women) randomly selected from a pool of 456 students enrolled in physical education classes in a university, which is located in central California. Of the participants, 44.7% majored in Physical Education and Kinesiology and the rest majored in Liberal Studies. The majority of these participants from the Physical Education and Kinesiology program were males (80%), while the majority of the participants from the Liberal Studies program were females (77.7%). The participants' ages ranged from 18 to 48 years (M = 22.3, SD = 3.94). The participants included African Americans (17.5%), Caucasians (31.3%), Hispanic Americans (44.1%), Asians (4.5%) and other races (2.6%). There was a large range in their physical activity level. The study was approved by the first author's Institutional Review Board and the informed consent was obtained from all participants.

> Number of participants randomly selected (not randomly assigned)

> Description of sample

> Indication of needed IRB approval

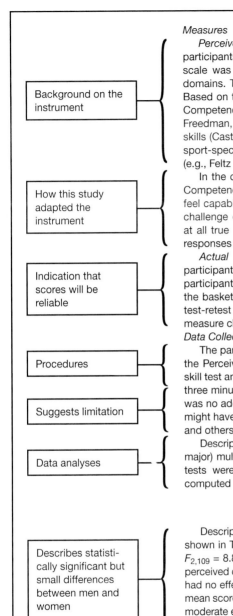

Measures

Perceived motor competence.—The Perceived Competence Scale was used to assess participants' perceived motor competence. Grounded from Self-Determination Theory, the scale was designed to assess individuals' perceived competence in relevant behaviors or domains. This questionnaire is a face-valid instrument that could be used in different areas. Based on their research purposes, researchers in different fields have adapted the Perceived Competence Scale to assess participants' perceptions on managing glucose levels (Williams, Freedman, & Deci, 1998), students learning interviewing (Williams, & Deci, 1996) and motor skills (Castelli, *et al.,* 2007). Additionally, researchers suggested that perceived competence is sport-specific and questions on perceived competence should be developed in specific sports (e.g., Feltz & Brown, 1984; Hopper, *et al.,* 1991).

In the current study, an adapted four-item questionnaire was used to measure Perceived Competence in Basketball, with items, "I feel confident in my ability to play basketball", "I feel capable of playing basketball", "I am able to play basketball", and "I feel able to meet the challenge of playing basketball." Items were rated on a 7-point scale, with anchors, 1: Not at all true and 7: Very true. Each participant's score was calculated by averaging his or her responses on the four items.

Actual motor competence.—The Control Basketball Dribble Test was used to measure participants' actual motor competence in basketball in the study. The test requires the participants to dribble a basketball as fast as possible around cones set in the paint area of the basketball court. The validity of this test has been reported to range from .37 to .91 and test-retest reliability from .88 to .97 (Safrit & Wood,1995). Researchers have used this test to measure children's basketball performance (French & Thomas, 1987).

Data Collection and Analysis

The participants took the Control Basketball Dribble Test immediately after they completed the Perceived Competence in Basketball Scale. Each participant took three trials during the skill test and the fastest time was taken as the measure of the skill. All participants spent about three minutes becoming familiar with the routine of the test before taking the test. While there was no additional training provided in basketball dribble before the test, a large range in times might have been observed among participants because some were Physical Education majors and others were Liberal Studies majors.

Descriptive statistics were calculated for each scale by gender and major. A 2 × 2 (gender × major) multivariate analysis of variance (MANOVA) and follow-up analysis of variance (ANOVA) tests were conducted. Additionally, Pearson's product moment correlation coefficient was computed on perceived competence in basketball and basketball dribbling time.

RESULTS

Descriptive statistics for perceived competence in basketball and basketball dribbling time are shown in Table 1. The MANOVA results indicted that gender differences existed (Wilk's lambda $F_{2,109} = 8.89$, $p < .002$, $\eta^2 = 0.12$), but the effect size was small. The univariate main effects of perceived competence in basketball and actual basketball dribbling time were examined. Gender had no effect on perceived competence in basketball ($F_{1,110} = 1.84$, $p = .18$, $\eta^2 = 0.02$), with the mean scores for men ($M = 5.83$) only slightly higher than for women ($M = 5.02$). Gender did have a moderate effect on basketball dribbling time ($F_{1,110} = 8.49$, $p < .005$, $\eta^2 = 0.07$), with the dribbling time for men ($M = 8.36$ sec.) faster than for women ($M = 10.28$ sec.).

Table 1

DESCRIPTIVE STATISTICS FOR PERCEIVED COMPETENCE AND RAW-SKILL SCORES BY MAJOR AND GENDER

| Measure | Physical Education Majors | | | | Liberal Studies Majors | | | |
| | Men ($n = 41$) | | Women ($n = 10$) | | Men ($n = 14$) | | Women ($n = 49$) | |
	M	SD	M	SD	M	SD	M	SD
Perceived competence	6.35	0.81	6.75	0.47	4.32	1.60	4.66	1.39
Basketball dribble test	7.90	0.87	8.70	0.86	9.70	1.50	10.61	1.52

Figure 1.8 Continued

The MANOVA showed a moderate overall effect for study major (Wilk's lambda $F_{2,109} = 56.01$, $p < .001$, $\eta^2 = 0.40$). The effect on perceived competence in basketball ($F_{1,110} = 56.21$, $p < .001$, $\eta^2 = 0.34$) was moderate: the mean score for Physical Education majors ($M = 6.43$) was higher than Liberal Studies majors ($M = 4.59$). The effect on basketball dribbling time was moderate ($F_{1,110} = 39.39$, $p < .001$, $\eta^2 = 0.26$); the mean basketball dribbling time for Physical Education majors ($M = 8.06$) was faster than for Liberal Studies majors ($M = 10.40$). The results supported Hypothesis 2. Additionally, the interaction effect of gender and major was very weak (Wilk's lambda $F_{2,109} = 1.00$, $p = .85$) and not statistically significant.

> Confidence interval

Perceived motor competence in basketball was statistically significantly and inversely related to basketball dribbling time ($r = -.55$, $p < .01$, 95% CI = -.49, -.85). That is, higher scores in perceived competence in basketball were associated with faster/shorter dribbling time, and lower scores in perceived competence in basketball were associated with slower/longer dribbling time. The results supported Hypothesis 3.

> Describes significant relationship among key variables

DISCUSSION

The current study examined the relationship between perceived and actual motor competence among college students. The findings of the study suggest that perceived motor competence in basketball is significantly associated with basketball dribbling time for college students. The result of the current study partially supports the results of the prior studies.

> Summary of purpose and findings

There are mixed findings in the literature on the relationship between perceived motor competence and actual motor competence among children and adolescents. Some reported perceived competence was statistically significantly associated with actual competence in object-control skill but not with actual competence in locomotor skill among children (e.g., Barnett, et al., 2008). Others reported that perceived competence was associated statistically significantly with actual competence in locomotor skills for boys and girls, but not in object control skills for girls (LeGear, et al., 2012). Castelli and colleagues (2007) reported that perceived motor competence was statistically significantly associated with the actual motor competence in throwing and paddle activity, but not with basketball skill. Moreover, one study indicates that statistically significant relationships were found among perceived soccer competence and soccer skill performances (Hopper, et al., 1991).

> How findings relate to other studies

Furthermore, the current study suggested that Physical Education majors had higher scores in both perceived competence in basketball and basketball dribbling time than Liberal Studies majors; these results could be attributed to the past experience in playing basketball (e.g., Horn, 2004). The results of the study also suggested that the male participants had higher scores in basketball dribbling time than female participants. However, one should be careful to interpret this result since there were more male than female participants majoring in Physical Education, and there were more female than male participants majoring in Liberal Studies. Given that actual motor competence is positively associated with perceived competence, enhancing an individual's actual motor competence may contribute to their perceived competence (LeGear, et al., 2012), which may encourage participation in physical activity.

> Explanation of findings

One limitation of the study is that only the Basketball Dribble Test was used to measure the actual motor competence in basketball, and the results of the test may not be a valid measure of participants' ability to play basketball. It would be helpful for future researchers to use more comprehensive and holistic assessment tools to measure basketball ability. Another limitation is that the current study only examined the relationship between perceived and actual competence in one sport, so results may not generalize. In the future, researchers need to examine the relationship between perceived and actual competence by using different sport or motor skills.

> Limitation

> Suggestion for future research

REFERENCES

Bandura, A. (1997) *Self-efficacy: the exercise of control*. New York: W. H. Freeman and Company.

Barnett, L. M., Morgan, P. J., Beurden, E. V., & Beard, R. B. (2008) Perceived sports competence mediates the relationship between childhood motor skill proficiency and adolescent physical activity and fitness: a longitudinal assessment. *International Journal of Behavioral Nutrition and Physical Activity, 5,* 40. DOI:10.1186/1479-5868-5-40. Available from: http://www.ijbnpa.org/content/5/1/40.

Castelli, D. M., Woods, M. K., Nordmeyer, E. E., Valley, J. A., Graber, K. C., Erwin, H. E., Bolton, K. N., & Woods, A. M. (2007) Perceived versus actual motor competence in children. *Research Quarterly for Exercise and Sports,* (78) A-51.

> References in "old" APA format

> Volume

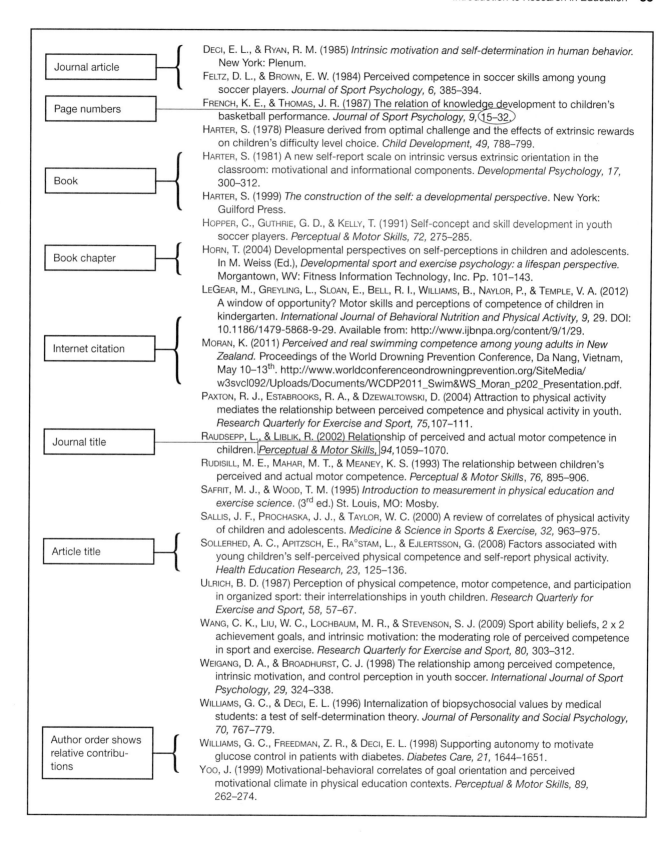

Journal article

Page numbers

Book

Book chapter

Internet citation

Journal title

Article title

Author order shows relative contributions

DECI, E. L., & RYAN, R. M. (1985) *Intrinsic motivation and self-determination in human behavior.* New York: Plenum.

FELTZ, D. L., & BROWN, E. W. (1984) Perceived competence in soccer skills among young soccer players. *Journal of Sport Psychology, 6,* 385–394.

FRENCH, K. E., & THOMAS, J. R. (1987) The relation of knowledge development to children's basketball performance. *Journal of Sport Psychology, 9,* 15–32.

HARTER, S. (1978) Pleasure derived from optimal challenge and the effects of extrinsic rewards on children's difficulty level choice. *Child Development, 49,* 788–799.

HARTER, S. (1981) A new self-report scale on intrinsic versus extrinsic orientation in the classroom: motivational and informational components. *Developmental Psychology, 17,* 300–312.

HARTER, S. (1999) *The construction of the self: a developmental perspective.* New York: Guilford Press.

HOPPER, C., GUTHRIE, G. D., & KELLY, T. (1991) Self-concept and skill development in youth soccer players. *Perceptual & Motor Skills, 72,* 275–285.

HORN, T. (2004) Developmental perspectives on self-perceptions in children and adolescents. In M. Weiss (Ed.), *Developmental sport and exercise psychology: a lifespan perspective.* Morgantown, WV: Fitness Information Technology, Inc. Pp. 101–143.

LEGEAR, M., GREYLING, L., SLOAN, E., BELL, R. I., WILLIAMS, B., NAYLOR, P., & TEMPLE, V. A. (2012) A window of opportunity? Motor skills and perceptions of competence of children in kindergarten. *International Journal of Behavioral Nutrition and Physical Activity, 9,* 29. DOI: 10.1186/1479-5868-9-29. Available from: http://www.ijbnpa.org/content/9/1/29.

MORAN, K. (2011) *Perceived and real swimming competence among young adults in New Zealand.* Proceedings of the World Drowning Prevention Conference, Da Nang, Vietnam, May 10–13th. http://www.worldconferenceondrowningprevention.org/SiteMedia/ w3svcl092/Uploads/Documents/WCDP2011_Swim&WS_Moran_p202_Presentation.pdf.

PAXTON, R. J., ESTABROOKS, R. A., & DZEWALTOWSKI, D. (2004) Attraction to physical activity mediates the relationship between perceived competence and physical activity in youth. *Research Quarterly for Exercise and Sport, 75,* 107–111.

RAUDSEPP, L., & LIBLIK, R. (2002) Relationship of perceived and actual motor competence in children. *Perceptual & Motor Skills, 94,* 1059–1070.

RUDISILL, M. E., MAHAR, M. T., & MEANEY, K. S. (1993) The relationship between children's perceived and actual motor competence. *Perceptual & Motor Skills, 76,* 895–906.

SAFRIT, M. J., & WOOD, T. M. (1995) *Introduction to measurement in physical education and exercise science.* (3rd ed.) St. Louis, MO: Mosby.

SALLIS, J. F., PROCHASKA, J. J., & TAYLOR, W. C. (2000) A review of correlates of physical activity of children and adolescents. *Medicine & Science in Sports & Exercise, 32,* 963–975.

SOLLERHED, A. C., APITZSCH, E., RA°STAM, L., & EJLERTSSON, G. (2008) Factors associated with young children's self-perceived physical competence and self-report physical activity. *Health Education Research, 23,* 125–136.

ULRICH, B. D. (1987) Perception of physical competence, motor competence, and participation in organized sport: their interrelationships in youth children. *Research Quarterly for Exercise and Sport, 58,* 57–67.

WANG, C. K., LIU, W. C., LOCHBAUM, M. R., & STEVENSON, S. J. (2009) Sport ability beliefs, 2 x 2 achievement goals, and intrinsic motivation: the moderating role of perceived competence in sport and exercise. *Research Quarterly for Exercise and Sport, 80,* 303–312.

WEIGANG, D. A., & BROADHURST, C. J. (1998) The relationship among perceived competence, intrinsic motivation, and control perception in youth soccer. *International Journal of Sport Psychology, 29,* 324–338.

WILLIAMS, G. C., & DECI, E. L. (1996) Internalization of biopsychosocial values by medical students: a test of self-determination theory. *Journal of Personality and Social Psychology, 70,* 767–779.

WILLIAMS, G. C., FREEDMAN, Z. R., & DECI, E. L. (1998) Supporting autonomy to motivate glucose control in patients with diabetes. *Diabetes Care, 21,* 1644–1651.

YOO, J. (1999) Motivational-behavioral correlates of goal orientation and perceived motivational climate in physical education contexts. *Perceptual & Motor Skills, 89,* 262–274.

Key Terms

Action research
Applied research
Basic research
Disciplined inquiry
Educational research
Empirical research
Epistemology
Evaluation research

Experimental research
Nonexperimental research
Research design
    Mixed methods
    Qualitative
    Quantitative
Research paradigm
    Interpretive/constructivist

Positivism
Postpositivism
Pragmatic
Transformative
Scientific
Theory

Discussion Questions

1. What are the strengths and weaknesses of different ways knowledge is accumulated about what works best in education?

2. How to the characteristics of "fox-like" and "hedgehog-like" thinking compare to principles of disciplined inquiry?

3. Why is empirical research more likely to find good signals than other ways of knowing?

4. What kinds of research problems or questions would be most suitable for qualitative rather than quantitative approaches?

5. What are the pros and cons of using different research paradigms as a basis for conducting educational research?

Application Exercise

1. Search a journal in your field of study and find an empirical research article that is of interest to you, then identify the major parts of the article. What is the type of research (quantitative, qualitative, or mixed methods)? What is (are) the research design(s) used in the research?

Check for Understanding Answers

1a. The *observed finding* is what the results look like. These results are influenced by the nature of the true signal but also by noise that impacts the results.

2a. Empirical research, unlike other ways of knowing, is characterized by gathering data and analyzing those data to come up with findings. It relies on a systematic set of "rules" for gathering and analyzing data that enhance the quality and credibility of what is reported.

2b. Take your pick of three: skepticism, control of personal bias, precision, parsimony, *tentative* conclusions, verification, openness to scrutiny, logic.

3a. Postpositivism relies heavily on the scientific method and generalized knowledge, while the interpretive/constructivist paradigm relies on the principles that knowledge is socially constructed and individualized.

3b. The main difference is that transformative studies are designed to gather data that will

promote positive change for marginalized peoples.

4a. Disciplined inquiry is critical because it establishes a set of conventions and standards for judging the quality of empirical studies.

4b. Research guided by fox-like thinking is stronger because it is better able to incorporate the realities of conducting educational research, with application of various sources of noise and different perspectives.

5a. Take your pick: use of numbers, measurement, statistics; use of deductive logic; structured design; detached researcher role; use of variables and hypotheses; postpositivist; seeks generalized knowledge.

5b. Experimental research includes an intervention that is under the direct control of the researcher; nonexperimental research lacks such direct control of an intervention.

Chapter 2
Ethical Issues, Principles, and Practices

by Lisa Abrams and James McMillan

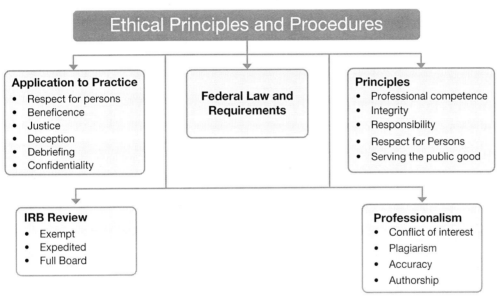

Ethical Principles and Procedures

Application to Practice
- Respect for persons
- Beneficence
- Justice
- Deception
- Debriefing
- Confidentiality

Federal Law and Requirements

Principles
- Professional competence
- Integrity
- Responsibility
- Respect for Persons
- Serving the public good

IRB Review
- Exempt
- Expedited
- Full Board

Professionalism
- Conflict of interest
- Plagiarism
- Accuracy
- Authorship

Source: Reprinted by permission from Lisa M. Abrams.

 Learning Outcomes

2.1 Understand the nature of ethics and how ethics and ethical standards are applied to educational research.

2.2 Describe how the federal government regulates and informs ethical requirements and policies.

2.3 Differentiate between respect for persons, beneficence, and justice as foundational ethical principles.

2.4 Explain why the purpose and procedures for informed consent, parental permission, and child assent are essential elements for conducting human subjects research with children.

2.5 Understand author ethical and legal standards for publishing.

Chapter Road Map

Whether you are a consumer or researcher (or both), ethical principles, researcher responsibilities, and legal requirements constitute increasingly important guidelines for conducting and reporting research. As a consumer, you need to be assured that appropriate professional and regulatory guidelines have been followed. More importantly, perhaps, you will need to use and cite research in a responsible and ethical manner. A researcher, of course, is obligated to conduct and report research in an ethical way, consistent with legal requirements and professional standards. This chapter explains these principles and describes the different ethical frameworks that influence educational research. It discusses how ethical principles get enacted and apply to research, and essential federal requirements that researchers must meet before starting research studies. You will learn what to think about and look for to be sure research is conducted according to the highest ethical and professional standards.

Introduction to Ethics and Ethical Decision Making

Learning Outcome 2.1   Understand the nature of ethics and how ethics and ethical standards are applied to educational research.

Without getting into a quagmire of definitions and philosophies, we need to begin by clarifying just what is meant by "ethics" in the context of educational research. **Ethics** are standards and principles that are used to guide conduct, to determine what is right or wrong, a virtue or vice, good or evil, often related to values and morals. The word *ethic* comes from the Greek word *ethos*, which refers to character or guiding beliefs. Current use of "ethics" refers to rules of behavior and questions of value or judgments that can be identified as good or bad, right or wrong.

Ethics as Applied to Educational Research

When applied to educational research, ethics inform our decision making about the conduct, reporting, and use of research findings. The main idea is that investigators and users of research will understand how ethical principles guide research design, and how ethical practices must be used to guide high-quality study implementation and valid interpretations of study findings. Research must be conducted in ways that are fair and beneficial to the participant groups and the study population of interest. This includes protecting study participants from harm and ensuring that that any benefits resulting from the study outweigh any potential risks associated with participation. In this sense, educational research ethics have a utilitarian bent, in which the potential benefits to participants, society, and the researcher are weighed against the risks associated with the procedures for conducting the research. An assessment of risk in educational research includes considering the potential harm, such as a breach in or a lack of confidentiality, for example if a study participant and their personal information become known to others, as well as considering the implications of the power and social dynamics that exist within classrooms and schools for data collection and recruitment.

Ethical considerations in educational research influence investigators' decisions about study design, recruitment, data collection strategies, and implementation, for which there are rarely absolute right or wrong answers. The following questions are just a few examples of the types of issues you might think about as you are reading published research or planning to conduct a study of your own.

- Is it right to randomly assign children to receive an educational intervention to improve reading, or should the resources be used for the lowest-performing students?
- Is it fair to intentionally deceive students so they do not catch on to the purpose of the research and, as a result, bias the study results?
- Should teachers be required to complete daily journal or log entries during school hours as part of a study of the type of feedback they give their students throughout the day?
- Should adolescents have an opportunity to decide whether they want to participate in a study even though their parents may have already given permission?
- Should student test scores of individual teachers be reported in presentations, papers, or reports?

To answer these types of questions, it is helpful to refer to a set of generally accepted professional ethical standards or codes of ethics. Such principles have been developed by many professions, including medicine and psychology, as well as education. These principles represent the broadest perspectives about what standards or guidelines should be considered in decision making. The principles are not intended to determine behavior in specific situations, but hopefully communicate a broad message about the fundamental considerations for all research. They are ideals, aspirational in nature.

Fundamental Ethical Principles for Professional Practice

As detailed in Table 2.1, there are six essential ethical principles for any type of research involving human participants. The principles are intended to provide guidelines that serve as the foundation for sound decision making, choices, and behavior of producers of educational research. At the heart of these principles is the notion of *integrity* and *respect* for your own work, the work of others, and for individuals who contribute to your research. *Professional competence* means that both producers and consumers of research are aware of their own professional knowledge and experiences, recognize the limitations in what they know and understand, and seek help and the expertise of others when needed, to ensure accurate information and higher-quality studies. Researchers can also expand their expertise and enhance their professional competence through professional development activities. For example, you may be in the process of building your professional competence and enhancing your understanding of and skills for interpreting published research studies by taking a graduate course in educational research. Even reading this chapter qualifies as professional development!

Integrity is concerned with issues of fairness and honesty, and requires trustworthy conduct. *Responsibility* communicates the importance of being accountable for one's work and ensuring that professional, scholarly, and research activities adhere to high standards of conduct. Similar to integrity, *justice* is also concerned with issues of fairness and sensitivity to research participants. The principle of justice demands that the results of research are reported in ways that are sensitive to different characteristics of the study participants or the populations that the results reflect. When study

Table 2.1 Ethical Principles for Educational Research

Principle	Definition	Examples
Professional Competence	Researchers understand work within their areas of competence and consult with others when needed.	• It would be unethical for a manuscript reviewer to make judgmental comments about a statistical procedure with which he or she was not familiar. • Ethical consumers do not judge research methods they do not understand.
Integrity	Researchers are honest and trustworthy, and promote accuracy. They do not cheat, steal, deceive, or misrepresent.	• A researcher who reported only the most positive findings would be unethical. • Ethical researchers do not over-generalize by simply saying "Research says . . ."
Responsibility	Researchers accept responsibility for their work. They are sensitive to the ethical behavior of colleagues.	• A researcher admits publicly that he or she made a mistake in reporting findings. • A reporter apologizes for attributing ideas or points to the wrong person.
Justice	Researchers are sensitive to the welfare of all individuals, take into account all perspectives in making decisions, and do not allow biases to result in unjust actions.	• A researcher is unethical if they fail to be sensitive to minorities in the language used to report results. • Users of research findings can use conclusions in an unjust manner, for example, when they are unaware of the impact of the results on overweight students.
Respect for People's Rights and Dignity	Researchers must respect the rights and dignity of all research participants and be sensitive to cultural, individual, sexual, ethnic, and role differences. All participants are held in high regard.	• An ethical researcher is able to word questions on a survey so that students with all gender identifications are not alienated. • It would be unethical for a reporter to show only poor results for Hispanic students and ignore poor results for other groups.
Serving the Public Good	Researchers are focused on what is good for the larger society and design and report research that results in the greatest public good.	• An unethical researcher should not be hired to conduct an "unbiased" study on charter schools by the Charter School Advancement Council. • It would be unethical to choose research to report results that support a single political view, ignoring other research.

results are reported by subgroups such as race/ethnicity, social economic status, or geographic region, the principle of justice requires that researchers consider how the reporting of results may affect these different populations in positive as well as harmful ways. Similarly, the principles of *respect for people's rights and dignity* and *serving the public good* are concerned with eliminating bias, being sensitive to differences among the populations studied, adhering to legal guidelines for the protection of study participants, and recognizing their social responsibility to contribute to the public good through professional and research activities.

These six fundamental principles serve as the foundation for commonly held standards for many professional organizations, including the American Educational Research Association (AERA), a national research organization that promotes research and inquiry to improve education. (This organization, founded in 1916, has more than 25,000 members, including university faculty members, educational researchers, graduate students, school administrators, instructional specialists, and classroom teachers [go to aera.net for more information]. You might want to think about joining!) The AERA Code of Ethics (AERA, 2011) is broadly applied and relevant to the professional work of all of its members. In 2014, AERA also endorsed the Singapore Statement on Research Integrity (singaporestatement.org), which offers guidance on the responsible conduct of research focused on honesty, accountability, professional courtesy and fairness, and good stewardship on behalf of others. Other education-related national organizations with ethical professional codes include the American Psychological Association (APA) and the American Evaluation Association (AEA).

A key ethical principle in all professional guidelines is *respect for persons*, and how study participants are treated throughout the research process. There are some good reasons for this. First, this principle has been violated in the past, with detrimental effects on participants. Second, in the United States, federal laws govern how research with human "subjects" must be conducted. These laws were developed to ensure that individuals who participate in research studies are protected from harm. A look at some of the historical events that led to the creation of current federal regulations for the protection of human subjects, and how these regulations are enforced and influence the practice of conducting research, is helpful in understanding the current standards governing research efforts.

Check for Understanding 1

1a. What aspects of conducting and reporting research need to be based on ethical principles?

1b. What are four of the six fundamental ethical principles for conducting and reporting educational research?

Federal Law and Legal Requirements for Conducting Ethical Research

Learning Outcome 2.2   Describe how the federal government regulates and informs ethical requirements and policies.

Most ethical standards for conducting research center on how researchers interact with and treat participants throughout the study, including before and after a study is completed. Ethical principles and standards are relevant to *all aspects* of how research is conducted, beginning with the nature of the research topic. For example, will the topic raise sensitive issues or address issues that parents may not want discussed with their child? Additional questions relate to the study procedures, and whether these procedures will in any significant way result in potential risks, including physical, psychological, or professional risks:

How are participants recruited and selected?
How are participants' privacy and confidentiality protected?
How do study participants experience interventions?
Will data collection and analysis procedures affect the well-being of the participants?

As we will see, formal ethical review procedures are in place at universities and other organizations, such as school districts, to ensure that research conducted by those affiliated with these institutions adheres to federal ethical guidelines.

A Brief History of Federal Ethics Codes

RESEARCH WITHOUT REGULATION   Research with human subjects (i.e., participants—ethical standards still use the term *subjects*) has had a troubled history. One of the most egregious examples of unethical research was the Tuskegee Study of Untreated Syphilis in the Negro Male, conducted by the U.S. Public Health Service over a 40-year period (1932–1972). This research was conducted to document and record the naturally occurring history of syphilis to investigate differences in the presentation of the disease and to develop treatment programs. (At the start of the study, there were no known effective treatments for the disease.) The researchers enrolled 600 men—399 with syphilis and 201 who did not have the disease—most of whom were illiterate and poor sharecroppers. All the men were told they were going to be treated for "bad blood," a common term at the time that was used to describe a variety of ailments, including syphilis, general fatigue, and anemia—but they weren't. By participating, the men received free medical exams, transportation to and from the clinics, free meals, medical treatment for minor complaints, and burial insurance. In 1972, the Associated Press (AP) broke a story condemning the Tuskegee Study. The news story described how the 40-year study left syphilis untreated among the study participants, even though penicillin was widely accepted as the preferred treatment for the disease as early as 1945. The withholding of penicillin from the study participants resulted in numerous unnecessary deaths and the needless infection of countless numbers of wives and other individuals. The uproar resulting from the AP story set into motion several actions that led to federal legislation that codified ethical principles and practice for research that involves human subjects (refer to Figure 2.1).

Figure 2.1 Timeline of Main Events Leading to the Creation of the Federal Ethical Guidelines for Research[1]

1932	1945	1964	1972	1974	1979
• Tuskegee Study starts • 600 Men enrolled	• Penicillin accepted as recommended treatment for syphilis	• World Medical Association develops a code of research ethics — *Declaration of Helsinki*	• July: AP story breaks about Tuskegee Study and withholding of treatment • October: Tuskegee Study ends	• Research Act passed • Creation of the National Commission for the Protection of Human Subjects of Biomedical and Behavioral Research	• The National Commission issues the *Belmont Report*

[1]This timeline highlights the key events that led up to the creation of federal ethical codes and guidelines. A more detailed timeline of events surrounding the 40-year implementation of the Tuskegee Study, medical developments, and research priorities that kept the study going can be found on the Centers for Disease Control and Prevention website, navigate to "The Tuskegee Timeline."

EMERGENCE OF FEDERAL RESEARCH REGULATIONS Public outcry about the Tuskegee Study demonstrated the need to change research practices so mistakes made in the study would not be repeated. There was a compelling need for ethical rules and regulations for the conduct of research involving humans. The National Research Act was passed in 1974. It established the National Commission for the Protection of Human Subjects of Biomedical and Behavioral Research, which was responsible for creating a code of ethics for research involving human subjects conducted in the United States. In 1979, the National Commission published a report, "Ethical Principles and Guidelines for the Protection of Human Subjects of Research," commonly known as the Belmont Report or the Belmont principles. These principles are the foundation for current ethical laws—the Code of Federal Regulations (CFR) Title 45, Part 46: Protection of Human Subjects. The ethical guidelines and requirements in the federal code apply to both social–behavioral research—which educational research is most often considered—and biomedical research. In 1991, Subpart A, the section of these regulations on the protection of human research subjects, was adopted by 15 federal agencies and became known as "the Common Rule." It is now the primary doctrine governing all research with human subjects. The Protection of Human Subjects code of federal legislation was most recently updated in 2018 and was adopted by 20 federal agencies. The 2018 revision to the Common Rule was designed to modernize and simplify current oversight systems while strengthening protections for individuals who volunteer to participate in research. The revised Common Rule brought about several changes to administrative oversight for those who conduct low-risk educational research.

Check for Understanding 2

2a. Why has the federal government established legal guidelines for the ethical conduct and reporting of research?

Application of Ethical Principles to Research Practice

Learning Outcome 2.3   Differentiate between respect for persons, beneficence, and justice as foundational ethical principles.

The Belmont Report identified three core principles that should govern all research and researcher–participant interactions: *respect for persons, beneficence*, and *justice*. These principles are ethical values that, when carried out or reflected in actions, are often considered the practice of "doing ethics." Table 2.2 summarizes how these three principles are applied to actual research studies. We examine each of them in some detail.

Respect for Persons

The *respect for persons* principle reflects the idea that individuals are autonomous and are entitled to make their own independent decisions about their actions. A key component of respect for persons is in the "voluntariness" of research. That is, participants should be free to decide for themselves whether they want to participate in a study and whether they want to end or discontinue their participation for any reason. We see respect for persons most clearly recognized in how we communicate information about the study either through an information sheet or through the **informed consent** process. The informed consent process usually takes the form of a written consent document that the researcher discusses with each potential study participant prior to their

Table 2.2 Belmont Principles and Applications for Research

Principle	Principle in Practice
Respect for Persons	Participants are provided with all information about the study to make an informed decision through the informed consent and/or child assent process; voluntary participation and withdrawal are supported.
Beneficence	Benefits of participation outweigh any potential risks; benefits are maximized and risks are minimized; researchers are obligated to ensure and protect the well-being of study participants.
Justice	Benefits and burden of the research are equitably distributed; participants are selected fairly; the group intended to benefit from the research should be similar to the group participating in the research.

involvement in the research. The document and consent discussion should include the following essential characteristics:

- Disclose to potential research participants all of the information needed to make an educated decision about participation.
- Ensure that the potential participants understand the information that describes the study and what participation will involve.
- Support the voluntary nature of the decision to participate.

An informed consent document is important for both the researcher and participant because it is essentially a contract designed to protect the participants. It also requires the researcher to describe the study in ways that are clear, easily understandable, and transparent. The federal Office of Human Research Protections (OHRP) provides a valuable informed consent checklist for being sure that everything that is required is included. The checklist for a social–behavioral study in Figure 2.2 includes all the required elements of informed consent. The checklist shows the information that should appear in consent documents and should be explained to potential research participants.

Figure 2.2 Informed Consent Checklist

✓ A concise overview of the purpose of the research study written in lay language
✓ A statement that the study involves research
✓ The expected duration of participation, procedures to be followed, and identification of any procedures that are experimental
✓ The approximate number of participants involved in the study
✓ A disclosure of appropriate alternative procedures, if any, that might be beneficial for the participant
✓ A description of any reasonably foreseeable risks or discomforts to the subject
✓ A description of any benefits to the participant or to others that may reasonably be expected from the research
✓ A disclosure of appropriate alternative procedures, if any, that might be beneficial for the participant
✓ A description of how the confidentiality of data and identifying information will be protected and any circumstances under which confidentiality may not be maintained (e.g., participant describes wanting to hurt self or others)
✓ Information about whom to contact for answers to questions about the research and research subjects' rights, and whom to contact in the event of a research-related injury
✓ A statement that participation is voluntary, refusal to participate will involve no consequences, and the subject may choose to discontinue their participation at any time without consequences.

As mentioned previously, the 2018 revisions to the common rule included changes to reduce administrative oversight for research considered low risk. Much of educational research involving the administration of tests or survey, or collecting data through interviews or focus groups where adults, such as teachers, administrators, and parents, are participants, would be considered low risk under the new common rule (most likely). In this situation it would be appropriate to use an information sheet, rather than an informed consent form. An **information sheet** avoids having a lengthy consent document and need to obtain a signature from participants while still including all of the information needed to make an informed decision about participating in a research study.

Figures 2.3 and 2.4 show examples of how the principle of consent was enacted as part of a recent study on student perceptions of science assessments. This study, conducted by a research team directed by one of the chapter authors, was designed to develop a self-report survey that could be answered by middle and high school students to gauge their reactions to the nature of a test they had taken. Before we could begin conducting our research, we needed to obtain permission, or consent, from parents to allow their child to be involved in the research and then obtain agreement or permission directly from each child/student to participate in the study in order to adhere to the ethical guidelines.

The 2018 Common Rule ensures consistent protections for children. Educational research often involves children (typically defined as individuals under 18 years of age). In investigations with children, researchers usually must obtain permission from parents or legal guardians for children to participate in a study. Obtaining parental permission, or consent, is very similar to the informed consent process. The same information is described and required, although permission, not consent, is sought. What does the parental permission process mean for respecting the autonomy of children? For example, adolescents or teenagers make important decisions about their well-being during the school day; after school; on social outings with friends; and as members of organizations, clubs, and sports teams. Would obtaining parental permission to study these areas respect the autonomy of the adolescents?

Figure 2.3 shows a parent consent form for the study on student perceptions toward classroom science assessments. Note that in this case the parents "opt out" their child, rather than give signed consent for their child to participate. You can see that parents only sign and return the form if they want to exclude their child from the study. This procedure is often used in low-risk research and works well with common school practices for obtaining parent signatures. Note that the opt-out procedure is still based on the idea of informed consent, but the signature or signed documentation of consent is waived.

Figure 2.3 Example of Parental Consent Form

PARENT CONSENT FORM

Dear Parents and Guardians,

Your child's school has been chosen to participate in a research study entitled, "Development and Validations of the Perceptions of Science Classroom Assessment Student Self-Report Survey." This study is being conducted as part of a collaborative partnership between Virginia Commonwealth University and Virginia County Public Schools.

The purpose of the study is to develop a student self-report survey that can be used to examine secondary school students' perceptions of tests and other classroom assessments they take in science classes.

Before we begin this study, your child's teacher will ask whether they are willing to participate. Students who agree to participate will participate in an interview [completing a short survey] about their attitudes toward science tests and other assessments. The interview [completing the survey] will be conducted with other students and last approximately 20–30 minutes. Information gathered from this study will be used to improve science assessment in the school division and research showing how perceptions of assessment are related to educational outcomes.

If you have questions or would like more information, you may call Dr. James McMillan at (804) 827-1332, or, e-mail him at jhmcmill@vcu.edu. If you have questions or concerns about your student's rights as a research participant, you may contact the VCU Institutional Review Board at (804) 827-2157.

Your child's participation in this study is voluntary. Participation in this study will have no effect on your child's grade in any subject area or his or her relationship with any teachers, the school, or Virginia Commonwealth University. No teachers or others in the school will know about individual student responses.

ONLY sign and return the form below with your child to give to their teacher (within 1 week of receipt of this letter) if you DO NOT want your child to participate in this study.

Sincerely,
James H. McMillan, Ph.D.
Lead Researcher

I do NOT want my child to participate in the Student Perceptions of Assessment study.
Name of Child (please print)

Name of Parent or Guardian (please print)
Signature of Parent or Guardian ——————— Date ———————

Should children be able to make an independent decision about participating in a research study? The answer to this question is clearly *yes*. The National Commission recommends that child consent, known as **child assent**, should be required at the age of 7 and older. However, federal regulations in the United States do not include specific requirements for informed assent similar to the requirements listed in Figure 2.2. It is generally recognized that researchers should inform children aged 7 and older of the research activities and provide an opportunity for assent to their participation in the study. Language that appears in the parental permission or consent form is modified for children so that it can be easily understood. A good approach is to use guiding questions, in which researchers would provide responses to the following types of questions:

What is this study about?
What will happen to me if I choose to be in the study?
Will you tell anyone what I say?
Do I have to be in this study?

Here, in Figure 2.4, is the child assent form used for the study on student perceptions toward science assessments. The assent document includes simple and clear language that is used to communicate the purpose of the study, the description of each student's involvement in the research and other essential ethical information.

Figure 2.4 Example of Child Assent Form

STUDENT ASSENT FORM

STUDY TITLE: Development and Validation of the Perceptions of Science Classroom Assessment Student Self-Report Survey

RESEARCHER'S NAME: James McMillan, Virginia Commonwealth University

Why are we meeting with you?

I am asking you take part in a research study. A research study is a way to learn more about something. You are being asked to join this research study because your opinions are important. After we tell you about it, we will ask whether you'd like to be in this study or not.

This form may have some words that you do not know. Please ask me to explain any words that you do not know. You may take this form home to think about and talk to your parents about before you decide whether you want to be in this study.

What is this study about?

This study is being done to develop a student self-report survey of attitudes toward science assessments (e.g., tests and projects) that you take in the classroom.

What will happen to me if I choose to be in this study?

If you agree to be in the study, you will be asked a number of questions about your recent science test. It will take no longer than 10 minutes to answer the questions.

Will you tell anyone what I say?

We will not tell anyone the answers you give us. We will not share your answers with your teachers, parents, or friends.

Do I have to be in this study?

You do not have to be in this study. It is up to you. You can say okay now and change your mind later. No one will blame you or get upset at you if you don't want to do this. All you have to do is stop.

Do you have any questions?

You can ask questions at any time. You can ask now or later. Just tell the researcher when you meet with them. Before you say **yes or no** to being in this study, we will answer any questions you have now. You may also contact the director of the research, Dr. James McMillan, if you have questions or would like more information, at (804) 827-2620, or, e-mail at jhmcmill@vcu.edu.

If you agree to participate in this study, please sign and return the following:
YOUTH ASSENT

_____   _____
Youth Participant's Name (Printed)   Date

_____
Youth Participant's Signature

_____
Name of Person Conducting Assent Discussion (Printed)

_____   _____
Signature of Person Conducting Assent Discussion   Date

_____   _____
Principal Investigator Signature (if different from above)   Date

The goal with this form is that each student would be sufficiently informed about key aspects of the study to make a decision about whether or not to cooperate. As you can see, the form describes the purpose of the study, the choice students make to participate, and what happens to their responses. An important point for students is that their answers will be anonymous. This not only helps to protect their identity but also encourages honest responses. In this way, adhering to ethical guidelines improves the study design and quality. Information sheets used for adult research participants would provide more detail than what you find in Figure 2.4.

The bottom line is that children need to understand the proposed research procedures and that they may discontinue their participation at any time, without any penalty. The researcher needs to communicate this in concrete language that is appropriate to the child's age and other considerations that may affect the child's comprehension of what they are assenting or agreeing to. The child needs to be allowed to ask questions and not feel undue pressure to participate. Including both parental permission and child assent ensures that researchers recognize the legal rights of the parents, as well as the autonomy of children, when it comes to making informed choices about participation in a research study.

In their research on literacy, Rogers, Labadie, and Pole (2016) describe how they balanced their commitment to ensuring ethical treatment and protection of their child participants with their participatory research design that encouraged authentic expression and voice. When research is focused on addressing or examining problems of educational practice or instruction, working in classrooms and schools is required. Oftentimes, the lines between instruction and research activities can become blurred, which adds to the complexity of school-based research activity with young children. These challenges were experienced by Rogers et al. as they conducted research to examine how "kindergarten students connect and respond to literature and read aloud focused on the theme of social class" (p. 37). To address their research question, the investigators used an action research model in one of the authors' classroom. They collected a variety of data, including "observations of read-aloud lessons with notes, video recordings and transcripts, photographs, teacher notes and reflections, 15 picture books focused on social class, privilege and poverty, student drawing and writing, and a class-constructed learning wall with artifacts representing their understanding of each of the books" (p. 38).

As the researchers analyzed the data, they explored how they could best ensure the confidentiality of the students while also presenting rich and detailed descriptions that were authentic to the children's voices and perspectives. To address this ethical concern, they created pseudonyms that reflected students' culture heritage as a way to balance authenticity of voice with the need to protect students identify and ensure confidentiality. Throughout their study Rogers et al. detailed how they made assent an ongoing process, paid attention to how students may be sharing nonverbal messages about their interest in participation, and used specific events such as setting up video cameras and additional researchers in the classroom as signals that research activities were occurring. Their work also demonstrates the complexity of doing research in schools with young children in ways that address instructional practices while simultaneously ensuring the protection of the young participants.

Beneficence

According to the principle of **beneficence**, researchers are obligated to protect study participants from harm and to act in ways that are in the best interest of the participants' welfare. Two key guidelines or rules illustrate the principle of beneficence: (1) *do not harm* and (2) *maximize the possible benefits and minimize the possible harms.* Research studies on educational issues, policies, and practices are often considered studies that involve "minimal risk," in which participants are not putting themselves at greater risk than they would ordinarily experience in the course of a typical day. That is, the possible "harms" tend to be minimal because interventions or data gathering are often nonintrusive study procedures that involve existing tests or noninvasive surveys, and results are typically reported in aggregate or summary form without any attribution to individuals.

The most common risk in educational research is some form of psychological stress. This may occur if the research topic is sensitive, or in situations in which there is accidental disclosure of private information or a breach in confidentiality. The public disclosure of an individual's participation in a study and the identification of private information could cause personal embarrassment and reputational harm.

DO NOT HARM   Perhaps you are familiar with the well-documented 1960s studies on obedience by Stanley Milgram. If you are, you are not likely to forget how the research was conducted. In a series of experiments, Milgram used what are now clearly recognized as unethical procedures to see how willing participants ("teachers") applied electrical shocks to "learners" (confederates, who volunteered to *appear* to be shocked), as encouraged by an authority figure.

The purpose of the study was to explore why average, everyday individuals may act in terrible ways that physically harm others just because the authority figure said it was all right. In the Milgram study, when the learners failed to answer a question correctly, the teachers were to administer shocks and were encouraged to do so by the lab assistant. The teacher participants were to continue to deliver greater amounts of shock treatments for wrong answers, despite protests from the learners. The teachers could only hear and not see the learners and believed that the learners were experiencing pain and suffering as a result of the continued and increasing severity of the shocks. The results showed that many of the teachers were willing to obey, believing that it was in the best interests of the learners to be given increasingly painful shocks of electricity. Although the findings "shocked" many, an important positive outcome was much greater sensitivity to the psychological damage studies can have on participants. In this case, there was evidence that some participants in Milgram's study did suffer psychological harm by tending to be less trusting in the future after they were told about what was actually being studied. It was one of several studies that led to the essential ethical principle that it is of utmost importance to *inflict no harm* and *minimize risks of harm* on participants.

When we consider the issue of "do not harm" in educational research and in classrooms, researchers need to think about the sensitivity of the research topic. Powell et al. (2018) found, not surprisingly, that parents, researchers, educators, and children (aged 7–14) had different views about what were sensitive topics for research involving children. Children reported that issues specific to health problems, individual's background, friendships and relationships, problems, and secrets were sensitive issues compared to the adult groups. These findings reinforce the importance of considering research involving children, from the child's perspective and not assuming that adults and children share similar views on the sensitivity of research in order to adhere to the "do not harm" principle.

In summary, it is unethical to ever put participants through an experience that could result in physical, psychological, or mental discomfort, harm, or injury. Even though it is unusual for educational studies to have a significant risk of harm, certain circumstances may reasonably be questioned and need to be approved by reviewers (review is discussed further in a later section). For instance, asking participants about deviant behavior that could make them feel uncomfortable or may stimulate further considerations and thinking (e.g., "Have you ever cheated on an exam?"), may need a review before implementation. Then, of course, there are direct interventions, or sometimes lack of intervention, that could be considered unethical due to the potential for harm. For example, would putting a student into a weight reduction program negatively affect self-esteem? Would it be ethical for a researcher to randomly select some students to receive a "failing" grade on a test to see their reaction to the low grade? Again, review is needed.

Another notable characteristic of Milgram's study was the use of **deception** to accomplish the research goals. As we learned from the discussion about respect for persons and informed consent, full disclosure is required to allow participants to make an informed decision about participation. Sometimes, though, if participants know the purpose, it makes the outcomes suspect. If Milgram's participants knew that the study was about obedience, they surely would not have given the shocks. In some research, then, the only way to provide credible results is to essentially deceive the participants about the purpose. Deception, though strongly discouraged, is sometimes the only way to conduct valid research, even in some educational studies. For example, if an observational study is investigating whether teachers' use of specific kinds of formative feedback affects student motivation, students' knowledge of why the observer was present could influence their behavior. They might fake their behavior to make the teacher look good.

If deception is used, it is necessary to *debrief* participants. **Debriefing** is a process of fully informing the participants about the actual nature of the study and why deception was necessary, and allows them to ask questions and discuss any concerns. Debriefing should occur immediately following data collection or the participant's completion of the study requirements. It is an essential component to minimize any potential negative consequences or harm that may have resulted from participation.

MINIMIZING RISK AND MAXIMIZING BENEFIT The risks associated with social–behavioral and educational research are different from those of biomedical research, though biomedical research is conducted in educational settings. Biomedical research could involve the study of a new drug treatment, assessment of the effectiveness of a new medical device such as those used to deliver insulin, or an intervention in which a participant is exposed to common cold germs or deprived of sleep. Think of the sleep and cold studies that are common on many college campuses. These examples suggest some physical risk or potential for injury associated with study participation. In contrast, educational research, by nature, rarely involves physical risk. As noted earlier, the types of risk most common in educational research are psychological, social, and reputational. Thus, researchers must weigh the potential risks involved with the study against the potential benefits of the knowledge gained. For research to be ethical, the benefits must be greater than any potential risk involved with participation. This can be called the *risk/benefit ratio* way of thinking, in which the risks are weighed against benefits. As illustrated in Figure 2.5, when risks outweigh benefits there is a poor ratio and you probably shouldn't be doing the study, whereas when benefits "weigh" more than risks, the ratio is good.

One way to support a positive risk/benefit ratio is to use **confidentiality**. To ensure the validity of research findings, participants need to be free to communicate their views, perceptions, or thoughts accurately and honestly. However, a breach in confidentiality or accidental disclosure of a participant's name or personally identifiable study information (e.g., responses on a survey or test scores) could have a detrimental impact on students' self-perceptions, schools' professional personnel, or community standing. Think about teachers who participate in a survey about the soundness of a controversial school policy. How would they likely feel, when the results were disseminated, if their answers were known by name to the school principal? They may be concerned about negative implications or ramifications as a result of their participation. For example, they may be concerned that their responses might affect their yearly professional evaluations.

Figure 2.5 Risk/Benefit Ratio Examples

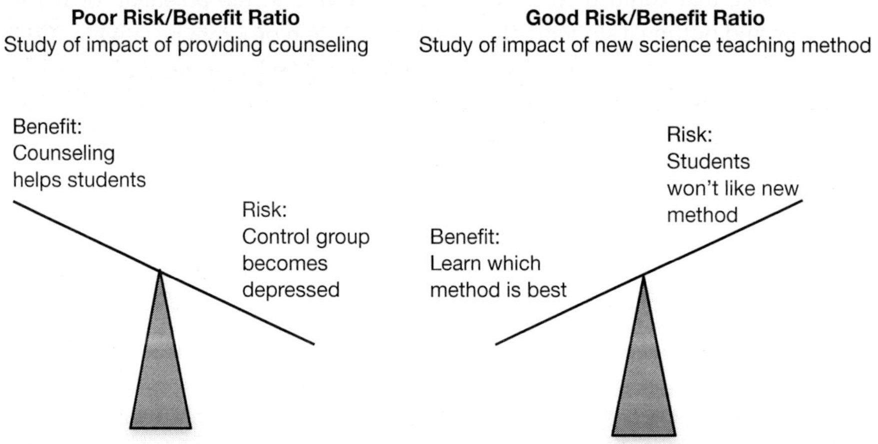

Poor Risk/Benefit Ratio	**Good Risk/Benefit Ratio**
Study of impact of providing counseling	Study of impact of new science teaching method

Benefit:
Counseling
helps students

Risk:
Control group
becomes
depressed

Risk:
Students
won't like new
method

Benefit:
Learn which
method is best

Protecting the confidentiality of participation and the privacy of personal information is essential to minimizing risk. In addition to providing assurances of confidentiality, researchers need to carefully consider how data are collected, stored, analyzed, and reported. One common way to do this is to assign each study participant an ID code so the researchers do not have to use participant's names on data collection forms or in databases. For example, participants can record something like the second number of their street address, third letter of their mother's maiden name, and fourth digit of their phone number. This allows you to match pretest with posttest scores. In qualitative research, researchers use pseudonyms, or fake names, to describe participants and research settings or sites (e.g., names of schools, school districts).

If a study is conducted in a way such that no names or identifiable information at all are collected, the data will be **anonymous**. Whether confidential or anonymous, the level of detail in reporting study findings should be sufficiently general or in summary form to protect the confidentiality of the participants and locations, to avoid possible identification in the future.

You might be wondering, what with our electronic databases, social media platforms, and well-documented snooping capabilities: How private is confidential information? Many do not believe that electronic surveys are *really* anonymous. A study at Harvard University proves this point. The university's Data Privacy Lab found that 87% of Americans can be identified using only three pieces of information: five-digit ZIP Code, gender, and birthday (Sweeney, 2000). Because participants may have privacy concerns, it is important to do everything possible to assure them that their privacy is protected. Depending on the software programs used, the topic, and the nature of participants, traditional paper surveys may provide a better assurance of privacy than electronic surveys.

In addition to developing procedures to maintain confidentiality, data security is an important privacy issue. This includes developing systems to properly store and secure electronic data and study documents. Using encryption software and password protections, locking down computers in research labs, avoiding storing data on laptops that can easily be stolen, and locking file cabinets and office doors are just a few ways to enhance data security and mitigate any potential breaches of confidentiality. Many colleges and universities have data safety and security standards to ensure that affiliated faculty and researchers are up to date on the best practice for securing their electronic data and records.

Author Reflection *Providing safeguards to assure no harm is no easy task. Sometimes it even seems so burdensome that there is question about whether it is worth the trouble to do the research. But, actually, that is the point—it needs to be worth the trouble! Research needs to be important and well designed, and the welfare of the participants is paramount.*

Justice

The final essential ethical principle is **justice**, which is really about fairness. The following question was posed in the Belmont Report: "Who ought to receive the benefits of research and bear its burdens?" The justice principle requires that the benefits and burdens of research are equitably distributed. This means that in research intended to benefit a specific segment of the population, study participants should be obtained from this same group. This principle guards against using samples of convenience, such as institutionalized or incarcerated individuals, for research that is not of direct benefit to them. An appalling example of disregarding justice was a study conducted on mentally disabled boys institutionalized at the State Residential School in Massachusetts, where the boys were intentionally fed radioactive iron and calcium in breakfast cereal to study adult nutrition and metabolism. In essence, there was no compelling reason to study children when the benefits were for adults. In this instance, children bore the brunt of the research, but were not the group intended to benefit from the study findings.

Figures 2.6 and 2.7 illustrate scenarios that show ethical concerns in conducting educational research. You will see that in each case studies are proposed, with accompanying ethical concerns related to the three key principles that have been discussed: respect for persons, beneficence, and justice.

Figure 2.6 Study Scenario A

- Educational researchers want to examine why beginning teachers decide to transfer to other schools, school districts, and out of teaching entirely. The researchers plan to administer a survey to all of the teachers in a school district. The survey includes questions about school climate, general job satisfaction, workload/expectations, and views on administrative policies and implementation.
- In addition, demographic information and employee ID numbers will be collected so that the researchers can track teachers who leave their present teaching position.
- Each school principal will distribute and administer the survey at a faculty meeting. The results will be reported to the school district and to the administrators at individual schools.

Scenario A: Ethical Concerns

Principle	Ethical Concerns
Respect for Persons	**Lack of informed consent process:** There are no plans to provide information about the study or informed consent. **Potential for non-voluntary participation:** Teachers may feel obligated, compelled, or even coerced to participate in the study because it is being distributed by their principal and completed in an open faculty meeting, and results are being shared with school principals.
Beneficence	**Lack of privacy:** Clear risks to participation are evident about participation decisions, as teachers who chose not to participate would be clearly evident during the data collection. **Risk associated breach of confidentiality:** As employee ID numbers are being collected in order to track teachers, any breach of confidentiality could identify teacher participants and have implications for current and future employment. The level of reporting also can potentially identify teacher participants.
Justice	**Benefits and burden of the research are not equitably distributed:** All teachers are being surveyed when the focus is on beginning teachers.

Figure 2.7 Study Scenario B

- A research team including educational researchers and physicians wants to understand how environmental factors may impact students' academic achievement in the middle and high school grades.
- The researchers arrange to conduct several fitness tests and obtain physiological measurements. They also plan to conduct group interviews with students, asking about home life, substance and physical abuse, levels of physical activity, and general diet.
- The school will provide the researchers with student transcript information and attendance records.
- The researchers propose using a parental opt-out procedure to notify parents about the study. Classroom teachers are asked to respond to any parent questions about the study and make arrangements for the researchers to conduct the group interviews.

Scenario B: Ethical Concerns

Principle	Principle in Practice
Respect for Persons	**Lack of parental consent process:** The plans for informing parents about the study and obtaining their permission for their child's participation are insufficient given the potentially sensitive nature of the research (e.g., home life, substance and physical abuse) and the release of federally protected student record information, including grades, transcript information, and attendance records. **Lack of child assent process:** No provisions for child assent are described and should be included given the age range of the potential child participants. **Role of classroom teachers:** Classroom teachers are not best positioned to answer questions about the research since they are not responsible for the implementation of the research study. Questions about the research study should be addressed by the research team directly.
Beneficence	**Benefits of participation do not outweigh the potential risks:** There are clear risks to participation given the sensitive nature of some of the topics under investigation. There is no mention of how research data will be protected and secured in order to maintain participant confidentiality.
Justice	It is **unclear whether the benefits and burden of the research are equitably distributed.** There is not a clear justification for the focus on the wide range of topics under investigation given the main goal of the research to examine the influence of environmental factors on students' academic achievement. For example, the collection of physical fitness tests and physiological measurements do not seem relevant and increase the burden on research participants.

The Hedgehog and the Fox Consider Whether or Not to Conduct a Study About a New Approach to Teaching Civics

I'm sure this is such a great new program that parents won't mind if their child is part of this experiment; besides, they will see the grades.

I have to make sure that I give students a choice of whether or not to get this new program and get parental permission. I also need to be sure there are no risks to students, especially since their work will be graded.

Check for Understanding 3

3a. What are the main differences between respect for persons, beneficence, and justice?

3b. Why is the risk/benefit ratio an important consideration in determining whether a study should be conducted?

Ensuring Ethical Research: The Role of Institutional Review Boards

Learning Outcome 2.4   Explain why different institutional review board procedures are essential elements for conducting human subjects research with children.

Even though few educational studies have severe potential negative consequences for the participants, much educational research has some level of small, or what is termed "minimal," risk. It is important to be sure that even in these circumstances the research is ethical. Minimal risk studies are generally ethical, but every study is unique and needs to be reviewed, just to be sure. Colleges, universities, hospitals, and other organizations where research is conducted are required to establish **institutional review boards (IRBs)**. These boards or committees are charged with the responsibility of protecting the rights and welfare of human subjects, and in doing so ensure that affiliated personnel who conduct research and the studies associated with the institution are compliant with the federal ethical regulations.

By design, IRBs are comprised of a diverse group of individuals, including scientists, non-scientists, and community members, representing different areas of expertise intended to reflect a broad range of perspectives. IRB committees review research before it begins to ensure that the study procedures, recruitment materials, informed consent, and assent documents meet the federal ethical requirements and reflect the principles of respect for persons, beneficence, and justice. As part of the review process, the IRB committee members weigh the benefits and risks involved in a study to determine whether the study should be approved and/or whether changes are required to further mitigate potential risks and afford greater protections to study participants. IRBs have an important role in helping to ensure that research is ethical, allowing for the enhanced validity of research findings and professional integrity.

There are three levels of institutional review, depending on the nature of the study. Prior to determining which of these levels is appropriate, there is a need to identify whether the proposed study is research that needs a review. This involves two considerations, one for what is considered "research" and one for "human subjects," as reflected in the following (adapted from the US Department of Health and Human Services [https://www.hhs.gov/ohrp/regulations-and-policy/regulations/revised-common-rule-regulatory-text/index.html]):

> A systematic investigation, including research, development, testing and evaluation, designed to develop or contribute to generalized knowledge (*research*), and obtaining information or biospecimens from a living individual through interaction with the individual or obtaining identifiable private information or biospecimens (*human subject*). (The 2018 Common Rule legislation extended the definition to biospecimens, given the growth and advances in genetic research).

If both of these conditions are not met, an institutional review may not be needed. This may suggest that, in some cases, pilot studies, program evaluation, and class assignments (e.g., an empirical investigation conducted in a research course) may not need to be reviewed formally, but ethical principles must still be adhered to! It is up to each institution to establish guidelines for determining whether proposed projects meet the definition of research and require review.

Authors' Reflection. *The new definition of "human subjects research" has opened the door to interpretations that many studies, e.g., of data already collected and de-identified, will not need IRB approval. But you need to be sure about possible harm, and this is best assured by others who are experts in ethical guidelines. Even if you think a study doesn't need IRB approval, it is wise to obtain assurance that this is the case.*

Once it is clear that an institutional review is needed, a study usually falls into three review categories: *exempt, expedited,* or *full,* depending on the level of risk involved in participation. Although we cannot go into all the complexities involved in deciding which type of review is needed, here is a brief overview.

In the **exempt** category, a study that very clearly has minimal risk is freed from federal regulations, but ethical principles still apply. The exempt determination must typically be made by IRBs. Exempt projects are very low risk and do not require a formal consent process. Researchers are required to provide potential volunteers with all of the information about the study to make a fully informed decision about participation. The 2018 Common Rule expanded the scope of exempt studies. Of the six categories of exempt research, three are most relevant to research in education, including educational research conducted in widely acceptable education settings involving normal education practices such as studies of curriculum or instructional strategies; use of surveys, interviews, educational tests, and public observations when the possibility of identifying specific individuals is unlikely; benign behavioral interventions; and studies involving the use of secondary or existing data that are publicly available or data that have been recorded so participants cannot be identified.

Studies that need an **expedited** review are also minimal risk but have greater participant involvement; the researchers may have more direct contact with study participants than in studies meeting exempt criteria. Most studies that involve children will, at a minimum, require expedited review. Expedited studies can include surveys, interviews, or classroom observations where personal identifying information is collected or recorded. These reviews are often conducted by an individual member of the IRB committee and do not require a review by the full board. Take a look again at Figure 2.3. The study described went through an expedited review by our institution's IRB. By comparison, studies that need a **full board** review typically involve greater than minimal risk, but do not meet the exempt or expedited review categories. Full board studies sometimes include specific "vulnerable" populations such as prisoners, children, or pregnant women. A full board review requires that a majority of the members of the IRB committee review and discuss the study at a panel or committee meeting. Diversity in the IRB committee membership is important so that the risk/benefit ratio is reviewed from differing perspectives, depending on committee members' expertise and background. Full board studies may involve the collection of blood and tissue samples, interventions that involve the consumption of alcohol to study driving impairment, or sensitive topics such as domestic abuse and violence.

The main point is that proposed research involving human subjects, regardless of review category, requires an external assessment to ensure that the legal and ethical requirements are met to safeguard potential research participants. The level of review depends on the level of risk associated with participation and the degree to which the target participants need additional protections.

Author Reflection *The IRB process can be perplexing and frustrating, sometimes taking weeks or months for approval before a study can be initiated. However, our experience is that it not only results in more ethical studies and safeguards for participants, but it also enhances the quality of the research. In this way, the IRB process helps to reduce potential noise in research introduced by unaddressed ethical issues, and enhances the signal or quality of research findings. It's a hurdle at times, yes, but an important one you need to learn more about.*

Check for Understanding 4

4a. What is the primary role of an institutional review board?

4b. What is the difference between exempt and expedited IRB reviews?

Ethical and Legal Standards in Authoring and Publishing

Learning Outcome 2.5 Understand author ethical and legal standards for publishing.

Both the AERA and APA have developed ethical guidelines related to being a researcher, writing about research, and publishing. The guidelines focus on three goals: *avoiding conflicts of interest, ensuring accuracy,* and *protecting intellectual property rights.* Each of these equally important guidelines will be discussed.

Avoiding Conflicts of Interest

It's not hard these days to read about research in which there are fairly obvious conflicts of interest. If the National Association of Year-Round Schooling sponsors, conducts, and reports "research" describing the benefits of year-round schooling, you should be cautious, at the very least, and probably suspicious. It is best if those doing the research do not have a vested interest in the nature of the results. What the National Association of Year-Round Schooling needs to do is identify others who are willing to do the research in a completely unbiased way, clearly without strings attached. Or suppose you want to do research on something that would benefit you financially. If there are any economic and/or commercial interests, it is really hard to be unbiased.

Some circumstances related to financial gains are obvious, such as having stock holdings in a company whose product is being evaluated, being a recipient of royalties from a new test that is developed, or providing data that would put you in a better position to get a grant. Other situations are less clear cut and should be IRB reviewed.

Conflicts of interest are not just a concern for researchers. Reviewers of research can also have a conflict of interest in that they may benefit if the review is positive or negative. In general, reviewers have an obligation to be unbiased, and should recuse themselves from a request to review if there is any conflict of interest. A potential conflict of interest should be discussed with the journal editor. In a similar vein, reviewers are obligated to keep reviewed manuscripts confidential.

Ensuring Accuracy

It is well documented that researchers have knowingly reported spurious data or results, or altered data, in a variety of fields, but it is not hard to understand why. Often a lot is riding on results, whether financial or professional, such as getting tenured and/or promoted at a university. Obviously, it is unethical to falsify data or results, or deliberately mislead, but it is more than that. *Duplicate publication*—in which data are misrepresented as original when they have previously been published—is generally prohibited, and it is unethical to submit essentially the same study for publication in two journals with different titles and slightly different wording or formatting. It is also best to avoid *piecemeal publication*, in which different parts of research are published separately, rather than together.

Protecting Intellectual Property Rights

Intellectual property of individuals, organizations, agencies, and other groups must be protected. There are two major principles involved: plagiarism and authorship.

PLAGIARISM   You know about plagiarism—claiming words or ideas of others as your own. The key determinant of plagiarism is that authors present something as if it were their own work, when in reality it is someone else's work. Using the same words that someone else wrote is pretty obvious and can often be detected easily by doing electronic searches of phrases. What is less clear is what you need to do when you paraphrase others' words or ideas. Paraphrasing is needed when other research and theory is discussed; just be sure that you include appropriate citations when that occurs. Give credit where credit is due, including from your own work (yes, there is *self-plagiarism*!).

Sometimes you will need to get permission to use others' work. Each journal has its own approach to permissions, which, we can tell you from experience, can sometimes be difficult and expensive. Generally, small quotes don't need permission; several paragraphs, tables, figures, and instruments usually do need permission.

AUTHORSHIP   Authorship can be a big deal, so you need to get it right. There are a few helpful ethical guidelines when multiple authors are involved. First, authorship should be bestowed only to those who have made a "substantial contribution" to a study and its publication. What "substantial contribution" means can vary, of course, but it typically means that each individual author has had a major role in and responsibility for contributing theory, deriving hypotheses, designing data collection, conducting interventions, and doing data analyses. Those providing lesser contributions, such as administering surveys or entering data, can be acknowledged in a footnote.

Principal authors are listed first, followed by others based on decreasing contribution. If authorship is alphabetical, that could mean equal contributions, but it should be so noted to be clear. With journal publications based on dissertations, the student is typically principal or sole author; faculty members are rarely listed. When you start a research project with others, take time to sketch out responsibilities and decide, to the extent possible, the author order of any products or presentations. It can be a little rough if that is not clear from the beginning. In the end, just remember that each author must make a substantial contribution to the work.

Check for Understanding 5

5a.   What are the three major goals of having ethical and legal standards for publishing.

Author Reflection *There is a great deal of pressure these days for professors to publish journal articles, so authorship can be an issue. An unethical individual might be tempted by having graduate students do a lot—perhaps even the majority—of the work, for which the faculty member wants to claim principal authorship. If you are a student, which is extremely likely if you're reading this, and you get involved with faculty research, be assertive about your rights!*

Figure 2.8 provides a checklist of considerations to make sure that the research process and reporting of results are ethical.

Figure 2.8 Ethical Considerations Checklist

✓ Has it been clearly determined whether the study involves human subjects research? If so, is appropriate IRB review included?
✓ Are participants protected from harm? Will participants benefit from the research?
✓ Are individuals respected by making informed decisions about participation? Can they stop their involvement in the study without penalty?
✓ Does the benefit of the research clearly outweigh the risks to participants? Are minors protected?
✓ Is participant privacy protected?
✓ Are conflicts of interest avoided?
✓ Are data accurate?
✓ Is plagiarism avoided?
✓ Are others' ideas and words appropriately cited?
✓ Does authorship accurately reflect substantial contributions of each individual, reflecting each person's role?
✓ Have all authors agreed about author order?
✓ Has appropriate permission been obtained for using substantial parts of others' work?

Key Terms

Anonymous	Deception	Exempt
Beneficence	Ethics	Expedited
Child assent	Information sheet	Full board
Confidentiality	Informed consent	Justice
Debriefing	Institutional review board (IRB)	

Discussion Questions

1. What is the nature of ethics, and why are ethics important for both consumers and researchers?
2. What are some examples of how essential ethical principles for conducting research are violated?
3. What is an example of research that could serve the public good but not respect the participants?
4. Why is it important for researchers to consider the justice principle in their studies?
5. Describe a hypothetical study in which the risks outweigh the benefits, then change the study so that the benefits outweigh the risks.
6. What is an example of a study that in one form would probably be exempt but with additional procedures be appropriate for an expedited review?
7. Why is it necessary to have IRBs?
8. What does it mean to "be an ethical educational researcher?"

Application Exercise

1. Go to your institutional website and locate pages that are concerned with human subjects research and IRB procedures. Review the website information and make notes about areas of agreement and possible disagreement with major points in the chapter. Indicate what is on the website that extends what is presented in the chapter.

Check for Understanding Answers

1a. Virtually all aspects of the research process, including design, implementation, and reporting of results; this is because all stages may contain practices that violate ethical principles.

1b. Take your pick: professional competence; integrity; responsibility; justice; respect for persons; serving the public good.

2a. Primarily because of past abuses and instances of egregious research practices; along with an increased sensitivity to protecting the welfare of others, especially vulnerable populations.

3a. Allowing individuals choice in whether or not to participate (respect for persons); benefits for the participants (beneficence); fairness (justice).

3b. Because for most research there are both benefits to participants and knowledge acquired, as well as risks, and it is important to clearly establish both to ensure that benefits outweigh risks.

4a. To provide an external, objective review, by experts in ethics, of whether an investigation will reflect ethical principles.

4b. An exempt review is done for studies with a very minimal risk to participants, often involving anonymity or confidentiality; an expedited review is done for studies with slightly more than minimal risk to and greater involvement of participants.

5a. To avoid conflicts of interest; assure accuracy in reporting; protect intellectual property.

Chapter 3
Research Problems and Questions

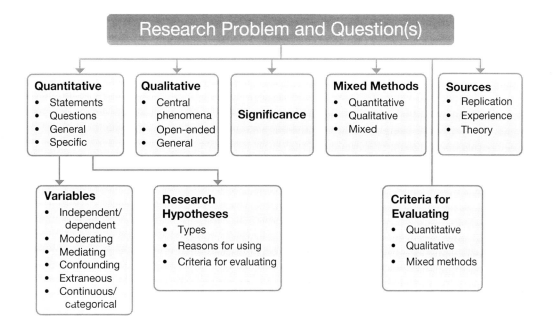

Research Problem and Question(s)

Quantitative
- Statements
- Questions
- General
- Specific

Qualitative
- Central phenomena
- Open-ended
- General

Significance

Mixed Methods
- Quantitative
- Qualitative
- Mixed

Sources
- Replication
- Experience
- Theory

Variables
- Independent/ dependent
- Moderating
- Mediating
- Confounding
- Extraneous
- Continuous/ categorical

Research Hypotheses
- Types
- Reasons for using
- Criteria for evaluating

Criteria for Evaluating
- Quantitative
- Qualitative
- Mixed methods

 Learning Outcomes

3.1 Know the nature and sources of general research problems.

3.2 Distinguish among types of variables used to formulate good specific research problem statements and questions, and research hypotheses, for quantitative studies.

3.3 Understand the nature of qualitative research problem statements and central questions.

3.4 Understand the nature of mixed methods research problem statements and questions.

Chapter Road Map

The first essential step in both conducting and understanding research—establishing the research problem and/or question—is discussed in this chapter. All studies begin with a general research problem that is usually refined into more specific questions. We will also learn about variables and research hypotheses, important concepts in quantitative and mixed methods studies, as well as central questions used in qualitative research.

Research Problems

Learning Outcome 3.1 Know the nature and sources of general research problems.

The **research problem** provides the context for why a study is important—the issue, concern, or need—and then indicates the goal or direction of the study that addresses the problem. The problem typically begins as a general topic and ends with a more specific statement of purpose. A good topic might be teacher evaluation. You could start with this as something you would like to study, make an argument for why the research is needed, then identify what specific aspects of teacher evaluation need to be investigated. All this is conveyed in the first few paragraphs of the study—using references, as appropriate, to support and justify the importance of researching the issue.

Research Problem Components

As illustrated in Figure 3.1, research problems consist of three components: context, significance, and purpose. *Context* explains the background or larger body of knowledge or area being investigated. For example, a researcher might say, "There has been growing interest in the assessment literacy of beginning teachers," or "For the past decade, researchers have investigated how classroom assessment practices affect student motivation," or "As a result of my experience in counseling pregnant high school girls, it has become clear that further study of their knowledge of pregnancy prevention needs to be explored." Excerpt 3.1 shows how context is described in an article, followed by an indication of the goal of the research. Excerpt 3.2 is a good example of how the first full paragraph of the study conveys the topic and context. Note the use of literature to support the importance of the topic, and the way the authors progress from a more general topic to a more specific issue—in this case too many community college students dropping out of school.

Figure 3.1 Components of Research Problems

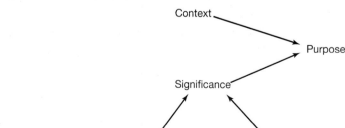

EXCERPTS 3.1 AND 3.2

Context in the Research Problem

In recent years there has been a growing concern regarding the current state of the educational system in the United States. For example, in comparison to other countries, high school students in the United States are falling behind students in other countries on various measures of academic achievement. . . . Given these concerns, one goal of this research was to examine the relative contributions of cognitive abilities to students' science achievement. (p. 161)

SOURCE: O'Reilly, T., & McNamara, D. S. (2007). The impact of science knowledge, reading skill, and reading strategy knowledge on more traditional "high-stakes" measures of high school students' science achievement. *American Educational Research Journal, 44*(1), 161–196.

Community colleges currently enroll about 34% of U.S. undergraduates, a disproportionate share of them from low-income families (Knapp, Kelly-Reid, & Ginder, 2009). At least half of these students will fail to earn a college credential, and success rates are even lower for students deemed in need of remediation (Attewell, Lavin, Domina, & Levey, 2006; Hoachlander, Sikora, & Horn, 2003). For many students, passing out of remedial math, in particular, proves an insurmountable barrier, with many dropping out before they even attempt a college credit-bearing transfer-level course (see Brock, 2010; Visher, Schneider, Wathington, & Collado, 2010; Visher, Wathington, Richburg-Hayes, & Schneider, 2008). (p. 298)

SOURCE: Butcher, K. F., & Visher, M. G. (2013). The impact of a classroom-based guidance program on student performance in community college math classes. *Educational Evaluation and Policy Analysis, 35*(3), 298–323.

Significance is the reason or need for the study—an argument for why the study is important. It is addressed by showing how the study will contribute to knowledge and/or practice because of a controversy, issue, or concern. For basic and applied research, a case is made about how the results will enhance an existing body of knowledge or practice. For evaluation and action research, the focus is on practice. The ideal is to be able to have several explanations for how the study will make a contribution. Often, authors will address what they think are "deficiencies" or shortcomings in the literature on a topic (sometimes called a "gap" in the literature or in specific studies) and indicate how their study will remedy the deficiency. My take on deficiencies is that just because something has *not* been studied does not necessarily mean it *should* be. Thus, it is more than something that has not been studied—*what* is studied must make a contribution. Significance often aligns with the way researchers come up with the topic, which we discuss in the next section.

Excerpt 3.3 shows how researchers indicate the significance of a study of school accountability and teacher motivation. In this case, there are contributions to both knowledge and practice, which is common with applied studies (note, too, that context is addressed).

Excerpt 3.4 shows the first two paragraphs of an article about student motivation. These paragraphs directly address the importance of the study, stating explicitly how the results will contribute to the literature.

EXCERPT 3.3
Research Problem Significance

This work attempts to move this larger body of research on school accountability policies forward by examining the influence of accountability policies on teacher motivation.... This empirical investigation of motivational theories in the SPS accountability context provides important insights into the motivation response of teachers to school accountability policies.... Understanding the factors that improve teacher motivation in low-performing schools... contributes to a broader knowledge based around improving teacher performance and, as a result, student performance. (p. 595)

SOURCE: Finnigan, K. S., & Gross, B. (2007). Do accountability policy sanctions influence teacher motivation? Lessons from Chicago's low-performing schools. *American Educational Research Journal, 44*(3), 594–630.

EXCERPT 3.4
Research Problem Significance

Previous research across various content domains ... suggests that when teachers provide students a sense of control and autonomy over their learning, there are positive results for student motivation (Guthrie & Alao, 1997; Guthrie et al., 2004; Guthrie et al., 2006; Perry, 1998; Turner, 1995). The study of autonomy in specific classroom contexts and domains is important because it aids in discerning what practices work at a given time and in a specific situation, thereby informing instructional practice.

In the field of literacy education, descriptive (e.g., Turner, 1995) and quasi-experimental studies (e.g., Guthrie et al., 2004) have shown the importance of teacher autonomy supports for increased reading motivation and reading achievement. However, these studies have neither examined students' perceptions of teacher autonomy supportive or suppressive practices nor related these to students' reading motivation. To further understand the role of autonomy in literacy instruction, it is necessary to examine how students' perceptions of teacher autonomy-enhancing and autonomy-suppressing behaviors relate to students' motivation for reading and learning in a specific literacy instructional context. Furthermore, given the attention to literacy development in the content areas, situating literacy instruction in a particular content domain will contribute the specificity of the context for autonomous learning. (pp. 22–23)

SOURCE: Barber, A. T., & Buehl, M. M. (2013). Relations among grade 4 students' perceptions of autonomy, engagement in science, and reading motivation. *The Journal of Experimental Education, 81*(1), 22–43. Copyright © by Taylor & Francis Group.

EXCERPT 3.5
Research Problem Significance

Although the educational setting is thought to be crucial for the development of these identities, scholars have primarily relied on evidence from comparisons of achievement among low- and high-achieving students at elite institutions and/or in developed countries (see Duckworth et al., 2007; Duckworth & Seligman, 2005; Fuller & Clarke, 1994). Yet students at nonelite institutions in developing countries also must learn to navigate straddling identities based on their gender and relative economic disadvantage. Still, we know very little about how nonelite institutions in developing nations, particularly those nations where gender roles may be relatively more restrictive than those of developed nations, can contribute to the educational achievement of their students, especially girls. In short, there is a need to understand how positive academic identities operate outside of the geographical and sociocultural contents in which they are typically studied. (p. 1310)

SOURCE: Nuamah, S. A. (2018). Achievement oriented: Developing positive academic identities for girl students at an urban school. *American Educational Research Journal, 55*(6), 1307–1338. Click here to enter text. https://doi.org/10%203102/0002831218782670

Finally, Excerpt 3.5 shows a paragraph from a study about how girls from an urban school in Ghana develop noncognitive skills, and the importance of those skills for achievement and for navigating gender-specific challenges that impede achievement. The significance of the study is to extend previous research in other settings with a new population, generating new knowledge that could lead to practical implications for helping girls in this context.

The *purpose* (research problem statement) is an indication of a more specific goal of the study. It is generally found in the first paragraph of an article, often at the end of that paragraph, as in Excerpt 3.1—although in some studies the statement will be located after the review of literature. Clearly stating the purpose is very important because it orients the reader early and helps in understanding how the literature is related to what is being proposed. It is a good initial guide to what will be investigated. This will help you determine whether a particular study will be helpful.

The research problem statement typically provides just enough information about the scope and purpose of the study to provide an initial understanding of the research. Often, the purpose is introduced using the following as a beginning, though there is no one correct or best way:

"The purpose of this study is to ... "

"The aim of the current investigation is to ... "

"In this study, we investigated ... "

"The goal of the research was to ... "

One of the most frequently used types of sentences is the first one: "The purpose of this study/investigation/research is to ... " For example:

- The purpose of this study is to determine factors predicting college student retention.
- The purpose of this investigation is to examine the relationship between student effort and attitudes.

- The purpose of this research is to understand beginning teachers' perspectives about having a mentor during their first year.
- The purpose of this research is to study adolescent loneliness.

Here are some further examples of research problem statements:

This research will investigate the social integration of adults with physical disabilities.

- This study investigates the relationship between school culture and student achievement.
- This research was designed to determine student perceptions of their high school experiences.

The research problem can also be framed as a question. Like most problem statements, these tend to be located at the beginning of an article/report, prior to the review of literature. For example:

- What is the relationship between school culture and student achievement?
- Is there a difference in motivation between homogeneously and heterogeneously grouped students?
- Do preschool teachers have different instructional styles?
- What explains the high rate of teacher absenteeism?

Some researchers may use the term *research problem* as synonymous with a more specific research problem statement or question. Thus, you will find some variety in the form, as well as in the location, of the research problem statement in an article or report. In some articles, the problem statement may be located at the beginning, with more specific questions later, whereas in other articles, the research problem may be communicated only by more specific questions or statements. The nature of these more specific statements and questions depends on whether they are for quantitative and mixed methods, or qualitative research, as we will see in later sections.

Sources for Research Problems

How do you come up with a good problem? What qualifies you as someone who can generate a problem that can be empirically investigated to make a contribution? Fortunately, there are many ways to begin the process of problem formulation, some of which are based on what you already know, have experience with, and can think about. This should help alleviate your concerns. At the same time, the process may be a rather arduous and time-consuming task. Ideas that seem promising initially typically need revision as literature related to the idea is analyzed and implications for research design are clarified. Many researchers begin to identify a topic by reading current books and journals in their area and by talking with knowledgeable professionals about current problems or issues. Once a broad area of interest is identified, further reading, reflection, and discussions with others leads to a more specific research problem.

Although there is no single strategy for identifying research problems that works best, the following strategies will help.

SKEPTICISM AND INTUITION   All of us are able to ask questions about what seems true based on overgeneralizations, traditions, or accepted practice. Here we use our ability to be skeptical and probing, as well as our intuition, to challenge common sense and "established" ways of doing things or "accepted" knowledge. You are essentially questioning common sense and what is currently "known" or done. For example, why must college courses be completed on a semester basis? Why should students attend school for 180 days—why not 200 days? Some would question why colleges and universities should prepare teachers; why not let school districts do that? Is it really best to publicly reward students for getting high test scores? Many assume that teachers are most motivated if they can receive monetary awards for showing high student achievement—is that correct? When students do poorly on a test, they feel bad—but is that really true? There are simply many accepted principles and practices—based on common sense, tradition, or logic—that can be questioned, and as you think about these principles and practices, using your inherent critical thinking skills and intuition, you will be able to generate some good research ideas.

INTERESTS AND EXPERIENCES   Some of the best sources of ideas come from your interests and practical experiences. A teacher encounters many problems and questions daily that may lead to researchable problems: concerns about teaching methods, grouping, classroom management, tests, individualization, grades, or standardized test data. Administrators may face problems in scheduling, communicating with teachers, providing instructional leadership, generating public support, or handling serious discipline. University professors may see that student teachers are encountering difficulties that must be resolved. In addition to personal experiences, each of us has interests and knowledge about our profession that can be the source of good problems. It may be a topic about which you are curious or have read in the professional literature, or it may be a long-standing interest in certain areas. Sometimes ideas generate from discussions with others, whether with colleagues at work or friends at the neighborhood barbecue.

APPLYING THEORY   A common source for research problems is from theories that have implications for educational practice. One approach is to take a theory in a related area, such as psychology or sociology, and develop a problem that extends it to an educational setting. Examples include using theories of reinforcement, attitude development, information processing, trauma, and communication to generate researchable ideas. In each case, the theories suggest implications that can be researched further in educational settings. For example, theories about motivation provide a rich source of possible research problems, such as how self-determination, autonomy, and purpose are applicable to teachers and college professors. You could do an exciting study comparing principals who emphasize these important influences to different degrees with teacher motivation. Another approach is to directly test, revise, or clarify an existing educational theory. Here, the intent is to develop and change the theory rather than to test its implications.

PREVIOUS RESEARCH   Probably the best way for you to find a good research problem is to read the professional literature in your area—especially primary sources, even if you cannot understand all the data analyses. When you read empirical articles and reports, you will find a rich source for new studies. The old adage about learning from experience is relevant here because you can learn from others' work and experience. Good research does not start from scratch; it builds on and is influenced by previous research. It is like coming up with a way to prepare a turkey—do you just start and experiment with various ingredients or methods, or do you ask others and read a few recipes?

REPRODUCING AND REPLICATING PREVIOUS RESEARCH   A special case of using previous research occurs when a study is reproduced or replicated. **Reproducibility** refers to a study in which an investigator uses extant data from a previous study and reanalyzes the data or uses new analyses to see whether there are different results. This type of study is becoming more popular with open science, open access, and greater transparency in reporting study details. **Replication** means that a new study is conducted that is the same or very similar to a previous study. *Direct* replication is when the new study copies the previous one, and a *conceptual replication* refers to a very similar subsequent study. Reproducibility is becoming more common with data sharing and open publications, but conceptual replications are most common.

Replication is an underappreciated approach, but one that is a key to good science. In fact, the lack of replication has been identified as one of "seven deadly sins" of psychological research (Chambers, 2017) because it is eschewed for novel or original research. According to Chambers less than 1% of published studies in psychology replicates previous research, but when replications *are* conducted many are unable to show the same results! Furthermore, replications in other fields, including sciences, also show dismal success in verifying findings (that isn't bad, by the way, because it often reveals noise in original studies).

The idea of a conceptual replication, which is most likely what you will find in the literature, is to repeat a study with relatively minor changes (e.g., different sample, instrumentation, procedures). It may seem that replication would not add new knowledge, as compared with doing something that has not been done before, but in fact just the opposite is true. Progress in building a body of knowledge and good practice depends on a series of replications to verify and extend initial findings. Here is a partial list of what replications can accomplish:

- Replications can confirm or disconfirm the validity of a study that produces new evidence or reports findings that challenge previous research or theory.

- Replications often use the same procedures but change the type of participants to see whether the original findings hold for different types of individuals. For example, much of Kohlberg's initial research on moral development was done with men. A good replication study would ascertain whether the findings hold for women as well. Studies that are originally limited in scope can justifiably be replicated to extend the findings to other people.

- Replications sometimes change the data gathering techniques and procedures or other aspects of the methodology to see whether the previous findings hold. Is what is found out about beginning teachers from observations the same as what is found from interviews? It is possible that a research finding may be unduly influenced by the way a variable is measured. For example, there are many ways to measure critical thinking. A particular study may report a "significant" result using one way to measure critical thinking, but the result may be limited by the way it was measured. Thus, a useful replication would repeat the study but change the instrumentation. The same is true for procedures in a study. Research that replicates and changes what may have been faulty methods, such as what the researcher says to the participants, may change the results.

- A very beneficial type of replication uses the same approach as a previous experimental study but changes the nature of the intervention. Perhaps a study of the effect of feedback changes the intervention from giving feedback immediately to giving it the next day. Often, interventions that have been investigated on a small scale or in laboratory settings are tested in less controlled settings.

- Replications can be used effectively to see whether initial findings hold over time. This type of replication is often done with attitudes, values, achievement, and other areas in which trend data are important.

Excerpt 3.6 is taken from a study on marijuana use and achievement-related student behaviors. Educational correlates of marijuana use have been well documented by previous research. Students who use marijuana more tend to have more negative

---

EXCERPT 3.6
Conceptual Replication Study

The present study examined the educational correlates of marijuana use but distinguished between general use and in-school use by comparing students who were non-users, general users, and school users of marijuana on school outcomes. The five educational correlates studied are indicators of student engagement (grades, class participation, attendance) or disengagement (cheating, discipline problems); all five have been found to be linked to student achievement. (p. 5)

SOURCE: Finn, K. V. (2012). Marijuana use at school and achievement-linked behaviors. *The High School Journal, 95*(3), 3–13.

---

perceptions of academic competence, lower grades, greater absenteeism, higher dropout rates, and less interest in school. This study examined many of these correlates, but extended the research to include different types of marijuana usage.

Another good strategy is to find an area in which different studies report contradictory findings. I have found seemingly contradictory findings on many topics in the literature. Some studies indicate one conclusion, and other studies investigating the same problem come to an opposite conclusion. These apparent contradictions present good sources for research problems. For instance, research on the effect of charter schools is very mixed. Some studies indicate that students attending charter schools outperform students in regular schools, whereas other studies conclude that there is no difference in student achievement. Why are there contradictions? By examining the studies, discrepancies in methodology or populations may be found that suggest further research to identify reasonable explanations.

Author Reflection   *Coming up with a good research problem statement or question is sometimes the hardest part of doing research. Time and energy are required to read literature and synthesize the information to know whether answering the problem or question is necessary. Sometimes there can be a series of psychological ups and downs if what seems at first to be a good idea turns out to be not so good after all, after further reading and reflection. The process can take months. It took me about a year to come up with my dissertation research questions and only a few months to complete the study. Check out Figure 3.2, which is my way of illustrating how the research problem process progresses psychologically.*

Figure 3.2 Psychological Outcomes During the Process of Research Question Formulation

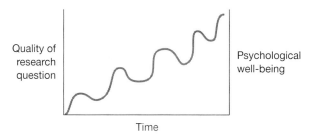

Check for Understanding 1

1a. Indicate why context and significance are important in formulating general research problems.

1b. Explain why each of three different common sources for coming up with general research problems is useful.

We now turn to quantitative research problems and the more specific types of research questions that are typically used with these kinds of studies.

Quantitative Research Problem Statements, Research Questions, and Research Hypotheses

Learning Outcome 3.2 **Distinguish among types of variables used to formulate good specific research problem statements and questions, and research hypotheses, for quantitative studies.**

In quantitative research, once the research problem is identified and literature searched, there is a need for clear, concise research problem statements and/or questions and hypotheses that indicate more specifically what will be studied. These questions are typically found after the review of literature, and, hopefully, convey the logic of the design.

One important aspect of research statements, questions, and hypotheses is to convey information about the variables that will be investigated. Understanding and using the term *variable* is fundamental to all quantitative studies. We discuss variables in some detail here before turning to specific quantitative research problem statements, questions, and hypotheses.

Variables in Quantitative Research

One of the most commonly used terms in quantitative research is *variable*. A **variable** is a label or name that represents a concept or characteristic. Concepts are nouns that stand for a class of objects, such as *tree, house, desk, teacher,* and *school*. A characteristic is a trait we use to describe someone, such as *tall, male, creative,* or *average*. Researchers use *variable* rather than *concept* or *characteristic* because what is studied varies—that is, it involves variations that can be described numerically or categorically. Thus, a variable is a type of concept or characteristic that can take on different values or be divided into categories. For example, intelligence, achievement, social class, and cognitive style each involve a range of values, which is usually expressed numerically. However, some variables are better described as containing two or more categories—for example, male and female, cooperative versus individualized instruction, or beginning teachers with or without student teaching experience.

Categorical variables are composed of *attributes* or *levels*. An attribute is the value or category that makes up the variation. Thus, for example, the variable *type of community* could have three attributes: *rural, urban,* and *suburban*. These categories may also be referred to as *levels*. For a variable such as learning style, the attributes or levels may be field dependent and field independent, or impulsive and reflective, depending on the conceptual definition. Here are some more examples of variables with corresponding attributes or levels:

Variable	Attributes or Levels
Socioeconomic status	High, middle, low
Grade level	Grades 7, 8, and 9; or elementary, middle, high school
Age	10–19, 20–29, 30+
Race	Caucasian, African American, Hispanic, Asian

Conceptual and Operational Definitions

A precise definition of each variable communicates clearly the researcher's intent and enhances the usefulness of the results. Vague definitions are difficult to interpret and usually lead to less meaningful results. Two types of definitions are commonly used in research: *conceptual* and *operational*. A **conceptual** (sometimes called *constitutive*) **definition** uses other words and concepts to describe the variable, as found in a dictionary. For example, *attitude* may be defined conceptually as "a predisposition to respond favorably or unfavorably toward a person, object, or event," and *value* may be defined as "the degree to which an event is perceived to be positive or negative." Conceptual definitions are important in communicating what is being investigated, but they may not indicate precisely what the variables mean. Another type of description, called an *operational definition*, is needed to provide this more precise meaning.

An **operational definition** indicates how the concept is measured or manipulated—that is, what "operations" are performed to measure or manipulate the variable. It is essential to understand operational definitions because researchers will use different ways of measuring or manipulating the same variable. Consequently, the meaning of the results depends on understanding the operational definition, not simply the more generic meaning implied by the conceptual definition. Suppose you are interested in learning about the relationship between parenting styles and children's loneliness. There are many definitions and ways of measuring both variables; you would need to examine the questions asked and the way the responses were scored to know what a particular researcher means.

Consider socioeconomic status (SES), in which the terms *high, middle,* and *low* often describe categories of this variable. These terms are meaningful only if one knows the rules for classifying individuals as "high," "middle," or "low." The same individual might be classified as "high" in one study and "middle" in another, depending on how the researcher defines these categories. Thus, to some extent, operational definitions are arbitrary and often are not explicitly stated. For example, if you are interested in knowing whether cooperative or individualized methods of teaching are most effective in promoting student achievement, knowing simply that a study of these two methods showed cooperative methods to be better is not sufficient. You need to know how the terms *cooperative, individualized,* and *achievement* are determined or measured.

The following are some examples of variables, with corresponding conceptual and operational definitions:

Variable	Conceptual Definition	Operational Definition
Self-concept	Characteristics used to describe oneself	Scores on the *Coopersmith Self-Esteem Inventory*
Intelligence	Ability to think abstractly	Percentile scores on the *Stanford-Binet test*

(Continued)

Variable	Conceptual Definition	Operational Definition
Feedback	Nature of information given to students following performance on tests	Findings revealed by examining written feedback with the *Robinson Scale of Feedback*
Digital information literacy	Ability to accurately interpret and critique information found on the Internet	Percentage correct scores from the *Tool for Real-time Assessment of Information Literacy* (TRAILS)

Types of Variables

It turns out that quantitative educational research uses numerous types of variables. Here we will consider the most important: *independent* and *dependent, confounding, extraneous, moderating, mediating,* and *continuous* and *categorical.*

INDEPENDENT AND DEPENDENT VARIABLES   In most quantitative research, one variable precedes another, either logically or in time. The variable that comes first and influences or predicts is called the **independent variable**. The second variable—the one that is affected or predicted by the independent variable—is the **dependent variable**. In an experiment, at least one independent variable is the presumed cause of differences between groups on the dependent variable. The independent variable is the antecedent (intervention), the dependent variable is the consequence (outcome). Predictions are made about what should happen to the dependent variable based on the independent variable. When we say, "If *X*, then *Y*," *X* is the independent variable and *Y* is the dependent variable. When we determine first which students receive particular teaching methods (intervention as an antecedent condition), we may see the effect on achievement (outcome as a consequence). In this example, teaching method is the independent variable; achievement is the dependent variable. In educational research, professional development for teachers, methods of instruction, and types of curriculum, are common independent variables (and sometimes dependent variables, depending on the design), and achievement, attitudes, values, self-efficacy, and student behavior are common dependent variables (and, you guessed it, sometimes independent variables). In the context of experiments, then, I hope you agree that it's pretty clear which variable is independent and which one is dependent.

In nonexperimental research, a variable may still be considered an independent variable if it clearly precedes the dependent variable, if it is used to create categories for comparison, or is explanatory. For example, a study of the effect of school size (independent variable) on achievement (dependent variable) may locate and use large, medium, and small schools, although it cannot manipulate or alter the size of a particular school. However, the logic is clear that school size precedes achievement. In correlational studies, several nonmanipulated variables may be considered independent because they "precede" the dependent variable. For instance, a school administrator may need to predict teaching effectiveness so he or she can hire the best teachers. Several variables are available for each candidate, including grade point average, supervisor's comments about student teaching, and an interview. If these variables are used to predict the outcome (effectiveness as a teacher), they are usually considered independent variables.

In some nonexperimental research, it is difficult to label variables as independent or dependent, particularly when one variable does not clearly precede the other. For instance, a study of the relationship between critical thinking and creativity may be conducted to show that they are distinct, unrelated concepts (small correlation). In this case, neither is an independent or dependent variable; it would be best to say that there are simply two variables in the study.

EXCERPT 3.7

Independent and Dependent Variables

The dependent variable in our study was student-counselor contact for college informa-tion [measured dichotomously—yes or no].... The student variables in this study were race/ethnicity, gender, mother's educational level, socioeconomic status (SES), and 10th-grade achievement.... Race/ethnicity was made up of six categories (American Indian/Alaskan Native, Asian/Pacific Islander, Black or African American, Hispanic, multi-racial, White).... The school background variables in this study were school setting, type of school, number of school counselors, school size, and percentage of students on free or reduced-price lunch.... [F]our composite variables measured parent involvement.... Counselor postsecondary aspirations for students was a primary independent variable. (p. 285)

SOURCE: Bryan, J., Holcomb-McCoy, C., Moore-Thomas, C., & Day-Vines, N. L. (2009). Who sees the school counselor college information? A national study. *Professional School Counseling, 12*(4), 280–291.

Nonexperimental, descriptive research may compare groups of individuals, and often the variable used to classify the groups is considered an independent variable. For example, a descriptive study of the attitudes of school principals toward school financing might divide the principals into groups depending on the size and location of each school. Here, attitudes would be the dependent variable and size and location of schools the independent variables.

A description of independent and dependent variables in a study is shown in Excerpt 3.7. In this investigation, student characteristics, school background, parent involvement, and school counselor aspirations were independent variables. Note that the term *categories* is used to refer to levels of different attributes of the independent variables.

CONTINUOUS AND CATEGORICAL VARIABLES   A **continuous variable** (or *mea-sured variable*) can theoretically take on an infinite number of values within a given range of scores. In other words, the value of a continuous variable could be any point on a continuum. The values are rank ordered, from small to large or low to high, to indicate the amount of some property or characteristic. Common continuous variables in educational research are achievement and aptitude test scores; self-concept, attitude and value measures; and height, weight, and age.

A **categorical variable** is used to assign an object or person to a group (level) that is defined by having specified characteristics. The simplest type of category has two groups (*dichotomous*) such as male/female, elementary/secondary, and morning/afternoon. Other categorical variables can have three or more groups—for example, grade level, nationality, occupation, and religious preference. It is also common to create categories on the basis of continuous scores. For instance, socioeconomic status is generally used as a continuous variable, but the scores can be grouped into cat-egories such as high, middle, and low SES. Thus, the designation of a continuous or categorical variable may depend on how the researcher uses the scores. The same vari-able can be continuous in one study and categorical in another. Also, although most dependent variables are continuous, both independent and dependent variables can be either continuous or categorical.

MODERATING VARIABLES   **Moderating variables** alter the strength and/or direction of the relationship or effect between the independent and dependent variables. A moderating variable, in other words, shows whether the relationship established with, say, two variables (one independent and one dependent) stays the same when a third moderating variable is introduced. For example, an often-used moderating variable is gender, with the idea that the influence of an intervention is different for females than males. Because most interventions, in fact, do depend on inherent characteristics of individuals, moderating variables are very important in establishing a complete understanding of the impact of the intervention.

MEDIATING VARIABLES   A **mediating** (or *intervening*) **variable** is one that helps explain how or why an intervention causes a change in the dependent variable. It is the mechanism or process that comes between the intervention and the outcome. For example, in a study on motivation, two groups of students could be given different types of homework problems (the independent variable with two levels), with achievement as the outcome. A possible mediating variable would be engagement or motivation, a dynamic that comes after the intervention that influences achievement. Similarly, the effect of watching violence on television (independent variable) on aggression (dependent variable) may be mediated by increased levels of adrenaline.

CONFOUNDING VARIABLES   A **confounding variable** is one that varies systematically with the independent variable due to the nature of the research design and influences the dependent variable. "Varies systematically" means that it is not possible to separate levels of the independent variable from the confounding one that has different values for each level of the independent variable. For instance, suppose you find a study comparing two methods of teaching reading: a totally phonics approach and a combined phonics/whole language approach. Two classrooms are used in the study, one classroom implementing each approach. However, because different teachers are in each class, "teacher" is a confounding variable because the style, personality, and knowledge of each teacher cannot be separated from each approach to teaching and will likely affect reading scores (dependent variable). Therefore, if one group of students did score better than the other, you would not know whether it was because of the method or the teacher. Think of confounding variables as having different values or degrees of influence in each group of participants. As you have probably surmised, confounding variables are prime suspects when it comes to noise. They can really distort the signal.

EXTRANEOUS VARIABLES   An **extraneous variable** affects the dependent variable but is either unknown or not controlled by the researcher. Extraneous variables are conditions, events, features, or occurrences that target a specific group or independent variable category, and, like a confounding variable, may affect the results. That is, they may provide an alternative explanation for the results—they "mess up" the study. Such factors are sometimes called *nuisance* variables. As "nuisance" implies, extraneous variables are also significant contributors to noise. An example would be that during a school-based intervention to diminish adolescents' use of smartphones, results of a major study showing harmful effects of too much smartphone use are widely disseminated on the Internet.

These major types of variables are defined, with further examples, in Table 3.1. The relationship among them is illustrated in Figure 3.3 in the context of an experimental investigation of the effect of different science teaching methods on student achievement and attitudes.

Specific Research Questions

We have already discussed general research problems as statements or questions that provide an indication of the direction of the research, a preview of what is to come. With these general statements of purpose and questions, you have some idea of what will be

Table 3.1 Types of Variables in Quantitative Research

Type	Definition	Example
Independent	The antecedent variable that affects or is related to the dependent variable	In a study of the effect of a new curriculum on student achievement, the new curriculum is the independent variable. If there are two new curriculums (A and B), there are two levels of the independent variable.
Dependent	The outcome, result, or consequence that is influenced or explained by the independent variable	In the preceding example, student achievement is the dependent variable.
Categorical	Mutually exclusive groups of participants	In this study, the categorical variables would be the male students and female students in each class that receives a new curriculum.
Continuous	Participants are assigned a range of possible values	The study uses test scores as a continuous measure of student achievement.
Moderating	Increases or decreases the relationship between the independent and dependent variables	It may be that, in this study, curriculum A works better with males and curriculum B with females. Gender is a moderating variable.
Mediating	Process or mechanism that explains how an intervention actually influences the dependent variable	In this study, it may be that one type of curriculum challenges students more, which leads to greater motivation, which, in turn, affects achievement.
Confounding	Something that is different for levels of the independent variable that affects the results	If this study assigned curriculum A to a class of high-achieving students and curriculum B to a class of low-achieving students, student ability would be a confounding variable.
Extraneous	External, uncontrolled incident or factor that differentially affects the dependent variable	In this example, if a student in one of the classes gets sick and distracts the class, that could be an extraneous variable.

Figure 3.3 Relationships Among Different Types of Variables

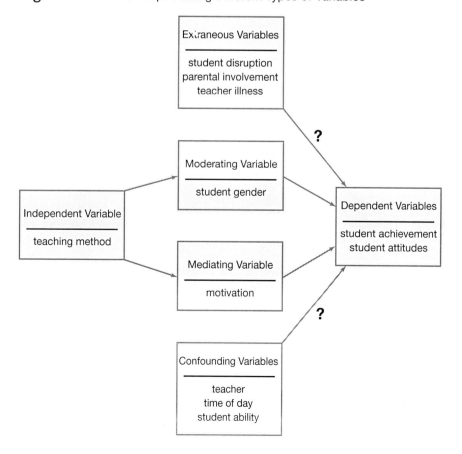

studied, but for quantitative studies these statements or questions may lack clarity, may contain ambiguous terms, and may not provide sufficient information to understand the logic of the study. They are fine as a beginning statement of purpose, but they eventually need to be more focused. These general problem statements and questions can be conceptualized as being on the Very General end of a specificity continuum:

Very General ◀——————————▶ Very Specific

At the other end of the continuum are statements and questions that contain more detail and information than is necessary. As a result, they are difficult to understand. An extreme example of a statement that is too specific is the following:

> The purpose of this study is to investigate whether seventh- and eighth-grade male and female teachers who teach in a predominantly middle-class school in a western Michigan suburb who are identified by principal ratings and the Teacher Effectiveness Inventory, given in the fall semester by trained observers, will have students who, matched by ability when entering school in the fall, differ in the level of achievement in mathematics and language arts as measured by the Iowa Test of Basic Skills.

The majority of appropriately specific quantitative research problem statements and questions are in the middle of the continuum. These sentences contain sufficient detail and information in one or more statements or questions that are clear and succinct. Following is an example of questions from a study that would be at the appropriate level of specificity (Excerpt 3.8). Also note how the authors justify the significance of the study, and the use of a moderator variable.

EXCERPT 3.8
Research Questions at Appropriate Levels of Specificity

The aim of this study was to extend the HDS model by exploring forms of parent involvement specifically suited to adolescents. Our study further contributes to this emerging literature by investigating distinctive patterns of parent involvement across diverse SES and racial/ethnic groups, and thus has the potential to move the field farther away from a one size fits all approach to understanding and working with diverse populations (Garcia, Coll, & Marks, 2009). Specifically, we explored three research questions:

Research Question 1: What are the key dimensions of parental involvement during this age period and are there racial/ethnic and SES differences across these dimensions of parent involvement?

Research Question 2: To what extent do parent sociodemographic variables, together with perceptions of school outreach efforts, parent satisfaction with the school, and parental motivational beliefs predict distinctive dimensions of parental involvement?

Research Question 3: Do parents' sociodemographic characteristics moderate the relationship of school outreach efforts, parent satisfaction, and parental motivational beliefs to parental involvement practices? (p. 108)

SOURCE: Park, S., & Holloway, S. D. (2013). No parent left behind: Predicting parental involvement in adolescents' education within a sociodemographically diverse population. *The Journal of Educational Research, 106*(2), 105–119.

In Excerpt 3.9 the authors use statements at the right level of specificity to clearly communicate the essential aims and multiple independent and dependent variables used in a correlational study.

EXCERPT 3.9

Research Problem Statements at an Appropriate Level of Specificity

To extend what we know about the relative contribution of language to mathematics performance, the present study investigates the associations between language ability and math performance in a sample of first- and second-grade students (N = 365). We first examine the associations between four indicators of language (syntax, morphology, vocabulary, and a general oral language screening tool) and latent mathematics performance. Then, we explore the differential contributions of language ability on three different mathematics problem types (calculations, addition problem solving, and equivalence). (p. 181)

SOURCE: Chow, J. C., & Ekholm, E. (2019). Language domains differentially predict mathematics performance in young children. *Early Childhood Research Quarterly*, 46, 179–186.

Consumer (and Researcher) Tips
Criteria for Evaluating Quantitative Research Problem Statements and Questions

1. **The problem should be researchable.** A researchable problem is one that can be answered empirically by collecting and analyzing data. Problems that are concerned with value questions or philosophical ideas are not researchable in the sense that a specific question has a correct answer. Many interesting questions in education require value or ethical analyses, but to be able to conduct research, the question must lend itself to the systematic process of gathering and analyzing data.

   Table 3.2 includes quantitative research questions in both general and specific language to illustrate the difference between nonresearchable and researchable questions. The specific questions are good because they communicate several aspects of the study, including the type of research (experimental, relationship, or descriptive), independent and dependent variables, and characteristics of the participants. Each of these will be considered in greater detail in discussing criteria for evaluating problem statements or questions.

Table 3.2 Researchability of Quantitative Problems

Nonresearchable	Researchable
Should we teach sex education in elementary schools?	What is the difference in knowledge and attitudes of fifth-graders who are taught sex education, compared with fifth-graders who are not taught sex education?
Do teachers need to have courses in test construction?	Will the classroom testing procedures used by teachers who take a course in test construction differ from those of teachers who have not taken the course?
Should the school day be longer?	What is the relationship between length of the school day and SAT scores of high school students?
Should students with disabilities be included in regular English classes as well as in physical education?	What is the effect of inclusion of fourth-grade students with learning disabilities into regular English classes on the self-concept, attitudes, and achievement of all students?

2. **The problem should be important.** The results of research need to have theoretical or practical significance. Theoretical importance is determined by the contribution of the study to knowledge as presented in existing literature. Are the results meaningfully related to what is already known? Do the results add new knowledge or change the way we understand phenomena? Practical importance suggests that the results will have immediate use in day-to-day activities or decisions.

3. **The research problem and questions should indicate the type of research.** The language used in the research problem(s) and question(s) should indicate whether the study involves a simple description, a comparison, a relationship, or a difference. A *simple description* is implied from such problems as these:

How many third-graders have computer experience?

What criteria are most important in placing children with autism spectrum disorder?

What are the social and personality characteristics of gifted children?

How do children react when parents separate?

A *relationship* study indicates how two or more variables may be related (remember—with either comparisons or correlations). For example, the following questions imply a relationship:

What is the relationship between achievement and self-efficacy?

Is there a relationship between effort in doing an assignment and attitudes about it?

Can leadership potential be predicted from high school grades, recommendations, and participation in extracurricular activities?

Comparative studies that use categories of one or more independent variables can also be nonexperimental. For example:

How do males and females differ in their attitudes toward freedom of the press?

Are elementary school teachers different from secondary school teachers in assertiveness?

What is the difference among sixth-, seventh-, and eighth-graders' self-concept of ability?

Excerpt 3.10 is from a study on the preparation, experiences, and self-efficacy of new counselors related to crisis intervention. The five questions include descriptive, comparative, and correlational aspects of the study.

Some research problems and questions imply more than a simple relationship or comparison—they suggest that one variable causes a change in another one. Here, the intent of the research is to test a cause-and-effect relationship between the independent and dependent variables. This includes all experimental research and some types of nonexperimental research. Typically, differences are emphasized in the problem statement, and often the word *effect* is used. (Unfortunately, some relationship studies that are not causal still use the term *effect*, which may be misleading.) Here are some difference questions that imply cause-and-effect relationships:

Will method A result in higher achievement than method B?

Is there a difference in attitude between students having peer teaching, and students who have traditional instruction?

What is the effect of small group instruction on the reading achievement of second-graders?

EXCERPT 3.10
Research Questions Illustrating Different Types of Research Logic

Specifically, our research questions were as follows:

1. How do new professional counselors rate their didactic preparation for a variety of crisis intervention tasks? [descriptive]
2. To what degree are new professional counselors called upon to engage in crisis intervention during pre- and postgraduation field experiences? What is their crisis-related self-efficacy? [descriptive]
3. Do new professional counselors' ratings of didactic crisis preparation and crisis self-efficacy vary by counseling setting or program accreditation status? [comparative]
4. To what degree are participation in crisis preparation activities, didactic crisis preparation, and crisis self-efficacy related? [relationship—both comparative and correlational]
5. What recommendations do new professional counselors have for counselor educators? [descriptive] (p. 258)

SOURCE: Wachter Morris, C. A., & Barrio Minton, C. A. (2012). Crisis in the curriculum? New counselors' crisis preparation, experiences, and self-efficacy. *Counselor Education & Supervision, 51,* 256–269.

---

4. **The research question should name the sample.** The sample is simply the people whom the researcher investigated. A good research question (or specific statement) identifies, in a few words, the most important distinguishing characteristics of the sample. Too much detail about the participants will unnecessarily repeat the full description in the data source section of the article or report. Hence, the description of the sample in the research question should be concise, yet informative. (Excerpt 3.8 provides a good example.) Here is a question in which the description of the sample is too vague:

   Do children who practice with calculators achieve more than those who do not practice with calculators?

   Here is the same question with a description that is too specific:

   Do fourth-grade, low-SES, low-ability students from Carpenter Elementary School who practice with calculators achieve more than those who do not practice with calculators?

   A good level of specificity would be this:

   Do low-ability, low-SES fourth-graders who practice with calculators achieve more than those who do not practice with calculators?

5. **The research question should specify the variables.** A good research question in a relatively simple study will name the variables and describe how they may be related in a single sentence or very few sentences. Often these will be independent and dependent variables. Variables are described with a moderate level of specificity. "A study of the effect of teacher workshops" is far too general; in fact, there is no dependent variable at all. "A study of the effect of teacher workshops on teacher morale as measured by the Smith Morale and Attitude Scale" does provide a dependent variable, but provides more detail than necessary about it and still does not communicate much about the independent variable (workshop). If two groups of teachers are being compared, one that attends the workshop and one that does not, a better, more informative question would be "Is there a difference in the morale of

teachers who attend a teacher workshop compared with that of teachers who do not attend?" Here, the independent variable is more than just named; it is described.

Research problems that are more complex by having several independent and/ or dependent variables may need to be stated in several questions. The first sentence typically includes either the main variables or a general term to represent several variables. It is followed by one or more sentences that describe all the variables:

> The aim of this study is to investigate the relationship between measures of aptitude and attitudes toward college among high school students. The measures of aptitude include scores from the SRA and SAT, high school grade point average, and class rank. Attitudes toward college are assessed by the Canadian College Attitude Scale, which reports four subscale scores: motivation, academic versus social climate, reputation, and expectations for success.

This study involves four independent and four dependent variables, and it would be cumbersome to try to include all of them in one sentence.

6. **The problem statement and research questions should be clear.** The importance of a clear, concise research problem statement and specific question(s) cannot be overemphasized. One purpose of the research problem statement is to communicate the purpose of the study, ensuring that the reader's understanding of the purpose is consistent with that of the researcher. In addition, a clear research problem reflects clear thinking by the researcher. A clear problem does not include ambiguous terms. Ambiguity occurs when different people, reading the same thing, derive different meanings from what is read. If a term or phrase can mean several things, it is ambiguous. Terms such as *effect, effective, achievement, aptitude, methods, curriculum,* and *students,* by themselves, are ambiguous or vague. They should be replaced or modified so that the meaning is clear. A vague statement such as "What is the effect of sex education?" needs much more specificity. What is meant by "effect" and "sex education"? What grade level is being studied? What type of study is it? A successful problem statement or question indicates unambiguously the what, who, and how of the research.

7. **Problem statements, research questions, and variables should be aligned to data analyses and reporting of results.** Research statements, questions, and variables are clearly aligned to the analyses and results when there is one-to-one correspondence between each question and statistical results. That is, it should be clear how each analysis reflects a specific statement or question, and all variables mentioned (and none that aren't) are included in reporting findings. Alignment also means that you can discern that the variables and logic in the statement or question are contained in the analyses. For example, if the question is "What is the difference in height between seventh-grade boys and girls?" the aligned analysis is to compare the mean of a sample of boys to the mean of a sample of girls. If the analysis also included race and ethnicity, there would be poor alignment.

Author Reflection *Writing good research questions is hard work. I've found that it's best to do some draft questions, using the above criteria, and then pair appropriate statistical analyses to each question. Often this process results in adding questions so that there is good alignment between questions and analyses. It's also good to have someone not familiar with your study review the draft questions for clarity. This almost always results in improved questions. For one of my studies I started with "How do teachers use accountability tests?" and eventually came up with "What is the relationship between when science teachers receive accountability test score results and use of the results to design specific instructional remediation strategies for ninth graders?"*

Research Hypothesis

A **research hypothesis** is a conjectural, declarative restatement of the research question that indicates the results the investigator expects to find. Research hypotheses are sometimes referred to as *working* or *substantive* hypotheses, and often simply as *hypotheses*. They are educated "guesses" or expectations about relationships or differences among independent and/or dependent variables. It is the investigator's prediction or expectation of what the results will show; a conjectural statement of the researcher's expectations about how the variables in the study are related, a prediction that is made *prior* to data collection.

Almost all research hypotheses are directional, in which the nature of the expected difference or relationship is stated. That is, a specified group is expected to score higher or lower than other groups, or a relationship is expected to be positive or negative. For example, a research hypothesis for an experiment would be

> Fifth-grade students participating in a computer-aided mathematics lesson will demonstrate higher achievement than students using a traditional paper-and-pencil lesson.

In a study of relationships, the research hypothesis might be

> There is a positive relationship between time on task and achievement.

Research hypotheses are used in some quantitative studies because they serve a number of important purposes:

1. **The research hypothesis provides a focus that integrates information.** Researchers often have hunches about predictions, based on experience, previous research, theories, and the opinions of others. By forming a research hypothesis, the investigator synthesizes the information to make the most accurate prediction possible. Usually, the researcher draws heavily on the related literature to formulate the research hypothesis, using previous studies of the same or similar variables, and theories.
2. **The research hypothesis is testable.** It provides a statement of relationships that can be tested by gathering and analyzing data.
3. **The research hypothesis helps the investigator know what to do.** The nature of the research hypothesis directs the investigation by suggesting appropriate sampling, instrumentation, and procedures. It helps the researcher keep a focused, specific scope.
4. **The research hypothesis allows the investigator to confirm or disconfirm a theory.** Research hypotheses help advance knowledge by refuting, modifying, or supporting theories. In fact, the strongest research hypotheses are based on theories that suggest specific outcomes. Theories are also helpful for establishing a rationale for a study, showing how the results are important for confirming or disconfirming the theory or suggesting modifications to the theory (e.g., a new moderating variable changing the impact of an intervention).
5. **The research hypothesis provides a framework for developing explanations that can be investigated scientifically.** Explanations that are not contained in a research hypothesis are metaphysical in nature and are not subject to scientific verification.
6. **When supported, the research hypothesis provides evidence of the predictive nature of the relationship between the variables.** Knowledge of a tested, confirmed prediction is more powerful evidence than an unconfirmed, untested observation.

7. **The research hypothesis provides a useful framework for organizing and summarizing the results and conclusions of the research.** It helps the reader understand the meaning and significance of the study.

Excerpts 3.11 through 3.13 provide a variety of research hypotheses from different studies, although you notice that the authors use the term *hypothesis* to mean research hypothesis, and that in Excerpt 3.11 the term *expected* is used to communicate anticipated findings. Note that, in each case, the direction of the difference or relationship is indicated. The literature imbedded in the hypotheses in Excerpt 3.11 is appropriate for providing a justification for the direction of the expected results.

EXCERPTS 3.11 AND 3.12
Research Hypotheses

The previous case studies literature suggests that teachers' disciplinary backgrounds and two nature-revealing courses may have significant effects on their substantive, syntactical, and pedagogical content knowledge in history. We use data from a survey on social studies teachers to quantitatively test their generalizability. Our research hypotheses are the following:

Hypothesis 1 (H_1): Teachers' historical knowledge, conceptions of history, and pedagogy would be positively related.

H_2: Teachers with history backgrounds would possess more historical knowledge, better conceptions of history, and pedagogy that is more in line with historical thinking abilities and is more varied.

H_3: Teachers who have taken historiography courses would possess more historical knowledge, better conceptions of history, and pedagogy that is more in line with historical thinking abilities and is more varied.

H_4: Teachers who have taken nontraditional history courses would possess more historical knowledge, better conceptions of history, and pedagogy that is more in line with historical thinking abilities and is more varied. (pp. 79–80)

SOURCE: Sung, P., & Yang, M. (2012). Exploring disciplinary background effect on social studies teachers' knowledge and pedagogy. *The Journal of Educational Research,* 106(1), 77–88. Copyright © by Taylor & Francis Group US Books.

We expected that the study strategy training would support the academic self-efficacy and study strategies development of students with and without a history of reading difficulty …We expected positive effects for students with no history of reading difficulty as well given that many university students struggle to develop effective study habits (Turner & Thompson, 2014) and that study strategy training has been shown to improve motivation and study habits in post-secondary settings (Hattie et al., 1996; Tremblay & Rodger, 2003; Tuckman & Kennedy, 2011). Based on findings that study strategy interventions tended to have larger effects for low- vs. high-achieving students (Hattie et al., 1996), we thought students with a history of reading difficulty may experience larger training effects compared to those with no history of reading difficulty. (p. 29)

SOURCE: Bergeya, B. W., Parrilab, R. K., Larochec, A., & Deaconc, S. H. (2019). Effects of peer-led training on academic self-efficacy, study strategies, and academic performance for first-year university students with and without reading difficulties. *Contemporary Educational Psychology, 56,* 25–39.

EXCERPT 3.13

Research Hypotheses for Several Dependent Variables

The hypotheses guiding our research were as follows: Relative to students receiving traditional reading lessons, students assigned to PALS will (a) achieve higher reading comprehension scores on experimenter-developed and standardized test tasks; (b) be more effective in mastering tasks specific to the taught strategies; (c) report greater knowledge about the respective strategies; and (d) indicate a better understanding of activities characteristics of self-regulated reading. (p. 291)

SOURCE: Spörer, N., & Brunstein, J. C. (2009). Fostering the reading comprehension of secondary students through peer-assisted learning: Effects on strategy knowledge, strategy use, and task performance. *Contemporary Educational Psychology, 34,* 289–297.

Table 3.3 shows the relationship among research questions and research hypotheses. The investigator begins with a research question and, based on a review of literature and/or personal experience, forms a research hypothesis.

Table 3.3 Research Questions and Corresponding Research Hypotheses

Research Question	Research Hypothesis
What is the effect of a mainstreaming workshop on the attitude of teachers toward mainstreaming?	Teachers' attitudes toward mainstreaming will improve as a result of attending a workshop on mainstreaming.
Is there a relationship between teachers' attitudes toward the curriculum and student achievement?	There is a positive correlation between teachers' attitudes toward the curriculum and student achievement.
Is there a difference in achievement between students who are given highly detailed written comments on their work, compared with students who are given grades only?	Students receiving highly detailed written comments on their work will show higher achievement than students given grades only.

Examples of research questions and hypotheses from a study of parents' teaching reading and mathematics to their children are illustrated in Excerpt 3.14. In Excerpt 3.15 you will find a statement of purpose, a slightly more specific research question, and then five research hypotheses that spell out in greater detail all of the specific variables and the analyses of interest.

EXCERPTS 3.14 AND 3.15

Research Questions and Hypotheses

Research Question	Corresponding Research Hypotheses
Does mothers' and fathers' SES predict their teaching of reading and mathematics during kindergarten and Grade 1?	Mothers and fathers with low SES would show more teaching of reading and mathematics than those with higher SES.
Do mothers' and fathers' self-reported learning difficulties predict the extent to which they teach reading and mathematics to their children?	Mothers and fathers who had experienced learning difficulties end up teaching their children more reading and mathematics than those without learning difficulties. (pp. 63–64)

SOURCE: Silinskas, G., Leppänen, U., Aunola, K., Parrila, R., & Nurmi, J. (2010). Predictors of mothers' and fathers' teaching of reading and mathematics during kindergarten and Grade 1. *Learning and Instruction, 20,* 61–71.

Purpose of the Study and Research Question

This study aimed at investigating the relationship between students' perceptions of their classroom assessment tasks, motivated learning strategies, and mathematics achievement for grade 11 students. The study was guided by the following research question: How do students' perceptions of the classroom assessment tasks predict their mathematics achievement after controlling for gender and motivated learning strategies?

The main research hypotheses for the investigation of the relationship between students' perceptions of their classroom assessment tasks, motivated learning strategies, and mathematics achievement for grade 11 students are presented below:

1. Gender; motivated learning strategies in terms of extrinsic goal orientation, task value, self-efficacy for learning and performance, rehearsal, and metacognitive self-regulation, and perceptions of assessment tasks in terms of congruence with planned learning, authenticity, student consultation, and transparency will explain a significant portion of the variance in mathematics achievement.
2. Congruence with planned learning will positively predict mathematics achievement after controlling for gender and motivated learning strategies.
3. Authenticity will positively predict mathematics achievement after controlling for gender and motivated learning strategies.
4. Student consultation will positively predict mathematics achievement after controlling for gender and motivated learning strategies.
5. Transparency will positively predict mathematics achievement after controlling for gender and motivated learning strategies. (pp. 521–522)

Source: Alkharusi, H. (2016). Predicting students' academic achievement: Contributions of perceptions of classroom assessment tasks and motivated learning strategies. *Electronic Journal of Research in Educational Psychology, 14*(3), 515–533.

Consumer (and Researcher) Tips
Criteria for Evaluating Research Hypotheses

1. **The research hypothesis should be stated in declarative form.** Because the research hypothesis is a possible explanation, it must be written in the form of a declarative sentence. A hypothesis should not be stated in the form of a question.
2. **The research hypothesis should be consistent with known facts, previous research, and theory.** The research hypothesis should follow from other studies and established theories. In general, it should not contradict previous research but rather should build on related literature; the results should contribute to the established body of knowledge. It is best for the research hypothesis to follow the review of literature. The reader should be able to understand why a particular hypothesis is put forth.
3. **The research hypothesis should follow from the research question.** It is confusing to use variables in the hypothesis that have not been identified by the research question. A general problem may include several variables, and, thus, several research hypotheses may be used to indicate all the anticipated relationships.

4. **The research hypothesis should state the expected relationship between two or more variables.** A hypothesis must have at least two variables and must indicate how the variables are related. A study that analyzes the relationship by a correlation coefficient will use the terms *positive relationship* or *negative relationship*. In a study that analyzes differences between groups, the relationship may be expressed as a difference (more or less, higher or lower). In either case, an expected relationship is stated. Most research hypotheses conjecture the relationship between just two variables. It can be awkward and confusing to include more than two variables in one sentence, with the exception of studies that have several dependent variables and one independent variable (e.g., "Students in the high technology class will show more positive attitudes toward learning, higher achievement, and less prosocial behavior than students in the low technology class.").

5. **The research hypothesis should be testable.** As pointed out previously, being testable means being verifiable; that is, data can be obtained to determine whether the hypothesis can be supported empirically. It is a matter of measuring the variables in such a way that the hypothesis can be confirmed or not confirmed. This means that the researcher must be able to obtain data that represent values of the variables. Operational definitions of the variables are needed (not necessarily as part of the hypothesis statement). Stated differently, the variables must be amenable to operational definitions that can be applied by using an instrument or observations to collect data. For example, the hypothesis "Children taking a unit on nutrition will be healthier" is not testable unless the independent variable, "taking a unit" and dependent variable, "more healthy," are operationally defined. That is, what does "taking a unit" mean? What measure is used to determine how healthy the children are?

6. **The research hypothesis should be clear.** As with the terminology used in research questions, the words, phrases, and descriptions in the research hypothesis should be unambiguous. A clear hypothesis is easier for the reader to comprehend and easier for the researcher to test.

7. **The research hypothesis should be concise.** Consistent with criteria for research questions, hypotheses should be sufficiently detailed to communicate what is being tested and, at the same time, should be as succinct as possible. A concise hypothesis is easier to comprehend.

Check for Understanding 2

2a. What is the difference between independent and dependent variables for experimental and nonexperimental research?

2b. Explain the difference between moderating and mediating variables.

2c. What is the difference between specific research questions and research hypotheses?

2d. Name three shared criteria for good research questions and research hypotheses.

The Hedgehog and the Fox Show Different Approaches to Study a New Idea to Improve Achievement

I'm going to show how well my new idea for improving student achievement works.

I'm interested in seeing whether or not my new idea for improving student achievement is successful and finding the conditions that influence its effectiveness.

Qualitative Research Problem Statements and Questions

Learning Outcome 3.3   Understand the nature of qualitative research problem statements and central questions.

In qualitative studies, researchers use overarching purpose statements or questions as a way to establish a beginning point for their study. Since the goal of qualitative research is to use a reflective process to better understand perspectives of people and social processes, initial broad problem statements and questions function as an opening to use ongoing data collection to suggest new and/or refined questions that meet the goals of the study. This reformulation and evolving of initial questions is needed to focus appropriately on the participants, processes, and context of the particular investigation. It is as if the researcher begins with an intellectual curiosity, interest, or idea, then frames an initial question or two that will point to appropriate theories, sources of data, and procedures for gathering data.

From the beginning, the logic and purpose of the questions used for qualitative research are different from quantitative research questions (refer to Table 3.4). Qualitative research problem statements and questions tend to be much more open-ended, less specific, evolving rather than static, and process oriented, initiating exploration and discovery. These differences result in unique usage of terms and language. For example, it is common for qualitative problem statements to use words such as *how, why, what, generate, understand*, and *explore*, rather than *relate, differ*, or *compare*. No predictions or expected results (e.g., hypotheses) characterize qualitative research problems and questions.

In some qualitative studies there are a number of subquestions that are initially framed to best capture all critical aspects of participant perspectives. This is illustrated nicely in a recent dissertation study conducted by one of my students. Her main focus, as stated in her prospectus, was "to understand undergraduate student attitudes about search data privacy in academic libraries and their preferences for how librarians should handle information about what students search for, borrow, and download" (Garieply, 2019, p. 8). She also listed four subquestions to initiate the development of an interview protocol to gather data to result in a deep understanding of student perspectives on privacy in academic libraries:

1. What are undergraduate students' attitudes about whether academic libraries should collect and maintain search data when using library resources, and why?
2. What are acceptable and unacceptable uses of students' library search data according to undergraduate students, and why?
3. In what ways do undergraduate student attitudes about search data privacy differ in the context of using academic libraries and commercial search engines such as Google?
4. What do students perceive as the risks and benefits of libraries collecting student search data, and how do these perceptions influence their search behavior?

This is an example of a qualitative study that relied on subquestions. Because her initial focus was on particular aspects of privacy, beginning with these subquestions was appropriate. In contrast, Excerpt 3.17 shows the use of a single research question.

Table 3.4 Differences Between Quantitative and Qualitative Research Problems

Quantitative	Qualitative
Specific	General
Closed	Open
Static	Evolving
Outcome oriented	Process oriented
Contains variables	Does not contain variables
Hypotheses	No hypotheses

Writing Good Qualitative Research Problem Statements and Questions

The first step in writing a qualitative problem statement or question is to identify the central phenomenon that is being studied. The **central phenomenon** is an issue or process that is being investigated (Creswell & Guetterman, 2019). Issues would be such things as teenage alienation, college student retention, bullying, or principal burnout. Processes could include the manner in which beginning teachers are inducted into the profession, how teachers integrate the demands of standardized high-stakes testing into their teaching, and the manner in which politicians develop their thinking about educational accountability. The general research problem statement or question—what Creswell & Guetterman (2019) call the *central question*—includes a single central phenomenon. As I've explained, the central question (or *foreshadowed* question) is relatively broad, in contrast to quantitative questions, which suggests an exploration of the central phenomenon. Two or more phenomena are not compared or related, as would be done in a quantitative study. (Comparisons and relationships can emerge from the data, but qualitative researchers typically do not go into the research with these already in mind.)

Similar to the general purpose statement for a quantitative study, the central "question" can actually be a statement of the overall aim or goal of the study, indicating in broad terms the purpose and focus of inquiry. A good example of a goal statement is illustrated in Excerpt 3.16. In Excerpt 3.17 the authors included both a general statement of purpose and a central research question, while Excerpt 3.18 illustrates yet another approach: stating a general goal followed by a more specific statement of intent.

EXCERPT 3.16

Qualitative Research Problem Statement

The current study captures the voices of three primary stakeholders in education (i.e., parents, teachers, and students) using qualitative methods, supported by quantitative indicators, to identify the goals and contexts for parental involvement in education, identify consistencies across stakeholders in the conceptualizations of parental involvement in education, and deepen our understanding of the types of involvement that matter for adolescents. (p. 12)

SOURCE: Hill, N. E, Witherspoon, D. P., & Bartz, D. (2018). Parental involvement in education during middle school: Perspectives of ethnically diverse parents, teachers, and students. *The Journal of Educational Research, 111*(1), 12–27.

EXCERPT 3.17

Qualitative Research Problem Statement and Central Question

In this article, we explore how social capital is manifested in an urban full-service community school's efforts to provide equitable educational opportunities for its racially/ethnically diverse students. We focus on the school as a source of social capital with bonding, bridging, and linking functions as well as threats to this capital.

The overarching question this article seeks to answer is:

> *Research Question*: What role does social capital play in achieving the transformative goals of full-service community schools for underserved students and families? (p. 145S)

SOURCE: Galindo, C., Sanders, M., & Abel, Y. (2017). Transforming educational experiences in low-income communities: A qualitative case study of social capital in a full-service community school. *American Educational Research Journal, 54*(Supp. 1), 140S–163S.

EXCERPT 3.18

Qualitative Research Problem Statements

The goal of this study is to understand how students' perceptions of school context, and family and peer environments help shape their college selection process. More specifically, we sought to understand how formal and informal social networks serve as a catalyst for students to gather information and engage in the college choice process. We use a qualitative approach to explore students' perceptions of access to and use of school, family, and peer networks as they glean information, and form and act on a postsecondary plan. (p. 1211)

SOURCE: Elliott, D. C., Brenneman, M. W., Carney, L., & Robbins, S. (2017). Social networks and minority male college access: The "Tip of the Iceberg" phenomena. *Urban Education, 53*(10), 1210–1237.

You may also find that different qualitative problem statements and questions align with qualitative research designs summarized in Chapter 1. Both Excerpts 3.16 and 3.18 suggest phenomenological studies, with an emphasis on participant perspectives, while 3.17 is a case study of selected schools.

Consumer (and Researcher) Tips
Criteria for Evaluating Qualitative Research Problem Statements and Questions

1. **The research problem statement/question should not be too general or too specific.** It is important that the central phenomenon not be too general or too focused. Qualitative research problem statements/questions that are too vague and broad give the impression that the research is more like a fishing trip than systematic inquiry, whereas those that are too narrow are inconsistent with the reason for doing qualitative research. If it is very general (e.g., a study on parental involvement in schools), it will probably not be able to provide information that results in a greater depth of understanding, which is the goal of a qualitative study. If it is too specific (e.g., a study of how parents perceive notes sent home to encourage participation in school lunches), the researchers may miss significant information because they are too narrowly focused. A middle ground is needed so that what is being investigated is clear, while at the same time it is not so specific that the researcher is unable to capture new and significant information when it arises.

2. **The problem statement/question should be amenable to change as data are collected.** It is important to write the initial problem statement/question so it is somewhat open ended and general. This allows for and encourages changes as the data are being collected. The continuing reformulation of a problem reflects the emergent design of the research. For example, beginning a study with a problem question such as "What are students' perceptions about tests required for graduation?" would be more amenable to change than something like "What do students say about whether graduation tests are fair?"

3. **The problem statement/question should not be biased with researcher assumptions or desired findings.** In qualitative research, the investigator's assumptions and biases must be considered in designing the study and interpreting the findings, but it is important to keep the central question as neutral as possible. All too often, researchers want to gather data to "prove" something to be true or advocate for an idea or position, and this threat to good research can easily occur in qualitative studies. Notice how a statement like the following suggests an assumption about what will be found: "The purpose of this study is to explore reasons college faculty give to explain a lack of multicultural awareness in their teaching." A better statement would be: "The purpose of the study is to explore multicultural awareness as reflected in teaching."

4. **The problem statement/question should be written using "how" and "what" to keep the focus on description of phenomena.** The most important goal of qualitative research is to be able to provide a rich description of the phenomenon that is being studied. This goal is best achieved if the researcher focuses on *what* occurs and *how* it occurs, leading to possible explanations. There should not be an emphasis on causal conclusions and relationships. You want to stay away from terms such as "impact," "determine," and "cause and effect."

5. **The problem should include the central phenomenon as well as an indication of the participants and the site in which the study is being conducted.** Good qualitative research problem statements and questions contain three elements: the phenomenon being studied, the participants, and the research site or

---

Table 3.5 Qualitative Research Problem Statements/Questions Associated with Qualitative Research Designs

Research Design	Associated Words and Phrases
Phenomenological	Describes the essence; understand perspectives
Ethnographic	Seeks to explore and understand; "what"
Grounded Theory	Seeks to discover, establish, or confirm
Case Studies	Explores a process; "how"
Critical Studies	Transform; transformative; change; critical inquiry; reflection; "lens"
Narrative Inquiries	Telling of stories; storytelling; personal accounts

---

setting. Creswell & Guetterman (2019) suggest using the following script: "What is (*the central phenomenon*) for (*participants*) at (*research site*)?" (p. XX). An example would be "What is athletic participation like for current seniors at James River High School?" This kind of statement is clear and concise and tells the reader about what is being studied, who is being studied, and the context of the study.

6. **Use language that conveys the nature of the design.** Certain words are used to suggest the main design that is used in the study. Words and phrases associated with six major qualitative research designs are summarized in Table 3.5.

Check for Understanding 3

3a. Why is it important for qualitative research questions to be general rather than specific?

3b. What is the primary difference between qualitative and mixed methods research questions?

Mixed Methods Research Problems and Questions

Learning Outcome 3.4 Understand the nature of mixed methods research problem statements and questions.

Because both quantitative and qualitative approaches are used in mixed methods studies, each type of design would need to have appropriate research problems and questions to reflect the connection between question and method. There is also a third kind of research question that is needed for mixed methods studies—one that combines or integrates the qualitative and quantitative components. This is important to establish the unique contributions that arise from having both approaches focused on the same general research problem. Consequently, it is common to find a general research problem that frames the intent of the study, followed by research questions that refer to separate quantitative and qualitative phases and research questions that combine the phases. The unique, third type of question is called the *mixed methods research question* to distinguish it from either the solely quantitative or qualitative questions.

For example, suppose a researcher is interested in studying students' perceptions of the assessments they take in school (this is actually a topic I have investigated). A mixed methods design is selected that uses initial student interviews to generate major themes in their perceptions. The research question for this phase of the study could be "What is the nature of middle school students' attitudes toward the tests they take in school?" At the same time, a quantitative phase could be implemented, based on questions such as "To what extent do middle school students believe multiple-choice tests are difficult?" and "To what extent do middle school students value feedback from teachers about their work?" This convergent design could then have a mixed methods question, such as "Do students' attitudes toward tests reflect the importance of receiving feedback from teachers?" The mixed methods research question ties the two approaches together, providing focus to why a mixed methods study was conducted in the first place.

The same would be true for either explanatory or exploratory sequential mixed methods studies. The mixed methods question would be framed to reflect the logic of the design. For example, Excerpt 3.19 illustrates an explanatory sequential mixed methods design logic by explaining how the qualitative component contributed to a better understanding of quantitative findings, whereas the questions in Excerpt 3.20 illustrates an exploratory sequential design.

EXCERPT 3.19
Explanatory Sequential Mixed Methods Research Questions

Our central questions were: (1) To what extent are adolescents' beliefs about competence control, and social belongingness stable over the transition from middle school to high school? The quantitative component assessed these beliefs through standard surveys of competence, control, and belongingness. The qualitative component assessed these beliefs through open-ended questions about students' concerns that were subsequently coded with regard to competence, control, and belongingness; (2) To what extent do changes in perceived competence, control, and social belongingness from the end of middle school (8th grade) to the beginning of high school (end of 9th grade) predict changes in emotional well-being over this same time period? This question was addressed with the two-year quantitative data and interpreted in light of the three waves of qualitative data. (p. 57)

SOURCE: Wentzela, K. R., Tomback, R., Williams, A., & McNeish, D. (2019). Perceptions of competence, control, and belongingness over the transition to high school: A mixed-method study. *Contemporary Educational Psychology, 56*, 55–66.

EXCERPT 3.20

Exploratory Sequential Mixed Methods Research Questions

Qualitative focus groups of college students examined how young voters interpret the salience of political advertising to them, and a quantitative content analysis of more than 100 ads from the 2004 presidential race focus[es] on why group participants felt so alienated by political advertising.... Three questions ... are addressed:

- How does the interaction between audience-level and media-based framing contribute to college students' interpretations of the messages found in political advertising?
- To what extent do those interpretations match the framing found in the ads from the 2004 U.S. presidential election?
- How can political ads be framed to better engage college students? (p. 186)

SOURCE: Parmelee, J. H., Perkins, S. C., & Sayre, J. J. (2007). "What about people our age?" Applying qualitative and quantitative methods to uncover how political ads alienate college students. *Journal of Mixed Methods Research, 1*(2), 183–199.

Consumer (and Researcher) Tips

Criteria for Evaluating Mixed Methods Research Problem Statements and Questions

1. **Keep in mind criteria for both quantitative and qualitative questions.** This includes being clear, being succinct, and including some indication of the nature of the participants.
2. **Clearly align appropriate research questions to each phase of the study.** It can be rather confusing if there is no clear alignment between each research question and the appropriate type of design, whether quantitative or qualitative. Remember that with qualitative research the questions can, and often do, emerge or change during data collection. It is best to place research questions in proximity to the matched phase of the design and analysis. The mixed methods research question typically follows the quantitative and qualitative ones, although the overall research question may suggest the integration of the methods.
3. **Be sure to include a separate mixed methods research question.** You may not see a separate mixed methods research question in a study, although it may be implied by the research problem. Inclusion of a mixed methods question strengthens the credibility of the study.
4. **Match the research problem and mixed methods research question with the logic of the design.** The research questions need to clearly convey whether the mixed methods design is explanatory sequential, exploratory sequential, or concurrent. This is accomplished by using phrases that show whether there is a logical sequence or whether the different elements converge.

Author Reflection   *Coming up with a separate good mixed methods research question is anything but easy. But it is important because, in coming up with that question, you focus on the reason for doing a mixed methods study rather than either a quantitative or qualitative one. Because mixed methods studies are typically more complicated and time consuming, you need to be sure that what you get out of using both in one study will pay off. In other words, you might ask yourself: Is it really necessary to use a mixed methods design? If you cannot come up with a good mixed methods research question, it may not be.*

Check for Understanding 4

4a. What is the difference between explanatory sequential and exploratory sequential research questions?

Key Terms

Central phenomenon
Replication
Reproducibility
Research hypothesis
Research problem
Variable

Categorical variable
Conceptual definition
Confounding variable
Continuous variable
Dependent variable
Extraneous variable

Independent variable
Mediating variable
Moderating variable
Operational definition

Discussion Questions

1. How is significance best established for research problems?
2. How is it possible for a research problem statement or question to be too specific?
3. Under what circumstances would it be helpful to state research hypotheses?
4. Why is it important to include operational definitions of variables?
5. Why are qualitative research questions tentative rather than fixed?
6. Why is it important to have a mixed methods research question in a mixed methods study, in addition to the quantitative and qualitative questions?
7. How and why are quantitative, qualitative, and mixed methods research questions different?

Application Exercise

1. Either by yourself or with another student, locate an example of a quantitative or qualitative study. For the quantitative study, see whether you can identify the general research statement of purpose, specific research questions, and/or hypotheses; for a qualitative study, look for the general research question or purpose, and central question. Evaluate the questions/purpose and/or hypotheses based on the criteria presented.

Check for Understanding Answers

1a. Context shows how the study fits with previous or existing circumstances and research; significance is critical to show how the study findings will contribute to the knowledge of the field, practice, and/or policy.

1b. Take your pick:
- Skepticism and intuition: Questioning the use of existing practices may lead to new, more effective practice.
- Interests and experience: Studies based on current interests and experiences are likely to be significant.
- Applying theory: Theory provides a powerful tool for explaining phenomena.
- Previous research: Alignment with previous studies suggests that the current study will contribute to a better understanding of the knowledge in a line of research.
- Reproducing and replicating previous research: Replication is able to confirm findings to result in more accurate conclusions about knowledge.

2a. In experimental research, the independent variable is always the one that is controlled (manipulated) to show its effect on the dependent variable; in nonexperimental research there is no intervention but the independent variable precedes the dependent variable or is used to establish groups that are compared.

2b. Moderating variables are used to see whether the effect of an independent variable is impacted by other factors; mediating variables explain why an independent variable causes a change in the dependent variable.

2c. Research questions are neutral with respect to outcomes; research hypotheses are predictions about the differences or relationships that are anticipated.

2d. Clear; testable/researchable; specify variables/expected relationship.

3a. Qualitative research questions are general because the researcher needs to be open minded about whatever the data show, purposefully exploring related areas and possible connections to new areas.

3b. Quantitative research questions are very specific and targeted and include variables; qualitative questions are general; mixed methods questions focus on what can be combined from quantitative and qualitative questions.

4a. Explanatory sequential questions state that qualitative data are used to explain quantitative findings; exploratory sequential questions state that the qualitative data are used to generate quantitative data.

Chapter 4
Locating and Reviewing Related Literature

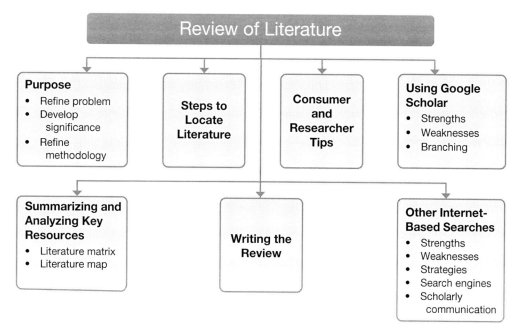

Review of Literature

Purpose
- Refine problem
- Develop significance
- Refine methodology

Steps to Locate Literature

Consumer and Researcher Tips

Using Google Scholar
- Strengths
- Weaknesses
- Branching

Summarizing and Analyzing Key Resources
- Literature matrix
- Literature map

Writing the Review

Other Internet-Based Searches
- Strengths
- Weaknesses
- Strategies
- Search engines
- Scholarly communication

Sergio Chaparro, Behavioral and Social Sciences Research Librarian, James Branch Cabell Library, Virginia Commonwealth University, provided helpful suggestions for the preparation of this chapter.

 Learning Outcomes

4.1 Describe how the review of literature is used to establish significance; to write research questions; and to identify appropriate sampling, data collection, and procedures.

4.2 Understand how to conduct a review of literature, including identification of key terms, databases, and search strategies.

4.3 Be able to synthesize related literature and write a review of literature.

Chapter Road Map

Once a research problem or general question has been identified, a review of the literature is essential. In this chapter I begin by summarizing the reasons for this, and I hope to convince you that the vast literature out there is both accessible and helpful—and even interesting. Then, we turn our attention to procedures for finding related studies, whether for quantitative, qualitative, or mixed methods research. This includes both primary and secondary sources. The chapter concludes with suggestions for organizing sources and writing the literature review section of a manuscript, article, proposal, or report.

Why Review Related Literature?

Learning Outcome 4.1   Describe how the review of literature is used to establish significance; to write research questions; and to identify appropriate sampling, data collection, and procedures.

When I teach my graduate students about research, the one topic that comes up over and over throughout the course is how existing literature can be used to first identify research questions and then inform methodology, results, interpretation, and conclusions. I have illustrated this in Figure 4.1 to emphasize how the literature contributes to all aspects of framing, understanding, conducting, and interpreting research.

Broadly stated, the initial purpose of the review is to relate previous research and theory to the problem under investigation. By showing how a current or proposed study compares with previous investigations, reviews of literature, and other scholarly discussions, the significance of the research problem can be established and placed in an appropriate context. The literature shows how the problem is aligned with the research questions. Subsequently, examining previous investigations helps researchers learn effective, as well as ineffective, methods. As we will learn in Chapter 16, good discussions interpret findings in light of previous studies. From a consumer's viewpoint, knowing the purpose of the review will contribute to an overall evaluation of the credibility of the research, as well as indicate whether the nature of the review is closely targeted to the reader's needs. Specific reasons for reviewing literature include the following:

- Refining the research problem
- Establishing the conceptual or theoretical framework
- Developing significance

Figure 4.1 How the Review of Literature Contributes to Empirical Studies

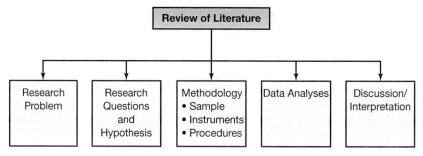

- Developing specific research questions and hypotheses
- Identifying methodological strengths and limitations
- Identifying contradictory findings
- Learning about new information
- Providing information for interpretation and discussion

Refining the Research Problem

By reviewing related studies and discussions of research in that area, you will learn how others have conceptualized and characterized the general problem. This will help you refine your initial problem. Ideas and examples will be found that help delimit the problem. The process of refining a research problem can be frustrating. Typically, your initial problem, which seems to have merit, must be changed as you review previous studies in the area. You formulate a new problem, and often it, too, needs revision as further literature is reviewed. This process can be repeated many times, so if you've experienced this, be patient—it's part of the process for establishing a good research problem.

Establishing the Conceptual or Theoretical Framework

By placing an investigation into a more general conceptual framework or theoretical orientation, a rationale is provided for the research question. The intellectual or scholarly perspective in which the problem is embedded is described. Establishing this framework is essential in quantitative and mixed methods studies. Some qualitative studies rely heavily on existing theories, whereas others take the perspective that it is best not to incorporate a particular theory because this could restrict or limit the inductive processes needed to analyze data. Finally, this part of the review helps to establish a logical link between the research questions and methodology. In Excerpt 4.1, from a study of the relationship between thinking styles and preferred interpersonal behavior, the author selects a specific theory of thinking styles to guide his research.

Developing Significance

Often it is not easy to see how some research is significant—how it contributes meaningfully to knowledge or practice. Making an argument without literature is tough; the existing literature can effectively establish significance by linking the proposed

---

EXCERPT 4.1

Using Theory in the Review of Literature

The theory of mental self-government (Sternberg, 1997) describes 13 thinking styles referring to people's preferred way of using the abilities that they have. Recent research conceptualizes that intellectual style is an overarching concept encompassing the meanings of all style constructs and distinguishes three types of styles. . . . Preferred thinking styles can be applied to different types of activities, including teaching and learning. (pp. 399–400)

SOURCE: Zhu, C. (2013). Students' and teachers' thinking styles and preferred teacher interpersonal behavior. *The Journal of Educational Research, 106,* 399–407.

Author Reflection *Sometimes researchers argue that a study is significant because of a "gap" in the literature or may contend that "little research" has been conducted in an area, or they may refer to a "paucity" of research (please consider not using the overused word paucity in your work and writing!). This may be fine, but be wary of "gaposis," which occurs when a researcher is so invested in filling a gap or doing something that has not been done that they imply that just because something has not been studied, it should be. Gaps by themselves do not indicate significance. What you want to identify is a "gap" in understanding.*

study to accumulated knowledge to indicate specifically how it will add to, expand, and build on this base. Previous studies will also help you identify new directions worth pursuing, determine needed replications, and avoid unnecessary duplication. Furthermore, researchers interpret results obtained from their study in relation to the findings from previous studies, making the conclusions more meaningful and enhancing the merit of the study.

Developing Specific Research Questions and Hypotheses

The existing literature is an excellent source for framing specific research questions and hypotheses. Examples of specific questions from other studies will give you ideas about wording and the number of questions that would be appropriate. Your own review will focus on the variables in your study so there is a clear and logical connection between the literature and the questions, showing the transition from the general problem to specific questions. Hypotheses should also be clearly related to what previous studies have found. The results from these studies provide justification for the direction of expected results. That is, previous research may suggest that a specific outcome is likely, and the new hypothesis is often consistent with that outcome. Therefore, a thorough review of literature is needed to find other empirical studies

EXCERPT 4.2

Using Literature to Develop Research Hypotheses

We based our predictions about the number and nature of the dimensions underlying students' attributions on the work of Wimer and Kelley (1982) and Weiner (1979, 1985). First, as Wimer and Kelley (1982) note, "researchers do not agree on a single set of attributional categories" (p. 1143). However, with few exceptions exploratory analyses of the structure of attribution have identified a locus of causality, or internal versus external, dimension. . . . Although less consistently, several investigations have also revealed a "good–bad" dimension (Passer et al., 1978; Ryan et al., 1981; Wimer and Kelley, 1982). Applied to an achievement setting, this view suggests that causes tend to be valenced: "good" causes increase the likelihood of success, whereas "bad" causes increase the likelihood of failure. We therefore expected to find evidence of both a locus of cause and a good–bad dimension in our analyses. (p. 161)

SOURCE: Forsyth, D. R., Story, P., Kelley, K. N., & McMillan, J. H. (2009). What causes failure and success? Students' perceptions of their academic outcomes. *Social Psychology of Education, 12*(2), 157–174.

and/or theories that can be used to formulate hypotheses. Sometimes, findings of studies from other fields are helpful. In Excerpt 4.2, a study from psychology is quoted to show the development of research hypotheses from the literature.

Identifying Methodological Strengths and Limitations

One of the best reasons to conduct a study is to investigate similar problems with different methods. By learning about the specific methods other researchers have employed to select participants, measure variables, and implement procedures, you can identify approaches that may be useful for your studies. Both successful and unsuccessful methods are usually found, and both help investigators identify new ideas and avoid past mistakes or difficulties. It is very helpful to identify measures and procedures that have been used successfully. This avoids the need for extensive psychometric work on new measures. Often, methodological weaknesses can suggest a need for research to be replicated with improvements in specific methods, as shown in Excerpts 4.3 and 4.4.

Identifying Contradictory Findings

A review of the literature may uncover studies or theories that contradict one another, as shown in Excerpt 4.5. As part of the review of literature for this study the authors cite conflicting previous research about the relationship between teacher retention and teacher gender. They go on to suggest that age may be a moderating variable that could explain the contradictory findings, providing justification for how the study will contribute to the knowledge base about teacher retention. Researchers find contradictory findings from previous studies a very fruitful area in which to conduct subsequent

---

EXCERPTS 4.3 AND 4.4
Identifying Methodological Limitations

Furthermore, for a number of reasons, the existing research is limited in its applicability to the case of a universal mandate, with which all schools are required to change their curricular offerings and all students are required to take college preparatory classes: First, virtually all prior studies have suffered from some degree of selection bias; second, prior research has paid little attention to differential effects by ability; finally, the findings developed from data on national samples may not generalize to schools with chronic low performance and weak instructional capacity. (p. 370)

SOURCE: Allensworth, E., Nomi, T., Montgomery, N., & Lee, V. (2009). College preparatory curriculum for all: Academic consequences of requiring algebra and English I for ninth graders in Chicago. *Educational Evaluation and Policy Analysis, 31*(4), 367–391.

Why is there so little agreement on the short-term effects of retention? There are three methodological reasons why studies differ in their conclusions about the short-term achievement effects of retention: (a) the point at which researchers estimate achievement effects; (b) the comparability of test scores across grades; and (c) the ability of researchers to construct adequate comparison groups of retained and promoted children and account for their prior characteristics. (p. 311)

SOURCE: Roderick, M., & Nagaoka, J. (2006). Retention under Chicago's high-stakes program: Helpful, harmful or harmless? *Educational Evaluation and Policy Analysis, 27*(4), 309–340.

EXCERPT 4.5

Identifying Contradictory Findings

Prior studies on the relationship between gender and teacher turnover have produced mixed results. Some studies find that women had higher turnover rates (migration or attrition) than did men (e.g., Ingersoll, 2001; Kirby, Berends, & Naftel, 1999), whereas other studies suggest that men are more likely to quit teaching or to transfer schools than women (e.g., Boyd et al., 2005; Ingersoll, 2001). Additionally, some research has found no gender differences in teacher turnover rates (e.g., Strunk & Robinson, 2006), while some scholars (e.g., Rees, 1991) have argued that men and women have similar exit behaviors before marriage but diverge after marriage due to childrearing and family obligations. It is possible, therefore, that patterns of exit behaviors may differ among men and women of different ages. We test this hypothesis in our model by incorporating interaction terms between gender and age indicators. (pp. 8–9)

SOURCE: Newton, X., Rivero, R., Fuller, B., & Dauter, L. (2018). Teacher turnover in organizational context: Staffing stability in Los Angeles Charter, Magnet, and regular public schools. *Teachers College Record, 120*(3), 1–36.

---

research. Possible reasons for the contradiction, such as the use of different types of participants, measures, or procedures, or additional variables can be identified, and research can be designed to resolve the contradiction.

Learning New Information

A review of literature almost always leads to new information and knowledge—in the topic of interest, related topics, or even unrelated areas. How often have you been reading research for one purpose and gotten distracted by other interesting ideas and findings? It happens to all of us when we do a lot of reading of the literature, and this is a good thing. Through the review of literature, you will also learn about journals, books, and other sources that publish information in your field of study.

Providing Information for Interpretation and Discussion

Once researchers report their findings, they need to interpret them, figure out what it all means. This is done in the discussion section of a research report. A good study integrates the literature into the discussion, showing how findings compare with what others have found and support or fail to support a theory or conceptual framework. This is often the most difficult part of doing really good research. But when you connect your findings to what others have found you can strengthen the significance of your study and show how it contributes to the literature.

Check for Understanding 1

1a. What are the major purposes of reviewing related literature?

1b. Explain how related literature is needed to establish the significance and credibility of a proposed study.

Steps to Find Related Literature in Established Literature Databases

Learning Outcome 4.2 Understand how to conduct a review of literature, including identification of key terms, databases, and search strategies.

As you are no doubt aware, the amount of information that is available on different topics is expanding exponentially, and our electronic capabilities allow us access to most of this information. This presents both challenges and opportunities. On the challenge side, how do researchers cull what is important from the vast amount of research that is out there? How can you be efficient and selective with your search so you can identify the research that will be most relevant and helpful? At the same time, it is likely that there is information out there on your topic of interest. Today, it is not so much finding studies that is the issue (not like the "old" days when folks like me went to the library and searched for articles by reading printed journals)—that is now easy—what is difficult, though, is identifying the most appropriate literature for your research problem and questions. This is best accomplished by following a few steps when searching for articles. By employing the steps, you will more efficiently find what will be most helpful.

There are two main approaches for finding related literature: using (1) established literature databases, and (2) Google Scholar. In addition, there are other Internet-based sources that may be helpful. In this section, steps for searching established literature databases are summarized, then we will consider Google Scholar and other Internet-based sources.

If you are just getting started with learning how to review the literature you probably will find it helpful to get oriented to the library you will use, including the organization of reference materials, the organization of the library website, and databases used. Most libraries offer very helpful instructional tools—seminars, webinars, and virtual lessons on various topics—that will help you get started in reviewing research. Most also offer tutorials available through the library website that are targeted toward specific fields. Often, reference librarians will specialize in a particular discipline, so if possible, seek out a person with experience in educational or social science literature. Don't be shy about asking your librarian about how to use available resources. It is important to learn how to identify, locate, and access the best sources for your topic efficiently, and a librarian can help immensely. Librarians *want* you to contact them.

By following four steps, outlined in Figure 4.2, you will increase the quality of your search using established literature databases and locate the most appropriate studies more quickly.

Figure 4.2 Sequence of Steps to Find Related Research in Established Literature Databases

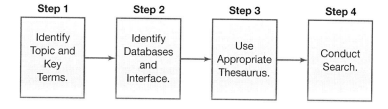

Step 1: Select a Topic and Key Terms

The first step in reviewing literature is to have some idea of the topic or subject in which you are interested. This could be rather general, such as "What teaching methods are best for students with learning disabilities?" or more specific, such as the research questions and hypotheses discussed in Chapter 3. Identify the most important terms in the problem and then think about other terms that are closely related. You will then use these terms in databases to find literature. For example, if you are interested in student motivation, it would be wise to use related terms, such as *engagement, effort, persistence, intrinsic motivation,* and *self-efficacy.* Your initial reading in an area will give you some idea whether the topic is closely related to a particular field of study outside education, such as health, psychology, sociology, or business. This will be helpful in completing Step 2.

Step 2: Identify Literature Database(s) and Interface

Research literature is stored in many different *literature databases.* A **literature database** is an organized and indexed grouping of publications and other scholarly documents in a field of study, one that is accessible electronically and allows searching for specific topics. Most databases have hundreds, if not thousands, of different journals and other types of sources, and there are hundreds of databases.

This means that you need to choose which databases will give you the best results. Although many journals are included in several databases, each database has its own unique sources. Just to give you an idea of the many databases that exist, here is a list of a few that are relevant to educators (those with an asterisk are clearly the most popular):

- ERIC—Education Resources Information Center*
- Education Research Complete*
- Dissertation Abstracts Online
- LexisNexis
- MEDLINE/PubMed
- PsycINFO*
- Sociological Abstracts
- Scopus (Elsevier's abstract and citation database)
- Social Sciences Citation Index (via the Web of Science)
- Teachers Reference Center

Most libraries also provide access to one or more multidisciplinary databases, such as Expanded Academic ASAP (Gale Cengage), Academic Search Complete (EBSCO), ProQuest Central (ProQuest), or the library's own single search platform, all of which can supply articles from scholarly journals, trade publications, and popular magazines from many fields.

Educational researchers usually find that ERIC, from the U.S. Department of Education, and PsycINFO, from the American Psychological Association, are the most helpful databases for finding relevant primary research articles. **ERIC**, an electronic database for finding relevant primary research articles in all areas of education, contains more than 1.3 million bibliographic records of journal articles, conference papers, reports, research syntheses, dissertations, books, and more. It is designed to provide a comprehensive, up-to-date, easily searchable database for anyone interested in educational research programs or issues. As such, ERIC is your best friend when it comes to finding the right literature.

The **PsycINFO** database contains documents, articles, dissertations, and books in psychology and related disciplines, including education. This database is also accessible online and contains more than 57 million cited references, covering mostly peer-reviewed journals, books, and dissertations. The InfoTrac Onefile database has access to more than 50 million articles, about half of which are available online and printed from your computer. This file combines scholarly and popular journals and magazines in all fields. Finally, a very useful database for conducting educational literature searches is Education Research Complete, from EBSCO. This database indexes and abstracts more than 2,400 education-related journals, books, and conference papers, and has full text for more than 1,400 journals and 500 books.

Both ERIC and PsycINFO will be available through one or more interfaces through a university library. These interfaces are selected by each library and provide somewhat different search options and screen layouts when you go to do your search, and also give slightly different results for the same search. Two common interfaces for ERIC are FirstSearch and ProQuest, although you can also go straight to ERIC on the government website, ERIC.ed.gov. Once you access the database, you are ready for Step 3.

Step 3: Use the Appropriate Thesaurus

Once you have identified key terms and a database, it is best to use a special *thesaurus* to help select the most appropriate words and phrases to use in your search. A **thesaurus** is a repository of words in a field of study that are used purposely to show how they are related, as well as to show synonyms and antonyms. You will want to use either the ERIC Thesaurus or the Thesaurus of Psychological Index Terms (accessed in the PsycINFO database with definitions and uses that are somewhat different than those in the ERIC Thesaurus). Find the *thesaurus* link when you open the database to begin a search, then type in the word or words of interest.

The thesaurus in ERIC has a "controlled vocabulary" of terms called *descriptors*. Descriptors are subject terms and are used to organize the index database materials by subject, regardless of the vocabulary used by the source authors. Professional indexers assign several descriptors to each record to represent the subjects covered in the article or document. Every record in ERIC will have assigned descriptors. The thesaurus is a great source of synonyms and alternative vocabulary, as it is organized in a hierarchical manner, showing broader, narrower, and related terms for each entry.

The thesaurus also uses *identifiers* (or *keywords*). Identifiers classify proper nouns, words, and phrases that are not yet descriptors and do not appear on every record. Keywords in FirstSearch match words found in the indexed record (title and abstract), whereas descriptors locate records that may not contain the specific keyword. This means that you need to search using both descriptors and identifiers/keywords.

You can search the ERIC Thesaurus by entering a specific term or phrase, or by browsing alphabetically or by category, to determine a match between how ERIC tends to define a term and your use of a term. A critical aspect of using different terms is to understand that a given topic will have broader or more narrow terms as well, as illustrated in Figure 4.3. When first beginning a search, it is best to use more general,

Figure 4.3 Specificity of ERIC Descriptors

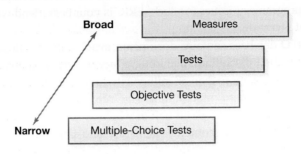

rather than more specific, terms. You can get an idea of the specificity of a term by pulling up the thesaurus record on it that shows other broader and narrower terms, as well as related terms. You can also see how ERIC has defined the term.

Suppose your topic is "the effect of using alternative assessment on student achievement." You enter "alternative assessment" in the thesaurus. The record shows that "evaluation" is a broader term and "performance-based assessment" is a narrower term. Interestingly, "authentic assessment" is not a related term, even though for many, this would be a type of alternative assessment. When I used "authentic assessment" to search in ERIC in January 2019, more than 1200 records were identified. This illustrates an important point in using key terms for your search: You must spend considerable time trying different searches with different terms, and you cannot assume that the way *you* think about and define terms is the same as the way the ERIC personnel who maintain the database think. Furthermore, key terms may change or be replaced by others.

Step 4: Conduct the Search

Although searches can be conducted in a number of different databases, we will limit our discussion of the literature search in education to ERIC in this section. The specific nature of the procedures to use to search ERIC depends on which interface you use. Each ERIC record has a number of searchable fields that can be incorporated into a search strategy to limit or narrow results. The placement of these fields for searching depends on the interface. Both EBSCO and ProQuest display most of the limiting fields on the Advanced Search screen, whereas ERIC.ed.gov displays these fields on the results page, after the initial search. (This means that ERIC.ed.gov requires an initial search to display them, whereas other interfaces give you options before your first search.)

Author Reflection *My experience in doing literature reviews is that the quality of studies has not changed appreciably for at least 20 years. Some topics were researched heavily many years ago with very good studies, so although it is important to use recent studies, don't be shy about using the older ones. I have found it more important to find other primary sources closest to what you want to research than to find something published recently.*

For example, you can limit your search to certain types of sources, such as journal articles, speeches, or reports. If you select "all" documents (even those not formally published in an article) you get the greatest number of records. You can select specific types of documents by checking as many as apply down the rather long list. If you check "journal article," for example, research disseminated as conference papers or reports will not be accessed. You can also limit searches by educational level (e.g., elementary, high school, or secondary education), targeted audience, and other screens.

Searches typically must be tailored until they can identify a reasonable number of sources that appear to be closely related to their research problem. The most common way of limiting a search is to use "and" to connect concepts or topics. Using *and* will reduce the number of records in the search because the computer will look for entries that are categorized by all the descriptors or keywords indicated. For example, a search of *teaching styles* and *elementary* would produce fewer hits than using only one of these terms. (*Teaching styles* by itself would include elementary, middle, and high schools, as well as colleges and universities.) If a third descriptor—say, *achievement*—is added, the search is further refined. This process of narrowing the search is illustrated in Figure 4.4, using descriptors "teaching style," "academic achievement," and "elementary education," completed in January 2019. If the delimiter "peer reviewed" is included (**peer review** means that experts in the field review the manuscript and make recommendations about revisions and acceptance) the final number was a very workable 27 records. You can use either sets (preferred) or Boolean logic (or, and) to construct a query. Put parentheses around sets, quotation marks around phrases or words you want to have together, and commas between terms. You can use an asterisk next to a term to retrieve all forms of that term (e.g., attitude* will also search for "attitudes").

Figure 4.4 Narrowing an ERIC Search

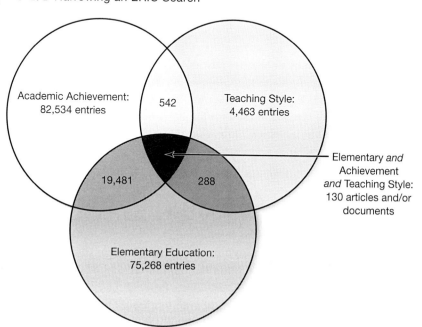

Once you construct a tailored search, you may wish to save the search, particularly when conducting ongoing research on a topic. It is best to check with your librarian for procedures that can be used to save searches.

The result of an ERIC search will be a list of records: articles and documents, summary information, and an abstract for each entry. You will find an ERIC number assigned to the entry. This number is permanent and will be the same across all versions of ERIC. If the number begins with EJ, it is a journal article; if it begins with ED, it is a nonjournal document.

One advantage of searching nonjournal documents is that conference presentations, proceedings, and federally funded research projects are included. Some of these presentations and projects may eventually be reported as articles, but there may be a significant time lag between submission of a manuscript to a journal for publication and the article appearing online or in print.

Once you have limited your search to a reasonable number of records—for instance, between 5 and 20—you need to obtain the articles or reports to examine each one in greater detail to determine whether they should be used in your review. Most journal articles are available electronically through your library, and you will be able to download them to a file or print them. In addition, I would recommend using RefWorks, Mendeley, EndNote, Reference Manager, Zotero, or some other type of citation management tool to organize and keep track of your records. These tools will allow you to move all your sources from different searches into a single database for later retrieval and use, and have the very important feature of formatting references into different output styles, including APA, MLA, and Chicago Style. Most libraries will have electronic links among these tools and databases that allow quick access. If you will be collecting much literature over a period of time, using these tools is a great help. Your library should have a citation management resource guide that will help in using these services.

The typical process, then, involves taking a large number of possible documents and reducing that number down to the relatively few that are appropriate to your review. For example, you might begin a study on science and mathematics teaching strategies with some 12,000 hits; reduce that number by restricting your search to a few years; reduce it again by accessing only journal articles; locate those articles; and then, finally, pick eight articles from among the 22 you obtained.

My recent ERIC searches have resulted in many articles from foreign-based journals and organizations. Many of these are credible, but many are not. Some are what we call "vanity" journals, in which the author(s) pay to have their work published. I would recommend sticking to known, high-quality journals first.

Google Scholar Searches

A relatively new and excellent tool for conducting literature reviews is Google Scholar. **Google Scholar** captures a wide range of sources from many different disciplines, including books, abstracts, articles, reports, court opinions, and other documents from academic journals, university websites, conference proceedings, professional societies, and academic publishers across the spectrum of scholarly fields. As a consequence, it is a very large and diverse set of scholarly literature. Furthermore, Google Scholar

Figure 4.5 Google Scholar Search Result

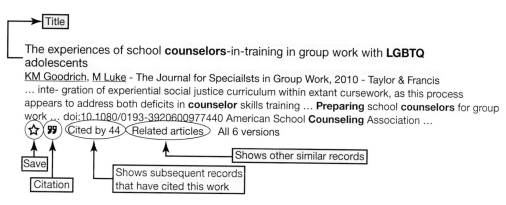

allows you to see how often an article or document has been cited by others, with links to those and other related records. A great advantage of Google Scholar is that it is linked to most academic libraries, so as a student when you identify a source of interest and want the full article, if the library subscribes to the journal the article can be easily retrieved for free (just like an article identified in ERIC or PsycINFO). Google Scholar also allows you to limit your search in several ways, including by author, publication dates, and relevance. On the downside, Google Scholar will give you hundreds if not thousands of hits to sort through (though it is still not comprehensive, nor are sources vetted by professionals). It is not clear what "scholarly" means, so the quality of the sources can vary greatly. Google Scholar also does not allow you to limit by "peer review." Finally, as a for-profit company, there may be concerns about whether material that could impact the bottom line is excluded.

A look at a typical Google Scholar output illustrates key advantages. In Figure 4.5 I have copied one record (out of 9590!) based on the terms 'counselor preparation and LGBTQ students.'

Not only was I able to obtain the full citation in one of several formats (e.g., APA, MLA, Harvard), when I clicked on 'Cited by 44,' it showed me 44 other records that have cited this article. This is a great way to follow up an article that is very close to what you want to review. These articles, in turn, are typically cited by others. Branching in this way allows a unique way of identifying closely related work that may not show up in the original list of hits. In addition to these 44 records, 110 more were identified in 'Related articles.' Using this branching approach is especially helpful with narrow topics, such as the example in Figure 4.5, and when you want to follow the work of particular authors. (Yes, you can search by author; this can be especially interesting and fun for those you know personally or have heard about.) Using ERIC with the same terms I got two hits, not including the one in Figure 4.5.

There is a key lesson to be learned here: You simply cannot do a good search by using *only* Google Scholar or *only* ERIC or some other database. Use both or many— you will find that this is the best approach for identifying the best literature related to your problem. Similarly, you can't be content with just a couple of searches using different terms and/or limiters.

The Hedgehog and the Fox Search the Literature

I've found several good studies of my topic in ERIC so I think I'm ready to write my review of literature.

I've found several good studies of my topic in ERIC, now I need to see whether there are other studies that can be identified in Google Scholar or PsycINFO.

Other Internet-Based Searches

While Google is a great source for finding literature, the Internet has much more to offer. Some of the most pertinent ways the Internet can be used are summarized in this section.

Strengths and Weaknesses of Using the Internet

The amount of information that is readily and quickly available on the Internet is truly amazing. Your challenge is to sift through thousands of web sources to find credible, helpful information. A careful consideration of the Internet's strengths and weaknesses will help you determine when and how to search the Internet for a specific topic. On the positive side, the Internet is particularly good at quickly delivering current and niche information, it can show you many articles and reports just by typing in the title, and it is conveniently accessed from almost anywhere. However, the Internet does not serve as an exhaustive source for searching educational literature. In addition, the Internet is not designed and organized for an educational researcher, nor are there uniform standards for accuracy and quality of the information. It is not a scholarly database. There is no indexing or quality control.

One of the most difficult aspects of using the Internet for educational research, including Google Scholar, is that, unlike databases such as ERIC, there is no standard, professionally determined vocabulary that facilitates a search. In ERIC you can depend on the subject headings, descriptors, and keywords to target needed information. There is no comparable system in place for the Internet, and there is no universal thesaurus to consult to determine the best search terms.

Everything that you find in ERIC has been through some type of professional review process. This does not mean that everything in ERIC is of high quality, but overall quality will be better than much of what is available from the Internet. Anyone (from a teenager to a respected scholar) can "publish" on the Internet. Although there is an appealing egalitarian characteristic to the Internet, it is crucial to evaluate the quality of Internet sources.

Even though ERIC offers a better-organized and peer-reviewed set of information about educational research, the Internet does have its advantages. If a journal has an online version, you will be able to browse the most recent publications—volumes that might take months to appear in ERIC. Also, online journals will often contain the full text of each article, whereas some ERIC articles and documents are limited to abstracts. Academic libraries, however, provide easy access to full-text articles, as they have electronic connections between ERIC search results and the library's collection of journals. You will also find useful information on the Internet beyond journal articles and research reports, such as statistics, e-mail links to experts, governmental information, datasets, organization websites, and discussion forums.

Fortunately, you are not limited in your research to either the Internet or journal databases like ERIC. In framing your research question, think about the type of information that each might offer. For example, you would certainly want to know what the research on your topic has looked like for the past 10 years as well as in the past months. By combining the Internet with the research tools that were presented earlier, you can capture a well-rounded and diverse portrait for your topic.

Internet Search Strategies

Once you have identified appropriate Internet search tools, pay attention to the various search options that each one offers, and construct your computer search accordingly. Each Internet search company (such as Bing, Yahoo!, or Google) compiles its own database of Internet sites. When you "search the Internet," you are really searching these databases. That is, your search does not go out onto the web and look at every page in existence. In choosing an Internet search tool, you want to look beyond the search screen and get some idea of the quality, content, organization, and scope of the data behind the scenes. The three primary types of Internet search utilities are *subject directories*, *search engines*, and *metasearch engines*. Understanding the differences among these will improve your Internet searching considerably.

SUBJECT DIRECTORIES   Internet **subject directories** are the "yellow pages" of the Internet, in which you are able to browse through lists of Internet resources by topic. Typically, each topic is located within a hierarchy of subjects. For example, in a subject directory there may be a choice for "Education," then numerous choices under that subject, such as "Universities," "K–12," "Government," "History," and so on. The advantage of subject directories is that the content has been reviewed and organized by a human! Subject directories rely on teams of editors who have knowledge of specific disciplines. Thus, under each category you will find a high degree of relevance and quality. Subject directories are often the quickest way to assemble a manageable list of Internet resources for a topic. Here are some research questions that would be especially good for a subject directory:

Where can I find a list of educational associations?
Where can I find the department of education from each state?
Where can I find a listing of online education journals?

Search Engines

Search engines are mechanisms to search thousands of web pages. Whereas subject directories are assembled and organized by human editors, search engines (e.g., Yahoo, Duck Duck Go, Google, Bing) are compiled in an automated fashion. Each search engine uses a "spider" or "robot" that trolls through the web from hyperlink to hyperlink, capturing information from each page that it visits. Therefore, the content of each search engine is dependent on the characteristics of its spider:

- How many pages has it visited?
- How often does it visit each page?
- When it visits, how much of the web page does it record?

This means that it is wise to try several search engines.

Because search engines index billions of web pages, they offer a quick way to search for specific words that may appear in web pages. Here are some research questions that would be especially appropriate for a search engine:

Are there any web pages that cover standardized testing in California?

Are there any web pages that deal with John Dewey's *Democracy in Education*?

SEARCH LANGUAGE   There is no standard search language that is consistent across all search engines. Some search engines understand logical connectors like "and," whereas others insist that you use a "+" before each word if you wish to limit your results to combined terms. Despite the lack of standards, there are several features that are common to most search engines. For example, even though some engines use "and," whereas others look for "+," the feature of combining more than one idea into a single search is available across all search engines. One of the best places to find out about each engine's search language is its online help page. It is advisable, even for seasoned Internet searchers, to periodically revisit the help pages of their favorite search engine. Google's searching tips are available at googleguide.com/. This site offers many tips to search more effectively and an online interactive tutorial that will help you get the most from the guide. Use the "advanced search" option with search engines to identify advancements and special search features such as limiting searches to location, language, and type of media.

RELEVANCY   In addition to search options, it is helpful to be familiar with the retrieval algorithms. **Retrieval algorithms** determine both how many pages each search retrieves and how the results of each search are ordered. The search algorithm is a mathematical formula that determines how many times and where your search terms appear in each document. For example, if you were searching for "cooperative learning," the web pages that appear at the top of your search results should be the most relevant. Perhaps these pages had both words as part of their title, whereas the web pages that appear at the very end of your search results might simply have the word "cooperative" somewhere in their text. If your results start to look less and less relevant, do not keep looking through the same list. Move on to a new search or a new search engine.

Metasearch Engines

A **metasearch engine** submits your search to multiple search engines at the same time. Examples of metasearch engines include Dogpile, Yippy, and Metacrawler. Metasearch engines can be especially useful since each search engine includes pages and records that others do not. On the other hand, no single metasearch engine includes all the major search engines. In addition, you cannot take advantage of the specific search language or features that are native to each search engine. For this reason, it is best to use search engines for your complex Internet searching, and rely on metasearch engines for searches that are very simple, having only one or two words. With metasearch engines it is especially important to pay attention to relevancy, as you have less control over how each search engine interprets your metasearch query. The following are examples of good questions for a metasearch engine:

Are there any sources that mention elementary school portfolio assessment?

Are there any sources that mention Jonathan Kozol?

Table 4.1 lists several subject directories and search engines that you will find helpful in using the Internet to find educational research and other information on contemporary educational issues (refer to thesearchenginelist.com/ for a complete list).

Open Access

Recently, **open access** articles and manuscripts have become important sources for reviewing research. Open access means that there is no charge to use the resources, nor is there a need for special permission. As the name implies, they are "open" to all. They also are free of copyright and licensing restrictions. Many traditional publishers now have a multitude of high-quality open access journals. OpenDOAR, the Directory of Open Access Journals (which contains about 500 education-related journals), OSF Preprints, SocArxiv, and OER Commons all provide lists of open-access journals. For example, the American Educational Research Association has an open access journal called AERA Open. Like more traditional journals, the highest-quality open access journals are peer reviewed.

Beyond Web Pages: Scholarly Communication Strategies

Perhaps the most revolutionary aspect of the Internet is its ability to connect people with shared interests. This is especially powerful in highly technical and specific areas of study in which geographical boundaries might otherwise hinder communication among a limited number of experts. For example, it might be hard to find a group of scholars in any one location who were all interested in the sociology of education. Through the Internet, however, scholars as well as practitioners are able to form

Table 4.1 Types and Descriptions of Internet Search Tools

Subject Directories	Description
Educator's Desk Reference	Provides high-quality resources and services, including lesson plans, links, responses to questions, theory, and research
Search Engines	
Google	Most popular and heavily used search engine, with extensive coverage of all types of sources
Bing	Large, comprehensive search engine sponsored by Microsoft
Yahoo! Search	Provides comprehensive searches of Yahoo! database
Ask	Allows you to access information by asking specific questions; some research included
Metasearch Engines	
Dogpile	Brings together searches from other leading search engines, including Google and Yahoo! Search, by relevance to the topic
Metacrawler	Searches other search engines, such as Google and Yahoo!, by relevance, sorted by commercial and noncommercial sites
Yippy	Provides consumer friendly results in clusters; good for blogs and personalized tabs
Surfwax	Shows results differently from other search engines, allows personalization

groups and discuss various issues specific to their field of study. Through the use of e-mail, mailing lists, newsgroups, blogs, social networks, and conferences, educational researchers have ready access to their peers and do not need to be isolated by location.

E-MAIL AND SOCIAL NETWORKING   Through e-mail it is possible to easily contact researchers, librarians, or institutions to get guidance on a specific research question. E-mail is also an excellent way to collaborate with colleagues on works in progress by sharing ideas, drafts, and files. You can locate experts on your topic by using Ask an Expert or the Directory of Educational Researchers and by searching university departments and schools of education that list faculty members and their research interests. Simply type the name of the college or university into a search engine, go to the web page of the appropriate school or department, and peruse the list of faculty, which usually includes e-mail addresses, or use the search feature on the university website.

One of the fastest-growing avenues for communication via the Internet is through social networking sites such as Facebook and LinkedIn. Social networking allows individuals to communicate individually and through participation in shared interest groups.

Author Reflection *Don't be hesitant about contacting researchers! Professors and other researchers are (almost) always pleased that students are interested in their work. A short, simple request will suffice.*

NEWSGROUPS, E-MAIL DISCUSSION GROUPS, BLOGS, AND LISTSERVS   There are literally thousands of newsgroups, mailing lists, and listservs on the Internet that cover every conceivable area of interest. Many newsgroups and discussion groups are very active in scholarly content and commentary, providing new viewpoints and new strategies for research as identified by others with similar interests. They are an excellent way to stay current in your area of interest.

USING KNOWN LOCATIONS   The third method for doing effective literature reviews on the Internet is to access known sources, authorities, and experts. A good starting point for online research is a library website. Virtually all libraries have begun developing resource or research guides or directories of websites classified by subject in order to make the Internet more accessible and better arranged for their users. Many universities have resource guides for most academic subjects, which will include one specific to education.

Check university and research center libraries that are known to be strong in the particular subject. Often, the websites for these organizations include unique information and resources. For example, the University of Illinois has a strong collection of children's literature, so if you were interested in that area, it would make sense to contact the University of Illinois library to see what has been done there to organize the topic.

In addition to libraries, federal and state government websites are excellent sources. A good starting place is the U.S. Department of Education's website (discussed in the next section), or the websites of state departments of education. These websites include not only a great variety of primary data, but also hyperlinks to other government sites and related websites. Other known sources of information include websites for national associations and organizations, companies focusing on educational products, nonprofit organizations, newspapers, and online journals.

FEDERAL GOVERNMENT   A good place for education professionals to begin their Internet research is at the U.S. Department of Education's website, ed.gov. This site contains current news and headlines, announcements about new projects and initiatives, related websites, and listings of the department's educational priorities and national objectives. It also includes budget information, policy issues, databases, funding opportunities, information on legislation that affects education, and websites for other departmental offices and contacts.

The Institute of Education Sciences (IES) is a particularly noteworthy part of the U.S. Department of Education. The IES plays a prominent role in educational research by conducting, collecting, and distributing research studies and statistics. The IES website homepage (ies.ed.gov) includes links to current educational research news, grant opportunities, statistics, publications, and other federally supported centers.

ASSOCIATIONS, ORGANIZATIONS, AND UNIVERSITY WEBSITES   All larger professional associations and universities have a substantial web presence. At each of these sites you can find useful information, such as lists of faculty, publications, resolutions, and links to other websites. By visiting these pages, you not only can gain knowledge of educational research, but can also get a feel for the culture and activity of each organization.

The American Educational Research Association (AERA) is particularly relevant. AERA (aera.net) is composed of divisions and special interest groups in all education areas (e.g., classroom assessment, teacher education, special education, mixed methods research). Researchers in these fields present their findings at a large conference each year, and there is electronic access to most of the papers that are presented.

> **Author Reflection** *Searching the Internet for educational research is now at the point that it actually makes sense to simply go online and try some things. There is so much out there that, in all probability, you will find something of value. It is especially helpful when searching for information on current issues and problems, even if much of what you find on these areas will be opinions, points of view, editorials, and positions, not empirical studies. To learn about contemporary topics quickly, however, the Internet is a great resource.*

Consumer (and Researcher) Tips

Evaluating Information from the Internet

Information obtained from the Internet can be an excellent complement to print research, but it can also be of low quality and even deceptive and misleading. Researchers using the Internet need to critically evaluate resources found online just as they would evaluate information found in a library, government office, center report, or journal. Remember that in most cases there is no peer review of information. As a result, the quality of the information varies considerably. Some of what you find may be of high quality and credible, whereas other information may be biased to present a particular point of view or may simply be of low quality. Your evaluation of Internet material will be strengthened by asking the following questions:

- Who is the author or publisher of the information? If an organization, is there an agenda?
- What is the author's reputation and what are the author's qualifications in the subject covered?

- Is the information objective or is there a noticeable bias?
- Are the facts or statistics verifiable?

When searching for contemporary topics, it is common to find center and nonprofit organization websites. Many of these organizations have a clear agenda that is promoted, so it is advisable to understand these points of view to detect bias and opinion rather than a more balanced, scholarly perspective. The key to evaluating any type of research is to carefully read and analyze the content. It is also helpful to find a variety of sources so you can compare and contrast them to get a fully informed view of any subject.

Check for Understanding 2

2a. What are the steps that need to be taken to conduct a good review of literature?

2b. What are the advantages and disadvantages of using ERIC and Google Scholar searches?

Read, Analyze, and Summarize Key Sources

Learning Outcome 4.3   Be able to synthesize related literature and write a review of literature.

You have found some articles and reports; now you need to decide how to use them for your review. This process begins with knowing whether the source is primary or secondary.

Identify the Source as Primary or Secondary

As you review literature, you will come across many different types of articles and reports. This can seem confusing because there are thousands of journals, agencies, and organizations that publish research reports. A good first step is to identify sources as *primary* or *secondary*. A **primary source** is an original article or report in which researchers communicate directly to the reader the data source, methods, analyses, and results of their studies. Primary sources provide first-hand or direct evidence of something.

Primary sources are reported in a wide variety of journals. In fact, hundreds of journals publish educational research, and they differ greatly in terms of quality. To understand these differences, consider how articles get published. The most common procedure is for the author(s) to write a manuscript that will be submitted to a journal for publication. If the format and topic of the article are appropriate, the editor will usually send the manuscript to two or three reviewers and/or associate or assistant editors to be evaluated. The evaluation is structured so that the reviewers, who are "experts" on the topic investigated, comment on the significance of the problem, methodology, data analysis, contribution of the findings and conclusions, and other criteria. Usually, the reviewers are asked to recommend one of four next steps: that the manuscript be published as submitted, revised slightly or some and resubmitted, revised with major revisions, or rejected. Rarely do they recommend to publish as submitted. The journal is said to be **refereed** if this peer-review procedure is followed. A **nonrefereed** journal does not use external reviewers to evaluate manuscripts. This feature is usually indicated on search databases.

Most journal articles have some kind of peer review, which tends to result in better quality than nonjournal documents. However, there are exceptions. Many journal articles, even with peer review, are not very credible, and many nonjournal documents are excellent.

The strength of the refereed process is that helpful suggestions from reviewers improve the quality of the manuscript. Most journals use a *blind review* process to control for reviewer bias. A **blind review** is one in which the names of the authors and their organizational affiliation are omitted. Clearly, a blind review process is desirable and is usually employed by high-quality journals. In the "publish or perish" culture of higher education, it is more prestigious to be published in higher-quality journals. As a result, many more manuscripts are submitted to these journals than are actually accepted. Indeed, the rejection rate is often used as a barometer of quality. The checklist in Figure 4.6 will help you determine journal quality.

One source that "objectively" evaluates journal quality is Journal Citation Reports, which provides statistical information based on articles' cited references, and publishes a "journal impact factor." Although not all journals are included in the Journal Citation Reports database, it is still an interesting source that gives some relative indicator of influence of many journals in a given field of study. Many other impact factor ratings are available, including Thomas Reuters, Scopus (Elsevier), and Google Scholar. The SCImago Journal Rank, contained on the Scopus website, includes four measures of quality for each journal. Also, you can see what the acceptance rate is for a journal, as well as its circulation. Obviously, journals with a small acceptance rate generally have better research that those with a high acceptance rate (a few education journals are less than 10%!). Remember though, just because research is reported in a journal that isn't rated high or has a high acceptance rate doesn't mean it can't be good research.

Figure 4.6 Checklist for Determining High-Quality Journals

✓ Is the journal refereed?

✓ Do the articles focus on a specific field of study or area, rather than wide or general coverage?

✓ Is there an editorial board, and do the board members have strong reputations?

✓ Is the journal indexed in multiple databases? (check *Ulrich's Periodicals Directory*)

✓ Does much come up with an Internet search of the journal?

✓ Is the journal supported by a specific professional organization?

✓ Is the acceptance rate low? (check *Cabell's Directories*)

✓ Is the journal highly ranked according to impact factor?

Author Reflection *In the past decade there has been a proliferation of new journals, most of which claim to publish "peer reviewed" articles. But some of these journals are closer to "vanity" than sound academic journals, and the quality of the articles varies greatly. The demand to publish, worldwide, is great, and these new journals are meeting the needs of graduate students and professors to establish a publication record. Just beware and be guarded—in my view there is a proliferation of low-quality research as a result of demand to be published. All the more reason to critically evaluate what you read!*

A **secondary source** is one that reviews, summarizes, or discusses primary research as well as theoretical frameworks or ideas. The author(s) provide(s) information and analysis, but it is not a firsthand gathering of data.

In earlier editions of this book I recommended that students begin a literature review by searching for appropriate secondary sources. Searching for secondary sources first is good because they provide an overview of the topic, often citing relevant research studies and important primary sources. Some examples of secondary sources are textbooks, scholarly books devoted to a particular topic, reviews of research in books or journals, yearbooks, encyclopedias, and handbooks. When using secondary sources, though, you should be aware that because they combine the information from other secondary sources and actual studies, it is possible that the author(s) did not accurately report the research. Furthermore, the review may be selective to support a particular point of view, or the author may have failed to locate some important studies.

There are three main types of secondary sources:

1. *Professional Books.* Scholarly books are written on many topics for other researchers and professionals in the area; therefore, they often contain more details about the research. Textbooks are also secondary sources, providing a nontechnical overview of several topics within a particular field of study. Written for students, they may lack detail but offer general overviews and references.

2. *Encyclopedias.* Encyclopedias (including Wikipedia) that contain short summaries of other literature are good sources during the initial stages of review.

3. *Reviews, Yearbooks, and Handbooks.* A number of sources include comprehensive, up-to-date reviews on specific topics. Many of the reviews are in books or monographs that are published annually (e.g., *Review of Research in Education*). Handbooks are more comprehensive than other secondary sources and more scholarly, as the target audience is other professionals and students. They can serve as a helpful resource for identifying research theories, authors' names, background material, and keyword search terms relevant to your research topic. Here are a few examples of handbooks:

   - *Handbook of Educational Psychology*
   - *Handbook of Reading Research*
   - *Handbook of Research on Curriculum*
   - *Handbook of Research on Educational Administration*
   - *Handbook of Research on Mathematics Teaching and Learning*
   - *Handbook of Research on the Teaching of English*
   - *Handbook of Research in Science Education*
   - *Handbook of Research on Teaching*
   - *Handbook of Research on School Supervision*

When searching for reviews in journals, you may come across what is called a *meta-analysis*, a review that quantitatively synthesizes previous studies. A **meta-analysis** is a procedure that uses statistical methods to systematically combine the results of a number of studies of the same problem. The studies are identified, and the results from all the studies are used to arrive at an overall conclusion. Most meta-analyses reported in reputable journals are characterized by a comprehensive search of the literature, clear inclusion and exclusion criteria, and sound statistical procedures (refer to Excerpts 4.6 and 4.7). Because there are many different ways of identifying the studies that comprise a meta-analysis, as well as different approaches to statistically

EXCERPTS 4.6 AND 4.7

Meta-Analysis

This meta-analysis reviewed research on summer reading interventions conducted in the United States and Canada from 1998–2011. The synthesis included 41 classroom- and home-based summer reading interventions involving children from kindergarten to Grade 8. Compared to control group children, children who participated in classroom interventions… enjoyed significant improvement on multiple reading outcomes. The magnitude of the treatment effect was positive for summer reading interventions that employed research-based reading instruction and included a majority of low-income children. (p. 386)

SOURCE: Kim, J. S., & Quinn, D. M. (2013). The effects of summer reading on low-income children's literacy achievement from kindergarten to grade 8: A meta-analysis of classroom and home interventions. *Review of Educational Research, 83*(3), 386–431.

Studies were located through computerized databases (e.g., PsycINFO, ERIC, Medline) using subject terms such as *grade retention, grade repetition, grade failure, nonpromotion, transition classroom, flunked*, and other synonyms. Reference sections of recent review articles also were reviewed to identify relevant articles. . . . Of 199 studies that were identified and carefully evaluated as described above, a total of 22 studies met study inclusionary criteria. . . . The search produced 22 studies and 207 individual achievement outcomes. (pp. 484–485)

SOURCE: Allen, C. S., Chen, Q., Willson, V. L., & Hughes, J. N. (2009). Quality of research design moderates effects of grade retention on achievement: A meta-analytic, multilevel analysis. *Educational Evaluation and Policy Analysis, 31*(4), 480–499.

combine them, it is necessary to examine the methodology to ensure credibility. For example, it would not make much sense if all studies, whether poorly conducted or well conducted, were included in the synthesis.

You may also come across an alternative to a meta-analysis that is called a **research synthesis** (or *best-evidence, narrative,* or *systematic* synthesis). In this type of review, both qualitative and quantitative research can be included (as well as mixed methods). Like a meta-analysis, this type of research synthesis is far more extensive and systematic than what is normally reported for a single research study. A summary of a research synthesis review of literature is shown in Excerpt 4.8. In this study, database searching led to 3,616 records. A first screening resulted in 462 records, of which 103 were eventually included for full coding.

Construct a Literature Matrix

Once you locate your primary sources, you will need to first decide whether they are worth retaining and using, and then, if they are, read them fully and summarize the information they contain. Begin by reading the abstract of the article, if there is one, and the purpose or research problem. Then read the results and decide whether it is worthwhile to read the article more carefully and take notes on it. Don't be too discouraged if some of the articles you locate are not useful. Part of the process of reviewing literature is to locate and read many more articles than you will eventually use.

EXCERPT 4.8

Research Synthesis Review of Literature

The purpose of this article was to systematically review the literature and identify common practice elements within EBPs and practices delivered by teachers designed to target social, emotional, and behavioral outcomes of young elementary students with and at-risk for EBD ... Four electronic databases were searched ...All studies were screened through two levels of inclusion criteria. The first level of inclusion/exclusion focused on participants and settings... Second, participants diagnosed with autism spectrum disorder were excluded...The second level of screening focused on study methodology...We identified 24 common practice elements ... describing a range of practices that teachers can use to promote the social, emotional, and behavioral development of elementary school students at risk for EBD...The identification of ... practice elements linked to target outcomes has the potential to help educators select evidence-based practices for use in authentic school settings. (pp. 78, 80, 83)

SOURCE: Sutherland, K. S., Conroy, M. A., McLeod, B. D., Kunemund, R., & McKnight, K. (2018). Common practice elements for improving social, emotional, and behavioral outcomes of young elementary school students. Journal of Emotional and Behavioral Disorders, doi: 10:1177/1063426618784009, p. 1.

You will need a strategy for recording notes on the articles as you read them. My recommendation for this is to use what is called a *literature matrix* or *literature map*. A **literature matrix** is a table that contains important information about each key study.

The literature matrix is a way to organize the key parts of each study in a single source, as illustrated in Figure 4.7, which I constructed for a study on student perceptions toward assessment. As you can see, the matrix has a number of columns that are used to summarize vital parts of each article. Doing a matrix allows you to begin to see how information from different sources is related as you summarize each article. This allows you to sort and organize questions, methods, and findings from different studies, a beginning step in synthesizing the sources. Note that in the last column are comments about my judgments pertaining to methods and implications of each article. This is also important because your goal is to analyze sources as well as summarize them. Be careful, though, to not put too much information in each column. Use bullets, abbreviations, and shorthand. This is a summary—you can access the full article for further detail.

Figure 4.7 Example of Part of a Literature Matrix

Author and Title	Journal/date	Question(s)	Sample	Method	Findings	Limitations/ Comments/ Connections
Alkharusi, H. *Development and datametric properties of a scale measuring students' perceptions of the classroom assessment environment*	*International Journal of Instruction,* 2011	What factors comprise students' perceptions of the classroom assessment environment?	450 tenth-grade Arabic language arts students	Likert scale self-report survey; principal components analysis; alpha reliabilities	Two scales with good reliability: (1) learning-oriented to improve learning and mastery of content; (2) performance-oriented purpose.	Supports importance of student perceptions toward learning and how that varies in the classroom; limited by nature of sarnple and single subject (English).

(Continued)

Author and Title	Journal/date	Question(s)	Sample	Method	Findings	Limitations/ Comments/ Connections
Brookhart, S. M., & Bronowicz, D. L. '*I don't like writing. It makes my fingers hurt'*: *Students talk about their classroom assessments*	*Assessment in Education, 2003*	What are students' perceptions about specific assessments in relation to interest, importance, self-efficacy, and goal orientation?	63 elem (3 & 5 grade) and 98 high school students from suburban & urban schools	Individual qualitative interviews over a year about specific assessments	• More similarities than differences across assessments • Student centered based on student needs, interests, and consequences • Interest = importance; converse not true • Heavy emphasis on effort and studying • Not concerned with others' perceptions • Mastery of goals important	Focused only on specific assessments; did not include middle school; asked only a few questions; most relevant to our last few questions; solid methodology; didn't find many subject area differences; has important similar framework and qualitative methods

A *literature map* is a bit more sophisticated, as you organize the sources by topic to show how they are related. The **literature map** is a graphic, visual presentation of the studies that shows how they are related and what they have in common. It helps you summarize major topical areas and understand how different studies overlap. I have illustrated a literature map for my research on student perceptions toward assessment (Figure 4.8) (based on the literature matrix in Figure 4.7 but with more studies). The matrix suggests three major themes—nature of perceptions, relationship of perceptions to motivation, and relationship of perceptions to achievement, and two minor themes—instrumentation and grade level.

Another approach—one that I used for many years, and still use sometimes—is to record your notes on index cards or separate pieces of paper. This facilitates easy organization of the sources in different ways. Begin taking notes by writing or typing bibliographic information, then summarize the research problem as briefly as possible. Next, similar to what is in the matrix, indicate in outline form the participants, instruments, and procedures used and then summarize the results and conclusions. Record interesting or insightful quotations; indicate any weaknesses or limitations in the methodology, analysis of the data, or conclusions; and indicate how the study may be related to your problem. You will find it useful to develop a code for indicating your overall judgment of the article. If you find it closely related to your problem and highly credible, you might give the article an A; if somewhat related and credible, a B; and so on. It will also help to develop a code that indicates the major focus of the study by topic or descriptor. For example, in reviewing studies on teacher awareness, you may find that some studies examine the effect of awareness on student achievement, some focus on strategies to improve awareness, and others emphasize different approaches to awareness depending on the type of students in the classroom. Each of these could have a code or notation on the card, such as "effect on ach.," "improv. awareness," and "approaches," to denote how they are different.

The best approach is the one that works for you! There is no single best way to summarize different studies. What you are most comfortable with is the one that will be most effective and efficient.

Figure 4.8 Literature Map for Student Perceptions of Assessment

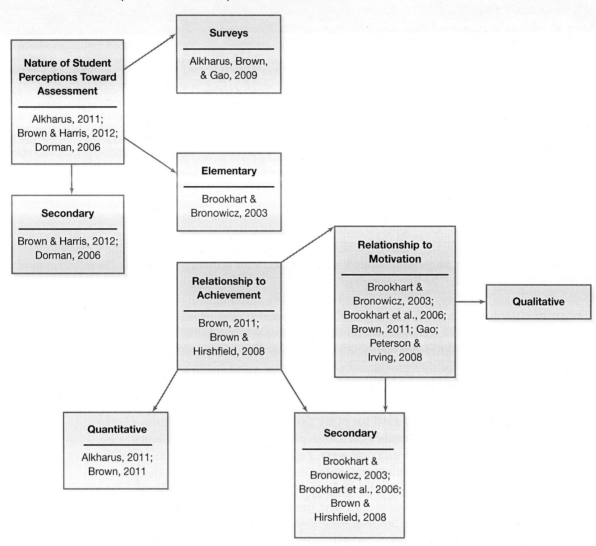

> **Author Reflection** *Doing a literature matrix is hard work, but it forces you to read each article carefully and focus on the most important information. You should feel free to use more or fewer or different columns. I think you will find doing one very helpful; it takes you to the next level.*

Writing a Review of Literature

After you have found the right articles and documents and constructed the literature matrix and/or map comes the challenging part: actually writing the review. Keep in mind that the review you write is selective (more comprehensive for a dissertation, though) and should emphasize the most relevant primary sources. For a more extensive discussion of writing about research, refer to Chapter 16. The basics for the review of literature are summarized here.

EXCERPT 4.9

Summarizing Results from Previous Studies

Surprisingly, studies that have directly compared elaborative feedback with correct answer feedback have found little or no benefit to increasing the complexity of the feedback message (for a review, see Kulhavy & Stock, 1989; for a meta-analysis, see Bangert-Drowns, Kulik, Kulik, & Morgan, 1991). For example, many studies have found that there is no benefit of providing explanation feedback relative to correct answer (e.g., Gilman, 1969... Whyte et al.). Similarly, other studies have shown that providing restudy feedback yields equivalent performance to correct answer feedback (e.g., Andre & Thieman, 1988; Kulhavy et al., 1985; Peeck, 1979). Critically, the content of the feedback message was manipulated as an independent variable in these studies, which allowed the unique effect of greater complexity (or lack thereof) to be isolated. (p. 291)

SOURCE: Butler, A. C., Godbole, N., & Marsh, E. J. (2012). Explanation feedback is better than correct answer feedback for promoting transfer of learning. *Journal of Educational Psychology, 105*(2), 290–298.

The aim is to write several paragraphs that accomplish three goals:

1. **Summarize findings from other related studies,** as illustrated in Excerpt 4.9.

2. **Analyze the quality of the findings.** The analysis is important because it suggests that you are not simply accepting the studies as credible; you are examining the methodology of the studies critically to make better judgments about the contribution of the results.

3. **Relate findings and previous methods to your study.** A critical examination enables you to show the relationship of the proposed or current study to previous literature. This step is essential for the results to contribute to our knowledge. It also generates many good ideas that will improve subsequent research.

Although reviews of literature can be organized in different ways, the most common approach is to group together studies that investigate similar topics or subtopics (thematic). The different topics are then put in order, beginning with articles related to the problem in a more general way, then turning to articles specifically related to the problem. Within each topic it may be possible to organize the studies by date, with the most recent studies last. This arrangement gives you a sense of the development of the research over time. Studies that are only generally related should be summarized briefly. If several of these studies have similar results, they should be grouped together; for example, "Several studies have found that teacher expectations are related to student achievement (Bae, 2015; Smith, 2019; Wylie, 2016)." Most reviews select representative general studies; there is no attempt to do an exhaustive review of all studies. Then one or two paragraphs can be written for each topic or grouping, with several studies cited in each paragraph. Since you will be using several citations in a paragraph, you will need to know how to format each citation (refer to Chapter 16). With a single reference, it is fine to write, "Lambiotte (2012) found that..." or "The positive relationship has been confirmed by Broda (2011)." With two or more references that have similar findings, they are listed together; for example, "Several studies have shown that hybrid online courses are more effective than courses that are entirely online (Koeneka, 2013; Olsen, 2010; Zumbrunn, 2009)" (note that these are alphabetical). Again, you'll need the APA manual or a similar source to be sure about how to format.

Putting several studies together in a single paragraph requires a synthesis of the sources; doing the synthesis requires some creativity and time. A good way to begin is to examine the literature matrix and map or spread out the sources on a table.

Here are a few more suggestions for writing (refer to Chapter 16). First, refrain from using long quotations or the same wording in discussing each study—for example, "A study by Brown (1987) indicated that…"; "A study by Smith (2000) indicated that…"; "A study by Jones (2001) showed that…" In general, quotations should be used sparingly and only when a special or critical meaning could not be indicated by your own words. Second, use short sentences as well as transition sentences, so there is a logical progression of ideas and sections.

The length of the review depends on the type of study, whether or not it is published, and the topic that is researched. The review of literature for an exploratory study may not be very long, whereas an exhaustive review in a thesis or dissertation can be as long as 30 or 40 or more typed pages. A lengthy review requires structuring with major and minor headings and periodic summaries.

The nature of the written review of literature will depend in part on whether the study is quantitative, qualitative, or mixed methods. Quantitative reviews are often very detailed and found in the beginning sections of an article. Qualitative reviews, in contrast, tend to be brief in the beginning but more integrated throughout the whole of the article, although this is a general tendency and many qualitative articles have an extensive review at the beginning. Rather than provide a detailed analysis of the literature prior to the methods section, the purpose of most qualitative reviews is to introduce the purpose and general or broad research questions. These foreshadowed questions provide a direction, but one that is purposefully general so that previous work does not limit, constrain, or predict what will be found. In this way, the review of literature is consistent with the discovery orientation and inductive approach of qualitative research. The approach is to state a general purpose or question so the views of the participants will emerge. Thus, the initial review of literature in a qualitative study is sometimes *preliminary* rather than complete. It provides conceptual frameworks by citing appropriate areas of scholarship and thinking from different perspectives, such as psychological or sociological. Together, the foreshadowed problems and conceptual frameworks are used to justify the need for a qualitative approach. Some qualitative researchers will not conduct an extensive review of the literature because they do not want what others have said about something to influence the openness that is needed or their own perspectives.

Once the qualitative study is under way and data are being collected, the researcher continues to read broadly in the literature. The additional literature reviewed enables the researcher to better understand what has been observed. The literature may provide meaningful analogies, a scholarly language to synthesize descriptions, or additional conceptual or theoretical frameworks to better understand and organize the findings. It helps the researcher to understand the complexities of what is observed and to illuminate subtle meanings and interpretations. Like good quantitative studies, the literature is integrated with the discussion and conclusion section of the article or report. At this point, additional new literature may be introduced to better explain and interpret the findings.

In mixed methods studies, the review of literature is usually presented in one section rather than having a separate review for the quantitative and qualitative sections. Although general reviews of literature in mixed methods studies typically are detailed and thorough, the review reflects the quantitative or qualitative emphasis of the study. With an exploratory sequential study, the review tends to be similar to those found in qualitative research, whereas explanatory sequential research uses a review similar to those in a quantitative study. Because mixed methods studies are much less standardized than either quantitative or qualitative research, the literature review section is also less standardized. This means that with these types of studies you will likely encounter quite different approaches to the review.

Figures 4.9 and 4.10 present reviews of literature—one for a quantitative article and the other for a qualitative article.

Consumer (and Researcher) Tips

Criteria for Evaluating a Review of Literature for an Empirical Article

You should consider several criteria when reading and evaluating the review of literature section of research studies or reports. First, identify which part of the article is the review of literature. Sometimes the review has a separate heading, but often it does not. Be sure to differentiate between an introduction, which provides a general overview or background, and the review, which should home in on empirical studies that are clearly related to the research problem. Once the review is identified, scan it to get an idea of the general structure and organization. When reading, highlight dates of references, places where findings from other studies are summarized, and analyses of the studies. In the margins of a copy of the article, you may find it helpful to write notes such as "sum" for summary and "an" for analysis, or even "+" to indicate places in the review that correspond to the criteria that follow. Finally, determine how well the review corresponds to these criteria. This can be recorded so when you review the overall credibility of the researcher and the study, the quality of the review can be a part of this summary judgment.

The following criteria will guide your evaluation of the review of literature:

1. **The review of literature should adequately cover previous research on the topic.** In reading research in an area with which you are familiar, you will be able to judge the scope of the review. Were important studies ignored? Does the number of studies in the review reflect research activity in that area? Often you will realize that there is far more research in an area than the review indicates. Do the authors of the article cite mainly their own research? Although it is sometimes quite appropriate for authors to use their own work as a major part of the review, it may also indicate investigator bias. If the authors limit their review to their own studies and do not include other related research, the credibility of the study could justifiably be questioned. Overall, then, you will typically have some sense of whether the review is sufficiently comprehensive. Based on length, a one- or two-paragraph review on a much-studied topic for a quantitative study is probably too brief, whereas reviews that cover several journal pages are probably more than adequate.

Figure 4.9 Example of a Review of Literature for Quantitative Research

Summary of previous research; theme is "hodgepodge grading"

Cross and Frary (1996) and Cizek, Fitzgerald, Shawn, and Rachor (2013) report similar findings concerning the hodgepodge nature of assigning grades. Cizek et al. (2018) found that although almost all teachers used formal achievement measures in grading, other "achievement-related" factors such as attendance, ability, participation, demonstration of effort, and conduct were used by at least half of the teachers. Cross and Frary surveyed 310 middle and high school teachers of academic subjects in a single school district. A written survey was used to obtain descriptions of grading practices and opinions regarding assessment and grading. Consistent with Brookhart (2017), it was reported that 72% of the teachers raised the grades of low-ability students if the students had demonstrated effort. One-fourth of the teachers indicated that they raised grades for high effort "fairly often." Almost 40% of the teachers indicated that student conduct and attitude were taken into consideration when assigning grades. Note that a very high percentage of teachers agreed that effort and conduct should be reported separately from achievement. More than half the teachers reported that class participation was rated as having a moderate or strong influence on grades. In an earlier statewide study, Frary (1993) used the same teacher survey that was used by Cross and Frary, and obtained similar results. More than two-thirds of the teachers agreed or tended to agree that ability, effort, and improvement should be included in determining grades.

Analysis of previous research; limitations

Another recent study, by Truog and Friedman (2017), further confirms the notion of the hodgepodge nature of grading. In their study, the written grading policies of 53 high school teachers were analyzed in relation to grading practices recommended by measurement specialists. In addition, a focus group was conducted with eight teachers to find out more about their reasoning behind their grading practices. They found that the written policies were consistent with the findings from earlier studies of teacher beliefs and practices. Nine percent of the teachers included ability as a factor in determining grades, 17% included attitude, 9% included effort, 43% included attendance, and 32% included student behavior.

One of the limitations of current research on the grading practices of secondary teachers is that the studies do not differentiate grading practices by ability level of the classes. This may be important in examining such factors as effort and improvement, and may reveal patterns that exacerbate existing achievement differences among students with varying ability levels. For example, Alarso and Pigge (1999) reported that teachers believe that essays provide better evidence of higher cognitive learning, and that students study harder for them. If it is demonstrated that higher-ability classes, such as honors and advanced placement classes, use more essays than basic classes, this may result in greater emphasis on thinking skills with higher-ability classes, whereas in lower-ability classes there would be more emphasis on rote memorization. Also, as with the research on assessment practices, most studies (e.g., Brookhart, 2011; Frary, 1993; Truog & Friedman, 1996) measure teacher beliefs, rather than actual practices or a reporting of what was actually used in a specific class.

Relates previous research to current study

Another limitation in the designs employed is that each of the factors used to assign grades has been considered separately. When put in the context of teaching, as pointed out by Stiggins, Frisbie, and Griswold (2019), it is more realistic to consider the joint effect of several factors. Only one study, Frary (1993), reported an analysis of how factors were grouped into meaningful components for secondary teachers. In their study, teacher opinions about the desirability of different grading and assessment practices were examined together using a Likert scale. Their findings focused on teacher attitudes toward the desirability of certain practices, but did not investigate whether there were underlying dimensions associated with actual grading and assessment practices of teachers.

The present study used a large sample of secondary school teachers (grades 6–12) to describe assessment and grading practices in a way that addresses limitations cited from the previous research. The critical role of effort and other nonachievement factors in grading was examined, as was the way these different factors cluster together in describing teachers' practices. The study was designed to document differences in actual assessment and grading practices conducted for a specific class taught by each teacher across a range of classes representing different student ability levels. Four specific research questions were addressed:

Figure 4.10 Example of a Review of Literature for a Qualitative Study

Social relationships among adolescents have been researched for many decades, beginning in the early 1900s. Early on, studies conducted at Michigan State University found that group dynamics and friendships were of great importance and provided rich descriptions of social behavior. The work of Gunther (1934) and Collins (1938) was particularly insightful. Their studies pioneered systematic observation as a method of gathering data. By going into schools and other settings, observational techniques were established that could provide rich descriptions of both group behavior and friendship patterns. Although these studies did not examine a large number of adolescents—only 30—the methodology they used and initial theoretical frameworks they established set the foundation for subsequent studies. More specifically, they found that groups in which adolescents worked on tasks cooperatively seemed to generate more genuine friendships as compared to groups in which the adolescents were working in a competitive environment. In addition, there seemed to be greater satisfaction and motivation.

> **Provides historical background**

These initial studies led to a greater emphasis on understanding the cooperative nature of group dynamics. Several researchers at the University of Minnesota (e.g., Johnson, 1975; Smith, 1977; and Zumbrunn, 1982), found that the quality of the social development mirrored the extent of the cooperation among members of the group. Their research extended observational methods developed earlier to provide an even richer description of group dynamics. They found that both single-sex and cross-sex friendships were equally affected. In contrast, groups that were more competitive seemed to mitigate friendships, particularly those between girls and boys.

Further scholarly efforts to understand adolescent social development were evident later in the 20th century. MacKenzie, Kronwall, and Wall (1990) found that explicit directions for working cooperatively greatly enhanced social development. Several investigators showed that friendships that were established in cooperative groups lasted in non-group settings (Miller, 1995; Smithfield & Collins, 1996; Stemhagen & Cauley, 1998; Zumbrunn, 1999). Others found that the richness and depth of the friendships went through a number of phases, and that sufficient time was needed for these developments. Gerber and Frederick (2003) also found that the effects could be long lasting.

> **Summary of general literature**

Although the research has found fairly consistently that cooperative groups develop friendships and enhanced social relationships, it is not at all clear how this process may be different for adolescents of different races. It is possible, for example, for racial stereotypes or cultural normative behavior, to affect comfort levels, trust, and freedom of expression. Most of the previous studies have been conducted with White students, with limited mixed-race groups. Given the importance of racial identification and awareness during adolescence, it is important to understand how cooperative groups of mixed races function, and how these processes may be unique. The depth of understanding that can be derived from a qualitative analysis of such groups will provide significant information of how the groups function and whether friendships are affected.

> **Introduction of phenomenon to be investigated**

Different perspectives on racial awareness will need to be included in the framework for the research. Durkin (2010), for example, emphasizes the importance of previous experiences with both same and different races. Wilhiem, Burns, and Stadler (2011) have found that percentages of different races in a group can make a difference in social relationships, with a tendency for same race adolescents to group together, whereas Admonson and Abrams (2014) showed that age is an important factor. They found that younger adolescent friendships were less affected by race than were friendships among older adolesc

> **Summarizes theoretical perspective**

Finally, it is interesting to note that adolescent group development may be very contextual and individualized. That is, personalities may be more important than either racial or sex differences, especially when groups have been appropriate support, time to develop, and common tasks that engage them in a meaningful way. For these reasons, the current study seeks to understand multiracial group dynamics in different contexts. There is an emphasis on understanding, from the adolescents' perspectives, what aspects of both the context and other group members are salient.

> **Justification for and direction of the current study**

2. **The review of literature should cite actual findings from other studies.** It is important for the review to be based on the empirical results of previous research, not on others' opinions about previous research or on the conclusions of previous research. To illustrate this point, consider Excerpts 4.10 and 4.11, which are reviews of literature citing results.

3. **The review of literature should be up to date.** The studies reviewed should include the most recent research on the topic. This does not mean that older studies are not relevant. Sometimes the best and most relevant research was conducted decades ago. You also need to consider that it may take a year or more to publish a study after it has been accepted for publication. But if you read a study published in 1999 and most of the citations are from work in the 1980s, the review is probably out of date. A quick glance at the references at the end of the study will provide you with a good idea of how contemporary the review is.

4. **The review of literature should analyze as well as summarize previous studies.** As noted, a good review interprets the quality of previous research. This analysis may be a critique of methodology or inappropriate generalizations, an indication of limitations of the study (e.g., to certain populations, instruments, or procedures), or a discussion of conflicting results. Notice how this is illustrated in Excerpts 4.10 and 4.11.

EXCERPTS 4.10 AND 4.11
Summary and Analysis of Previous Research

One Australian study that focused on the role of parents in reducing children' s experiences of bullying victimization involved a randomized control trial utilizing a targeted (vs. universal) cognitive-behavioral parenting program, which also aimed to develop children' s social and emotional skills (Healy & Sanders, 2014). This parenting program assisted parents ($n = 111$) of victimized children to work with schools to support their children' s social development and interactions with peers. The program resulted in significant decreases in these children' s victimization experiences, internalizing symptoms and aggression, with increases in their positive attitudes to school and peers. These findings suggest that targeted school-based interventions with strategies to strengthen partnerships between parents could be effective in reducing harms from bullying. However, the targeted study involved only children who were chronically bullied (Healy & Sanders, 2014), and it is unclear if a more universal approach to enhancing parent capacity to help their children prevent harm from bullying could also be effective. (p. 256)

SOURCE: Cross, D., Lester, L., Pearce, N., Barnes, A., & Beatty, S. (2018) A group randomized controlled trial evaluating parent involvement in whole school actions to reduce bullying, *The Journal of Educational Research, 11*(3), 255–267.

Annis (1983) conducted the only study found in which the effects of teaching expectancy and actually teaching were directly compared. In the experiment, participants either read a history passage with the expectation of later being asked to recall the material or the expectation of tutoring another student on the material. Of those expecting to tutor, some participants actually tutored the material to someone else, whereas some participants only prepared to tutor someone else. The results provided some evidence that expecting to tutor may enhance learning beyond studying normally, and further, that tutoring another student enhanced learning beyond only preparing to tutor. Although this finding provides

(Continued)

early evidence of an added benefit for tutoring, there are important limitations of Annis' study that are in need of further investigation. From a theoretical standpoint, one limitation is that the students who tutored interacted with another student (e.g., answering questions, providing and receiving feedback). According to Bargh and Schul (1980), interactions with students represent an additional stage of learning by teaching beyond only explaining to others. Therefore, it is unclear whether the added benefits of tutoring can be attributed to explaining material to another student or the various interactions that take place with the other student. (p. 282)

SOURCE: Fiorella, L., & Mayer, R. E. (2013). The relative benefits of learning by teaching and teaching expectancy. *Contemporary Educational Psychology, 38*(4), 281–288.

5. **The review of literature should be organized logically by topic, not by author.** A review that devotes one paragraph to each study usually fails to integrate and synthesize previous research. A well-done review is organized by topic. Typically, several studies may be mentioned together in the same paragraph, or may be cited together. For example, rather than using a separate paragraph to summarize and analyze each study, a good review might be something similar to the one in Excerpt 4.12.

EXCERPT 4.12
Literature Review Organized by Topic

In a study of pre-service teachers' development of formative approaches to assessment throughout a four-year initial teacher education programme, Cowan (2009) found that formal assessment courses, coupled with classroom practicum placements, supported pre-service teachers' development of formative approaches to assessment. However, at the end of the pre-service programme, these teachers were primarily implementing straightforward formative assessment practices (e.g. sharing learning goals and success criteria, using questioning) and rarely implementing more complex formative assessment practices (e.g. self- and peer-assessment, providing feedback to students). In a related study, Smith, Hill, Cowie, and Gilmore (2014) compared the assessment beliefs of first and third year pre-service teachers across four teacher education programmes. Their findings showed that pre-service teachers' beliefs shifted from primarily summative to more formative conceptualizations by the end of the programme. In particular, pre-service teachers became more aware of the role of students in the assessment process (i.e. assessment informs both teaching and learning) and began to negotiate the challenges associated with contemporary approaches to assessment within accountability-driven frameworks. These studies suggest that teacher candidates can begin to extend their conception of classroom assessment beyond strictly a summative orientation to include formative practices. As current classroom assessment demands include the use of formative, summative, and diagnostic elements, developing teachers' comprehensive understandings across these elements is critical. (p. 358)

SOURCE: DeLuca, C., Valiquette, A., Combs, A., LaPointe-McvEwan, D., & Luhanga, U. (2018). Teachers' approaches to classroom assessment: A large-scale survey. *Assessment in Education: Principles, Policy & Practice, 16*(3), 355–375.

6. **The review of literature should briefly summarize minor studies and discuss major studies in detail.** Minor studies are those that are related to one or two aspects of the study, or those that provide a general overview. Major studies are directly relevant to most aspects of the study or have important implications. A good review concentrates on major studies. It may be informative to mention minor studies, but the focus of the review should be on an analysis of the most closely related studies.

7. **The review of major studies should relate previous studies explicitly to the research problem or methods.** It is important to emphasize how the major studies relate to or contribute to the research problem or the methods of the current study. For example, the author might say, "These findings suggest that it is important to include gender as an independent variable in the study" or "This study adopts the methodology successfully used by Mendoza and Jones (2019)." It should be clear to the reader why a particular analysis or finding is important or helpful to the current study.

In Excerpt 4.13, the author effectively connected previous research to methodology:

8. **The review of literature should provide a logical basis for the hypothesis.** If there is a hypothesis, it should be based on the review of literature. This provides evidence that the hypothesis is based on reasonable logic supported by others, rather than on the researcher's whim. If the review of literature is unclear or provides

---

EXCERPT 4.13

Explicitly Relating Previous Research to Methodology

Conley (2012) examined patterns of motivation profiles among 7th grade students in mathematics, that included achievement goals as well as expectancy-value perspectives and self-efficacy beliefs. A seven-profile solution was identified, including a low profile (low on all motivational indices), three average clusters (average ratings with an emphasis on mastery, cost, or across motivational indices), and 3 high clusters (high ratings on competence beliefs, cost, or high across motivational indices) (Conley, 2012). The profiles characterized by average endorsement on the achievement goal, task value, and self-efficacy belief factors were associated with higher academic achievement and positive affect (Conley, 2012). Of note, a high mastery oriented profile commonly found in other person-centered studies was not identified (e.g., Jang & Liu, 2012; Tuominen-Soini, Salmela-Aro, & Niemivirta, 2011). Possible explanations for this discrepancy include the domain of study (mathematics) and developmental stage of participants (middle school) that together is associated with lower levels of mastery goals (Conley, 2012). Therefore, when making comparisons across motivation profile studies, in addition to the achievement goal model and grade level, the role of content domain may also be an important feature to consider. In fact, several scholars have argued that attention to subject area in person-centered studies is particularly relevant during the secondary years when subjects become more differentiated (Madjar & Chohat, 2017; Shim & Finch, 2014, 2006). (pp. 92–93)

SOURCE: Bae, C. L., & DeBusk-Lane, M. (2018). Motivation belief profiles in science: Links to classroom goal structures and achievement. *Learning and Individual Differences, 67,* 91–104.

conflicting predictions, the researcher may still state a hypothesis, though justification should be provided. Overall, there should be clear connections among the problem, review, and hypothesis.

9. **The review of literature should establish a theoretical or conceptual framework for the problem.** For basic and most applied research the review should provide the theoretical context for the study. A good theoretical context enhances the significance of the study and shows that the researcher is aware of the theory and has used it in framing the questions and methodology. Often, the theoretical framework is provided as a foundation for reviewing specific studies as illustrated by Excerpt 4.14. In Excerpt 4.15, the theory of social capital is explicated to provide an approach for a study of low-income educational communities.

EXCERPTS 4.14 AND 4.15

Providing a Conceptual or Theoretical Framework

The theoretical basis for the present work draws from Bronfenbrenner's bioecological model (Bronfenbrenner & Morris, 1998, 2006). This model considers four sources of influence on children's development: process, person, context, and time. . . . Proximal processes investigated herein refer to the reciprocal interactions between teachers and children; such interactions are hypothesized to be the primary mechanism by which children learn in classrooms. . . . Use of this framework to investigate teacher–child interactions may uncover the mechanisms through which teachers influence their students' development (Rutter & Maughan, 2002). (p. 913)

SOURCE: Curby, T. W., Rimm-Kaufman, S. E., & Cameron, C. (2009). Teacher–child interactions and children's achievement trajectories across kindergarten and first grade. *Journal of Educational Psychology, 101*(4), 912–925.

Thus, while empirical studies on full-service community schools underscore their potential benefits, more research is needed to better understand the conditions that facilitate or hinder these schools' effectiveness.

Accordingly, this article uses social capital as a theoretical lens to explore the interrelationships between school personnel, families, and community partners within an urban full-service community school.

Social capital is a complex but highly useful construct for understanding the role of relationships in various domains. Since Coleman's (1988) influential paper nearly three decades ago, the theory of social capital has evolved and spread across the social sciences. This evolution has led to a typology of social capital that highlights common structural and conceptual features, including its components and functions (Halpern, 2005). One distinct component of social capital is an intentionally constituted network of individuals (Bourdieu, 1986). The size of the network; its structure in terms of positions, hierarchies, and types of relations; and the amount of resources possessed by its members have important implications for the opportunities it offers (Lin, 2001). Another component is shared norms, values, and expectations as well as sanctions that help to maintain social network functioning by reinforcing cohesiveness and trust and reducing negative behaviors (Coleman, 1988). . . .

> Social Capital as a Key Theoretical Construct

(Continued)

> Further, Orr (1999) argued that there is a racial/ethnic dimension to the functions of social capital. Based on his ethnographic study of school reform in Baltimore, Maryland, he concluded that when communities are constituted by different racial/ethnic groups, it is important to distinguish between intergroup and intragroup social capital. Orr conceptualized intragroup social capital as a type of ethnic bonding where relations and organizations within a given ethnic group protect members' interests and expand their access to opportunities. In contrast, he defined intergroup social capital, a form of bridging social capital, as relations and networks across racial/ethnic groups that are embodied in alliances and coalitions (Orr, 1999). Thus, intergroup social capital is especially important in reducing isolation among communities and facilitating the exchange and dispersion of goods. (p. 142S–143S)
>
> SOURCE: Galindo, C., Sanders, M., & Abel, Y. (2017). Transforming educational experiences in low-income communities: A qualitative case study of social capital in a full-service community school. *American Educational Research Journal, 54*(Supp. 1), 140S–163S.

10. **The review of literature should help establish the significance of the research.** The significance of a study is usually established by the nature of previous studies, which suggest that further research would be helpful or informative. However, as previously mentioned, be careful with studies you read that imply significance because of a "paucity of research" in an area. The significance of most investigations is based on what other, previous research has reported, not on the fact that few or no studies could be found on a topic.

Check for Understanding 3

3a. Why is it important to use primary sources, rather than secondary sources, for the review of literature?

3b. Why is it best to organize a review of literature by topic rather than by date of publication?

3c. Describe how making a literature map would provide a way to organize the review of literature.

3d. What are four criteria for evaluating a review of literature?

Author Reflection *Writing a literature review is no easy task, so do not be surprised if it takes a while to complete it. I find that it is best to use a large table and spread out summaries of different studies like a fan. That seems to help in the synthesis process, which is essential to being able to write a review that does much more than simply list what other studies have found. I also find it helpful to construct an outline before actually writing. You may find it necessary to step away for a few days and then come back. Finally, when you get in a productive writing groove, keep with it as long as you can.*

Key Terms

Blind review
Literature database
  ERIC
  PsycINFO
Literature matrix
Literature map
Meta-analysis

Nonrefereed
Open access
Peer review
Primary sources
Refereed
Research synthesis
Retrieval algorithms

Search engine
  Google Scholar
  Metasearch engine
Secondary source
Subject directories
Thesaurus

Discussion Questions

1. Why is it important to use the review of literature to inform all aspects of a study, including the discussion section?
2. How can sources be used to frame the context and general problem of the research?
3. Why is it actually good to find contradictory findings from previously reported research?
4. How are key terms best identified and used in a search of the literature?

5. What are the best ways of both delimiting and expanding a search of the literature?
6. How is using the Internet for searching literature different from an established database such as ERIC?
7. How does the review of literature for a qualitative study differ from a quantitative study?

Application Exercises

1. Using the same topic and key terms, conduct a review of literature for the past 10 years separately using ERIC and Google Scholar. Compare the results of the searches to determine what records were common, how the searches differed, and make an argument for which was most helpful.

2. Using just five articles, construct a literature matrix and corresponding literature map. Show how the five articles are similar as well as different, and how they would be grouped together for writing the review of literature.

Check for Understanding Answers

1a. Broadly, to relate previous research and theory to the problem. More specifically, to refine the problem, establish a conceptual/theoretical framework, establish significance, develop research questions/hypotheses, identify method strengths/weaknesses and contradictory findings.

1b. The review is used to establish significance by showing how it is important in making a contribution to existing literature, practice, or policy; by filling a gap in understanding. The review is used to establish credibility by showing how proposed

methods build upon successful and unsuccessful methods used in previous studies.

2a. Select topic, select key terms and databases, use thesauruses, conduct searches.

2b. ERIC uses criteria, review, and a controlled vocabulary that increases hits and quality, but is not as comprehensive as Google Scholar. Google Scholar is extensive and inclusive, allows branching (e.g., cited by others), is linked to libraries, is current, is accessible, but is not organized with controlled vocabulary, and is without uniform standards or indexing for quality control.

3a. Primary sources provide specific questions, methods, and findings that will best support significance and the identification of appropriate methods and analyses.

3b. Because it shows how different studies converge and differentiate, allowing for an effective synthesis. It is also more engaging, less tedious.

3c. The literature map will show similarities and differences, how studies are related, and the flow of knowledge generated from one or more studies to others.

3d. Take your pick: adequate coverage; cite findings; current; analyze; topically organized; summarize minor studies less and major studies more; relate to problem or methods; basis for hypotheses; establish conceptual/theoretical framework; establish significance.

Part II

Quantitative Research

For many decades educational research was dominated by what is now called a "quantitative" approach. Based on principles of scientific inquiry, quantitative research seeks to use measurement and statistics to "objectively" identify relationships among different phenomena. While "measurement and statistics" may conjure up something like the bubonic plague, the reality is that with computer capabilities, "big data," and increasingly sophisticated statistical tools, quantitative research is plentiful and important.

It takes six chapters to provide justice to quantitative methods. Chapter 5 covers sampling and how the nature of participants may impact and limit findings. We then turn to two chapters on measurement. The first reviews fundamental principles of descriptive statistics. These are absolutely essential to comprehend for an informed analysis of quantitative studies, and for understanding how data are measured (Chapters 6 and 7). Armed with knowing how to collect data, and from whom, the next step is to identify and employ the right design. Chapter 8 is devoted to nonexperimental designs (these are the popular ones), and Chapter 9 focuses on experimental designs, the types of studies that use an intervention to see whether one factor will cause changes in outcomes.

The final chapter in this section, Chapter 10, is an introduction to how researchers use statistics to make inferences about what may be a signal. Here, the logic of what is found statistically is emphasized, not calculations. You will also notice a healthy skepticism about what inferential statistics can tell us. It turns out that limitations in these procedures, as well as misconceptions, suggest that other, more practical ways of making meaning from the numbers need to be included.

Chapter 5
Participants and Sampling for Quantitative Designs

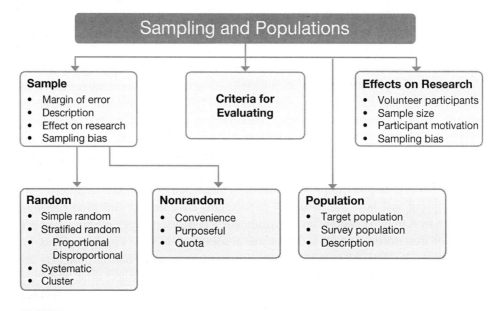

Sampling and Populations

Sample
- Margin of error
- Description
- Effect on research
- Sampling bias

Criteria for Evaluating

Effects on Research
- Volunteer participants
- Sample size
- Participant motivation
- Sampling bias

Random
- Simple random
- Stratified random
  - Proportional Disproportional
- Systematic
- Cluster

Nonrandom
- Convenience
- Purposeful
- Quota

Population
- Target population
- Survey population
- Description

∨ Learning Outcomes

5.1 Describe the differences between samples and populations, and how sample statistics are used to approximate what is true for the population.

5.2 Contrast random with nonrandom sampling procedures; distinguish among random selection procedures.

5.3 Distinguish among types of nonrandom sampling procedures and possible sources of bias.

5.4 Explain how factors related to sampling can influence, even bias, findings; know and apply the criteria for evaluating sample and participant sections of research articles and reports.

Chapter Road Map

The stage is set—you know what you want to study and why, with appropriate research questions. The next step is making decisions about the methodology. As you (hopefully) recall, methodology consists of participants or data source(s), technique(s) (e.g., measures) for gathering data, procedures, and, for some studies, one or more interventions. In this chapter, we consider the participants component for quantitative studies—and in the following two chapters, techniques for gathering data. Following Chapter 7, we examine, separately, the procedures used for different types of quantitative, qualitative, and mixed methods designs. This chapter is divided into three major sections to help you understand the different ways in which researchers find participants from whom data are collected. Then we examine how sampling affects research. First, though, we start with a few words about what sampling is all about and why it is important.

What Are Participants and Samples?

Learning Outcome 5.1 Describe the differences between samples and populations, and how sample statistics are used to approximate what is true for the population.

Learning Outcome 5.2 Contrast random with nonrandom sampling procedures; distinguish among random selection procedures.

Every empirical investigation collects data from someone or something, what is often referred to more broadly as the *source of evidence* or *unit of study*. These terms refer to the individuals, groups, documents, sites, events, or other sources from which data are gathered. As we will see, it is critical to describe these sources and understand their effect on studies and how we can use the results. The most common source of evidence is the individual, who is now commonly called a *participant* (in some quantitative studies, the term *subject* is still used), and groups of individuals, which is where we focus our attention in this chapter.

Simply put, a **participant** (subject) is someone from whom data are collected or someone whose past behavior, performance, trait, or characteristic is used in the study. Much research is designed to plan and then collect new data from participants (e.g., give a test or survey, conduct an interview, make an observation), but many studies use existing data or look back at previously generated documents or other artifacts. When participants, or other units of study, are described, it does not really matter whether the data are generated or already exist. For example, in experiments, each individual who experiences the intervention and whose behavior is measured is considered a participant; or if a researcher uses last year's fourth-grade test scores as data, each fourth-grader included is considered a participant. Either way, you need to know how those participants were selected, their characteristics, and how the characteristics of the participants could affect the results.

Collectively, the group of participants from whom data are or have been collected is referred to as the **sample**. As we will see, you have many choices about how to select your sample(s), i.e., the methods that need to be matched to the purpose of the study and carried out so the results are credible. It turns out that these choices are identified by different types of sampling, typically described with one or more adjectives such as *random* sampling, *stratified random* sampling, or *convenience* sampling.

Table 5.1 Types of Sampling for Quantitative Studies

Random	Nonrandom
• Simple Random	• Convenience
• Stratified Random	• Purposeful
• Systematic	• Quota
• Cluster	

Table 5.2 Types of Random and Nonrandom Sampling

Type	Description	Example
Random		
Simple Random	Every numbered population element has an equal probability of being selected.	From a population of 400 college freshmen, 40 are selected randomly for the sample.
Systemic Sampling	A list of members of the population is used so that each nth element has an equal probability of being selected.	A list of 900 students attending a community college is used to select each eighth student on the list to form a random sample of 112 students.
Stratified Random	Elements are selected randomly from strata that divide the population.	Two hundred preschool students are first divided into boys and girls, then random groups of 25 boys and 25 girls are selected from each of the two groups.
Cluster Sampling	Equal groups are identified and selected randomly, and participants in each group selected are used as the sample.	Five of 25 city blocks, each containing a high percentage of low-socioeconomic status families, is selected randomly, and parents in each selected block are surveyed.
Nonrandom		
Convenience	Participants with the needed characteristics are selected on the basis of availability.	Students in Dr. Simon's introductory special education class are used to examine the effectiveness of using technology to teach principles of inclusion.
Purposeful	Sample is selected from participants who have desired characteristics.	Students from six schools who are planning to go to college are surveyed to examine the relationship between type of college selected and participation in high school co-curricular activities.
Quota	Sample is selected from groups so it approximates characteristics of the population.	Fifty assistant professors and 20 full professors are surveyed about their professional needs, reflecting the larger population of 1000 assistant professors and 400 full professors.

Sampling procedures for quantitative research are typically categorized into one of two types—by whether the procedure for selecting participants is *random* or *nonrandom* (refer to Table 5.1). Specific types of random and nonrandom sampling are described in Table 5.2, with examples.

Before moving on to random sampling procedures I need to introduce two principles of quantitative research that are indispensable to doing good studies, *variability* and *sensitivity*, and explain how these are affected by sampling.

In quantitative studies, because there is typically some measure of relationship, the sample must be selected so that there will be *variability* of responses. This is because variability is essential for showing statistical measures of relationship. **Variability** is the spread or distribution of the scores, how much the scores range above and below the mean or median. For instance, if a researcher wanted to examine a relationship between personality traits and attitudes toward going to college, the sample must include students who will show a wide range of scores from measuring each variable. If the sample consisted solely of students who are taking advanced placement classes and think very highly about college, the results on the attitude variable will not have sufficient variability to show a relationship to personality traits. The sample needs to include students who vary in their attitudes toward college. Likewise, if you select only students who volunteer to answer questions about self-efficacy, and that leads to mostly high self-efficacy scores (lack of variability), it will be difficult to show relationships between self-efficacy and other variables. In either case, the lack of variability is noise in the sense that it is much more difficult to find relationships. What is reported would be a smaller relationship than the true signal.

Sensitivity, with respect to sampling, is the degree to which the participants being studied in an experimental or longitudinal design are capable of showing changes on the dependent variable, or, in a nonexperimental study, likely to show variability of scores. That is, the participants need to be *able* to be changed by the intervention or to show change over time, or to show differences. If you wanted to show how a specific program enhanced high school students' grit, you would have a hard time showing that if the sample consists of students who already have high grit scores. There would be limited room for improvement (ceiling effect). Likewise, if you sample high socio-economic students each year over a 10-year period, there is less likelihood of showing improvement from the program. A sample taken from the middle or low end of the distribution would be more likely to show change. In other words, a sample would be described as *insensitive* if there is inadequate *possible* variation.

With that said, let's get into specific sampling techniques.

The Hedgehog and the Fox Select a Sample to Study Service Learning

I'm going to use a group of college freshmen and sophomores taking introductory social work for my sample because they are socially conscious and will answer positively about service-learning courses.

It will be important for me to use a heterogeneous group of college students who are quite varied in their level of social consciousness since I know that can relate to how they may rate the value of service learning.

Random Sampling

The intent of some quantitative studies is to study a relatively small group of participants (the sample) that represent a well-defined larger group of individuals. The larger group of individuals (technically called *elements*, which could also be classes, schools, objects, or events) is called the **population**. This larger group is also referred to as the **target population** or *universe* (designated by N). The specification of the population begins with the research problem and review of literature, through which a population is described conceptually or in broad terms—for example, seventh-grade students, beginning teachers, principals, special education teachers, and so forth. A more specific definition is then needed, based on demographic characteristics. These characteristics are sometimes referred to as *delimiting* variables. For example, in a study of first-grade minority students, there are three delimiting characteristics: students, first grade (age), and minority.

It is important to distinguish the target population from the *survey population* (or *sampling frame or accessible population*). For example, as illustrated in Figure 5.1, the target population may be beginning teachers across the United States, in all types of schools. The **survey population** is the group from whom data could be collected (e.g., a list of first-year public school teachers obtained from 40 states). The sample (designated by *n*) is drawn from that list. Although the intent may be to generalize to all beginning teachers, the generalization in this case would be most accurately limited to first-year public school teachers in the 40 states.

Figure 5.1 Relationship Among Target Population, Sampling Frame, and Sample

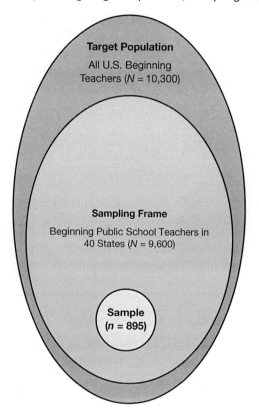

It is also important to remember that the sample selected from the population may not be the same as the participants who provide data—that is because often not all individuals in the sample respond (more about this problem later).

When investigating a large population, it is often impractical and usually unnecessary to gather data from all the elements in the population. Typically, a relatively small number of participants or cases is selected from the larger population. The goal is to select a sample that will adequately represent the population, so what is described in the sample will also be approximately true of the population. The best procedure for selecting such a sample is to use some type of **random sampling** (selection), or what is commonly known as *probability sampling*. This is a method of sampling in which each of the individuals in the population has a known chance or likelihood of being selected (remember—random *selection* is a type of sampling; random *assignment* is used for some experimental designs).

Random selection implies that each member of the population as a whole or of subgroups of the population has a known chance of being selected. The steps taken in random sampling are illustrated in Figures 5.2 and 5.3. As long as the number of cases selected is large enough, it is likely that a small percentage of the population, represented by the sample, will provide an accurate description of the entire population. A word of caution: Just because an initial number of participants is selected randomly, that doesn't mean the final sample is a good representation of the population. For example, in many survey studies, only a small portion of randomly selected individuals cooperate and return the survey.

Figure 5.2 Steps in Random Sampling

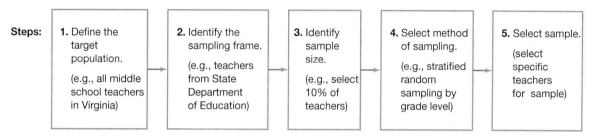

Figure 5.3 Sampling and Margin of Error

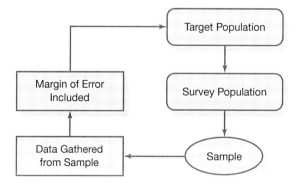

Author Reflection *Getting down the difference between random sampling and random assignment requires careful consideration of how researchers use these and related terms. If a researcher said, "I have taken a random selection of students from the total to be in each group," this means random assignment, not random selection. (I know, "random selection" is supposed to mean random sampling.) Also, when you see random, randomized, or randomization, be sure you know what is being described.*

Note, however, that there is always some degree of error in random sampling, and that error must be considered in interpreting the results. In probability sampling, this calculation can be made precisely with some statistical procedures. Consider a population of 1000 third-graders, from which you will randomly select 5%, or 50, to estimate the attitudes of all the third-graders toward school. If the attitude score was 75 for the sample of 50 individuals, 75 can be used to estimate the value for the entire population of third-graders. However, if another sample of 50 students is selected, their score might be a little different—say, 73. Which one is more correct? Because not all 1,000 students have been tested to obtain the result, we do not know for sure, but the results can be used to estimate the error in sampling. This is basically the technique that political polls follow when it is reported that the vote is 45% ± 3%. The plus or minus 3 is the estimate of error in sampling. For example, it is common to report what is called a *margin of error* in polling. The **margin of error** indicates an interval within which the true population value probably lies. In polling, there is typically a 95% probability that the population value is within the interval that is provided. Thus, for 45% ± 3, there is a 95% chance that when the entire population votes, the result will be between 42 and 48. This also means that for a very small number of studies the actual population value that is presumed to be true, based on sample statistics, will be outside the margin of error.

The four major types of random sampling procedures in educational research are *simple random, systematic, stratified,* and *cluster.*

Check for Understanding 1

1a. What is the difference between the target population and the survey population?

1b. What is margin of error in sampling? Why is it important?

Simple Random Sampling

In **simple random sampling**, every member of the sampling frame has an equal and independent chance of being selected for the sample. This method is often used with a population that has a small number of cases—for example, putting the names or numbers of all population members into a hat and drawing some out as the sample. Once the names are in the hat or other container, they are mixed thoroughly and then one is selected, then mixed, then selected, and so on until you have the number of elements needed for the sample. The downside of this method is when you have a large population, you will have many pieces of paper! A great example of simple random sampling occurred in 1970, the first year the military draft was reinstituted since 1944, for all men born between 1944 and 1950. Every day of the year was the population, and 366 blue plastic capsules, each containing a date, were put in a large drum. The drum was rolled, and dates were picked out randomly. The first date picked was given the number one draft number, the second date selected the number two draft number, and so on. The process was televised and rather dramatic, as young men with birthdays selected early, and thus with low numbers, mostly were drafted to go to Vietnam. Interestingly, later studies showed that the selections were not really random after all, owing to insufficient mixing of the capsules.

Researchers rarely use hats or drums to select random samples. For many years, one could use a table of random numbers, found in statistics books or other sources. There are typically pages of columns of numbers, as in Figure 5.4. Suppose, for example, that you had a population of 100 third-graders and wanted to select 20 by simple random sampling. First, each third-grader in the population is assigned a number from 001 to 100. Second, the researcher randomly selects a starting point in a table of random numbers and then reads all three-digit numbers, moving either across rows or down columns. The researcher would follow the row or column until coming across 20 of the third-graders in the population. This is illustrated in Figure 5.4 for 5 of the 20 third-graders by showing those selected (bolded) going down the first three digits of each column. This results in having participants with numbers 100, 52, 53, 5, and 31.

Figure 5.4 Selecting Participants from a Table of Random Numbers

46614	20002	17918	23470	**031**64
16482	**052**17	54102	74619	60137
91677	62481	**053**74	88283	99205
62855	62660	20186	46018	30106
10089	96487	59058	33251	93872
45638	73291	11859	**005**10	20167

The most common way of selecting a simple random sample from a large population is by computer. There are computer programs that will assign numbers to each element in the population, generate the sample numbers randomly, and then print out the names of the people corresponding to the numbers. You can use websites such as random.org or randomizer.org, or statistical software packages such as SPSS.

Simple random sampling is illustrated in Excerpt 5.1.

EXCERPT 5.1

Simple Random Sampling

The population of the study is undergraduate university students of Jammu and Kashmir (India). The participants in this research were 900 undergraduate university students in Kashmir province of Jammu and Kashmir, who were selected via simple random sampling technique. This technique has been selected for some benefits; including ease of use, accuracy of representation and exhibit low sampling error (Singh, 2008). (p. 61)

SOURCE: Bashir, H., & Bala, R. (2018). Development and validation of academic dishonesty scale (ADS): Presenting a multidimensional scale. *International Journal of Instruction, 11*(2), 57–74.

Systematic Random Sampling

In **systematic random sampling**, every nth element is selected from a list of all elements in the sampling frame, beginning with a randomly selected element. Thus, in selecting 100 individuals from a population of 50,000, every nth element would correspond to every 500th individual. The first element is selected randomly. In this example, that would be some number between 1 and 500. Suppose 240 was randomly selected as a starting point. The first individual chosen for the sample would be the 240th name on a list, the next individual would be the 740th, then the 1240th, and so on until 100 individuals were selected.

An example of systematic sampling is illustrated in Figure 5.5. In this case, there is a sampling frame of 80 students. The researcher needs a sample size of 10% (8 cases). This means that every 10th student will be selected from the list (80/8), beginning with a randomly selected number between 1 and 10.

Figure 5.5 Systematic Random Sampling

Random start

1 2 3 4 5 **6** 7 8 9 10 11 12 13 14 15 **16** 17 18 19 20 21 22 23 24 25 **26** 27 28 29

Every 10th student

30 31 32 33 34 35 **36** 37 38 39 40 41 42 43 44 45 **46** 47 48 49 50 51 52 53 54 55

56 57 58 59 60 61 62 63 64 65 **66** 67 68 69 70 71 72 73 74 75 **76** 77 78 79 80

Sample: 6   16   26   36   46   56   66   76

There is a possible (though uncommon) weakness in systematic sampling if the list of cases in the population is arranged in a pattern so only individuals with similar characteristics or those who come from similar contexts are selected. For instance, if a list of fourth-graders in a school division is arranged by classroom and students in the classrooms are listed from high to low ability, there is a cyclical pattern in the list (referred to as *periodicity*). If every *n*th student selected corresponds to that pattern, the sample would represent only a certain level of ability and would not be representative of the population. Alphabetical lists do not usually create periodicity and are suitable for choosing individuals systematically. Systematic sampling can be better than simple random sampling if the individuals can be rank ordered on a variable that is related to the dependent variable. This would occur if you were studying the relationship of class size to achievement. If you could select the classes systematically from an ordered list from largest to smallest, the systematic sample would be less likely to miss some class sizes.

Stratified Random Sampling

Stratified random sampling is a modification of either simple random or systematic sampling in which the population is first divided into homogeneous subgroups. Next, individuals are selected from each subgroup, using simple random or systematic procedures, rather than from the population as a whole. The strata are the subgroups. Researchers may sometimes indicate that stratified sampling is used first, followed by simple random sampling.

In Figure 5.6, stratified random sampling is illustrated with male and female subgroups. Stratified sampling is used primarily for two reasons. First, as long as the subgroups are identified by a variable related to the dependent variable in the research (e.g., socioeconomic status in a study of achievement) and results in more homogeneous groups, the same-sized sample will be more representative of the population than if taken from the population as a whole. This result reduces the margin of error and allows a smaller sample to be chosen.

Figure 5.6 Stratified Random Sampling

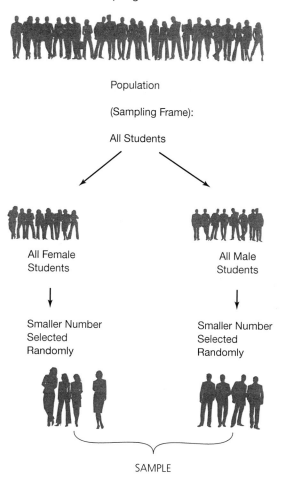

Population

(Sampling Frame):

All Students

All Female
Students

All Male
Students

Smaller Number
Selected
Randomly

Smaller Number
Selected
Randomly

SAMPLE

Second, stratified sampling is used to ensure that an adequate number of individuals is selected from different subgroups. For example, if a researcher is studying beginning elementary school teachers and believes that there may be important differences between male and female teachers, using simple random or systematic sampling would probably not result in a sufficient number of male teachers to study the differences. It would be necessary in this situation first to stratify the population of teachers into male and female teachers and then to select individuals from each subgroup.

The stratified samples can be selected using one of two methods. **Proportional stratified sampling**, or *proportional allocation,* is used when the number of individuals selected from each stratum is based on the percentage of individuals in the population that have the characteristic used to form the stratum. That is, each stratum is represented in the sample in the same proportion as it is represented in the population. Thus, if 20% of the population of 200 elementary teachers is male, 20% of the sample would also be male teachers. Proportional stratified random sampling is illustrated in Excerpt 5.2.

Using proportional stratified sampling, however, does not always ensure that a sufficient number of individuals will be selected from each stratum. A second approach, referred to as **disproportional stratified sampling**, mitigates this problem

---

EXCERPT 5.2

Proportional Stratified Random Sampling

The participants in this study consisted of 2,100 adolescents.... Participants were chosen using a proportional stratified random sampling method.... The sample was first stratified in terms of participant's area of residence (urban or rural) and the type of institution (middle school, high school, or juvenile corrective institution).... The sample size was adjusted and allocated to ensure representativeness in terms of each stratification parameter. (pp. 441–442)

SOURCE: Kim, H. S., & Kim, H. S. (2008). The impact of family violence, family functioning, and parental partner dynamics on Korean juvenile delinquency. *Child Psychiatry and Human Development, 39,* 439–453.

---

by typically taking the same number of individuals from each stratum, regardless of the percentage of individuals from each stratum in the population. For instance, if only 10% of a population of 200 elementary teachers is male, a proportional sample of 40 would include only four male teachers. To study teacher gender, it would be better to include all 20 male teachers in the population for the sample and randomly select 20 female teachers. When disproportional sampling is used, the results of each stratum need to be weighted to estimate values for the population as a whole.

In Excerpt 5.3, disproportional stratified sampling is used with three levels of stratification, in which three groups of students are compared with regard to mathematics instruction. Note that an equal number of students was selected from each stratum. Excerpt 5.4 also shows disproportional stratified sampling, in which 50 cases were selected randomly from each of three groups of higher education institutions, based on enrollment.

EXCERPTS 5.3 AND 5.4

Disproportional Stratified Random Sampling

Once we obtained the most complete [population] possible, we attempted to stratify our sample based on race of the student, socioeconomic status, parent education, and type of school. Specifically, we randomly selected (a) White non-Hispanic non-ELL ($n = 100$), (b) Hispanic non-ELL ($n = 100$), and (c) Hispanic ELL ($n = 100$) students from ... 3,487 fifth grade student participants. One hundred students were selected for each subgroup due to the limited [population] size of ELL status and race/ethnicity. (p. 175)

SOURCE: Valle, M. S., Waxman, H. C., Diaz, Z., & Padron, Y. N. (2013). Classroom instruction and the mathematics achievement of non-English learners and English learners. *The Journal of Educational Research, 106*(3), 173–182.

First, using the Carnegie Classification of Institutions of Higher Education, we obtained three lists of 4-year, not-for profit colleges and universities: small (enrollment of 1,000–2,999; $n = 683$), medium (enrollment of 3,000–9,999; $n = 480$), and large (enrollment of least 10,000; $n = 285$). Using a Web-based random number generator, we drew a random sample of 50 schools from each list, for a total N of 150. Within this sample, 52% ($n = 78$) of institutions were public, and 48% ($n = 72$) were private. (p. 258)

SOURCE: Holland, K. J., Cortina, L. M., & Freyd, J. J. (2018). Compelled disclosure of college sexual assault. *American Psychologist, 73*(4), 256–268.

Disproportional stratified random sampling is further illustrated in Figure 5.7. In this case, the population is first divided into three strata based on age, then each age group is further stratified into groups of male and female students.

Cluster Sampling

When it is impossible or impractical to sample individuals from the population as a whole—for example, if there is no exhaustive list of all the individuals—*cluster sampling* may be used. **Cluster sampling** involves the random selection of naturally occurring groups or units (clusters), and then using individuals from the chosen groups for the study. Examples of naturally occurring groups would be universities, schools, school districts, classrooms, city blocks, and households. For example, if a researcher were conducting a state survey on the television viewing habits of middle school students, it would be cumbersome and difficult to select children at random from the state population of all middle schoolers. A clustering procedure could be employed by first listing all the school districts in the state and then randomly selecting 30 school districts from the list. One middle school would then be selected from each district, and all students from each school, or a random sample of students, would be included in the survey. Although cluster sampling saves time and money, the results are less accurate than those based on other random sampling techniques.

Figure 5.7 Example of Disproportional Stratified Random Sampling with Two Strata

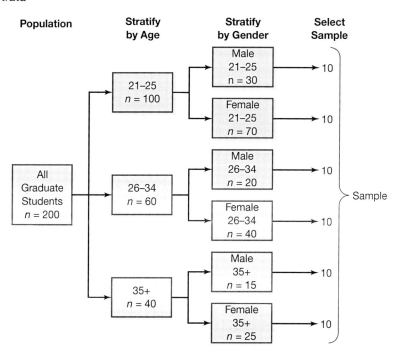

A two-stage cluster sampling procedure is illustrated in Excerpt 5.5. The first cluster is school type and the second cluster is classroom. Each of these was selected randomly, then all students in each selected class were used in the analyses.

EXCERPT 5.5

Cluster Sampling

A random sample from each school type was drawn from four federal states in Germany. Within each school, two seventh-grade classes were randomly. (p. 155)

SOURCE: Von Keyserlingk, L., Becker, M., & Jansen, M. (2019). Academic self-concept during the transition to upper secondary school. *Contemporary Educational Psychology, 56*, 152–160.

Check for Understanding 2

2a. Why is it important to know how participants were identified or sampled?

2b. What is the difference between stratified random, systematic, and cluster sampling? When would you want to use each one, and why?

Nonrandom Sampling

Learning Outcome 5.3   Distinguish among types of nonrandom sampling procedures and possible sources of bias.

In many research designs, it is unnecessary, not feasible, or not desirable to obtain a random sample. Often, for example, researchers are not interested in generalizing to a larger population. In these situations, a *nonrandom* sample is used. **Nonrandom sampling** is one in which the selection of the participants is based on the judgments of the researcher. Even if there is a desire to have some level of generalizability to others that could be used to make a case that the sample is "representative," that generalization is logical or based on how similar the sample is to the population. It is also quite common for the population to be the same as the sample, in which case there is no immediate need to generalize to a larger population. In fact, much educational research reported in journals (especially experimental studies) uses a group of individuals that has not been selected from a larger population.

There are several types of nonrandom sampling procedures used in quantitative studies. We will consider the three types that are used most commonly: *convenience, purposive,* and *quota.*

Convenience Sampling

A **convenience sample** is one that is simply available (so often it is called an *available sample*). Here, the researcher uses a group of individuals because they are accessible. Of course, this does not mean just anyone. Presumably, the sample will have characteristics that are targeted by the study. As indicated earlier, this means that the participants have some level of variability or spread of scores on each variable. Suppose you wanted to see whether there is a relationship between class size and student achievement, but you could not randomly select the classes. However the sample was selected, it would need to contain classes of different sizes. Thus, if the only available classes have about the same size, you may as well not do the study! Another consideration, with experiments, is whether the participants *can* show changes or differences (sensitivity). If you are studying the effect of a new curriculum and the only participants available are all high achievers, there may not be much chance of showing a change.

Often, what is convenient or available is based on circumstances and who knows whom. For example, many studies are done with college students, usually because they are conveniently accessed. The classrooms of teachers who are enrolled in a graduate class or the schools of principals who are participating in a workshop are often asked to be participants or provide participants. In a dissertation conducted at my university a few years ago, the researcher happened to be talking to a school superintendent, mentioned that she was doing her study, and ended up using the middle school students and their parents in that school district as the participants.

As you might surmise, the nature of the convenience sample may bias the results. For example, if the available sample for studying the impact of college is the group of alumni who return on alumni day, their responses would probably be quite different from those of all alumni. Similarly, research on effective teaching that depends on the participation of teachers in a particular geographic area because they are available may result in different findings than research done in other geographic areas. Often, a *volunteer* sample, a type of convenience sample, is used, which has obviously potential bias. Say you asked a group of athletes whether some would volunteer to be in a study about sleep and performance. The individuals who agree to participate may represent only female students, those from a particular sport, or those from just one or two classes. You get the idea—not only is generalizability severely hampered with volunteers, but there is also a decent chance of getting biased results with that group.

Although we should be wary of convenience samples (sometimes these samples are negatively referred to as *accidental* or *haphazard*), often this is the only type of sampling possible, and the primary purpose of the research may not be to generalize but to better understand relationships that may exist. Suppose a researcher is investigating the relationship between creativity and intelligence, and the only available sample is a single elementary school. When the study is completed, the results indicate a moderate relationship: Children who have higher intelligence tend to be more creative than children with lower intelligence. Because there was no random sampling, should we conclude that the results are not valid or credible? That decision seems extreme. It is more reasonable to interpret the results as reasonable for children who are similar to those studied. For example, if the children in the study are from a school that serves a low-socioeconomic area, the results will be useful for children in similar schools but less useful for those from schools that serve middle- or high-socioeconomic levels. The decision is not to dismiss the findings, but to limit them to the type of participants in the sample. As more and more research accumulates with different convenience samples, the overall credibility of the conclusions is enhanced. Just remember, the participants are not randomly selected from a larger population, so strict statistical estimates of what is likely to be true for others is not possible.

Although a researcher may not state explicitly that a convenience sample was used, it usually will be obvious from the data source subsection of the article. If some type of random sampling procedure was used, it will be described. Thus, in the absence of random sampling particulars, you can assume that the sample was an available one. Excerpts 5.6 and 5.7 illustrate convenience sampling.

EXCERPTS 5.6 AND 5.7

Convenience Sampling

Participants were recruited from a local elementary school located in one of the largest school districts in the southeast United States. The school was chosen due to the close proximity to researchers and the active gaming department at the university. A total of 57 of 81 children (*M* age = 8.7 ± 1.2 years; age range = 7–11 years) in Grades 3, 4, and 5 volunteered to participate in this study. (pp. 353–354)

SOURCE: Millecker, R. R., Witherspoon, L., & Watterson, T. (2013). Active learning: Educational experiences enhanced through technology-driven active game play. *The Journal of Educational Research, 106,* 352–359.

Participants (*N* = 39) were adult graduate students attending a CACREP-accredited counselor training program at a comprehensive, regional university in Pennsylvania. Participants consisted of a nonprobability convenience sample of all students enrolled in one of two courses. (p. 34)

SOURCE: Wilkerson, K., & Eschbach, L. (2009). Transformed school counseling: The impact of a graduate course on trainees' perceived readiness to develop comprehensive, data-driven programs. *Professional School Counseling, 13*(1), 30–39.

Purposeful Sampling

Purposeful (or *purposive*) **sampling** is done so the sample is "representative" of the types of participants needed to conduct the study. The reason for selecting certain individuals is that they will have the characteristics that will be studied or to whom the results will be generalized. Often there is a population of interest, and the researcher selects participants nonrandomly so they have about the same characteristics as the population. For instance, if you wanted to compare charter school student achievement to public school student achievement, you would want to select some students at both charter and public schools. If you could not do that randomly, you would want to identify and use a sufficient number of each type of school, perhaps from different geographical areas (urban and suburban). The percentages of schools in each group are typically not in the same proportion as what is present in the population. Thus, if 10% of all schools are charter schools, the researcher may select 20 charter schools and 20 public schools for the sample.

Note in Excerpt 5.8 how the researchers identified certain types of schools that needed to be in the sample.

EXCERPT 5.8

Purposeful Sampling

The sample comprised 643 elementary and high school students from 15 schools on the east coast of Australia.... [Schools] were selected on the basis of their emphasis on one or more of the five major arts areas (art, dance, drama, film/media, and music) so that across the sample, each arts form was well represented.... Based on these sample attributes, the selection of students and schools for this study can be considered a broad cross-section of schools in its spread of type, region, prior achievement, socioeconomic status, language background, and gender composition. (p. 714)

SOURCE: Martin, A. J., Mansour, M., Anderson, M., Gibson, R., Liem, G. A. D., & Sudmalis, D. (2013). Role of arts participation in students' academic and nonacademic outcomes: A longitudinal study of school, home, and community factors. *Journal of Educational Psychology, 105*(3), 709–727.

Quota Sampling

Quota sampling is used when the researcher is unable to take a probability sample but still wants a sample that is representative of the entire population. Different composite profiles of major groups in the population are identified, and then individuals are selected, nonrandomly, to represent each group. This is akin to stratified random sampling, but the selection from each stratum is nonrandom. Often, the quota sample is carefully selected so that the percentage of participants in each stratum in the sample is about the same as the percentages in the population. For example, if you wanted to investigate political affiliations of college students and knew that major would be a consideration, you would first determine the percentages of students in different majors in the population, then find individuals to survey so the sample shows the same percentages of students in different majors as the population. In other words, if in the population 60% of college students are humanities majors, 20% science majors, and 20% engineering majors, then students would be selected nonrandomly so that the sample would also contain 60% humanities majors, 20% science majors, and 20% engineering majors. In quota sampling, the goal is to be able to generalize to the population, but the individuals are not selected randomly from different strata.

Description of the Sample

Regardless of the type of sampling procedure, it is important for the researcher to describe the characteristics of the group of participants or cases that provided information used in the data analyses of the study (e.g., age, gender, grade level, race, ethnicity, primary language).

Why Description of the Sample Is Needed

A good description of the sample is important for three reasons. First, characteristics of the sample may show differences from the population, indicating, as previously discussed, possible bias. Second, characteristics may help explain why certain results were obtained. For example, if a group of college student respondents were mostly math and science majors, the relationship between their attitudes toward statistics and achievement would probably be different from a group of humanities majors. Third, a good description is needed to generalize the results, suggesting how the results could apply to other groups of individuals. The studies in Excerpts 5.9 and 5.10 are both examples of good descriptions of samples.

Identification of Race, Ethnicity, Gender, and Disability

It is very common for researchers to use race, ethnicity, and gender in both describing populations and analyzing data, and much research is conducted with people with special needs. Consider race/ethnicity. Often, researchers use some variation of four major racial/ethnic minority groups for the United States: Asian American/Pacific Islander, persons of African descent, Latinx, and American Indian/Alaska Native. The challenge is in knowing and interpreting what is meant more specifically by such labels and whether other terms (e.g., Black, Hispanic not White, Latino) have different meaning. Ethnicity, for example, is based on having a common origin or culture with shared language, ancestry, and race. (The term *race* alone refers to common physical

EXCERPTS 5.9 AND 5.10

Descriptions of Samples

Participants. Six hundred ninety-seven students from four middle schools in a midsize Midwestern city completed the WHBS during the spring semester. The sample included all students enrolled in eighth grade, English/language arts (ELA) classes ... 692(99.7%) were eighth graders ... 327(47.3%) were boys. Mean reported age ($n = 692$) was 13.8 years. Overall, approximately 62% of the participating students reported their racial-ethnic status as Caucasian, 10% as African American, 8% as Latino/Latina, 5% as Asian American, and 15% as multiracial or another ethnicity. Five hundred eighty-two (83.5%) reported that English was the primary language spoken at home; 110 students (16.5%) reported languages other than English primarily being spoken at home. The proportions of students participating in free or reduced lunch programs in the four participating schools were 76%, 66%, 51%, and 23% (overall proportion in district middle schools = 38.1%). (pp. 29–30)

SOURCE: Bruning, R., Dempsey, M., Kauffman, D. F., McKim, C., & Zumbrunn, S. (2013). Examining dimensions of self-efficacy for writing. *Journal of Educational Psychology, 10*(1), 25–38.

A total of 298 school counselors completed the survey. Their ages ranged from 25 to 67 ($M = 43.88$, $SD = 11.37$). By gender, 35 participants (11.7%) identified as male and 263 identified as female (88.3%). By race and ethnicity, 275 (92.3%) participants identified as Caucasian, with the remaining participants identifying as African American ($n = 13$), American Indian/Alaskan Native American ($n = 3$), Hispanic American ($n = 3$), or multiracial ($n = 3$), and with one participant declining to answer. By education level, 279 respondents (93.6%) had completed a master's degree in school counseling, nine had completed either a PhD or EdD (3.0%), eight had completed an EdS degree (2.7%), and two individuals (0.7%) declined to answer. Reports of years of experience as a school counselor ranged from 1 year to 39 years ($M = 11.18$, $SD = 8.01$) with caseloads of students ranging from 30 to 1,800 ($M = 448.74$, $SD = 238.39$). Regarding the geographic location of the schools, 96 respondents (32.2%) worked in a rural setting, 114 (38.3%) in a suburban setting, and 60 (20.1%) in an urban setting; 28 (9.4%) declined to answer. A large majority of the sample (92.3%, $n = 275$) worked at a public school. Lastly, less than a third (30.2%, $n = 90$) of the sample noted they had implemented the ASCA National Model at their school. (p. 351)

SOURCE: Fye, H. J., Gnilka, P. B., & McLaulin, S. E. (2018). Perfectionism and school counselors: Differences in stress, coping, and burnout. *Journal of Counselling & Development, 96*, 349–360.

features, such as skin tone; *racial identity* involves a sense of belonging to a common culture.) In reality, both race and ethnicity as categories are contextual in nature and evolving over time. This means that, for a particular population or sample, the meaning of racial and ethnic terms may not be the same as how those in different populations or samples interpret the categories.

Since gender is a term that refers to social roles within a culture, and there are now many more categories of sexuality (biological sex and/or sexual orientation) than male/female, using only a dichotomous interpretation may not appropriately describe the population or sample. Similarly, in describing people with special needs, there are many categories of disabilities. The best description will be as specific as possible, with both conceptual and operational definitions provided for such labels as "learning disability" "visual impairment," "emotional disturbance," and "autism spectrum disorder." Specific definitions are also needed for gender/gender identity and race/

ethnicity. This means that it is important to be aware that descriptions of samples and populations using these labels will not necessarily be the same for different studies. It also means that good research recognizes the complexity of use of the labels and strives to be as clear and targeted as possible.

Check for Understanding 3

3a. What is the difference between quota, convenience, and purposeful sampling?

3b. What is the primary advantage and disadvantage of using convenience sampling?

3c. Why is it important to have a good description of the participants?

The Effects of Participants and Sampling on Quantitative Research

Learning Outcome 5.4 Explain how factors related to sampling can influence, even bias, findings; know and apply the criteria for evaluating sample and participant sections of research articles and reports.

In reading and interpreting research, you need to be conscious of how the sampling procedures may have affected the findings and how the characteristics of the participants affect the usefulness and the generalizability of the results. When evaluating the sampling used in a quantitative study, it is helpful to keep in mind the advantages and disadvantages of the sampling strategy that has been used (refer to Table 5.3). That will allow you to better critique the effect of the sampling on the results and conclusions.

Volunteer Participants

A continuing problem in educational research, as well as in much social science research, is the use of volunteers as participants. It is well documented that volunteers differ from nonvolunteers in important ways. Volunteers tend to be better educated, on a higher level socioeconomically, more intelligent, more in need of social approval, more sociable, more unconventional, less authoritarian, and less conforming than nonvolunteers.

Volunteers are commonly used in research because the availability of participants is often limited by time and resources. There have been thousands of studies with teachers who volunteer their classes for research. Much research on school-age children requires written permission from parents, and this necessity can result in biased samples. Suppose a researcher needed parents' permission to study their involvement in the education of their children. Chances are good that parents who are relatively involved would be most likely to agree to be in the study, affecting a description of the nature of parental involvement for "all" students. In this case, the volunteer sample will provide a biased result. **Nonresponse bias** occurs when the participants who volunteer to provide data are systematically different from the larger population and show findings that are not true for the population.

Table 5.3 Strengths and Weaknesses of Quantitative Sampling Methods

Method of Sampling	Strengths	Weaknesses
Random		
Simple	1. Usually representative of the population 2. Easy to analyze and interpret results 3. Easy to understand	1. Requires numbering each element in the population 2. Larger sampling error than in stratified sampling
Systematic	1. Same as above 2. Simplicity of drawing sample	1. Periodicity in list of population elements
Proportional Stratified	1. 1–3 of simple random 2. Allows subgroup comparisons 3. Usually more representative than simple random or systematic 4. May be costly and difficult to prepare lists of population elements in each subgroup 5. Fewer participants needed 6. Results represent population without weighting	1. Requires subgroup identification of each population element 2. Requires knowledge of the proportion of each subgroup in the population
Disproportional Stratified	1. Same as above 2. Ensures adequate numbers of elements in each subgroup	1. Same as above 2. Requires proper weighting of subgroup to represent population 3. Less efficient for estimating population characteristics
Cluster	1. Low cost 2. Requires lists of elements 3. Efficient with large populations	1. Less accurate than simple random, systematic, or stratified 2. May be difficult to collect data from all elements in each cluster 3. Requires that each population element be assigned only one cluster
Nonrandom		
Convenience	1. Less costly 2. Less time consuming 3. Easily administered 4. Usually ensures high participation rate 5. Generalization possible to similar individuals	1. Difficult to generalize to other individuals 2. Less representative of an identified population 3. Results dependent on unique characteristics of the sample
Quota	1. Same as above 2. More representative of population than convenience or purposeful	1. Same as above 2. Usually more time consuming than convenience or purposeful
Purposeful	1. 1–5 of convenience 2. Assures receipt of needed information	1. 1–3 of convenience

Another way in which volunteers impact research, especially with large-scale studies that employ listservs, e-mail lists, or other sources to contact a large number of potential participants, is that only a percentage of volunteer individuals are likely to respond. Often, the percentage is unknown due to a lack of knowledge about the number of initial contacts, and very often the percentage is very small. Excerpt 5.11 is a good example of this type of sampling. Note that it is not clear what the total number of those contacted was, so calculating a percentage who volunteered is not possible. In this case, since "professional associations" could easily mean thousands of individuals; only a very small number returned usable surveys. What does this suggest about the veracity of the findings? Some indication of whether the sample is at least somewhat representative of the larger population can be determined by comparing the participant demographics to those of the population, if known. Another approach

---

EXCERPT 5.11

Volunteer Sample

The initial sample consisted of 693 teachers with 404 teachers completing the entire survey. The sample included teachers from select regions across Canada and the United States. Participants were invited to complete the ACAI through email and list-serve invitations. Specifically, teachers were targeted through professional associations and groups including social and web media sites. (p. 360)

SOURCE: DeLuca, C., Valiquette, A., Coombs, A., LaPointe-McEwan, D., & Luhanga, U. (2018). Teachers' approaches to classroom assessment: A large-scale survey. *Assessment in Education: Principles, Policy & Practice, 25*(4), 355–375.

---

is to follow up with a randomly selected group to see whether their responses are different from those who did respond.

In some cases, however, volunteers will provide a biased result. For example, if you are describing the amount of time adolescents use YouTube, asking for volunteers might result in mostly individuals who like YouTube and consequently report a greater amount of time usage than the population of adolescents as a whole.

Sample Size

An important consideration in judging the credibility of research is the size of the sample. In many studies there are restrictions that limit the number of participants, although it is difficult to know when the sample is too small. Most researchers use general rules of thumb in their studies, such as having at least 30 participants for correlational research and at least 15 participants in each group for experimental research. However, in many educational studies conducted in the field, higher numbers of individuals are needed. In surveys that sample a very large population, often a very small percentage of the population needs to be sampled—for example, less than 5% or even 1%. Of course, if the survey sample is too small, it is likely that the results obtained cannot characterize the population. Generally, if you want to have a representative sample from a population of 50, you need almost all the individuals—at least 40. For a population of 100, at least 70 participants may be need to be in the sample. As the population size increases, the percentage needed for the sample decreases. Any random sample of 800 or more is typically adequate for any size population. Small sample size is rarely an issue with large data sets (big data). With these studies the focus needs to be on whether a large sample size results in distorted "significance" of findings (more about this important issue in Chapter 10).

Formal statistical techniques can be used to determine the number of participants needed, even if these techniques are not used in many educational studies. As long as the researcher knows how precise the results need to be (that is, something like margin of error), and knows about the likely spread of scores, the number of participants needed can be calculated, resulting in something called *power*. (We take a closer look at this intriguing concept in Chapter 10.)

In educational research, a major consideration with respect to sample size is the interpretation of findings that show no difference or relationships, particularly in studies that use small samples. For example, suppose you are studying the relationship between creativity and intelligence and, with a sample of 20 students, found that there was no relationship. Is it reasonable to conclude that in reality there is no relationship?

Probably not, because a plausible reason for not finding a relationship is that such a small sample was used, and this limited what was found. In addition to the small number of participants, it is likely that there may not be many differences in either creativity or intelligence, and without such differences it is impossible to find that the two variables are related. That is, with a larger sample that has different creativity and intelligence scores, a relationship may exist. This problem—interpreting results that show no difference or relationship with small samples—is subtle but very important in educational research because so many studies have small samples. As we will see in Chapter 10, it is possible to misinterpret what is reported as a "significant" difference or relationship with a very large sample. Furthermore, a sample that is not properly drawn from the population is misleading, no matter what the size.

Author Reflection *Small sample size is a deliciously intriguing situation for quantitative studies because large samples, often available with big data, which you think would be a good thing, sometimes result in misleading conclusions just because the sample is huge, whereas the failure to find relationships with small samples does not mean that they don't exist. This may seem confusing, but it is an important principle for interpreting results. We'll flush it out in Chapter 10.*

Participant Motivation

Sometimes participants will be motivated to respond in certain ways. Clues for this phenomenon will be found in the description of how the participants were selected. For example, if a researcher was interested in studying the effectiveness of computer simulations in teaching science, one approach would be to interview teachers who used computer simulations. The researcher might even want to select only science teachers who had used the simulations for more than 2 years. Understandably, the selected teachers, because they had been using the simulations, would be motivated to respond favorably toward them. The response would be consistent with the teachers' decision to use simulations. Conversely, psychology students may be motivated to give inaccurate responses in studies conducted by their disliked psychology professor.

Sampling Bias

In selecting a sample from a population, there is always some degree of sampling error (margin of error). This error (which is expected and precisely estimated as part of random sampling) is the discrepancy between the true value of a variable for the population and the value that is calculated from the sample. A different type of error is due to **sampling bias**, a type of error that is often controlled or influenced by the researcher to result in misleading findings. The most obvious deliberate bias is selecting only individuals who will respond in a particular way to support a point or result. For instance, if a researcher is measuring the values of college students and wants to show that the students are concerned about helping others and being involved in community service, bias would result if the researcher deliberately selected students studying education or social work and ignored students in majors that might not be so altruistically oriented. Selecting friends or colleagues may also result in a biased sample.

An even more flagrant type of bias occurs when a researcher discards some individuals because they have not responded as planned, or keeps adding participants until the desired result is obtained. Sampling bias also occurs nondeliberately, often because of inadequate knowledge of what is required to obtain an unbiased sample and the motivation to "prove" a desired result or point of view.

Bias can also result from selecting participants from different populations and assigning them to different groups for an experiment or comparison. Suppose a researcher used graduate sociology students to receive an intervention in an experiment and graduate psychology students as a control group. Even if the samples were selected randomly from each population, differences in the populations—and, consequently, the samples—in attitudes, values, knowledge, and other variables could explain why certain results were obtained.

When conducting a survey, the investigator typically sends questionnaires to a sample of individuals and tabulates the responses of those who return them. Often, the percentage of the sample returning the questionnaire will be 50% to 60%, or even lower. Much like with volunteering, the nature of the results depends on the types of persons who respond, and generalizability to the target population is compromised. The specific effect of a biased sample on the results depends on the nature of the study. For example, a study of the relationship between educational level and occupational success would be likely to show only a small relationship if only those who are most successful respond. Without some participants in the sample who are not successful, success cannot be accurately related to level of education.

Consumer (and Researcher) Tips

Criteria for Evaluating Quantitative Sampling Procedures and Participant Descriptions

1. **The participants in the study should be clearly described, and the description should be specific and detailed.** Demographic characteristics, such as age, gender, socioeconomic status, ability, and grade level, should be indicated, as well as any unique characteristics—for example, gifted students, students enrolled in a psychology class, or volunteers.
2. **The population should be clearly defined.** It is especially important that a specific definition of the population be provided in studies using random sampling. Vague descriptions, such as "retired workers" or "high-ability students," are inadequate. The characteristics of each stratum in a stratified sampling procedure should also be included.
3. **The method of sampling should be clearly described.** The specific type of sampling procedure, such as simple random, stratified, cluster, maximum variation, or convenience, should be explicitly indicated in sufficient detail to enable other researchers to replicate the study.
4. **The response rate for survey studies should be clearly indicated.** In addition, it is helpful to indicate procedures used to keep the response rate high, as well as an analysis of how nonrespondents compare with those who did respond, to determine possible bias. With a low response rate, there is a need to directly address possible limitations.
5. **The selection of participants should be free of bias.** The procedures and criteria for selecting participants should not result in systematic error. Bias is more likely when a researcher is "proving" something to be true, with convenience samples, and when volunteers are used as participants.

6. **Selection procedures should be appropriate for the problem being investigated.** If the problem is to investigate science attitudes of middle school students, for example, it would be inappropriate to use high school students as participants. If the problem is to study the characteristics of effective teaching, the work of student teachers would probably not be very representative of effective teaching behaviors.

7. **There should be an adequate number of participants.** If the sample is selected from a population, the sample size must be large enough to represent the population accurately. There must also be a sufficient number of participants in each subgroup that is analyzed. Studies with small samples that report no differences or no relationships should be viewed with caution because a higher number or a better selection of participants may result in meaningful differences or relationships. Studies that have a very large number of participants may report "significant" differences or relationships that are of little practical utility.

Author Reflection *I have found that the quality of quantitative research depends heavily on the nature of the sampling. The sources of data are critical, whether some kind of random sample is selected, a volunteer sample is used, or criteria are used to select participants. This is because the responses of individuals depend heavily on who they are and what they have done. I have also found that some quantitative studies ignore individual differences when searching for overall group effects.*

Check for Understanding 4

4a.   How can volunteer samples result in misleading findings?

4b.   How do you know if there is an adequate number of participants?

4c.   What criteria should be used in judging the adequacy of a data source section in a report or sampling procedure?

Key Terms

Margin of error
Nonrandom sampling
  Convenience sample
  Purposeful sampling
  Quota sampling
Nonresponse bias
Participant

Population
  Survey population
  Target population
Random sampling
  Cluster sampling
  Simple random sampling
  Stratified random sampling

Disproportional stratified sampling
Proportional stratified sampling
Systematic random sampling
Sample
Sampling bias
Sensitivity
Variability

Discussion Questions

1. How is the "sample" different from the "population?"
2. Why is "margin of error" an important principle of sampling?
3. Under what circumstances would a random sampling procedure be needed?

4. Why should researchers be wary of using convenience samples?
5. How can volunteer participants bias a study? What can researchers do to address possible bias?
6. How can sampling result in greater noise in determining the relationships among phenomena?

Application Exercises

1. Use blocks, circles, arrows, and lines to draw a cognitive map of different kinds of sampling for quantitative studies. Include as much terminology as possible to identify each block, circle, arrow, and line.

2. Hank the hedgehog used a convenience sample of college sophomores and surmised that most students (60%) thought that the academic advising they received was either "very good" or "excellent." What would Frank the fox think about this conclusion?

Check for Understanding Answers

1a. The target population is the theoretical group to which you hope to generalize; the survey population is the group from which the sample is selected.

1b. Margin of error in sampling describes an interval in which the actual value of the population lies. It is important in interpreting the meaning of the result, keeping in mind the sample has some degree of error.

2a. Because you need to know about possible bias, lack of variability or sensitivity, and generalizability of the results.

2b. Stratified random first divides the population into subgroups then samples from the subgroups, systematic selects from a list of population elements, and cluster uses all participants from randomly selected units of participants. Stratified random is used to reduce the margin of error and include adequate numbers from each subgroup; systematic and cluster are used for convenience.

3a. Purposeful samples are selected according to criteria, convenience samples are available, and quota samples include minimum numbers with specific characteristics.

3b. The advantage is that it is easy to access; the disadvantage is that it may not be sensitive or show variability, or may have limited generalizability.

3c. To consider reasons for findings and generalizability.

4a. By self-selecting with biased perspectives, abilities, or other characteristics.

4b. By using established rules of thumb, previous studies, and power calculations.

4c. Clear description of sample, population, method of sampling, and response rate; free from bias; appropriate to the problem; adequate size.

Chapter 6
Foundations of Educational Measurement

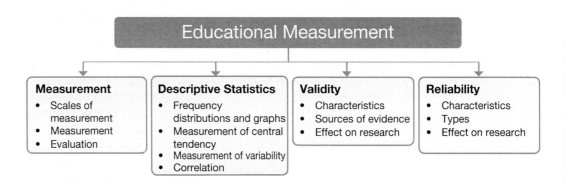

Educational Measurement

Measurement
- Scales of measurement
- Measurement
- Evaluation

Descriptive Statistics
- Frequency distributions and graphs
- Measurement of central tendency
- Measurement of variability
- Correlation

Validity
- Characteristics
- Sources of evidence
- Effect on research

Reliability
- Characteristics
- Types
- Effect on research

 ## Learning Outcomes

6.1 Describe the nature of measurement and how measures are used in quantitative research.

6.2 Understand fundamental descriptive statistics that are used in quantitative research, including frequency distributions, measures of central tendency and variability, and correlation.

6.3 Explain the meaning of measurement validity, sources of evidence to support validity arguments, and the effect of validity on research.

6.4 Explain the meaning of measurement reliability, sources of evidence to estimate reliability, and the effect of reliability on research.

Chapter Road Map

This is the first of two chapters that focus on gathering data for quantitative and mixed methods research, although even some qualitative studies use descriptive statistics to summarize data. Initially, important fundamental principles of measurement and descriptive statistics are reviewed, then we look at measurement validity and reliability as technical aspects that affect the quality of data that are gathered.

Introduction to Measurement

Learning Outcome 6.1   Describe the nature of measurement and how measures are used in quantitative research.

Measurement is one of the key building blocks of quantitative research. This section explains more precisely what is meant by the term, its purpose, and scales of measurement.

What Is Measurement?

Measurement can be defined as an appraisal of the amount of something. Determining the "amount" is typically done by assigning numbers to indicate different values of a variable. Some researchers may also use the term to refer to all aspects of quantitative data collection. In other words, *measurement* is used to quantitatively describe how much of a trait, attribute, or characteristic an individual, object, or event possesses. Numbers are used to describe and differentiate attributes or characteristics. **Measures** are specific items, techniques, or instruments used for measurement. These are often tests and questionnaires that provide objective, quantifiable data. For example, a specific reading test may be used to provide measurement of reading ability; a student self-report survey could measure attitudes toward grades.

   Assessment is a word that is sometimes used synonymously for measurement. The shorter term, *assess,* is a synonym for the verb *measure.* When researchers say they "assessed" something, they mean that they measured it. Sometimes *assessment* means "evaluation," and sometimes it refers to the more specific process of diagnosing of individual difficulties, such as assessing for learning disabilities. Some measurement specialists use *assessment* to refer to procedures used to obtain information about student performance. This is similar to how I have defined the term *measures.* In the context of classroom assessment, *assessment* refers to the entire process of measurement, evaluation, and, finally, use of the information by teachers and students (e.g., formative assessment).

The Purpose of Measurement for Research

The purpose of measurement is to quantitatively describe the variables and units of study that are being investigated (e.g., participants, settings, traits, objects). In education, this includes variables such as intelligence, achievement, aptitude, classroom environment, attitudes, and values. Measurement is a critical component of quantitative research because it provides a systematic, objective procedure for recording observations, performance, or other responses of individuals, and because it provides the basis for a quantitative summary of the results from many participants. The information collected through measurement provides the basis for the results, conclusions, and significance of the research. Quantitative research is credible to the extent that measurement is accurate. Simply put, good quantitative research must have sound measurement.

   There is a close relationship between the names and definitions of the variables being studied and the nature of their measurement. In practice, the variable is defined by how it is measured (*operational definition*), as well as by how it is labeled or given a constitutive definition by the researcher (*conceptual definition*). This distinction is especially important for consumers of research who want to use the results. For example, if you were reading research on improving students' critical thinking, you would find that there are many ways to define and measure critical thinking. It would be important to read the instruments section of the research to determine the specific manner in which critical thinking was measured to see how well it matches the critical thinking you want to promote with your students. You would not want to scan the results of various studies about critical thinking and employ the teaching methods that are reported to be effective without examining the measures used in each study carefully.

Measurements are used to describe participants. Often there is an indication of the number and percentages of participants with different characteristics, using traits such as gender, race, and age. Participants are also described quantitatively on variables such as socioeconomic status, ability level, and pretest scores.

Finally, measurement is a means by which we can differentiate between participants on dependent variables. If the measure of the dependent variable is correctly selected or developed, the results will show a good distribution of scores on the variable. Another way to think about this purpose is through the concept of *variability*, which is discussed later in this chapter.

Scales of Measurement

Measurement requires that the values of variables be differentiated. The nature of differentiation can vary, from a simple dichotomy, such as male/female, to more elaborate measures, such as scores on aptitude tests. There are four basic ways in which the variables and numbers from measures differ, depending on the nature of the information that is provided. These four methods are referred to as *scales of measurement*. Because the scales are arranged hierarchically on the basis of power and complexity, they are often called *levels of measurement*. **Measurement scales** are important for research because they help determine the nature of the quantification needed to answer research questions, and help the researcher select the appropriate method of statistical analysis.

Figure 6.1 shows the four measurement scales. As you can see, the scales differ on four characteristics—unique unrelated categories, rank ordering, equal size intervals, and true ratio. These four characteristics will be explained in the description of each measurement scale.

NOMINAL The simplest scale of measurement is termed *nominal*, or *classificatory*. A **nominal scale** is one in which there are mutually exclusive categories, without any order or relationship implied. Mutually exclusive categories are those in which all observations assigned to the same category have a similar characteristic, and they differ on the basis of a specific characteristic from observations in other categories. Examples of nominal data in research are gender, race, type of school, and nature of community (e.g., rural, suburban, urban). Numbers are sometimes assigned arbitrarily to different categories for statistical purposes, without any value or order being placed on the categories. For example, male could be coded "1" and female "2."

In research, the term *nominal* is also used to describe the nature of the data that are collected. Data are referred to as nominal if the researcher simply counts the number of instances, or frequency of observations, in each of two or more categories. The following are examples: counting the number of male and female students; the number of fifth-, sixth-, and seventh-graders; the number of times a teacher uses different types

Figure 6.1 Characteristics of Measurement Scales

Feature	Nominal	Ordinal	Interval	Ratio
Unique categories	✓	✓	✓	✓
Rank ordering		✓	✓	✓
Equal size intervals			✓	✓
True ratio				✓

of reinforcement; and the number of tenured and untenured teachers voting "yes" or "no" on a proposal to abolish tenure.

ORDINAL   An **ordinal scale** is one in which the categories are rank ordered. Each category can be compared to the others in terms of *less than* or *greater than*, but in an ordinal scale there is no indication of the magnitude of the differences. In other words, the categories are ordered but the degree of difference between the categories is not specified. A good example of an ordinal scale is the ranking of debate teams on their performance. The results show who is best, next best, and so forth, but not the magnitude of the difference between rankings, for instance, between first and second best. Other examples of ordinal scales include grades, percentages, and socioeconomic levels.

Ordinal scales are used extensively in educational research because many of the traits measured can be defined only in terms of order. Thus, students may be characterized as more or less mature, serious, ethical, altruistic, cooperative, competitive, or creative. The scores obtained from ordinal measurement can be interpreted to mean that one score is higher or lower than another, but the *degree of difference between the scores* is not known. Suppose we have rank-ordered four students on the basis of competitiveness. We know who is in each place, but not *how much* they differ from one another. The most competitive student could be only marginally higher than the student ranked second, whereas the other students might be much lower.

INTERVAL   An **interval scale** is ordinal and has equal intervals between categories or scores. The characteristic of equal intervals allows us to compare directly one score to another in terms of the amount of difference. For instance, if John scores 90 on a test with an interval scale, June scores 80, and Tim scores 70, we know that the distance between Tim and John is twice the distance between John and June or between June and Tim. We also know that the distance between the scores of 50 and 60 is equal to the distance between 80 and 90. Examples of interval scales include temperature and SAT and IQ scores.

RATIO   A **ratio scale** is one in which ratios can be used in comparing and interpreting the scores. This use is possible if the trait being measured has a true zero point; that is, none of the trait is present. Height and weight are examples of ratio data because there is a true value for zero, which corresponds to no height or weight at all, and there are equal intervals between different heights and weights. We can say, for instance, that Liam, who weighs 150 pounds, is twice as heavy as Dylan, who weighs 75 pounds. Few measures in educational research are ratio in nature, however.

Although identifying the scale of measurement of some variables is not always easy, it is especially important to distinguish among nominal, ordinal, and interval, because the appropriateness of statistical procedures depends on the scale of measurement for each variable. In fact, there are "assumptions" about the scale of measurement that should be met to accurately calculate many types of statistical procedures (more about those in Chapter 10). In addition, it is easy to interpret ordinal scale data as having equal intervals, which can be misleading. Suppose, for instance, that you have a measure of income, which translates into five levels—extremely high, very high, high, medium, and low. It would be a mistake to conclude that a "very high" income is twice the amount as "high" income. "Low" income could be 20 times lower than "extremely high."

Check for Understanding 1

1a.   How is measurement different from evaluation and assessment?

1b.   Why is measurement important in determining the quality of educational research?

1c.   What is the purpose of different scales of measurement?

Descriptive Statistics and Graphs

Learning Outcome 6.2 Understand fundamental descriptive statistics that are used in quantitative research, including frequency distributions, measures of central tendency and variability, and correlation.

Because measurement involves the use of numbers, basic principles of descriptive statistics and simple graphs are introduced now to help you understand subsequent principles of measurement presented in this chapter. We will also see that relatively straightforward and easily understood descriptive statistics are essential for conducting, reporting, and understanding quantitative research—certainly as important, in my mind, as the more complex inferential statistics.

Statistics are mathematical procedures used to summarize and analyze data. In quantitative studies, the data are collected by the researchers, who apply statistical techniques to better understand the meaning of the numbers. In this sense, statistical procedures are applied after data collection to obtain the results of the study. **Descriptive statistics** transform a set of numbers into indices that summarize data about or from a sample. Common descriptive statistics include the frequency of scores, percentages, means, and standard deviations, as well as graphs such as histograms and frequency polygons. These statistics and graphs communicate characteristics of the data as a whole and estimate the characteristics of the population. (The characteristics of a population are called *parameters*, rather than statistics.)

Descriptive statistics also represent principles and are the basis for a vocabulary used in measurement. For instance, a *distribution* can be a statistical result from a study; it can also describe concepts related to measurement (e.g., "The distribution of scores from a norm-referenced test is normal").

> **Author Reflection** *I used to think that descriptive statistics were a second cousin to more sophisticated inferential statistics, but after "just a few years" of analyzing all kinds of quantitative data, I have great respect for these seemingly simple, almost "primitive" procedures. I think it is a matter of how easily descriptive procedures more directly and concretely characterize what is being studied, which, in turn, improves understanding by both researchers and consumers. Clearly, descriptive statistical procedures are absolutely fundamental to good quantitative research.*

Frequency Distributions

Suppose you are interested in studying science achievement with a class of eighth-graders. You administer an instrument to measure performance on a biology test to 36 students and obtain the following scores, one for each student:

```
15 24 28 25 18 24 27 16 20 22 23 18
22 28 19 16 22 26 15 26 24 21 19 27
16 23 26 25 25 18 27 17 20 19 25 23
```

When the results are in this form, it is difficult to understand how the students performed as a group or to have some idea of the number of students who obtained different scores. To understand the results, the researcher would first create a **frequency distribution**, which organizes ungrouped data by indicating the number of times (frequency) each score or group of scores was obtained. There are three types of frequency distributions that you can use to summarize the 36 scores: simple, grouped, and cumulative. Let's take a look at each one of these.

SIMPLE FREQUENCY DISTRIBUTION   In a **simple frequency distribution**, individual scores are typically rank-ordered from highest to lowest, and the frequency of each score is indicated. The simplest type of frequency distribution is a frequency table, in which the values of the scores and the frequencies are listed vertically. Table 6.1 shows a frequency table for the set of critical thinking scores given earlier. As you can see, the scores are rank ordered from the highest score, 28, to the lowest score, 15. The number of individuals obtaining each score is in the second column, here designated by f (frequency), though it could also be n. Sometimes a frequency table also includes a third column to indicate the percentage of individuals who obtained each score.

GROUPED FREQUENCY DISTRIBUTION   If there is a large number of different scores, a simple frequency distribution can be cumbersome and difficult to interpret. When there are more than 10 different scores, as in Table 6.1, it is useful to display the frequencies by creating mutually exclusive groups of scores, or intervals, and then showing the number of scores in a **grouped frequency distribution**. Typically, you will find five to eight groups with equal intervals. This is illustrated in Table 6.2, which shows the critical thinking scores in seven groups.

CUMULATIVE FREQUENCY DISTRIBUTION   In some studies, it is helpful to point out the number and/or percentage of scores that are at or below a specific score. This is accomplished by adding a third column, which gives a running total to show the number of participants with a specific score or a lower score. This type of **cumulative frequency distribution** is illustrated in Table 6.3 (*CF* is used for cumulative frequency).

Table 6.1 Simple Frequency Distribution Table

Score	f
28	2
27	3
26	3
25	4
24	3
23	3
22	3
21	1
20	2
19	3
18	3
17	1
16	3
15	2

Table 6.2 Grouped Frequency Distribution Table

Score	f
27–28	5
25–26	7
23–24	6
21–22	4
19–20	5
17–18	4
15–16	5

Table 6.3 Cumulative Frequency Distribution Table

Score	f	CF
27–28	5	36
25–26	7	31
23–24	6	24
21–22	4	18
19–20	5	14
17–18	4	9
15–16	5	5

Frequency Graphs

Another way to present frequencies for continuous data is to construct a two-dimensional graph, in which the frequencies are indicated on the vertical dimension and the scores or score intervals are on the horizontal dimension. The number of students who obtained each score is then indicated in the graph. In this graphic form, the data can be presented as a *frequency polygon* or a *histogram*. A **frequency polygon**, illustrated in Figure 6.2 for the biology scores, is a series of lines that connect the observed frequencies for each score to show a graph of the distribution.

The shape of a distribution reveals some important characteristics of the scores at a glance: the most and least frequently occurring scores, whether the scores are bunched together or spread out, scores that may be isolated from the others, and the general

Figure 6.2 Example of a Frequency Polygon

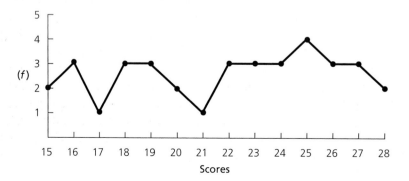

Figure 6.3 Examples of Different Shapes of Frequency Distributions

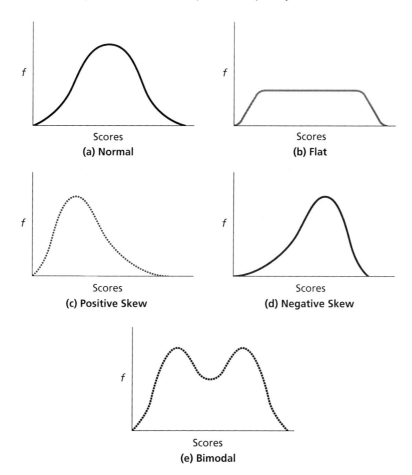

shape of the distribution. Figure 6.3 illustrates some common general shapes of distributions with single, smoothed lines. The **normal curve** is perhaps most widely used with large data sets. It is symmetrical and shaped like a cross section of a bell (hence the "bell curve"). It tells us that the majority of scores tend to cluster around the middle, with the same number of scores above and below the middle point. Because the normal curve characterizes many naturally occurring phenomena and has standard properties, it is used extensively for research and statistical procedures. In a flat, or rectangular curve, the scores are widely spread out from the middle. Distributions that concentrate scores at the high or low end of the distribution, with fewer at the opposite end, are called *skewed*. In a **positively skewed** distribution (or distribution with a positive skew), the scores are concentrated at the low end of the distribution, with fewer high scores; in a **negatively skewed** distribution, the majority of the scores are at the high end of the distribution, with fewer low scores. (I know, the definitions for positive and negative skew seem logically the opposite of what it should be. Actually, *positive* and *negative* refer to the effect of the scores on the mean score, relative to the median. That is, in a distribution with a positive skew the mean is higher, or to the right, relative to the median.)

For example, in a study of administrators' salaries, the distribution would be positively skewed if most of the salaries were relatively low and a few of the salaries were very high. Negatively skewed distributions are common in standards-based classroom assessment, in which, typically, most of the students score high and a few students score low.

Frequency distributions are also important in identifying unusually high or low scores. Such scores, if they are very different from others, are *outliers*. **Outlier scores** are so atypical that their inclusion may distort the findings. Whenever researchers use quantitative data, they must look carefully for outliers and decide how to handle them. Sometimes outliers are bad data, perhaps because of a data entry error; sometimes they represent inaccurate responses. The easiest outliers to identify are those that are outside of the response scale (e.g., if the response scale has five points, a score of 6 or 7 would be bad data. Often, we will look for scores that are extremely high or low.

Author Reflection *There was a time when I thought that you had to include all your obtained scores—that ethically it was expected. I have learned that what you really want are accurate data. Therefore, you should never include known bad data in a study! Outliers are indicators of possible bad data, as are specific patterns of participant responses. Look at and check data carefully. Bad data are noise—not only do they make it harder to find the signal, they make for misleading results and conclusions.*

Frequency data are also often presented graphically in what is called a *histogram*. A **histogram** is a two-dimensional graph that uses vertical columns to show the frequency of each score (or score intervals). This is illustrated with our critical thinking data in Figure 6.4. The relative difference in the heights of the vertical columns makes it easy to detect patterns and differences, especially with grouped data or data intervals.

The *bar chart* is another kind of frequency graph that is very common in the popular literature. A **bar chart** or graph also uses columns, but the ordering of the columns is arbitrary (i.e., nominal data). An example of this type of display of data would be to show how students at private colleges differ in their loan amounts to attend

Figure 6.4 Histogram of Biology Test Scores

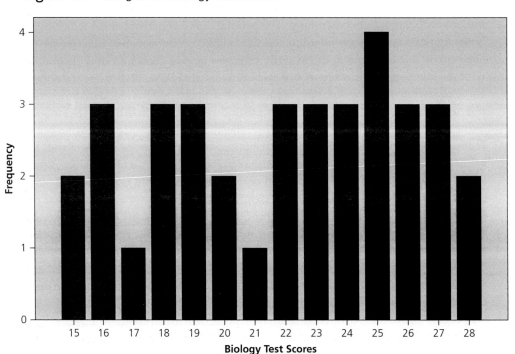

Figure 6.5 Bar Chart of Students Attending Institutions of Higher Education

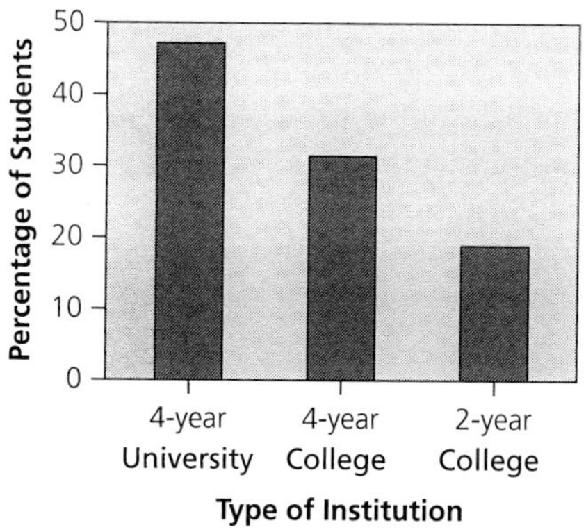

higher education compared to students in public colleges. In contrast to histograms, bar charts do not have continuous data on the dimension that is used to begin the bars. The units used as categories can be almost anything that needs to be compared (e.g., states, schools, boys and girls, racial groups), and the bars can be solid colors or even depict what is being studied. Often, percentages are placed at the end of the bar rather than on one axis or the other. Figure 6.5 is an example of a bar chart showing the percentages of high school students attending different types of institutions of higher education. Note that in a bar chart there is generally more space between the different categories than in a histogram.

Another type of graph that depicts percentages is a *pie chart* or *pie graph*. **Pie charts** use wedges of a circle to show relative proportions. The area of each wedge is proportional to the percentage of cases that is represented by the wedge. Pie charts are very effective as long as there aren't many small wedge slivers, use only two dimensions, avoid legends, and are not too busy. Often, however, a bar graph can present the data more effectively.

Measures of Central Tendency

Although it is useful to know the pattern of the scores as indicated by the frequency distributions and graphs, it is also important to be able to use a single score to characterize the set of scores. The three most commonly used **measures of central tendency**—the mean, median, and mode—provide statistics that, respectively, indicate the average, middle, or most frequently occurring score in the distribution.

MODE   The **mode** (or modal value) is simply the score in the distribution that occurs most frequently. It is a crude index of central tendency and is seldom used in research. Sometimes distributions have more than one most frequent score; such distributions are designated bimodal, trimodal, or multimodal. These terms also describe a distribution that may technically have only one mode; for example, two scores in different parts of the distribution clearly occur more frequently than the rest in a bimodal distribution. There is no mode in distributions in which each score occurs the same number of times. In a normal distribution, the mode is at the top of the curve.

MEDIAN   The **median** is the middle score of the distribution—the midpoint that divides a rank-ordered distribution into halves containing an equal number of scores.

Thus, 50% of the scores lie below the median and 50% lie above the median. The median is unaffected by the values of the scores. This characteristic is an advantage when the distribution contains atypically large or small scores, such as measures of "average" income and the "average" cost of a new house. It is much more reassuring to know, for instance, that 50% of the houses available for purchase are priced below $200,000, rather than hearing that the mean price of a new house, skewed higher by a relatively few number of very expensive houses, is $280,000. The median is symbolized by *Mdn* or *Md*. In some studies, the median score is used to split groups into two classifications or subgroups.

MEAN The **mean** (or *arithmetic mean*) is the arithmetic average of all the scores in the distribution. It is calculated by adding all the scores in the distribution and then dividing this sum by the number of scores. For example, if a distribution contains the scores $5, 7, 8, 10, 10, 12, 14, 15, 15, 17$, the mean would be 11.3 ($5 + 7 + 8 + 10 + 10 + 12 + 14 + 15 + 15 + 17 = 113$; $113/10 = 11.3$) or for the distribution of biology test scores in Table 6.1, the mean is 21.92 ($789/36$). The mean is used extensively in research, symbolized by $\bar{x}$, $\overline{X}$ or M for the sample mean and μ for the mean of the population. The mean may be misleading as a typical or representative score in skewed distributions that contain extremely high or low scores because it is pulled toward the extreme scores (as in housing prices as described above). Thus, in a positively skewed distribution, such as personal income, the mean income is higher than the most typical income because some very high incomes are used in the calculation. In this case, the median income is more typical. Conversely, in a negatively skewed distribution, the mean is lower than the median (refer to Figure 6.6).

Measures of Variability

Although a measure of central tendency is an adequate statistic of the most typical or representative score in a distribution, to obtain a full description of the scores you also need to know something about how they tend to cluster around the mean or median. **Measures of variability**, or *indices of dispersion*, show how spread out the scores are from the mean, or how much "scatter" exists in the scores. If there is a large degree of dispersion—that is, if the scores are very dissimilar—we say that the distribution has a large or high *variability*, or *variance*. If the scores are very similar, all clustered together, there is a small degree of dispersion and a small variance.

Figure 6.6 Skewed Distribution Locations of Mean, Median, and Mode

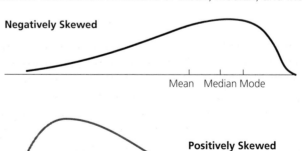

Figure 6.7 Distributions with the Same Mean but Different Variability

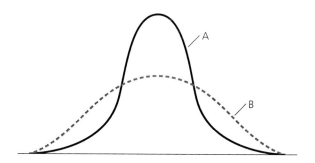

The need for a measure of dispersion to describe a distribution is illustrated by comparing the different types of distributions in Figure 6.7. Distributions A and B would have the same mean but represent different distributions. The scores in distribution B show greater variability. It is necessary to add a measure of variability to provide a more complete description. We will discuss two measures of variability, the range and the standard deviation, which provide more specific statistics than such general terms as *small, large, great,* or *little.*

RANGE   The **range** is simply the numerical difference between the highest and lowest scores in the distribution. It is calculated by subtracting the lowest score from the highest score. The range is a rough measure of dispersion because it is based on only two scores in the distribution, and it does not tell us anything about the degree of cluster. The range is particularly misleading in highly skewed distributions.

STANDARD DEVIATION   The measure of variability used most often in research is the **standard deviation** (*SD*), a statistic that indicates whether the scores are clustered close to the mean or deviate broadly from the mean. Standard deviation is a statistic that is calculated using the mean and all scores in the distribution. The first step is calculating the distance of each score from the mean. These are the *deviation* scores, which tell us how much each score deviates, or differs, from the mean (x – mean). Then the deviation scores are used to calculate the standard deviation. If all the deviation scores in a normal distribution were added, the result would be zero, so the scores are squared, then added and divided by $n - 1$; the square root of that number (the *variance*) is the standard deviation. It is really not too complicated, as illustrated in Figure 6.8. This figure shows seven steps that can be used to determine the *SD* for a set of scores. In this example there are 10 participants, each providing a single score.

For each unique set of scores, the standard deviation will pertain to the distribution of the scores in that set. Thus, the standard deviation of one distribution may be .72; for another distribution, 16; and for yet another, 35. Once the standard deviation is computed, it is reported by indicating that one standard deviation equals a number; for example, 1 *SD* = 12.7, or 1 *SD* = 3.25. (Two other symbols are also used for standard deviation: *s*, which indicates the sample standard deviation, and the lowercase Greek letter sigma, *σ*, which indicates the population standard deviation.)

The standard deviation is particularly useful because of its relationship to the normal distribution. In a normal distribution, a specific percentage of scores falls within each standard deviation from the mean. For example, if the mean of a

Figure 6.8   Steps in Calculating Standard Deviation

Step 1	Step 2	Step 3	Step 4	Step 5	Step 6	Step 7
Rank order scores	Calculate the mean	Subtract each score from the mean $(x - \bar{x})$	Square each deviation score $(x - \bar{x})^2$	Add squared deviation scores $\Sigma(x - \bar{x})^2$	Divide by $N - 1$ $\dfrac{\Sigma(x - \bar{x})^2}{N - 1}$	Take the square root $\sqrt{\dfrac{\Sigma(x - \bar{x})^2}{N - 1}}$
20	$\Sigma x = 130$	7	49	120	$120/9 = 13.33$	$\sqrt{13.33} = 3.65$
15	$N = 10$	2	4			
15	$\bar{x} = 13$	2	4			
14		1	1			
14		1	1			
14		1	1			
12		−1	1			
10		−3	9			
8		−5	25			
8		−5	25			

distribution is 40 and the standard deviation is 10, we know that about 34% of the scores of the distribution fall between 40 and 50. Similarly, we know that about 34% of the scores fall between 30 and 40. Thus, in normal distributions, regardless of the values of the scores, we know that about 68% of the scores fall between −1 and +1 *SD* (refer to Figure 6.9). Furthermore, we know that about 14% of the scores fall between −1 and −2 *SD* and between +1 and +2 *SD*, and that about 2% of the scores fall between −2 and −3 *SD* and between +2 and +3 *SD*. These properties of the normal curve and standard deviation, illustrated in Figure 6.9, allow researchers to compare distributions by knowing the standard deviations. Two distributions may have similar means, but if one has a standard deviation of 36 and the other 8, the former is far more variable. As already indicated, the square of the standard deviation is called

Figure 6.9 Normal Probability Curve

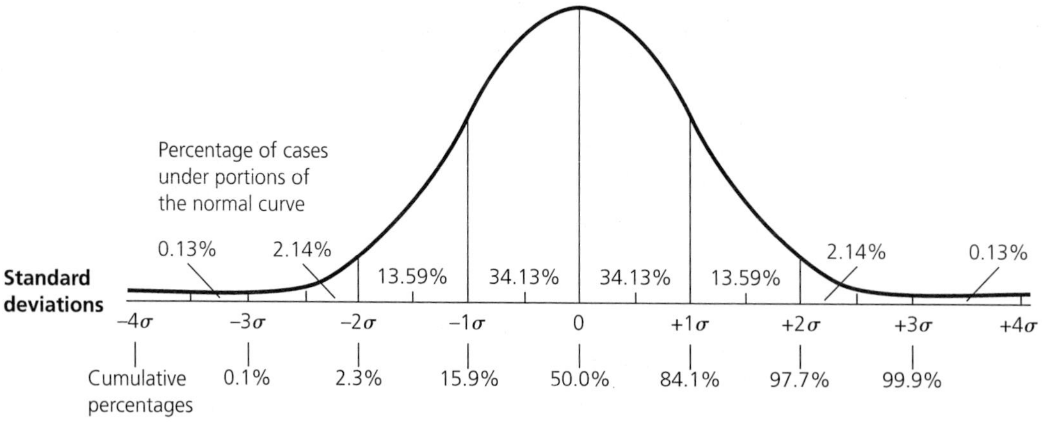

the variance, although this term is also used more generally to mean dispersion or spread of scores.

Standard deviation is related to another important term in measurement, *percentile rank*. The **percentile rank** indicates the percentage of scores at or below a particular score. For example, if 17 is at the 64th percentile, 64% of the scores in the distribution are the same or lower than 17. In a normal distribution, a score at $+1$ SD is at the 84th percentile. In other words, 84% of the scores in a normal distribution are at or below $+1$ SD. Similarly, -1 SD is at the 16th percentile, $+2$ SD is at the 98th percentile, and -2 SD is at the 2nd percentile. (Percentiles for the normal curve are indicated as cumulative percentages in Figure 6.9.)

Percentile rank is used with what is called the *interquartile range*, which is the difference between the scores at the 25th and 75th percentile (middle 50% of the scores), to construct a graph of the scores called a *box-and-whisker* plot, or more simply *boxplot*, which shows the spread of scores. In Figure 6.10, the ends of the box are at the 25th and 75th percentiles. The bar near the middle of the box is the median (50th percentile), and the whiskers extend to the 10th and 90th percentiles, or beyond. Scores beyond the ends of the whiskers are singled out. These are often identified as outliers.

Bivariate Correlation

Correlation is a statistical measure of the degree to which two or more variables are related. A **bivariate correlation** is a measure of the linear relationship between two variables. A relationship means that the values of the variables vary together; that is, if there is a correlation, the value of one variable can be predicted to some extent by knowing the value of the other. For example, we would expect that there is a relationship between age and weight among a group of 3- to 10-year-olds— by knowing a child's age we can predict the child's weight. Thus, we can predict that most 10-year-olds weigh more than most 3-year-olds. In this case we have a **positive correlation**, in which an increase in one variable is accompanied by an increase in the other variable. This is also called a *direct* relationship. A positive correlation is illustrated graphically in Figure 6.11 in the form of a **scatterplot** for age and weight. The values of each variable are rank ordered, and the intersections of the two scores for each subject are plotted in the graph. Scatterplots are useful

Figure 6.10 Box-and-Whisker Plot

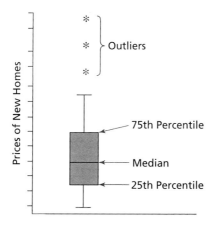

in identifying scores that lie outside the overall pattern, such as point I in Figure 6.11, and indicate whether the relationship is linear (in more or less a straight line) or curvilinear.

Correlation is often depicted numerically by the *correlation coefficient*. A **correlation coefficient**, or *bivariate* correlation, is a number between –1 and +1 that indicates the direction and strength of the relationship between two variables. The correlation coefficient is calculated by a formula and is reported as, for example, $r = .45$, $r = -.78$, $r = .03$, and so on. A positive correlation coefficient will have a positive value; for example, $r = .17$ or $r = .69$. The strength, or magnitude, of the relationship is the degree to which the variables are related. For a positive correlation the strength increases as the number increases. Hence, a correlation of .85 is stronger than a correlation of .53, which is stronger than .37. In general, correlations between .10 and .30 are referred to as small or low positive relationships, .40 to .60 as moderate positive relationships, and .70 and above as high positive relationships.

Although there are several types of correlation coefficients, the one you will encounter most is the Pearson product moment coefficient, or Pearson's *r*.

A **negative correlation** indicates that as one variable increases, the other variable decreases. This is also referred to as an *inverse* relationship. Examples of negative correlations include the relationship between absenteeism and achievement and between amount of practice and number of errors in tennis. A negative correlation coefficient always has a negative sign (–). The strength of a negative relationship increases as the absolute value of the correlation increases. Thus, a correlation of –.75 is a stronger relationship than –.52. In other words, the strength of any relationship is independent of its direction. A correlation of –.63 indicates a stronger relationship than .35. Correlations between –.10 and –.30 are considered small; between –.40 and –.60, moderate; and between –.70 and –1.0, high. Correlations between –.10 and .10 generally indicate a very small or no relationship.

Figure 6.11 Scatterplot

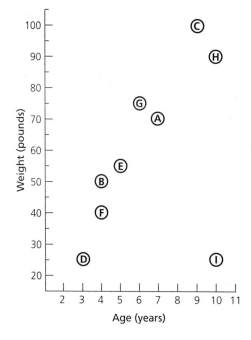

Subject	Age	Weight
A	7	70
B	4	50
C	9	100
D	3	25
E	5	55
F	4	40
G	6	75
H	10	90
I	10	25

Figure 6.12 Scatterplots of Different Correlations

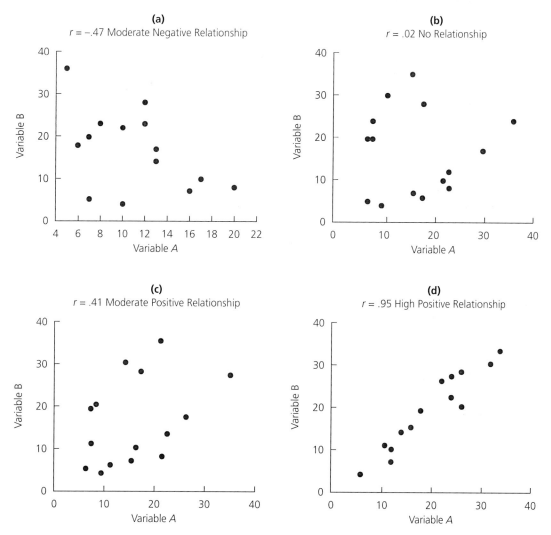

Several different scatterplots with associated correlation coefficients are shown in Figure 6.12. Note that even with what would be a moderate relationship (a and c), your ability to predict the value of one variable from the other is not too good. That is, a range of possible values of one variable is predicted from a single value of the other variable.

Check for Understanding 2

2a. What are the common shapes of frequency distributions?

2b. In what ways are the mode, median, and mean different?

2c. Explain the concept of standard deviation. Why is it important for research?

2d. Why is a scatterplot important in examining relationships?

Measurement Validity

Learning Outcome 6.3 Explain the meaning of measurement validity, sources of evidence to support validity arguments, and the effect of validity on research.

This section discusses *validity*, the first of two technical characteristics of measurement used to judge overall quality and appropriateness of the scores. *Reliability*, the second characteristic, is discussed in the next section.

What Is Measurement Validity?

Measurement validity (or, more simply, **validity** in the context of measurement, or what is often called test validity) is an overall evaluation of the extent to which theory and empirical evidence support interpretations that are implied in given uses of the scores. In other words, validity is a judgment of the appropriateness of a measure for the specific inferences, interpretations, claims, or conclusions that result from the scores generated by the measure. It is the *inference* that is valid or invalid, not the measure.

You may be familiar with a long-standing definition of validity that is something like "Does the test measure what it purports to measure?" That is a good start, but the emphasis in that phrase is on the measure and not the inference. If you say "the test is valid" you imply that this is true, without consideration of the use. The reality is that we always use test scores to make claims about something. My point is that the same results can be valid in one circumstance or for cne claim or use, and invalid for another. For example, tests of beginning teacher competency may be valid for judging how much a prospective teacher knows and understands about classroom management, child development, learning, motivation, and curriculum, but it may be invalid as a predictor of teaching effectiveness. Similarly, most standardized achievement tests are not valid for evaluating the effectiveness of a specific curriculum in a school because such tests are constructed to measure a broad range of curricula, not a unique one. Five important characteristics of measurement validity are summarized in Table 6.4.

Sources of Measurement Validity Evidence

Measurement validity is established by presenting evidence that the inferences are appropriate. There are seven major sources of evidence, each based on a different kind of logic and data: *content, internal structure, convergent/discriminant evidence based*

Table 6.4 Characteristics of Measurement Validity

1. Measurement validity refers to the *appropriateness* of the interpretation of the results, not to the procedure or measure itself. Saying "the validity of the test" is not as correct as saying "the validity of the inference."

2. Measurement validity is a *matter of degree;* it does not exist on an all-or-none basis. Some inferences are rock solid, whereas others are based on weak evidence.

3. Measurement validity is *specific* to some particular use or interpretation. No measure is valid for all uses or purposes. Each interpretation may have a different degree of validity.

4. Measurement validity is a *unitary concept.* It is a single concept that is based on accumulating and integrating different types of evidence. There are different types of evidence, depending on the nature of the inference, not different types of validity.

5. Measurement validity involves *an overall evaluative judgment.* Your professional judgment, given the evidence presented and the nature of the interpretation, is needed to determine the extent to which the inference is valid.

Source: Based on Miller, Linn, & Gronlund (2013).

EXCERPTS 6.1 AND 6.2

Content-Related Evidence for Validity

One common practice for establishing content validity is to employ the judgment of subject-matter experts and use the resulting feedback to provide evidence supporting claims of validity. It the panel endorses an item, it can be considered to have construct validity, whereas the panel's rejection of an item can lead to the item being either discarded or rewritten. Although there are several methodological approaches to analyzing the resulting data in such investigations, we provide two: (a) a simple aggregation of responses in the form of averages, with an a priori threshold for the determination of what will be considered acceptable, and (b) a method established Lawshe (1975) that is more rigorous and grounded in statistics. Both approaches evaluate the degree to which any individual item is endorsed by the panel of experts and provide aggregated indexes. (pp. 60–61)

SOURCE: Pearl, C. E., Vasquez III, E., Marino, M. T., Wienke, W., Donehower, C., Gourwitz, J., ... Duerr, S. R. (2018). Establishing content validity of the Quality Indicators for Classrooms Serving Students With Autism Spectrum Disorders instrument. *Teacher Education and Special Education,* *4*(1), 58–69.

This assessment was reviewed by several experts in the field of early literacy to ensure that the content was accurate and research based. Each community-college instructor reviewed the assessment for content validity and alignment with the course syllabus. On the basis of their comments, revisions were made.... Results from this pilot were analyzed using item analysis to identify the best items for further analysis and inclusion in the assessment of teacher knowledge. (pp. 544–545)

SOURCE: Neuman, S. B., & Cunningham, L. (2009). The impact of professional development and coaching on early language and literacy instructional practices. *American Educational Research Journal, 46*(2), 532–566.

---

on relationships with other variables, concurrent relationships to other variables, predictive relationships to other variables, response processes, and consequences of testing. Each source represents a different type of argument. Under ideal conditions, the nature of evidence used is consistent with the use of the results to provide support for the intended interpretation of the scores. Establishing sound validity involves an integration of information from these different types of evidence to show that the intended interpretation of the scores is appropriate and reasonable. We will consider the first five types of evidence here, because they are the most used and reported for conducting educational research.

EVIDENCE BASED ON CONTENT   In general, **evidence based on content** (or *content-related evidence*) demonstrates the extent to which the sample of items or questions in the instrument is representative of an appropriate definition, universe or domain of content, tasks, or hypothetical construct (e.g., motivation. attitude). This type of evidence is usually accumulated by having experts examine the contents of an instrument and indicate the degree to which the items measure predetermined descriptions, criteria, or objectives. Experts are also used to judge the relative criticality, or importance, of various parts of the instrument. For example, to gather evidence for a test of knowledge for prospective teachers, it is necessary to have experts examine the items and judge their representativeness (e.g., is a question about Piaget representative of what needs to be known about child development?) and whether the percentage of the test devoted to different topics is appropriate (e.g., 20% of the test is on classroom management, but maybe it should be 40%). Evidence based on

> ### EXCERPT 6.3
> # Validity Evidence Based on Internal Structure
>
> This study examined the internal structure, convergent validity, and reliability of the student self-report Special Education Classroom Climate Inventory (SECCI) in a sample of 325 students attending special education classes in six (semi) secure residential settings and in two youth prisons in the Netherlands. Both exploratory factor analysis (EFA) and confirmatory factor analysis (CFA) provided evidence of a theoretically based four-factor model—with Teacher Support, Positive Student Affiliation, Negative Student Interactions, and Unstructured Classroom Environment as dimensions—showing an adequate fit to the data, providing preliminary support for validity of the SECCI. (p. 736)
>
> SOURCE: Beld, M. H. M., van der Voort, D., van der Helm, G. H. P., Kuiper, C. H. Z., de Swart, J. J. W., & Stams, G. J. J. M. (2018). Assessing classroom climate in special education: A validation study of the special education classroom climate inventory. *Journal of Psychoeducational Assessment, 36*(7), 736–749.

test content is essential for achievement tests. Also, the domain or universe that is represented should be appropriate to the intended use of the results. This type of evidence is also used for measures of attitudes, interests, and dispositions by having experts review whether important aspects of the conceptually defined construct are included.

Recently, a doctoral student at my university used this type of evidence in establishing a measure of teacher demoralization. She contacted several experts (professors) and asked them to review 20 items, some of which did fit her definition of teacher demoralization, along with other items that did not. Even though she did not personally know the individuals (i.e., "experts" who had published in the field), most responded! The items projected to measure demoralization were confirmed by the ratings.

Unfortunately, evidence based on content for validity for locally devised instruments is rarely reported. When standardized instruments are used, you need to refer to previous research, reviews of the instrument, or technical manuals. Excerpts 6.1 and 6.2 demonstrate how researchers report content-related evidence for validity.

EVIDENCE BASED ON INTERNAL STRUCTURE   The *internal structure* of an instrument refers to how items that measure the same thing relate to one another, and how items measuring different things are, hopefully, not related. **Evidence based on internal structure** is provided when the relationships between items and parts of the instrument are empirically consistent with the theory or intended use of the scores. Thus, if a measure of self-concept posits several "types" of self-concept (e.g., academic, social, athletic), then the items measuring the academic component should be strongly related to one another and not as highly related to the other components. In the measurement section of an article, *factor analysis*, as reported in Excerpt 6.3, is a technique used to establish internal structure evidence. Here the authors summarize data that support the internal structure of students' perceptions of classroom climate. The analyses supported four distinct factors.

EVIDENCE BASED ON CONVERGENT/DISCRIMINANT RELATIONSHIPS An excellent way that validity of interpretations is established is by showing how scores from a given measure relate to different measures of similar as well as different traits, with what is called *evidence based on relations to other variables*. There are several ways this can be done. The most complete approach is to provide **evidence based on convergent/discriminant relationships**. When scores from one instrument correlate highly with scores from another measure of the same trait, we have what is called *convergent* evidence. For example, scores from the *Test of Early Reading Ability* could be correlated to another measure of reading ability, the *Reading Aptitude Assessment*. Or, if teacher ratings of altruism match what is shown by student self-reports about altruism, there is convergent evidence.

Discriminant evidence exists when the scores do not correlate highly with scores from an instrument that measures something different. Thus, we would expect that scores from a measure of self-concept would correlate highly with other measures of self-concept (convergent) and show less correlation to related but different traits, such as anxiety (divergent). Convergent and discriminant data are often used as evidence of "construct validity." The term *construct validity* was used prior to the current categories of validity evidence; some researchers will say something like "the construct validity of the instrument."

EVIDENCE BASED ON CONCURRENT RELATIONSHIPS Another approach to gathering evidence based on relations to other variables pertains to the extent to which the test scores or measures are related to scores on what is called a *criterion measure*. Two approaches are used to obtain test-criterion evidence: predictive and concurrent. **Concurrent criterion-related evidence** is established by correlating two measures of the same trait that are given to the same individuals at about the same time. The logic is that if two different approaches to measuring the same variable are related, it is likely that they are assessing a similar trait. This type of evidence is illustrated in Excerpt 6.4, in which validity evidence was gathered as part of the study.

EXCERPT 6.4

Evidence Based on Concurrent Relationships

The criterion-related or more specifically the concurrent validity of the UGAS and its three subscales was assessed by correlating them with the FSMAS and three of its subscales. A strong positive correlation ($r = .702$, $p < .001$) was found between the UGAS and the FSMAS. In addition, strong positive correlations were found on the corresponding confidence subscales ($r = .651$, $p < .001$), on the corresponding usefulness subscales ($r = .670$, $p < .001$), and between the enjoyment scale of the UGAS and the effectance motivation scale of the FSMAS ($r = .658$, $p < .001$). (p. 93)

SOURCE: Utley, J. (2007). Construction and validity of geometry attitude scales. *School Science and Mathematics, 107*(3), 89–93.

EVIDENCE BASED ON PREDICTIVE RELATIONSHIPS With **predictive criterion-related evidence**, the criterion is measured in the future, after the instrument has been administered. The evidence pertains to how well the earlier measure can predict the criterion behavior or performance. For instance, in gathering evidence on a new measure to select applicants for leadership positions, the scores on the instrument would be correlated with future leadership behavior. If persons who scored low on the test turned out to be poor leaders and those who scored high were good leaders, predictive criterion-related evidence would be obtained.

Keep in mind that measurement validity is a matter of degree and is not an "all-or-none" proposition. Rarely will a measure capture 100% of a defined construct. The goal is to use validity evidence that focuses on as much of the construct as possible, without contaminating it with other variables. Researchers need to show that for the specific inferences they make in their study, evidence for validity exists. Consumers, however, may have their own uses in mind, and therefore need to base their validity judgments on how they intend to use the results.

For established, published instruments existing evidence on validity has probably accumulated (but validity of the inferences is a not a given just because an instrument is established). Locally devised instruments, with little or no history of use or reviews by others, need to be evaluated with more care. Furthermore, if an instrument has specific procedures for administration—for example, qualifications of the person who administers it, directions, and time frame—the results are valid only if these procedures have been followed. For instance, some instruments are appropriate for certain ages, but use with other ages would be invalid.

Although measurement validity is a key concept in research, you will find a great deal of variability in the amount of information given about it in articles and research reports. It is not uncommon to find that there is no mention of validity or very little reference to it.

The five major types of evidence for measurement validity that are used in educational research are summarized in Table 6.5. Even though you will encounter slightly different terminology for these, the important point is to understand the logic of the evidence and how that logic makes sense for the specific nature of the study and conclusions that are researched.

Table 6.5 Types of Evidence for Measurement Validity

Type of Evidence	Description	Example
Evidence Based on Content	The content of the measure is consistent with what is more generally described or conceptualized.	A measure of knowledge of descriptive statistics includes scales of measurement, measures of central tendency, and measures of relationship.
Evidence Based on Internal Structure	All items measuring the same trait or characteristic are related to one another; items measuring separate factors in the same instrument are less related.	Students answer the five items measuring the nature of correlation in the same way, and differently from the way they answer the questions about graphs of descriptive data.

(Continued)

Type of Evidence	Description	Example
Evidence Based on Convergent/ Discriminant Relationships	Item responses from different measures linked to the same traits are highly related, whereas answers to items measuring other traits are less related.	Students' answers to questions about correlation from both the test and project are strongly positively related, whereas answers to questions about graphs from the tests are less related to those about correlation.
Evidence Based on Concurrent Criterion-Related Relationships	Results from a measure of a trait are highly related to the criterion measure that is given at about the same time.	A self-report measure of popularity is positively correlated to friendship group composition.
Evidence Based on Predictive Criterion-Related Relationships	Results from a measure of a trait are highly related to a criterion measure that is given later.	A measure of musical aptitude is positively related to subsequent years' musical performances.

The Hedgehog and the Fox Consider Using a Questionnaire

I found some literature that says my questionnaire is valid and reliable, so it's the best one to use for my study.

I found some literature that reports some evidence of validity and reliability, but I need to know what kind of evidence and the participants sampled to determine whether the questionnaire will be appropriate for my study.

Check for Understanding 3

3a. What is the fundamental meaning of measurement validity?

3b. Why is it important for researchers to know about different types of evidence used in validity arguments?

3c. Why is measurement validity an important principle for high-quality quantitative research?

Measurement Reliability

Learning Outcome 6.4 Explain the meaning of measurement reliability, sources of evidence to estimate reliability, and the effect of reliability on research.

An important concept in conducting and interpreting research is understanding that there is rarely if ever a perfect indication of the trait, skill, knowledge, attitude, or whatever is being assessed. That is, there is almost always error in measurement—basically noise—and this error must be taken into consideration. It is not a question of whether error exists, only what type and how much. This is something that we have all experienced—scores that did not very accurately reflect our knowledge, attitude, or ability.

Measurement reliability, or, more typically, simply **reliability** (or *reliability/precision*), is the extent to which participant, rater, and observer scores are free from error. If a measure consistently gives the same scores, it has high reliability and greater precision; there is relatively little error in the scores. If the scores are inconsistent, there is greater error and less precision, and the reliability is low. Reliability is often defined as "the consistency of the scores," though my emphasis is on the idea of error or noise. Let's see why.

Many factors (refer to Table 6.6), both random and systematic, contribute to the imperfect nature of measurement (e.g., questions may be ambiguous; students may not try hard, be fatigued or sick, be unfamiliar with the types of questions asked, or simply guess incorrectly on many items). Whatever the reasons, participants will answer somewhat differently on one occasion than on another or on questions designed to measure the same thing. Noise is a reality! We simply do not have measures of traits such as ability, self-efficacy, motivation, interests, or even achievement, without noise. It's like saying that if you take the same 30-item test on types of validity evidence on two different days, your scores probably will not be exactly the same—there is noise that accompanies the results each time even if your actual or real knowledge doesn't change.

The actual amount of error is combined with the true or actual value of the trait to give you an observed score. Since we know, then, that error is part of the observed score, our estimates of error, both statistical and logical, are critical in determining the veracity of the scores. From a statistical perspective, we use estimates of error based on the variance of observed scores. These estimates are then calculated as reliability coefficients.

Types of Reliability Estimates

An estimate of the amount of error in measurement is determined empirically through several types of procedures. As with validity, different types of evidence are used to indicate the error. These are called *estimates of reliability*. Each estimate measures certain kinds of hypothetically random errors. The estimates are reported in the form of a **reliability coefficient**, which is an index that ranges between .00 and .99. If the index is high—say, .78 or .85—the reliability is adequate, or even good. This means that there is not too much random error (noise). Correlation coefficients below .60 generally indicate inadequate, or at least weak, reliability (unacceptable high level of random error).

Table 6.6 Sources of Measurement Error

Sources Associated with Test Construction and Administration	Sources Associated with Participants
Observer differences	Test anxiety
Changes in scoring	Reactions to specific items
Changes in directions	Illness
Interrupted testing session	Motivation
Race of test administrator	Mood
When the test is taken	Fatigue
Sampling of items	Luck
Ambiguity in wording	Attitudes
Misunderstood directions	Test-taking skills (test wiseness)
Effect of heat, lighting, ventilation of room	Reading ability

Five specific estimates of reliability are used in educational research: *stability, equivalence, equivalence and stability, internal consistency,* and *agreement*.

STABILITY A **stability** estimate of reliability is obtained by administering one measure to one group of individuals, waiting a specified period of time, and then readministering the same instrument to the same group. The correlation of the two sets of scores is then calculated. This type of estimate is also called *test–retest* reliability. What is being measured is the consistency of the individuals' responses over time. If the trait or skill that is being measured changes between the first and second administration, the correlation, and the reliability, will be low. Consequently, stability estimates should not be used with unstable traits, such as mood, and when it is used, any changes that may have occurred between the administrations should be noted. The value of the correlation will also vary with the length of time between administrations. Other things being equal, a longer time interval will result in a lower correlation. It is best, therefore, to report the time interval with the correlation coefficient. On the other hand, if the interval is too short, participants may remember their answers and simply reproduce them, making the reliability estimate higher than it would be if there was a longer interval.

Stability estimates are used for many aptitude tests, tests in the psychomotor domain, and some achievement tests. As illustrated in Excerpt 6.5, stability estimates are written in a straightforward manner, so they are easy to identify.

EQUIVALENCE A measure of **equivalence**, or what is sometimes called *alternate-forms reliability*, is obtained by administering two forms of the same measure to one group of individuals and then correlating the scores from the two forms. This type of reliability estimate is often used in research on achievement when both a pretest (Form A) and a posttest (Form B) are administered to show how much the achievement of the individuals changed. Rather than giving the same test twice, the researcher gives alternate but equal tests. The estimate of reliability is calculated prior to the research that uses the pre- and posttest.

EQUIVALENCE AND STABILITY An **equivalence and stability** estimate is obtained by administering one form of an instrument and then a second form after a time interval to the same group of individuals. This method combines equivalence (alternate forms) with stability (time interval). This is the most stringent type of reliability estimate. It is especially useful when researchers are concerned with long-range prediction (the strength of stability) and need to generalize to a large domain of knowledge or aptitude (the strength of equivalence).

EXCERPT 6.5
Stability Estimate of Reliability

Test-retest reliability: ASPeCT-DD total scores collected in October of 2007 were compared with scores collected in January of 2006 . . . for the school-based portion of the sample. Sixty-one of the 77 students for whom ASPeCT-DD scores were available in October of 2007 also had scores recorded in January of 2006. Approximately 56% of the 61 students rated in 2006 were rated by the same informant in 2007. The correlation between these two sets of scores was fair ($r = 0.56$), and significant at the $p < 0.01$ level (one-tailed). (p. 438)

SOURCE: Woodard, C. (2009). Psychometric properties of the ASPeCT-DD: Measuring positive traits in persons with developmental disabilities. *Journal of Applied Research in Intellectual Disabilities, 22,* 433–444.

INTERNAL CONSISTENCY   **Internal consistency**, easily the most widely used estimate of reliability, indicates the degree to which individuals' answers to items measuring the same trait are consistent. Unlike the other estimates, only one form of an instrument is given once to one group of individuals. There are three common types of internal consistency estimates: *split-half, Kuder-Richardson,* and *coefficient alpha* (*Cronbach's alpha,* or simply *alpha*). In split-half reliability, the items in a test are divided into equal halves, and the scores of each person on the two halves are correlated for the reliability coefficient. The Kuder-Richardson method is used in tests for which each item has a right and wrong answer. The coefficient alpha method is used with instruments that use a scale for answering each question. This means that there is a range of possible answers for each item, such as agree–disagree, that constitute a scale, rather than right/wrong scoring.

You will want to use internal consistency when the purpose of your instrument is to give you a status measure of a single trait. To allow calculation of the index, several items are used to measure the same trait. Thus, in some instruments, it seems as though the same or very similar questions are being asked over and over. To have internal consistency, a rule of thumb is that there must be at least three questions about the same trait, and preferably five or more. In instruments in which there are subscales or subtests, a separate measure of internal consistency should be reported for each subscale. Of all the estimates, internal consistency is easiest to obtain and usually gives the highest reliability.

As shown in Excerpts 6.6 through 6.8, the accepted convention in reporting internal consistency is simply to state that it has been used, along with the index.

EXCERPTS 6.6–6.8
Internal Consistency Estimate of Reliability

The alpha coefficient is regularly used to measure the internal consistency.... the reliability was measured by interpreting the obtained value of Cronbach's Alpha (Cronbach, 1951) to assess the internal consistency of the scale.... the internal consistency score for each of the scales ranged from moderate to high.... Cronbach's Alpha for the overall scale was found to be .831... this illustrates a high degree of internal consistency among the items. (p. 66)

SOURCE: Bashir, H., & Bala, R. (2018). Development and validation of Academic Dishonesty Scale (ADS): Presenting a multidimensional scale. *International Journal of Instruction, 11*(2), 57–74.

Before implementing the actual study, the questionnaires were pilot-tested using 57 high school students in a single school to examine its reliability. The questionnaires were internally consistent indicating adequate reliability (Cronbach' s alpha) as follows:
(a) Psychological Sense of School Membership scale, .79; (b) commitment, .78; (c) control, .71; and (d) challenge, .76. The respondents were encouraged to describe any problems or ambiguities in the survey. The respondents gave positive feedback toward the general structure and presentation of the questionnaires. (p. 347)

SOURCE: Abdollahi, A., & Noltemeyer, A. (2018). Academic hardiness: Mediator between sense of belonging to school and academic achievement? *The Journal of Educational Research, 111*(3), 345–351.

Cronbach's alpha was used to compute internal consistency reliability estimates for the pretest and posttest Value Scale and Difficulty Scale; these estimates ranged from .63 to .94. Table 3 displays the internal consistency reliability estimates for the pretest and post-test value and difficulty scales (note that scales with just three items have lower reliability than those with 15 items). (p. 107)

Table 3 Internal Consistency Reliability (Cronbach's Alpha for Pretest and Posttest Value and Difficulty Scales Associated with Attitudes and Perceptions Related to the Integration of Mathematics Science, and Technology Education ($n = 81$))

Variables	Number of items	Cronbach's alpha
Pretest value scale	15	.87
Posttest value scale	15	.94
Pretest difficulty scale	3	.65
Posttest difficulty scale	3	.63

SOURCE: Berlin, D. F., & White, A. L. (2010). Preservice mathematics and science teachers in an integrated teacher preparation program for grades 7–12: A 3-year study of attitudes and perceptions related to integration. *International Journal of Science and Mathematics Education, 8,* 97–115.

AGREEMENT There are three situations in which some type of *coefficient of agreement* exists, expressed as either a correlation or as a percentage of **agreement**. The usual procedure is to assess the extent to which different raters agree on what they observe or score. That is, when two or more raters independently observe the same behavior, will they record it in the same way? Will two raters scoring an essay give the same score? Typically, raters are trained until they reach a desired level of agreement. A statistic termed *kappa* is used to report the results, rather than a bivariate correlation, as reported in Excerpt 6.9.

EXCERPT 6.9

Interrater Reliability

There were four observers. They were all experienced researchers who were familiar with working in schools and able to explain the research and put teachers and pupils at their ease. The basic aim was to avoid passing judgments and to use the schedule as intended. All observers had initial training in which they were provided with an observation manual of categories, conventions, and procedures, as well as tips acquired during previous use. Conventions were discussed, and there was work on videotapes, accompanied by periodic checks of accuracy and understanding of how to use categories. This was followed by at least a day's observation in a class not involved in the study and then a follow-up training session to discuss field visits and iron out difficulties.... Reliability coefficients for the main sets of mutually exclusive categories were high. Setting; subject; teacher-child social setting, child role, teacher content; and child-to-teacher child contribution, child content, and not interaction all had reliability coefficients (kappas) greater than 0.80. Kappa for child-child content was 0.77. (p. 459)

SOURCE: Blatchford, P., Bassett, P., & Brown, P. (2005). Teachers' and pupils' behavior in large and small classes: A systematic observation study of pupils aged 10 and 11 years. *Journal of Educational Psychology, 97*(3), 454–467.

Table 6.7 Procedures for Estimating Reliability[1]

[1]A and B refer to different forms of the same test; R1 and R2 refer to rater 1 and rater 2.

	Time 1	Time 2
Stability	A	A
Equivalence	A B	
Equivalence and Stability	A	B
Internal Consistency	A	
Agreement	R1 R2	

These five methods for estimating reliability are compared in Table 6.7 according to two criteria—the number of forms of the instrument, and when the instruments are administered to gather the evidence—and summarized with examples in Table 6.8.

Table 6.8 Types of Reliability

Type of Reliability	Description	Example
Stability	The same measure is given to the same group of individuals over time.	The Bream Measure of Self-Confidence is given to students during the first and then the fifth week of the semester.
Equivalence	Two different forms of the same measure are given to the same group of individuals at about the same time.	Form A of the Bream Measure of Self-Confidence is given to students on Monday and Form B is given to the same students on Tuesday.
Equivalence and Stability	Two different forms of the same measure are given to the same group of individuals over time.	Form A of the Bream Measure of Self-Confidence is given to students during the first week and Form B is given to the same students during the fifth week.
Internal Consistency	A single form of the measure is given to the individuals once.	The Bream Measure of Self-Confidence is given to students during the first week.
Agreement	The extent to which different raters' or observers' answers agree.	Observer A rank orders the students on self-confidence in about the same order as Observer B.

It is important for the type of reliability evidence to be consistent with how the results are used. If you wish to use test results for prediction or selection for special programs, stability estimates of reliability are needed. If you are interested in programs to change attitudes or values, internal consistency estimates are appropriate. When pilot testing or when relying on previously reported results, reliability should be established with individuals who are similar to the participants who will be used in the research. If you intend to study elementary-level students, use elementary students for the pilot. Similarly, if previous studies report good reliability with middle school students and you intend to use the instruments with elementary school students, the reliability may not be adequate.

You will read some research in which reliability is not addressed, yet the results of the research show what are called "significant differences" or "significant relationships" that have resulted from statistical calculations. This is an interesting situation in research because it is more difficult to find relationships or differences between groups with scores that have low reliability. It is as if relationships or differences were observed despite what *may* have been low reliability. Of course, it is possible that the scores were reliable, even though no reliability estimates were reported. This is likely to occur in research in which the participants are responding to questions that are so straightforward and simple that reliability is assumed. For example, in much research, the participants report information such as age, gender identification, occupation, and other questions that are relatively straightforward. For these types of data, statistical estimates of reliability are generally not needed.

Reliability is enhanced in a number of ways. One is based on the length of a test or questionnaire: An instrument with more items measuring the same trait is more reliable than a shorter one. That doesn't mean, though, that instruments need to have a large number of items. Often relatively few items, three to five, can provide good reliability. Reliability is also a function of the heterogeneity of the group. Internal consistency estimates are higher for groups that are more heterogeneous on the trait that is being measured.

The nature of the trait that is being measured is important. Some variables, such as most measures of achievement, have high reliabilities, whereas measures of attitudes and other dispositions, have lower reliabilities. Consequently, a reliability of .80 or above is generally expected for achievement variables, whereas estimates of .70 are usually acceptable for measuring personality traits. By comparison, then, an attitude instrument reporting a reliability coefficient of .90 would be judged excellent, and an achievement test with a reliability of .70 would be seen as weak. A much higher reliability is needed if the results will be used to make decisions about individuals. Studies of groups can tolerate a lower reliability, sometimes as low as .60 in exploratory research. Measures of young children are usually less reliable than those of adolescents and adults.

Reliability is higher with standard conditions of data collection. All respondents should be given the same directions, have the same time frame in which to answer questions at the same time during the day, and so on. Error is often increased if different individuals administer the instruments. It is important to know whether there are any unusual circumstances during data collection because these may affect reliability. The instrument needs to be appropriate in reading level and language to be reliable, and respondents must be properly motivated to answer the questions. In some research, it is difficult to get participants to be serious—for instance, when students are asked to take achievement tests that have no implications for them. Reliability can also suffer when respondents are asked to complete several instruments over a long period of time. Usually, an hour is about all any of us can tolerate, and for children less than half an hour is the maximum. If several instruments are given at the same time, the order of their administration should not be the same for all participants. Some should answer one instrument first, and others should answer the same instrument last (this is called *counterbalancing* the instruments).

Similar to validity, reliability is not a characteristic of a test or other instrument. Rather than saying "the reliability of the instrument was adequate," it would be more accurate to say, "the reliability of the scores was adequate." This is important because the conditions of administering the instrument, as well as participant mood and motivation, can vary from one situation to another. Thus, it is the scores that are obtained from a specific administration that have noise specific to that situation and the respondents at that time. Good researchers are keenly aware of such factors when collecting data—often this knowledge contributes logically based estimates of error (in addition to the reliability coefficient). For example, if you know students are tired or bored, that would likely lower reliability previously reported for a measure of achievement.

Finally, reliability is a necessary condition for validity. That is, scores cannot be valid unless they are reliable. However, a reliable score is not necessarily valid. You can obtain a very reliable score of the length of your big toe, but that would not be valid as an estimate of your intelligence!

Author Reflection *Measurement specialists have admonished researchers to use the language "the validity of the inferences and reliability of the scores, not the instruments" for many years, but with limited success. Most of the time there is wording such as "the reliability and validity of the test." I have been somewhat perplexed by this, as the "new" definitions have been around for more than 25 years! So, you will probably hear or read the "old" language; I would advise interpreting it with the "new" definitions.*

Check for Understanding 4

4a. How is reliability different from validity?

4b. What are some common sources of error in educational measurement?

4c. How can researchers assure good reliability with the measures they employ for their studies?

Key Terms

Bar chart
Correlation
  Bivariate correlation
  Correlation coefficient
  Negative correlation
  Positive correlation
  Scatterplot
Frequency distribution
  Cumulative frequency distribution
  Grouped frequency distribution
  Simple frequency distribution
Frequency polygon
Histogram
Measurement
Measures
Measures of central tendency
  Mean
  Median
  Mode

Measures of variability
  Range
  Standard deviation
Measurement scales
  Interval scale
  Nominal scale
  Ordinal scale
  Ratio scale
Negatively skewed
Normal curve
Outlier scores
Pie charts
Percentile rank
Positively skewed
Reliability (measurement reliability)
  Agreement
  Equivalence
  Equivalence and stability

Internal consistency
Reliability coefficient
Stability
Statistics
  Descriptive statistics
Validity (measurement validity)
  Concurrent criterion-related evidence
  Predictive criterion-related validity
  Evidence based on content
  Evidence based on convergent/ discriminant relationships
  Evidence based on internal structure

Discussion Questions

1. What are some real-life examples of variables that would be normally distributed, negatively skewed, positively skewed, and curvilinear?
2. What are some examples of how different ways of measuring the same variable would give results with either a small or large variance?
3. Does a curvilinear relationship, as illustrated in a scatterplot, overestimate or underestimate the signal? Why?
4. What is the relationship between reliability and validity?
5. Why is it important to match the nature of evidence for the validity argument with the claim that is made from the results?
6. What are some good measurement procedures that can be used to enhance reliability?

Application Exercises

1. Make a dataset that has 20 more or less random numbers between 1 and 10. Use that dataset to calculate the mean and median, and prepare a frequency distribution and histogram. Estimate the variance of the scores by looking at the average deviation scores. Add a second set of random numbers for each member of your "sample" and show a scatterplot of the correlation.
2. Hank the hedgehog has a sample of a few students who really like math (all scored a 5 on a 5-point scale) and many students who don't like math at all (scoring mostly 1 and 2). Hank concludes that, on average, students have a decent attitude toward math (the overall mean was 3). What would Frank the fox say about these data?

Check for Understanding Answers

1a. Measurement simply provides numbers to differentiate; evaluation and assessment use the numbers for a specified purpose.

1b. To determine the accuracy and precision with which a variable is measured; to use for reporting results; to determine appropriate statistical procedures.

1c. To know how to interpret the results based on measurement and to determine appropriate statistical analyses.

2a. Normal, positively skewed, and negatively skewed.

2b. The mode is the most frequently occurring score, the median the middle score, and the mean the average score.

2c. Standard deviation represents the spread or dispersion of scores in relation to percentile rank; it is important in describing distributions and for use in calculating inferential statistics.

2d. To identify outliers and curvilinear relationships.

3a. The extent to which evidence supports an argument that the inference based on a measure is reasonable and appropriate, depending on how the scores are used.

3b. Because the type of evidence should correspond to the way the scores are interpreted and used.

3c. Measures without evidence of validity may not be sensitive to the construct being investigated, leading to results that underestimate the signal.

4a. Reliability is concerned with the consistency of scores; validity with the reasonableness of the inferences and uses of the scores.

4b. External factors, such as room conditions, distractions, guessing, and researcher/rater bias; internal such as mood, illness, response set, and motivation.

4c. By aligning the type of reliability coefficient (e.g., internal consistency or stability) with the nature of the inference from the scores; by gathering evidence prior to the actual study; by gathering evidence from administration of the instrument in the study; by awareness of factors that could impact the scores during administration.

Chapter 7
Quantitative Data Collection Techniques

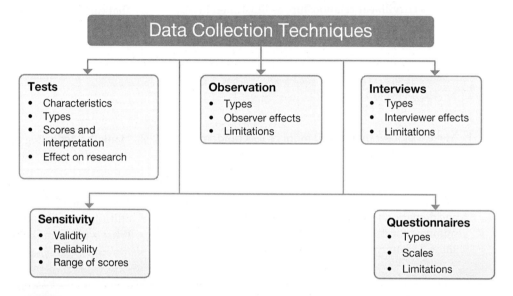

Data Collection Techniques

Tests
- Characteristics
- Types
- Scores and interpretation
- Effect on research

Observation
- Types
- Observer effects
- Limitations

Interviews
- Types
- Interviewer effects
- Limitations

Sensitivity
- Validity
- Reliability
- Range of scores

Questionnaires
- Types
- Scales
- Limitations

∨ Learning Outcomes

7.1 Understand how measurement sensitivity is affected by validity, reliability, and variability of observed scores, and how sensitivity impacts quantitative research.

7.2 Describe the characteristics of standardized tests, how they differ from locally developed tests, and how they are used in research. Know how to interpret scores reported from standardized tests.

7.3 Distinguish among different types of questionnaires and item formats. Know how to construct self-report questionnaires to provide valid and reliable information.

7.4 Distinguish among different forms of interviewing and observation techniques used to collect quantitative data and know how to address limitations of each approach.

Chapter Road Map

Once you have decided that a quantitative or mixed methods design is appropriate, and have identified your sample, the next step is to choose the best technique to gather the data you need. Making the right choice is critical; you will need to understand not only the strengths and weaknesses of different techniques, but also how the measure used affects the nature of the results, interpretations, and conclusions.

First Things First: Is the Measure Sufficiently Sensitive?

Learning Outcome 7.1 Understand how measurement sensitivity is affected by validity, reliability, and variability of observed scores, and how sensitivity impacts quantitative research.

Imagine if you were a sail maker and wanted to see whether a new type of sail would make a difference in the speed of sailboats. What kind of "measure" would be best to see how it works? One option is to use a measure of time that records how long it takes, in hours, to sail 2 miles, comparing the new sail to the old one with a fleet of boats. Other options would be to measure time in minutes, or even in seconds. What would you get with hours as the unit of measurement? Assuming a decent breeze, it would be highly likely that every boat would receive the same score—less than 1 hour! Using minutes would give you a greater range of scores and a better opportunity to show a difference, and using seconds, even tenths of seconds, the best measure to find that the new sail is better. If you use hours, the measure would be *insensitive*—unable to detect differences. Measuring by minutes or seconds is more sensitive and provides the *capability* of finding differences. **Sensitivity**, then, is the ability or capacity of a measure to identify and discriminate differences. Finding relationships among variables, which is paramount in quantitative research, depends on sensitivity. Measures that are insensitive are much less likely to show relationships and differences, or, for that matter, to provide an adequate, accurate simple description. Let's see how this plays out in educational research. What we will see is that you want to avoid insensitivity to reduce noise.

Suppose you have decided to investigate the relationship between self-efficacy and achievement. Measures of both variables will need to be selected; ones that are more sensitive will provide the greatest opportunity to demonstrate the relationship. As illustrated in Figure 7.1, you have some choices. You could pick measures of a general sense of self-efficacy and achievement that simply categorizes participants into two groups for each variable, high and low self-efficacy and pass/fail on achievement. This would be very *in*sensitive because you would not be able to discriminate much for either variable. If you select more targeted, specific measures of self-efficacy—say, as related to performance on a test in a class using a scale from 1 to 10—and examine achievement as measured by the test, giving you a wide range of scores for both variables, you now have very *sensitive* measures, and you are much more likely to find a relationship, if one exists. In other words, you need to use measures that provide a variety of scores—that show variability. The question is: How will you know whether the measure you use, one you develop or select, will be sufficiently sensitive? Three considerations are most important: validity, reliability, and the range of obtained scores.

Figure 7.1 An Illustration of Sensitivity

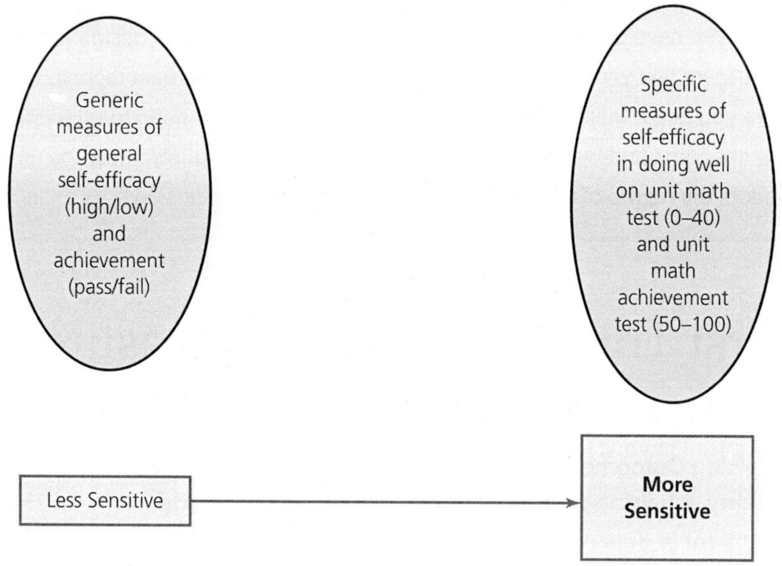

Validity

You need to use measures that provide valid scores. You wouldn't use a measure of height to assess intelligence! In the same way, if your measure does not clearly focus on the trait in which you are interested, it will not be sensitive. How do you know whether a measure used in a study has good validity? Of course, there are sources of evidence used for this purpose, as described in the previous chapter. The validity goal from a sensitivity perspective is that the trait or construct being measured is assessed directly and completely, without being influenced by other factors. If you are measuring something that is supposed to change, the instrument needs to be sensitive enough to show the change. For example, suppose you want to study the relationship between preservice teachers' knowledge about teaching and actual teaching effectiveness. You know each of your two variables needs to provide valid scores. If your measure of teachers' knowledge is either incomplete or contains irrelevant information, you lose sensitivity. An incomplete test of knowledge might not include much on effective assessment techniques. In this case, there is an *underrepresentation* of the construct "teachers' knowledge." If the test includes complicated, long reading passages, it could be measuring more than just teachers' knowledge—it might also be measuring reading ability or general aptitude. Or, the test could include some questions about things that have little to do with teaching effectiveness, such as knowing the specific steps to hold a conference with a parent. In these two cases, the test contains *extraneous* information, and, as a result, it is less sensitive. More irrelevance occurs if the emphasis on specific topics is not correct, such as too much emphasis on child development and not enough on classroom management.

The lack of sensitivity from a validity standpoint helps us understand why educational research is so difficult. The variables we are often interested in, such as motivation, achievement, classroom environment, engagement, and values, are hard to specify, especially if we use measures that appear to be important but may not be sensitive. This occurs frequently with the use of "established" instruments. For example,

Figure 7.2 Influence of Extraneous Factors on a General Measure of Critical Thinking That Lessens Sensitivity to Relationships with Instructional Methods

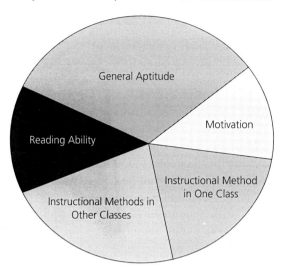

there are several very fine tests of general critical thinking ability, which tend to not be tied to specific subjects. If one of these tests is used at the end of the year, as a dependent variable, in relation to an instructional method used in one student's class, the test will not be very sensitive because of all the other factors that influence an individual's general ability to think critically. The most sensitive measure of critical thinking is one that is most directly and specifically related to what was done in class. In other words, a sensitive test would be very targeted to what was emphasized in the class in a single subject. Another way to think about this is to imagine all the factors that influence a measure of general critical thinking skills, some of which are illustrated in Figure 7.2. As you can see, the general measure is affected by many factors, which makes it less possible for you to find a difference or relationship to something from a single class that can be only part of the total score.

Reliability

As you now know, reliability is related to error in measurement. If scores are influenced by error, then that means that less of the score is directly measuring the trait you have targeted. That is, the less reliable, the more error, and the lower the sensitivity. One way to think about this is that if an instrument has low reliability, you need to subtract what is accounted for by the noise before you can hope to show relationships to other variables. You need to find direct links and alignment, and that can be accomplished only for the accurate part of what is being measured. For low reliability scores, then, there is so much noise that you can't "hear" the relationship.

Range of Observed Scores

Simply put, you need a measure that will provide a good distribution of scores to show relationships and differences. If all your participants get the same score on the dependent variable, your study is doomed. For instance, when you measure achievement with a test, you do not want to have such difficult questions that you get a floor effect, nor do you want questions that are so easy that everyone gets a perfect score, a ceiling effect. You want scores to vary, to be different. For measures that use scales, which we consider in more detail shortly, this means that all or most of the points on the scale need to be used. Here is an example of a question with an extremely insensitive scale:

Do you use effort to grade students?   Yes   No

A more sensitive question would be:

How much do you use effort to grade students?
Always   Often   Sometimes   Rarely   Never

The second question is more sensitive because respondents can discriminate more finely, presumably more in line with their practice than what could be measured in the first question. Sometimes we need to add points to one end of a scale to get more variability. A good case for that would be for questions students use to evaluate teachers. Rather than giving just four response categories (e.g., poor, average, good, excellent), which could easily result in a ceiling effect if most teachers are good or excellent, you could extend the ceiling: poor, average, good, very good, excellent, outstanding, best ever.

How do you know if a measure will give you an adequate spread of scores? There are two answers: (1) find evidence of a good distribution of scores in previous studies; and (2) do a pilot test with individuals similar to those you intend to study. If you intend to use a previously developed and used instrument, search the literature for studies using that instrument for evidence of variability. For a newly developed instrument, a pilot test is a must. The pilot, even with a small number of people, will give you some idea of whether you are likely to get an adequate spread of scores in your study. Pilots are actually almost always a good idea, even when using established instruments.

With sensitivity as a backdrop, we now consider specific types of quantitative measures, starting with tests. Each type of measure has characteristics that are important for planning, conducting, and evaluating research.

Author Reflection *If you can't tell, I just love sensitivity. Maybe it's because it relates well to my affective sense of the world, but mostly I am enamored by it because it is so darn important. I see study after study that lack sensitivity to sensitivity, and I think this contributes greatly to why so many educational studies do not show significant findings—or, when they do show significance, it's not much.*

Check for Understanding 1

1a. Describe how an insensitive measure, compared to a sensitive one, would affect a study.

1b. Explain how validity and reliability contribute to insensitivity.

Tests

Learning Outcome 7.2   Describe the characteristics of standardized tests, how they differ from locally developed tests, and how they are used in research. Know how to interpret scores reported from standardized tests.

For our purposes here, a **test** is a measure that requires individuals to complete a cognitive task by responding to a standard set of questions (tests are also used for measuring skills and personality). In a study, the answers to the questions are summarized to obtain a numerical value that represents targeted knowledge, understanding, ability, or skills of each participant. All tests measure performance at the time the test is given. Tests differ in how the results are used, in their development, and in the types of evidence for validity and reliability that are established. The major differentiating characteristics are whether tests have norm- or criterion-referenced/standards-based interpretations, whether they are measuring achievement or aptitude, and whether they are standardized or locally developed.

Norm- and Criterion-Referenced/Standards-Based Interpretations

A critical aspect of testing is the interpretation of the results. When a score is obtained, what does it convey? How do you interpret it? What does it mean, for example, when the average score is 70% correct? Measurement specialists have identified two approaches to interpretation to derive meaning from the scores: norm-referenced and criterion-referenced/standards-based. In **norm-referenced** interpretation, individual scores are compared with the scores of a well-defined norming group of others who have taken the same test. Ideally, the norm has the same characteristics, such as age and grade level, as the participants in the study. Performance is described as relative position (e.g., percentile rank). There is less emphasis on the absolute amount of knowledge or skill demonstrated. What matters most is the comparison group and the test's ability to distinguish among individuals on the trait being measured.

Because the purpose of a norm-referenced test is to differentiate among individuals, it is desirable to obtain a distribution of scores that shows high variance. It would be difficult to say much about relative standing if the scores were all about the same! To achieve high variability, the test items are often designed to differentiate the final scores. This is accomplished with some tests by having a single group of items that tend to be moderately difficult. Easy items, ones that most know the answer to, and very difficult items, ones that few can answer correctly, are used sparingly. The emphasis on items with moderate difficulty may affect what is covered on the test, which, in turn, would affect the interpretation of the results. A newer approach to testing, called *computer adaptive testing*, is able to tailor the items to each individual's ability, by giving progressively more difficult items. This method of testing is used widely today because it requires far fewer items than previous test methods and can provide more accurate scores for higher as well as lower ability.

It is also necessary to attend carefully to the nature of the norm or reference group in interpreting the results. Proper interpretation requires knowing what the scores are being compared against. It is like being in a class with an instructor who grades on a curve (each student's grade depends on how others in the class did on the test). If the class contains mostly very bright, motivated students, you can learn a lot and still look bad by comparison.

On the other hand, if you are in a class with students who have low ability and are unmotivated, you can look good even though you have not learned much. National standardized tests usually report national norms, so the scores are compared with those of students across the nation. However, there are different ways of obtaining a "national" sample. An accurate interpretation can be made only if the characteristics of the norm group are understood. In addition, evidence of reliability and validity established with the norm group may be inappropriate for individuals not represented in the norm group.

An important implication of reporting school or school district achievement or aptitude test results based on national norms is that the socioeconomic nature of the school or district population can make it relatively easy or difficult to obtain scores that show positive results. This is because of the relationship between socioeconomic status and aptitude, which is positive. For low socioeconomic schools, comparing students with others with higher socioeconomic status is problematic–they invariably score lower. The opposite is true for high socioeconomic schools. It is easy for these students to score high when the comparison group, overall, has a lower socioeconomic status. From an interpretation standpoint, then, if a low socioeconomic school scores at the national average or above, that is quite an achievement! A low-scoring high

Author Reflection *Norm-referenced comparisons can be rather interesting, to say the least. American students' performance on international tests is a great example. Many other countries do better than America on these tests—but remember, these results depend heavily on the nature of the groups being compared (not to mention curriculum and cultural differences).*

socioeconomic school, on the other hand, would raise a few eyebrows. For some tests, you can ask for special norms that will provide a more similar comparison group. Often, it makes most sense to compare apples to apples and oranges to oranges.

The purpose of a **criterion-referenced/standards-based** interpretation is to show how an individual's performance compares with an established level of performance or skill. Here, the score is interpreted by comparison with a standard or criterion, rather than with the scores of others. The result is usually reported either as a percentage of items answered correctly or as falling within categories such as *pass, proficient*, and *advanced*. Examples of criterion-referenced/standards-based measurement include grading scales—such as 95 to 100 = A, 88 to 94 = B, and so on—and competency tests, in which the emphasis is on making sure that students know certain concepts and principles and have certain skills. The results from some criterion-referenced/standards-based tests show a highly negatively skewed distribution. This characteristic lessens variability, which may make it difficult to find relationships between the test results and other variables. This is often the case with classroom assessments. However, most large-scale criterion-referenced/standards-based tests, such as state accountability tests, have essentially normally distributed results.

With standards-based interpretations, professional judgment is used to set the passing or mastery score. There are many ways to make these professional judgments, with quite different results. In the end, someone has to decide where to set the "cut" points to designate the levels of performance. Who are the individuals setting the standards? What perspectives and abilities, or even motives, do they bring to the process? Although "high" standards may mean that students must answer most questions correctly, simply getting the correct answer does not tell the whole story. There are easy and hard items, so to accurately interpret the meaning of achieving a "proficient" or "advanced" designation, you need to examine the items.

Table 7.1 Characteristics of Criterion-Referenced/Standards-Based and Norm-Referenced Interpretation

	Criterion-Referenced/ Standards-Based	Norm-Referenced
Purpose	To describe levels of performance in relation to set criteria.	To discriminate between individuals; indicate relative standing.
Content Tested	A well-defined, delimited domain.	Typically, a large domain.
Item Difficulty	Items tend to be relatively easy.	Items tend to be moderately difficult, with fewer very easy or difficult items.
Interpretation	Categorical, based on how levels of performance are established.	Based on comparison to a clearly defined norm group.

Source: Based on Miller, Linn, & Gronlund, 2013.

The differences between norm- and criterion-referenced/standards-based interpretations are summarized in Table 7.1.

Large-Scale Standardized Tests

A **standardized test** has set procedures for administration and scoring. Directions specify the procedures for giving the test, such as qualifications of the person administering the test, time allowed to answer the questions, materials that can be used by the participants, and other conditions. The scoring of responses is usually objective, with specific instructions for scoring that do not involve the tester's personal judgments. Most standardized tests have been administered to a norming group, which is helpful in interpreting the results, and most are prepared commercially by measurement experts. This means that careful attention has been given to technical aspects such as cultural bias, reliability, validity, clarity, and item analysis.

Large-scale standardized tests are intended to be used in a wide variety of settings. (Obviously, commercial test publishers want to sell as many tests as possible.) The traits and skills measured by these tests are usually defined in broad, general terms. Consequently, the test may not be specific enough for use in a particular setting. For example, suppose a teacher is investigating the effect of different instructional methods on 11th-grade students' achievement in English. A standardized test of English (e.g., a test of national English standards) may be available, but it may not be consistent with the specific reading materials this teacher intends to use. In this case, the standardized test would probably not be sensitive enough to the different materials to show positive results. Thus, a trade-off exists in using standardized tests for classroom-oriented research. Although there may be established technical qualities, the test may not focus directly on what is being studied.

STANDARDS-BASED TESTS Accountability testing, based on learning standards for students, is now universal. These measures are often called **standards-based tests**. They are standardized achievement tests with criterion-referenced/standards-based interpretations. As such, they are influenced both by what students learn in school and by what students learn at home and in the community. Students are typically judged to be "proficient" or "not proficient" on the basis of their scores on the tests. These tests are *domain-referenced*. A sample of content and skills is selected from a larger domain of standards. Because results from standards-based tests are very visible for both students and schools, they are often used to evaluate school programs and methods of instruction. This may be appropriate as long as inferences are limited to the domain that is tested, and as long as the influence of home and community is recognized.

These tests also have high stakes, often determining whether a student can be promoted to the next grade or can graduate from high school, deciding whether schools can be accredited, and, more recently, evaluating teachers. We know that in a high-stakes environment test score increases often result from other factors (e.g., test-wiseness by students, a narrowed curriculum, drill-and-kill instruction, multiple-choice classroom assessment that mimics the accountability test), rather than an increase in knowledge or skills. As with other standardized tests, what is measured tends to be broad and general and may not be the best measure when research has targeted more specific dependent variables. For example, it would not be appropriate to use a high school end-of-course science test (one that covers the entire year) when an intervention in an experiment consists of a specific 4-week unit. Once again, this illustrates a lack of sensitivity.

Author Reflection *A great amount of research has been conducted that relates student growth to teacher effectiveness by using "value-added" analyses. The idea is to use standards-based test scores as pre and post measures to make conclusions about the quality of teaching over that period. That sounds like pretty good logic, except for one important reality—the student scores are affected by far more than what the teacher has done. There are influences such as the home environment, parents, siblings, peers, group dynamics in the classroom, and many other factors. Thus, the teacher will have an impact on achievement, but by no means will be responsible for all of it. Also, the teacher is influential in many other ways—on such important traits, for example, as self-efficacy, attitudes, responsibility, and interpersonal skills. Considering these two well-known caveats (as well as others), there are clear limitations in what student accountability test scores tell us about teacher effectiveness.*

STANDARDIZED ACHIEVEMENT TESTS A **standardized achievement test** is a large-scale, commercially prepared test. It measures present knowledge and skills of a sample of relevant content. The emphasis is on recent school learning—what has been learned by the student—measuring proficiency in one or more areas of knowledge.

The type of achievement test selected for research depends on the purpose of the study. If the investigation is concerned with a single topic, a test that measures only that area would be preferable to a comprehensive battery of many topics. If the purpose is to compare schools on achievement, a norm-referenced achievement test would be best. Evaluations of overall school performance are best assessed with survey batteries.

When existing standardized achievement tests do not match well with the purpose of the research, a locally developed test is needed. These "homemade" or informally developed tests can be designed to be more targeted to what is being investigated, and in that sense have greater sensitivity (although there may be technical limitations). Many tests now being used at a school or school-district level, such as "common" or "benchmark" tests, are large-scale in implementation but are locally developed. Important differences between large-scale standardized and locally developed achievement tests are summarized in Table 7.2.

STANDARDIZED APTITUDE TESTS A **standardized aptitude test** is a commercially prepared measure of knowledge, ability, or skills that is used to predict future performance. The difference between an achievement test and an aptitude test is in the way the results are applied. The actual items can be very similar, especially in tests for

Table 7.2 Characteristics of Large-Scale Standardized Tests and Locally Developed Tests[1]

	Large-Scale Standardized Tests	Locally Developed Tests
Sensitivity	Low	High
Technical quality	High	Low
Quality of test items	High	Low
Administration and scoring	Specific instructions	Flexible
Score interpretation	Compared to national norms	Limited to local context
Content tested	General	Specific to local context

[1]This table shows general trends. Some locally developed tests, for example, have high-quality items, and some standardized tests are highly relevant to the research.

young children. Often, the terms *intelligence* and *ability* are used interchangeably with *aptitude*. Actually, *aptitude* is a more general term that refers to the predictive nature of the instrument. *Intelligence* usually means some indication of an individual's capacity to understand, process, and apply knowledge and skills in thinking or problem solving. It involves many different aptitudes.

Aptitude tests are widely used in education and are useful in predicting performance on many tasks. Some tests, such as the *Otis-Lennon School Ability Test* and the *Cognitive Abilities Test*, are given to large groups of students; others, such as the Stanford-Binet and the Wechsler scales, are given on an individual basis.

Because aptitude tests are concerned with predicting future behavior, it is important to establish predictive criterion-related evidence for validity. It is also best to have a stability estimate of reliability. These technical qualities are important in tests that are used to select individuals for special programs that attract a large pool of applicants.

Interpreting Norm-Referenced Scores

A characteristic of norm-referenced interpretation is that different types of scores are reported and used in research, each having unique characteristics. Two of the most common are *standard scores* and *grade equivalents.*

STANDARD SCORES Most publishers of standardized, norm-referenced tests report at least two types of scores. One is the actual number of items correct—the raw score—and another, the *standard score*, is calculated from these raw scores. **Standard scores** are transformed raw scores that have a distribution in the same shape as the raw score distribution but with a different mean and standard deviation. The most basic standard score is called a linear **z-score**, which has a mean of 0 and a standard deviation of 1. The formula is

$$z = \frac{\text{raw score } - \text{ mean}}{\text{standard deviation}}$$

Every raw score can be transformed to a z-score with known percentile ranks, as illustrated in Figure 7.3.

Many other derived standard scores, such as SAT and IQ scores, are then calculated from z-scores. When interpreting these types of standard scores, consider two important points. First, the unit of standard deviation is determined arbitrarily and does not reflect "real" differences between subjects. For instance, the SAT composite score has a standard score mean of about 1060 and a standard deviation of about 210. One individual may score 1200 and another 1240, but the 40-point difference is only in standard score units. In fact, the 40 points may represent a difference of only a few

Figure 7.3 *z*-Scores and Percentile Ranks

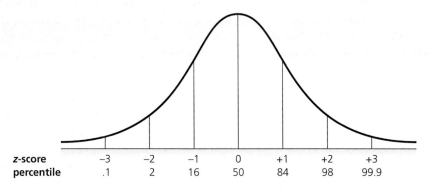

z-score	−3	−2	−1	0	+1	+2	+3
percentile	.1	2	16	50	84	98	99.9

correct answers. Second, in distributions of a small number of individuals, and in any raw score distribution that is not normal, scores are sometimes "normalized"—that is, forced into a normal distribution and reported as standard scores. This practice may distort the meaning of the scores. Despite these limitations, standard scores are often used in research because the data are in a form that can be used in statistical analyses of the results. Furthermore, with standard scores, it is easier to compare groups who have taken different tests.

GRADE EQUIVALENTS   Grade equivalents (GEs) are sometimes used for reporting achievement, even if they are often misinterpreted. A **grade equivalent** score indicates how an individual compares with others in a norm group in terms of grade level. For example, a student who scores 5.0 has achieved the median score for all beginning fifth-graders *in the norm group*, whereas the score 3.2 is equivalent to the average score of third-graders in November. The most serious misinterpretation is the belief that a student who scores, say, 6.0, should be in the sixth grade, or knows as much as a sixth-grader. Grade determination is based on local school policy and the level of achievement of students in a particular school, whereas the GE is based on a national norm.

Check for Understanding 2

2a.   What is the difference between "off-the-shelf" and "locally developed" tests? Why would a researcher want to use a locally developed test rather than one that has already been developed and used?

2b.   What is the difference between criterion-referenced/standards-based and norm-referenced interpretations?

2c.   Why are changes in scores and differences between groups difficult to obtain with many standardized tests?

Questionnaires

Learning Outcome 7.3   Distinguish among different types of questionnaires and item formats. Know how to construct self-report questionnaires to provide valid and reliable information.

The questionnaire is used widely in educational research. A **questionnaire** contains written prompts or questions that are used to obtain an individual's perceptions, attitudes, beliefs, values, perspectives, and/or dispositions (on paper or in electronic format).

Questionnaires are used extensively because they provide an efficient way to obtain information from surveys of large populations to reactions of students to different instructional methods. (Sometimes a "survey" can mean a questionnaire, although "survey research" uses both questionnaires and interviewing; some questionnaires are delivered orally.) Questionnaires can be used to assess different kinds of traits and can take several formats.

Personality Assessment

Psychologists have been concerned with measuring personality for many decades. Although there are different definitions of personality, a common theme is that it involves the total individual—so-called noncognitive, affective traits, styles, and temperaments, as well as cognitive characteristics, that are similarly manifest in various settings and situations. As such, personality is relatively stable (unlike, for example, self-confidence to ride a bike). This holistic emphasis is evident in standardized personality instruments that assess general adjustment, such as the *Minnesota Multiphasic Personality Inventory* (MMPI). The MMPI is a self-report questionnaire for adults aged 16 and above. Fourteen scales are reported, including paranoia, hysteria, social introversion, schizophrenia, and depression. Another well-known personality assessment is the *Myers-Briggs Type Indicator* (MBTI), which reports extraversion/introversion scores along with other traits.

Questionnaires that are used by teachers and educational researchers that may be related to personality are not typically standardized. Rather, they measure important individual traits related to learning and motivation, such as self-efficacy, self-regulation, and cognitive style. The instruments are designed so that educators without clinical training can understand and use the results.

One personality trait that is studied extensively in educational research is self-concept. Self-concept, or self-image, can be defined as the way one characterizes oneself. It is a description formed by self-perceptions and beliefs. Although it is possible to measure a single, global self-concept, most questionnaires are designed to assess many different self-concepts, such as descriptions about the physical, social, academic, moral, and personal self. The items in the instruments require self-report perceptions.

Typically, short statements are presented that describe various aspects of self-concept. Participants answer each item by indicating whether it is true for them, or whether they agree or disagree that the statement is like them. For example, respondents would be directed to answer "yes" or "no" or "true" or "false" to the following statements:

1. I am tall.
2. I get mostly average grades in school.
3. I am often nervous when taking tests.

Often the scoring of the instruments indicates a positive or negative self-concept, an interpretation that has an evaluative component termed *self-esteem*. Self-esteem has to do with how individuals *feel* about their self-concepts. In the literature, *self-concept* and *self-esteem* may be used interchangeably, so it is necessary to examine the nature of the items to understand what is being measured.

Another commonly assessed trait is self-efficacy. *Self-efficacy* is the judgment of the person's capabilities to undertake appropriate action that results in successful performance. With strong self-efficacy, students are empowered to be more engaged and motivated to do well, and to persist in the face of difficulties. With low self-efficacy, students are more likely to avoid tasks with which they may not be successful and to give up more quickly. Self-report measures are used to assess self-efficacy and use items similar to those found in Figure 7.4.

Attitude, Value, and Interest Questionnaires

Attitudes, values, and interests are generally thought of as *noncognitive* or *affective* traits that indicate some degree of preference toward something. *Attitudes* are defined as predispositions to respond favorably or unfavorably to an object, group, or place. They reflect likes and dislikes and generally predict behavior. Like attitudes, interests are concerned with preferences. Both are related to favorable or unfavorable responses toward something. *Interests,* however, are feelings and beliefs about an activity rather than an object, concept, or person. Like attitudes and interests, *values* can be defined in a number of ways, so it is necessary to examine items in a value survey to know what is being measured.

When reading research that investigates attitudes, values, and interests, three types of items are commonly used: scales, checklists, and ranked items.

Types of Scales

A **scale** is a progressive series of gradations of something. The most typical format for a scaled item is to follow a question or statement with a scale of potential responses. Individuals indicate their attitudes or values by checking or circling the appropriate place on the scale that best reflects their feelings and beliefs about the question or statement. The **Likert scale** (pronounced LICK-ert) is the most widely used example. In a true Likert scale, the statement includes a value or positive or negative direction, and the respondent indicates agreement or disagreement with the statement.

An example might be:

It is very important to go to college.

| strongly agree | agree | neither agree nor disagree | disagree | strongly disagree |

Likert-*type* rating scales, which have a different form, begin with a neutral statement, and the direction or gradation is provided in the response options:

Mrs. Calder's classroom management is

| outstanding | excellent | good | fair | poor |

Figure 7.4 Scale for Assessing Self-Efficacy

	Always	Almost Always	Often	Sometimes	Never/ Rarely
I am confident that I can complete most schoolwork successfully.	A	AA	O	S	NR
Science is easy for me.	A	AA	O	S	NR
I am confident in my ability to do well in my English class.	A	AA	O	S	NR
No matter how hard I try, I have trouble with math.	A	AA	O	S	NR

Likert-type scales are useful for measuring traits other than attitudes. Such measures are usually referred to as rating scales. Statements and response options can be selected for a wide variety of needs, for example,

How often does your principal visit your classroom?

| every day | 2 or 3 days a week | once a week | once every 2 weeks | once a month |

How often does your teacher give praise?

| Always | most of the time | sometimes | rarely | never |

How did you feel about your performance on the exam?

| very satisfied | somewhat satisfied | somewhat dissatisfied | very dissatisfied |

Note that the number of possible responses on a Likert-type scale is not always the same. There is usually a minimum of four options, and there can be as many as seven or eight (though rarely more than seven). Some questions will have a middle option, and others will have an even number of options to "force" the individual to one side of the scale or the other. However, if a neutral or middle choice is not provided and this is the real attitude or belief of the person, the individual will be forced to give an inaccurate response (or may choose not to respond at all).

A good example of a study in which I participated used Likert-type items to survey teachers about their grading and classroom assessment practices for a specific class and survey students about their motivation to be engaged in the class and to work for high grades. The purpose of the study was to determine relationships between teacher practices and student motivation. Some of the items for both the teacher and student surveys are illustrated in Figure 7.5. Both questionnaires used a 5-point scale.

Excerpt 7.1 shows how a Likert-type scale was used for developing an instrument that would measure prosocial behavior. Note that the authors indicate use of a "7-point Likert scale," which is actually a Likert-type scale. This is not at all rare. You will often find researchers say "Likert scale" and use a variation of the true scale approach of an agree–disagree continuum.

Another type of scale is the **semantic differential**, which has adjective pairs that provide a series of scales. Each adjective acts as an end anchor, and the respondent checks a point between each end anchor of each scale to indicate attitudes toward some person, concept, or idea. Although the true semantic differential uses the same set of

---

EXCERPT 7.1

Use of a Likert-Type Scale

{W}e worded the instructions to ask respondents to assume that the opportunity to enact each behavior presents itself and set the time frame to the general future. Each item was rated on a 7-point Likert scale ranging from 1 (definitely would not do this) to 7 (definitely would do this). Items included behaviors such as, "Care for a sick friend or relative." All items were coded positively, with higher scores indicating stronger intentions to perform the behaviors. (p. 4)

SOURCE: Baumsteiger, R., & Siegel, J. T. (2018). Measuring prosociality: The development of a prosocial behavioral intentions scale. *Journal of Personality Assessment, 12*, 305–314.

EXCERPT 7.2

Use of a Semantic Differential

The researchers developed a 20-item, five point semantic differential to measure attitudes and perceptions related to the concept of "mathematics, science, and technology education integration" using bipolar adjectives previously used in their research that had exhibited high internal consistency reliability (e.g., bad-good, boring-exciting, weak-strong, strange-familiar, hard-easy). Students responded to the series of bipolar adjectives by marking an X on one of five spaces to reflect their attitudes and perceptions. (p. 106)

SOURCE: Berlin, D. F., & White, A. L. (2009). Preservice mathematics and science teachers in an integrated teacher preparation program for grades 7–12: A 3-year study of attitudes and perceptions related to integration. *International Journal of Science and Mathematics Education, 8,* 97–115.

adjective pairs in the three clusters, changing the object or concept that is being studied and changing the adjective pairs as appropriate are common in educational research.

An example of using a semantic differential for measuring the science attitudes of preservice teachers is illustrated in Excerpt 7.2.

A **checklist** provides the respondent with a number of options from which to choose. The checklist can require a choice of one of several alternatives. Here's an example:

Check one: The research topic I enjoy most is

☐ measurement
☐ qualitative designs
☐ quantitative designs
☐ reviewing literature

Or, respondents can check as many as apply:
Check as many as apply. The topics in research that I find very useful are

☐ measurement
☐ qualitative designs
☐ quantitative designs
☐ reviewing literature

Checklists are also used when asking participants to answer yes or no, or to check the category to which they belong, for example:
Are you a full-time student?

☐ Yes
☐ No

Indicate the appropriate category:

☐ single, never married
☐ married
☐ separated
☐ divorced
☐ widowed

Figure 7.5 Examples of Likert-Type Items

To what extent did you use the following grading and assessment practices *in the class you are currently teaching?*	Not at ALL	Minimally	Some	Quite a Bit	Extensively
1. feedback (written or verbal) on performance that was given privately to each student	1	2	3	4	5
2. feedback (written or verbal) that contained suggestions for further learning	1	2	3	4	5
3. checklists to evaluate student work (**not** rubrics)	1	2	3	4	5
4. formative assessments (i.e., assessment given during instruction to check student learning; anecdotal or structured)	1	2	3	4	5
5. assessments that measured student deep understanding (e.g., exploration, inquiry, and problem solving)	1	2	3	4	5
6. tests and other assessments of moderate difficulty	1	2	3	4	5

Rate each item by how true it is for you.	Not at All True for Me		Somewhat True for Me		Very True for Me
1. I'm certain I can understand the ideas taught in this class.	1	2	3	4	5
2. It's important to me that I learn a lot in this class.	1	2	3	4	5
3. It's important to me that other students in my class think I am good at my class work.	1	2	3	4	5
4. **I don't** want my teacher to think **I** know less than other students in class.	1	2	3	4	5
5. One of my goals is to gain a lot of new skills in this class.	1	2	3	4	5

In a **rank-ordered** item, the respondent is asked to place a limited number of categories into sequential order. The sequence could be based on importance, liking, degree of experience, or some other dimension. Asking individuals to rank-order may provide different results from those provided by a Likert item or semantic differential. For example, if a researcher is interested in determining the importance of different staff development topics, a Likert-type item format could be used. For each topic, the teachers check or circle "critical," "very important," "important," or "not important." If most of the teachers check or circle "important" for each topic, then there is limited information about which of the topics should be given priority. However, if the teachers rank-order the topics by importance from 5 for most important to 1 for least important, an average rating can be found that will more likely identify which topic should be given priority.

The Hedgehog and the Fox Contemplate Which Scale to Use

I intend to use the standard Likert scale for my questionnaire. It's the one I've found used the most so it's appropriate.

I'm not sure, but the Likert scale may be best for my study. I need to see whether it needs to be modified to best fit my questions and pilot test the scale to be sure the respondents will clearly understand. The pilot will also be used to check for sensitivity. Maybe a different scale will be better.

Constructing Questionnaires

Researchers often need to construct a questionnaire for their study. As you can imagine, this results in a range of quality, from instruments that are excellent to those of, shall we say, lesser quality. Whether you are reading a study in which a questionnaire has been developed, or constructing your own, knowing the right steps is a good basis for being sure that the quality and credibility of the instrument are sound. These steps are illustrated in Figure 7.6.

The first step is to develop a sound rationale and justification—a reason for why you need to construct the questionnaire. This depends on a thorough review of literature to determine whether existing instruments are available or can be borrowed from. Justification for a constructed questionnaire is strengthened to the extent that theory and previous research support its development and use. The goal is to connect the instrument to established conceptual distinctions, knowledge, and theory, which provides a basis or foundation for what is measured, analyzed, and interpreted. A good example would be the way in which "student use of results" is conceptualized

Figure 7.6 Steps in Constructing Questionnaires

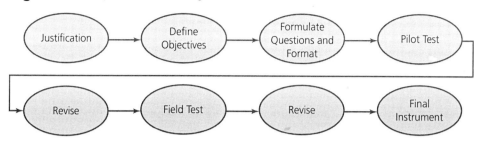

EXCERPT 7.3

Justification for Developing an Instrument

I developed the LSPI using research conducted by Dunn and Dunn (1992), who classify individuals as analytical or global learners. Dunn and Dunn found that analytical learners are more successful when information is presented step-by-step in a cumulative, sequential pattern that builds toward a conceptual understanding.... Global learners have the opposite set of characteristics, learning more easily when they master a concept first and then concentrate on the details.... I developed an instrument to quickly assess these two major learning-style elements. (pp. 227–228)

SOURCE: Pitts, J. (2009). Identifying and using a teacher-friendly learning-styles instrument. *The Clearing House, 82*(5), 225–231.

---

as the basis for a measure of feedback. There are differences in the way "feedback" is defined, so a particular instrument needs to be clearly aligned with the definition. Note in Excerpt 7.3 how the researchers used previously reported research and theory to develop their instrument.

Justification is followed by identifying important objectives that will be achieved. There needs to be a clear link between the research questions and items. Once the objectives are determined, items and an appropriate scale are developed to match the objectives. The format of the questionnaire—how the items are arranged—is designed. The items and format are then pilot tested with individuals who are similar to those who will be used in the research. The purpose of the pilot is to obtain feedback on the clarity of the items and response scale. This step leads to revisions to result in an almost final form that can also be given as a field test to appropriate individuals to obtain more feedback and establish data for reliability and validity. Further revision is completed to result in the final instrument.

Let's take a closer look at step three—formulating questions and designing the format. There is an extensive survey literature that has established some excellent "rules" about writing good items. I have summarized these suggestions in the form of a checklist in Figure 7.7. It is important to tailor items to characteristics of the respondents in a manner that captures the variation of what is being measured. This means that, as pointed out earlier about whether there should be a "neutral" choice with Likert items, there must be clarity for the respondents, shared interpretations, and opportunities to accurately reflect their feelings or beliefs. For example, if the scale that is selected does not allow for the most extreme attitudes, by using only "agree" or "disagree" as

---

Figure 7.7 Checklist of Criteria for Constructing and Evaluating Questionnaire Items

✓ Are the items short, simple, and clear? (e.g., avoid slang, technical terms, ambiguous terms, and jargon)

✓ Is the language specific rather than abstract?

✓ Are any of the questions double-barreled? (e.g., What is your attitude toward math tests and homework?)

✓ Does the response scale match the question? (e.g., How often have you volunteered to tutor? Agree–Disagree)

✓ Are respondents capable of answering the question? (e.g., asking a sample of American third graders to respond to how difficult it is to do well on the SAT)

✓ Are negatively worded items used sparingly, if at all?

✓ Are double negatives avoided altogether?

✓ Are biased, leading items avoided? (e.g., Studying hard is good for learning and will make me better prepared for life—agree or disagree)

✓ Are response options exhaustive?

✓ Are response options mutually exclusive? (e.g., How much do you study? 2–4 hours or 4–6 hours?)

✓ Does each point on the scale have a clear meaning?

✓ Is a midpoint included? (it's usually better to include a midpoint)

✓ Are "Don't Know" or "Not Applicable" options included to avoid missing data?

✓ Are socially desirable items avoided? (e.g., Students should do their homework; Agree–Disagree)

---

options (rather than, for example, "strongly agree" and/or "very strongly agree"), true attitudes may not be recorded. Scales need to represent the full continuum of possible responses to enhance sensitivity.

Most items in constructed questionnaires are **selected response** (closed-ended), in which individuals select an answer from choices. **Constructed response** (open-ended) questions, in which respondents write in answers, can provide rich information, especially if there is a need to understand what is paramount or of most importance. For example, in evaluating a character-building curriculum, a survey could ask in an open-ended fashion, "What is most important in how you treat others?" rather than using a series of closed-ended questions about caring and trust (e.g., "How important is it to care about others?"). The open-ended question may give a better indication about what is believed without the respondent being prompted.

There are also some well-established principles for how the questions should be organized (Dillman, Smyth, & Christian, 2014, and Fanning, 2005, provide more details). These suggestions are summarized in Figure 7.8. The guiding principle is that the flow and sequence of questions make logical sense to the respondent, encourage answering all questions, and make it easy to respond. Appropriately designed questionnaires motivate respondents and result in more accurate data.

Both the format and clarity of specific items are examined in the pilot test. This can be accomplished by allowing those in the pilot to check specific items that are not clear and answer specific questions about the directions and overall organization. The pilot also provides an opportunity to see how long it takes to complete the questionnaire. The field test should be conducted just like the collection of data in the actual study. This allows for a check on the procedures and provides an opportunity to gather evidence for validity and reliability.

Notice in Excerpt 7.4 how the questionnaire was organized by topic areas, although in this case the researchers put the demographic questions first. The items were appropriately based on questions used in previous studies that aligned with the conceptual frameworks for motivation, metacognition, and self-regulation.

Figure 7.8 Checklist of Criteria for Questionnaire Format

✓ Are the directions clear?
✓ Are the first few questions easy to answer?
✓ Are important questions presented near the beginning?
✓ Are questions on the same topic and those using the same response scale grouped together?
✓ Are more difficult and sensitive questions placed near the middle or end?
✓ Are questions that don't apply filtered?
✓ Are headings and sections clear and appropriate?
✓ Are there too many questions?
✓ Are there mostly closed-ended questions?
✓ Does item order affect responses? (e.g., asking about general life satisfaction after answering questions about raising children could suggest that general life satisfaction doesn't include raising children)
✓ Are demographic questions placed at the end?
✓ Is the questionnaire uncluttered?
✓ Is the layout professional looking? (e.g., fonts, spacing, spelling)

EXCERPT 7.4

Questionnaire Construction

The self-report survey was divided into four major sections. In the first, students responded to individual items used to determine their age, sex, ethnicity, and their academic level at the university. The remaining three sections assessed students' motivational beliefs and attitudes, learning strategies and procrastination, and their use of motivational regulation strategies. All of the self-report items in these final three sections were constructed so as to measure students' beliefs, attitudes or behaviors with respect to the specific history or human development course in which they were currently enrolled. All items used a 7-point Likert scale. For the motivational, learning strategies and procrastination items, the scale ranged from 1 (*strongly disagree*) to 7 (*strongly agree*). . . . Using items derived from Pintrich et al. (1993) and from Midgley et al. (1998), four aspects of students' motivation were assessed. . . . Participants' use of cognitive and metacognitive strategies were assessed with items originally derived from Pintrich et al. (1993) and used previously in Wolters (2003b). (p. 206)

SOURCE: Wolters, C. A., & Benzon, M. B. (2013). Assessing and predicting college students' use of strategies for the self-regulation of motivation. *The Journal of Experimental Education, 81*(2), 199–221.

Internet-Based Questionnaires

The pervasiveness of the Internet has led researchers to this medium as a way to gather questionnaire data. These could be called Internet- or web-based questionnaires, online surveys, electronic surveys, or Internet surveys. Usually, researchers will use an existing software program for constructing and distributing the questionnaire and for setting up an initial database (e.g., SurveyMonkey; Inquisite). These programs make the process simple and straightforward. Typically, respondents agree to complete the questionnaire and are directed to a website to access it, answer the questions, and submit.

Internet-based surveys are becoming the standard approach for gathering self-report information; no doubt you have taken a few. Most people are familiar with them and comfortable answering the questions, and an electronic format saves money and time. Research comparing web-based to paper-and-pencil questionnaires shows that they are equally reliable and provide the same results in most cases. The ability to easily create a database is an important feature. In general, online surveys are effective because they present questions in an attractive format, are able to access distant populations, and make it easy to answer questions. The main disadvantages are a low response rate, especially compared with having a captured sample in a room, and that respondents may be concerned about confidentiality and, as a result, give biased responses. It is also difficult to know whether the person who responded is the targeted participant or someone else. (More detail about Internet-based surveys is presented in the next chapter.)

Author Reflection *My experience with Internet-based surveys is mixed. The ones that have worked best are targeted to specific populations that have a vested interest in the topic. In other words, the less meaningful, the lower the return rate. Would you be likely to respond to questions about how, as a student, you went to different types of restaurants over the past month?*

Check for Understanding 3

3a. Identify two factors that affect the measurement of "noncognitive" traits and explain how each one affects the results.

3b. What are two criteria that should be used to evaluate the quality of questionnaires?

Interviews

Learning Outcome 7.4 Distinguish among different forms of interviewing and observation techniques used to collect quantitative data and know how to address limitations of each approach.

The **interview** is a form of data collection in which specific questions are asked orally and participants' responses are recorded, verbatim and/or summarized (in person, by phone, or through digital portals such as Zoom). For quantitative studies, the steps in developing what is called an interview *protocol*, which is essentially a script for conducting the interview—with procedures, questions, and prompts results in essentially an oral questionnaire. The questions, as well as possible response options, are predetermined and standard for all participants. There is direct verbal interaction between the interviewer and the respondent, which has both advantages and disadvantages compared with tests and self-report questionnaires. By establishing a proper rapport with the interviewee, a skilled interviewer can enhance motivation and obtain information that might not otherwise have been offered. More accurate responses are obtained as the interviewer clarifies questions that the respondent may have and follows up leads (probing). The interview allows for greater depth and richness of information. In face-to-face interviews, the interviewer can observe nonverbal responses and behaviors, which may indicate the need for further questioning to clarify verbal answers. Interviews can be used with many types of individuals, such as those who are illiterate or too young to read or write. The presence of an interviewer tends to reduce the number of "no answers" or neutral responses, and the interviewer can press for more complete answers when necessary. Compared with questionnaires, interviews usually achieve higher response rates; often as many as 90% or 95% of the individuals will agree to be interviewed.

One disadvantage of interviews is that because they are expensive and time-consuming compared with other methods of data collection, the sample size is often small. With small samples, a high response rate is needed to avoid bias in the nature of the sample. The advantages of flexibility and the opportunity for probing and clarification allow for a certain degree of subjectivity in summarizing what is heard for open-ended questions. This subjectivity may lead to biased interpretation of responses. Another disadvantage is that there is lack of anonymity. This may result in respondents being less than fully truthful or prone to give socially acceptable or researcher anticipated answers (more on that later in the chapter).

Types of Interview Questions

There are three types of interview questions used in quantitative studies: *structured*, *semistructured*, and *unstructured*. **Structured questions** give the participant choices from which an answer is selected. They are essentially selected response. For example, in a study of student attitudes, the interviewer may ask, "How important is it to you to obtain high grades in school? Is it critical, very important, important, or not very important?"

Semistructured questions, which are used in both quantitative and qualitative studies, do not have predetermined, structured choices. Rather, the question is open-ended yet specific in intent, allowing individual responses. For instance, an interviewer may ask, "What are some things that teachers you like do to keep you interested?" The question is reasonably objective, yet it allows for probing, follow-up, and clarification.

Unstructured questions, which are open-ended and broad (a mainstay of qualitative research) are used sparingly in quantitative studies. The interviewer has a general goal in mind and asks questions relevant to this goal. Thus, there is some latitude in what is asked, and often somewhat different questions are used with each participant. This lack of standardization can be a problem.

Interviewer Effects

The ideal role of the interviewer in a quantitative study is to act as a neutral medium through which information is transmitted. The interviewer should not have an effect on the results, except to make it possible for the participant to reveal accurate answers. However, because of the one-on-one nature of the interview, there are several potential sources of error. Interviewers must be careful that preexisting bias does not influence what they hear or record. Contamination can also occur if the interviewers have knowledge of facets of the study. **Leading questions** that encourage a desired response (e.g., Wouldn't you agree that Mrs. Jones is an excellent teacher?) can bias responses. With experiments, interviewers should not be aware of which participants are receiving special interventions or whether certain results will have positive benefits. Obviously, interviewers need to be trained so that many of these potential sources of error will be mitigated.

There is some evidence that certain interviewer characteristics may influence the results of in-person interviews. For example, matching interviewers and interviewees on demographic variables such as age, socioeconomic status, race, and gender may result in more valid results. Generally, most inhibition in responding occurs with persons of the same age but different gender. Interviewers should dress according to existing norms or in a fashion familiar to the respondents, and not in such a way that the interviewees would sense that particular responses are desirable.

Additional error may occur from the way the in-person interview is conducted. It is important for the interviewer to be pleasant, friendly, and relaxed in establishing a relationship with the interviewee that is conducive to honest interchange and little inhibition. This result is often accomplished by beginning the interview with "small talk." Probing should be anticipated and planned for in the training of the interviewers, and specific types of probes should be identified for certain situations.

The manner in which the interviewer records responses may affect the results. At one extreme, a tape recorder can provide a verbatim record of the answers. The tapes can then be analyzed by different individuals to increase validity, as is typically done with qualitative research. This method is most useful with semistructured and unstructured questions, which lend themselves to greater subjectivity on the part of the interviewer. However, the mere presence of a tape recorder may inhibit certain types of responses from some individuals. At the other extreme, the interviewer can wait until the interview is over and then write notes that summarize the results. This procedure is more prone to error because it is easier for interviewer bias to affect what is remembered and recorded. To reduce this source of error, most interviewers take some notes during the interview. Typically, they write brief notes for each question during the interview that can be expanded after the interview is over.

I have summarized some important criteria for conducting a good quantitatively oriented interview in Figure 7.9. The major goal is to preserve the objectivity needed for quantitative data and at the same time provide additional, valuable information that could not be gathered through a self-report questionnaire.

Observations

Tests, questionnaires, and interviews are similar in that they rely on participants' direct answers. While relatively economical and easy to use, they have limitations that may bias the results, such as response set, participant motivation, and faking. Another major type of data collection used in quantitative studies, which does not rely on self-reports, is **observation**. Although observational techniques also have limitations, recording behavior as it occurs yields firsthand data without the contamination that may arise from self-reports. Moreover, observation allows the description of behavior as it occurs naturally. Any kind of self-report introduces artificiality into the research. Observation of behavior in natural settings also allows the researcher to take into account important contextual factors that may influence the interpretation and use of the results.

Figure 7.9 Checklist of Criteria for Conducting Effective Quantitative Interviews

✓ Are interviewers trained?
✓ Is the interview tape-recorded?
✓ Is rapport established between the interviewer and respondent?
✓ Is there a standard protocol?
✓ Does the interviewee understand the questions and feel comfortable answering?
✓ Are probes and other follow-up questions used when needed?
✓ Is the interviewer biased?
✓ Is the interview rushed?
✓ Are interviewer evaluations and interpretations recorded?
✓ Is the interview done the same way for all participants, in similar settings?

Observational data-gathering techniques for quantitative studies vary in several ways. Some observations are made in natural settings and others in controlled settings. Some observations may be guided by a general problem and there may be flexibility about what and whom to observe, whereas other observations may be specific and highly structured. Observers may be "detached" from the participants, even unknown to them, or they may have some type of relationship. Quantitative observations are controlled and systematic, and rely on numbers to summarize what has been observed.

On the Nature of Inference

A major factor in observational research is the extent to which the person who is observing and recording the behavior makes inferences, or judgments, about what is seen or heard. Although there will always be some degree of inference, the amount can vary considerably. At one extreme, as illustrated in Figure 7.10, the observer may record specific, easily identified behaviors such as "asks a question" or "wrote objectives on the board." These are called **low-inference** observations because the observer does not have to interpret (very much, at least) what is seen and heard. Either the behaviors are present or not, and the observer makes no judgment about their meaning. The recorded behaviors are then summarized and interpreted, often by someone else; most of the inference is made after all the data have been gathered. At the other extreme are observations that require the observer to make and record a judgment or interpretation. This approach, referred to as **high-inference** observation, requires the observer both to see relevant behaviors and to make inferences about their meaning. A common example of high-inference observation is that of a principal who, on the basis of visits to a classroom, rates a teacher as excellent, good, adequate, or poor on dimensions of teaching such as "classroom management" or "formative assessment."

With low-inference observation, reliability is usually high, but you need to understand how the recorded behavior is translated into conclusions. Translation can be a complex process and will involve some degree of arbitrary judgment. For example, in a study of motivation, how many times does a teacher need to give helpful feedback to be judged competent in encouraging appropriate motivation? Or, how many student questions during a class period indicates acceptable student engagement? Critics of low-inference systems also point out that teaching and learning may not be understood well by a simple recording of specific behaviors, without considering context.

The most structured observational techniques are found in controlled settings and use a systematized observational schedule to record specific behaviors. A detailed form or procedure, identified before the study begins, is used to record specific

Figure 7.10 High and Low Observational Inference

Low Inference	High Inference
• Number of times a counselor asked empathy questions	• Effective questioning by a counselor
• How often the principal solicited feedback from teachers	• Appropriate leadership style
• Number of instances teachers paired specific comments with notice of incorrect answers	• Good use of feedback

behaviors. Low-inference observations are made, and methods of summarizing and analyzing the observations are specified in advance. The emphasis is on objectivity and standardization.

In high-inference observation, the competency of the observer in making correct judgments is critical. Training high-inference observers is more difficult, and reliability is often lower, as compared with low-inference observation. You should look for any factors that may bias a high-inference observer, such as the researcher also acting as the observer or observers knowing about the expected results of the study.

Some observations fall between the low- and high-inference extremes. One such approach is to make high-inference ratings and indicate the specific behaviors and contextual factors that led to the inference implied in the judgment.

Most observational studies in education take place in the field, in schools and classrooms where behavior occurs naturally. From a quantitative perspective, the typical approach is to define the behaviors to be observed, identify a system of coding and recording them, train observers to use the system, and go to the school or other setting and make the observations. The intent is to measure the frequency and/or duration of predetermined behaviors.

The behaviors can be recorded in several ways. The most common approach is to indicate the number of times a behavior occurs during a specified time period (event-based frequency). The observer has a list of behaviors that may be observed, and every time a behavior is seen, a tally mark is placed next to that behavior. Sometimes the observer will observe for a short time, such as 1 to 3 minutes, then record all the behaviors seen in that time; sometimes the recording is done continuously. Excerpt 7.5 describes how low inference observational data, using frequencies from several items, were combined for more globally described subscales (also notice the use of Cronbach's alpha for estimating internal consistency reliability).

Observer Effects

The observer is the key to observational research, and the quality of the results depends to a great extent on how the observer and the procedures for observing affect the participants. We consider several potential limitations here.

EXCERPT 7.5
Frequency-Based Observational Data

More specifically, observed student behaviors were the key outcomes of interest in the current study. Observers documented the frequency of negative student behaviors, and included any student acts of noncompliance, horseplay, physical aggression, verbal aggression, and profanity observed. The global ratings include the following student subscales: aggression (5 items; e.g., students argue with peers, students verbally harass and threaten others; α = .65), and positive student behaviors (6 items; e.g., students consistently follow rules appropriate to settings, treat their peer with respect; α = .87)... items were marked on a 0 to 4 point scale (for aggression, never occurred [0 times], rarely occurred [1 time], occurred a few times [2-3 times], sometimes occurred 4-6 times], often occurred 6+ times]; for positive student behaviors, never, seldom, some of the time, a lot of the time, and almost continuously). (p. 107)

SOURCE: Cash, A. H., Debnam, K. J., Waasdorp, T. E., Wahl, M., & Bradshaw, C. P. (2018). Adult and student interactions in nonclassroom settings. *Journal of Educational Psychology, 111*(1), 104–117.

OBSERVER BIAS **Observer bias** is a type of error that occurs because of the background, expectations, or frame of reference of the observer. For example, if an observer of counselor techniques has a predetermined idea that a particular approach is best (e.g., cognitive behavioral therapy), and the counselor who is observed does not use this style, the observer may have a tendency to bias the observations in a negative direction. On the other hand, bias in a positive direction may occur when observers record the behavior of a style of counseling they believe to be most effective.

There are three procedures researchers use to reduce potential observer bias. First, there should be evidence that the observer has been trained and will provide reliable results. Second, if possible, two or more observers should independently observe at least some of the same behavior. Third, it is important to anticipate and control prejudice, including prejudice toward or against certain races; toward gender; and toward other characteristics such as physical attractiveness, social class, and exceptionalities.

CONTAMINATION **Contamination** occurs when the observer has knowledge of one or more aspects of the study, and this knowledge affects subsequent observations. One type of contamination results from knowledge of the study's hypothesis. If the observers know which group is "expected" to do best, for example, they may unconsciously favor that group. Contamination also occurs if the same observer is assigned to more than one type of group. For example, if an observer begins with a group of known "expert" teachers and then observes "poor" teachers, the second group will probably receive lower ratings than they deserve because of the comparison. Contamination is less likely to occur when specific behaviors are targeted for observation, observers are trained, the observers do not know about expected outcomes, and they are not told which groups are experimental and control.

HALO EFFECT The **halo effect** occurs when an observer allows an initial impression about a person or group to influence subsequent observations. For example, an initial positive impression about a teacher, based on the way the teacher begins a class, may create an overall positive "halo" so ratings of subsequent behaviors, such as questioning or monitoring of classroom activities, are higher than they should be. The halo effect is an inappropriate generalization about all aspects of the observation. It is suspected in ratings of different behaviors when all the ratings are the same. The halo effect, like other sources of errors in observation, is reduced with adequate training.

Similar to questionnaires on different topics and areas of study, hundreds of observation schedules have been developed for quantitative data gathering. Furthermore, as with questionnaires, it is best to access these to either find one that fits well with what you want to study, or modify one. Previously used observational instruments and procedures will likely have evidence for reliability and validity, and have a tested protocol.

Excerpt 7.6 is from a study that measured children's engagement with structured observation. Notice how the researchers identified specific behaviors that were used for measuring engagement.

EXCERPT 7.6
Structured Observation of Children

As part of this procedure, the percentage of children engaged in one of four main activity categories was determined. The activity categories, along with two subcategories were: engagement with adults (attention or interactional), with peers (attention or interactional), with materials (premastery or mastery), and nonengagement (active or passive). Children were scored as engaged when they displayed certain behaviors, such as visually attending to a peer or adult (attentional engagement) or interacting with a peer or adult (interactional engagement). Children involved with materials, whether the involvement was developmentally or situationally appropriate, were counted as engaged. *Active non-engagement* was defined as behaviors that were physical (e.g., running across the room, jumping on the couch, crying without caregiver's support), whereas *passive nonengagement* included times when the child was involved in aimless wandering, staring off into the distance, and so on. . . . Observations were conducted in the programs during free play, once a week for 4 weeks. Each observation lasted 30 minutes and was conducted by graduate students in child development. During this time, the child engagement measure was completed. To complete the group engagement measure, observers stood/sat in an unobtrusive location in the program as to not disturb the routine, play, or interactions, but where they could see and hear the children. If a program used more than one space as a learning environment, the observer followed the children. The observer used a stopwatch to time 5-minute intervals. At the end of each five-minute interval, the coder coded each child's current engagement. The process continued for six intervals. (p. 65)

SOURCE: Ota, C. L., Baumgartner, J. J., & Berghout Austin, A. M. (2013). Provider stress and children's active engagement. *Journal of Research in Childhood Education, 27*(1), 61–73. Copyright © Taylor and Francis Group.

Problems in Measuring "Noncognitive" Traits and Dispositions

Compared with cognitive measures such as achievement and aptitude tests, noncognitive instruments generally have lower reliability and less evidence for validity. One difficulty with noncognitive measurement is clearly defining what is being assessed, based on an adequate conceptual framework. There are different definitions of terms such as *attitude, belief, value,* and *personality.* Thus, the same labels can be used, but what is being measured can be different. An "attitude" toward mathematics can mean one thing in one study and something different in another study. Consequently, when reading research that uses noncognitive instruments, it is important to examine the *operational* definition of the trait that is being measured, which is best accomplished by reading the actual items in the scale or schedule. The results are most meaningful in regard to the way in which the trait is measured, not by how the researcher labels or communicates the findings in titles or conclusions.

Most noncognitive measures are susceptible to two sources of error: response set and faking. **Response set** is the tendency of the participant to respond in the same way, regardless of the content of the items—for example, always selecting the neutral category or the "strongly agree" category in a Likert scale or marking the favorable adjectives on a semantic differential. An especially troublesome type of response set is **social desirability**. This is the tendency to respond to the items in a way that is socially acceptable or desirable, regardless of the true or real attitudes or beliefs of the individual. For example, if a question asks students about their alcohol consumption, the responses may be influenced by what the students think is socially accepted. Or, students may indicate an interest in attending college because that is more desirable socially than not attending college. Response set tends to be more prevalent on Likert-type inventories, with ambiguous items, and in situations in which the respondents are not motivated to give honest answers. In evaluating noncognitive instrumentation, it is best to look for techniques that lessen response set, such as forced-choice responses, short inventories, an approximately equal number of positively and oppositely worded items, alternating positive and negative adjectives in the same column on a semantic differential, ensurance of anonymity or confidentiality, and motivation of participants.

Faking occurs when participants give deliberately inaccurate indications of their attitudes, personality, or interests. Faking usually depends on the purpose of the test and the consequences of the results. Sometimes it occurs if the researcher indicates that certain results will have positive consequences; sometimes participants fake responses simply to please the researcher (which is why someone other than the researcher probably should administer the instrument or conduct the observation). In other situations, faking occurs because the results have important consequences for the individual—for example, to determine admission to college or selection for a management training program. Occasionally, participants will fake to provide a more negative picture. Faking can be controlled by establishing good rapport with the participants and proper motivation, by disguising the purpose of the instrument and research, and by using a forced-choice format. There are also techniques to detect faking. Whatever the approach, it is best for the instrument to be pilot tested with similar individuals to ensure that problems such as response set and faking are controlled as much as possible.

A summary of problems faced by researchers using questionnaires, interviews, and observations for obtaining noncognitive information is provided in Table 7.3. Look for these problems when determining the quality of the measurement.

Table 7.3 Problems for Researchers Measuring "Noncognitive" Traits

Questionnaire

Multiple sources of error, especially over time.

Unclear definitions of the trait.

Response set, especially social desirability.

Faking; participant motivation to respond seriously and honestly.

Interview

Depends on skills of the interviewer.

Interviewer bias.

Low sample size.

Contamination.

Expensive and time-consuming.

No anonymity for participants.

Halo effect.

Interviewer characteristics may influence participants.

Procedure for recording responses may not be accurate or may influence participants.

Observation

High inference depends on quality of observers to make judgments; may be less reliable.

Low inference reliable but often too artificial.

Observer bias.

Contamination, especially if observer knows which group is experimental and which is control.

Halo effect.

Check for Understanding 4

4a.   What are three characteristics of preparing for and conducting good interviews?

4b.   Under what circumstances would it be better to use observation rather than using questionnaires or interviews?

Author Reflection   *Which method of collecting quantitative data is best? I have used all the approaches in this chapter and have found that the richest, most relevant data come from well-done interviews. There is simply no substitute for engaging another person in a face-to-face setting. Yes, it is time-consuming, but the advantage of being able to probe and observe nonverbal communication is invaluable. There is something about direct personal interaction that is compelling, even when determining what someone knows and can do from an achievement standpoint.*

Furthermore, my experience is that respondents are generally very honest. This is what I have found with adults, children, and adolescents, whether audio-recorded or not. Generally, people—especially most education professionals—want to be helpful. As long as you have the resources, interviewing is a great way to obtain great data.

Sources for Locating and Evaluating Existing Instruments

Literally thousands of instruments have been used in educational research over the past 50 years. When you read research, you will encounter many different measures. How will you know whether they are providing valid and reliable information? Often, there is insufficient information in an article to make an informed judgment. And if you need to construct a questionnaire or test, it is important to see what already exists. You can find descriptions and reviews for a number of existing instruments. Check the sources in Table 7.4. Some of these sources may seem dated, but they can still provide useful examples of well-done instruments. Some of the sources summarize the instruments; others provide a critique as well.

In addition to these sources, an excellent way to obtain information about an instrument is to contact its developer. The developer may be able to send you a technical manual and may know about other researchers who have used the instrument. Technical manuals are almost always available for published tests.

Finally, you may want to try a computer search of journal articles that have up-to-date information on critical evaluations of validity and reliability and other studies that have used the instrument. In the ERIC database, a proximity search is one alternative. In a proximity search, terms that make up the name of the instrument, or related terms, are used to locate relevant articles. Google Scholar is also an excellent source for identifying instruments, as is the Internet more generally. For example, to find instruments that assess student attitudes toward testing, try typing in "measures of student attitudes about testing" and similar phrases.

Table 7.4 Sources of Information About Available Instruments

Source	Information Provided
Index to Tests Used in Education Dissertations (Fabiano, 1989)	Describes tests and test populations used in dissertations from 1938 to 1980; keyed by title and selected descriptors.
ERIC	The ERIC database can be used to locate instruments in two ways. One approach is to find research articles and reports that include a measure of a construct that can be used as a keyword or descriptor in the search. Another good strategy is to go to the Advanced Search web page, enter your keyword or descriptor, and then go to the Publication Type or Document Type pull-down menu and click on "Tests/Questionnaires."
ETS Test Collection and Test Link Database	Test Link is a database that contains descriptions of more than 25,000 previously administered tests, surveys, and assessment tools that are contained in the Educational Testing Service (ETS) Test Collection. This library contains instruments collected from the early 1900s to the present and is the largest such compilation in the world. The database can be searched by author, title, topic, or date. Each record contains information about the test, including an abstract. Once identified, a test can be ordered from ETS. The collection also includes materials that accompany tests, such as administration guidelines, scoring procedures, and psychometric information.
Tests: A Comprehensive Reference for Assessments in Psychology, Education, and Business, 6th ed. (Maddox, 2008)	Provides a description of more than 2,000 published tests from more than 164 publishers in psychology, education, and business, including purpose, cost, scoring, and publisher.
Test Critiques, Vols. 1–10 (Keyser & Sweetland, 1984, 1994)	Gives evaluations for widely used, newly published, and recently revised instruments in psychology, education, and business. Contains "user oriented" information, including practical applications and uses, as well as technical aspects and a critique by a measurement specialist. The companion, *Test Critiques Compendium,* reviews major tests from *Test Critiques* in one volume.
Handbook of Family Measurement Techniques (Touliatos, Perlmutter, Straus, & Holden, 2001)	This three-volume set provides overviews and reviews of hundreds of instruments used to measure family dynamics, including marital interaction, parenthood, child and parent adjustment, and roles.
Mental Measurements Yearbooks (MMYs), Buros Institute of Mental Measurements	Provides critical reviews of commercially available tests. References for most of the tests facilitate further research. The MMYs have been published periodically for 70 years (20th edition in 2017). Each new MMY edition provides reviews of only new or revised tests. The MMY contains descriptions of newly released or revised instruments. Thus, if a test has not been revised recently, information could be obtained by consulting an earlier edition. The MMY evaluations are available on Test Reviews Online, also sponsored by the Buros Institute. Test Reviews Online is a subscription service that allows searching by title, purpose, publisher, acronym, author, and scores. The database contains nearly 4000 commercially available tests.
Tests in Print (TIP)	Also published periodically by the Buros Institute. TIP provides a comprehensive index to the MMY by including brief descriptions of over 4000 commercially available instruments, intended uses, and a reference list of professional literature about each instrument. Tests in Print IX was published in 2016.
Handbook for Measurement and Evaluation in Early Childhood Education (Goodwin & Driscoll, 1980)	A comprehensive review of affective, cognitive, and psychomotor measures for young children.
Handbook of Research Design and Social Measurement, 6th ed. (Miller & Salkind, 2002)	Reviews and critiques popular social science measures.
Directory of Unpublished Experimental Mental Measures, Vol. 9 (Goldman & Mitchell, 2008)	Describes nearly 1,700 experimental mental measures that are not commercially available. Includes references, source, and purpose on topics ranging from educational adjustment and motivation to personality and perception.
Health and Psychosocial Instruments (HaPI)	Database that can be searched to identify published and unpublished instruments in health, education, and psychology.
APA databases	Search the PsycINFO database using the field category "tests and measures" and the PsycTESTS database to search for instruments by trait, names of tests, or author.
ProQuest Dissertations and Theses	Search this dissertation database for specific instruments as well as to identify instruments used to measure traits that have been used in dissertations.

Consumer (and Researcher) Tips
Criteria for Evaluating Quantitative Instrumentation

1. **Evidence for validity should be stated clearly.** Researchers should address validity by explicitly indicating the type of evidence that is presented, the results of analyses that establish validity, and how the evidence supports the inferences that are made. For evidence that does not match well with the participants or situation of the investigation, it is best to indicate why it is reasonable to believe that the results are appropriate and useful. References should cite previous research that supports the validity of the inferences. If possible, it is best to collect evidence for validity in a pilot or field test.

2. **Evidence for reliability should be stated clearly.** The reliability of all scores that are used in data analyses should be indicated, including the type of reliability estimate used. Reliability should be established in a pilot or field test with participants similar to those used in the research, and also reported for a study that shows original data. High reliability is especially important for results that show no "statistically significant" difference or relationship.

3. **The instruments should be clearly described.** Sufficient information about the instrument should be given to understand how the participants gave their responses. This information includes some idea of the type of item, which is often accomplished by providing examples. It is also necessary to indicate how the instrument is scored.

4. **The procedures for administering the instrument should be described clearly.** You need to know when the instrument was given and the conditions of its administration. Who gave the instrument to the participants? What did they know about the study? What were the participants told before they answered the questions? Did anything unusual happen during the administration? Was a script or protocol used? Did the participants understand the directions for completing the instrument? These questions are especially critical for standardized tests.

5. **Norms should be specified for norm-referenced interpretations.** The norms used to determine the results need to be clearly indicated. What is the nature of the norm group? Is it appropriate to the type of inferences that are made?

6. **Procedures for setting standards should be indicated for criterion-referenced/standards-based interpretations.** It is necessary to know how standards that are used to judge the results are set. Were experts consulted to verify the credibility of the standard? What is the difficulty level of the items in relation to the standard?

7. **The scores used in reporting results should be meaningful.** For many tests, standard scores or some type of derived scores are used in reporting the results. Whatever the scores, they should not distort the actual differences or relationships, either by inflating or deflating the apparent differences or relationships.

8. **Measures should avoid problems of response set and faking.** Researchers need to indicate how response set and faking are controlled for when measuring personality, attitudes, values, and interests. Special attention should be given to the manner in which the participants are motivated.

9. **Observers and interviewers should be trained.** Researchers must show that the observers and interviewers in studies have been trained to avoid such problems as bias, contamination, and halo effect. Interviewers need to know how not to ask leading questions and how to probe effectively. Interobserver reliability should be indicated.

10. **In high-inference observations, the qualifications of the observers to make sound professional judgments should be indicated.** With low-inference observations, reliability is usually high, but if high-inference observations are used, the characteristics and training of the observer are more important and should be specified.

11. **The effect of the interviewer or observer should be minimal.** Examine the characteristics of the interviewers. Could these traits create any error in the nature of the responses obtained? Were appropriate steps taken to establish a proper rapport with the participants? Any possible effects of the interviewer or observer on the participants should be noted.

Key Terms

Constructed response
Faking
Interview
  Leading questions
  Semistructured questions
  Structured questions
  Unstructured questions
Observation
  Contamination
  Halo effect
  High-inference
  Low-inference

Observer bias
Questionnaire
  Checklist
  Rank-ordered
  Response set
Scale
  Likert scale
  Semantic differential
Selected response
Sensitivity
Social desirability

Test
  Criterion-referenced/
    standards-based
  Norm-referenced
  Grade equivalent
  Standard score
  z-score
Standardized test
  Standardized achievement test
  Standardized aptitude test
  Standards-based tests

Discussion Questions

1. Why are locally developed instruments typically more sensitive with respect to validity but less sensitive with respect to reliability?

2. Why would a standardized test of problem-solving ability be less sensitive if used for a study about a new science curriculum compared to one that was specific to science?

3. Why is measuring "noncognitive" traits and dispositions so difficult?

4. Under what circumstances would it be better to use an interview rather than a questionnaire with fifth-grade students?

5. What would you look for in a methods section of an empirical article to evaluate the quality of the data collection method and procedures?

Application Exercise

1. With another student, identify a "noncognitive" trait or disposition that you would like to measure. Assuming that no existing measures are available, draft both a 10-item questionnaire and an interview protocol that could be used to gather the data. Use the questionnaire to gather data from 10 college students; use the interview to gather data from six other college students. What did you find? Compare the results and evaluate the quality of the items to determine which would be most credible. What changes would you make to revise both the questionnaire items and interview questions?

Check for Understanding Answers

1a. An insensitive measure would make it much less likely to find the signal: significant relationships or differences.

1b. Validity impacts sensitivity because if the measure is not clearly focused and specific to the variable, there are other traits that are included in the scores so that there is less likelihood of capturing the construct and more noise. Measures that are not reliable lessen validity and contribute greater amounts of noise.

2a. Off the shelf" tests are previously prepared with good technical evidence and often standardization; "locally developed" are constructed by the researcher and may have greater sensitivity.

2b. With criterion-referenced/standards-based interpretations, the basis of the result depends on a level of performance, while a norm-referenced interpretation shows comparison to others who have taken the test.

2c. Because they may be insensitive.

3a. Take your pick: there are multiple sources of error; vague trait definitions; response set; social desirability; taking; participant motivation; honesty.

3b. Take your pick from Figures 7.7 and 7.8 and explain each (e.g., a cluttered format may create confusion; double-barreled questions lead to unreliable scores).

4a. Take your pick: Having a structured interview guide; pilot testing; training; audio-recording; establishing rapport; using a standard protocol; using standardized contexts; using probes; eliminating interviewer bias; allowing adequate time.

4b. Observation is best when naturally occurring behavior needs to be recorded; when it is helpful to consider context; when it is difficult to operationalize variables.

Chapter 8
Nonexperimental Quantitative Research Designs

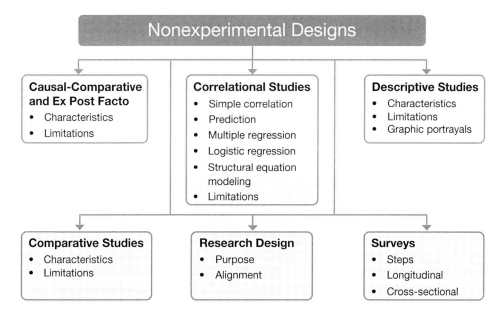

Nonexperimental Designs

Causal-Comparative and Ex Post Facto
- Characteristics
- Limitations

Correlational Studies
- Simple correlation
- Prediction
- Multiple regression
- Logistic regression
- Structural equation modeling
- Limitations

Descriptive Studies
- Characteristics
- Limitations
- Graphic portrayals

Comparative Studies
- Characteristics
- Limitations

Research Design
- Purpose
- Alignment

Surveys
- Steps
- Longitudinal
- Cross-sectional

Learning Outcomes

8.1 Identify and explain the importance of two key principles of effective quantitative research designs.

8.2 Understand the essential characteristics and limitations of using descriptive and comparative designs to investigate relationships.

8.3 Understand the essential characteristics and limitations of using correlational and predictive designs to investigate relationships.

8.4 Know the characteristics and limitations of causal comparative and ex post facto studies.

8.5 Identify the steps taken to design and employ an effective paper or electronic survey.

Chapter Road Map

Now we move on to commonly employed quantitative research designs. In this chapter, we consider four types of nonexperimental research designs: *descriptive, comparative, correlational,* and *ex post facto.* Identifying and understanding these designs will enable you to know whether they are appropriate for answering your research question and what to look for and ask about to understand research weaknesses, limitations, and mistakes. We also take a look at survey research designs.

Quantitative Research Design

Learning Outcome 8.1   Identify and explain the importance of two key principles of effective quantitative research designs.

Research design refers to the plan, structure, and procedures of the study to collect data, and in the case of experiments, to implement interventions. It involves a number of key decisions that need to be made by the researcher, including how variables are conceptualized and measured, when and how data are collected or identified, the sample, and how interventions are carried out. To help you understand how these aspects work together, researchers use different categories or types of designs, which fall under the broad categories of quantitative/qualitative and experimental/nonexperimental. The specific designs help you know the essential purpose of the study as well as the logic of the analysis. Thus, for example, if you see that the study is experimental, you know the purpose is to test a causal relationship. If it is a simple correlational design, it will not examine a causal relationship.

Two key principles should be kept in mind in considering research designs:

1. Is the research design clearly aligned with the research question, nature of the variables, and the way results are analyzed?
2. Is the design conceptualized and carried out to give you the best opportunity to find the signal about what is described, related, or predicted?

Aligning the research design with the research question is really important. Suppose the question is something like "What is the difference among first-year teachers' attitudes toward implementing a merit pay system?" The purpose and logic of this question is simply to gather data to describe attitudes. If your design is experimental—seeing whether an intervention to *change* teachers' attitudes was successful—the design would not be aligned with the question. Similarly, if the purpose of the research is to predict which teachers are most likely to receive excellent student ratings, without an intervention, the purpose and logic would still be nonexperimental, so an experimental design would be *un*aligned.

Likewise, the data analysis and way of presenting results need to be aligned. If you are looking at whether fourth-grade boys have a more positive attitude toward math than fourth-grade girls, the analysis should compare these two, showing whether they are different. If you want to examine the relationship between attendance and achievement using continuous measures of both, you will want to use a correlational analysis. This relates to the nature of the variables—primarily whether they are categorical or continuous—and the scale of measurement. These characteristics often determine data analysis, and also need to be aligned. For example, you obviously wouldn't use a mean score to describe gender.

The second principle is the key to doing good quantitative research. It is so critical that I want to highlight it as follows:

> *A good design provides the best prospect of finding what is true about what is studied (the signal).*

The reason this is so important is that it guides the decisions you make about the design so that noise is limited, and the results are important because they approximate what is real. This means that the nature of the result is essentially less important than the design, at least in the sense that, as a researcher, you are not trying to prove that something is true (like a biased study might), but you *are* searching for the true signal. That is, knowing that there really is *no* relationship can be just as important as knowing that there is a relationship. As long as the design is well conceptualized, the results are worthwhile, however they turn out. On the other hand, if the study is poorly designed, the results are problematic. There will be too much potential or actual noise to accurately portray the signal.

Author Reflection *So how do you know if you'll have the right design? In my experience, your best guidance, beyond applying principles of good design, is to work with others or at least have colleagues give you feedback. My designs are almost always improved with comments from others, no matter how good I initially think they are!*

Check for Understanding 1

1a. Explain why alignment between the research question and design is needed.

Types of Nonexperimental Research Designs

There are several types of nonexperimental research designs. Actually, you will find that there are different ways to categorize these designs, and no one right way to do it. I have identified four types that make sense to me; others might choose a different conceptualization (e.g., not differentiate between descriptive and correlational designs, or might consider correlational one type of descriptive. Some would contend that anything that is not experimental is descriptive). No matter—what is important is to understand how the nature of the design guides your judgments about credibility of the conclusions.

The essence of quantitative nonexperimental designs is that the researcher has no *direct* control over an intervention (treatment). This means that the researcher does not implement and monitor a planned intervention. The emphasis on lack of direct control is critical. There are many research opportunities in which there is an identified intervention, but it is not controlled by the researcher. I refer to these as *causal–comparative*, rather than experimental designs, because of the absence of active, intentional control. Also, sometimes we can look back at what has happened differently to groups we want to compare because they experienced different interventions (ex post facto), but there is also no direct control. Therefore, more than anything else, nonexperimental designs are those in which there is no explicitly conceived and managed intervention that occurs as part of the ongoing study.

Another reason for this way of defining nonexperimental is that, as you may have already figured out, the issue of "cause" is a separate consideration. Not too long ago, "nonexperimental" was characterized as a type of research that you could only rarely use to make causal conclusions, in contrast to what you do with experiments. But there are now many ways in which nonexperimental designs can examine causal explanations. Think about medical research that, nonexperimentally, examines the relationship between asbestos exposure and cancer. You cannot study this with an experiment by exposing some people to asbestos and comparing subsequent rates of cancer to a control group! The best you can do is look at the relationship nonexperimentally; there are ways to do that to uncover the truth about what the exposure probably means for developing cancer. (Remember, science is rarely settled—that is one of its major tenets.)

In one sense, then, nonexperimental studies investigate the current or past status of something. This general purpose leads to other reasons for nonexperimental designs—reasons based on relationships, comparisons, predictions, and causal explanations—which, in turn, are used to characterize the different types. You also need to recognize that in most nonexperimental studies there may be two or more purposes, with different data analyses. Part of a study could be descriptive and another part correlational. Therefore, as we consider the different types, keep in mind that more than one can be used in a single study.

Table 8.1 provides a summary of the nonexperimental designs we will consider, based on purpose and data analysis. Keep in mind that nonexperimental studies can be planned and carried out by collecting and analyzing data, or conducted by examining and analyzing data that have already been collected. The latter is often called **secondary data analysis**, meaning subsequent analyses after the data have been collected by someone else for some other purpose. Secondary data analysis has become very popular with the increasing availability of large data sets and developments in statistical analyses that can be used to parse out meaningful relationships, including causal explanations.

A word or two is needed about the difference between *descriptive data*, on the one hand, and *descriptive analyses*. Descriptive data are simple indices for indicating frequencies, percentages, central tendency, and variation that are calculated from a set of numbers, or data elements. These tools for data simplification are then used to characterize a phenomenon with descriptive analyses, often showing meaningful patterns in the data. Whether identified as descriptive research or descriptive analyses, the goal is to summarize data meaningfully to answer research questions focused on an accurate depiction of "what is" (Loeb et al., 2017), whether that is a characterization of something, patterns, trends, relationships, or explanations. In other words, a descriptive research study "stands alone" as an investigation. Descriptive data are the indices that summarize sets of numbers. So, a database would not be descriptive data or descriptive analyses. (But given the increasingly rich and available sets of databases there are many opportunities to use those data elements for meaningful descriptive analyses).

Both descriptive data and descriptive analyses are essential for all kinds of quantitative research, including experiments (e.g., descriptive analyses often elucidate why an intervention causes change). As we will see, they are needed for appropriate interpretations of more complex statistical findings. Descriptions are also needed to portray the context and conditions of research that are important for interpretation and generalization of the findings.

Author Reflection *Sometimes my students get hung up over categorizing and labeling the different types of designs. I understand this, but the reality is that there are few absolute rules, and what one researcher considers causal–comparative might be considered ex post facto by another researcher. As is often said, the devil is in the details. What matters most is what the researcher does, not what it is called.*

Table 8.1 Types of Nonexperimental Research Designs

Design	Purpose	Typical Data and Analyses
Descriptive	To provide a description of the what and how much of a phenomenon	Frequencies, percentages, means, medians, range, graphic depictions
Comparative	To compare dependent variable values of two or more levels of an independent variable	Comparing means or medians
Correlational	To show how two variables are related, using a correlation coefficient	Using bivariate and other correlational procedures
Predictive	To show how well one or more variables predict something	Correlational, using regression
Causal–comparative	To suggest causal explanations by comparing groups that receive naturally occurring interventions	Comparing means
Ex post facto	To suggest causal explanations by comparing groups that received different interventions in the past	Comparing means

Descriptive Designs

Learning Outcome 8.2   Understand the essential characteristics and limitations of using descriptive and comparative designs to investigate relationships.

As noted, descriptive research or analysis refers to a wide range of studies, from those that simply examine what or how much of something exists, to some that show patterns and relationships. I have used the term descriptive design to refer to research that focuses solely on the "what" or "how much" questions of descriptive research, addressing such questions as

"What strategies do college professors use to prepare for lectures?"
"How much time, on average, does it take for students to graduate from college?"
"How have adolescent attitudes changed over the past five decades?"
"What percentage of students attend different types of after-school programs?"

The description is usually in the form of statistics such as frequencies or percentages, averages, and sometimes variability. Often, graphs and other visual images of the results are used.

Descriptive designs are particularly valuable when an area is first investigated. For example, there has been much research on the nature of classroom culture and its relationship to student attitudes and learning. A first step in this research was to describe adequately what is meant by "classroom culture," initially by a clear constitutive definition and conceptual framework, then operationally. Student self-report surveys, which assess characteristics such as how students talk and act toward one another; how they feel about the teacher and learning; and feelings of openness, acceptance, trust, respect, rejection, hostility, and cooperation, are used to describe culture. Once this understanding was achieved, the research then moved on to see whether various dimensions of culture could be related to student learning and teacher satisfaction, and, ultimately, whether culture could be controlled with interventions to examine causal relationships. However, the first step was to have really good descriptions. Or, suppose you want to do a study on the relationship between principals' leadership styles and teachers' attitudes. You need to be sure that you have an adequate description of *leadership styles* of principals and *attitudes* of teachers, and it may take several descriptive studies to get to that point.

Here are additional examples of questions that can be investigated appropriately with descriptive research designs:

What do teachers think about magnet schools?

How often do students write papers?

What is the nature of the papers students are required to write?

What percentage of students score above 1200 on the SAT?

What forms of communication are used in the school district?

How often are higher-order questions used in the classroom?

What type of feedback do teachers use, and when do they use it?

Excerpts 8.1 and 8.2 illustrate descriptive designs. Excerpt 8.1 is a summary of some of the descriptive findings from a survey of teachers' approaches to classroom

EXCERPTS 8.1 AND 8.2
Descriptive Nonexperimental Designs

Part Two of the ACAI, Perceived Skill in Classroom Assessment, asked teachers to identify their perceived level of perceived skill in assessment (Table 4). The two items with the highest means were, 'I provide useful feedback to students to improve their learning' ($M = 3.82$, $SD = .92$), and 'I provide timely feedback to students to improve their learning' ($M = 3.77$, $SD = .95$). The two items with the lowest means were, 'I engage students in monitoring their own learning and using assessment information to develop their learning skills and personalised learning plans' ($M = 3.15$, $SD = 1.10$), and 'I communicate purposes and uses of assessment to parents/guardians when appropriate' ($M = 3.04$, $SD = 1.41$). This suggests that teachers have the greatest perceived skill about providing useful and timely feedback to students, and least perceived skill about engaging parents and students in the assessment process. (pp. 365–367)

SOURCE: DeLuca, C., Valiquette, A., Coombs, A., LaPoint-McEwan, D./, & Luhanga, U. (2018). Teachers' approaches to classroom assessment: A large–scale survey. *Assessment in Education: Principles, Policy & Practice, 16*(3), 355–377.

Participants were asked about their use of common instructional activities using a 4-point Likert scale indicating whether they use the activity frequently, often, seldom, or never. The instructional activity used frequently by the largest number of participants (18.0%) was the use of technology/internet to inquire about and explore specifc topics of interest. This activity was also selected as being used often by the largest number of participants (37.5%). Three instructional activities were used seldom by the largest number of participants, including cooperative learning projects (38.0%), simulation including role-playing and case studies (41.5%), and peer revision writing groups (42.9%). Thirty percent (30.6%) indicated they never use simulation, including role-playing and case studies during instruction. (p. 40)

SOURCE: Henry, L. (2013). Literacy content knowledge expertise among adult education providers in Kentucky. *Journal of Research and Practice for Adult Literacy, Secondary, and Basic Education, 2*(1), 36–48.

assessment, using means and standard deviation in the presentation of results. The goal of the study in Excerpt 8.2 was to obtain a description of Kentucky adult education programs, using a survey. Some of the results are shown in the excerpt, using simple percentages of respondents.

Consumer (and Researcher) Tips
Criteria for Evaluating Descriptive Designs

1. **Make sure there is alignment between questions and analyses.** See whether there is a clear connection between each of the research questions and the analyses. It is confusing if there are results that are not well aligned, such as when new questions are introduced in the results section. You could spot this if the results narrative said something like, "In addition, we decided to examine the relationship…" This suggests an ad hoc analysis, which, though occasionally justified, should be thought through before conducting the study.

2. **Conclusions about relationships among variables should be made with caution.** An important limitation of descriptive studies is that relationship conclusions *generally* are not warranted from simple descriptive data. It is easy to make assumptions from simple descriptions about how two or more variables may be related, but be wary. For instance, suppose a study describes the types of questions students and teachers ask in a classroom and reports that teachers ask "low-level" questions and students do not ask questions at all. It would be tempting to conclude that there is a relationship between these variables—namely, the more teachers ask "low-level" questions, the fewer questions students ask. However, to address the question of relationship, teachers would also have to ask "high-level" questions.

3. **Participants and instrumentation should be well described.** When evaluating descriptive research, pay particular attention to participant selection and instrumentation. You should know whether the sample was made up of volunteers, whether the results would have been different if other individuals had been included, and whether the participants were sensitive to what was being measured. The instrumentation section should have documentation of validity and reliability, and a clear and complete description of the procedures for gathering the data. It is important to know when the data were collected, by whom, and under what circumstances. For example, an observational description of what is occurring in a class may differ, depending on the role of the observer (e.g., teacher, principal, or parent).

Relationships in Nonexperimental Designs

Before we examine comparative and correlational designs, a word or two is needed on the nature of relationships among variables. All quantitative research that is not simply descriptive is interested in relationships. (Remember, though, some use "descriptive" as a category that includes correlational and comparative.) A **relationship**, or *association*, is found when one variable varies systematically with another variable. Relationship is illustrated in Figure 8.1. Here, the variables of interest are grade level and self-concept. You can see that a relationship exists between grade level and self-concept because there are progressively fewer students with a high self-concept as grade level increases. This example shows how relationship can be investigated by comparing different groups. In this case, there is a negative relationship because as one variable increases (grade level), the other variable decreases (number of students with high self-concept). Relationships are, of course, also investigated with correlational designs.

Relationships are important in our understanding of educational phenomena for several reasons. First, relationships allow us to make a preliminary identification of possible causes of students' achievement, teachers' performance, principals' leadership, and other important educational outcomes, and patterns of relationships help us identify causal explanations. Second, relationships help us confirm that certain variables may fruitfully be investigated in experiments. Before seeking to find whether an intervention is effective with an experiment, examine relationships first. If there is a weak relationship, it is unlikely that you will find a causal relationship. For example, you would be well advised to study the simple relationship between class size and achievement before randomly assigning students to large and small classes to see whether their achievement differs. Third, relationships allow us to predict the value of one variable from the values of other variables. Predictions are very important, without isolating causes (e.g., knowing what factors predict whether students will graduate helps identify individuals who may benefit from selected interventions).

Perhaps most important, the language of quantitative research is dominated by the term *relationship*, so you need to be fully informed about what is meant, how relationships can be examined, and what relationship studies can and cannot tell us. In the text that follows, you will see that relationships can be studied with both comparative and correlational designs. It is also helpful to understand that predictive, causal–comparative, ex post facto, and experimental studies all include examination of relationships. Thus, in one sense, all designs except simple descriptive ones investigate relationships of one kind or another.

Figure 8.1 Relationship Between Grade Level and Self-Concept

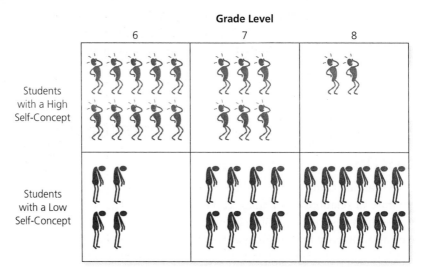

Comparative Designs

The purpose of **comparative designs** is to investigate the relationship of one variable to another, by simply examining whether the value of the dependent variable(s) in one non-intervened group is the same as or different from the value of the dependent variable(s) of other non-intervened groups. In other words, a comparative design contrasts two or more groups on one or many variables in the absence of an intervention. A simple example is a study of the relationship between gender identity and school grades. A sample of identified female students' grades could be compared with the grades of a sample of identified male students. The question is answered by comparing males to females on, say, grade point average for the same courses. The results show how differences in one variable, gender identity, "relate" to differences in another variable, grade point average. If the results show that females have a higher grade point average, this indicates that there is a relationship between the two variables. Notice, however, that this is not a *causal* relationship. We can predict, to a certain extent, whether females or males have a higher grade point average, but we do not know how being male or female affects or *causes* grade point average. That is, a relationship between two variables does not necessarily reveal an underlying cause or that one variable affects or changes another variable.

If the independent variable is changed from gender to grade level, the idea of "relationship" makes more sense. Then you could conclude, for example, that grade point average decreases as grade level increases. In this instance, both the variables are ordinal, which corresponds more clearly to the idea of relationship.

Another example is a study of the relationship between personality type and achievement. Suppose there are four types or categories of personality and a measure of reading achievement. A sample of students representing each personality type can be obtained, and the average reading achievement of the students in each group

Figure 8.2 Diagram of a Relationship Study Examining Group Differences

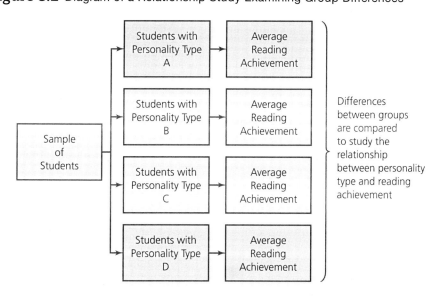

EXCERPTS 8.3 AND 8.4

Comparative Research Designs

Tables 2 and 3 present data describing the career survival of 4,788 elementary and 8,467 secondary teachers at their first assigned schools, hired by the LAUSD, who were observed between 2002–03 and 2008–09. The numbers indicate whether or not, and if yes, when these teachers exited the first assigned schools between the first year of observation period and 2008–09, which was the last year of observation period... both elementary and secondary school teachers were at the highest risk of leaving their initially assigned schools during the first year of teaching at their schools. This risk of exit in general decreases over time for both elementary and secondary teachers. In addition, the risk (i.e., the hazard probabilities) was slightly higher among secondary teachers than elementary teachers. (pp. 20–21)

SOURCE: Newton, X., Rivero, R., Fuller, B., & Dauter, K. (2018). Teacher turnover in organizational context: Staffing stability in Los Angeles charter, magnet, and regular public schools, *Teachers College Record, 120*(3), 1–36.

This study was designed to investigate counseling self-efficacy of graduate students in counselor education programs to determine whether Bandura's (1986) self-efficacy theory applies. Specifically, we investigated the relationship between the training background of graduate students and counselor self-efficacy.... In other words, we examined whether students from CACREP-accredited and non-CACREP-accredited counselor training programs would demonstrate differences in counseling self-efficacy. (p. 73)

SOURCE: Tang, M., Addison, K. D., LaSure-Bryant, D., Norman, R., O'Connell, W., & Stewart-Sicking, J. A. (2004). Factors that influence self-efficacy of counseling students: An exploratory study. *Counselor Education and Supervision, 44*, 70–80.

can be compared. This method also provides a measure of the differences among the groups, which represent a relationship between personality and achievement. Be careful, though, not to conclude that the personality *causes* differences in achievement. At best, we can predict that students with a particular type of personality will have higher or lower achievement. Personality may affect or influence achievement, but our relationship study does not give us a good measure of cause and effect. (Note that experimental studies are "comparative" too in the sense that dependent variable values are compared.) This hypothetical study is diagrammed in Figure 8.2.

Comparative designs were employed in Excerpts 8.3 and 8.4. In Excerpt 8.3, teachers from Los Angeles were compared with respect to grade level and type of school. In Excerpt 8.4, the study examined whether graduate students from a CACREP (an accrediting agency for school counseling programs) program have stronger counselor self-efficacy than graduates of non-CACREP programs.

Consumer (and Researcher) Tips
Criteria for Evaluating Comparative Designs

1. **Participants, instrumentation, and procedures should be well described.** As in descriptive designs, it is important to clearly and completely describe the participants, instruments used, and procedures for gathering the data. In comparative designs, it is also important to know whether individuals who are in different groups have unique characteristics that could better explain differences on the dependent variable than could be determined by the independent variable. For

example, suppose a researcher drew a sample of first-grade students from one school and compared the students to second-graders from a different school on attitudes toward reading. Even if more positive attitudes were found for the second-graders, this result may have been because of differences between the student populations (e.g., one school serving a higher socioeconomic level, or one school being private, the other public) rather than grade level.

2. **Specify the criteria for establishing different groups.** It is important to know how the different groups that are compared are formed. In some studies, the criterion or procedure for forming the groups is self-evident, such as studies that compare males to females, but in many studies, the procedure used to form the groups is important for interpretation of the results. For example, suppose a study is designed to compare participation in athletics of low-ability students and high-ability students. How the researcher identifies "high ability" and "low ability" is important. What measure, if any, was used to assess ability? How were the groups formed? One approach would be to take all the students and divide them into two ability groups on the basis of the median ability score of the group as a whole (median split technique). Or, the researcher could take the highest and lowest third or quartile of students. Another approach would be to establish groups by how the students compared with the national norms, rather than just each other. You can see that several approaches are possible. Even though none of them is necessarily better or more correct than the others, some are more sensitive to finding differences. It is more likely, for instance, to find differences in athletic participation if the groups represent the lowest and highest third, based on ability, rather than by splitting the groups into two halves based on the median.

3. **Rarely infer causation from comparative research designs.** It is important to refrain from concluding that a causal relationship exists as a result of findings from a comparative design. The most accurate result with a comparative design is that a relationship does or does not exist, or that there are or are not significant differences between the groups, but significant relationships or differences do not necessarily suggest a *causal* relationship. This principle is easy to overlook because some comparative designs seem to logically establish a causal connection between the independent and dependent variables. For instance, suppose it is reported that students from private schools outscore students from public schools on measures of achievement. It is tempting to conclude that the reason, or cause, of the difference is the nature of the school (private or public). However, there are many other possible explanations, such as differences in parental involvement, socioeconomic status of students, curriculum used, and quality of teachers.

Here is another example. You want to see whether watching violence on TV affects the amount of aggressive behavior that is exhibited. You identify two groups of children, one that watches a lot of violence and one that watches little violence, and then you measure aggressive behavior. There is no intervention; you are simply comparing these two groups. You find a positive relationship—the group of children watching more violence have more aggressive behavior. Causation, which might seem logical, cannot be determined. There are two reasons, illustrated in Figure 8.3. First, you do not really know whether watching violence caused aggressive behavior, or whether aggressive behavior caused a change in how much TV violence was watched. Second, there may be additional variables associated with either TV watching or aggressive behavior that could better explain the relationship. For instance, the children who watch more violence may live in neighborhoods that have more crime, which causes more aggressive behavior. Or perhaps the crime rate influences TV viewing habits far more than being aggressive does. The key is that the design does not enable you to

Figure 8.3 Two Reasons That Causation Cannot Be Concluded from a Comparative Design

1. The direction of the impact is not known.

Does watching violence cause aggressive behavior?

Or does aggressive behavior cause watching more violence on TV?

2. Are there other variables associated with watching TV violence and/or aggressive behavior?

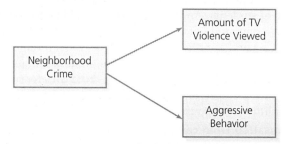

cull out these possible explanations, so you just do not know. At the same time, it is possible that watching TV does cause more aggression. You just cannot conclude that from this type of comparative design.

4. **Graphic presentations should not distort the results.** Because graphs are used frequently to present comparative results, you need to be careful in interpreting the image that is displayed. That is because you are more likely to remember the image than the numbers used to construct it. This is fine when the image is a reasonable representation of the numbers, but numbers can be manipulated in a graph to present different images. One type of distortion to look for is in the vertical dimensions of the graph, which typically shows values of the dependent variable. The size of the interval between different scores on this dimension is set by the researcher (sometimes based on what the computer program automatically creates). It turns out that this interval size greatly affects the resulting image. In fact, a crafty, if unethical, researcher can make fairly substantial differences appear quite small by decreasing the size of the intervals between scores or other measurement units. The researcher can also make small differences look large. For an illustration, examine the two graphic presentations in Figure 8.4. Although each graph has summarized the same data about expenditures per pupil, the visual results are different because the size of the interval between amounts is much smaller in one graph than in the other. Knowing the importance of size of interval can be really critical in presenting longitudinal data. If you want trends to look steeper, simply increase the intervals along the vertical axis.

Another example of how to show the same data that provides a completely different visual is shown in Figure 8.5, which shows changes in the percentages of students scoring proficient in a school division. Which one of these would the

Figure 8.4 Expenditures Per Pupil

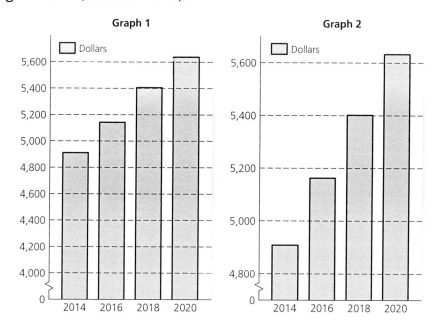

Figure 8.5 Percentage of Students Scoring Proficient on Accountability Test

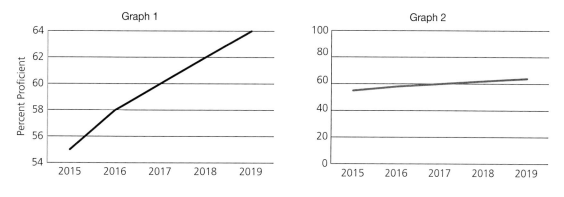

Figure 8.6 Corrected Graph of Percentage of Students Scoring Proficient on Accountability Test

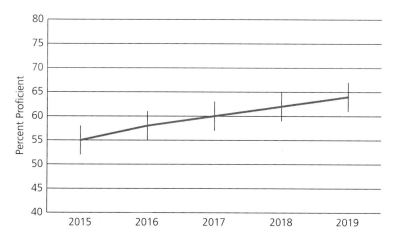

superintendent use? I think the answer is obvious. The "correct" image, one not as dramatic as Graph 1 nor as nearly a straight line in Graph 2, would include a measure of variability at each year to indicate gain beyond what occurs by chance variation (Figure 8.6). The results suggest a meaningful change from 2015 to 2018 and 2019, and from 2016 to 2019 (where the error bands don't overlap).

> **Author Reflection** *Over the years, I have seen many students conduct seemingly simple descriptive, comparative, or correlational studies and then become overwhelmed by the large number of analyses, tables, and variables. It is easy to include many variables and just "a few more" questions on a survey. Often, these variables or questions are "interesting" but are not directly related to the main purpose of the research. My experience is that you will learn more by focusing on a few variables or questions in depth than by measuring many variables with many questions and then spending arduous hours organizing and interpreting the results.*

Check for Understanding 2

2a. What are two reasons for not implying causation with a simple comparison of different groups?

2b. How does the way in which groups are defined affect the results of comparative studies?

Correlational Designs

Learning Outcome 8.3 Understand the essential characteristics and limitations of using correlational and predictive designs to investigate relationships.

Like the term "relationship," "correlation" is used extensively in quantitative research. The word can refer to a specific data analysis procedure and, as I have done in this chapter, as a way of describing a type of nonexperimental design. We examine three types of correlational designs here: simple, complex, and predictive.

Simple Correlational Designs

In a simple **correlational design**, two or more variables are related with the use of one or more correlational statistical procedures. As you recall from Chapter 6, correlational relationships are indicated by obtaining at least two scores from each participant. The pairs of scores are used to produce a scatterplot and to calculate a correlation coefficient. For example, variables such as self-efficacy, socioeconomic status, previous achievement, time on task, and amount of homework completed can be related to achievement, attitudes, self-concept, and motivation. Grades in student teaching can be related to principals' ratings of effective teaching. In each case, a correlation coefficient expresses the nature of the relationship between the variables.

Correlations are used in Excerpts 8.5 and 8.6 to report results. The first examined the relationship between school counselor demographic characteristics and leadership practices (note that gender must be converted to an ordinal variable); the second measured correlations among the quality of school facilities, school climate, and student achievement.

EXCERPTS 8.5 AND 8.6

Using Bivariate Correlations to Report Nonexperimental Results

Bivariate correlations (Pearson product-moment and Spearman's rank–order) were used to determine any relationships between school counselor demographics (gender, age, professional training, experience, and work setting) and leadership practices.... Negative relationships were indicated between leadership practices and graduate training... the year the most recent degree was obtained... and the number of school counselors employed in the school. (p. 112)

SOURCE: Mason, E. C. M., & McMahon, H. G. (2009). Leadership practices of school counselors. *Professional School Counseling, 13*(2), 107–115.

As Table II indicates, all three components of AC were positively correlated with SA in language, Pearson correlation coefficients ranging from 0.39 to 0.25. The correlations between both AP and DC and SA in language were higher than between UIT and SA in language. A similar pattern appeared with SA in math. Student SES had a significant correlation with SA in language but not math.

The three variables hypothesized to form the generalized latent variable, AC, were correlated with each other. The correlation between DC and instructional time (0.75) was higher than the other two correlations (0.60 and 0.65). This result supports our original rationale for creating AC, of which each of these three variables is a key component. Students' SES was positively related to AP (0.28) but not to DC or instructional Time. (p. 356)

SOURCE: Leithwood, K., Sun, J. (2018). Academic culture: A promising mediator of school leaders' influence on student learning. *Journal of Educational Administration, 56*(3), 350–363.

There are some important influences that impact the strength of correlation coefficients. When highly reliable scores are used, correlations are stronger. Conversely, if reliability is low, correlations are weak. Consequently, the researcher should demonstrate evidence of reliability for the types of individuals from whom data are collected. As indicated in Chapter 7, it is critical for the instrument to provide a range of responses from a sufficient number of individuals. That is, the scores on the measures need to show good dispersion. If the scores are about the same on a variable, it is difficult to relate the variable to anything else. For example, if a study examines the relationship between ratings of teacher effectiveness and teaching style and all the teachers in the sample are rated as excellent, there would be no chance of finding a relationship. Similarly, it is difficult to find relationships between achievement of gifted students and other variables because of the lack of variability of achievement among these students.

Lack of variability can result when an instrument fails to differentiate along a continuum, or when the individuals in the sample are too homogeneous on one of the traits being measured. If either is the case, you will need to be careful in your interpretation of relationship studies that fail to find significant relationships. If there is a lack of variability, you will not know whether there really is no relationship or, because of a small range of responses, a particular study was unable to demonstrate the relationship.

There is also a limitation on finding significant relationships in a study that has a very large number of participants and/or variables. Some researchers, using what is sometimes called "fishing" or the "shotgun" approach, measure a large number of

Figure 8.7 Example of Correlation Matrix

Table 1. Correlations Among Demographic, Student Motivation and Achievement Variables

Variable	1	2	3	4	5	6	7	8
1. Self-efficacy	(.88)							
2. Performance goals	.50	(.75)						
3. Engagement	.55	.38	(.58)					
4. Math achievement	.67	.34	.45	(.89)				
5. Reading achievement	.72	.62	.53	.62	(.93)			
6. Gender[a]	.30	.17	.22	−.55	.63	NA		
7. Race[b]	.22	.67	−.20	.33	.16	.44	NA	
8. Age	.10	.44	.72	.29	.11	.25	.31	NA

Note: Correlations above .60 are significant at $p < .05$. Reliability coefficients are shown on the diagonal in parentheses.
[a]Gender is coded 1 = male and 2 = female
[b]Race is coded 1 = White and 2 = African American

Results: The correlations among the variables identified several significant relationships. Math achievement showed a positive relationship with self-efficacy, though not with either performance goal orientation or engagement. Reading achievement, however, was positively related to both self-efficacy and performance goal orientation. Females had higher reading scores than males. African American students showed stronger performance goal orientation than White students, and age was positively related only to engagement—older students were more engaged than younger students.

variables with the hope that at least some of the many correlations that are calculated will be significant. However, in such studies some of the correlations will be statistically significant by chance alone, and without a theoretical or practical reason for inclusion, the results will be difficult to interpret. When thousands of participants are used, it is also possible to calculate statistically significant correlations that are actually quite small. Consequently, the relationship that is reported may be very small and of little value. We will discuss this limitation later in this chapter.

Figure 8.7 shows how several simple correlations can be reported in the form of a *correlation matrix.* Can you follow the results narrative that is below the matrix? The statements come directly from the correlations in the figure.

Complex Correlational Designs

Although simple, bivariate correlations are very helpful—indeed, essential—in understanding relationships among variables, it is also possible to examine several independent variables in one analysis to see how, together, they may show a relationship to the dependent variable. Correlations are also used together to show patterns of relationships. In both these cases, researchers are hoping to find explanations for relationships—sometimes even causal explanations. We look at two such approaches here: *multiple regression* and *structural equation modeling.*

MULTIPLE REGRESSION In a **multiple regression**, or *multiple correlation,* two or more independent variables are used to predict values of a continuous dependent variable (in *bivariate regression,* one independent variable is used to predict one dependent variable). The idea is that the predictive power of the independent variables can be combined into a set to see how all of them together predict the dependent. It is also possible to see the contribution of each of the independent variables. Let's examine how this works, because it is a very common way to examine relationships and it has many useful applications.

The approach taken with a regression is that an equation is derived to show how the independent variables, when combined, associate with the dependent variable. This is called a *regression equation.* This is what the equation looks like in a case with two independent variables (X_1 and X_2), each with a *regression coefficient* (b_1 and b_2), and a single dependent variable (Y):

$$Y = (a + b_1 \cdot X_1 + b_2 \cdot X_2) + \text{error}$$

The idea is to use the equation with all the independent and dependent variable scores to predict values of the dependent variable (resulting in the **coefficient of multiple correlation**, R). If there is a strong relationship among independent and dependent variables, there will be a good prediction. By being able to combine the predictive power of several independent variables, a stronger prediction or explanation is achieved than could be found with a single independent variable. In addition, you can find out how much a single variable, such as X_2, which comes after X_1 in the equation, predicts Y after the influence of X_1 is accounted for, or "controlled." This feature, it turns out, is very valuable, as it allows us to see the amount of relationship left after considering variables that need to be "controlled" (more accurately *adjusted* for). Let's consider an example to see how all this works.

Suppose you are interested in whether there is a relationship between exercise and obesity, after "controlling" for caloric intake. That is, you want to hold caloric intake constant, then see whether exercise is related to obesity. You gather data for the dependent variable, obesity, and the two independent variables, caloric intake and exercise. The regression equation that results could look like this (actual regression coefficients are calculated from the data):

$$Y = 6.42 + 4.08 \, (X_1) + 15.56 \, (X_2) + \text{error}$$

where
    Y = obesity
    X_1 = calories
    X_2 = exercise

If the overall R is .70, then the square of that (.49) is called "amount of variance accounted for," for both independent variables together, which is interpreted to mean that 49% of the variance in obesity is explained by the two independent variables. Furthermore, you might find that after "controlling" for diet, exercise accounts for 20% of the variance found in obesity. Also, an individual's actual caloric intake can be plugged into the formula to see how much additional difference exercise makes in the relationship to obesity for that person.

Hopefully, you can see how useful regression is for educational research. It is important, and often essential, to make predictions on the basis of many factors, and to see how much a factor can explain after accounting for other variables. Suppose you are interested in seeing whether there is a relationship between class size and achievement. You have a sample of classes, but the students have different levels of ability by class. However, you have access to students' ability test scores. These scores can be used in a regression to "control" for the effect of ability, allowing you to see whether class size is related to achievement.

There are several different types of regression. One type that is becoming increasingly popular is called **logistic regression**. With logistic regression, the dependent variable is categorical, usually with two levels. The results are reported with something called the *odds ratio*, which is often an easy way to explain results. For example, a study using logistic regression might conclude that students who take service learning courses in college are "twice as likely" to choose a non-business career than students who do not take service learning courses.

Excerpt 8.7 is from a study that looked at how amount of physical activity was related to body mass index (BMI) and perceived benefits and barriers. Note how the variables are examined to highlight their "unique" contribution to explaining physical activity. Excerpt 8.8 explains how logistic regression was used in a study of women's interest in STEM careers.

STRUCTURAL EQUATION MODELING Another useful nonexperimental kind of analysis that can be used to study causal explanations with many variables is **structural equation modeling** (SEM), which is a common type of what is called *causal modeling*. This approach hypothesizes that the independent variables are related to each other in certain ways, and then to the dependent variable, and uses the correlations among the variables to test the hypothesized model. The logic is to see whether the data are consistent with theory that predicts certain relationships. Although I cannot go into detail here about this procedure, it provides a technique for using nonexperimental data to make causal conclusions A very simple causal model is illustrated in Figure 8.8. Using dropping out of high school as the dependent variable, several variables are hypothesized to be important in explaining the factors that may cause students to drop out.

EXCERPT 8.7
Multiple Regression

A stepwise multiple regression analysis was carried out to test the effects of BMI and the perceived benefits and barriers on physical activity. BMI was entered in the first regression equation, and it accounted for 23% of the variance in physical activity (adjusted $R^2 = .23$). Then... BMI and the perceived benefits and barriers were entered as variables, and these variables together explained 48% of the variance in physical activity. The incremental increase in R^2 for this regression model (R^2 change $= .32$, $p = .01$) indicated that some of the perceived benefits and barriers were statistically significant even after taking BMI into account (better outlook, weight control, feeling confident, physical dissatisfaction, lack of competence). (p. 987)

SOURCE: Kim, Y. (2013). Differences in physical activity and perceived benefits and barriers among normal weight, overweight, and obese adolescents. *Perceptual & Motor Skills: Exercise & Sport, 116*(3), 981–991. Copyright © 2013, Ammons Scientific, Ltd.

EXCERPT 8.8
Logistic Regression

Because of the binary dependent variable (STEM career interest; no STEM career interest), logistic regression models were used (Pedhazur, 1997; Grimm and Yarnold, 1995; Tabachnick and Fidell, 1996). Significant predictor variables were interpreted via odds ratios, giving the reader a more intuitive understanding of how the variables were associated with STEM career interest (Pedhazur, 1997). Lastly, interactions of independent and control variables were examined (Pedhazur, 1997). SPSS 23.0, a statistical analysis software package, was used to create our logistic regression models. (p. 259)

SOURCE: Dabney, K. P., Johnson, T. N., Sonnert, G., & Sadler, P. M. (2017). STEM career interest in women and informal science. *Journal of Women and Minorities in Science and Engineering, 23*(3), 249–270.

Figure 8.8 Example of a Causal Model

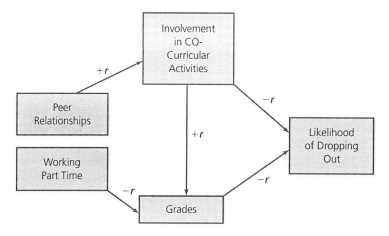

As you might imagine, because many independent variables are related to important dependent variables the models can become very complex. Remember, too, that these are correlational data, and unaccounted-for additional variables may be overlooked or not included. A nonexperimental correlational study that employed SEM is described in Excerpt 8.9.

Prediction Study Designs

With a **prediction study design**, a regression analysis is used to show how one variable can predict the dependent variable that occurs at a later time. Whereas in a simple or complex relationship study variables are measured at about the same time, a predictive study shows how one or more variables can predict the value of the dependent variable measured *in the future*. Predictions like these are made constantly in education. Suppose you are director of admissions at a selective university. You must choose a small number of students from the large pool of applicants. How should you select the students to be admitted? You decide to use some criteria to predict which students are most likely to succeed. Because one predictor is probably previous achievement,

---

EXCERPT 8.9

Structural Equation Modeling

The purpose of this study was to (a) test the relationships between sense of belonging to school, academic hardiness, and academic achievement and (b) examine the mediating role of academic hardiness (including commitment, control, and challenge) on the association between sense of belonging to school and academic achievement. Five hundred and twenty 15–21-year-old high school students (245 young women and 275 young men) from eight high schools in Tehran, Iran, participated in the study by completing a series of validated questionnaires... structural equation modeling provided evidence that commitment, control, challenge, and sense of belonging to school were positively associated with academic achievement. Commitment, control, and challenge partially mediated the relationship between sense of belonging to school and academic achievement. (p. 345)

SOURCE: Abdollahi, A., & Noltemeyer, A. (2018). Academic hardiness: Mediator between sense of belonging to school and academic achievement? *The Journal of Educational Research, 111*(3), 345–351.

you look at the high school grade point average (GPA) of each applicant. If it turns out to be correlated with college GPA, you have identified a variable that can be used to predict success in college. High school students with a high GPA are likely to have a higher college GPA than high school students with a low GPA. Because high school GPA precedes college GPA, it is called a *predictor variable*. College GPA would be termed the *criterion variable*.

In a prediction study, then, it is necessary to collect data on a group of individuals over some length of time. Data collection can be longitudinal—that is, first collecting predictor variable data with a sample, waiting a specified amount of time, and then obtaining criterion variable data with the same sample. This approach for the preceding example would involve recording the GPA of high school students before they started college, then waiting, say, for a year and recording their first-year college GPA.

An example of this kind of study is provided in Excerpt 8.10, which examines the predictive relationship between the quality of teacher–child relationships and child social and academic outcomes a year later. In the next study (Excerpt 8.11), researchers also followed individuals over time, in this case to see whether selected variables predicted achievement.

In some studies, the predictive relationship is "tested" with another sample of individuals. The tested prediction (which will be lower than the original one) is the relationship that most closely indicates how well the predictor variable will predict the criterion variable with future groups of individuals.

Several factors influence the accuracy of the predictions. One, like simple and complex correlations, is the reliability of the scores obtained from the predictor and criterion variables (higher reliability results in better predictions). Another factor is the length of time between the predictor and criterion variables. In most cases, predictions involving a short time span are more accurate than those involving a long time span because of the general principle that the correlation between two variables decreases

EXCERPTS 8.10 AND 8.11
Predictive Studies

The current study examines whether teacher-child relationship quality as perceived by both teachers and children is associated with child socio-emotional and academic outcomes over one school year and whether these associated are moderated by the quality of classroom emotional climate. Participants included 526 Grade 3-5 students and their 35 teachers from six urban public elementary schools. Higher child-reported relationship quality with teachers predicted lower child-reported depressive symptoms in spring, controlling for fall levels... higher quality classroom emotional climate may mitigate risk of aggression for children with poor-quality teacher relationships. (p. 992)

SOURCE: Rucinski, C. L., Brown, J. L., & Downer, J. T. (2018). Teacher–child relationships, classroom climate, and children's social-emotional and academic development. *Journal of Educational Psychology, 110*(7), 992–1004.

This was a longitudinal, correlational study that was conducted in two phases. In the first phase (during students' first semester in college) students completed measures of achievement motivation and their general achievement goals for college. We obtained students' transcripts 2 years later. (p. 116)

SOURCE: Diurik, A. M., Lovejoy, C. M., & Johnson, S. J. (2009). A longitudinal study of achievement goals for college in general: Predicting cumulative GPA and diversity in course selection. *Contemporary Educational Psychology, 34*, 113–119.

as the amount of time between the variables increases; furthermore, with more time there is a greater opportunity for other variables to influence the criterion variable, which would lower the correlation. Finally, criterion variables—such as success in college, leadership, a successful marriage, and effective teaching, which are affected by many factors—are often not very sensitive. They are more difficult to predict than relatively simple criterion variables such as success in the next mathematics class.

Consumer (and Researcher) Tips
Criteria for Evaluating Correlational Designs

1. **Causation should rarely be inferred from correlation.** The most important principle in evaluating correlational research is that it typically does not establish causation. This is not as easy as it sounds, for many relationships based on correlations seem as if they *do* infer causation, and many do provide reasonable explanation. For example, if you find a positive predictive relationship between academic time on task and achievement, it is easy to falsely assume that increasing academic time on task will increase achievement. Although this *may* be true, it should not be concluded from a correlational finding for the two reasons I summarized earlier, and that are illustrated in Figure 8.3. First, the direction of possible causation is not clear. That is, it may be that higher achievement causes students to be on task more. Second, other variables associated with time on task that are not included in the study may affect the relationship and may, in fact, be causally related. For instance, perhaps students who spend more time on task have a higher aptitude for learning, better motivation for learning, and more parental support than students who spend less time on task; teachers may interact differently with students who are on task compared with students who tend to be off task.

This principle is illustrated more clearly in a relationship between student achievement and per-pupil expenditures. Although a positive relationship may exist, it would be a mistake to think that achievement can be affected simply by spending more money because many other variables also related to per-pupil expenditure, such as family background, are causes of student achievement.

As a final example of this important principle, consider the following "true" statement: There is a positive relationship between students' weight and reading achievement. Unreasonable, you think? Examine Figure 8.9. There is a positive relationship between the two factors because a third variable, age, is related to weight. Obviously, there is a positive relationship between age and reading achievement. If you were puzzled by the first conclusion, *you were probably thinking causation*, which would lead to the conclusion that achievement could be improved by fattening up the students!

2. **The *reported* correlation should not be higher or lower than the *actual* relationship.** You need to be aware of factors that may spuriously increase or decrease a correlation. One factor is the nature of the sample from which the correlation

---

Author Reflection   *There is an old admonition in research, something like "never infer causation from correlation." Well, it turns out that recently developed statistical procedures, mostly variations of structural equation modeling, render this staple obsolete. There are many correlational studies that do suggest credible causal explanations.*

Figure 8.9 "Relationship" Between Weight and Reading Achievement

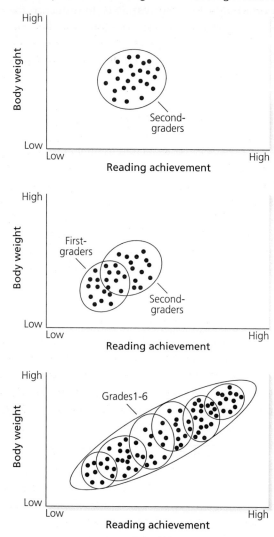

is calculated. If the sample is more homogeneous than the population on one of the variables, the correlation will be lower than for the population as a whole. Conversely, if a sample is more heterogeneous than the population on the variable, the correlation will be higher than would be true for the population as a whole.

A second factor is the range of scores on the variables that are correlated. If the variability of scores on one variable is small, the correlation will be low. This is sometimes referred to as **restriction in range**, or more simply, *restricted range*. If the range is restricted, the variability is reduced, and without adequate variability, the correlation will be low. Thus, in some research in which the range is restricted, the actual relationship is higher than that reported.

A third factor relates to the reliability of the scores obtained of the correlated variables. As noted, correlations are directly related to reliability—the lower the reliability, the lower the correlation. A lowering of the correlation because of unreliability is called **attenuation** and is sometimes "corrected" statistically to show what the correlation would be if the scores were more reliable.

3. Practical significance should not be confused with statistical significance.
Researchers use the word "significant" in two ways. In one sense, it refers to a

statistical inference, which means that the coefficient that is calculated is probably different from zero—that is, concluding that there is a relationship. (Chapter 10 discusses this concept in greater detail.) Thus, a researcher may report that "a correlation of .30 is significant." This type of phrase is associated *only* with the *statistical* meaning of significance. Another meaning of significance implies importance or meaningfulness of the practical value of the correlation. This is a more subjective judgment. One important principle of correlation needs to be considered in making this judgment. Because correlations are expressed as decimals, it is easy to confuse the coefficient with a percentage. However, the correlation coefficient is not an indication of the percentage of "sameness" between two variables. The extent to which the variables share common properties or characteristics is actually indicated by the square of the correlation coefficient (similar to the squared *R* in a regression analysis). This is called the **coefficient of determination**, which is a much better indicator of practical or meaningful significance than the correlation coefficient. For example, a correlation of .50, squared, indicates that the variables have 25% in common, or 25% "explained" of what can be accounted for, which leaves 75% unexplained. Thus, if the correlation between achievement and some other variable is .70, which is regarded as a "high" correlation, about 50% of what can vary with respect to achievement is not predicted or accounted for by the correlation.

In Excerpt 8.12, the phrase "percentage of variance predicted" is used to interpret the results of correlations between school readiness (preschool and kindergarten academic/cognitive and social/behavioral assessments) and similar measures after the first and second grades. The authors use the term **effect size** in their discussion, which is a common term when addressing practical significance. In this case, effect size is synonymous with coefficient of determination. (It is also common to use the correlation coefficient as effect size.)

4. **The size of the correlation should be sufficient for the use of the results.** Much larger correlations are needed for predictions with individuals than with groups. Crude group predictions can be made with correlations as low as .40 to .60, whereas correlations above .75 are usually needed to make predictions for individuals. In exploratory studies, low correlations (e.g., .25 to .40) may indicate a need for further study, but higher correlations are needed for research to confirm theories or test hypotheses. In studies using regression analysis, correlations between .20 and .40 are common and usually indicate some practical significance.

5. **Studies with prediction designs should report accuracy of prediction for a new sample.** To use the results of prediction research, consumers must know the

---

EXCERPT 8.12

Interpretation of Correlation Coefficients

The moderate estimates of effect size found for the academic/cognitive domain indicate that, on average, 25% of variance in early school academic/cognitive performance is predicted from preschool or kindergarten academic/cognitive status.... In contrast, social/behavioral assessments at preschool or kindergarten age account for 10% or less of the variance in social/behavioral measures in kindergarten, first grade, or second grade. (p. 474)

SOURCE: LaParo, K. M., & Pianta, R. C. (2000). Predicting children's competence in the early school years: A meta-analytic review. *Review of Educational Research, 70*, 443–484.

accuracy of the predicted relationship. This is found by testing a presumed predictive relationship with a new, different group of persons.

6. **Correlational design studies that claim explanations should be examined for other influential factors.** Complex correlational studies, such as those using regression or causal modeling, need careful scrutiny for the influence of unaccounted-for variables on the correlation. Such explanations are commonly found with multiple correlation studies. Typically, researchers claim that most known variables are used, resulting in the dependent variable being explained by differences in the independent variable. Such claims, however, are always tentative. Something not included could influence the relationship between the targeted independent variable and dependent variable, so the search for additional influential factors is essential.

Author Reflection *Often my students get confused about the differences between "prediction" and "relationship." Every correlation can be used for prediction in the sense that one variable predicts the other because they are related. The analysis advances to prediction when the research question and theory suggest a clear antecedent (predictor as independent variable) and consequence at a later time (outcome as dependent variable). It goes back to alignment between the questions and analyses.*

Check for Understanding 3

3a. What are two reasons for not implying causation with a simple correlation between two variables?

3b. Why is a good spread of scores on each variable needed for correlational studies?

3c. What are two reasons for using a multiple or logistic regression?

The Hedgehog and the Fox Interpret Nonexperimental Findings

This study shows that the amount of time students spend with homework assigned is associated with higher test scores. This means I need to assign my students more homework.

This study shows that the amount of time students spend on homework is associated with higher test scores. I wonder how "amount of time" was operationalized, and if any other factors, such as student ability, were controlled. Maybe students who score higher on tests *decide* to spend more time on homework on their own?

Causal–Comparative *and* Ex Post Facto Designs

Learning Outcome 8.4   Know the characteristics and limitations of causal comparative and ex post facto studies.

There are two additional nonexperimental designs that look very similar to experimental studies and are structured to investigate cause-and-effect relationships: causal–comparative and ex post facto.

Causal–Comparative Designs

The hallmark of an experimental study, as I've emphasized, is that the researcher has direct control of the intervention. In some situations, though, there is an intervention *without* direct control. This kind of design may be called a "natural" experiment in the sense that something occurs differently for one group of participants compared with others. Even though there is no *direct control* of the intervention, it is possible to monitor what occurs and measure outcomes that compare the groups. I choose to call these designs **causal–comparative** to distinguish them from experiments.

Suppose you were interested in determining the impact of attending preschool on first-grade performance. The intervention, attending preschool, is the independent variable. You cannot really control the intervention, but you can measure the extent to which it is implemented. A comparison group of children not attending preschool could be used in this design to investigate whether attending preschool results in greater first-grade achievement (dependent variable). The quality of the design depends on how well the comparison group is matched to the intervention group, and how well you can understand how the intervention may have caused an increase in achievement.

There are many types of "interventions" that can be studied using causal–comparative designs. For example, different approaches to mentoring beginning teachers, different curricula, staff development, different ways that principals evaluate teachers, group counseling compared to individual counseling, and providing special advising tools for college students would lend themselves to investigation using a causal–comparative design because in each case it would be difficult for the researcher to control the program or strategy that is implemented.

The obvious weakness of a causal–comparative study is lack of researcher control of the independent variable. The researcher cannot determine the nature of the intervention, just note that it has or has not occurred. It is very important in these designs to choose comparison participants who are as similar as possible in the intervention group. This is typically accomplished by matching or using homogeneous groups. If random assignment of participants is possible, many of the extraneous/confounding variables can be accounted for, but there is still lack of control over the intervention and what happens within each group as the intervention is experienced. Some statistical adjustments can be used as well.

Ex Post Facto Designs

In **ex post facto** designs, the investigators examine whether one or more different *pre-existing* "interventions" have caused subsequent differences when participants who experienced one type of condition are compared with others who experienced a different condition (the phrase *ex post facto* means "after the fact").

EXCERPT 8.13
Ex Post Facto Design

The institution's Office of Admissions and Records generated individual reports... that contained the entry information for first-year students... enrolled in each section of the freshman-year experience.... In order to match students in the control group... student data on all of the pertinent class lists were coded to show the specific combination of courses in which an individual student was enrolled during his or her first semester on campus. Once the final sample of students in the experimental and control groups was identified, the completion rate for the first academic year... [and] the percent of general education courses completed were determined by reviewing each student's transcript.... Findings from the ex post facto investigation were based on the academic characteristics for the experimental group ($n = 431$) and the control group ($n = 431$). (p. 436)

SOURCE: Sidle, M. W., & McReynolds, J. (2009). The freshman year experience: Student retention and student success. *NASPA Journal, 46*(3), 288–300.

In ex post facto designs, like causal–comparative ones, there is no active control of the independent variable because, with this design, it has already taken place. In an ex post facto study, then, the researcher investigates an intervention that has already occurred, whereas in a causal–comparative design, the researcher is able to monitor and observe the intervention as it occurs.

In conducting an ex post facto study, you would select participants who are as similar as possible, some of whom experienced the intervention, others who did not. For example, in a study of the effect of physical education on elementary students' achievement, you need to locate groups of students who are similar in all respects except whether they have or have not taken physical education. In making the final selection of the students, you need to be aware of possible extraneous variables that make causal conclusions problematic. Thus, the students should not differ in grade level, ability, motivation, socioeconomic status, or other factors that could influence achievement. Often in ex post facto designs these possible confounding variables are "controlled" statistically.

In Excerpt 8.13, the researchers used an ex post facto design to study the extent to which a specific freshman year course was responsible for increased student retention and academic success. Students who had enrolled in the course over 3 years were compared to similar, matched students who did not enroll in the course. Note that the authors use the terms "experimental" and "control" groups to describe their design, even though there is no direct manipulation, which technically means, in my view, it is not an experiment. Student records were used to compare students who took the course to other students who did not take the course (different conditions) in previous years.

Consumer (and Researcher) Tips
Criteria for Evaluating Studies Using Causal–Comparative and Ex Post Facto Designs

1. **The primary purpose of the research should be to investigate causal relationships when an experiment is not possible.** The experiment is usually the best method for studying the causal impact of an intervention, so causal–comparative and *ex post facto* studies should be used only when it is not possible or feasible to conduct an experiment. There should be sufficient evidence in prior research to indicate that relationships exist between the variables and that it is appropriate to

study causal relationships. Without existing empirical evidence of relationships, a strong theoretical rationale is needed.

2. **The presumed causal condition should have already occurred in an ex post facto study.** It is essential for the condition represented by the independent variable to have occurred before data are collected on or recorded for the dependent variable. The "intervention" must have already taken place for a study to be classified as ex post facto.

3. **Potential confounding and extraneous variables should be recognized and considered.** It is critical to show that potential confounding and extraneous variables have been considered. Because existing groups are usually used in the comparison, these nuisance variables usually consist of differences in characteristics of the participants, but other factors may also be problematic. You need to present evidence that the groups being compared differ only on the independent variable. Failure to do this suggests that the groups have not been carefully selected to avoid the influence of extraneous variables.

4. **Differences between groups being compared should be controlled.** When it is clear that there are measurable differences between individuals in the groups being compared (e.g., gender, age, ability), use appropriate procedures to control their effect. Matching participants is one procedure; statistical techniques can also be used.

5. **Causal conclusions should be made with caution.** Even when all potential extraneous variables have been controlled, which is rare, it is best to accept results that seem to suggest a causal relationship *with caution*. Researchers should indicate possible limitations and frame the finding as "suggesting" a causal relationship. In almost all causal–comparative studies, there will be sufficient reason to be tentative in concluding cause-and-effect relationships.

Check for Understanding 4

4a. What is the difference between causal–comparative and ex post facto designs?

4b. What are two major limitations of causal–comparative and ex post facto designs?

Survey Research Designs

Learning Outcome 8.5   Identify the steps taken to design and employ an effective paper or electronic survey.

As I explained briefly in Chapter 7, the term *survey* can have two different meanings. It can connote a specific measure, like a questionnaire, or it can refer to a more comprehensive type of research or research design. **Survey research** is a well-established nonexperimental method of collecting information from a designated population or sample, using questionnaires or interviews. The results are typically presented as statistical summaries. As you know from reading about polls of various sorts, survey research is used frequently in business, government, public health, politics, psychology, sociology, and transportation, as well as in education. The key purpose is to use the data to depict traits or other characteristics of a clearly defined sample or larger population. Some questions suitable for survey research would be the following:

What are teachers' self-identified needs for professional development in applications of technology?
What do parents think about using public funds for private charter schools?
What types of financial assistance do college students of color access?

What is the trend in spending per pupil for public education?

To what extent do businesses use SAT scores in evaluating applicants for new positions?

Survey research is popular because of versatility, efficiency, and generalizability. Surveys are versatile in being able to address a wide range of problems or questions, especially when the purpose is to describe the attitudes, perspectives, and beliefs of a large population, and they can be conducted economically with written questionnaires or interviews. It is relatively easy to reach individuals from remote locations, and many questions can be answered quickly. An important value of survey research is that probability sampling from a population can be used to result in fairly accurate generalizable conclusions about the larger population. Even for very large populations, good sampling and response rates of as few as 800 individuals can provide accurate descriptions of the population. For example, national polls of political preference or voting intentions, which may include 800 to 1,500 adults, are usually (but not always) fairly accurate indicators of the nation as a whole.

Steps in Conducting Survey Research

Survey research is effectively implemented with the following steps:

1. *Define the purpose, objectives, and research questions.* List each pertinent objective or research question that will be addressed and only collect information that has a direct bearing on the objectives or questions. Refrain from asking questions that "would be nice or interesting to know about," or any questions that are not clearly tied to the way in which the data will be used.

2. *Identify the target population and sampling frame.* You need to know, with as much specificity as possible, the characteristics of the population you want your results to represent. This is typically a larger population that cannot be completely surveyed, or it may be a nonrandom sample that you hope will be representative of a larger population. Then the sampling frame needs to be identified. Statistically, results are most valid for the sampling frame, so comparing that to the target population is important.

3. *Select the sampling procedure.* Once the target population and sampling frame are defined, the best sampling procedure can be identified. The specific method, whether random or nonrandom, will depend on the characteristics of the sample and how individuals can be reached, and which procedure will give you the most accurate results. Some "captured" populations, such as students in a school, can easily be sampled with random methods. Other target populations, such as parents of students, are more difficult to reach. You could try something random with parents, such as sending letters home with students to a randomly selected sample of parents, but you will probably get a very low response rate. You might be better off surveying all the parents who attend back-to-school night, but then you have to worry about sampling bias.

4. *Determine sample size.* Generally, the larger the sample, the more accurate the survey results. (If you include the entire population, there is no sampling error.) Typically, however, surveys use some kind of random sampling, and the usual question is "How many respondents do I need?" This is a complex question—one that depends on a number of factors, including the homogeneity of the population (the more homogeneous, the smaller the sample), type of trait being measured (more abstract traits need larger samples), the size of the population (the percentage of the population you need to survey increases from 50% for a

population of several hundred to only 1,200 for a very large population), likelihood of nonresponse, how much error you are willing to live with (the larger the sample, the less the error), and what minimum numbers are needed to show relationships (what is called "power"). In the end, sample size can vary dramatically for different studies, and there is much disagreement about what size is needed for good results. For large populations, a random sample of 800 is not uncommon. For small populations—say, 100—some would say you need 70%, whereas others would be happy with 40%. For many educational surveys, a sample size of 20% or 30% is not uncommon.

5. *Choose an appropriate survey method.* Surveys are either paper- or web-based written questionnaires, phone interviews, or personal interviews, as discussed in the previous chapter. Each method has advantages and disadvantages (refer to Dillman, Smyth, & Christian, 2014). The most important advantages of the written survey are that many questions can be asked, respondents can be assured of anonymity, the cost is lower, and it is possible to reach a fairly large sample. Interviews are used when there is a need to have a very high response rate, to probe (particularly with nonverbal feedback), when many open-ended questions exist, and when there are just a few questions.

6. *Construct directions.* It is important to have clear instructions so there is no ambiguity about how and where to respond, and what to do when completing the survey. It is best to give the directions at the beginning of the survey and in each section with a different response scale, not in a cover memo or e-mail. Directions should include information about confidentiality and IRB requirements.

7. *Develop a letter/message of transmittal.* The letter or message of transmittal is crucial to obtaining a high response rate. The letter/message should be brief and professional in appearance. The following elements should be included:

   - Credibility of the researcher and sponsoring institution or organization
   - Purpose of the study
   - Benefits of the study for the researcher, respondent, and profession
   - Importance of a high response rate
   - Protections related to anonymity and confidentiality
   - Time limit for responding (typically, a few days to a week is fine)
   - Request for cooperation and honesty
   - Opportunity for respondents to receive results of the study

8. *Pilot test.* As you know, I am big on pilot testing. With a written questionnaire, the entire process needs to be pilot tested, from selecting the sample to actually surveying 10 to 20 respondents from the sample, or persons very similar to the sample, to obtain feedback about the directions, questions, and process. In the pilot test, the respondents should read the directions and complete the survey. When finished, they can comment on the clarity and format of the survey. The pilot helps you know how long it will take to complete the survey.

9. *Analyze nonrespondents.* One of the most serious limitations of survey research is a low response rate. The smaller the response rate, the more likely that the results will be biased. If possible, nonrespondents should be analyzed to determine whether they are systematically different from the respondents on anything that could impact the results. This is often accomplished by seeing whether the nonrespondents differ from respondents in their demographic characteristics. Demographics of the respondents can be compared to the entire population. Sometimes special efforts are made to follow up with nonrespondents to see whether, as a group, their responses differ from respondents.

Response rates can be increased by the following:

- Use a well-designed, professional, attractive, and easy-to-complete survey.
- Use several contacts with the sample, including a pre-notification, reminder, and reissuing of the survey.
- Use first-class mail for paper surveys; certified mail and express mail are best for long surveys.
- For mailed surveys, include return postage and a return envelope.
- Use a transmittal letter that clearly indicates the benefits of the survey.
- Use telephone follow-up.
- Use financial or other incentives.

Survey research is conducted with one or more samples or populations at one time (cross-sectional) or are given more than once to the same or similar individuals over a specified length of time (longitudinal). These differences have important implications for interpreting results.

Cross-sectional Survey Designs

In a **cross-sectional** survey, information is collected from one or more samples or populations at one time. There are two types of cross-sectional surveys. One type simply studies a phenomenon as it occurs at one time—for example, political surveys and surveys that study an attitude or characteristic of a group. A good illustration is the annual Gallup Poll of the Public's Attitudes Toward the Public Schools, published in *Phi Delta Kappan*. The purpose of this poll is to estimate the attitudes of the adult civilian population in the United States toward many aspects of schooling, including the perceived biggest problems facing public schools, inner-city schools, part-time work by high school students, length of the school year and day, and parental choice.

Another type of cross-sectional survey is intended to compare individuals of different ages to investigate possible developmental differences or relationships. For example, if researchers are interested in changes in students' self-concepts between sixth and twelfth grades, and factors that may affect self-concept at various ages, a cross-sectional survey could be designed in which samples of current sixth- through twelfth-grade students are selected and questioned. All participants could be asked the questions at about the same time (e.g., October 2020).

Cross-sectional surveys are convenient and allow some tentative conclusions about how individuals may change over time. However, caution is advised for two primary reasons. First, there may be important differences between the individuals who are sampled in each grade or in each age category. For instance, if the sampling is done within a school, an assumption is that the type of students attending the school has not changed. If current sixth-graders are different in important ways, besides age, from twelfth-graders, conclusions about changes over time are affected. Second, because the data are obtained at one time, what may show as a "difference" from sixth to twelfth grade may not represent a change. It could be that twelfth-graders did not, when in sixth grade, have the same responses of current sixth-graders.

Longitudinal Survey Designs

With a **longitudinal** survey, the same or a similar group of individuals is studied over a specified length of time. For example, a longitudinal study of changes in students' goal orientation might begin in 2015 with a survey of sixth-graders and continue until

2020 for the same students, who would now be in the eleventh grade, when another survey is administered.

There are variations of longitudinal surveys, depending on the individuals who are sampled or used to make up the "same group." In what is called a *trend* study, the same population is studied over time, although the participants are sampled from the population each year or time of data collection (e.g., studying trends in children's texting behavior as they grow older). In a *cohort* study, groups with very similar characteristics are sampled each time, such as surveying a sample of sixth graders in 2019 and comparing those results to a sample of sixth graders in 2020. A *panel* study is a cohort investigation in which the same individuals are surveyed each time data are collected. Excerpts 8.14 gives an example of a panel longitudinal survey study. In this investigation, students were surveyed twice over 2 years. The students provided the first two letters of their surname, the first two letters of their given name, their month of birth, and the last two digits of their home phone number to match responses and encourage a sense of anonymity. Excerpt 8.15 is from a cohort study that examines differences in adolescent behaviors from the 1970s to the 2010s.

EXCERPTS 8.14 AND 8.15
Longitudinal Survey Designs

We sought to address the following research questions: (a) What is the link between arts participation and academic (e.g., motivation) and nonacademic (e.g., self-esteem) outcomes, beyond sociodemographics and prior achievement? (b) What is the relative salience of specific forms of arts participation—school (arts tuition, engagement), home (parent–child arts interaction, arts resources), and community (external arts tuition, participation and attendance in arts events)—in predicting academic and nonacademic outcomes? In attending to these research questions, we implemented a longitudinal survey-based design (two measurement waves, 1 full academic year apart) with students from Grade 5 to Grade 11 in 2010 and then to the same students from Grade 6 to Grade 12 in 2011. (p. 713)

SOURCE: Martin, A. J., Mansour, M., Anderson, M., Gibson, R., Liem, G. A. D., & Sudmalis, D. (2013). The role of arts participation in students' academic and nonacademic outcomes: A longitudinal study of school, home, and community factors. *Journal of Educational Psychology, 105*(3), 709–727.

In this article, we investigate birth cohort differences in U.S. adolescents' engagement in adult activities, examining whether adolescents in recent years pursue a faster or slower developmental path than adolescents did in previous decades. To do this, we draw from seven large, nationally representative data sets ($N = 8.44$ million) that have surveyed U.S. adolescents (ages 13–19) since the 1970s, 1980s, or 1990s and into the 2010s, allowing the comparison of several generations of young people. These data sets each examine one or more adult activities such as having sex, dating, drinking alcohol, working for pay, going out without one's parents, and driving. (p. 639)

SOURCE: Twenge, J. M., & Park, H. (2017). The decline in adult activities among U.S. adolescents, 1976-2016. *Child Development, 90*(2), 638–654. https://doi.org/10.1111/cdev.12930

A disadvantage of longitudinal designs is loss of participants, which occurs with studies that extend over a long period of time and with populations that are difficult to track (e.g., following high school or college graduates). Not only will the sample size sometimes become too small for adequate generalizations, but also there may be a systematic loss of certain types of participants. For example, a longitudinal study of attitudes of high school students, from 9th to 12th grade, should consider the fact that

Figure 8.10 Cross-sectional and Longitudinal Designs

			May 2021
Cross-Sectional			Samples of fourth-, fifth-, and sixth-grade students taken.

	May 2019	May 2020	May 2021
Longitudinal	Sample of fourth-grade students taken.	Sample of fifth-grade students taken.	Sample of sixth-grade students taken.

some of the sample will have dropped out, leaving mainly those who, in all probability, have more positive attitudes than all ninth-graders would have had.

The differences between longitudinal and cross-sectional studies are illustrated in Figure 8.10.

Internet-Based Survey Research

As pointed out in Chapter 7, Internet-based questionnaires are now commonplace. In survey research, this is a very economical way to obtain a sample from a large population.

TYPES OF INTERNET-BASED SURVEYS   There are essentially two types of Internet-based survey research: e-mail with an attachment, and web-based, using electronic links. An e-mail survey that is attached typically looks much like a paper survey. The more common web-based survey directs the respondent to the survey, typically with a link. Web-based surveys are typically designed with available software. There are dozens of choices, including SurveyMonkey, which can be used for small surveys for free, Qualtrics, SurveyGizmo, and SurveyAnyplace (for mobile devices). Survey software will differ, of course, in cost as well as features, but most offer administrative flexibility, customization of format, and some type of reporting. (More sophisticated software, such as Qualtrics, offers extensive statistical analyses and reporting options.) The surveys are usually very attractive, using graphics and sometimes multimedia resources. Respondents often answer only a few questions on each screen, and then simply "click" to the next set of questions. They are very easy to complete. If you are in a position to select the software, go simple and less expensive for short and straightforward surveys. Check carefully for ease of use and support. While there may be some restrictions related to format and response scales, most survey software products mimic what can be gathered in paper format.

ADVANTAGES AND DISADVANTAGES   The advantages of digital surveys are fairly obvious: reduced cost and time, easy access, quick responses, and ease of entering responses into a database. Electronic surveys are most effective with targeted professional groups, with "in-house" groups, when they are short and simple, and when a password can be used to ensure anonymity. Of course, there are also disadvantages. Samples are limited to those with access to the technology—both hardware and software—which may lead to bias. For example, there are some disparities by socioeconomic status with respect to Internet access. Even when access exists, the respondents need to feel comfortable with the procedures and Internet tools that are used. Perhaps the most serious limitation is that respondents may not believe that their answers will be confidential. Confidentiality and privacy issues are very important; many will be reluctant to be honest because, even with the use of passwords and assurances from the researcher, there may be a lingering feeling that any electronic response can be traced to the individual. (Table 8.2 provides a summary of advantages and disadvantages.)

Table 8.2 Advantages and Disadvantages of Internet-Based Survey Research

Advantages	Disadvantages
Costs less	Low response rate
Fast response	Response bias
Takes less time to distribute	Lack of confidentiality and privacy
Respondents enter answers directly for each question	Confidence that participant and not someone else answered the questions
Provides enhanced presentation through color and graphics (especially for children)	Potential information overload, such as too many questions
Immediate database construction	Participants must be skilled in computer usage
Convenient	Hardware compatibility
Increased accuracy of responses	Hard to inform participants about their ethical rights
Easy follow-up	Hard to provide incentives
Easy access to geographically diverse samples	Sampling limited to those with access to computers

DESIGNING INTERNET-BASED SURVEYS Many of the previously summarized suggestions about effective questionnaire are applicable to Internet-based surveys. There are some additional considerations related to technology. Essentially, a simple, clear layout without clutter is needed for easy navigation. Some further suggestions include the following:

- Show only a few questions on each screen, unless there is a matrix of items with the same response scale.
- Show both question and response categories on the same screen.
- Avoid excess scrolling.
- Limit the use of matrix format questions.
- Direct respondents to simply click on their response to closed-ended questions.
- Use error messages that refer to a specific location needing attention.
- Use graphics, hypertext, and colors.
- Indicate progress toward completing the survey.

Check for Understanding 5

5a. What are three advantages and three disadvantages in using electronic rather than paper surveys?

5b. When is a pilot test used in creating or using a survey?

Anatomy of a Quantitative Nonexperimental Article

The following example of a published nonexperimental quantitative study (Figure 8.11) is included to show you how such an investigation is designed and reported, and how it should be interpreted. This particular nonexperimental study is an example of comparative and correlational relationship research.

Figure 8.11 Anatomy of a Nonexperimental Study[1]

Psychological Reports: Sociocultural Issues in Psychology
2012, 111, 3, 761–764. © Psychological Reports 2012

STUDENTS' PERCEPTIONS OF SCHOOL CLIMATE AND TRAIT TEST ANXIETY [2,3]

YANG YANG LIU

Department of Psychology
Nanjing University, China

┌ Indicates relationship study

Summary.—In a sample of 916 Chinese high school students, the relations among the students' perceptions of school climate and their trait test anxiety were examined. The results indicated that students' perceptions of teacher-student relationships and student-student relationships negatively predicted their trait test anxiety. Furthermore, girls had higher scores on trait test anxiety than boys.

┌ Introduction

Based on the framework of Bronfenbrenner's (1979) ecological model, school climate is a concept that has been researched for many years. In previous research, school climate has been widely linked to students' academic performance (McEvoy & Welker, 2000) and adjustment problems (Loukas & Murphy, 2007). Recently, some researchers have suggested that the learning

┌ Review of literature

environment influences students' academics-related appraisals of subjective control and subjective values and that these appraisals are significantly related to their emotional experiences (Frenzel, Pekrun, & Goetz, 2007). In empirical research, some studies have supported this hypothesis. For instance, Hembree (1988) showed that students' relationships with their teachers were significantly related to their test anxiety scores. Students' perceptions of peer esteem were negatively associated

┌ Purpose

with their anxiety scores (Frenzel, *et al.,* 2007). However, no studies have examined the effects of school climate on Chinese students' test anxiety. Therefore, the present study seeks to contribute to the literature by examining the relationship between Chinese high school students' perceptions

┌ Research hypothesis

of school climate and their trait test anxiety. It was hypothesized that Chinese high school students' perceptions of school climate would significantly predict their trait test anxiety scores.

METHOD

Participants

┌ Convenience sample

Participants were recruited from three urban senior high schools located in Jiangsu province. Ethical approval for the study was granted by the author's institution. High school students

┌ Description of participants

($N = 916$; 508 girls) provided their agreement to participate in the study. Students were distributed about equally by grade: 307 students were in Grade 10, 299 students were in Grade 11, and 310 students were in Grade 12. The mean age of the participants was 17.6 yr. ($SD = 0.6$).

Procedure

┌ To ensure confidentiality

Students completed a 20-min. survey during classroom time. They were told that no teacher would have access to their questionnaires. Graduate students in psychology carried out the administration of the measures. Informed consent was obtained from students and one of their parents.

Measures

┌ Description of instrument

School climate.—Students' perceptions of school climate were assessed with a 27-item scale adapted from Cemalcilar's (2009) scale on school climate and validated for use in China (Liu & Lu, 2011). The scale has four subscales measuring teacher-student relationship, student-student relationship, physical features, and supporting resources. Responses are scored on a four-point scale, with anchors 1: Strongly disagree and 4: Strongly agree. Negatively keyed items were

┌ Cronbach alpha

reverse-coded and a mean score was computed for each subscale. The internal consistencies of the subscales were adequate ($\alpha = .85$ for teacher-student relationship; $\alpha = .80$ for student-student relationship, $\alpha = .70$ for physical features, and $\alpha = .91$ for supporting resources, respectively).

[1]**SOURCE:** Liu, Y. Y. (2012). Students' perceptions of school climate and trait test anxiety. Psychological Reports: Sociocultural Issues in Psychology, 111(3), 761–764. Reprinted by permission of the publisher.

[2]Address correspondence to Yang Yang Liu, Department of Psychology, Nanjing University, Hankoulu #22, Nanjing, China or e-mail (Liuyangyang661@sina.com).

[3]We are grateful to the Fundamental Research Funds for the Central Universities and Programs for the Philosophy and Social Sciences Research of Higher Learning Institutions of Jiangsu (2012SJD190007) for supporting this study.

Test anxiety.—Test anxiety was measured by the Test Anxiety Inventory (TAI; Spielberger, 1980). The scale has been widely used to measure students' test anxiety (Keith, Hodapp, Schermelleh-engel, & Moosbrugger, 2003). A Chinese study suggested that the two dimensions of the scale were highly correlated with the sum score of the scale ($rs = .90$ and $.91$, respectively; Ye & Rocklin, 1988). Hence, a sum score of the scale was computed in this study. Studies indicated that the Chinese version of the scale had good validity and reliability (Ye & Rocklin, 1988; Wang, 2003). The present study revealed that the internal consistency of the scale was excellent ($\alpha = .94$).

Table 1 Means, Standard Deviations, and Pearson Correlations Among Variables ($N = 916$)

Variable	M	SD	1	2	3	4
1. Teacher-student relationship	3.19	0.53				
2. Student-student relationship	3.31	0.56	.42†			
3. Physical features	2.84	0.64	.53†	.35†		
4. Supporting resources	2.67	0.81	.46†	.25†	.59†	
5. Trait test anxiety	2.17	0.65	−.17†	−.17†	−.11†	−.08*

*$p < .05$. † $p < .01$.

RESULTS

Means, standard deviations, and inter-correlations of the variables are presented in Table 1. Boys ($M = 2.09$, $SD = 0.64$) had lower scores than girls ($M = 2.23$, $SD = 0.66$) on Test Anxiety ($t = 3.14$, $p < .01$, Cohen's $d = 0.22$). Multiple regression analysis indicated that students' perceptions of teacher-student relationship $\beta = −.12$, $p < .01$) and student-student relationship ($\beta = −.13$, $p < .01$) significantly and negatively predicted their trait test anxiety scores, whereas the other two dimensions of school climate were not significant predictors.

Table 2 Regression of School Climate Variables to Predict Test Anxiety

Model	Unstandardized Coefficients			Standardized	t	p
	B	95% CI B	SE	Coefficients β		
Teacher-student relationship	−.31	−.53, −.09	.11	−.12	−2.80	<.001
Student-student relationship	−.57	−.91, −.25	.17	−.13	−3.42	<.001
Physical features	−.08	−.43, .27	.18	−.02	−0.45	.65
Supporting resources	.03	−.13, .19	.08	.01	0.35	.73

DISCUSSION

This study significantly adds to the literature by examining the relationship between Chinese high school students' perceptions of school climate and their trait test anxiety. Results supported the hypothesis and revealed that Chinese high school students' perceptions of teacher-student relationship and student-student relationship negatively predicted their trait test anxiety scores. These findings suggest that the findings in Western samples (Frenzel, *et al.,* 2007; Hembree, 1988) of a relationship between students' perceptions of school climate and test anxiety can be generalized to Chinese students. The findings also suggest that school interpersonal climate is more likely to be related to students' trait test anxiety scores than to other dimensions of school climate. Additionally, the findings imply that improvement of students' teacher-student and student-student relationships may reduce their trait test anxiety.

REFERENCES

Brofenbrenner, U. (1979) *The ecology of human development.* Cambridge, MA: Harvard Univer. Press.

Cemalcilar, Z. (2009) Schools as socialisation contexts: understanding the impact of school climate factors on students' sense of school belonging. *Applied Psychology,* 59, 243–272.

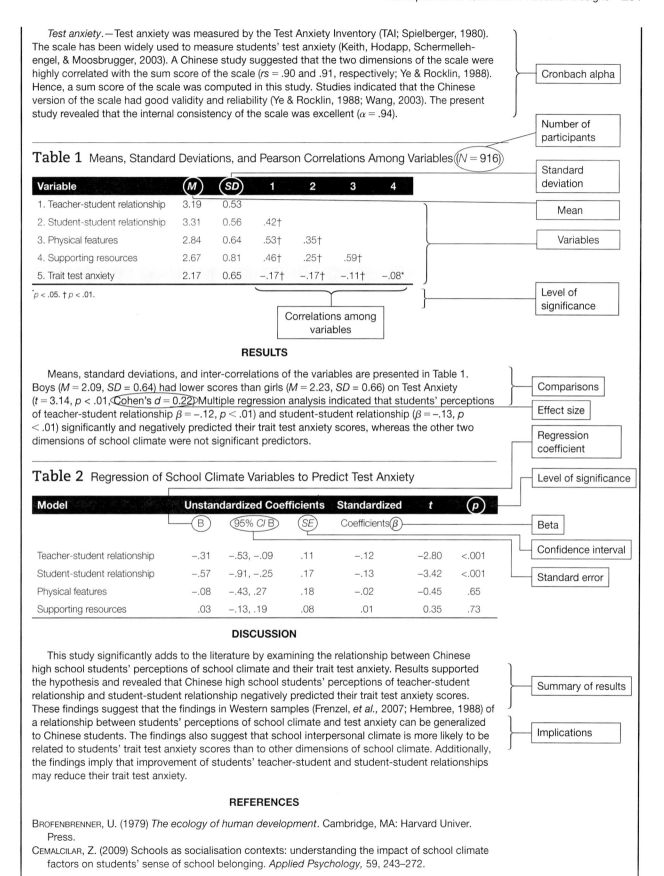

FRENZEL, A. C., PEKRUN, R., & GOETZ, T. (2007) Perceived learning environment and students' emotional experiences: a multilevel analysis of mathematics classrooms. *Learning & Instruction,* 17, 478–493.

HEMBREE, R. (1988) Correlates, causes, effects and treatment of test anxiety. *Review of Educational Research,* 58, 47–77.

KEITH, N., HODAPP, V., SCHERMELLEH-ENGEL, K., & MOOSBRUGGER, H. (2003) Cross-Sectional and longitudinal confirmatory factor models for the german test anxiety inventory: a construct validation. *Anxiety, Stress, & Coping,* 16, 251–270.

LIU, Y., & LU, Z. (2011) Students' perceptions of school social climate during high school transition and academic motivation: a Chinese sample. *Social Behavior and Personality,* 39(2), 207–208.

LOUKAS, A., & MURPHY, J. L. (2007) Middle school student perceptions of school climate: examining protective functions on subsequent adjustment problems. *Journal of School Psychology,* 45, 293–309.

McEVOY, A., & WELKER, R. (2000) Antisocial behavior, academic failure, and school climate: a critical review. *Journal of Emotional & Behavioral Disorders,* 8,130.

SPIELBERGER, C. (1980) *Test Anxiety Inventory: preliminary professional manual.* Palo Alto, CA: Consulting Psychology Press.

WANG, C. (2003) (TAI)[The reliability and validation of the Chinese Version of the Test Anxiety Inventory]. *[Chinese Journal of Clinical Psychology]*, 11, 69–70.

YE, R., & ROCKLIN, T. (1988)[A cross-cultural study of test anxiety]. *Psychological Science Report,* 3, 25–29. *Accepted October 22, 2012.*

Key Terms

Attenuation

Causal–comparative

Comparative designs

Coefficient of determination

Correlational design

Logistic regression

Multiple regression

Coefficient of multiple correlation

Prediction study design

Structural equation modeling

Effect size

Ex post facto

Relationship

Research design

Restriction in range

Secondary data analysis

Survey research

Cross-sectional

Longitudinal

Discussion Questions

1. Why is it important to choose the right kind of research design?
2. When would it be most appropriate to use a descriptive or correlational design?
3. What differentiates a comparative from a correlational design?
4. Why would a causal–comparative or ex post facto design be employed, rather than an experimental design?
5. Why is it important to pilot test a survey?
6. When would it be more appropriate to use a paper survey rather than an electronic survey?

Application Exercise

1. Locate a recently published nonexperimental study in your area of expertise that used a survey to gather data. Classify it with respect to type of design(s), determine whether the questions align well with the design and analyses, and identify limitations to study. Identify the strengths and limitations of the survey.

Check for Understanding Answers

1a. The design needs to align with the question to establish the appropriate logic of the study and to show that the procedures are best for estimating the signal.

2a. Because the direction of influence is not known, and other confounded variables could better account for causal effects.

2b. Since group membership is determined by decisions of the researcher, differences could easily be masked if techniques do not show sufficient variability.

3a. The direction of a possible cause is not known; other confounded variables could be causes.

3b. To provide a reasonable opportunity to find a relationship.

3c. To provide an explanation of how many variables are related to a dependent variable; to predict values of a criterion variable gathered at a later time.

4a. Causal–comparative designs are like natural experiments in which the intervention occurs in the future; ex post facto designs examine interventions that have occurred in the past.

4b. Potential confounding or extraneous variables; no control over the intervention.

5a. Take your pick from Table 8.2.

5b. Pilot testing should be used for any newly designed survey or sample, and when new procedures are used.

Chapter 9
Experimental Research Designs

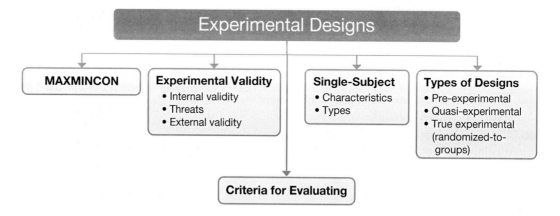

Experimental Designs

- **MAXMINCON**
- **Experimental Validity**
  - Internal validity
  - Threats
  - External validity
- **Single-Subject**
  - Characteristics
  - Types
- **Types of Designs**
  - Pre-experimental
  - Quasi-experimental
  - True experimental (randomized-to-groups)

Criteria for Evaluating

Learning Outcomes

9.1 Explain why researchers need to MAXimize differences between interventions (reasonably), MINimize error, and CONtrol extraneous and confounding variables in designing good experimental research.

9.2 Distinguish among the threats to internal and external validity of experimental designs.

9.3 Identify and apply different types of experimental designs.

9.4 Understand criteria for evaluating experimental studies.

9.5 Know characteristics and limitations of single-subject designs.

Chapter Road Map

While some nonexperimental designs can lead to causal explanations, the venerable experiment gives us the best opportunity to show how an intervention can impact educational outcomes. You know about experiments in science and in other fields, but it is really hard to do good experimental research in education, especially in field settings like schools and colleges. In this chapter, I want to give you the essential principles of good experimental educational research, illustrate the principles with a few fundamental designs, and explain the noise that makes it difficult to find the signal.

Characteristics and Goals of Experimental Research

Learning Outcome 9.1   Explain why researchers need to MAXimize differences between interventions (reasonably), MINimize error, and CONtrol extraneous and confounding variables in designing good experimental research.

In this section we will review the two distinguishing characteristics of experimental research and show how the goal of this type of research, to show a causal link between the intervention and outcome, is best obtained with designs that follow MAXMINCON principles.

Characteristics

In my mind, there is one essential characteristic of all **experimental research**: direct control of an intervention. Direct control means that the researcher treats participants in a pre-planned way (hence, the term *treatment* that is often used when discussing experimental research). That is, the researcher decides on and carries out the specific intervention (or treatment) for one or more "groups" of participants. Most educational experiments compare participants who have received different interventions, in which the researcher must be able to "manipulate" what occurs during the time these different interventions are received or experienced. One simple intervention, for instance, is to give one type of feedback to one group of participants, based on their performance, and compare their progress with individuals who received a different type of feedback. The independent variable is feedback, with two levels, and the researcher determines when and how the "experimental" participants experience it. In educational research, experimental interventions in the field are typically designed as something that can realistically impact outcomes, such as method of instruction, type of rewards given to students, curricula, type of grouping, amount of learning time, and assignments.

A second ubiquitous characteristic of experiments is "control" of extraneous and confounding variables. In an experiment, the researcher seeks to keep all conditions, events, and procedures the same, except the intervention(s). Keeping such factors constant eliminates them as explanations of the results. In other words, the effect, which is measured by differences in the dependent variable, should be differentially influenced only by the intervention(s). That is, control of confounding and extraneous variables is necessary to conclude that an intervention is causally related to the outcome. Although such control is relatively easy in contrived laboratory experiments, it is difficult to achieve in applied educational research.

Control is established by either eliminating possible extraneous or confounding variables, or keeping the effect of such variables constant for all groups. Depending on the design, there may be extraneous or confounding variables that cannot be eliminated. For example, in an experiment designed to investigate which of two methods of instruction is most effective, different teachers may be assigned to a particular method. This would mean that it would be very difficult to separate the effect of different teachers from the impact of the instruction.

A third characteristic that is critical in experiments in which two or more groups are compared is determining that there are no systematic differences between the individuals of one group and those of comparison groups. Differences could include achievement, gender, attitudes, backgrounds, and a host of other characteristics. The goal is to have statistical "equivalence" of the groups. This is most effectively achieved with random assignment of a sufficient number of participants to each group. The use of random assignment is so important that some researchers regard it as an essential characteristic, that a study should not be classified as an experiment without random assignment. My view is less strict—there are many good studies of interventions without random assignment.

> **Author Reflection**   *I should point out that sometimes confusion exists about what an "experiment" is because of how science is taught. In some science "experiments," there is simply observation following an intervention or influence, such as mixing two chemicals. Other science "experiments" have a control or comparison group. My take for understanding educational research is that as long as there is researcher control of the intervention, and you measure change or differences, that qualifies as an experiment.*

Goals

The main goal of an experiment is to establish a cause and effect signal—to be able to say that the dependent variable was or was not clearly affected only by the intervention. The challenge is the part about being able to show a change or difference, then say it's the intervention and not something else that caused it. One way to think about this from a design perspective is to consider noise as a possible influence. As a researcher, you want your experiment to give you the best and clearest signal. In the end, though, as with measurement, you get only the *observed* signal. The *real* signal is affected by noise (error and other factors). As with other educational research designs, you need to minimize the noise. That's the hard part with experiments. You already know about measurement noise from Chapters 6 and 7, which surely will exist in most educational studies; now you must be concerned with noise caused by other factors influencing the dependent variable and the nature of the intervention. There will be noise; it's only a matter of how much.

You will get the clearest signal if you design experiments with three goals:

1. MAXimize the systematic variation between comparison groups or times.
2. MINimize the error variance.
3. CONtrol the variance due to extraneous and confounding variables.

These three goals can be put together to make the word **MAXMINCON**. It's a great acronym to remember what every experimental design is trying to achieve. *MAXimizing systematic variation* simply means giving yourself the best chance to show a difference (similar to my favorite, *sensitivity*). For example, a study of the effect of small group instruction would have a better chance of showing a difference if groups of 8 or 9 were compared with groups of 20 to 25, rather than comparing groups of 8 or 9 to groups of 11 or 12. Or consider a study on the effect of diet on weight. You wouldn't do it for 1 day and expect an effect! The caveat with MAXimizing systematic variation is that while the differences between the levels of the independent variable need to be clear, those differences also need to be reasonable. It wouldn't make sense to compare class sizes of 3 or 4 to 20 or 25 because the difference is unreasonable.

Error variance is MINimized by standardization in the intervention procedures and context in which the study takes place. CONtrol is achieved by being aware of possible extraneous and confounding variables, then taking action to remove, or at least lessen, their influence. These goals will be further elucidated in the following sections in our discussion of different designs.

Check for Understanding 1

1a.   What is the overall goal of experimental research?

1b.   How does maximizing systematic variation, minimizing error variance, and controlling confounding variables impact the design of good experiment?

Experimental Validity

Learning Outcome 9.2   Distinguish among the threats to internal and external validity of experimental designs.

In the language and jargon of experimental research, two concepts are used to describe the level of credibility that results from the studies: *internal validity* and *external validity*. We will consider internal validity first because the primary purpose of experiments relates most closely to this concept.

Internal Validity

Internal validity is the sine qua non of experiments. It refers to the extent to which the intervention, and not extraneous or confounding variables (noise), produced the observed effect. A study is said to be *strong* in internal validity if extraneous and confounding variables have been controlled; or, conversely, if something other than the intervention was responsible for the effect, the study has *weak* internal validity. As we will see, there are many ways to design experiments, and each design controls for different extraneous/confounding variables. As a result, at the outset, some designs are relatively strong in internal validity, whereas other designs are comparatively weak.

Most possible extraneous/confounding variables fall into one of several major categories. These categories, often referred to as "threats" to internal validity, comprise factors that may weaken the argument that the intervention was solely responsible for the observed effects. We will discuss these threats briefly and then consider them within the context of different experimental designs. These factors represent the most important aspects of an experiment in interpreting the quality of the research. When you read an experimental study, you should keep each threat in mind and ask: Is this a *plausible* threat to the internal validity of the study? The word *plausible* is key. To be a plausible threat to internal validity, two conditions must be met: (1) the factor must influence the dependent variable, and (2) the factor must be different in amount or intensity across levels of the independent variable. This means that if a factor is present to the same extent at all levels of the independent variable, it is not a threat to internal validity, even if it does affect the dependent variable.

In identifying plausible or likely threats to internal validity, it is helpful to first eliminate threats that are not even possible, or are very unlikely. As we will see, these are typically determined by the specific design that is used. For threats that are possible or potential, and not controlled, it is then necessary to consider whether the threat is plausible or probable. This determination is made by examining how the study was carried out. In Figure 9.1 a decision tree is illustrated to help guide you through the process of determining the plausibility of threats to internal validity.

Keep in mind that the names of these various threats to internal validity that I have used should not be interpreted literally. Often, the names have a broader meaning than the term may at first suggest. While some of the threats are unique to this book, most were established many years ago by Campbell and Stanley (1963) and have stood the test of time. Some of the factors identified for both internal and external validity have been applied to nonexperimental studies as well.

In the end, it is most important to know what factors can constitute plausible rival explanations for a particular study, not categorizing them correctly. On now to the terrible 12 threats to internal validity.

DOSAGE   As you are probably aware, clinical trials in medicine are typically searching for the right dosage of a treatment or drug. There are clearly important reasons for finding the right amount of an intervention, such as how much radiation is needed – there needs to be a sufficient amount to kill cancer but not cause too many undesirable side effects. In education, **dosage** of an intervention refers to its intensity and duration. What might not be effective in a small dose might work well in larger doses. Consider the impact of small group counseling to alleviate adolescent anxiety. How many sessions are needed? Just one or two might be insufficient to show changes in anxiety. Research could easily show that if the groups met eight times anxiety would be lessened. The failure of finding an effect, then, is because of inadequate dosage.

Figure 9.1 Decision Tree for Determining Threats to Internal Validity

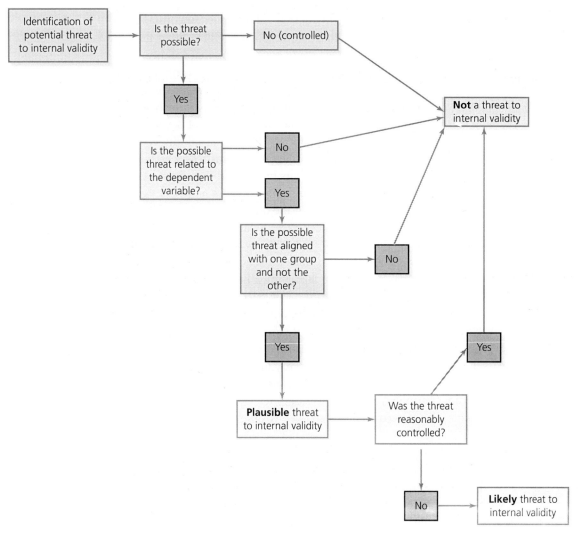

HISTORY   In an experiment, some amount of time elapses between the onset of the intervention and the measurement of the dependent variable. Although this time is necessary for the intervention to take effect and influence the participants, it allows for other events to occur that may also affect the dependent variable. **History** is the category of uncontrolled and/or unanticipated events or conditions that occur during the intervention that influence the dependent variable. If some event does occur during the study that is plausibly related to the dependent variable, it is difficult to know whether the independent variable, the event or condition, or some combination of the two produced the result. In this sense, the event or condition is confounded with the independent variable; the two cannot be separated.

History threats can occur "within" the study as participants are affected by something that happens in conjunction with the intervention (internal history), or from something "outside" the experimental setting (external history). Internal history is illustrated in a situation where an unexpected disciplinary event that distracts a class receiving a method of instruction could adversely affect the influence of the lesson. Students in this class might score lower than other classes, but the researcher does not know whether this result was caused by the distraction or the method of instruction.

External history could be a threat if during a unit studying the Middle East a major international crisis occurs in Syria. If the students are affected by knowledge of the crisis, which in turn influences the way they respond to a multicultural attitude questionnaire, this event, external to the experimental setting, constitutes a plausible history threat to the internal validity of the study. Figure 9.2 illustrates a history threat to internal validity for a single group study on the effect on students' multicultural attitudes of teaching a unit about Russia.

Conditions that vary systematically with different groups can also be problematic. Let's say one intervention group is in a room that is very hot, the other in a room with normal temperature. This condition difference in temperature is a confounding variable and could influence the results. Similarly, consider an experiment that compares two methods of instruction. One intervention is in the morning and the other is in the afternoon. A confounding variable, time of day, would constitute at least a possible threat to the internal validity of the study. In general, if both groups in an experiment have the same experiences, in very similar conditions, history would probably not be a threat to internal validity.

SELECTION   In experiments in which two or more groups of participants are compared, special attention to the characteristics of the participants in each group is needed. In some experiments, **random assignment** is used to determine which participants will receive each intervention. This procedure helps ensure that the different groups of participants are comparable on such characteristics as ability, socioeconomic status, motivation,

Figure 9.2 History Threat to Internal Validity

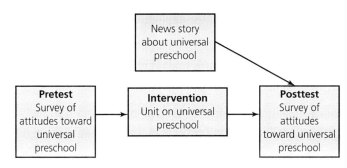

Figure 9.3 Selection Threat to Internal Validity

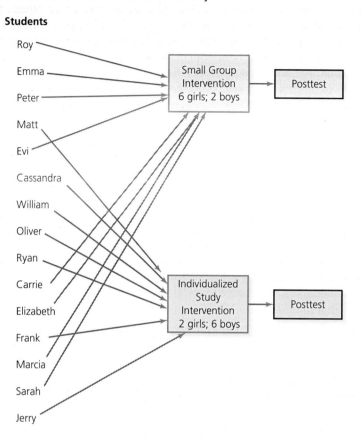

attitudes, and interests. However, in other experiments the participants are not randomly assigned, and sometimes only a few participants or groups are randomly assigned. In these circumstances, it is possible that systematic differences will exist between the groups on characteristics of the participants. If these differences are related to the dependent variable, there is a threat of **selection** to internal validity (sometimes called *selection bias* or *differential selection*; note that this is not the same as selection of participants from a population). For example, suppose one class is assigned to receive the blue health curriculum and another class receives the red health curriculum. The students are not randomly assigned to the classes; in fact, the students who have the blue curriculum are more capable academically than the students in the other class. At the end of the experiment, the students who had the blue curriculum did better on a test of health concepts than the other class. Surprised? Obviously, the result is related to the initial differences between the classes, and the study would be judged to have very weak internal validity.

Figure 9.3 shows why selection can be a threat to internal validity even with random assignment. The students in the class are randomly assigned to either the small group intervention or the individualized study intervention. Though not likely, when the random assignment was completed, the small group intervention had many more girls than boys. Differences due to gender, then, would constitute a potential threat to internal validity.

MATURATION As stated earlier, there is some passage of time in an experiment. Just as history events may affect the results, changes that may occur *within* the participants over time may also alter the results. These changes are called **maturation** threats. People develop in naturally occurring ways that, over a sufficient period of time, can influence the dependent variable separately from a treatment condition. These can include physical, social, and mental development. For example, in an experiment on the effect of a new orientation course on the adjustment of college freshmen, the researcher may measure adjustment before college begins and then again at the end of the first year, after an orientation class. Although it would be nice to attribute positive changes in adjustment to the orientation course, you would need to consider the natural maturation process of 18- and 19-year-olds and how much adjustment would have been influenced by this process.

Maturation also includes relatively short-term changes in people as they become tired, bored, hungry, or discouraged. Imagine that a researcher who needs to measure the attitudes of third-graders toward science, mathematics, reading, and art asks the children to answer questions for an hour to complete the questionnaire. What do you suppose the children will be doing after the first 20 minutes or so?

PRETESTING   A *pretest* is a measure of the dependent variable that is given before the intervention begins. When the pretest is used in an experiment, it is possible for the participants to act differently *because they took the pretest*. For example, if two groups are given a pretest measuring self-concept, the participants may be sensitized to issues concerning the development of self-concept because they took the pretest. Although one group may receive an intervention to improve self-concept, those in another group may become motivated to do some outside reading that they otherwise would not have done; this reading would probably affect changes in their self-concept and the results of the study. This threat is termed **pretesting** or *testing*. Pretesting is also a threat when a pretest given to single group of participants influences responses on the posttest. In a study of changes of achievement, this is likely if there is a pretest of knowledge, a short lesson, and then the same posttest. If a study seeks to determine the effect of a lesson on attitudes, and an attitude questionnaire is used as a pretest, simply reading the questions might stimulate the participants to think about the topic and change their attitudes.

INSTRUMENTATION   The quality of the measurement used for the dependent variable can affect the results of research in several ways. **Instrumentation** refers to threats to internal validity because of unreliability in measurement. Instrumentation also refers to changes in the measures or procedures for obtaining data. For example, if a researcher in an observational study has one set of observers for one group of participants and a second set of observers for another group, any differences between the groups may be due to the different sets of observers. Observers or interviewers can also become bored or tired or change in other ways that affect the results.

INTERVENTION REPLICATION   In an experiment, the intervention should be repeated so each participant of one group receives the same intervention *separately* and *independently* of the other members of the group. Actually, the idea is that there really is no "group" as if everyone is together for the intervention. "Group" means only that some individuals are assigned one intervention, and other individuals the other intervention, and that they are statistically analyzed by a group mean. They are a "group" only because they get the same intervention. For example, if you test a new method of instruction with a class, teaching them as a group together, you have only one "replication" of the intervention; that is, the intervention is conducted once. In this case, the group is considered a single participant, so several classes are needed to do the experiment properly. **Intervention replication** is a threat to internal validity to the extent that the reported number of participants in the study is not the same as the number of replications of the intervention. Suppose a video intervention is shown once, to the entire group at the same time. This type of group intervention is a single replication. However, if each student went to a separate room and viewed the video alone, the number of interventions would be equal to the number of students.

In Excerpt 9.1, the authors describe how small groups of students, rather than individual students, are used as the number of replications.

EXCERPT 9.1

Appropriate Attention to Intervention Replication

Each group consisted of 3 participants, resulting in 15 control groups and 15 experimental groups.... All analyses... are based on the group level. Analysis on the group level was necessary because the individuals in a group were not independent of each other. (pp. 274, 282)

SOURCE: Engelmann, T., Tergan, S., & Hesse, R. W. (2010). Evoking knowledge and information awareness for enhancing computer-supported collaborative problem solving. *The Journal of Experimental Education, 78*, 268–290.

PARTICIPANT ATTRITION **Participant attrition** (some researchers refer to this threat as *mortality* or *differential attrition*, or simply *attrition*) occurs when participants systematically drop out of or are lost from the study, and their absence affects the results. This is most likely to be a problem in research that extends over a long period of time, but it can also be a threat to short experiments if one of the interventions causes participants to drop out. Consider a study that compares two weight loss interventions. If the group with mandatory exercise has attrition of half the participants, whereas the group with a different diet experienced little attrition, participant attrition is a threat to internal validity. In this instance, the groups would no longer be comparable at the end of the study, even if there was random assignment. (As you may have already surmised, participant attrition is also an important threat to nonexperimental longitudinal research).

In Excerpt 9.2, the researchers analyzed attrition because approximately 42% of the initial sample of college students were not available at the completion of the study.

STATISTICAL REGRESSION **Statistical regression** (sometimes called *regression toward the mean, regression effect,* or *regression artifact*) refers to the tendency of groups of participants who score extremely high or low on a pretest to score closer to the mean on the posttest, regardless of the effect of the intervention. That is, a group of very low pretest scores is likely to be higher on the posttest, and a group of very high pretest scores is likely to be lower on the posttest (refer to Figure 9.4; 40 is the mean score of the low group on the first test, 150 is the mean score of the high group). Statistical regression is a result of measurement error and a function of mathematical probability. It is a threat when groups are selected for research *because* they have high or low

---

EXCERPT 9.2

Analysis of Participant Attrition

We conducted attrition analyses to examine whether students who were not available at follow-up ($n = 403$) differed on variables of interest at baseline from those who remained in the study. We observed no significant differences between attriters and nonattriters on baseline alcohol use measures, but some differences did emerge on normative perceptions .... Cross-tabulation of attriters by treatment type revealed no evidence of experimental mortality ... 44% attriters in the SSNC condition and 45% in the ISNC condition. (p. 53)

SOURCE: Reilly, D. W., & Wood, M. D. (2008). A randomized test of a small-group interactive social norms intervention. *Journal of American College Health, 57*(1), 53–60.

Figure 9.4 Illustration of Statistical Regression

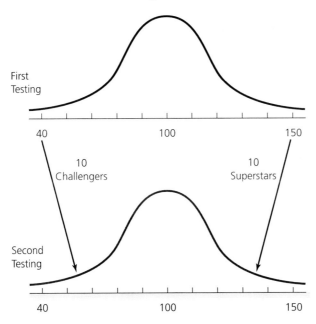

scores. For example, in studies of programs to help low achievers or students with low self-concept, the participants could very well be initially selected on the basis of low pretest scores. It would be expected that mathematically, without any influence of a treatment, the posttest scores of these students, *as a group*, will be higher because of statistical regression. Wily researchers know this—to show a positive change, pick the lowest-scoring individuals with no control or comparison group, and watch them improve!

DIFFUSION OF INTERVENTION   In experiments with two or more groups, it is best if the groups do not know about the other interventions. If a control or comparison group does come into contact with an intervention group or knows what is happening to that group, the effects of the intervention could spread (or, to use the more specific "scientific" term, *ooze*) to the other group. **Diffusion of intervention** is a threat if an intervention given to one group affects other groups that do not receive that intervention. Suppose a researcher tests the effect of preschool on children by randomly assigning one twin from each family to a preschool. Diffusion of treatment is a threat because it is probable that any influence of the preschool is "diffused" to the other child when they are together at home.

EXPERIMENTER EFFECTS   **Experimenter effects** refers to attributes, expectations, or behaviors of the researcher that influence the results. In an ideal experiment, the researcher has no effect on the responses of the participants; they would be detached and uninvolved. Attributes of the experimenter include such characteristics as age, sex, race, status, hostility, authoritarianism, and physical appearance. Participants may respond differently to certain characteristics. For example, studies suggest that female counselors are likely to elicit more self-disclosure from the client than male counselors are.

Experimenter expectancy refers to deliberate or unintentional effects of bias on the part of the experimenter, which is reflected in differential treatment of the participants—e.g., being more reassuring to the group the experimenter "wants" to do better. If the experimenter is involved in the research as an observer, as an interviewer, or in implementing the intervention, the procedures reported should show that bias has not influenced the results. For example, if the experimenter is observing beginning teachers who have been assigned a mentor, which is hypothesized to result in more effective teaching compared with beginning teachers who do not have a mentor, the experimenter's expectation that mentoring helps may influence what is observed and recorded. In fact, this potential source of error is true for all observers and interviewers, whether or not they are the researchers conducting the study. Observers and interviewers should be unaware of the specifics of the research. They should not know the hypothesis of the study or which participants are the "experimental" ones.

PARTICIPANT EFFECTS   In an ideal experiment, as well as a nonexperiment, participants respond naturally and honestly. However, when people become involved in a study, they often change their behavior simply because they understand they are "participants," and sometimes these changes affect the results. **Participant effects** (also called *subject effects* and/or *reactivity*) refers to changes in behavior, initiated by the participants themselves, in response to being in the experiment. If participants have some idea of the purpose of the study or are motivated to "do well," for example, they may alter their behavior to respond more favorably. Participants will pick up cues from the experimental setting and instructions, which may motivate them in specific ways (these cues are called *demand characteristics*).

Participants in many studies will also want to present themselves in the most positive manner. Thus, positive self-presentation, or *social desirability*, may affect the results. For instance, most people want to appear intelligent, competent, and emotionally stable, so they may resist interventions that they perceive as manipulating them in negative ways, or they may fake responses to appear more positive. Some participants may increase positive or desirable behavior simply because they know they are receiving special treatment (this is termed the *Hawthorne effect*). Control group participants may try harder because they see themselves in competition with a treatment group or may be motivated because they did *not* get the treatment (this is termed the *John Henry effect* or *compensatory rivalry*). Other participants, when they realize that they were not selected for what they believe is a preferred treatment, may become demotivated (this is called *resentful demoralization*). Finally, many individuals will react positively, with increased motivation or participation, because they are doing something new and different (this is termed the *novelty effect*).

I know this is a pretty long list of possible threats to internal validity, but it is important to keep them in mind. Knowing them will help you design a good experiment (remember, CONtrol), and when you read studies you will be able to spot potential noise. As we review some of the most frequently used experimental designs, you will see that some of these threats are of greater concern in some designs than in others. Other potential threats are related more to how contrived the study is, rather than to the design itself, and some threats are never completely controlled. In the end, internal validity is a matter of professional judgment about whether it is *reasonable* that *possible* threats are *likely* to affect the results (that is, become plausible or probable rival hypotheses). This kind of judgment is essential. In the excellent words of noted researcher Lee Shulman (2005):

> Truth is, research is all about exercising judgment under conditions of uncertainty, and even experimental designs don't relieve us of the judgmental burdens. The acts of designing experiments themselves involve value judgments, and interpreting the results always demands careful judgment. (p. 48)

Table 9.1 Summary of Threats to Internal Validity

Threat	Description	Example
Dosage	Inadequate amount of the intervention	A short performance assessment is not effective; a long performance assessment is effective.
History	Unplanned events or different conditions that occur during the research	Fire drill occurs in the middle of a study on the effect of a computerized lesson.
Selection	Different characteristics of participants in groups that are compared	Students from a private school who have strong parental support are compared with students from a public school who have weak parental support.
Maturation	Maturational or other natural changes in the participants	Change in critical thinking of college students is attributed to a rigorous curriculum.
Pretesting	Taking a pretest that affects subsequent behavior	Students take a pretest on their opinion toward creationism, read and discuss a book, then are posttested.
Instrumentation	Differences in results due to unreliability or changes in instruments, raters, or observers	One rater graded all the intervention group tests and a second rater graded all the control group tests.
Intervention replications	Only a small number of independent, repeated interventions	A new method of instruction, using group games, is administered in three classes.
Participant attrition	Loss of participants	More participants drop out of the study from the intervention group, which was required to have strenuous exercise, than control participants.
Statistical regression	Scores of extreme groups of participants moving closer to the mean	Students with the worst free-throw-made percentage are used to test a new strategy for improving the accuracy of making free throws.
Diffusion of intervention	Intervention effects influencing control or comparison groups	Fifth-grade students not able to participate in a new book club (control group) are resentful of the intervention group.
Experimenter effects	Deliberate or unintended effects of the researcher	A teacher unconsciously helps experimental students get higher test scores.
Participant effects	Changes in behavior generated by the participant by virtue of being in a study	Students give the professor high evaluations because they know he is up for tenure and their evaluations are key evidence.

Table 9.1 lists the 12 categories of threats to internal validity, with definitions and examples. Although these names will help you remember specific kinds of threats, the bottom line is being able to recognize what might be messing up a study.

Author Reflection *I often suggest to my students that they need to list these threats, and tape the list to their bathroom mirrors. Some have actually told me that it helped! These threats are really important, so whatever you can do to memorize them will put you ahead of the game. It's an excellent cost/benefit ratio.*

External Validity

The second concept that is used to describe the usefulness of findings from an experiment is *external validity*. **External validity** refers to the extent to which the results can be generalized to other participants, measures, interventions, procedures, and settings. Factors to consider in making appropriate generalizations are summarized in Table 9.2. To be able to make appropriate generalizations, you will need to attend carefully to the specific procedures for implementing an intervention, just as you need to know about the participants' age, gender, socioeconomic status, and other characteristics to

Table 9.2 Factors Affecting Generalizability

Factor	Description
Participants	Characteristics of participants, such as socioeconomic status, age, gender, race, and ability. Whether and how participants are selected from a larger population; conclusions based on group averages may be inappropriately assumed true for individuals or subgroups within the sample; participants' awareness of the research.
Situation	Characteristics of the setting in which the information is collected (e.g., naturally occurring or contrived, time of day, surroundings).
Time	Some explanations change over time (e.g., years or decades).
Interventions	Characteristics of the way in which an experimental intervention is conceptualized and administered.
Measures	Nature and type of measures used to collect information.

generalize appropriately to other individuals or groups. Similar to internal validity, external validity is described along the weak to strong continuum, depending on the specifics of the study's design. It is quite possible for a study to be strong in internal validity and weak in external validity. In fact, because the primary purpose of experiments is to control extraneous variables, external validity is often weak.

Usually, external validity refers to generalizing *from* a sample or set of conditions *to* a population or other individuals or contexts. It may also be inappropriate to make generalizations *within* the sample. Generalizing within the sample means that the researcher inappropriately attributes the effect on the whole group to subgroups of individuals. For example, if a class of sixth-graders was used in an experiment and the class as a whole showed a positive gain in achievement, it may not be accurate to generalize the findings to subgroups such as the males or high-aptitude students. There would need to be specific analysis of these groups to draw this conclusion. In other words, what may be true for the class as a whole may not be true for a subgroup.

Check for Understanding 2

2a. What is the difference between internal validity and external validity?

2b. What two conditions are needed for a confounding variable to be a legitimate threat to internal validity?

2c. Why is establishing strong internal validity difficult for educational experiments that are conducted in the field?

Types of "Group" Experimental Designs

Learning Outcome 9.3   Identify and apply different types of experimental designs.

We now turn our attention to six fundamental "group" experimental designs. These designs will illustrate how some threats to internal validity are controlled by specific design features, and how other threats are not controlled. This gives you a good initial idea of which threats to consider.

Experimental designs include four essential components: (1) interventions, (2) pretests and posttests, (3) the number of "groups" in the study, (4) the presence or absence of random assignment. These components will be represented with the following notation system:

R	Random assignment
X	Intervention(s) (subscripts indicating different interventions)
O	Observation (pretest or posttest; subscripts indicating different dependent variables)
A, B, C, D	Groups of participants

Single-Group Designs

There are two types of experimental single-group designs. (Remember, group refers to individuals, each of whom experiences an intervention or serves as a control.) These two designs, and the next one, are often called *pre-experimental* because they usually have inadequate control of many threats to internal validity. In some circumstances the designs can provide good information, but, as we will see, this occurs only in special conditions.

In the **single-group posttest-only design** the researcher identifies participants, administers an intervention to each participant, and then makes a posttest observation of the dependent variable. It can be represented as follows:

$$\frac{\text{Group}}{\text{A}} \longrightarrow \frac{\text{Intervention}}{X_1} \longrightarrow \frac{\text{Posttest}}{O_1}$$

This is the weakest experimental design because without a pretest or another group of participants, there is nothing that the posttest result can be compared to. This design is useful only when the researcher can be sure of the knowledge, skill, or trait that will be changed before the intervention is implemented, and when no extraneous events occur at the same time as the treatment that could affect the results. For example, suppose your research class instructor conducted an "experiment" by having you learn about statistical regression or something even more exciting, like construct irrelevance. It may be reasonable to assume that you had little knowledge about these concepts if this is your first research course, and it is unlikely that there would be any extraneous events or experiences that would also affect your knowledge of the concepts. In this circumstance, the single-group posttest-only design can give you credible information.

The **single-group pretest–posttest design** differs from the single-group posttest-only design by the addition of a pretest:

$$\frac{\text{Group}}{\text{A}} \longrightarrow \frac{\text{Pretest}}{O_1} \longrightarrow \frac{\text{Intervention}}{X_1} \longrightarrow \frac{\text{Posttest}}{O_1}$$

A single group of participants is given a pretest, then the intervention, and then the posttest, which is the same as the pretest. The results are determined by comparing the pretest score to the posttest score. Although a change from pretest to posttest could be due to the intervention, other causal factors must be considered. Suppose an experiment is conducted to examine the effect of an in-service workshop on teachers' attitudes toward gifted education. An instrument measuring these attitudes is given to all teachers in a school division before 2-day workshops are conducted and again after the workshops (one workshop for each school). What are some possible threats to the internal validity of this study?

First, because there are no control or comparison groups, we cannot be certain that extraneous events have not occurred, in addition to the workshop, that would change attitudes. Perhaps an article that appeared in the local paper during the 2 days of the workshop changed some attitudes, or maybe some of the teachers in some groups gave moving testimonials. Second, if the teachers began with negative attitudes for some reason, statistical regression would be a threat. There would likely be some positive change even if there were no intervention. Third, pretesting is a significant threat in this study because awareness from completing the pretest questionnaire may affect attitudes. Fourth, attrition would be a problem if a significant number of teachers who do not like the workshop fail to show up for the posttest. Fifth, maturation is a potential threat if the teachers are tired at the end of the second day. Finally, experimenter and participant effects are definitely threats in this type of study if the teachers want to please the person conducting the workshop. With this number of plausible threats, the study would, in all likelihood, be very weak in internal validity.

The single-group pretest–posttest design will have more potential threats to internal validity as the time between the pretest and posttest increases and as the intervention becomes less controlled. The design can be good for studies in which participant effects will not influence the results, such as aptitude tests, and when history threats can be reasonably dismissed. The design is strengthened if several pretest observations are possible, thereby providing an indication of the stability of the trait. (If there is a sufficient number of both pretests and posttests, the study may be called an *abbreviated time series* design.)

Suppose you want to study a new technique for increasing student attendance, which involves having teachers make targeted phone calls to the parents of students who tend to be absent. All teachers in the school participate. Attendance (O_1) is taken each week for 4 weeks prior to initiating the calls. After a week of calling, attendance is taken again. The study could be diagrammed as follows:

Group	Pretests (attendance)	Intervention (phone calls)	Posttest (attendance)
A $\longrightarrow$	$O_1 O_1 O_1 O_1 \longrightarrow$	$X_1 \longrightarrow$	O_1

By having several "pretests," a stable pattern of attendance can be established so that it would be unlikely that a particularly "good" or "bad" week as a pretest would influence the results.

In Excerpt 9.3, the authors describe both the name of the design and the nature of the analysis of results that illustrate a single-group pretest–posttest experiment. Note, too, the attention to design features intended to help rule out experimenter and participant threats.

EXCERPT 9.3

Single-Group Pretest–Posttest Design

The study utilized a single-group pretest/posttest design. In such a design, each participant serves as his or her own control.... All data (pre and post) were entered at the conclusion of the study to reduce potential experimenter and subject effects.... Pretest to posttest results were analyzed to determine whether the course content had a positive

(Continued)

impact on school counselor trainees' perceptions of their readiness to implement the ASCA National Model.... Results indicate that participants' scores increased significantly. (p. 33)

SOURCE: Wilkerson, K., & Eschbach, L. (2009). Transformed school counseling: The impact of a graduate course on trainees' perceived readiness to develop comprehensive, data-driven programs. *Professional School Counseling, 13*(1), 30–37.

Nonequivalent-Groups Designs

The third "pre-experimental" design has a comparison or control group but no pretest. Here is a diagram of the **nonequivalent-groups posttest-only design**, with a control group:

Group	Intervention	Posttest
A $\longrightarrow$	X_1 $\longrightarrow$	O_1
B	$\longrightarrow$	O_1

One group of participants (A) receives the treatment, whereas the other group (B) acts as a control, receiving no intervention. In some nonequivalent-groups posttest-only designs, two or more groups receive different treatments:

Group	Intervention	Posttest
A $\longrightarrow$	X_1 $\longrightarrow$	O_1
B $\longrightarrow$	X_2 $\longrightarrow$	O_1
C $\longrightarrow$	X_3 $\longrightarrow$	O_1

The crucial feature of this design is that the participants in each group may be different in ways that will differentially affect the dependent variable (selection threat). That is, one group may be brighter, more motivated, better prepared, or in some other way different from the other groups on a trait that affects the dependent variable because there are different individuals in each group. Without a pretest, it is difficult to control for such selection differences. For example, if teachers in a single school received an analytic form that was used to evaluate their teaching during the year, and teachers in another school used a holistic form, you might conclude that if teachers in the first school were judged to be more effective, it was because they used analytic forms. However, it may be that the teachers in the first school were *already* more effective! It is also possible that extraneous events in one school affected the results. Therefore, this design is best employed when groups of participants are comparable and can be assumed to be about the same on the trait being measured before the interventions are given to the participants.

Author Reflection *I remember first learning about pre-experimental designs (now quite a few years ago) as being essentially useless, that at the very least one needed to use a quasi-experimental design. Now, I'm convinced that this was too dogmatic. Every experiment, regardless of design, has the potential to contribute important information. As long as the experimenter is sufficiently aware of and considers threats to internal validity, some studies with pre-experimental designs can be credible.*

A second type of nonequivalent-groups design adds a pretest and becomes what is called a **nonequivalent-groups pretest–posttest design**. This design, which is often referred to as a **quasi-experimental design** (because it closely approximates the most desirable randomized experimental designs; there are other quasi-experimental designs), is commonly used in educational research. The design with a control group looks like this:

Group	Pretest	Intervention	Posttest
A $\longrightarrow$	$O_1 \longrightarrow$	$X_1 \longrightarrow$	O_1
B $\longrightarrow$	$O_1 \xrightarrow{\hspace{4cm}}$		O_1

In this diagram, there are two groups of participants, A and B. One group (A) takes the pretest (O_1), receives the intervention (X_1), and then takes the posttest (O_1); the other group (B) takes the pretest, receives no intervention, and takes the posttest. In this diagram, group B is considered a "control" group because it does not receive any type of intervention. In other nonequivalent designs, two or more different interventions may be compared, as indicated in the following diagram (this is a comparison group design):

Group	Pretest	Intervention	Posttest
A $\longrightarrow$	$O_1 \longrightarrow$	$X_1 \longrightarrow$	O_1
B $\longrightarrow$	$O_1 \longrightarrow$	$X_2 \longrightarrow$	O_1
C $\longrightarrow$	$O_1 \longrightarrow$	$X_3 \longrightarrow$	O_1

As a hypothetical example, suppose Mr. Mendez, a social studies teacher, wants to see whether a new way of praising students is more effective than the method he currently uses. Because it would be awkward to use different approaches in the same classroom, Mr. Mendez decides to use the new type of praise in his morning class and to use an afternoon class as a comparison group. At the beginning of the same new unit on the Civil War, Mr. Mendez gives his students a pretest of their knowledge. He then uses the new approach to praising students in the morning class and continues to use the same approach he has been using with his afternoon class. Both classes take the unit posttest at the same time.

The most serious threat to the internal validity of this study is selection (not the only threat, as we will see). For example, Mr. Mendez may find that students do better with the new type of praise, but this may be because the students in the morning class are brighter or more motivated than those in the afternoon class. Even though there is a pretest, which helps to reduce the threat of selection, differences in the participants must be addressed. Sometimes, researchers will use measures of other characteristics of the participants, in addition to the pretest, to show that even though the groups are not "equal," there are probably no significant differences between them.

The nonequivalent-groups pretest–posttest design is often used when participants are available in existing, or "intact," groups, such as classes. In the example with Mr. Mendez, two intact classes were used. This procedure, using intact groups, creates problems other than selection. If the classes meet at different times of the day, as did Mr. Mendez's classes, time of day is a confounding variable. In this example, the same teacher conducted both interventions. Although, in one respect, this is a good condition—because if different teachers were in each class, teachers would be a confounding variable—it also increases the potential for experimenter effects. Perhaps the most serious limitation is that there is only one intervention, given by class, so other

EXCERPT 9.4

Nonequivalent-Groups Pretest–Posttest Design

The present study followed a nonequivalent pretest-posttest control group design involving three instructional conditions: (a) a treatment group with 12 sixth-grade dyads from four primary schools using CL [Cooperative Learning] instruction and practices based on a 2-year staff development CL program, … (b) a control group with 6 sixth-grade dyads from two primary schools using CL instruction and practices based on a 1-year staff development CL program, … and (c) a control group with 6 sixth-grade dyads from one primary school not using CL.(p. 120)

SOURCE: Veenman, S., Denessen, E., van den Akker, A., & vander Rijt, J. (2005). Effects of a cooperative learning program on the elaborations of students during help seeking and help giving. *American Educational Research Journal, 42*(1), 115–151.

extraneous events associated with that one replication may affect the results. Thus, treatment replication is a potential threat to internal validity. Even though a pretest is used in this design, pretesting is not likely to be an extraneous variable since its effect is probably the same for both groups.

Excerpt 9.4 shows how to summarize a nonequivalent-groups pretest–posttest design. This study investigated the effect of a cooperative learning intervention on student achievement. Two equivalent versions of a math test were given to students—one version as the pretest and the other version as the posttest.

A strong indicator that groups are not significantly different, even though there is no random assignment, occurs when the groups are essentially equal on a pretest. That does not rule out other selection differences, but it does help to reduce the likelihood that selection is a plausible threat to internal validity.

In Excerpt 9.5, a nonequivalent pretest–posttest design was used to study the effects of a peer helping program. A diagram of the study would look like this:

Group	Pretests	Intervention	Posttests 1	Posttests 2
A $\longrightarrow$	$O_1 - O_5$ $\longrightarrow$	X_1 $\longrightarrow$	$O_1 - O_5$ $\longrightarrow$	$O_1 - O_5$
B $\longrightarrow$	$O_1 - O_5$ $\longrightarrow$		$O_1 - O_5$ $\longrightarrow$	$O_1 - O_5$

EXCERPT 9.5

Nonequivalent-Groups Pretest–Posttest Design with Multiple Dependent Variables

A pretest, post-test experimental design, involving a treatment and control group, was carried out…. At the end of the training program, both the treatment and the waiting-list control group participants were administered the post-test instruments…. The follow-up-test instruments were administered to both groups six months later…. Results indicate that there was a significant difference between treatment and control groups in specific measures of empathic and reflection skills, but not in communication skills as a general measure. Significant improvements also were found in the treatment group participants' self-esteem and self-acceptance in regard to time. (pp. 255, 261)

SOURCE: Aladag, M., & Tezer, E. (2009). Effects of a peer helping training program on helping skills and self-growth of peer helpers. *International Journal of Advanced Counseling, 31*,255–269.

Randomized-to-groups Designs

These designs are termed **true** (pure) **experimental designs** because the participants have been randomly assigned to different interventions or to an intervention and control condition. In the **randomized-to-groups posttest-only design**, participants are first randomly assigned to the different intervention or control conditions, separately given the intervention (or no intervention, if control), and then given the posttest. There are different individuals in each group. Thus, if the study starts out with 60 participants, 30 of them would be assigned randomly to each group. The design, with a control group, is represented by the following diagram:

Random Assignment	Groups	Intervention	Posttest
R	A	X_1	O_1
	B		O_1

If a comparison group is included, rather than a control group, the design looks like this:

Random Assignment	Groups	Intervention	Posttest
R	A	X_1	O_1
	B	X_2	O_1

In most educational experiments, there is a comparison group rather than a control group because of limited resources and time to work with students, and often there is more than one comparison group:

Randomized-to-Groups		Pretest	Intervention	Posttest
R	A	O_1	X_1	O_1
	B	O_1	X_2	O_1
	C	O_1	X_3	O_1

Random assignment means that each participant has the same probability of being in either the intervention or comparison or control group. Random assignment is used to help ensure that there are no systematic differences in the characteristics of individuals in different groups. This "equalization" can be assumed when a sufficient number of individuals is randomly assigned to each group (generally, 15 or more). The obvious strength of random assignment is the control of selection as a threat to internal validity, as well as many other threats. It is assumed that the participants in each group are essentially "equal" on any characteristics that may affect the dependent variable. However, there are potential threats that are not controlled by random assignment, including diffusion of treatment, experimenter effects, participant effects, intervention replication, and extraneous events within a group of participants, and these need to be considered.

Careful attention needs to be paid to how "randomization" is carried out. If a researcher includes individual participant scores in the analysis, the "unit" of the analysis is the individual. As long as the randomization was done so each participant could be assigned to each group, and there was independent replication of the intervention

EXCERPTS 9.6 AND 9.7

Clustered Randomized-to-Groups Design

This article reports on a small-scale cluster randomized trial of the Johnsons' approach to cooperative learning (Johnson et al., 2013) as an intervention to prevent bullying and victimization in middle school.... The sample was derived from a small-scale randomized trial of cooperative learning in 15 rural middle schools in the Pacific Northwest. Schools were matched based upon size and demographics (e.g., free and reduced-price lunch [FRPL] percentage) and randomized to condition (i.e., intervention vs. wait-list control). (p. 1194)

SOURCE: Van Ryzin, M. J., & Roseth, C. J. (2018). Cooperative learning in middle school: A means to improve peer relations and reduce victimization, bullying, and related outcomes. *Journal of Educational Psychology, 110*(8), 1192–1201.

In order to isolate the causal effect of teacher-family communication on student engagement, we designed a cluster randomized trial that addressed concerns about both equity and potential spillover effects. We began by randomly assigning students to their class-taking groups. We then randomly assigned seven of the 14 class-taking groups to either the treatment or control condition so that students in the treatment group would only attend classes with their treatment-group peers. By assigning treatment at the class-taking-group level, we eliminate the potential for any spillover effects due to students in the treatment group interacting with their control-group peers in the same classroom. (p. 124)

SOURCE: Kraft, M. A., & Dougherty, S. M. (2013). The effect of teacher–family communication on student engagement: Evidence from a randomized field experiment. *Journal of Research on Educational Effectiveness, 6*(3), 199–222.

for each participant, then it is a randomized-to-groups design. In contrast, a study in which there are four existing classes of students, two of which are randomly assigned to the treatment and two to the control condition, is not a randomized-to-groups design. In this case, randomly assigning only two cases to each group is not sufficient to be defined as a true experiment.

In many large-scale experiments, random assignment is commonly done by class or school. In these studies, students are considered "clustered" or "nested" within each larger unit. These units create new sources of influence on the results that need to be considered, both statistically in how results are analyzed, and by knowing the potential influences of differences between the units. Both Excerpts 9.6 and 9.7 illustrate cluster designs. The study in Excerpt 9.6 examines the effect of cooperative learning on bullying and victimization with randomization by school. In Excerpt 9.7, students are individually randomized but then the intervention is accomplished through "class-taking groups." Note in Excerpt 9.6 that matching is used to reduce the threat of selection differences.

A second type of true experiment, the **randomized-to-groups pretest–posttest design**, has both a pretest and a posttest. Otherwise, it is the same as the randomized-to-groups posttest-only design. A pretest is used to further "equalize" the groups statistically, in addition to what random assignment provides. Researchers use a pretest with random assignment when there may be small, subtle effects of different interventions, when differential participant attrition is possible, and when there is a need to analyze subgroups that differ on the pretest. Participants can be randomly assigned before or after the pretest. In some studies, the pretest scores are used to match participants, and then one participant from each pair is randomly assigned to each group. Excerpt 9.8 describes a randomized pretest–posttest experiment that used four different pretests.

Table 9.3 summarizes threats to internal validity of the previously described six designs. Although the "scoreboard" will give you a good start in evaluating the credibility of an experiment, each study must be judged individually. Overall, credibility is determined not so much by the particular design but by how well the researcher understands and controls for possible threats to internal validity. In essence, an experimenter must be an "anthropologist" of the study, knowing as much as possible about the intervention *as experienced*.

Factorial Designs

All the designs we have considered in this chapter so far have one independent variable. Many experiments, like most nonexperimental studies, will have two or more independent variables (or one independent variable and a moderator variable) and employ what are called **factorial designs**. There are two primary purposes for using factorial designs. One is to see whether the effects of an intervention are consistent across participant characteristics, such as age, gender, or aptitude. The second is to examine what are called **interactions** among the independent variables and moderator variables. Interactions are investigated to see whether the effect of an intervention is moderated or influenced by other interventions or participant characteristics. If a study is testing the effect of two methods of instruction—for example, computerized compared with lecture—it might be desirable to know whether the effectiveness of the methods was the same for males as for females. Thus, the study could have one independent and one moderator variable, each with two levels. The study may be diagrammed in different ways, as illustrated in Figure 9.5. Figures 9.5b and 9.5c show that the students were first divided into groups of males and females and then randomly assigned to the two instructional methods.

A numerical notation system used with factorial designs tells you about the number of independent variables and the number of levels within each independent variable. In the previous example, the notation would be 2×2. Each number indicates a single independent or moderator variable with two levels. If a study has one

Table 9.3 Internal Validity Scoreboard

Threats to Internal Validity

Design	Dosage	History	Selection	Maturation	Pretesting	Instrumentation	Intervention Replications	Participant Attrition	Statistical Regression	Diffusion of Intervention	Experimenter Effects	Participant Effects
Single-Group Posttest-Only	?	–	–	–	NA	?	?	?	–	NA	?	?
Single-Group Pretest-Posttest	?	?	?	–	–	?	?	?	–	NA	?	?
Nonequivalent-Groups Posttest-Only	?	?	–	?	NA	?	?	?	?	NA	?	?
Nonequivalent-Groups Pretest-Posttest	?	?	?	?	?	?	?	?	+	?	?	?
Randomized-to-Groups Posttest-Only	?	?	+	+	NA	?	?	?	+	?	?	?
Randomized-to-Groups Pretest-Posttest	?	?	+	+	?	?	?	?	+	?	?	?

In this table, a minus sign indicates a definite weakness, a plus sign means that the threat is controlled, a question mark indicates a possible source of invalidity, and NA means that the threat is not applicable to the design.

Figure 9.5 Diagrams of 2 × 2 Design

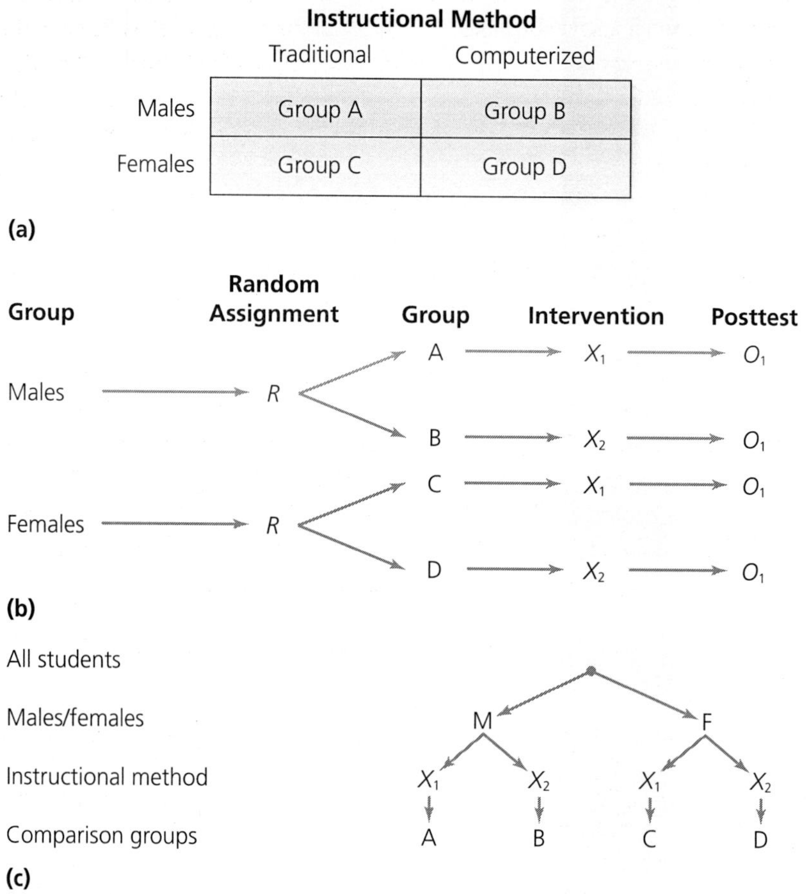

Instructional Method

	Traditional	Computerized
Males	Group A	Group B
Females	Group C	Group D

(a)

Group	Random Assignment	Group	Intervention	Posttest
Males	R	A	X_1	O_1
		B	X_2	O_1
Females	R	C	X_1	O_1
		D	X_2	O_1

(b)

All students	
Males/females	M F
Instructional method	X_1 X_2 X_1 X_2
Comparison groups	A B C D

(c)

Figure 9.6 Notation for a Study of the Effect of Three Types of Teacher Feedback in Grades 2–5

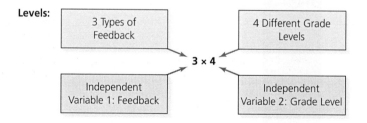

independent variable with three levels and one with four levels, it would be designated as 3 × 4 (refer to Figure 9.6). If a third variable were added, with two levels, it would be 2 × 3 × 4.

Interactions are very important because much of what we do in education is based on the assumption that we should match student characteristics with appropriate instructional methods. What may work well for one type of student may not work well for other students. Factorial designs allow us to test these assumptions. Interactions occur when the effect of one variable differs across the levels of the other variable.

In other words, the effect of a variable is not consistent across all levels of the other variable. Applying this definition to the example in Figure 9.5, we would have an interaction if the difference between males and females for computerized instruction was not the same as the difference between males and females for lecture instruction. This result would show that the effect of the method of instruction depends on whether we are studying males or females. In this example, then, gender is moderating the effect of the interventions, and as such is important to understanding the differential effects of computerized and traditional instruction. This kind of thinking reflects the reality in education much better than single variables do.

An important aspect to consider in interpreting results is that because of possible interactions, what may not be true for a total group may be true for certain participants in the population. That is, for example, if a study shows that for all fourth-graders together, it makes no difference whether they have homework assignments or not, an interaction might show that some low-ability students benefit greatly from homework compared with other low-ability students who receive no homework.

An example of a factorial design is summarized in Excerpt 9.9. In this study, students were randomly assigned to either an intervention or control group, and gender was included as a moderating variable. Note that there was a pretest, how gender was important in explaining the results, and how clustering occurred.

EXCERPT 9.9
Example of Factorial Experimental Design

In September 2005, the school committed three teachers to serve as program instructors and designated 16 senior students to be trained as peer leaders. This allowed for a total of eight program groupings (two peer leaders conducting each group), with 12 first-year students included per group. Incoming ninth-grade students were randomly assigned to the program group ($n = 94$). The remaining 174 students were designated as part of the control group. There were approximately equal proportions of young women and young men in the program and control groups.... All 268 participants completed a baseline survey during the orientation day, in small group administrations, prior to the start of their freshman year.... Results... demonstrated that male students who participated in the program during Grade 9 were significantly more likely to graduate from high school within 4 years than male students in the control group (81% vs. 63%). (pp. 186, 189)

SOURCE: Johnson, V. L., Simon, P., & Mun, E. U. (2014). A peer-led high school transition program increases graduation rates among Latino males. *The Journal of Educational Research, 107*(3), 186–196. Taylor & Francis Group US Books.

Check for Understanding 3

3a.   Why are true experimental designs stronger in internal validity than quasi-experimental designs?

3b.   How is threat of selection "controlled" in the nonequivalent-groups pretest–posttest design?

3c.   Why is a factorial interaction among independent/moderator variables important in experimental research?

Consumer (and Researcher) Tips
Criteria for Evaluating Single-Subject Designs

Learning Outcome 9.4   Understand criteria for evaluating experimental studies.

1. **The primary purpose is to test causal hypotheses.** Experimental research should be designed to investigate cause-and-effect relationships that are anticipated with clear research hypotheses, consistent with theory. The hypothesis implies that there is sufficient descriptive and relationship evidence to warrant an experiment, and gives the researcher a better basis for interpreting the results.

2. **There should be direct control of the intervention.** An essential feature of an experiment is that the researcher controls the intervention(s)—the nature and duration of what the participants experience. If it is not clear that such control has occurred, the ability to make causal interpretations is limited.

3. **The experimental design should be clearly identified.** Although it is not necessary to use the specific terminology in this chapter to identify a design (e.g., randomized-to-groups posttest-only), it is important that sufficient details about the design are provided to enable you to understand what was done to which participants, and the sequence of measurement and interventions. In fact, there should be enough detail so that you could essentially replicate the study. As noted, the threats you need to focus on to evaluate the study depend to a certain extent on the design. If you cannot understand the design, the researcher may not have understood it either!

4. **The design should provide maximum control of extraneous/confounded variables.** The researcher should indicate how specific aspects of the design control possible extraneous and confounding variables. Obvious threats, such as selection in the nonequivalent-groups designs, need to be addressed. If obvious threats are not controlled by the design, the researcher should present a rationale for why a particular threat is not a plausible alternative explanation for the results.

    Use Table 9.4 to systematically evaluate the possibility and plausibility of threats to internal validity. For any given study or design, check first whether the threat is possible, then identify any of those that would be likely. Finally, depending on the specifics of the design, indicate whether any of the likely threats would be considered "fatal flaws."

Table 9.4 Evaluating Threats to Internal Validity

Threat	Possible?	Likely?	Fatal Flaw?
Dosage			
History			
Selection			
Maturation			
Pretesting			
Instrumentation			
Intervention replications			
Participant attrition			
Statistical regression			
Diffusion of intervention			
Experimenter effects			
Participant effects			

5. **The intervention should be described and implemented as planned.** The key features of interventions and procedures need to be described in sufficient detail to allow other researchers to compare it to similar intervention studies, and to allow for research syntheses such as a meta-analysis. A complete description also allows you to connect the theory behind the intervention with what was implemented. Most interventions use labels that can be operationalized in different ways, in much the same way constructs are in measurement. For example, there are several ways of operationalizing "small class," "benchmark testing," "formative assessment strategies," and other interventions. You need enough detail to know what was actually done, not simply the label or general description. At the very least, the key features of the intervention should be completely described.

In field studies, it is important to document that the *planned* intervention was what was *actually* implemented. This can be called a *check on the intervention, adherence, treatment fidelity, treatment integrity, fidelity of implementation,* or *intervention fidelity.* **Intervention fidelity** is strong when evidence is presented that the *enacted* intervention is consistent with *intended* intervention. The evidence could consist of observations, surveys from participants, daily logs of activities, and/or interviews. In a study of the use of feedback to motivate students, for instance, observers in the classroom could determine whether the nature of the feedback provided was consistent with what was planned. A more detailed study of the intervention helps researchers identify whether the level of intervention was constant or fluctuated across implementers. This analysis leads to a better understanding of the conditions in which the intervention is effective.

Excerpts 9.10 and 9.11 show how researchers have addressed intervention fidelity. The first excerpt is from a well-known experiment on class size. The second is from a study that investigated whether university students' academic self-efficacy and achievement could be impacted from participating in workshops on improving study strategies.

EXCERPTS 9.10 AND 9.11
Intervention Fidelity

In the STAR experiment, the primary treatment of interest is the manipulation of class size. The intent of the STAR experiment was to compare the achievement of students in small classes (13–17) with that of students in larger classes (22–26 students) and in larger classes with full-time aides. However, as in any field experiment, it is important to determine how well the treatment was implemented, because implementation is never perfect at all sites. Thus, in evaluating the STAR experiment, it is important to determine the actual size of the classes to see if the intent of the experimenters was realized. (p. 128)

SOURCE: Nye, B., Hedges, L. V., & Konstantopoulos, S. (2000). The effects of small classes on academic achievement: The results of the Tennessee class size experiment. *American Educational Research Journal, 37,* 123–151.

After each workshop, peer coaches completed a written report in which they documented if and how workshops deviated from the planned lesson, identified what worked well, what did not go as planned, and other reflections on the perceived effectiveness of instructional decisions. . . . According to the written and oral reports, there were no substantial deviations from planned lessons and most reports indicated lessons were executed exactly as designed. (p. 31)

SOURCE: Bergey, B. W., Parrila, R. K., Lrocher, A., & Deacon, S. H. (2019). Effects of peer-led training on academic self-efficacy, study strategies, and academic performance for first-year university students with and without reading difficulties. *Contemporary Educational Psychology, 56,* 25–39.

EXCERPT 9.12

Single-Group Pretest–Posttest Design with a Whole Group Intervention

Sixteen ESL students participated in the study... the students were split and assigned into two groups... the groups met for an hour after school once a week for five weeks... the authors compared pre- and post-group scores on the Coopersmith Self-Esteem Inventory-School Form (CSEI-SF) to examine the effectiveness of the group intervention on ESL students' self-esteem. (pp. 65–66)

SOURCE: Shi, Q., & Steen, S. (2012). Using the achieving success everyday (ASE) group model to promote self-esteem and academic achievement for English as a second language (ESL) students. *Professional School Counseling, 16*(1), 63–70.

---

6. **The determination of *n* should be the same as independent replications of the interventions.** In a classic experiment, each participant is randomly assigned to interventions and experiences the intervention independently from others. In some studies, participants are randomly assigned to groups and then all the participants in each group receive one intervention together. Technically, each group in this situation is one "*n*." If each person experiences the intervention separately from the others, each person is one participant. However, if only one intervention is given to a group of people, the group should be identified as one "participant." In reading an experimental study, you should look for the number of times the intervention is replicated, which should be the same as the number of participants in the study. (As discussed in Chapter 10, the statistical results are highly dependent on the number of participants.)

   Excerpt 9.12 is taken from a single group pretest–posttest experiment that investigated the effect of a particular type of group intervention on the self-esteem of English as a second language (ESL) students. Notice how the description of the procedures indicates that there were two groups, each one participating in the intervention. This means that the intervention was replicated twice, once for each group. Consequently, intervention replications pose a serious threat to internal validity. Participants are "clustered" together in each group, creating unique dynamics quite apart from the influence of the intervention. A better way to test the impact of the intervention would be to implement it in many groups. Each group, not each individual, would be considered a "participant."

7. **The measure of the dependent variable must be sufficiently sensitive to capture the change caused by the intervention.** The measurement of the dependent variable needs to be sensitive to change because of what has been implemented from the intervention. That is, it may be difficult to show change in scores on some standardized tests of ability or reasoning, or with relatively stable traits such as self-efficacy or cognitive style. For example, an intervention that focuses on critical thinking in a science class might not be detected by a broad measure of critical thinking that is not specific to science.

8. **The design should be consistent with MAXMINCON.** An experiment will have the best opportunity to show a causal relationship if MAXMINCON is adhered to. You want to be sure that the differences between the interventions have been maximized (though not to a ridiculous degree), that error is minimized, and that threats to internal validity have been accounted for.

The Hedgehog and Fox Interpret the Results of an Experiment

This randomized study shows that when a group of students is asked to make concept maps their learning is improved. I think I'll use concept maps more in my class.

My first impression is that concept maps may help with student achievement for my class, but I need to be sure there are no plausible threats to internal validity. If this was done with just a few classes, the results would be suspect, and even if significant I have to be sure of what worked with those students and whether the method of doing concept maps would work with my students.

Check for Understanding 4

4a. Why is it important for researchers to establish good fidelity of implementation?

4b. What threats to internal validity are most associated with experiments in which the intervention is administered to the whole group rather than individually?

Single-Subject Designs

Learning Outcome 9.5   Know characteristics and limitations of single-subject designs.

In the designs we have considered so far in this chapter, participants are studied as "groups" in the sense that group means are used for data analyses. By conducting experiments with groups, individual differences are pooled and the results can be generalized to other persons who, as a group, are like the participants. However, in some circumstances it may be necessary to administer an intervention to very small numbers of participants. In these situations, researchers conduct their experiments with individuals through **single-subject (or** *single-case*) **designs,** which use one or just a few participants to study the influence of an intervention. The approach of the design is to repeat measures of the dependent variable before and after an intervention is implemented. The basis of comparison is the difference in behavior prior to and then after initiation of the intervention. Single-subject designs are used extensively in research with children and adolescents with special needs, where the focus of change is on individuals rather than on groups.

Characteristics of Single-Subject Research

McMillan and Schumacher (2010) summarize five characteristics of single-subject research:

1. *Reliable measurement:* Because these designs involve multiple measures of behavior, it is important for the instrumentation to be standardized to provide reliable scores. Conditions for data collection, such as time of day and location, should be

the same, and observers must be trained. Consistency in measurement is especially crucial in the transition before and after the intervention.

2. *Repeated measurement:* The same behavior is measured over and over again. This step is different from most experiments, in which the dependent variable is typically measured only once. Repeated measures are needed to obtain a clear pattern or consistency in the behavior over time. This controls for the normal variation of behavior that is expected within short time intervals. This aspect of single-subject designs is similar to abbreviated time series studies, which investigate groups rather than individuals and do not provide for a return to conditions that were present before the intervention was implemented.

3. *Description of conditions:* A clear, detailed description of the conditions of measurement and the nature of the intervention is needed to strengthen internal and external validity.

4. *Baseline and intervention conditions:* Each single-subject study involves at least one baseline and one intervention condition. The **baseline** refers to a period of time in which the target behavior (dependent variable) is observed and recorded as it occurs prior to the intervention. The baseline behavior provides the frame of reference against which future behavior is compared. The term *baseline* can also refer to a period of time following an intervention in which conditions match what was present in the original baseline. The intervention condition is a period of time during which the experimental manipulation is introduced and the target behavior continues to be observed and recorded. Both the baseline and intervention phases of the study need to be long enough to achieve stability in the target behavior.

5. *Single-variable rule:* During a single-subject study, only one variable should be changed from baseline to intervention conditions. In some studies, two variables are changed together during the same intervention condition. This is an interaction in single-subject research.

Types of Single-subject Designs

Although some single-subject designs can be rather complex, most are easily recognized variations of an A–B–A or multiple-baseline design.

A–B–A DESIGN Single-subject designs use a notation system in which A refers to a baseline condition and B to a treatment condition. The order of the letters indicates the sequence of procedures in the study. Thus, an **A–B design** contains one baseline and one intervention condition. In an A–B–A design, the intervention condition is followed by another baseline, as indicated in the following diagram:

Baseline	Intervention (treatment)	Baseline

$$X_1 X_1 X_1 X_1 X_1$$
$$O_1 O_1 O_1 O_1 O_1 O_1 O_1 O_1 O_1 O_1 O_1 O_1 O_1 O_1 O_1$$

This design is called an **A–B–A withdrawal design**. The intervention is introduced after a number of observations of the baseline behavior, and is stopped to return to the same condition that was present during the original baseline measurement. The design allows a strong causal inference if the pattern of behavior changes with the addition and withdrawal of the intervention. Without the second baseline phase, it is possible that extraneous events that occur at the same time as the intervention may account for changes in the behavior.

For example, suppose a teacher is interested in trying a new procedure to reinforce a student, Mary, to increase Mary's time on task (time actually engaged in studying and learning). The dependent variable is time on task. The teacher would observe the

Figure 9.7 Results of A–B–A Single-Subject Design

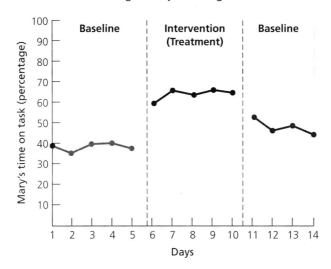

percentage of time Mary is on task for several days to establish a baseline. Then the teacher would introduce the new reinforcement technique and continue to record the percentage of Mary's time on task. After a few days of the new procedure (when the behavior is stable), the teacher would withdraw the new reinforcement technique and record the percentage of time on task for this second baseline period. Figure 9.7 shows how the results would be graphed and indicates evidence that the new technique is affecting Mary's time on task. Given the positive benefits of the new type of reinforcement, the teacher would want to reinstitute it.

One limitation of the A–B–A design is the difficulty in interpreting a positive change that is not altered during the second baseline. In this situation, the intervention may be so strong that its effect lasts a long time, or something else may have occurred with the intervention that affected the behavior and did not stop when the intervention did.

MULTIPLE-BASELINE DESIGNS In a single-subject **multiple-baseline design**, observations are made on several participants, different target behaviors of one or more participants, or different situations. Thus, multiple baselines are conducted across participants, behaviors, or settings. A design that has more than one participant may implement the intervention with each participant or use one or more participants as a control condition. Different behaviors are studied when an intervention is applied to more than one target behavior. For example, the effectiveness of using time-out for

---

EXCERPT 9.13

Single-Subject Multiple-Baseline Study across Behaviors Design

A multiple baseline design across behaviors was employed to evaluate the effects of a randomized group contingency program on students' homework accuracy rates....
Baseline data were collected for 3 weeks, the intervention was implemented for 6 weeks, and follow-up data were obtained for 8 weeks. (p. 474)

SOURCE: Reinhardt, D., Theodore, L. A, Bray, M. A., & Kehle, T. J. (2009). Improving homework accuracy: Interdependent group contingencies and randomized components. *Psychology in the Schools, 46*(5), 471–488.

individuals with attention-deficit disorder can be observed for several types of behavior, including taking food from others and hitting others. If a study examines the effect of the same procedure on behaviors in several different settings or situations, such as different classes, a multiple-baseline across-settings design is employed. For instance, an investigator may be interested in whether time out is as effective with an individual in math class as it is in science class.

Excerpt 9.13 is from an article in which accuracy was examined across three subjects—spelling, mathematics, and reading comprehension—for six fourth-grade students. This resulted in three A–B-A analyses for each individual.

Consumer (and Researcher) Tips
Criteria for Evaluating Single-Subject Designs

1. **There should be reliable measurement of the target behavior.** It is important for the measurement to be standardized and consistent. Evidence for reliability should be presented in the procedures section of the study. If more than one observer is used, interobserver reliability should be reported.

2. **The target behavior should be clearly defined operationally.** There should be a detailed definition of the dependent variable, described operationally in terms of how it is measured.

3. **Sufficient measurements are needed to establish stability in behavior.** There should be enough times behavior is measured to establish stability in the behavior. Typically, a minimum of three or four observations is needed in each phase of the study to provide results that show a small degree of variability. This step is especially important for the baseline condition because this is the level of behavior against which behaviors occurring during the treatment are compared, but it is also necessary for the intervention condition. Often, there is the same number of measures during each phase of the study.

4. **Procedures, participants, and settings should be fully described.** Because the external validity of single-subject designs is relatively weak, the usefulness of the results depends to a great extent on the match among the procedures, characteristics of the participants, and settings in the study with other participants and settings. The best judgments of the extent of this match are made when there is a detailed description of what was done, to whom, and where.

5. **A single, standardized intervention should be used.** The procedures for administering the intervention should be standardized so that precisely the same procedure is given each time. Only one intervention or one combination of interventions should be changed from the baseline to treatment phases of the study.

6. **Experimenter or observer effects should be controlled.** Because of the heavy reliance on a single observer—who, in many cases, is the experimenter—it is important to indicate how potential bias is controlled.

7. **Results should be practically significant.** The results of most single-subject studies are analyzed by inspecting their graphic presentation and judging whether the patterns of behavior in different phases of the study appear to be different. This judgment should be based on graphs that do not distort differences by artificially increasing the intervals used to describe the behaviors. Clear differences should be evident, and they should be significant in practical terms, showing enough of a difference to clearly affect the behavior of the subject. Some single-subject studies use a statistical analysis of the results, but a "statistically significant" difference still needs to have practical significance.

Author Reflection *Is it really worth it to conduct experimental research in education? Sometimes it seems that so many possible and plausible threats to the design exist that it would be nearly impossible to say that there is strong internal validity, especially for field experiments. My perspective on this issue is that yes, field experiments can be very helpful, even with limitations. As long as the researcher is aware of possible threats before conducting the experiment and applies fox-like thinking, the design can be sufficiently strong to be able to make valid causal conclusions about the signal. What is most problematic is when the results show no difference. Then it is hard to know whether some limitation in the design led to the result or whether, in fact, the intervention was not effective. We explore this intriguing aspect of research in the next chapter.*

Check for Understanding 5

5a. What characteristics would you look for in a good single-subject design?

Anatomy of an Experimental Research Article

The article reproduced in Figure 9.8 is an example of how an experimental study is designed and reported.

Figure 9.8 Anatomy of an Experimental Study

The Effects of Metacognitive Reflective Assessment on Fifth and Sixth Graders' Mathematics Achievement

John B. Bond
Seattle Pacific University

Arthur K. Ellis
Seattle Pacific University

The purpose of this experimental study was to investigate the effects of metacognitive reflective assessment instruction on student achievement in mathematics. The study compared the performance of 141 students who practiced reflective assessment strategies with students who did not. A posttest-only control group design was employed, and results were analyzed by conducting one-way analysis of variance (ANOVA) and nonparametric procedures. On both a posttest and a retention test, students who practiced reflective strategies performed significantly higher than students who did not use the strategies. A within-subjects ANOVA was also conducted six weeks following the intervention to assess how the factor of time affected retention levels. No significant difference was found between the posttest and retention test results for the experimental groups or the control group.

At least since Socrates, learners have been counseled to reflect on what they know. Socrates taught that the unexamined life is not worth living. In the Meno, there is the familiar story of Socrates teaching a slave boy the Pythagorean Theorem. The point of the story is that teaching involves to a considerable extent the teacher's willingness to give the learner an opportunity to reflect on what the learner knows. With regard to learner empowerment, Socrates is quoted in Theaetetus as saying, "... the many fine discoveries to which they cling are of their own making" (Plato, 1952, pp. 150–151). Socrates' lament was that teachers spend far too much time telling and too little time allowing students to think about what they are learning, an argument that continues to be heard to this day. Recent reforms in mathematics education have included, among other things, the recommendation that students spend more time studying problems in depth and less time covering wide ranges of topics (Kaye, 2005). Also noted in the current literature is the recommendation that students be allowed opportunities to

General introduction and context

Figure 9.8 Continued

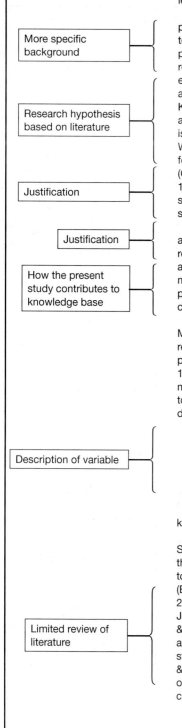

practice formative self-assessment as a means of clarifying their thinking about what they are learning (Marzano, 2009; Shepard, 2008).

Daily reflection by students on the material they are taught represents formative assessment, primarily designed to afford students a sense of their progress. Whether systematic opportunity to practice reflective assessment about what is being taught to them enhances academic performance is an empirical question. The oftabsent integration of formative assessment and reflective activity as part of the lesson routine contrasts sharply and ironically with the current emphasis upon standardized testing. Assessment is often viewed by teachers and students alike as a process separate from teaching and learning (Gulikers, Bastiaens, Kirschner, & Kester, 2006; Herman, Aschbacher, & Winters, 1992). As a consequence, knowledge and skills are often taught as preparation for assessment but not as the corollary, that is, assessment is construed as ongoing informer of knowledge and skills (Perrone, 1994; Simmons, 1994; Wiggins, 1993; Wragg, 1997). It is hypothesized in the present study that lesson-integrated formative assessment rather than merely as a separate and often judgmental process (Chappuis, 2005; Earl & LeMahieu, 1997; McTighe & O'Connor, 2005; Stiggins, 2008; Wiggins, 1993) has a positive effect on achievement. Students are often required to think in order to solve problems, but the deeper stage of thinking about their thinking, or metacognition, is seldom solicited as part of their problem solving.

The extent to which elementary school children (in the case of the present study, children age 10–12 years) are capable of exercising the executive function needed to benefit from reflective practice is a question that invites further inquiry. Research by Michalsky, Mevarech, and Haibi (2009) with fourth-grade students who studied scientific texts and who practiced metacognitive learning strategies provides evidence that such practice is beneficial. The present study focuses on slightly older children and their ability to reflect meaningfully on concepts and skills in mathematics.

The relationship between metacognition and reflective assessment is a close one. Metacognition literally means thinking (cognition) after (meta) and in that sense represents reflection on experience. Metacognition has been defined as an awareness of one's thinking patterns, learning characteristics and techniques (Schneider, Borkowski, Kurtz, & Kerwin, 1986) and is commonly referred to as "thinking about thinking" (Costa, 2001). The term, metacognition, was introduced into the literature of educational psychology by John Flavell to indicate self-knowledge of cognitive states and processes (Flavell, 1976). Beyond mere definition, Flavell offers this description:

> Metacognition refers to one's knowledge concerning one's own cognitive processes or anything related to them, e.g., the learning relevant properties of information or data. For example, I am engaging in metacognition if I notice that I am having more trouble learning A than B; if it strikes me that I should double check C before accepting it as a fact (Flavell, 1976, p. 232).

Brown (1978) offers the corollary of "secondary ignorance" (p. 82) as not knowing what you know.

The literature is rich (Bandura, 1997; Chappuis, 2005; Dewey, 1933; Earl & LeMahieu, 1997; Stiggins, 2008; Tittle, 1994; Wiliam & Thompson, 2008) with philosophy and opinion regarding the value of metacognitive practice for students, but few empirical studies designed specifically to measure such effects have been published. Although a number of empirical investigations (Blank & Hewson, 2000; Black & Wiliam, 1998; Conner & Gunstone, 2004; Dignath & Büttner, 2008; Gulikers et al., 2006; Gustafson & Bennett, 2002; Hartlep & Forsyth, 2000; Naglieri & Johnson, 2000; Schneider et al., 1986; Schunk, 1983; Wang, Haertel, & Walberg, 1993; White & Frederiksen, 1998) have reported positive effects of metacognitive activities on student achievement, these findings are typically embedded as one of several components of such studies. While not all research on this topic has found significant results (Andrade, 1999; Kurtz & Borkowski, 1984), a pattern of findings appears to be developing that supports the inclusion of reflective assessment strategies in learning activities. The present study is an effort to contribute to the body of research.

Purpose and Research Questions

The purpose of this study was to investigate the effects of metacognitive reflective assessment instruction on the mathematics achievement of fifth- and sixth-grade students. The following research questions guided the investigation: (a) What are the effects of using reflective assessment strategies on the mathematics achievement of fifth- and sixth-grade students? (b) Does the use of reflective assessment strategies enhance student retention of mathematics concepts over time?

METHOD

This investigation of student reflective assessment and its effects upon mathematics achievement employed an experimental posttest-only control group design (Campbell & Stanley, 1963; Shadish, Cook, & Campbell, 2002). The independent variable was reflective assessment strategies, which were practiced only by Experimental Group I. The dependent variable was the mathematics scores for Experimental Group I, Experimental Group II, and the Control Group, as measured by a researcher-designed instrument.

A posttest-only control group design was selected for this study, rather than a pretest-posttest design, for several reasons. First, a stable enrollment at the school in which the investigation was conducted indicated that participant mortality would not be a serious threat to internal validity, which is a weakness of posttest-only designs (Shadish et al., 2002). Second, since the study was embedded within an ongoing mathematics curriculum pilot, the posttest-only design allowed the researcher to disguise the purpose of the study in order to control for teacher effects (Bingham & Felbinger, 2001). Thus, teacher and student participants were not exposed to the test content through the four weeks of the investigation, which controlled for their possible sensitivity to the purpose of the research (Chong-ho & Ohlund, 2010). In particular, not having a pretest kept the control group teachers blind to the mathematical content that comprised the dependent variable. Since the six randomly assigned teacher participants worked in close proximity in the school, not having a pretest minimized the risk for conversation about the study content and potential experimental treatment diffusion. Third, the effects of pretesting were a concern because of the four-week duration of the study and the repeated administration of the instrument as a retention test. In a pretest-posttest design the retention test would have been the third administration of the instrument over a 10-week period, which would have called for development of an alternate instrument.

The study was conducted in conjunction with a curriculum pilot of mathematics materials that were being considered for a school district adoption. Since the study did not interfere with the normal course of study, there was no resistance to the random assignment of students.

Participants

A sample of 141 fifth- and sixth-grade student participants from a suburban elementary school were randomly assigned to three experimental conditions (reflective assessment, nonreflective review, and control) delivered to two reconstituted classes for each condition. Six teacher participants were randomly assigned to one of the three treatments. Each group was comprised of two subgroups of approximately 24 participants each for total group sizes of 47, 48, and 46. Random assignment of participants resulted in balance among the three groups regarding gender, ability level, socioeconomic status (SES), and ethnicity. Socioeconomic status was estimated by participation in the free or reduced meal program (see Table 1). The sample was drawn from a predominantly White, middle-class school population (see Table 1) and was comprised of 61 males, 80 females, 61 fifth graders, and 80 sixth graders. Fifteen of the student participants, 10.6% of the sample, belonged to subgroups commonly accepted in educational literature as at-risk factors to academic performance. Seven students received special education instruction for both reading and mathematics, four were English Language Learners (ELL), and five qualified for free or reduced lunch. Of the four ELL students, Spanish was the first language of three students, and Russian was the first language of one student.

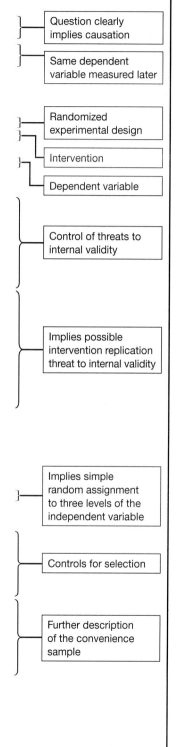

Question clearly implies causation

Same dependent variable measured later

Randomized experimental design

Intervention

Dependent variable

Control of threats to internal validity

Implies possible intervention replication threat to internal validity

Implies simple random assignment to three levels of the independent variable

Controls for selection

Further description of the convenience sample

Figure 9.8 Continued

Table 1 Achievement and Demographic Percentages

	Study Site	Pilot Site 1	Pilot Site 2
Met standard on state test			
Reading	85.7	80.6	83.0
Math	62.8	70.1	77.7
Writing	59.7	64.2	69.1
Race/ethnicity			
American Indian/Alaskan Native	0	1.7	.9
Asian/Pacific Islander	9.4	12.2	11.8
African American	3.8	2.4	.7
Hispanic	10.6	4.4	4.6
White	76.2	79.4	82.0
Special programs			
Free or reduced-price meals	8.3	9.4	10.7
Special education	14.7	14.3	11.3
ELL	5.6	.6	1.1
Migrant	0	0	0

Measures

The posttest questions were drawn from *Connected Mathematics: Data About Us* (Lappan, Fey, Fitzgerald, Friel, & Phillips, 2002b) on which the lessons were based for the experimental groups. Objectives for each of the 16 scripted lessons taught by the Experimental I and II groups were stated in multiple choice questions. A pilot test of 38 questions was administered in two classrooms at schools not involved in the study to determine the reliability of the test items. The pilot schools and classes were selected to closely match the achievement, diversity, mobility, and at-risk factors of the school in which the study was to be conducted (see Table 1).

Item analyses of the pilot test resulted in two questions being discarded. Cronbach's alpha and split-half coefficients of .72 and .71, respectively, were found on the remaining 36 posttest items, indicating satisfactory reliability (Vogt, 2005). In addition to instrument reliability analyses, the face and content validities of the instrument were examined by two assessment experts, one a university professor of statistics and the other a school district assessment director. Independently, they reported that both the face validity and content validity of the instrument appeared to be high. The 36-item multiple choice test on probability and statistics was administered following the intervention and again six weeks later as a retention test.

A priori power analysis for a one-way analysis of variance (ANOVA; posttest-only design with approximately *40 cases* per cell) was conducted using G*Power 3 (Faul, Erdfelder, Lang, & Buchner, 2007) to determine a sufficient sample size using an alpha of .05, a power of .70, a small effect size ($d = .4$), and one tail.

Procedures

Scripted lesson plans were provided for the teachers of the experimental and control groups. All lesson scripts were derived from the *Connected Mathematics Program*. A probability and statistics unit was the focus of lessons for the experimental groups (Lappan et al., 2002b), while the control group was taught a unit on area and perimeter (Lappan, Fey, Fitzgerald, Friel, & Phillips, 2002a). Students in the experimental groups were taught identical statistics lessons, except for the reflective intervention. At the closing of each class session, students in the Experimental I Group practiced a reflective activity regarding what they had learned in the class session. This reflection served as the independent variable in the study. Teachers in Experimental Group II closed each class session with a five-minute review of the lesson activities and objectives in order to ensure that equal time on task existed for the two experimental groups. Control Group lessons focused on area and perimeter, which was another mathematics unit being piloted.

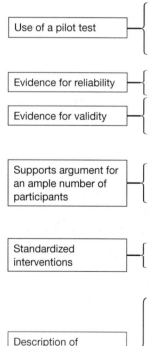

Use of a pilot test

Evidence for reliability

Evidence for validity

Supports argument for an ample number of participants

Standardized interventions

Description of interventions

Table 2 Posttest and Retention Test Means, Medians, and Standard Deviations

Standard Deviation

	Posttest				Retention Test			
	Mean	Median	SD	N	Mean	Median	SD	N
Reflection group	29.40	31.00	4.33	47	29.18	30.00	3.54	44
No reflection group	26.92	29.00	5.61	48	26.77	27.00	5.54	48
Control group	22.30	22.00	4.37	46	22.42	22.50	4.45	45
Total	26.24	27.00	5.61	141	26.12	27.00	5.36	137

Table 3 Between-Subjects Effects: Posttest and Retention Test

Level of significance   Effect size

	df	Mean square	F	p	Partial η²
Posttest					
Corrected model	2	602.538	25.962	<.01	.273
Error	138	23.208			
Retention test without missing values					
Corrected model	2	524.064	24.606	<.01	.269
Error	134	21.299			
Retention test with missing values imputed					
Corrected model	2	544.882	26.347	<.01	.276
Error	138	20.68			

Two separate reflection strategies were combined to form the independent variable: a written "I Learned" statement and a verbal "Thinking Aloud" strategy. These reflective strategies are efficient ways for teachers to facilitate student reflection on what has been learned while finding out if their lesson objectives have been attained. During the last five minutes of the lesson, students in the Experimental Group I were asked to think about what they had learned during the class period and then to write a sentence that began with the phrase "I learned." Students were then prompted by the teacher to talk about what they had written with another student, the "Think aloud" strategy, and finally to edit as appropriate their "I learned" statement. The written statements were then collected by the teacher each day and submitted to the researchers.

Description of interventions

Prior to the start of the investigation, the researchers provided training for teacher participants that emphasized the need to precisely follow the lesson scripts and prescribed time allotments. Teacher participants agreed not to discuss the investigation until its completion. The researcher closely monitored progress throughout the investigation to ensure that lesson scripts were followed, confidentiality was maintained, and disruptions were avoided.

Helps control diffusion of interventions

Intervention fidelity

RESULTS

A one-way ANOVA was conducted to evaluate the effects of the reflective strategy intervention on participant achievement on the mathematics test. An alpha level of .05 was used for all statistical tests. Three participant groups (reflective assessment, nonreflective review, and control) were administered a posttest at the end of the study, and again six weeks later as a retention test (see Table 2). Significant main effects were found in both administrations of the mathematics test (see Table 3). Effect size calculations indicated a medium effect of the reflection strategy (see Table 3).

Three group means compared statistically

Figure 9.8 Continued

<table>
<tr><td>"Statistically significant" results</td><td>Follow-up tests were conducted to evaluate pairwise differences among the means. For both the posttest and the retention test, Tukey HSD procedures indicated that the mean scores were significantly different between the Experimental I and II Groups (posttest, $p = .035$; retention test, $p = .036$). Significant difference $(p < .01)$ was found in all pairwise comparisons with the Control Group on both administrations of the mathematics test. These results indicate that the reflective strategy intervention did indeed lead to higher achievement, related to the first research question.</td></tr>
</table>

Table 4 Within-Subjects ANOVA: Descriptive Statistics

	Missing Values Omitted			Missing Values Imputed		
	Mean	SD	N	Mean	SD	N
Reflection group	29.86	3.91	44	29.18	3.42	47
No reflection group	26.77	5.54	48	26.77	5.54	48
Control group	22.27	4.41	45	22.42	4.40	46
Total	26.34	5.62	137	26.12	5.31	141

Table 5 Repeated Measures: Missing Value Comparisons

	N	Wilks' ¶	F	p	Partial η^2
Time					
Without missing values	137	.998	.222	.64	.002
Missing values imputed	141	.999	.110	.74	.001
Interaction					
Without missing values	137	.989	.492	.69	.011
Missing values imputed	141	.998	.106	.96	.002

Shows different standard deviations

On the retention test Levene's Test of Equality of Error Variance found nonhomogeneity among the groups $(F[2, 134] = 3.28; p = .041)$. During the six weeks between the posttest and retention test administrations, four students withdrew from school causing unequal sample sizes. Since this could have violated an assumption that all groups were the same, a Dunnett's C-test was conducted, which also found significant mean differences between the Experimental I and II Groups $(p < .05)$ and in comparisons with the control group $(p < .05)$. In addition, leptokurtosis $(Ku = 2.45)$ was found in the reflection group posttest scores, although the sample size likely was large enough to yield fairly accurate alpha values (Green & Salkind, 2007).

Response to some assumptions not being met about the data

Further nonparametric procedures were calculated in response to the nonhomogeneity issue discussed above. A Kruskall–Wallis test was found to be significant on both the posttest $(\chi^2 [2, N = 141] = 41.95, p < .01)$ and on the retention test $(\chi^2 [2, N =137] =41.25, p < .01)$. Mann–Whitney U tests conducted for pairwise comparison among the three groups found significant results that the Experimental I Group (reflection) performed significantly higher than the Experimental II Group (nonreflection) on both the posttest and the retention test (posttest $[z = -2.37, p = .018]$; retention test $[z = -2.29; p = .022]$). On both tests, the reflection and nonreflection groups scored significantly higher $(p < .01)$ than the control group. These findings verified the results of the one-way ANOVA.

Addresses second research question

A repeated measures analysis of variance was conducted in which the within-subject factor was time (post and retention test occasions), and the between-subjects factor was experimental condition (reflective assessment, nonreflective review, and control). The dependent variable was performance on the mathematics test. This analysis was conducted first with the four missing retention test scores omitted, and then with missing values imputed (see Table 4). No significant difference between the posttest and retention test results was found in either of the repeated measures ANOVAs (see Table 5). There was also no significant interaction found between the test factor and the treatment factor (see Table 5).

> Means no change from first to second posttest

Mauchly's Test of Sphericity was not significant for both analyses indicating that variance differences were roughly equal. These results indicate that reflective strategies do not necessarily result in higher retention over time, since both the Experimental I and II groups sustained their levels of performance after six weeks. While the Experimental I (reflection) Group learned significantly more, both groups equally sustained what they had learned. As expected, the retention test scores for the Control Group scores were only slightly different than the posttest results.

DISCUSSION

The results of this study support the theory that student reflection during learning activities enhances achievement (Bandura, 1997; Black & Wiliam, 1998; Costa, 2001; Dewey, 1933; Marzano, 2009; Stiggins, 2008; Wiliam & Thompson, 2008). Students who practiced reflective strategies performed significantly better when compared to students who did not. In addition to the statistical significance, medium to large effect sizes were found that give support for reflective strategies as a practical classroom learning tool.

> Findings related to literature

> Practical significance

These results provide an answer to the first research question in demonstrating that the inclusion of reflective strategies in mathematics lessons did indeed cause greater learning. The findings are consistent with previous empirical research (Michalsky et al., 2009; Naglieri & Johnson, 2000) that has supported reflective strategies. This is reason to advocate for increased application of reflective strategies as embedded formative assessment in daily classroom activity.In response to the second research question, the within-subjects ANOVA results indicate that reflective assessment strategies do not lead to enhanced retention of learning over time. It had been expected that students who practiced reflective strategies would retain more what they had learned than students who did not reflect. This did not prove to be the case. In fact, all three groups—reflective, nonreflective, and control—sustained their levels of performance on the second administration of the mathematics test. Additionally, the absence of interaction shows that the retention test results were not significantly influenced by exposure to the instrument six weeks earlier.

> Conclusion

Strengths

As with any research conducted in a school, this study was tailored to match the situation. As expected, the posttest-only control group design controlled for anticipated threats to internal validity of pretesting and teacher effects. In addition, this design avoided the need to develop an alternate instrument that would have been desirable had a pretest been administered in addition to the other two assessments. For this study, these strengths out-weighed the risk of student attrition that is an inherent problem with posttest only designs (Shadish et al., 2002). While the stability of student enrollment led the researcher to choose a posttest-only design, in an area of moderate or high student mobility, a pretest-posttest control group design would be appropriate.

Several strengths to this investigation give confidence in the findings. These include the study's experimental design, with random assignment of student participants and of teachers to groups, which provided assurance of balanced groups and consistency of instruction (Gall, Gall, & Borg, 2007). First, as anticipated, mortality of student participants was not an issue during the four weeks of the study, which supported the choice to use a posttest-only control group design. Therefore, the absence of a pretest, a design weakness according to Shadish et al. (2002), did not prove to be a problem in the major component of the investigation regarding the effects of reflective strategies on learning mathematical concepts. Teacher differences were further controlled by the provision of lesson plans that included verbatim scripts, time allotments, and materials. Adherence to the scripted lesson plans was closely monitored by the researcher throughout the investigation, and experimental treatment diffusion did not appear to be a cause for concern. Equal time on task for the experimental groups was accounted for in the lesson plans, including an alternate closure activity for the nonreflection group. In addition, teacher and student participants were blind to the purpose of the study (Bingham & Felbinger, 2001), which was conducted during a curriculum pilot.

> Justification for credible findings

Figure 9.8 Continued

Providing a meaningful experience for the Control Group was an important aspect to this study. Since these students were also participants in the mathematics curriculum pilot, their experience during the four-week study was equally desirable to that of the other groups. Feedback from Control Group teachers contributed to school district decision making regarding the piloted mathematics curriculum, just as did that of Experimental Group I and II teachers.

Limitations

The limitations of this study include mortality of student participants for the retention test, the use of a researcher-designed instrument, and the generalizability of the findings. First, it was not expected that homogeneity of groups would prove to be a limitation of this investigation considering the stability of student enrollment and the initial efforts to ensure balance among groups. Participant attrition, in fact, was not a concern during the four weeks of the investigation and the subsequent posttest. However, mortality did prove to be a minor problem six weeks later for the retention test. While the overall attrition rate for the retention test was only 2.8%, four of the 141 participants, three participants withdrew from the Experimental Group I. While imputation of the missing values confirmed the findings related to research question 2 (see Tables 4 and 5), participant attrition limited the validity of retention test results. For the retention test component of this study, a pretest-posttest design would have better accounted for the mortality issues.

Threat to internal validity for second research question

The use of a researcher-designed instrument is another potential limiting factor for this study. Since the opportunity to implement an experimental design depended on doing so during a curriculum pilot, the choice of curricular content was beyond the researcher's control. For this reason a researcher-designed instrument was developed that aligned with the lesson objectives found in the piloted mathematics curriculum. Even though the pilot study found instrument reliability to be adequate, the use of a standardized instrument would have been preferable.

Limitations of using a locally designed instrument

Use of a standardized instrument would be less sensitive

The sample for this study was representative of a suburban, middle class population, and thus, any generalizing of results should be done with this in mind (see Table 1). Since the posttest findings are causal, external validity is required in order to be of use to other settings (Briggs, 2008). Caution, therefore, should be exercised when applying the findings to schools of high poverty, urban situations, or cultural and ethnic diversity. In addition, generalizing the results to at-risk populations, such as special education or ELL students, should be carefully considered. While the results of this study offer promise that other populations of students will benefit from practicing reflective strategies, the findings should be generalized with high confidence only to schools with similar demographics as those represented in the study (see Table 1). Future research is needed to demonstrate the effectiveness of reflective strategies in diverse student populations.

Limitations related to external validity

Conducting the study in one school where student and teacher participants had contact outside of the randomly assigned treatments is another limiting factor (Shuttleworth, 2009). This was a major factor in the selection of the posttest-only control group design, however, stronger control for potential contamination of the results could have been provided if several schools had been included in the study. Due to the structure of the curriculum pilot in which the study was embedded, the research was limited to one elementary school.

CONCLUSION

In an era of high-stakes testing and increased pressure on classroom teachers to improve student achievement, the results of this study offer proof of the effectiveness of reflective assessment strategies in improving student learning. Mathematics teachers, especially, can leverage these findings to support the incorporation of student reflection as an integral part of lesson activity. Standing out among the findings of this study is the positive impact on student learning when reflective assessment strategies are included in daily mathematics instruction. That this innovation can be easily implemented at low cost and with minimal impact on classroom instruction makes reflective assessment a highly practical innovation. At a time when public education faces the dual dilemmas of increased expectations and diminishing resources, reflective assessment is an innovation that should be broadly embraced for it addresses both issues.

Practical implications of findings

The results of this study were statistically significant and causal, which offer mathematics practitioners strong rationale for applying the findings in the classroom. The findings also inform practice in other content areas and provide reason to delve deeper into how reflection can be harnessed in all classrooms to enhance student learning. Further research should be conducted with diverse student populations, in other subject areas, at different grade levels, and with a variety of reflective strategies. It will be especially important to conduct research in schools of high poverty, where reflective strategies will provide effective small-scale assessment tools that are usable by both teachers and students.

Suggestions for further research

The Connected Mathematics Project (CMP), whose curriculum was used in this research, has developed a substantial evidence base regarding effective mathematics curriculum, instruction, and assessment. The results of this study contribute to the growing body of empirical evidence regarding mathematics instruction and assessment that is being developed and compiled by CMP-affiliated researchers.

In addition, more research is needed on how long-term memory is impacted by the inclusion of reflective strategies in learning experiences. While this study did not find differences in the retention levels of the three groups, it may be that six weeks was too short a time period to find retention differences among the three groups. Future studies should include several repeated assessments over longer time spans to determine how reflection impacts long-term memory.

Suggestions for further research

An important outcome of this study is that it demonstrated that experimental research can be conducted in the schoolhouse without major disruption. This occurred because the study was conducted as part of a school district curriculum pilot. Collaboration with school districts on curriculum adoptions offers opportunity to conduct empirical research without interfering with the scope and sequence of an instructional program. In this study, for example, it is not likely that the school district would have allowed random assignment of students had a curriculum pilot not been in progress.

The results of this study lend support to the theoretical view that student reflection on material taught increases the probability that the student will learn the material. The results provide support for the incorporation of reflective assessment strategies into daily classroom activities. The statistically significant findings of this study contribute empirical evidence to the argument in the metacognitive literature that supports reflective strategies as an effective practice and provide reason for continued research on the topic.

Overall summary

REFERENCES

Andrade, H. G. (1999). *Student self-assessment: At the intersection of metacognition and authentic assessment.* Paper presented at the Annual Meeting of the American Educational Research Association, Montreal, Quebec, Canada.

Bandura, A. (1997). *Self-efficacy: The exercise of control.* New York: W. H. Freeman and Company.

Bingham, R. D., & Felbinger, C. L. (2001). *Evaluation in practice: A methodological approach* (2nd ed.). New York: Chatham House Publishers/Seven Bridges Press.

Black, P., & Wiliam, D. (1998). Inside the black box. *Phi Delta Kappan, 80(2),* 139–148. Retrieved from http://www.pdkintl.org/utilities/archives.htm

Blank, L. M., & Hewson, P. W. (2000). A metacognitive learning cycle: A better warranty for student understanding? *Science Education, 84(4),* 486–506.

Briggs, D. C. (2008). Comments on Slavin: Synthesizing causal inferences. *Educational Researcher,* 37(1), 15–22.

Brown, A. L. (1978). Knowing when, where, and how to remember: A problem of metacognition. In R. Glaser (Ed.), *Advances in instructional psychology* (Volume *1,* pp. 77–165). Hillsdale, NJ: Lawrence Erlbaum Associates, Publishers.

Campbell, D. T., & Stanley, J. C. (1963). *Experimental and quasiexperimental designs for research.* Boston, MA: Houghton Mifflin Company.

Chappuis, J. (2005). Helping students understand assessment. *Educational Leadership, 63(3),* 39–43. Retrieved from http://www.ascd.org/publication/educational-leadership/nov05/vo16 3/num03/HelpingStudents-Understand-Assessment.aspx

Chong-Ho, Y., & Ohlund, B. (2010). Threats to validity of research design. Retrieved from http://creative-wisdom.com/teaching/WBI/threat.shtml

References continue

APA format

Key Terms

Experimental research
External validity
Factorial designs
Interactions
Internal validity
   Diffusion of intervention
   Dosage
   Experimenter effects
   History
   Instrumentation
   Intervention replication
   Maturation
   Participant attrition

Participant effects
Pretesting
Selection
Statistical regression
Intervention fidelity
MAXMINCON
Nonequivalent-groups
   posttest-only design
Quasi-experimental designs
   Nonequivalent-groups
      pretest–posttest design
Single-group posttest-only design

Single-group pretest–posttest
   design
Single-subject designs
   A–B design
   A–B–A withdrawal design
   Baseline
   Multiple-baseline design
True experimental designs
   Random assignment
   Randomized-to-groups
      posttest-only design
   Randomized-to-groups
      pretest–posttest design

Discussion Questions

1. Quasi-experimental designs are common in educational settings. What are important considerations to lessen threats to internal validity with these designs?
2. Why is it important for researchers to be more concerned with internal validity than external validity in designing experiments?
3. What are some examples of experimental designs in which moderator variables are needed to obtain credible results?
4. What is an example of a true experiment with one intervention variable (three levels) and one moderator variable (two levels)?
5. How is the MAXMINCON principle helpful for designing experiments?

Application Exercises

1. Hank the hedgehog and Frank the fox have decided to study impact of new intervention designed to promote greater social awareness skills among college students. First show Hank's design for a quasi-experimental study with an additional moderator variable (the intervention is the independent variable with two levels). Then show Frank's design with the same variables. In addition to the design, state the research questions and statistical analyses.
2. A researcher wants to find out whether cooperative learning groups, in which students' learning depends on the achievement of other students, is better than individualized instruction for developing prosocial behavior (helping, supporting, and encouraging others). Two teachers agreed to participate in the experiment. One teacher used the cooperative method and the other teacher used the individualized method. Prosocial behavior was measured by the researcher based on observations of out-of-class interactions. What design was used in this study? What threats to internal validity are possible, plausible, and probable?

Check for Understanding Answers

1a. To establish a sound argument that an intervention, and only the intervention, has caused a change in the dependent variable.

1b. By employing these principles, the researcher will provide the best opportunity for approximating the true signal.

2a. Interval validity is concerned with what has caused a change in the dependent variable. Strong internal validity is present when possible threats (alternative hypotheses) are ruled out. External validity addresses generalizability of findings to other individuals and conditions.

2b. One, the variable needs to be present in different amounts in different levels of the independent variable; two, the variable needs to impact the dependent variable.

2c. Primarily because it is difficult to design experiments to control for selection and intervention replications, as well as other confounding and extraneous variables.

3a. Primarily because of random assignment of participants that controls for selection and other threats to internal validity.

3b. By use of pretest scores and other information about the participants that could be used to show they have few differences.

3c. Because it provides a way to see whether interventions are consistent across levels of other variables, and whether there are interactions.

4a. Because if the intervention is not experienced as projected it is more difficult to understand what caused the change. Good intervention fidelity also allows a better understanding of which aspects of the intervention may have been most impactful.

4b. Intervention replications and history.

5a. Consistent, reliable measurement; discrete baseline and intervention conditions; stable patterns of behavior; study of a single variable.

Chapter 10
Understanding Statistical Inferences

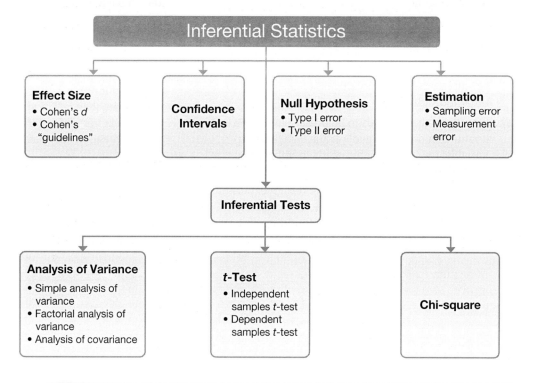

Learning Outcomes

10.1 Describe the nature of estimation based on sampling and measurement error.

10.2 Understand the use of the null hypothesis and level of significance with inferential statistics.

10.3 Explain why effect size and other indicators of practical significance are essential in communicating the results of studies.

10.4 Know how to use specific inferential tests to analyze data, including *t*-tests, analysis of variance, chi-square and multivariate statistics.

Chapter Road Map

Chances are good that you are not particularly eager to get to this chapter! There is usually a perception that complex mathematics are involved in understanding statistical principles, which can seem intimidating, with little practical value. Although it is true that most statistical procedures require complex calculations, the computer handles these very efficiently. We will focus on the logic and meaning of the procedures (which will not require sophisticated mathematics), on how different statistical tests relate to research questions, and on understanding and evaluating the use of the procedures in research reports and articles.

The Purpose and Nature of Inferential Statistics

Learning Outcome 10.1   Describe the nature of estimation based on sampling and measurement error.

As indicated in Chapter 6, statistics are mathematical procedures used to summarize and analyze numerical data. In this chapter, the focus is on procedures that use statistics to make inferences or estimates about characteristics of a population from a sample, and what is likely to be true when comparing and analyzing sample data, given the inexact nature of measurement. That is, descriptive data from a particular sample in a study (sample statistics) are used to draw conclusions about what is probable about phenomena in the population. These procedures, called **inferential statistics**, are necessary to understand the *imprecise* nature of descriptions, relationships, and differences based on the data collected in a particular study. They give us some sense of noise and reinforce the need for fox-like, probabilistic thinking.

Uncertainty (Noise)

It would be nice (not to mention profitable) if we could be certain about our predictions. How likely are we to win the lottery? How certain is a principal that a particular kind of teacher evaluation procedure will provide credible information on which to base merit salary increases? Are you confident in your ability to predict who will win a race or an election? If we know that a small sample of sixth-graders will pass an accountability test, how certain can we be that *all* sixth-graders will pass it? The degree to which we can be certain in each of these circumstances, and in others, will vary. There is almost always some degree of *uncertainty* in the questions addressed in quantitative educational research, and inferential statistics indicate in a precise way what we can, for the most part, be confident about. The degree of confidence depends on the amount of error (noise) in sampling and measurement, as well as noise that is contributed by confounding and extraneous variables.

Estimation in Sampling and Measurement

Sampling was discussed in Chapter 5 as a procedure for studying a portion of a larger population. Individuals in the sample are measured to obtain descriptive statistics *for the sample*. Inferential statistics are then used to *infer* conclusions about the entire population (refer back to Figure 5.4). Suppose you are interested in the attitudes of seventh-graders toward learning and school. The population is large—say, 1,000 seventh-graders—so you select a sample of 100 seventh-graders randomly and have these students respond to the attitude questionnaire. Then you would use the results from the sample to make an inference about the attitudes of all 1,000 seventh-graders. Because there is some degree of error in sampling (as well as measurement), this error must be taken into account in making the inference to the population. That is, even with a random sample, the mean attitude of the sample drawn is not likely to be exactly the same as the mean for the entire population. A second or third random sample of 100 students would result in somewhat different means. Likewise, the attitudes of your sample of 100 seventh-graders will not be exactly right (the true signal) since there is measurement error. If you took 30 different random samples of seventh-graders from the population you would have a normal distribution of means.

If you do take three random samples of 100 seventh-graders, which one of the three is most correct? Which one can you be most certain will provide the most accurate estimation of the population? As illustrated in Figure 10.1, suppose one random sample results in a mean of 25, a second random sample results in a mean of 23, and a third random sample mean is 26.

Fortunately, inferential statistics are designed so that you can estimate, on the basis of *one* sample, the error (noise) that should be considered in characterizing the attitudes of the entire population of 1,000 seventh graders. This is based on an assumption that the mean from this single sample is the mean of the population. Thus, if the mean attitude of the single sample was 25, on a scale of 10 to 35, and there was little error, you might estimate the population attitude (the signal) to be somewhere between, say, 23 and 27. If there was a large amount of error, the estimate might be between 21 and 29. You use inferential statistics to indicate the precise range in which the actual mean attitude for the 1,000 students probably lies. In other words, you use inferences, based on specific premises and procedures, to make conclusions about the attitudes of the population.

Suppose you use the entire population of 1,000 students, rather than a sample. Would the survey result be the "real" or "actual" value of the trait for the population (the signal)? Although now there is no sampling error, there *is* measurement error, which also needs to be taken into consideration. In educational research, our variables are such that we almost always make inferences from imperfect measurement. Just as in sampling error, each time you measure a group on variables such as attitudes,

Figure 10.1 Illustration of Taking Several Samples from a Population

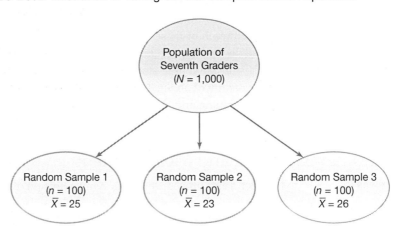

achievement, and motivation, the result will be somewhat different, depending on the validity and reliability of the scores. If the scores are highly valid and reliable, and other factors well controlled, there will be little measurement error, but if validity and reliability are low, the results could vary considerably each time, especially for small samples. Therefore, we need to take measurement error, as well as sampling error, into account. This is what is done with inferential statistics, giving us an indication of the *probable* "real" or "actual" values. If your variable is measured without virtually any error, such as determining weight, only sampling error is a concern.

The manner in which most researchers use inferential statistics is based on a set of procedures developed by Ronald Fisher, back in the 1920s. Although there are actually different approaches to statistical inference (notably, Bayesian statistics), Fisher used a method of deductive logic that is ubiquitous. The logic starts with something called the *null hypothesis*, to which we turn next.

Author Reflection *Statistics seem to be more important than ever—especially with "big data," secondary data analysis, corporate collection of data, data analytics and metrics, and the use of more complex statistical procedures. Basic inferential statistics are now commonplace in mathematics standards for public school education. The problem, in my view, is accepting statistical results as the signal. In fact, there are significant limitations to Fisherian-based statistics that lead to many misconceptions and mistakes. Even though I cannot go into all of the reasons in detail here, one key principle is that "statistically significant" results with a large number of cases may have little practical value. Keep in mind that statistics are just a tool to help us understand better what may or may not be true. Statistics do not give final answers; they help us make tentative answers and know what else to ask. My advice? Think like a fox, don't be overly persuaded by them.*

Check for Understanding 1

1a. What is the difference between descriptive and inferential statistics?

1b. Explain how both sampling and measurement error contribute to inexact estimate of what is true from data gathered for a specific study.

The Null Hypothesis

Learning Outcome 10.2 Understand the use of the null hypothesis and level of significance with inferential statistics.

In a study that compares two groups on a measure of achievement, the question that is investigated is the likelihood that there is a difference between the groups. Because we know error exists, it is more accurate to conclude that there *probably* is or is not a real difference. In Fisherian logic, the procedure for making the decision about whether it is likely that there is or is not a difference begins with a **null hypothesis** (H_0). The null hypothesis is a statement that no difference exists between the populations that are being compared on the basis of a selected dependent variable. (Note, though, that not all null hypotheses are stated as "no difference.") In a relationship study, the null hypothesis would indicate that there is no relationship. The researcher uses inferential statistics to determine the probability that the null hypothesis is untrue, or false. If the null is probably untrue, the researcher concludes that there probably *is* a relationship

Table 10.1 Examples of Research Questions, Null and Alternative Hypotheses

Research Question	Null Hypothesis (H_0)	Directional Alternative Hypothesis (H_1)
Is the stress level of students living on campus less than students living off campus?	There is no difference in the stress level of students living on or off campus.	Students living on campus show a lower level of stress compared to students living off campus.
Is there a relationship between preservice teachers' supervisor ratings and student achievement?	There is no relationship between supervisor ratings and student achievement.	There is a positive relationship between supervisor ratings and students' achievement.
Do female students show greater grit than male students?	Female and male scores on grit are the same.	Females show stronger grit than males.

or difference between groups. Thus, if we "reject" the null hypothesis, it is likely that we are not wrong in saying that there is a difference. In other words, the null hypothesis is probably not true. If we "fail to reject" the null hypothesis, we conclude that there may be no difference (not that the null is true, however).

The logic behind the null hypothesis is based on the notion that in science we seek to falsify the idea that there is a difference, then see whether the data fail to support that conclusion. That is, the idea is that it is best to begin with an assumption of "no difference" or "no relationship," then show evidence that this assumption is probably not true. In other words, researchers use null hypothesis significance testing (NHST) as a starting point and then collect data to show it is likely to be wrong. If the null is likely to be wrong, then the **alternative hypothesis** (H_1), which is usually a statement of a difference or relationship that is consistent with the research hypothesis, can be tentatively "accepted." While alternative hypotheses can be either nondirectional (simply a difference or relationship, $H_0 \neq H_1$), or directional ($H_0 < H_1$), most suggest a specific directional result. Note the differences in how null and directional alternative hypotheses are stated in Table 10.1.

The double and even triple negatives expressing interpretations of null hypotheses can be tricky. Here is a sequence of phrases that may help:

Null hypothesis: no difference (same)
Reject null hypothesis: difference (not the same)
Wrong in rejecting the null hypothesis: mistake to say that there is a difference

In Excerpt 10.1, note how the authors first expressed the null hypotheses, then showed how that null hypothesis was rejected. Note, though, in most published studies null hypotheses are implied and not explicitly stated.

EXCERPT 10.1

Null Hypothesis

Correlational research was employed to determine if there was a relationship between DL and teacher affective commitment. One hypothesis was tested. The null hypothesis stated that there is no significant correlation between DL and teacher affective commitment.... The null hypothesis was rejected. The positive correlations between teacher affective commitment and the dimensions (TL, SL, and OL) of DL align with Liou's (2008) research results that individuals are more committed when there is a sense of belonging to the organization. (pp. 163, 165)

SOURCE: Ross, L., Lutfi, G. A., & Hope, W. C. (2016), Distributed leadership and teachers' affective commitment. *NASSP Bulletin, 100*(3), 159–169.

Level of Significance

Inferential statistics is used to indicate the probability of being wrong in rejecting the null hypothesis. Initially, the researcher sets what is called a **level of significance** or **alpha level** (*a*) that will be used after crunching the data to determine whether or not the null hypothesis is rejected. Often, the level of significance is set at .05 (a 5% probability that the difference is due to chance; that is, a 5% chance of making a mistake if the null is rejected). This decision is made on the basis of the data analysis, which results in what is indicated by the small italic letter *p* ("*p*-value"). It is usually reported as $p = x$ or $p < x$ (.05 or less than .05). Thus, if $p = .20$, there is a 20% probability that the difference is due to a chance variation. A *p* of .20 is too great a chance to accept in research. Typically, researchers will not conclude that there is likely to be an actual difference in the populations unless the probability of obtaining the difference by chance is equal to or less than 5% ($p \leq .05$). This is a convention that is often translated to mean a "statistically significant" difference (although this is actually an arbitrary decision—there are many situations when a 5% chance of being wrong is too high, and, in reality, there is little difference between a $p < .05$ and $p < .06$). If the level of significance is .001, there is only 1 chance out of 1,000 that the difference obtained is due to chance.

What we need to know is whether the decision, based on comparing the *p*-value to level of significance (to reject or not reject) is true. If the decision is to reject the null hypothesis when it is, in fact, true (no difference in the populations), the researcher has made what is called a **Type I error**. A Type I error is a false positive—it is concluded that there is a difference or relationship when in reality there is no difference or relationship (like crying wolf when there is no wolf). The probability of making this type of error is equal to the *p*-value. It is also possible to fail to reject the null hypothesis when it is, in fact, not true and should have been rejected. This is called a **Type II error** (a false negative). That is, the conclusion is that there is no difference or relationship (*p* greater than the level of significance) when in fact there is one. As we will see, Type II errors are very problematic in education because of all the factors (noise) that can make finding a significant difference or relationship difficult.

In some studies, the researchers will not indicate the level of significance of rejecting each null hypothesis. Because there is no absolute rule or standard in what constitutes "statistical significance," it is necessary to interpret summary narrative statements in the context of the actual *p*-values. Typically, in the absence of a level of significance general conventions are used (e.g., $p < .05$ is statistically significant). Sometimes a *p*-value between .10 and .05 is called "marginally" significant. In exploratory studies, a *p*-value of .10 may be judged sufficient to conclude that further research is justified.

The *p*-value is determined by three factors, as illustrated in Figure 10.2 in a simple case of comparing two groups. The first is the difference between the groups being compared. The greater the difference between the groups, the smaller the *p*-value. The second is the degree of sampling and measurement error. The lower the error, the smaller the *p*-value. The third factor is the size of the sample. If a very large sample is used, the *p*-value will be smaller than if the sample size is small. In fact, in some studies a seemingly small difference may be reported as "significant," because of the large *n*. (If you increase the sample size enough, almost any result will be statistically significant!)

The *p*-value and level of significance help us make a *statistical* decision related to the null hypothesis, but it does not tell us anything about *why* there was a difference. When the null hypothesis is rejected, we examine the design of the study to see

Figure 10.2 Determinants of p-Value

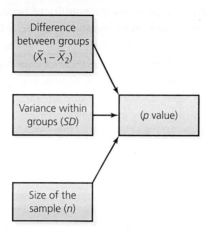

whether there are extraneous variables that may explain the results. If the null hypothesis is not rejected, we are tempted to conclude that there is, in reality, no difference or no relationship *for this particular study*. In a well-designed study, failure to reject the null hypothesis is just as important, scientifically, as rejecting it. This suggests that the actual signal is no difference or relationship. The problem is that in many studies that find "no significant differences," there are often noise factors in the design that may have contributed to the finding—for example, low reliability, sampling error, low number of participants, diffusion of treatment, and other threats to internal validity. With these studies, we simply do not know whether there is really no difference or whether the study, as designed, fails to show a difference that, in fact, does exist.

In Excerpt 10.2, the results of an experiment (notice "treatment" and "control group") led to a statistically significant result. No more than three decimal places are needed for reporting p-values.

Check for Understanding 2

2a. What is the difference between the null and alternative hypotheses?

2b. What data are used to establish the p-value?

2c. What is the difference between a Type I and a Type II error in hypothesis testing?

2d. How is a p-value of .01 best interpreted?

EXCERPT 10.2

Reporting p-Value

For the sixth-grade spring GRADE [Group Reading and Diagnostic Evaluation] NCEs [normal curve equivalents], the unadjusted means for the treatment and control groups are 31.0 and 29.8, respectively. However, the estimate of the HLM-adjusted means for spring NCEs is 30.0 for treatment and 27.2 for control. This indicates an estimated impact of 2.76. Sixth-grade students in the targeted intervention significantly outperformed sixth-grade students in the control group ($p = .034$). (p. 266)

SOURCE: Cantrell, S. C., Almasi, J. F., Cater, J. C., Rintamaa, M., & Madden, A. (2010). The impact of a strategy-based intervention on the comprehension and strategy use of struggling adolescent readers. *Journal of Educational Psychology, 102*(2), 257–280.

Author Reflection *If the logic of null hypothesis testing, statistical signifi-cance, and types of error seems convoluted, join the club. I too have struggled with these concepts. Part of the reason is that there are double negatives. My advice it to get together with others and practice verbalizing what "reject-ing" and "failing to reject" the null hypothesis means, using different terms as descriptors, then give each other examples of a p-value that is interpreted for hypothetical results with actual designs. I promise that with practice and experience any initial feelings of confusion lessen; eventually it comes together and makes sense.*

Beyond Significance Testing

Learning Outcome 10.3 Explain why effect size and other indicators of practical significance are essential in communicating the results of studies.

There is a now long-standing debate among researchers about the value of null hypoth-esis statistical significance testing. Some have argued, in fact, that such tests should be banned (which might make your student life a little easier!). Essentially, many believe that making a simple dichotomous yes/no decision based on an arbitrary level of sig-nificance (e.g., the magical $p < .05$ is completely arbitrary) is fundamentally flawed. This is because, in many studies, assumptions for using a specific statistical test may not be met, high sample sizes may obscure the meaningfulness of the results, statisti-cal significance may be interpreted to mean something noteworthy, good, or desirable, and noise may not be given appropriate attention.

  Of course, as you know from reading quantitative research articles and reports, null hypothesis testing is everywhere. Clearly, it is not going away any time soon. However, it is important to understand the limitations of this kind of reasoning, and to supplement inferential significance testing with other analyses that can ameliorate these limitations. There are three primary ways of doing this: carefully examining descriptive statistics, using confidence intervals, and reporting effect size. Descriptive statistics have already been presented. Simple descriptive statistics, particularly those in the same metric that was used in the measurement of variables, are absolutely essential to be able to under-stand a statistically significant result based on inferential statistics. Scatterplots and graphs are also very helpful. We consider the other two procedures here in greater detail.

Confidence Intervals

A **confidence interval** provides a range of values in which the population or "real" trait value lies, within the parameters of specific probabilities. It is calculated with the same data used for significance tests, but there is no p-value or a specific cutoff point for deci-sion making. This is how it works: Taking the sample data, the researcher calculates a measure of variability called the **standard error of the mean** ($SE_{\bar{x}}$). This value is then used to create score-based intervals around the sample mean that correspond to the prob-ability of obtaining a population value in that interval. Essentially this shows the margin of error. For example, if a sample mean is 60, a researcher might have a 95% confidence in-terval of 48–72. This means that there is a 95% chance that the population or "true" mean is somewhere in this interval. By presenting confidence intervals, researchers use vari-ability in reporting results and remind readers that there is error involved. Confidence intervals are also used when comparing groups to show how much the intervals of each group overlap. This gives you a sense of how likely it is that the population values differ.

EXCERPT 10.3
Reporting Confidence Intervals

Changes in the targeted teacher practices are presented in Table 3. The greatest increase was in the percentage of lessons taught outdoors (+34.6%, 95% confidence interval [CI; 15.4, 53.9]). The average percentage of time spent in motor content during PE lessons increased by 8.4% (95% CI [0.3, 16.5]). Conversely, the greatest decrease was in the percentage of time lines were observed (−33.9%, 95% CI [−48.7, −19.0]). One teacher practice changed in an undesirable direction (teacher verbal promotion of physical activity; −2.4%, 95% CI [−6.1, 1.4]) but did not reach statistical significance. Students were also off-task or uninvolved in lesson content more often at outcome than at baseline (increase of 11.2%, 95% CI [4.8, 17.6]). (p. 364)

SOURCE: Weaver, R. G., Webster, C. A., Beets, M. W., Beets, M. W., Brazendale, K., Chandler, J., … Aziz, M. (2018). Initial outcomes of a participatory-based, competency-building approach to increasing physical education teachers' physical activity promotion and students' physical activity: A pilot study. *Health Education and Behavior, 45*(3), 359–370.

A 95% confidence interval is equal to two standard errors from the mean (similar in interpretation to two standard deviations since in both cases a normal distribution of scores is assumed). The 95% interval is the default in most research unless otherwise stated. Occasionally a 99% (three standard errors) or 68% (one standard error) interval is used. But if not specifically indicated, it is likely the 95% interval.

The use of confidence intervals is illustrated in Excerpt 10.3. This is a pretest–posttest evaluation of the effectiveness of a professional development workshop on physical education teachers' physical activity promotion and students' actual physical activity. The first confidence interval suggests that the increase in percentage of lessons taught outdoors was between 15.4% and 53.9%.

Effect Size

The null hypothesis and level of significance refer *only* to statistical significance to provide a measure of chance variation. It is up to each consumer and researcher to judge the practical importance or usefulness of what may be "statistically significant." This judgment is made by examining the *magnitude* of differences or relationships that are called statistically significant, and considering the context in which the results are used. For example, a very small but statistically significant difference in the reading achievement of students (small magnitude) may not justify changing the method of instruction if teachers' attitudes toward the new approach are negative. It is also possible that a large magnitude difference accompanies statistical nonsignificance, which may suggest further study and consideration. That is, in some cases statistical significance is not needed to have important practical significance. In the end, only the reader or consumer can determine what is practical and meaningful in using the results. In this sense, your conclusions are more important than those stated by the researchers!

Several procedures are used to quantify the practical significance of results. In correlational studies, the correlation coefficient or coefficient of determination is used. In studies that compare different groups, as with experiments, a procedure called *effect size* is reported. The **effect size** is a way of quantifying the degree of difference between two groups. (Some researchers use *effect size* to refer to any of several procedures for determining the magnitude, importance, or practicality of a difference or relationship.) Other terms that are used include *effect magnitude, magnitude effect,* or even *magnitude of effect.* For our purpose here, effect size will be restricted to the comparison of two groups.

The logic of effect size is that the difference between means is best understood for practical significance in the context of variance of the scores. This point is illustrated in Figure 10.3. It shows how the means of two groups can be the same but the amount of overlap, or variance, is quite different. When there is little overlap, as illustrated in the top half of Figure 10.3, the effect size is greater.

A simple formula, called Cohen's *d,* is often used with two groups, where $\overline{X}_1$ is the mean of one group, $\overline{X}_2$ is the mean of a second group, and *SD* is a measure of variance (pooled from the groups or from the control group):

$$d = \frac{\overline{X}_1 - \overline{X}_2}{SD}$$

With this formula, *d* represents the difference between two groups as a function of variance. In other words, *d* expresses the difference in terms of standard deviation units. Thus, if the difference between the means is 3 and the standard deviation is 3, $d = 1$. If the difference is 2 and the standard deviation is 4, then $d = .5$. Note that this formula does *not* include sample size. This is a key difference from statistical significance testing.

In reading research, you will find reference to a rule of thumb established by Cohen that has been used to label different values of *d* into "small," "moderate," and "large" effects. This general guideline is presented in Table 10.2, along with correlations that correspond to different effect sizes. However, it is important to know that these rules of thumb often underestimate practical significance in educational studies. A good guideline for education has been established by the federal government's What Works Clearinghouse, which labels an effect size equal to or greater than .25, often regarded as "small" according to Cohen's guideline, as "substantively significant." This is saying that a difference of one-quarter of a standard deviation shows practical significance, which is often true in education. It is essential, then, that the description of a *d* according to Cohen's guidelines is *not* what is automatically used to make a conclusion about practical significance. In other words, the size of the *d,* or any other measure of effect size, is only a beginning and part of a judgment about practical significance.

Figure 10.3 Effect Size Estimates

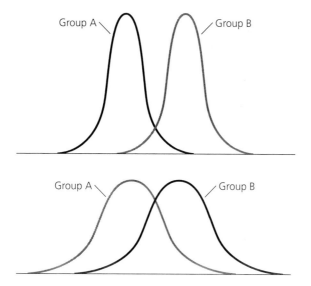

Table 10.2 General Rules of Thumb for Interpreting Cohen's d, Correlation, and Eta[2] Effect Sizes

	Cohen's d[1]	Pearson r	Eta squared[2]
Small	.20	.10	.02
Moderate	.50	.30	.13
Large	.80	.50	.26

[1]Used to compare means of two groups.
[2]Used to compare means of three or more groups in simple ANOVA.

Effect size is best applied when the effect can be stated as a measure that has direct practical application. For example, when an effect size of .33 is converted to percentile ranks for a group average, it is like saying that one group's average is at the 50th percentile, the other at the 63rd percentile. This kind of difference would probably have important implications for high-stakes accountability testing. An effect size of 1.0 is one group at the 50th percentile and the second group at the 84th percentile. This is a very large increase and would clearly have practical value.

Thus, it is important to remember that the meaning of a specific effect size is ultimately a matter of professional judgment, depending on previous research, circumstances, context, costs, and benefits. For example, finding that a small group of students who fail a high-stakes test and participate in a new computerized individualized instructional approach, which increases the likelihood of their passing the retest by 30%, may be very important, even though the increase may not be statistically significant. Waiting to obtain a $p < .05$ result could be unfair to these students.

The following two excerpts illustrate the use of effect size using two different statistics. In Excerpt 10.4, Cohen's d is used with a meta-analysis (refer to Chapter 4). The SE refers to standard error, which gives you a sense of how much the effect size might vary. In Excerpt 10.5, confidence intervals are used along with Cohen's d. Confidence intervals also give you a sense of variability, as the calculated effect size is only an estimate.

EXCERPTS 10.4 AND 10.5

Reporting Effect Size

Research studies have implicated executive functions in reading difficulties (RD). But while some studies have found children with RD to be impaired on tasks of executive function other studies report unimpaired performance. A meta-analysis was carried out to determine whether these discrepant findings can be accounted for by differences in the tasks of executive function that are utilized. A total of 48 studies comparing the performance on tasks of executive function of children with RD with their typically developing peers were included in the meta-analysis, yielding 180 effect sizes. An overall effect size of 0.57 ($SE = 0.03$) was obtained, indicating that children with RD have impairments on tasks of executive function. However, effect sizes varied considerably suggesting that the impairment is not uniform. (p. 133)

SOURCE: Booth, J. N., Boyle, J. M., & Kelly, S. W. (2010). Do tasks make a difference? Accounting for heterogeneity of performance of children with reading difficulties on tasks of executive function: Findings from a meta-analysis. *British Journal of Developmental Psychology, 28*(1), 133–176.

(Continued)

In general, results show that living on campus had statistically significant and positive effects on all seven dependent variables, especially when compared to living farther than walking distance from campus (Table 4). However, because *p*-values are highly sensitive to sample size, the regression coefficient is a better effect size for interpreting the practical significance, or magnitude, of the relationships. The most popular frame of reference is a set of benchmarks offered by Cohen (1988, 1992). Cohen described small effects as those that are hardly visible, medium effects as observable and noticeable to the eye of the beholder, and large effects as plainly evident or obvious. He suggested that r values of about 0.1, 0.3, and 0.5 would represent small, medium, and large effects, respectively. Using this standard, we can identify which are the more meaningful effects in our results and which are perhaps too small to be of any consequence. Using Cohen's references, results show that three of the models had at least a small effect. First, although living on campus had a small positive effect (0.07) on engagement in Collaborative Learning compared to living within walking distance, it had a medium positive effect (0.26) compared to living farther than walking distance. Second, living on campus had small effects (0.13 and 0.15) on engagement in discussions with diverse others relative to all students living off campus, no matter their proximity to campus. (p. 262)

SOURCE: Graham, P. A., Hurtado, S. S., & Gonyea, R. M. (2018). The benefits of living on campus: Do residence halls provide distinctive environments of engagement? *Journal of Student Affairs Research and Practice, 55*(3), 255–269.

Author Reflection *Being tied to Cohen's effect size guidelines has led to much misunderstanding about real effects. When all you see in an article is "according to Cohen's guidelines," the researcher has missed the true meaning of effect size. Recently a noted researcher at a conference I attended claimed, quite appropriately, that the effect size of .13 he obtained was important because it represented a 25% increase in student achievement. Effect size must be interpreted in light of the context and situation, stated in numbers that convey meaningful differences.*

The Hedgehog and Fox Interpret a Cohen's *d* Effect Size

According to Cohen's guidelines, my small effect size of .25 shows little practical significance.

The effect size of .25, while considered small according to Cohen's guidelines, shows that students in the experimental group gained an average percentile rank of 58%, compared to 50%. This represents nearly a one-third growth in achievement over the year, clearly a substantial and important difference.

Check for Understanding 3

3a. What is the difference between statistical and practical significance?

3b. Why is it important to *not* use only Cohen's guidelines for interpreting effect size estimates?

Some Specific Inferential Tests

Learning Outcome 10.4 Know how to use specific inferential tests to analyze data, including *t*-test, analysis of variance, chi-square, and multivariate statistics.

There are many different inferential procedures. Each is used to analyze the results of particular research designs. Thus, depending on the design, a specific statistical formula is used to obtain a level of significance appropriate to the null hypothesis(es). Most of the procedures you will read about are **parametric statistics**. These statistics are used when certain assumptions can be made about the data, such as having a population that is normally distributed, equal variances of each group, and interval level measures. If these assumptions cannot be met (and even sometimes when they are met), researchers may use **nonparametric statistics**. The interpretation of the results is the same with both types of statistics, but parametric statistics have greater power to detect significant differences. The computational equations are different, but both test a null hypothesis and report a level of significance. We will consider two commonly used parametric procedures, *t*-tests and analysis of variance, and one nonparametric statistical tool, chi-square.

The *t*-Test

The ***t*-test** (also '*t* test') is most often used to test the null hypothesis that the means of two groups are the same. The *t*-test is also used to see whether a correlation coefficient is significantly different from zero (no correlation), to compare a mean to a set value, and to compare a pretest score with a posttest score. In comparing two means, the researcher uses the two sample means and the group variances to generate a number called the *t* value or *t* statistic. The *t* value is determined by a simple formula in which the difference between the two means is the numerator and the standard error of the mean is the denominator. The numerator is akin to the signal, the denominator the noise. The larger the difference between the means and the smaller the standard error mean (noise), the greater the chance of rejecting the null hypothesis. That is, the less noise, as represented by the standard error of the mean (error variance), the stronger the potential for identifying the signal.

The *t* value is then used with sample size to obtain a *p*-value for rejecting the null hypothesis that the population means are the same. It is important to recognize that the sample size is actually directly related to the level of significance that is obtained. This means that the more subjects in the study, the greater the chance that the null hypothesis will be rejected (e.g., the same *t* value with 20 subjects that shows a *p* = .08 may show a *p* = .01 with 30 subjects). In most studies the researcher will report the *t* value for each *t*-test, with corresponding *p*-values. The *t* values may be in a table or in the narrative of the results section. For studies with several dependent variables there will often be a table of the means of each group, with accompanying *t* and *p*-values. You will see *t*-tests used for both experimental and nonexperimental studies.

Figure 10.4 Use of *t*-Tests for Experimental and Nonexperimental Designs

Independent samples *t*-test for experiment to impact science achievement, with or without random assignment:

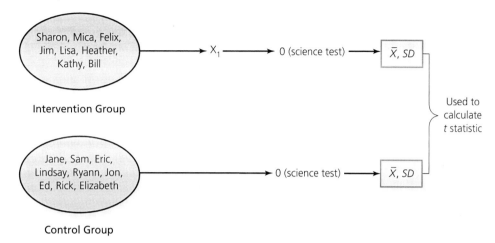

Dependent samples *t*-test for a single-group pretest–posttest design:

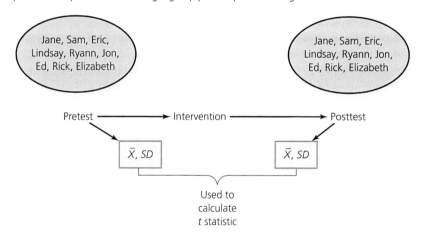

Nonexperimental design use of independent samples *t*-test:

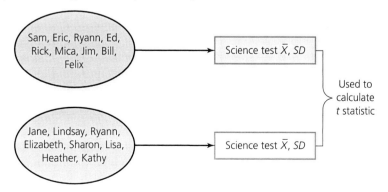

EXCERPT 10.6

Independent Samples *t*-Tests

With respect to declarative knowledge, the skill-training group achieved higher ratings than the control group in the posttest, $t(142) = 3.00$, $p = .002$, $d = 0.79$, as well as in the delayed posttest, $t(134) = 3.04$, $p = .002$, $d = 0.81$ (medium effects). With respect to procedural knowledge the skill training group achieved higher ratings than the control group after the intervention, $t(142) = 2.34$, $p = .010$, $d = 0.70$ (medium effect). However, one week after the experiment, this effect on procedural knowledge could no longer be found, $t(134) = 1.42$, $p = .079$. Finally, the skill-training intervention also fostered argument quality, $t(142) = 3.04$, $p = .002$, $d = 0.74$ (medium effect). (pp. 336–337)

SOURCE: Hefter, M. H., Renkl, A., Riess, W., Schmid, S., Fries, S., & Berthold, K. (2018). Training interventions to foster skill and will of argumentative thinking. *The Journal of Experimental Education, 86*(3), 325–343.

There are two forms of the *t*-test. One, the **independent samples *t*-test**, is used in designs in which there are different individuals in each group, as illustrated in Figure 10.4. When the groups being compared have different participants the design may also be called a *between-subjects* design. For example, a randomized-to-groups posttest-only design with two levels of the independent variable and a single dependent variable would use an independent samples *t*-test. In a nonexperimental study, the independent variable would also have two levels; the single dependent variable would be continuous (refer to Figure 10.4 and Excerpt 10.6). If the participants in the groups are paired or matched in some way, a second form of the *t*-test is used. This may be called a **dependent samples *t*-test**, *correlated t*-test, or *matched t*-test. It is commonly used in the single-group pretest–posttest design when the same group of individuals is given both the pretest and posttest (refer to Figure 10.4 and Excerpt 10.7). This type of design may also be called a *within-subjects* or *repeated-measures* design.

The *df* in the examples refers to **degrees of freedom**. This number is used to calculate the level of significance and is approximately the same as the number of participants in the study. It may be indicated in parentheses after the *t* without the letters *df*. In some reports degrees of freedom may be implied or indicated in a table of results, not in the narrative.

EXCERPT 10.7

Dependent Samples *t*-Test

A matched-sample t test was utilized to test the first null hypothesis: H0: There will be no difference in the number of science integrating learning objectives within the CTE teachers' courses of study before and after the engagement of the cooperative learning group process (see Table 6; $H_{0number}$: $\mu_{pre} = \mu_{post}$). The results indicate that the number of science integrating learning objectives ($M = 60.84$, $SD = 14.23$) within the CTE teachers' courses of study following the CLG process was significantly greater ($t = -11.56$, $p = .0001$) than the number of science integrating learning objectives ($M = 44.75$, $SD = 9.06$) in the CTE teachers' courses prior to the CLG process. In this case, the null hypothesis was rejected and difference between the means represents a large practical effect ($d = 1.08$). (p. 166)

SOURCE: Spindler, M. (2016). A cooperative learning group procedure for improving CTE and science integration. *Career and Technical Education Research, 41*(3), 157–173.

Analysis of Variance

Analysis of variance (abbreviated ANOVA) is a parametric procedure that has the same basic purpose as the *t*-test: to compare group means to determine the probability of being wrong in rejecting the null hypothesis. Whereas the independent samples *t*-test compares two means, each from a different group of individuals, ANOVA compares two or more different group means. In effect, ANOVA is an extension of the *t*-test that allows the researcher to test the differences between more than two group means. We'll consider two common types of ANOVA: simple and factorial.

SIMPLE ANALYSIS OF VARIANCE In **simple analysis of variance** (also called *one-way* ANOVA), a single independent variable is analyzed with a single dependent variable. For instance, if a researcher compares three types of students—high, medium, and low socioeconomic status (SES)—on a measure of self-regulation, there are three levels of the independent variable. ANOVA would test the null hypothesis that there is no difference among the means of all three groups. It would be referred to as a 1 × 3 ANOVA (one independent variable with three levels). The ANOVA equation uses the variances of the groups to calculate a value, called the *F* statistic (or *F* ratio—signal divided by noise). The *F*, analogous to the *t* value, is a three- or four-digit number employed to obtain the *p*-value that the researcher uses to reject or fail to reject the null hypothesis. If the *F* value is large enough, with a sufficient number of participants, the null hypothesis can be rejected with confidence that at least two of the group means are not the same. ANOVA is also used for experimental studies when the design is posttest-only with a single dependent variable and the independent variable has more than two levels. This is illustrated in Figure 10.5, along with a nonexperimental example.

In the nonexperimental example in Figure 10.5, let's assume that the science test means for each group are as follows: Group A, 30; Group B, 23; and the control group, 22. The null hypothesis that is tested is that the means from each group are the same (30 = 23 = 22). If the *F* statistic calculated with ANOVA is 4.76 and the *p*-value is .01, the null hypothesis would be rejected. Like *t*-tests, the *p*-value is directly influenced by the number of subjects (more subjects results in greater significance). However, this analysis does not indicate *which* pair or pairs of means are different. In some studies, the results are such that the different pairs are obvious (as in this example), but in most studies there is a need for further statistical tests to indicate those means that are significantly different from other means. These tests are called **multiple comparison procedures** (or post hoc or follow-up comparisons). There are several types of multiple comparison procedures, including Bonferroni, Fisher's LSD, Duncan's new multiple range test, the Newman-Keuls, Tukey's HSD, and Scheffe's test. The selection of which to use depends on several factors, considerations beyond what I am able to present here. I should also point out that these post hoc tests will sometimes show significant differences between two or more groups even when the overall *F* statistic is not significant.

The results of simple 1 × 3 ANOVAs are illustrated in Excerpts 10.8 and 10.9. The results of an ANOVA can be summarized as part of the narrative, as with Excerpt 10.8, or presented in an ANOVA table, as illustrated in Excerpt 10.9. In Excerpt 10.8 the three levels of the independent variable are three parent groups: African American, Euro-Americans, and Latinos. The table in Excerpt 10.9 shows various numbers that are used to calculate the level of significance. The "between groups" factor shows the variance between the group means, whereas "within groups" is an estimate of variance for each group. In good research, between-groups variance is maximized (like the MAX in

Figure 10.5 Use of ANOVA for Experimental and Nonexperimental Designs

ANOVA for experiment to impact science achievement, with or without random assignment:

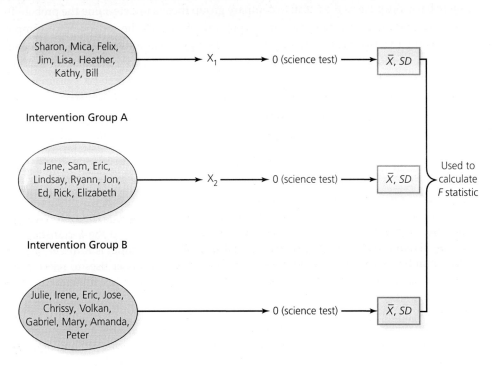

Intervention Group A

Intervention Group B

Control Group

ANOVA for nonexperimental study that compares different groups

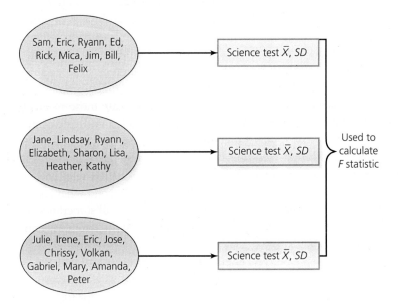

MAXMINCON), while within-groups variance is minimized (MIN). Between-groups variance is enhanced when the differences between the levels of the independent variable are enhanced. For example, suppose you decide to compare three "self-efficacy" groups to see whether they differ in achievement, choosing the top third as one group, the middle third as the second group, and the lowest third as the last group. That procedure probably would not produce as much between-groups variance as choosing the lowest 10%, middle 10%, and highest 10%.

EXCERPTS 10.8 AND 10.9

One-Way ANOVA with Post Hoc Tests

However, there were ethnic differences in parental self-efficacy, $F(2, 55) = 3.60, p < .05$; school-based involvement, $F(2, 55) = 7.35, p < .001$; and parents' reports of the quality of their relationships with teachers, $F(2, 59) = 3.64, p < .05$. African American parents ($M = 5.08, SD = 0.54$) reported higher levels of parental efficacy than did Euro-Americans ($M = 4.87, SD = 0.47$) or Latinos ($M = 4.48, SD = 0.92$); who were not different from each other. African Americans ($M = 0.95, SD = 0.52$) and Euro-Americans ($M = 0.96, SD = 0.47$) reported being more frequently involved at school than did Latinos ($M = 0.33, SD = 0.44$). African Americans ($M = 3.05, SD = 0.69$) reported higher quality relationships with their youths' teachers than did Latinos ($M = 2.72, SD = 0.69$). Euro-Americans were not different from Latinos or African Americans in their ratings of the quality of their relationships with their youths' teachers ($M = 2.82, SD = 0.79$). Finally, there were no ethnic differences in students' reports of cognitive competence, $F(2, 61) = 1.87, p = $ ns. (p. 17)

SOURCE: Hill, N. E., Witherspoon, D. P., & Bartz, D. (2018). Parental involvement in education during middle school: Perspectives of ethnically diverse parents, teachers, and students. *The Journal of Educational Research, 111*(1), 12–27.

Education majors had the highest attitude score ($M = 3.48, SD = .72$) and Business Administration majors had the lowest attitude score ($M = 2.95, SD = .92$). Mathematics majors had a mean of 3.21 ($SD = .67$). The overall mean for all three majors was 3.35 ($SD = .78$). The ANOVA showed significant differences between groups (Table 4).

The Scheffe post hoc procedure was conducted to determine which groups differed. The results from the Scheffe procedure indicated that the difference between Education majors and Business Administration majors was statistically significant ($p = .000$). No other differences between groups were found. These results illustrate that Education students had a more positive attitude towards group work than Business Administration majors but there were neither differences between Education and Math majors, nor between Math and Business Administration majors.

Table 4 Analysis of Variance for Student Attitude

Source	SS	df	MS	F
Between Groups	12.38	2	6.19	10.77*
Within Groups	163.92	285	.58	
Total	176.31	287		

Note: N = 288. * $p < .001$

SOURCE: Gottschall, H., & Garcia-Bayonas, M. (2008). Student attitudes towards group work among undergraduates in business administration, education, and mathematics. *Educational Research Quarterly, 32*(1), 3–29. Copyright © Educational Research Quarterly. (p. 15)

FACTORIAL ANALYSIS OF VARIANCE designs have more than one independent variable and allow the investigation of interactions among the independent variables. The statistical analysis of such designs requires the use of **factorial analysis of variance**. The most common factorial ANOVA has two independent variables and is therefore referred to as a *two-way* ANOVA. In a two-way ANOVA, three null hypotheses are tested: one for each independent variable and one for the interaction between the two independent variables. Consequently, there are three F ratios, one for each null hypothesis. The test for each independent variable, sometimes called a *main effect*, is similar to a one-way ANOVA for that variable by itself. Thus, there will be an F ratio and corresponding p-value for each independent variable. If one variable in a factorial design has two levels and another variable has three levels, the analysis would be a 2×3 ANOVA. A $3 \times 3 \times 4$ ANOVA would mean that there are three independent variables, two with three levels and one with four levels.

Suppose you are interested in whether class size affects freshman college students' writing skills, *and* whether the effect of class size is related to, or varies, according to how well students write when they begin college. In this experimental design class size is the independent variable and writing proficiency is a moderator variable. You decide to have three different class sizes (10–12, 18–20, and 28–30), so you have an intervention variable with three levels. Before you randomize entering students to one of the three class sizes, you divide them into high and low proficiency levels based on a test of writing skills they take in the summer. This gives you a moderator variable, with two levels. At the end of the semester, all the students take a writing test, which is the dependent variable. Your design, for analysis purposes, looks like this:

		Class Size		
		Small	Medium	Large
Beginning Writing Proficiency	High			
	Low			

As you can see, there are six different groups of participants: three groups of high-proficiency students, each in a different-sized class, and three groups of low-proficiency students, also in different classes. This means that there are different students in each of the six groups (a between-subjects design). Now, the logic of the statistical analysis is whether there are differences between high- and low-proficiency students (one of two main effects), differences between students according to class size (second main effect), and whether students high or low in proficiency achieve the same, regardless of class size (interaction effect). To do this, you examine the mean scores in each of the six groups. You can think of each of the six groups as being in cells, and in which a mean and variance is calculated for the students in each group. Beyond these six means, you can see what the average mean would be for each level of each independent variable. This is accomplished conceptually by calculating column and row means, which essentially gives you results so you can examine group differences for one independent variable without the influence of the other one.

Let's see how this works with some actual numbers. Figure 10.6 depicts the individual cell means, as well as the total row and column means. Take a minute to examine how each column and row mean was derived ($\overline{X}_7 - \overline{X}_{11}$). Now, the first step is analyzing each of the main effects. This is accomplished by comparing the row means for writing proficiency and the column means for class size. Thus, $\overline{X}_7$ is compared to $\overline{X}_8$, with the null hypothesis that the means are not different ($80.67 = 68.67$). A main

Figure 10.6 2×3 ANOVA Cell, Row, and Column Means

		Class Size Low	Medium	High	Row Means
Writing Proficiency	High	$\overline{X}_1 = 82$	$\overline{X}_3 = 80$	$\overline{X}_5 = 80$	$\overline{X}_7 = 80.67$
	Low	$\overline{X}_2 = 81$	$\overline{X}_4 = 65$	$\overline{X}_6 = 60$	$\overline{X}_8 = 68.67$
Column Means		$\overline{X}_9 = 81.1$	$\overline{X}_{10} = 72.5$	$\overline{X}_{11} = 70$	

effect statistical test is calculated, resulting in an F statistic and corresponding p level for writing proficiency, independent of class size. In this example, the means are very different, showing that the high-proficiency students ($\overline{X}_7$) scored significantly higher than the low-proficiency students ($\overline{X}_8$). For examining class size, without regard for entering proficiency, the column means ($\overline{X}_9, \overline{X}_{10}, \overline{X}_{11}$) are compared with what is like a 1×3 ANOVA. When you look at these means, it is pretty clear that students in small classes do better than students in medium or large classes, with not much of a difference between medium and large classes. Here, the overall F statistic would be significant, and a post hoc test would be used to confirm which groups are different from each other.

The third statistical test is the interaction, which in null form states that there is no interaction. No interaction would mean that the effect of class size is the same for both high- and low-proficiency students. If the statistical test for the interaction is significant, however, you examine the cell means to see what is going on. This is accomplished by looking at the differences between high- and low-proficiency students for each class size. In our example, that would mean comparing the difference between $\overline{X}_1$ and $\overline{X}_2$ (small class), which is –1 (80–81), to the difference between $\overline{X}_3$ and $\overline{X}_4$ (15) and between $\overline{X}_5$ and $\overline{X}_6$ (20). Because –1 is very different from both 15 and 20, there would be a significant interaction. When you look at the direction of the differences, it is pretty clear that in small classes students achieve about the same, regardless of writing proficiency, but with larger classes low-proficiency students do much worse. One conclusion, then, would be that for low-proficiency students class size makes a big difference, whereas for high-proficiency students class size does not seem to matter.

In interpreting factorial ANOVA studies, you will find that significant interactions are often presented in a graph, which is constructed to show how the means of all the groups compare. The values of the dependent variable are placed along the vertical axis of the graph, and levels of one of the independent variables are on the horizontal axis. The means of all the groups are then indicated in the graph by reference to the second independent variable. For example, Figure 10.7 illustrates a significant interaction. The two independent variables are student effort (high or low) and type of reward (intrinsic or extrinsic). The results of the 2×2 ANOVA indicate that, overall, high-effort students did better on achievement, a main effect for effort, and that there was a significant interaction—high-effort students who received an intrinsic reward did better than high-effort students who received an extrinsic reward. For low-effort students, it did not matter whether they received intrinsic or extrinsic rewards. A 2×2 factorial design is illustrated in Excerpt 10.10, with two interventions, each with two levels. In Excerpt 10.11, an interaction between gender and two levels of the intervention is reported.

Figure 10.7 Graph of Hypothetical 2 × 2 ANOVA and Interaction

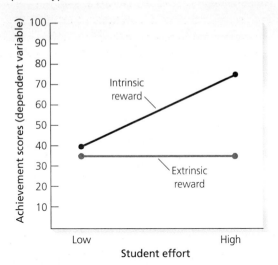

EXCERPTS 10.10 AND 10.11

2 × 2 Factorial Designs

A 2 × 2 between-subjects ANOVA was calculated, comparing the effects of certification route (i.e., traditional and alternative) and level of experience (i.e., 1–10 years and 11 or more years) on the dependent variable self-efficacy. The main effect for certification was not statistically significant, $F(1, 139) = 1.00$, $p = .32$, indicating that self-efficacy scores for TCMTs ($M = 58.15$, $SD = 3.86$) were similar, on average, to self-efficacy scores for ACMTs ($M = 56.96$, $SD = 4.68$). There was a statistically significant main effect for level of experience, $F(1, 139) = 16.57$, $p < .01$, with a medium to large effect size ($\eta^2 = .11$), indicating meaningful practical differences in the music teacher self-efficacy of early career music teachers ($M = 55.89$, $SD = 4.36$) and mid- to late-career music teachers ($M = 59.23$, $SD = 3.21$). Finally, the interaction between certification and level of experience was not statistically significant, $F(1, 139) = 0.22$, $p = .90$, indicating that the self-efficacy similarities in TCMTs and ACMTs remained consistent across levels of experience (see Figure S1 in online supplementary material). (pp. 103–104)

SOURCE: West, J. J., & Frey-Clark, M. L. (2019). Traditional versus alternative pathways to certification: Assessing differences in music teacher self-efficacy. *Journal of Music Teacher Education, 28*(2), 98–111.

There was a significant interaction between instructional method and blocked preassessment scores on transformed postassessment scores for males, $F(2, 99) = 5.35$, $p = .01$. Simple main effects analysis showed that there were no significant differences between instructional methods' postscores for the low males' ($p = .56$) and medium males' ($p = .28$) blocked preassessment scores. However, there was a statistically significant difference between instructional methods' postassessment scores for high blocked preassessment males' scores ($p < .01$) in favor of the control group. (p. 343)

SOURCE: Wilhelm, J., Jackson, C., Sullivan, A., & Wilhelm, R. (2013). Examining differences between preteen groups' spatial-scientific understandings: A quasi-experimental study. *The Journal of Educational Research, 106*(5), 337–351.

There are many variations of factorial designs and many terms are used to describe specific types of analyses. You may read such terms as *split plot, randomized block, within subjects,* or *repeated measures* in the results sections of articles. Regardless of the language, the results are interpreted in basically the same manner. There is some type of null hypothesis that needs to be tested, and the *F* ratios are used to see whether there were statistically significant differences.

Author Reflection *I have found that students often struggle with understanding the results of a factorial ANOVA, so if that is the case for you, again, join the club. The best antidote is to work through example after example, using different cell means and different levels of the independent variables. Once you get the hang of it, it sticks.*

ANALYSIS OF COVARIANCE   A common and useful variation of ANOVA (both one-way and factorial) is **analysis of covariance** (ANCOVA). ANCOVA is used in experimental studies in which participant differences between groups prior to an intervention can be used to statistically adjust the dependent variable results so the analysis is more powerful and accurate. That is, it adjusts posttest scores statistically, based on initial group differences, which reduces the influence of that difference on the results. Adjustments are made by one or more *covariates*. These are variables that literally *covary* with the dependent variable (that is, they are related). In the case of experiments, they measure pre-intervention differences. (Covariates are also used in regression to minimize the influence, to "control" for the effect of variables that could be related to the dependent variable but need to be "equalized.") Suppose a researcher uses two groups in an experiment to see which type of counseling, individual or small group, is most effective for reducing anxiety. Because participants cannot be randomized to the types of counseling, the individualized group, from Calder University, has less-anxious students than the students from Greene University, who are in a small-group intervention. To account for this difference, which could have an obvious impact on the dependent variable, a measure of anxiety is given to participants in both groups before counseling begins. (Yes, this is a nonequivalent-groups pretest–posttest design!) If the Calder University students' group score on the pretest is 15, and the Greene University students' 20, the covariate (pretest) is used to adjust the posttest scores statistically to compensate for the five-point difference between the groups. This adjustment results in more accurate posttest comparisons. In this design, it would be a 1×2 ANCOVA. Note that the analysis does not compare the pretest/posttest score difference for each group, using *t*-tests. ANCOVA is the better analysis. Other types of covariates can also be used in a study, such as socioeconomic status, aptitude, attitudes, and previous achievement, but the covariate must be related to the dependent variable to be useful. Excerpt 10.12 offers an illustration of how covariance analysis is used.

Multivariate Statistics

Each of the preceding parametric statistical procedures represents what is termed a **univariate** analysis, because a single dependent variable is used. However, in many complex social settings, such as schools, there is often a need to study two or more dependent variables simultaneously. For example, a teacher may be interested in comparing two teaching methods on two attitudes, one toward learning and one toward school. A principal may want to determine the effect of a new homework policy on parent involvement, student confidence, and achievement in each of several different

---

EXCERPT 10.12

Analysis of Covariance

Because prior research suggests that reading comprehension and vocabulary respond differently to summer reading interventions... we conducted an analysis of covariance (ANCOVA) on each of the three GMRT posttests with pretest scores serving as the covariate.... An ANCOVA on the total reading scores revealed a nonsignificant main effect of condition, $F(2, 307) = 0.40$, *ns* [nonsignificant], suggesting that there was no difference in covariate-adjusted total reading scores among children in the three experimental conditions. When we analyzed treatment effects by subtests on the GMRT, we found no significant main effect in reading comprehension, $F(2, 309) = 0.35$, *ns*, or reading vocabulary, $F(2, 310) = 2.22$, *ns*. These findings suggest that opportunities solely to read 10 books or in combination with a family literacy intervention did not produce significant improvements in children's reading comprehension or vocabulary scores. (p. 25)

SOURCE: Kim, J. S., & Guryan, J. (2010). The efficacy of a voluntary summer book reading intervention for low-income Latino children from language minority families. *Journal of Educational Psychology, 102*(1), 20–31.

---

subject areas. In such situations, it may be inappropriate to analyze each dependent variable separately, with a different ANOVA or *t*-test. Rather, a **multivariate** statistical procedure may be warranted. Multivariate statistics analyze all the *related* dependent variables in a single procedure, which is important in accounting for the relationships among the dependent variables. For each of the univariate statistical procedures, there is a multivariate analog (e.g., Hotelling's *T* for the *t*-test, and MANCOVA for ANCOVA).

Multivariate procedures are commonly reported in the literature. Although the computations and interpretation of multivariate tests are complex, they employ the same basic principles for rejecting the null hypotheses. It should also be pointed out that some researchers have a somewhat different definition of the term *multivariate,* which may refer to any study that has more than one variable, either independent or dependent. With this definition, multiple correlation would be considered a multivariate procedure. Note in Excerpts 10.13 and 10.14 that MANOVAs were used initially to analyze the results; once significance was shown, additional analyses were needed to complete the statistical procedures.

EXCERPTS 10.13 AND 10.14

Multivariate Analysis of Variance

We used a MANOVA to determine mean differences in ratings of didactic preparation, crisis self-efficacy at graduation, and current crisis self-efficacy for participants who had and had not completed a course dedicated to crisis intervention. Assumptions for normality and homoscedasticity were met. Results showed a statistically significant multivariate effect for course, Λ [Wilks lambda] = .86, $F(3, 188) = 10.63$, $p < .001$, partial η^2 [eta squared] = .15. Univariate F tests showed that those who had completed a crisis course rated didactic preparation ($F = 21.50$, $p < .001$, $R^2 = .14$), crisis self-efficacy at graduation ($F = 9.35$, $p < .01$, $R^2 = .05$), and current crisis self-efficacy ($F = 6.11$, $p = .01$, $R^2 = .03$) more favorably than those who did not complete a crisis course. (p. 263)

SOURCE: Wachter Morris, C. A., & Barrio Minton, C. (2012). Crisis in the curriculum? New counselors' crisis preparation, experiences, and self-efficacy. *Counselor Education & Supervision, 51,* 256–269.

We performed a multivariate analysis of variance on perceptions in four dependent variable domains: (a) quality of relationship with their supervising teacher, (b) knowledge of school policies and procedures, (c) perception of teaching ability, and (d) adequacy of time to prepare for profession. The independent variable was type of student-teaching experience, which consisted of two levels: extended year-long and traditional semester-long internship. With the use of Hotelling's criteria, the association between the combined dependent variables and the type of internship experience was statistically significant.... We conducted a series of independent *t*-tests to examine the nature of the relationship. (p. 267)

SOURCE: Spooner, M., Flowers, C., Lamber, R., & Algozzine, B. (2008). Is more really better? Examining perceived benefits of an extended student teaching experience. *The Clearing House, 81*(6), 263–269. Copyright © Taylor & Francis.

Chi-Square Test of Independence

As a reminder, the statistical procedures I have summarized so far are in the *parametric* family, used when certain assumptions about the nature of the distributions are met (e.g., normal distribution) and type of data (e.g., interval). When the assumptions are not clearly met, a *nonparametric* procedure may be used. The most typical type of nonparametric technique is used when you are interested in the number of responses or cases in different categories, using nominal level data. For example, you might be interested in studying whether there is a relationship between race and gender. These are both nominal variables. In this situation, a procedure called a **chi-square test of independence** (or often simply *chi-square*) is used to analyze the results (there are other types of chi-square tests, such as chi-square test for variance or for homogeneity). The null hypothesis is that there is no difference between an observed number and an expected number of responses or cases that fall in each category. For our race and gender example, that would mean that there is no relationship—that the percentage of males and females is the same for each race. The expected number is usually what would be expected by chance alone. Suppose an administrator wanted to see whether there is a difference between the number of junior-level and senior-level students who take advanced placement courses. The expected number by chance alone would be an equal number of juniors and seniors in advanced placement courses. The administrator would use the chi-square test to determine whether the actual number of male students taking advanced placement courses was significantly different from the number of female students taking advanced placement courses.

As final example, suppose you are interested in investigating the relationship between gender and choices of types of books for a book report. There may be several types of books, such as romance, adventure, mystery, and biography. You would count the number of males and females who choose each type of book and analyze the results with a chi-square to determine whether the null hypothesis—that there is no relationship between gender and book choice—can be rejected. This type of chi-square may be referred to as a *contingency table*—in this example, a 2 × 4 table. The result is often reported with a single measure of relationship called a *contingency coefficient*, which is interpreted in the same way as a correlation coefficient.

The results of a chi-square will usually be reported in a table that shows either the number and/or percentage of responses or cases in each category, or what are called *residuals*. If the number of expected observations is less than five in any single cell, the chi-square test needs to be "corrected" statistically. This correction adjusts the numbers to provide a more valid result.

In Excerpt 10.15, note that percentages were compared to see whether there were relationships between principal characteristics, such as gender, and the value they placed on teacher applicants with different types of degrees. The gender by degree analysis was a 2 × 3 chi-square. Can you determine what the "3" means? Excerpt 10.16 is from a study that investigated the relationship between gender and various binge drinking behaviors among college students.

EXCERPTS 10.15 AND 10.16

Chi-Square Test of Independence

A national survey of high school principals ($N = 683$) was used to assess the acceptability of job applicant qualifications that included degrees earned either online, partly online, or in a traditional-residential teacher-training program.... Chi square tests were used to assess whether certain respondent characteristics had any relationship to applicant selection. Results indicated that applicant selection differed significantly based on certain respondent characteristics. For example, male principals were significantly different from female principals in their applicant selection in both Situation 1, $\chi^2 = 4.577$, $df = 1$, $p = .032$, and Situation 2, $\chi^2 = 6.946$, $df = 1$, $p = .008$, with female principals more likely to choose an applicant with a degree earned in a non-traditional setting.

Principals' responses differed significantly by school type (i.e., public vs. private) in both Situation 1, $\chi^2 = 15.617$, $df = 1$, $p < .001$, and Situation 2, $\chi^2 = 5.121$, $df = 1$, $p = .024$. Interestingly, principals who work in private schools were more likely to recommend Applicant C than were their public school counterparts. One of the more interesting findings made in this section of analysis is that neither the respondents' age nor the number of years they had worked as principals were significantly associated with applicant selection in either hiring situation. (pp. 408, 414)

SOURCE: Adams, J., Lee, S., & Cortese, J. (2012). The acceptability of online degrees: Principals and hiring practices in secondary schools. *Contemporary Issues in Technology and Teacher Education*, *12*(4), 408–422. Copyright © Association for the Advancement of Computing in Education.

In support of our first hypothesis, results indicated that, among counseling center clients who engaged in frequent binge drinking, men were overrepresented (48%) and women were underrepresented (52%) compared to their expected frequencies within the entire sample, $\chi^2(1, 427) = 38.61$, $p < .001$.

In support of our second hypothesis, the observed number of clients who engaged in frequent binge drinking who endorsed *never* when asked if others had expressed concern about their alcohol use (43%) was significantly lower than chance expectation based on the whole sample, $\chi^2(3, 279) = 437.71$, $p < .001$. Relative to the entire sample, the NC group was just as likely to endorse *never* (74%) as would be expected based on chance, $\chi^2(3, 62) = 6.09$, $p = .11$, although the NC group's *never* received concern at a rate higher than expected among the high-risk group, $\chi^2(3, 62) = 28.00$, $p < .001$. The EC group was significantly less likely to endorse *never* (6%) than the whole sample, $\chi^2(3, 35) = 211.56$, $p < .001$. The EC group, however, was significantly less likely to endorse *never* (6%) than what was expected based on the distribution of *never* responses within the high-risk group, $\chi^2(3, 35) = 20.46$, $p < .001$. (p. 268)

SOURCE: Graceffo, J. M., Hayes, J. A., Chun-Kennedy, C., & Locke, B. D. (2012). Characteristics of high-risk college student drinkers expressing high and low levels of distress. *Journal of College Counseling*, *15*(3), 262–273.

Table 10.3 Parametric and Analogous Nonparametric Procedures

Parametric	Nonparametric
Pearson product-moment correlation coefficient	Spearman rank-order correlation coefficient
	Phi correlation coefficient
Independent samples *t*-test	Median test
	Mann–Whitney *U* test
Dependent samples *t*-test	Sign test
	Wilcoxon test
One-way ANOVA	Median test
	Kruskal–Wallis ANOVA

The chi-square test of independence is one of several nonparametric statistical procedures. A few more common nonparametric ones are listed in Table 10.3.

Check for Understanding 4

4a. What results, other than the number of participants, determine the *p*-value with *t*-tests and ANOVA, and how are these factors related to the signal and the noise?

4b. When is it best to use an independent samples *t*-test, a simple ANOVA, and a factorial ANOVA?

4c. Under what circumstances would it be appropriate to use chi-square for the analysis?

Author Reflection *While inferential statistics are commonly reported in quantitative research, there are good reasons to be sceptical of conclusions, especially when "significance" statistically is equated to mean "significant" results and conclusions. The best way to use inferential statistics is to give you guidance in using descriptive statistics to understand what the numbers suggest.*

Consumer (and Researcher) Tips
Criteria for Evaluating Inferential Statistics

1. **Basic descriptive statistics are needed to evaluate the results of inferential statistics.** Remember, the results of an inferential test rely on the descriptive data that were gathered—the means, variances, frequencies, and percentages. Although inferential statistics provide important information about the probability that conclusions about populations, or "true" values, are not due to chance, the interpretation of the results depends on the descriptive statistical results. It may be misleading to rely solely on the conclusions of the inferential test results. *You should always look at the more basic descriptive data to derive meaning from the results.*

2. **Inferential analyses refer to** *statistical,* **not** *practical,* **significance.** It is easy to confuse statistical with practical significance. The results of inferential analyses should not be the sole criterion for conclusions about changing a practice or other decisions. The use of inferential tests should be kept in balance with other considerations relative to the use of the results, primarily whether the magnitude of the difference or relationship is sufficient to have practical importance.

3. **Statistical significance is determined in part by the number of participants.** Remember that one of the determining factors to get "statistically significant" results is the number of participants. In fact, there is a direct relationship, so if the n used is in the thousands, it is fairly easy to find statistical significance.

4. **The level of significance should be interpreted correctly.** Remember that the level of significance indicates the probability that the difference or relationship is not due to chance. It is not a definitive statement that there either is or is not a difference or relationship. A high p-value (e.g., .20 or .40) does not necessarily mean that there is no difference or relationship in the population or in reality. Nonsignificant findings may result from inadequate design and measurement.

5. **Inferential analyses do not indicate internal validity.** The extent to which a result shows a causal relationship depends on how the data were gathered and design of the intervention(s). The inferential test is used as the first and necessary step to conclude that an intervention caused a change in the dependent variable. Once the statistics show that there is a relationship or difference, you need to analyze the design and procedures to determine whether there is adequate internal validity to derive a causal conclusion.

6. **Inferential analyses do not necessarily indicate external validity.** Although we use inferential statistics to infer population values from sample values, generalizability to other individuals and settings depends on whether the participants were randomly selected, the characteristics of the participants, and the design of the study.

7. **The results of inferential tests depend on the number of intervention replications.** If there are many independent replications of the intervention, a very small difference or relationship can be statistically significant; if only a few replications are used, what appears to be a large difference or relationship may not be statistically significant. This phenomenon is especially important in experimental studies in which there is a difference between the number of participants and replications of the treatment. If a researcher uses the number of participants, when it is clear that the number of independent replications of the intervention is much smaller, the inferential test that leads to a conclusion to reject the null hypothesis may be invalid. In fact, there is a whole family of statistical procedures that can capture variation due to participants being in groups that receive interventions. Google *hierarchical linear models* or *nested designs* and you will find very interesting approaches to handling this troublesome source of error. It is also important in many studies that examine existing databases, which can have very large numbers of individuals. This makes it very easy to find statistically significant results.

8. **The appropriate statistical test should be used.** It is important to use a statistical test that is appropriate to the design and questions of a study. Most journal reviewers and editors evaluate studies to be certain that the appropriate tests were employed. However, it is likely that some studies that are published have used the wrong statistical test. The most likely mistakes are to use a parametric procedure when the assumptions for using such a test are not met, and to use many univariate tests when a multivariate test would be more appropriate.

9. **Be wary of statistical tests with small numbers of individuals in one or more groups or categories.** Whenever there is a small number of participants in a group, there is a good chance that the statistical test may provide spurious results. When only a few numbers are used to calculate a mean or variance, one or a few atypical scores may significantly affect the results. It is best to have at least 10 individuals in each comparison group, and 30 in calculating a correlation. The results of studies that use a small number of participants also have less generalizability.

10. **Be wary of studies that have scads of statistical significance tests in a single study.** If you run enough random samples from the same population, some will be statistically significant by chance alone. In fact, if you are willing to live in a world of $p = .05$, 5 of 100 would be significant by chance alone! So when you see many, many significance tests, as you do with some correlational studies, be careful.

Author Reflection *For many students, perhaps including yourself, just contemplating inferential statistics is akin to fear of sky diving. Hopefully, by this point, anxiety has been replaced by confidence in knowing the basics of such tests and how the descriptive results are actually more important. Only a very small percentage of people are statisticians, and the number of statistical procedures out there is growing. But the fundamental purpose of any of the tests is to simply help us focus on what, in a more practical sense, may be useful. And, statistics don't replace design... factors such as threats to internal validity are separate and more important.*

Key Terms

Alpha level	Degrees of freedom	Parametric statistics
Alternative hypothesis	Effect size	Standard error of the mean
Analysis of variance	Inferential statistics	*t*-Test
Analysis of covariance	Level of significance	Dependent samples *t*-test
Factorial analysis of variance	Multiple comparison procedures	Independent samples *t*-test
Simple analysis of variance	Multivariate	Type I error
Chi-square test of independence	Nonparametric statistics	Type II error
Confidence interval	Null hypothesis	Univariate

Discussion Questions

1. Why is it necessary to examine descriptive statistical results carefully when interpreting inferential statistical results?
2. What are two reasons why researchers need to be very careful in their use of inferential statistics to imply "significance?"
3. How does sample size effect inferential statistics? Specifically, how does it affect the level of significance?
4. Why is it important for researchers to report both practical as well as statistical significance? When would practical significance be more important than statistical significance?
5. What does a factorial ANOVA tell us that a one-way ANOVA cannot?

Application Exercise

1. Design a hypothetical experimental study that has a single independent variable with two levels, and indicate the appropriate statistical analysis. Expand the design to include the same independent variable

with three levels and indicate the appropriate analysis. Expand the study again to include a moderator variable with two levels; create a table of hypothetical means that will show one main effect and an interaction.

Check for Understanding Answers

1a. Descriptive statistics are used to summarize data gathered from a group of participants; inferential statistics are used to approximate what is true for the population or signal.

1b. Sampling contributes error because only a portion of the population is used to calculate descriptive statistics; measurement error is present each time that data are collected from the participants.

2a. The null hypothesis states that there is no difference; the alternative hypothesis states that the groups will be different.

2b. The value of p is determined by knowing group means, variance, and number of participants.

2c. Type I error is being wrong in rejecting the null; Type II error is being wrong in accepting the null.

2d. That there is a 1 in 100 chance that rejecting the null is a mistake.

3a. Statistical significance indicates the probability that the results are due to chance; practical significance indicates the magnitude and importance of the results without consideration of number of participants.

3b. Cohen's estimates are not specific to education where smaller effect sizes tend to have greater practical value.

4a. Differences between the means and within-group variance; the greater the difference between the means and the less the variance (noise), the more accurate the inference about the signal.

4b. Use the t-test when comparing two means; ANOVA for two or more means; factorial ANOVA for two or more categorical independent variables.

4c. When comparing the frequency counts of participants in one or more categories.

Part III
Qualitative Research

Research design takes a considerable turn with qualitative investigations. Based on a different epistemology about how to best understand phenomena, the qualitative approach has grown to become an accepted and well-respected set of strategies and analyses. There are many educational issues and research questions that are best aligned with qualitative methods. The ability of qualitative research to provide deep understanding and explanations that can take into account individuals' lived experiences in context is a unique feature that is rarely achieved with quantitative methods. In these three chapters, we examine major types of qualitative designs, how qualitative data are gathered and analyzed, and how qualitative findings are reported.

The first chapter in this section explores the distinctive characteristics of qualitative research in detail, followed by a listing of threats the validity. These threats, akin to threats pertaining to quantitative research, are key considerations in judging the credibility of a qualitative study. They also frame critical considerations in designing a sound qualitative study. Six popular qualitative approaches are then described. Each is used for different purposes, much like different quantitative designs, all with the central goal of insightful understanding of naturally occurring phenomena.

Chapter 12 focuses on qualitative data collection techniques. This chapter shows how to conduct qualitative interviews, observation, and document review. For each, it is important to know how to enter the field with a specific role, and to collect information with protocols that will address threats to validity. The final chapter in this section describes how qualitative data are analyzed and reported. This includes the coding of data that leads to identification of patterns and themes, establishing validity/trustworthiness, and the use of participant voices in reporting results.

Chapter 11
Qualitative Research Designs

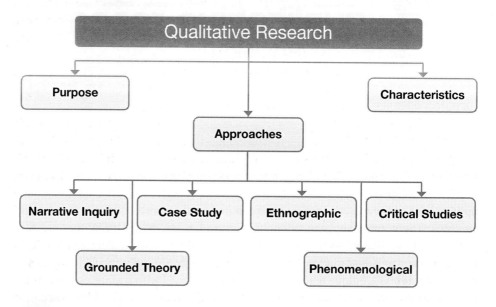

Qualitative Research

Purpose

Characteristics

Approaches

Narrative Inquiry   Case Study   Ethnographic   Critical Studies

Grounded Theory   Phenomenological

⌄ Learning Outcomes

11.1 Describe the nature and characteristics of qualitative research.

11.2 Know how threats to validity/trustworthiness can compromise the integrity, credibility, and value of qualitative findings.

11.3 Differentiate six major approaches to conducting qualitative research.

Chapter Road Map

This chapter is a rather abrupt change from the previous four, not only in research methods and data analysis but also with respect to philosophical assumptions about how it is best to understand what is being studied. We begin by reviewing the nature of qualitative research and characteristics that are common to most qualitative studies, then discuss validity/trustworthiness. Six approaches to qualitative research are presented. In the next chapter, we will look at strategies to collect qualitative data, and in Chapter 13 we discuss how to analyze qualitative data, ensure validity/trustworthiness, and recognize credible conclusions.

Introduction to Qualitative Research Designs

Qualitative research has gone mainstream. Once a rather scarce—and even diminished—approach to research, qualitative studies are now commonplace in social science fields, education, and health sciences. This includes psychology, a field that was initially based on principles of quantitative science. Like research in psychology, much educational research has historically been quantitative, so the transition of the field of research more generally to include qualitative approaches has led to new concepts. This has resulted in some challenges related to terminology. Some of the same terms developed and used for quantitative research are applied to qualitative research but with slightly different meanings, and new terms have been used in qualitative research but have meanings similar to some quantitative concepts. If this sounds confusing, it is! Furthermore, new qualitative approaches are being developed; old ones refined.

With these caveats in mind, it is important to remember that qualitative methods are no less "scientific" than quantitative methods, and many of the same principles apply to both. Qualitative researchers maintain that their approach is scientific with respect to being *systematic* and *rigorous*, just as quantitative approaches are. What is most different for qualitative studies are epistemological assumptions about the nature of the information that is needed to arrive at credible findings and conclusions, as well as the primary purpose. Researchers using a qualitative approach believe that multiple realities are represented in participant perspectives, and that context is critical in exploring and understanding the phenomenon being investigated. The key words here are *exploring* and *understanding*. The purpose of qualitative research is to explore and understand social phenomena, social constructs, theories, societal injustices, and historically disenfranchised populations, and to describe participants' perspectives (Levitt et al., 2018). In contrast, a quantitative study assumes that there is a single objective reality that can be measured, documented, and summarized numerically.

Qualitative approaches are characterized by an assumption that the researcher's biases and perspectives must be understood and included in interpreting findings, whereas in a quantitative study, researcher bias is a threat to internal validity. Qualitative research is focused on natural settings and verbal reports, rather than numbers. Participants' language, based on social contexts, is central to data analysis. The bottom line is that both quantitative and qualitative approaches have advantages and disadvantages, strengths and weaknesses. The key is to use whichever approach is most appropriate, separately or in combination, by beginning with the research question, then aligning methodologies that will provide results closest to the signal.

Characteristics of Qualitative Research

Learning Outcome 11.1 Describe the nature and characteristics of qualitative research.

Qualitative research can be described as a tradition of research techniques, as well as a philosophy of knowing. The term *qualitative* refers to a number of approaches that share some common characteristics, with somewhat different philosophical and theoretical emphases. It is also helpful to remember that there are many terms associated with qualitative research, such as *field research, naturalistic, participant observation, ecological, constructivist, interpretivist, ethnomethodology,* and *case study*. The exact definition and use of these terms, as well as "qualitative," vary according to their disciplinary roots (anthropology, sociology, psychology, political science, and philosophy). Educational researchers are likely to use "qualitative" in a generic sense, as a methodology that has some or all of a few key characteristics. Let's begin with contemporary definitions.

Two recent definitions of the term *qualitative research* are helpful in understanding the nature of this type of research and how it is different from quantitative studies. The first is from an American Psychological Association task force that recently reported standards for reporting qualitative research in journals. Here is the quote from the report (Levitt et al., 2018, p. 27):

> The term qualitative research is used to describe a set of approaches that analyze data in the form of natural language (i.e., words) and expressions of experiences (e.g., social interactions and artistic presentations). Researchers tend to centralize the examination of meanings within an iterative process of evolving findings—typically viewing this process as driven by induction (cf. Wertz, 2010)—and viewing subjective descriptions of experiences as legitimate data for analyses.

Another contemporary and inclusive definition is offered by Creswell & Poth (2018, p. 8):

> Qualitative research begins with assumptions and the use of interpretive/theoretical frameworks that inform the study of research problems addressing the meaning individuals or groups ascribe to a social or human problem. To study this problem, qualitative researchers use an emerging qualitative approach to inquiry, the collection of data in a natural setting sensitive to the people and places under study, and data analysis that is both inductive and deductive and establishes patterns or themes.

Both of these definitions describe qualitative research as having a number of characteristics. These main characteristics are summarized next (refer to Table 11.1), before moving on to descriptions of six specific types of qualitative designs.

Table 11.1 Key Characteristics of Qualitative Research

Characteristic	Description
Natural contextualized setting	Study of behavior as it occurs naturally in specific contexts.
Direct data collection	Researcher collects data directly from the source.
Rich narrative descriptions	Detailed narratives provide in-depth understanding of contexts and behaviors.
Process orientation	Focus is on why and how behaviors occur.
Inductive-(deductive) data analysis	Generalizations are induced from synthesizing gathered information.
Participant perspectives	Focus is on participants' understanding and meaning.
Socially constructed meaning	Knowledge is based on experience and social interactions with others.
Emergent research design	Research design evolves and changes as the study takes place.
Researcher reflexivity	Researcher awareness of positionality and constant use of reflection on the impact of position on data gathering and interpretation.

Natural Contextualized Settings

A distinguishing goal of most qualitative research is to understand that behavior and perceptions occur naturally, and that it is important to capture what is natural as it occurs in specific contexts. There is no manipulation or control of behavior or settings, nor are predetermined constraints imposed. Rather, the setting is such that external influences are mitigated. For some qualitative research, this means that observation of behavior occurs in an actual classroom, school, playground, clinic, or neighborhood. This is why qualitative research is often described as *field research;* much of it takes place in the field or natural setting. For example, a qualitative approach to studying beginning teachers would be to conduct observations in a few schools and classrooms in which these individuals were teaching. In contrast, a quantitative approach might use a questionnaire to gather the perceptions, beliefs, and practices of a sample of beginning teachers.

There are two reasons for conducting research in the field. One is that behavior and perceptions are best understood as they occur without imposed constraints and control; a second is that the situational context is very important in understanding behavior and perceptions from the participants' point of view and meanings. Both of these reasons are based on the belief that setting influences the way humans think, feel, and behave. Therefore, it is not possible to understand the behavior without taking the situational characteristics into account. The phenomena that are studied are about an individual or group *in a particular setting*. This could be thought of as *context sensitivity*. It is essential for both understanding individuals' thoughts and actions, and for suggesting how the findings could apply to other similar contexts.

Direct Data Collection

In qualitative studies, the investigator has a direct role in obtaining narrative-based information as either the interviewer, an observer, or as the person who studies artifacts and documents. Information is obtained directly from the source, without intermediaries. This is accomplished by spending a considerable amount of time in direct interaction with the settings, participants, and documents that are studied. There is a reluctance to use other observers or measurement techniques developed by others because the researchers are then not as "close" to the data as they need to be for a full understanding. Prolonged, direct engagement with the phenomena enhances the depth of understanding and credibility of the findings (Berger, 2015).

Excerpt 11.1 shows how a researcher spent years in direct interviewing and observation to understand girls' educational achievement at a government-subsidized school in Ghana.

EXCERPT 11.1

Direct Data Collection

In Year 1, I conducted in-depth, semi-structured interview with random students in their third year of high school... I also conducted multiple interviews with the headmistress and assistant headmaster.... I also collected in-depth observational data over a three-month period on the school's various activities to better understand the school culture and how students operated within that environment.... In the second year of my study, I returned to the school and conducted follow-up interviews.... I also continued to collect observational data on the various activities occurring before, during, and after school.... I then returned to Ghana one year later for one month to closely follow the home lives and post-high school experiences of 12 of the girls examined in the second and third years of my study as prepared for their next steps. (p. 1315)

SOURCE: Nuamah, S. A. (2018). Achievement oriented: Developing positive academic identities for girl students at an urban school. *American Educational Research Journal, 55*(6), 1307–1338.

Rich Narrative Descriptions

Qualitative research approaches participants, situations, and documents with the assumption that nothing is trivial or unimportant. Every detail that is recorded may contribute to a better understanding of behavior. The descriptions are in the form of words or pictures rather than numbers, although simple numerical summaries are used in some qualitative studies. The intent is to provide rich, detailed descriptions that cannot be achieved by reducing pages of narration or images to numbers. Rather, the descriptions capture what has been observed or heard in the same form in which it occurred naturally. Nothing escapes scrutiny or is taken for granted. The detailed approach to description is necessary to obtain a complete understanding of the context and to accurately reflect the complexity of human emotions, thinking, and behavior. To accomplish these goals, qualitative studies may extend over a long period of time and require intense involvement, and they typically culminate in extensive written reports. Often, much in the reporting is based on extensive memoing by the researcher as the study unfolds.

Process Orientation

In contrast to when researchers use quantitative approaches, qualitative methods look for the *process* through which behavior occurs, not just the outcomes or products, to understand *how* and *why* emotions, thinking, and behavior occur in a specific context. For example, whereas quantitative research can document the effect of teachers' expectations on student achievement, qualitative studies would be appropriate for understanding *how* teachers' expectations affect students' achievement and behavior. The emphasis would be on how expectations are formed and how they play out in the nature of teacher interactions with students, in a specific context. The emphasis on process allows for conclusions that explain the reasons for results. For instance, suppose a state is interested in how teacher professional development affects student behavior. A quantitative approach could be to objectively record student behavior before and following professional development, whereas a qualitative inquiry would focus on how the teachers changed as a result of the professional development experienced in a particular school and how this change affected student behavior as observed in the classroom.

Inductive-(Deductive) Data Analysis

Quantitative research employs a deductive logic to guide hypothesis generation and data gathering to test hypotheses. In qualitative research data are gathered first and then synthesized inductively to generate generalizations, models, or frameworks. Conclusions are developed from the "ground up," or "bottom up," from the detailed particulars, rather than from the "top down." This approach facilitates being open to new ways of understanding (e.g., finding new, unexpected signals). Predetermined formal hypotheses limit what data will be collected and what results will be reported.

The main process used in qualitative research is like an upside-down funnel (refer to Figure 11.1). In the beginning, the data may seem unconnected and too extensive to make much sense, but as the researcher works with the data, progressively more specific findings and deeper understandings and connections are generated. Once themes are developed, deductive reasoning is used to constantly check and challenge as new data emerge. Deductive reasoning is also used to establish initial coding criteria based on existing theory, working hypotheses, or assumptions.

Figure 11.1 Steps in Inductive Data Analysis

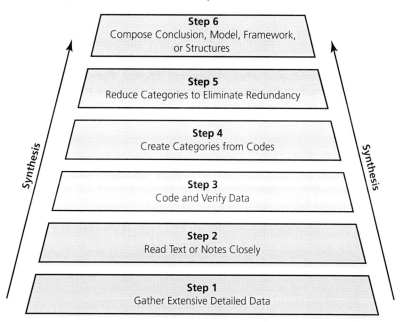

Participant Perspectives

This is perhaps the most important characteristic of most qualitative educational research—and certainly the most essential. Qualitative research reconstructs reality *as the participants they are studying demonstrate or see it*. It is not a matter of applying predetermined definitions or ideas about how people will feel, think, or react. For example, a quantitative study may assume that a teacher's feedback is interpreted by students in a certain way, whereas a qualitative investigation would be interested in how the participants (students) actually interpreted the feedback. The goal in qualitative research is to gain deep understanding from *participants'* points of view and/or behavior. In other words, the focus is on the meaning of events and actions as expressed or demonstrated by the participants. This often results in multiple perspectives and meanings. Thus, in a qualitative study of what motivates students, it would be important to focus on what the students said and did—to describe motivation using the words and actions of the students, not the researcher.

Notice in Excerpt 11.2 how the researchers were very deliberate in their quest to capture authentic **participant perspectives**, in this case of 12 Black male engineering students, over a 6-year time frame.

Socially Constructed Meaning

Another key characteristic of qualitative research that is based on participant perspectives is the belief that participants *actively construct their own reality*. They develop meaning from their social experiences and their own way of describing this meaning. Knowledge, then, for each individual, is built on their lived experiences and situation-specific interactions with others. Meaning is "socially constructed," arising from interactions with others. This suggests that the meaning of "reality" is individualistically constructed. Likewise, the meaning of different situations is individualized.

> ## EXCERPT 11.2
> # Participant Perspectives
>
> A second round of data analysis specifically focused on participants' perspectives on being Black and male in an engineering graduate program. The aim of this intersectional analysis was to ensure that participants' racialized and gendered experiences were accounted for. Codes were emergent in that no preexisting codes based on a priori findings were used to generate the codes in this study.... we used to data, the voices of student participants, to determine the patterns of gendered racialized experiences they were reporting. (p. 979)
>
> SOURCE: Burt, B. A., Williams, K. L., & Smith, W. A. (2018). Into the storm: Ecological and sociological impediments to Black males' persistence in engineering graduate programs. *American Educational Research Journal, 55*(5), 965–1006.

A theory of knowledge closely related to social constructivism is called *interpretivism*. This theory lies at the heart of qualitative research and provides the fundamental notion of how qualitative research differs from quantitative research. The following quote from a noted qualitative researcher describes this approach very nicely:

> Interpretivist theories are fat with the juice of human endeavor... with human contradiction, human emotion, human frailty.... [They] are derived from pure lived experience... replete with multiple levels of understanding; assembled from many "ingredients"; and patched together to form new patterns, new images, new languages, rather than extracting what are believed to be a priori patterns. (Lincoln, 2010, p. 6)

Emergent Research Design

As in quantitative research, qualitative designs have a plan for conducting the research. The difference is that in a qualitative study, researchers enter the investigation "as if they know very little about the people and places they will visit. They attempt to loosen themselves from their preconceptions" (Bogdan & Biklen, 2007, p. 54). Because of this perspective, the study does not begin with a precise, detailed, and complete research design. As the researchers learn about the setting, people, and other sources of information, they discover what needs to be done to fully describe and understand the phenomena being studied. Thus, a qualitative study will begin with a well-thought-out plan that represents *some* idea about what data will be collected from whom and the procedures that will be employed, but a full account of the methods is given *retrospectively*, after all the data have been collected. The design is emergent in that it remains flexible and evolves during the study.

Researcher Reflexivity

In qualitative research it is important for the researcher to understand their own background and perspectives so that they can "position" themselves when conducting data gathering, analyses, and interpretations. This requires a degree of self-reflection and self-analysis to discern how their cultural experiences and ideas inform or affect the nature of the information gathered and their interpretation of what that information means. This is often described as the researcher's *positionality*. **Positionality** allows for **reflexivity** to occur throughout the study and writing of the report.

Before going on to validity/trustworthiness in qualitative research and more specific approaches to conducting qualitative studies, I want to stress again that the preceding characteristics are typically present *to some degree* in any single qualitative investigation. The extent to which each characteristic is included depends on the particular design and the orientation of the researcher. In some qualitative studies, especially ethnographies and case studies, all these characteristics may be present, whereas in other qualitative studies only some of them are present (e.g., there is a great amount of qualitative research that is based exclusively on interview data. Interviews are not exactly naturally occurring behavior!).

Check for Understanding 1

1a. Name and describe at least five characteristics of qualitative research.

1b. Explain how the purpose of qualitative research is different from what quantitative research seeks to achieve.

1c. What is the primary difference between qualitative and quantitative research designs? Why is this difference important?

Author Reflection: *It is important, in my view, to separate the idea of conducting research that is qualitative from being a qualitative researcher. In my mind, knowing how to do quantitative studies well helps you do good qualitative research, and vice versa. It is more a matter of being fox-like—knowing the strengths and limitations of different approaches—than identifying as being a certain "type" of researcher.*

Qualitative Research Validity/ Trustworthiness

Learning Outcome 11.2 Know how threats to validity/trustworthiness can compromise the integrity, credibility, and value of qualitative findings.

As I've often emphasized, all research is conducted with the goal of obtaining results that reflect the signal—the truth and reality about something. The degree of truthfulness in quantitative research is referred to as *validity*; this much-used term has the same general meaning with qualitative studies. I should note, though, that qualitative literature is mixed about whether to use the term "validity" at all, or whether other terms would be more appropriate to emphasize what is unique to qualitative methods. Some would argue that completely different terms are needed, such as "trustworthiness" and "credibility." Levitt (2019), for example, in writing guidelines for reporting qualitative research in American Psychology Association journals, defines trustworthiness as a concept that communicates "the value of qualitative research... [to] help consumers of research discern whether the claims made in a project are warranted" (p. 30). This sounds a lot like validity, right? I concur with Creswell and Poth (2018) that it is appropriate to use the term "validity" with qualitative studies as an overall sense of whether the assertions represented in results and conclusions are warranted, but expand this term to *validity/trustworthiness*.

Table 11.2 Threats to the Validity/Trustworthiness of Qualitative Research

Threat	Description	Example
Context insensitivity	Insufficient description of the context and lack of consideration of contextual factors in the findings.	A study of racial relationships among high school students fails to include a complete history of events in the school that could influence current relationships.
Inadequate participant perspectives	Scant consideration of actual participant voices, language, and meanings in understanding the phenomena.	An investigation of teachers' views of using students' academic progress to evaluate their effectiveness did not include specific quotes from teachers.
Researcher bias	The researcher—often the same person who gathers information—allows assumptions and predispositions to affect what data are gathered and how the data are interpreted.	A researcher who believes that uniforms are best for elementary students asks parents to give reasons why it would be good to use uniforms.
Inadequate transparency	A lack of information about how a study was conducted, how decision making occurred, and how interpretations were made.	In a report of a study on college students' sexual preferences, there is no indication why the researcher decided to only interview on-campus students.
Inauthenticity	A characteristic that suggests that the findings are not genuine, actual, or real.	A study of dorm life of college students doesn't include actual observations of a variety of dorms, what they look like, and what students do.
Instrumentation	The nature of data collection skews results.	An observer of bullying in schools has a specific definition of what constitutes bullying and, as a result, misses instances of what many others would consider bullying.
Confirmability	Occurs when findings are not verified in some way, typically by others.	After interviewing a number of provosts, the researcher summarizes her findings but includes only her own interpretations of the meanings suggested in the transcripts.
Sampling	How the nature of the individuals in the study could affect the findings.	To better understand the role of associate deans, the researcher uses snowball sampling to identify those most likely to participate.
Reactivity	Participants providing less than authentic responses because they are in a research situation.	An interviewer with ties to the school coaches asks athletes about how they are motivated to perform.

The essential **validity/trustworthiness** question with qualitative research is: Do the data, findings, interpretations, and conclusions portray authentic reality? It is a matter of believability—is there sufficient rigor to results in agreement among researchers and readers about whether the findings are accurate and the conclusions reasonable? A related term, *credibility*, is often used as a validity/trustworthiness concept in qualitative research. **Credibility** refers to whether the results accurately reflect the views and meanings of the participants. Credibility, then, in this sense, is specific to whether claims about what the researchers report about participants is accurate. It is more targeted than validity/trustworthiness.

Like quantitative research, the quality of qualitative studies depends on methods that minimize the impact of factors that could lead to errors and misunderstandings (noise). In the spirit of internal validity for quantitative research, I think it makes sense to also keep in mind several "threats" to the validity/trustworthiness of qualitative research in the sense that "alternative explanations" could compromise the extent to which the conclusions reflect truth. As we will see in Chapter 13, there are specific procedures to address the threats.

Here is my list of important threats to the validity of qualitative research, summarized in Table 11.2; keep them in mind whether designing or critiquing qualitative studies. The goal is to sample, collect data, and analyze data in ways that minimize the threats.

Context Insensitivity

Context insensitivity occurs when the researcher does not give adequate attention to how the context within which the data are gathered influences the interpretation of results. This could include time periods, cultural mores, organizational priorities, what occurs prior to and after observations, laws, other adults present, neighborhoods, schools, playgrounds, and other contextual dimensions of what is being heard, seen, and recorded. If there is inadequate description of the context, the researcher may be missing important clues that help in understanding the data. The phase "put it into context" is what rules. In education, context is a critical dimension in research because outcomes such as achievement, motivation, and attitudes are almost always a function of situational differences. The same curriculum used in a warm, supportive, and trusting climate is different from the one implemented in a cold, unsupportive, and competitive climate. Appropriate context sensitivity is displayed in the attention to contextual factors and in providing sufficient, detailed descriptions. This results in what qualitative researchers call a "thick" description.

Inadequate Participant Perspectives

As you are now well aware, rich participant perspectives are paramount in doing good qualitative research. It makes sense, then, that if the reporting of these perspectives is scarce, incomplete, or cursory, important understandings may be missed. The goal is to go beyond the surface, to get into some depth and complexity of perspectives. The result of having **inadequate participant perspectives** is that too much attention is given to the researchers' interpretations and not enough attention given to the meaning behind participants' words and actions. When participant perspectives are rich, detailed, and abundant, deeper understanding and more insights result, and the true meanings of the participants are revealed.

Researcher Bias

Researcher bias is an old friend by now. It occurs in all types of research, although some qualitative researchers do not like or use the term. However, because qualitative studies are more exploratory, open-ended, and flexible, and basically less objective than other types of research, bias is a constant worry. Bias occurs when you do a qualitative research project and you more or less find what you are looking for, rather than a search for the signal. Suppose you are concerned about teacher morale—a definite issue with all the testing, regulation, and teacher record keeping required. You interview some teachers about their morale, but because you are pretty much already convinced that it is bad, your questions are slanted and your probes anything but neutral. You thus confirm your expectations and find that teachers' morale is poor! Or if you think charter schools are the bane of education, observing the culture of such schools could result in recording mostly negative issues and circumstances. Bias must be addressed, typically by first recognizing it, then with reflexivity in which there is continuous critical self-reflection of the effects of predispositions.

Inadequate Transparency

Transparency is a key qualitative principle. It refers to the need to provide explicit, clear, and complete information about all aspects of the research, particularly how and why decisions were made about design, procedures, data collection, and data analysis, including the theoretical values, perspectives, and assumptions that provide the basis for the study. This is particularly important for qualitative research because, as noted, the methods evolve during the study. Transparency provides the detail needed to judge the overall validity/trustworthiness of the study. **Inadequate transparency** is reflected in unclear, missing, or scant explanations about the whys and hows of the study, as well as the interpretations that are posited.

Inauthenticity

Inauthenticity is a threat that strikes at the heart of qualitative research—the need to provide results that are genuine, real, accurate, and complete, in original voices and other data. Your qualitative study will be authentic by presenting key differences and views, not cherry-picking the ones you want, and using participant and document language to convey a frank and honest portrayal of what was found. You get a sense of authenticity by the way researchers align their interpretations with illustrations from participant and document language and visuals. For example, in a description of low-income home environments, it may not suffice to rely solely on participant descriptions. A more authentic portrayal may be found when participant perspectives are combined with firsthand observations of all aspects of the home.

Instrumentation

This threat has essentially the same meaning here as it does for quantitative studies. **Instrumentation** refers to the nature of data collection and the procedures used to gather information. This includes who collects data and the methods of gathering information. If there are limitations or weaknesses in these procedures, the threat to validity/trustworthiness grows. For interviews, this might mean a lack of training for the individuals conducting the interviews, a failure to do a pilot interview, not using a set protocol that allows flexibility in asking follow-up questions, and not having time after the interview to record observations and insights. For observations, the threat could occur by not having observer training, by not specifying the role of the observer in the setting, or through errors in recording.

Confirmability

Confirmability is all about verification. The idea is that researcher findings need to be verified or confirmed in some way. We don't simply take for granted that the interpretations are correct without evidence that others find essentially the same things. This is accomplished by showing original data and audit trails so others can understand the process and decision making, confirming that they are appropriate. A good example of confirmability is the use of what is called "member checking." With member checking, researcher notes and interpretations are shared with participants who review them and "confirm" that they accurately represent what they said, their experiences, and their perspectives. Other researchers can confirm the coding of data and whether themes that are generated seem reasonable.

Sampling

Because most qualitative research depends heavily on just a few individuals or sites for data, the nature of the sample is critical to the findings. There are many approaches to selecting samples for qualitative studies (e.g., criterion, typical case, maximum variation, snowball)—all some form of **purposeful sampling**. Maxwell (2013) lists five criteria for good purposeful sampling: (1) to provide examples that provide authentic representation of the phenomenon being studied; (2) to offer some heterogeneity in perspectives; (3) to be able to test theory (e.g., search for negative cases); (4) to be able to make comparisons between participants; and (5) to provide assistance in data collection. These criteria help ensure that the sampling will result in comprehensive, authentic data. Unlike random sampling, which is rarely used in qualitative studies, the goal is to identify a sample that results in a rich and accurate understanding of the phenomena.

Obviously, the type of individuals accessed will affect what is found. This is both a blessing and a curse. Although targeting certain individuals allows for greater depth of understanding, what can be generalized to others is often limited—sometimes rather dramatically. The key way to avoid **sampling** as a threat in qualitative studies is to have a clear description of the sample and how it was obtained, and to consider characteristics of the sample in interpreting the results. I experienced this threat recently in a qualitative study I conducted about students' perceptions of classroom assessments. Even though I tried hard to get a maximum variation sample, based on ability and achievement, the final sample was skewed toward the higher end. What would that mean when I found that most of the students thought that assessments provided valuable information, didn't dislike them much, and looked forward to challenging tests? Would I find the same thing for different types of students? Did the schools provide access to students who had particular ideas about assessment that were unique? What is important is knowing how the nature of the individuals may influence and restrict conclusions.

Reactivity

A final threat to validity/trustworthiness of qualitative research is called *reactivity*. **Reactivity** occurs when the presence of the researcher influences participant answers to questions and behaviors. Similar to participant effects in quantitative studies, reactivity creates noise by diminishing authenticity. Reactivity is lessened by establishing a trusting relationship with participants. Remember, the goal is for participants to disclose honest thinking and emotions, and to display natural behavior. Researchers need to be sensitive to any conditions that would encourage reactivity (e.g., not answering questions about feedback received on a paper because the participant was concerned that their teacher might know about their answers; having a very positive relationship so that participants tell the researcher what they perceive the researcher wants to hear).

Author Reflection *These nine so-called "threats" to the validity/trustworthiness of qualitative studies are my own invention. You probably won't find them in other texts, nor are you likely to be able to Google them for some additional explanations or examples. My main intent is to get you to think like a fox—to consider all aspects of a study that could jeopardize whether the interpretations and conclusions are reasonable.*

Check for Understanding 2

2a. Describe what "validity" refers to in qualitative research and explain why it is important.

2b. What are at least five key threats to the validity/trustworthiness of qualitative research?

The Hedgehog and the Fox Think About Sources of Data for a Qualitative Study

According to what these middle school students said about their after-school experiences in a focus group, it seems like there needs to be a lot of structured activities for them.

I wonder whether I would have heard something different in individual interviews. How much of an influence is the context of the school these students attend? Would observations of students engaging in after-school activities suggest anything different? Maybe students are telling me what I want to hear. I wonder whether results would have been different if the focus groups were more homogenous.

We now examine six specific approaches to conducting qualitative research. The nature of each approach has implications for the research design, types of data collection, data analysis, and which threats to validity/trustworthiness should receive particular attention.

Six Approaches to Qualitative Research

Learning Outcome 11.3 Differentiate six major approaches to conducting qualitative research.

There are many different approaches to conducting qualitative research. Furthermore, there is overlap, and in some studies more than one approach is used. Here I describe six types of studies that cover most of what you will find in educational literature. We begin with ethnography, which, in my mind, while not as common as other approaches, is the quintessential qualitative methodology because it encompasses most of the characteristics discussed earlier in the chapter.

Ethnographic Studies

An **ethnographic** qualitative study (or *ethnography*—I'll use this term interchangeably with ethnographic, although others reserve ethnography to mean a comparative study of cultural groups) is an in-depth, comprehensive description and interpretation of cultural patterns and meanings within a culture or social group or system. The goal is to take a holistic, emergent learning approach to better understand sociocultural contexts and interpersonal processes within identified, bounded cultural systems. Shared patterns of behavior, norms, and thinking are documented. These shared patterns establish mores, rules, and expectations that characterize the group. For many years, ethnography has been the primary mode of study in anthropology for investigating primitive cultures, including such aspects of culture as religious beliefs, social relations, child rearing, marriage, and language. The approach to gathering data in these studies is to (1) observe the culture for weeks, months, or even years; (2) interact with and interview members of the culture; and (3) analyze documents and artifacts. These three methods of gathering data—observation, interviews, and document analysis—remain the primary methods of data collection for ethnographic studies in education.

Whatever the mode of data collection, the researcher engages in extensive work in the naturally occurring setting or context, the *field*. Ethnography involves **fieldwork**—actually being present in settings where participants' day-to-day behavior can be studied. In education, this is typically the school, university, or classroom. The logic is that the researcher will obtain a complete understanding of the educational system, process, or phenomena only through prolonged experience in the field. In the field, ethnographers employ many different types of data collection, including casual conversations, informal observation, content analysis of visual material, spatial mapping, and interviews. But the mainstay method is prolonged, intense observation.

As mentioned, the hallmark of an ethnographic study is its emphasis on *culture*, or *subculture*. Culture can be defined as shared patterns of beliefs, normative expectations and behaviors, and meanings. The emphasis is on what is characteristic of a group. The key concept in culture is what is *shared*. What is individualistic is not culture. A group must adopt very similar meanings and normative behaviors and expectations for all individuals over time to be defined as having a culture. Although it is possible for a group to consist of only two individuals, the minimum number is more typically 6 to 10, and can range to 50 or more. Regardless of how it is defined, the group must have interacted for a sufficient period of time to establish shared patterns of thinking and behavior. Of course, there is still individual variation in behavior and beliefs, but in an ethnographic study the main emphasis is on groups and the cultural themes that characterize the group. Integrating characteristics of individuals with how they come together to establish a cultural group is called a *holistic* perspective. For example, if observations and interviews of students at risk of failing identify common traits, such as the need for a social support system, this could be viewed as culture. A specific social support system that may be true for only a few students, however, such as going to church, is not a group cultural trait. In the end, educational ethnographers study specific *cultural themes*, such as the induction of beginning teachers, student–teacher relationships, persistence of athletes, sexual abuse with college students, and teacher decision making about classroom assessment and grading practices.

You may find researchers referring to specific types of ethnographies. There are many (e.g., *ethnohistory, autoethnography, critical ethnography, realist ethnography, feminist ethnography, microethnography*). These more specific approaches are characterized by distinctive paradigms and/or methods. For instance, feminist ethnographies may capture the theme of cultural systems that oppress women. Critical ethnographies focus on culture as related to marginalized groups, based on characteristics such as race, gender, and socioeconomic class.

A good example of an ethnographic study of a specific group, focused on a cultural theme, is a relatively recent study of middle school "nondominant" girls as they engaged in science-related activities, both in and out of school. Note how, in Excerpt 11.3, the authors explain the wide range of data collected, across different contexts, to understand the nature of identity development shared among these individuals.

Another description of an ethnographic study is illustrated in Excerpt 11.4. In this study, the group included members of a chemical engineering group of students. Notice that, as in the previous excerpt, there are many approaches to collecting

EXCERPTS 11.3 AND 11.4

Ethnographic Studies of Specific Groups

We followed the... girls into science class, science clubs, other figured worlds of their choice (e.g., math, English, and music classes), and informal spaces (e.g., cafeteria, club, and home). Most of the data were collected during the 2010–2011 and 2011–2012 school years.... [As] primary data, we generated per year: (a) 56 to 90 hours of observation per girl across the three sites (home, school, and club), (b) interviews (2 hours/girl), (c) science artifacts from across the three sites, and (d) yearly digital "science and me" stories (see Table 1). Additionally, as supplementary data, we conducted interviews with teachers who worked with the girls in school and/or afterschool clubs and with the parents whom we could approach during the data collection either formally or informally.... Research sites were deliberately selected based on historical relationships, allowing for depth of knowledge regarding schooling and science institutional and cultural narratives. (p. 46)

SOURCE: Barton, A. C., Kang, H., Tan, E., O'Neill, T. B., Bautista-Guerra, J., & Brecklin, C. (2013). Crafting a future in science: Tracing middle school girls' identity work over time and space. *American Educational Research Journal, 50*(1), 37–75.

This study offers a more holistic, and thus, more nuanced, exploration of the ways individuals, practices, and individual factors and experiences shape the professional of those in a chemical engineering research group... data collection included 13 months of fieldwork.... Ethnographic methodology guided data collection... fieldwork in the present study involved observations and formal and informal interviews to understand the culture of the Houston Research Group and its influence on members' professional intentions... sustained engagement in a research site over extended periods can promote greater rapport with participants, resulting in more authentic insights as well as richer and thicker descriptions of the cultural phenomena of interest... observations provided a holistic understanding of participants' research and of group members' roles, interactions, relationships, and rituals... fieldnotes were taken during observations to capture the cultural tools used in the research group.... Other data sources included lesson plans, transcripts, and student artifacts. (pp. 295, 297, 298)

SOURCE: Burt, B. A. (2018). Toward a theory of engineering professional intentions: The role of research group experiences. *American Educational Research Journal, 56*(2), 289–332.

data. Also, notice the emphasis on culture, sustained engagement, rapport with participants to lessen reactivity, holistic understanding, and "thicker descriptions."

Although there is considerable variation in the way ethnographies are conducted, there are some essential steps, as illustrated in Figure 11.2. The steps typically begin with a relatively wide focus, then narrow during data collection and analysis (which occur concurrently). Because the design is emergent, there must not only be provisions for making changes, but new points of emphasis must also be encouraged as the researcher learns more about the culture being studied. In the end, as in all qualitative research, the process is inductive, showing how themes are generated from more specific data.

Case Studies

A qualitative **case study** is an in-depth analysis of one or more real-life "entities"—events, settings, programs, social groups, communities, individuals, or other "bounded systems" in their natural context. The "boundaries" clarify the nature of the case or

Figure 11.2 Steps in Conducting Ethnographic Studies

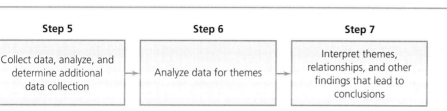

cases, carefully defined and characterized by time and place. Examples of single cases include a classroom, school, bullying prevention program, academic department at the university, or event, such as the introduction of laptop computers for students. The case is used as an illustration of a phenomenon that can be described, explored, and understood.

An entity could be an investigation of a program in one school or setting (a single exemplar), which would be a *within-site* or *intrinsic* single-case study. If the program is studied in a number of different schools, it would be a *multisite, multiple,* or *collective* case study. Whatever the number of sites or cases, the intent is the same: What can be learned about the system through a holistic approach involving the detailed description of the issue or setting?

Excerpt 11.5 contains text from an article that used a single-case study approach to investigate the efforts of African American parents to increase parental involvement and student success in a single high school. Note the extensive descriptions in the excerpt of both context and researcher role. Context needs to be detailed for both establishing the "boundaries" and understanding what is studied. In this study, the researcher is also a teacher in the school, so the consideration of researcher role is very important, ensuring transparency and noting possible researcher bias.

EXCERPT 11.5
Single Case Study

[A] unique case study [is presented] in which a group of African American parents banded together in an effort to increase their own involvement, increase the involvement of other African American parents, and work to increase the success of African American students at one public high school....[T]he goals of this research are to (a) understand [the involvement of] this parent group...and (b) identify [factors] that inhibited this parent group's involvement in the school.

Context

This study was conducted at...[a public high school] located in...[O]f the student population, 24% identify as African American, 24% identify as Caucasian, 18% identify as Hispanic, 18% identify as Asian American....Nearly 41% of the student body qualified for free or reduced price lunch.... students were successful in school.... however, [for African American students] the rate of success is much different.

Role of the Researcher

For five years prior to conducting this research and throughout its duration, my role as teacher [in the school] and my role as researcher were often blurred. . . . [T]he time I spent working as a teacher ...undoubtedly shaped my thoughts, interactions, and data that I collected. . . . My position as both a teacher and a researcher ... also shaped the data that I collected from individual teachers. (pp. 197–198)

SOURCE: Wallace, M. (2013). High school teachers and African American parents: A (not so) collaborative effort to increase student achievement. *High School Journal, 96*(3), pp. 197–198. Copyright © University of North Carolina Press.

In Excerpt 11.6, a collective case study of two teachers and their classrooms in two high schools in New Zealand is described. A multisite case study is illustrated in Excerpt 11.7.

EXCERPTS 11.6 AND 11.7
Collective and Multisite Case Studies

An interpretivist-based methodology was used, and this comprised a multiple case study approach.... In the first case study a total of 12 one-hour lessons were observed... while in the second fewer lessons were observed.... A case study approach was used in order to facilitate a holistic, interpretive investigation of events in context with the potential to provide a more complete picture of the science curriculum students were experiencing compared to other modes of research.... The interpretive analysis concentrated on their [students'] perspectives of classroom reality. (p. 274)

SOURCE: Hume, A., & Coll, R. K. (2009). Assessment of learning, for learning, and as learning: New Zealand case studies. *Assessment in Education: Principles, Policy & Practice, 16*(3), 269–290.

The aim of this... study was to gain a detailed understanding of the interplay between adolescent needs and secondary school structures that may promote developmentally responsive school environments.... Studying both structured and unstructured aspects of the middle and high school environment provided a holistic picture of what students experienced as they entered high school.... [T]his constructivist, multi-site case study highlighted student and school personnel voices that expressed their realities of how both Ford and Westshore fostered school environments that supported adolescents' needs. (p. 175)

SOURCE: Ellerbrock, C. R., & Kiefer, S. M. (2013). The interplay between adolescent needs and secondary school structures: Fostering developmentally responsive middle and high school environments across the transition. *High School Journal, 96*(3), 170–194.

I should note that case studies can also be conducted with quantitative approaches. Often, both qualitative and quantitative methods are used in the same case study. In my summary here, however, I will restrict usage of case study to qualitative research.

Once you decide to use a case study approach, a now-familiar series of steps is used to conduct the investigation. The first step, as in any study, is to establish research questions that align well with the case study methodology. The questions need to focus on description and understanding of a unique, special, and carefully defined entity. A question such as "How do tenured, associate professors adapt to changing expectations for promotion to full professor?" would be appropriately addressed with a case study. A full description of what occurs, within context, would be needed.

The second step would be to determine the more specific nature of the type of case study that would be undertaken. There are many approaches, each targeted to specific needs (refer to Table 11.3). The choice depends on the focus of the study and availability of the sites and participants. The most commonly used types in education are *intrinsic, instrumental*, and *collective* (psychology uses *explanatory, exploratory*, and *descriptive* types of case studies). Intrinsic case studies are used extensively when the focus is on a single exemplar of something to gain a better understanding, particularly for new and emerging phenomena, but it could also be a single person. In an instrumental case study, the emphasis is more on using the study to understand something that is represented by or elucidated by the case (e.g., studying student self-regulation by examining a specific implementation of formative assessment use in a single school). Collective case studies are used when the best understanding is derived by synthesizing the results from several sites or instances. Contrasts between sites or events are helpful in providing convergence of findings, as well as learning how differences between contexts affect the results. For instance, it might be most fruitful to examine the formation of several charter schools, not a single one, if the intent is more about generalization of principles than detailed description.

Although case studies are great for detail, thoroughness, and deep understanding (good for authenticity, context sensitivity, and transparency), they are limited in several ways. First, they are time consuming and resource intensive. Typically, there are multiple data collection strategies and prolonged involvement. Even when only a single case is involved, the researcher could spend weeks or months observing, interviewing, analyzing documents, and gathering other types of data. Multiple site studies require even more time. By using multiple data sources, researchers are able to "triangulate" results, showing how more than one source suggests the same interpretation, insight, or conclusion. Negative cases are sometimes searched for to illustrate where a theme or finding does not hold.

Table 11.3   Types of Case Studies

Type	Description
Intrinsic (within)	A single, targeted entity or phenomenon is described in detail to provide in-depth understanding and insight.
Instrumental	Use of a single case to study a phenomenon, theme, or issue.
Collective	Use of two or more sites and/or participants to generate principles and other generalizations.
Historical organizational	Focus is on a specific organization over time, often tracing the organization's development.
Holistic	Emphasis is on phenomenological description.
Embedded	Study of a subunit that is part of a larger study.
Multisite	Use of multiple sites as different units of analysis.

Case studies are difficult to replicate and may have weak generalizability, especially intrinsic investigations of unique persons, events, or issues (confirmability). Sometimes, researchers will try to identify a "typical" case to study. If so, they are concerned with at least some generalization to a larger group or other situations as traditionally defined. However, this is difficult in education because it is not very feasible to find a single exemplar that is representative of others. For example, doing a case study of a single classroom to investigate how a beginning teacher functions will provide in-depth descriptions of that classroom and teacher, but it is unlikely that other classrooms or teachers will be the same. The best to hope for is that the readers will come to their own conclusions regarding generalizability (or what qualitative researchers call *transferability*). Finally, sampling is critical, and researcher bias is a concern, particularly if the study is conducted by one person.

> **Author Reflection** *The term "case study" has been around a long time in social science research, particularly in sociology, and the approach is used in many disciplines, including business and law (however, it is not the same as the teaching strategy called "case method"). It seems to me that many qualitative researchers have adopted it as their own. My perspective is that case studies can involve quantitative as well as qualitative components—whatever is needed to gain an in-depth understanding.*

Phenomenological Studies

The purpose of conducting a classic **phenomenological** study, or *phenomenology*, is to describe, clarify, and interpret the everyday life experiences (what are called *lived experiences*) of participants to understand the "essence" of the experience *as consciously perceived by and described by the participants*. The basis of phenomenology is that knowing how something is experienced by several individuals provides data that can lead to a deep understanding of common meaning. That is, whereas each participant provides primary data (participant perspectives), the focus is on commonality in real-life experience, not on different contexts or individual characteristics. For example, a few years ago I conducted a phenomenological study of national board-certified teachers' perspectives on the use of measures of students' academic progress for teacher evaluation. I interviewed the teachers to understand deeply what "commonalities" existed among their experiences with this phenomenon, regardless of what grade level or subject they taught. I was interested in what phenomenologists call the "invariant structure" in the meanings given by the teachers. Other examples of phenomenological studies include the following:

- Grief experienced by high school students upon the death of a classmate
- Minority students' cross-race friendships
- Female assistant professors balancing family and work expectations and demands
- Regular teachers' perceptions of challenges working with autistic students
- Beginning teachers' experiences with mentors

Some phenomenological research may seek to incorporate differences in context or individual characteristics with what is called *interpretative phenomenological analysis* (IPA). This more recent approach examines individuals' experiences in different situations to understand how context affects meaning.

The first step in conducting a phenomenology is to make sure that the topic or issue is best investigated by examining shared experiences of different people, and that the best way to understand the "essence" of it is to gather evidence of lived experiences from each individual. This leads to development of the central phenomenon that is investigated. The second step is identifying the participants. Obviously, this is critical. You need individuals who have clearly "lived" the experience and are able to "relive" their thoughts and feelings about the phenomenon, and, importantly, communicate those to you (so your selection of participants needs to include a willingness and ability to communicate). Typically, unstructured or semistructured interviews are conducted by the researcher, although it is also possible to ask participants to "think aloud" while doing something, observe, analyze documents, or supplement individuals' perspectives in other ways. Participants can also review videotapes and talk about their thoughts and feelings at different moments. Once data are collected, they are coded, analyzed, and organized to identify key statements and phrases, then themes that synthesize the information. Analysis includes a detailed description of what was experienced and how it was experienced.

Note in Excerpt 11.8 how the researchers provided a justification for using the phenomenological approach. Note, too, how the study identified a clear phenomenon to be studied: motivation and enculturation of older students returning to a traditional university.

EXCERPT 11.8
Example of Phenomenological Study

Following the phenomenological tradition, this study sought to understand and interpret the lived experiences of seven students participating in the senior (62+) reduced tuition program at a large Southeastern university. Phenomenological methodologies attempt to "see reality through another person's eyes," and as such, they provide the researcher with different perspectives through which to identify problems and solutions (Bernard, 2000). In this way, qualitative studies following this tradition are of particular utility as initial investigations which can be further developed and explored in later research with quantitative methods (Stake, 2000). (p. 64)

SOURCE: Parks, R., Evans, B. & Getch, Y. (2013). Motivations and enculturation of older students returning to a traditional university. *New Horizons in Adult Education & Human Resource Development, 25*(3), 62–75.

Grounded Theory Studies

A **grounded theory** study is characterized by a unique purpose: to discover or generate theory from real-world data that explain central phenomena. The intent is to focus on theory *generation*, rather than theory *confirmation*. Theory-making is the goal. By gathering views of participants and applying systematic procedures for data analysis, the theory emerges. In this sense, the theory is "grounded in" or derived from data collected in the field. It takes phenomenology one step further by using participant perspectives, as well as other sources of information, about a common experience, process, or situation, to build an explanation that shows how something has occurred. The theory that is generated is not usually bound by a particular context or set of participant characteristics.

Suppose you wanted to generate a theory that could explain how at-risk students show resilience—how they turn things around and become successful. There might be some ideas in the literature about this, but nothing that is based on the real-life experiences of the at-risk students. Thus, the purpose would be to use the perspectives of the at-risk students, not what someone else observed or hypothesized, to generate the theory. This is an ideal issue for conducting a grounded theory study. By interviewing students, you could learn about what experiences, events, and people the students thought were important for their success. You might come up with a theory about how all the students found purpose, which translated to activities, which led to success and avoidance of negative influences. A theory about resilience emerges! Or imagine wanting to explain why some students are bothered by bullying and others not so much. If a theory could be developed based on the perspectives of bullied students, perhaps protective mechanisms could be identified and taught.

What one hopes to create with the theory is a causal explanation, not just a description. Based on initial interviews, factors that may be responsible for creating or affecting the phenomenon are suggested. The emerging ideas are "tested" or researched further through additional participant interviews, what is essentially an iterative process of the researcher generating ideas, going back to the field and gathering more data, then refining and verifying ideas to come up with a reasonable theory. (The continuous interplay among data, researcher analysis, and theory is called *constant comparison*.) The emphasis is on theory building, gathering sufficient data to explain causes and consequences. It takes a "theoretically sensitive" researcher to know when to go back into the field, what follow-up questions are best, and how additional data contribute to a deeper understanding of causal links. Consequently, the skill of the researcher is critical, with researcher bias a significant threat to validity/trustworthiness. Confirmability is also a critical threat to validity/trustworthiness—did the researcher gather sufficient data to confirm initial ideas and hypotheses?

In Excerpt 11.9, the researchers use grounded theory to identify factors that are important for successful physics laboratory work, eventually generating a theory of how the factors influenced student work.

EXCERPT 11.9
Grounded Theory Study

In the present study we applied the principles of grounded theory to frame a set of factors that seem to set major challenges concerning both successful work in the school physics laboratory and also in the preparation of lessons that exploit practical work. The subject groups of the study were preservice and inservice physics teachers who participated in a school laboratory course. Our results derived from a detailed analysis of tutoring discussions between the instructor and the participants in the course, which revealed that the challenges in practical or laboratory work consisted of the limitations of the laboratory facilities, an insufficient knowledge of physics, problems in understanding instructional approaches, and the general organization of practical work. Based on these findings, we present our recommendations on the preparation of preservice and inservice teachers for the more effective use of practical work in school science and in school physics. (p. 393)

SOURCE: Nivalainen, V., Asikainen, M. A., & Sormunen, K. (2010). Preservice and inservice teachers' challenges in the planning of practical work in physics. *Journal of Science Teacher Education, 21*(4), 393–409. Copyright © Springer Science.

Author Reflection *I've noticed that there is often a difference between a substantive grounded theory study—one that generates a substantive and useful theory—and qualitative studies that use "grounded theory methods," such as constant comparison. The full benefit of grounded theory research occurs when you get the whole enchilada, not just the beans and rice.*

Critical Studies

Critical studies are distinguished by a researcher role as advocate to respond to the themes and issues of marginalized individuals. These studies are based on the transformative research paradigm, focused on systems of power and control, privilege, inequity, inequality, dominance, and influence based on race, gender, and socioeconomic class. The central issue that is studied is typically the struggle of targeted groups to enhance their power and influence, "emancipating" them from the more dominant culture. Typically, theories of marginalized groups are used, such as critical race theory, queer theory, and feminist theory. For example, a researcher might focus on the inequitable treatment of students with learning disabilities, or students whose primary language is not English. Data, primarily in the voice of participants, would be gathered to challenge the status quo and to initiate action to ameliorate injustices. Essentially, the researcher applies a critical "lens" through which data are gathered and analyzed (e.g., feminine, gender).

Two critical studies are illustrated in Excerpts 11.10 and 11.11. In the first study, a phenomenological approach was used with indigenous youth to investigate the use of applied community theatre to address homelessness. In the second, a feminist, poststructural perspective was used to study masculinity among adolescent boys. Excerpts 11.1 and 11.2 also illustrate critical studies.

EXCERPTS 11.10 AND 11.11

Examples of Critical Studies

We employed a contextualist approach (Braun & Clarke, 2006), which attends to the importance of both individual subjective meaning-making of lived experiences, as well as the broader social ecologies in which this process occurs, bridging phenomenological and constructionist methodologies. On a theoretical level, we intended to better understand the lived experiences of Indigenous youth, who are or have dealt with homelessness, and the intersections of educational and social services, with the meanings they attach to these experiences, as well as through critical considerations of the systemic and structural factors influencing these experiences. (p. 54)

SOURCE: Ansloos, J. P., & Wager, A. C. (2020). Surviving in the cracks: a qualitative study with indigenous youth on homelessness and applied community theatre. *International Journal of Qualitative Studies in Education, 33*(1), 50–65.

This study stems from a yearlong qualitative inquiry examining the influence that gender ideologies exercised in the lives of four young men in the high school setting. Utilizing a feminist, post-structuralist perspective (Davies 1997, 1989; Connell, 1996, 1997, 1989; Martino, 1995), it analyzes how masculinity constructs itself through discursive practices. The study involves four adolescent boys, Michael, Peter, Aiden and Jack, all friends and

> classmates in a small, Midwestern high school comprised mainly of working class and farming families. This study examines each boy's idiosyncratic positioning within dominant discourses of masculinity, specifically questioning its ability to shape, influence and possibly constrain posture and performance in the classroom setting. (p. 101)
>
> **SOURCE:** Heinrich, J. (2012). The making of masculinities: Fighting the forces of hierarchy and hegemony in the high school setting. *High School Journal, 96*(2), 101–115. Copyright © University of North Carolina Press.

Narrative Inquiry Studies

The sixth and final major type of qualitative study has a long history in some fields but is a relative newcomer to education, as well as to other social sciences. It's called *narrative inquiry*. **Narrative inquiry** has a single distinguishing characteristic that makes it easy to remember—*human stories*. Each of us lives a "storied life"—in other words, there are stories in our life that capture important experiences, perceptions, influences, beginnings, and endings. Essentially, we have "lived stories" and can tell them to others. The goal of narrative inquiry is to use individuals' actual lived stories to provide a deep and rich understanding of a specific phenomenon, often best communicated as a story that can be compelling. Narrative research is used to establish and study meaningful stories.

Although there are several types of narrative designs, including oral and life history, autoethnography, bibliographical, and psychological, there are a number of characteristics that are usually included. These include the following:

- *Continuity of experience,* in which stories are organized and communicated temporally, in a logical and meaningful sequence and chronology.
- *Use of several sources of data,* including participant stories, such as observation, documents, work samples, and others' viewpoints.
- *An emphasis on context and situation,* noting how stories are related to social culture; narratives occur in specific places and situations.
- Exploration of *identity formation,* in which participants define themselves.
- An emphasis on *turning points,* critical moments that elucidate meanings.
- *Collaborative relationship* between the researcher and participant(s), in which stories are co-constructed.

Conducting a narrative study requires a "fluid" research design. Although typically narrative studies begin with one to three participants telling their stories, you need to be very flexible in what and how additional data are collected so important elements needed for a credible study are included. For example, there are "told" stories and "lived" stories, and both provide needed information. "Told" stories emanate directly from the participant, through both formal and informal conversations, whereas "lived" stories may involve a broader description based on context, supporting documents such as memos or photographs, family members' thoughts, and researcher observations as he or she "lives with" the participant. Here, the researcher places stories within contextual factors such as where the stories transpire (e.g., home, school, work) cultural dimensions, and time frames. Once sufficient data (or *field texts*) are collected, you would analyze the stories and context and organize them into a framework that identifies key themes and insights temporally. That is, information that is gathered may not show a clear sequence, so it is the job of the researcher to "restory" the information—to organize it into a sequence of events and experiences that are used to infer themes and meanings, the "essence" of the phenomenon. The end product is much more than reporting a compelling story; it's fully understanding the story. Acute and adroit analysis and interpretation are needed to go beyond the story and communicate the meaning it has for others.

Narrative research is challenging, to say the least. It depends heavily on the researchers' skill in deciding what information to gather, how that information is analyzed, and what themes arise. Because the design is not static, justifications for whatever procedures and decisions are made need to be clear. Since there is a relational quality to narrative studies between the researcher and participant, strong interpersonal skills, an ability to establish a trusting relationship, and good communication are a must. With the importance of context, the small number of participants, and researcher skills, nearly all the threats to validity/trustworthiness in Table 11.2 apply to narrative studies. Pay particular attention to researcher bias, context insensitivity, and sampling.

In Excerpt 11.12, the researchers use narrative inquiry to investigate the phenomenon "collaborative curricular making" among middle school physical education teachers. Note the emphasis on context, fluid design, and multiple sources of data.

The six approaches to qualitative studies presented in this chapter are summarized and compared in Table 11.4. Keep in mind that the different types of qualitative studies will overlap in many respects to some degree, and that the general characteristics summarized at the beginning of the chapter will apply to each type.

EXCERPT 11.12
Narrative Inquiry Study

The relational quality of narrative inquiry research (Craig and Huber, 2006), coupled with the fluctuations within teachers' contexts of teaching, makes narrative inquiry a difficult research process to explain and an even more difficult method to live (Clandinin et al., 2006). This is largely because it follows no pre-set research design. Simply put, the research process emerges as each narrative inquiry unfolds. The relational quality of narrative inquiry research (Craig and Huber, 2006), coupled with the fluctuations within teachers' contexts of teaching, makes narrative inquiry a difficult research process to explain and an even more difficult method to live (Clandinin et al., 2006). This is largely because it follows no pre-set research design. Simply put, the research process emerges as each narrative inquiry unfolds.... The curriculum making stories we feature in this work emerged from the many devices we used to conduct our narrative inquiry: (1) teacher interviews; (2) focus group discussions; (3) participant observation of classes and field trips; (4) videotapes of classes and field activities; (5) participant observation of department meetings; (6) audiotapes of department meeting conversations; (7) analysis of curriculum documents; and (8) summaries of archival materials. All of these tools produced field texts from which the research texts were crafted. The research texts coalesced around the following themes: (1) Physical Space Story, (2) Physical Activity Story and (3) Human Relationship Story. (pp. 173, 176)

SOURCE: Craig, C. J., You, J., & Oh, S. (2013). Collaborative curriculum making in the physical education vein: A narrative inquiry of space, activity and relationship. *Journal of Curriculum Studies, 45*(2), 169–197.

Author Reflection *This last sentence needs some explaining. Unlike most quantitative studies, qualitative investigations often mix and match, using different aspects of various approaches in unique ways. This can be confusing! Keep your focus on the extent to which essential characteristics of good qualitative research are included.*

Table 11.4 Characteristics of Six Approaches to Conducting Qualitative Research

	Purpose	Typical Design	Nature of Results
Ethnography	Describe a cultural group	Primarily observations and interviews	Description of cultural behavior
Case study	In-depth analysis of single or multiple cases	Use of multiple sources of data	In-depth description of case(s)
Phenomenology	Understand the essence of experiences	Extended interviews with participants	Description of essence of the experience from participants' perspectives
Grounded theory	Develop a theory from field data	Recursive, iterative process of gathering and analyzing data	A set of propositions, hypotheses, or theories
Critical studies	Advocate for marginalized individuals	Use of multiple sources of data	Assertions based on inequity or inequality
Narrative inquiry	Stories used to describe meanings of participant experiences	Participant stories of lived experiences that are analyzed for understanding	Summary narrative developed to communicate themes and meanings

Check for Understanding 3

3a. What are the key differences between ethnographic and narrative inquiry approaches to qualitative research?

3b. What are the steps researchers take in conducting either a case study or ethnographic study?

3c. Why would an ethnography be more difficult to conduct than a phenomenological study?

Anatomy of a Qualitative Research Article

I have included in Figure 11.3 an example of a critical qualitative study, using critical race theory, and a phenomenological approach, based on interviews of African American graduate students.

Figure 11.3 Anatomy of a Qualitative Research Article

Received 05/15/12
Revised 11/11/12
Accepted 11/14/12
DOI: 10.1002/j.1556-6978.2013.00033.x

Counselor Preparation

A Phenomenological Investigation of African American Counselor Education Students' Challenging Experiences

Malik S. Henfield, Hongryun Woo, and Ahmad Washington

This study explored 11 African American doctoral students' perceptions of challenging experiences in counselor education programs. The authors identified the following themes using critical race theory: feelings of isolation, peer disconnection, and faculty misunderstandings and disrespect. Implications for counselor education programs and policies are discussed.

Attracting, enrolling, and retaining a diverse body of students is a growing concern at U.S. universities—particularly predominantly White institutions (PWIs; Harper & Patton, 2007; Lett & Wright, 2003). According to the *2009 Standards* of the Council for Accreditation of Counseling and Related Educational Programs (CACREP), accredited counselor education (CE) programs must demonstrate "systematic efforts to attract, enroll, and retain a diverse group of students and to create and support an inclusive learning community" (p. 4). To assess the degree to which programs are prioritizing this initiative specific to African Americans, Johnson, Bradley, Knight, and Bradshaw (2007) surveyed 29 CACREP-accredited doctoral programs and found that 148 (17.9%) of 825 students were African American. Considering that African Americans comprised 6.9% of all doctorates in 2009 (National Science Foundation, 2010), these results suggest adequate representation. | **Background and context**

Despite this representation, there is minimal literature on the experiences of African American doctoral students in CE programs. Henfield, Owens, and Witherspoon (2011), in a qualitative study, outlined various forms of human agency that African American doctoral students use as they navigate their respective programs. Unfortunately, there is no research to date that focuses exclusively on the challenges that African American doctoral students encounter while enrolled in CE programs. The challenges confronting African American students often promote feelings of frustration and dissatisfaction that can complicate the doctoral process (Daniel, 2007; Shealey, 2009). Without such information, it is virtually impossible to understand the steps required to retain students as CACREP Standards (2009) clearly dictate. | **Need for research**

Malik S. Henfield, Hongryun Woo, and Ahmad Washington, Department of Rehabilitation and Counselor Education, University of Iowa. Correspondence concerning this article should be addressed to Malik S. Henfield, Department of Rehabilitation and Counselor Education, University of Iowa, N352 Lindquist Center, Iowa City, IA 52242 (e-mail: mailk-henfield@uiowa.edu).

(continued)

Figure 11.3 (Continued)

Critical study; purpose	Using a critical race lens, the purpose of this phenomenological study was to explore African American students' self-identified challenges and any program structural and cultural practices that affect successful retention and matriculation. The use of the voice of marginalized students is consistent with critical race research and is frequently used to engender a more inclusive and less alienating environment for members of racial and ethnic minorities (Ladson-Billings & Tate, 1995; Solorzano, Ceja, & Yosso, 2000; Yosso, 2005). A brief discussion of African Americans' perceptions of doctoral program experiences and student retention considerations are presented first.

African Americans' Perceptions of Doctoral
Program Experiences

Research in related areas	Scholarship from other academic disciplines and programs concerning African American students' doctoral program experiences offers some insight, particularly related to obstacles students encounter while enrolled in doctoral programs. Difficulty associated with combining personal culture with program culture or cultural integration (Chavous, Rivas, Green, & Helaire, 2002; Protivnak & Foss, 2009; Rendon, Jalomo, & Nora, 2000) and feeling a sense of academic and social isolation from the rest of the university body (Daniel, 2007; Johnson-Bailey, Valentine, Cervero, & Bowles, 2009; Protivnak & Foss, 2009; Shealey, 2009) are two salient themes in the literature on African American students at PWIs. For example, Lewis, Ginsberg, Davies, and Smith (2004), in a qualitative study, reported that eight currently enrolled and recently graduated African American students in education-related doctoral programs experienced numerous bouts of social isolation, often described as invisibility. This concept has been found in other qualitative studies related to African Americans' experiences at PWIs (Ellis, 2001; Gasman, Hirschfeld, & Vultaggio, 2008; Gay, 2004). Related to social isolation, qualitative studies have indicated that African American students report a lack of involvement in mentoring relationships with faculty and meaningful relationships with peers (Ellis, 2001; Gildersleeve, Croom, & Vasquez, 2011; Shealey, 2009).
Conceptual framework	Not surprisingly, social and academic isolation as a function of difficulties associated with cultural integration may incline African American students to gravitate toward racially similar support systems to navigate the doctoral process. Gay (2004) posited that African American doctoral students, in particular, value connections with their ethnic communities. These connections can be relationships African American students maintain with their communities of origin (L. D. Patton, 2009) or solidarity with other African American students through membership in African American organizations on campus (L. D. Patton, 2009; Shealey, 2009), which may be challenging when transitioning to the dominant culture of university settings and the professoriate. However, although the discontinuity to which Gay alludes can be construed as a function of African American students' connection to their ethnic community, it is perhaps more attributable to the discomfort they experience within their academic programs.

Student Retention

Justification	Researchers across disciplines have been dedicated to understanding the student-centered variables that mediate difficulties associated with cultural integration and isolation experiences and contribute to low retention rates of African American college students (Gay, 2004; Quezada & Louque, 2004; Rodgers & Summers, 2008). Frequently, these student-centered concerns have emphasized the importance of, for instance, financial, academic, and personal support systems and how these concerns contribute to academic success (L. D. Patton, 2009; Oseguera & Rhee, 2009; Rodgers & Summers, 2008; Shealey, 2009). From a practical standpoint, attention has also been dedicated to understanding how students use self-advocacy strategies to persist and succeed academically. Henfield et al. (2011) detailed the personal (e.g., assertiveness) and collective (e.g., the formation of or participation in social organizations) strategies students used for successful completion of their doctoral studies. This is the only scholarly work to date to examine how African American students' personal attributes (e.g., assertiveness, resiliency, collectivism) and the self-agency strategies students use to combat issues were associated with cultural integration and isolation in their respective programs. Perhaps CE programs' efforts to retain African American students could be optimized if they also included a critical examination of program policies and practices that have been found to be salient in the educational experiences of African American doctoral CE students (Henfield et al., 2011; Hill, 2003).

Method

The phenomenological tradition is constructivist in its approach to qualitative research (Hays & Wood, 2011), allowing one to identify prevalent themes that emerge from individuals who share a particular lived experience (Kline, 2008). In terms of utility as a research tradition, phenomenology allows scholars to "understand the individual and collective internal experience for a phenomenon of interest and how participants intentionally and consciously think about their experience" (Hays & Wood, 2011, p. 291). We entered the study with the explicit intention of asking questions that were focused on participants' experiences with respect to their race. In line with this intent, a critical race theoretical (CRT) framework was used to expose the salience of race in students' perceptions. According to Solorzano and Ornelas (2002), "CRT represents a paradigm shift in discourse about race and racism in education.... [It] seek[s] to identify, analyze, and transform the structural and cultural aspects of education that maintain subordinate and dominant racial positions in and out of the classroom" (p. 219). The following research questions served as a guide for this study: (a) What challenges confront African American students in CE programs? and (b) How, if at all, do CE programs' structural and cultural practices contribute to students' challenges?

> Integration of critical race and phenomenological approaches

> Research questions

Researcher Bias

The research team consisted of one African American counselor educator who received his doctoral degree from a PWI and two doctoral candidates (one Asian woman and one African American man) currently enrolled in a PWI. All three are affiliated with the same institution. Each member of the research team has conducted multiple qualitative studies, and one member is writing a qualitative dissertation. In addition, each member has published a number of manuscripts focused on African American students at different stages of education.

> Descriptions of researchers

The phenomenological research tradition requires one to refrain from imposing any perspectives other than those of the participants (i.e., bracketing; Wertz, 2005). Given that two research members identified with the role of African American students at some point and both experienced multiple challenges associated with race at all points along the educational pipeline (e.g., racism, low expectations), we bracketed our major assumption that other African American students would report these challenges (i.e., that it would be virtually impossible for an African American student to be enrolled in CE programs and graduate without experiencing some race-related challenges). The other research team member (i.e., Asian female) held similar biases given her background scholarship related to African American students. Bracketing was also used throughout the data analysis process as a means to prevent our personal biases from interfering with data analysis. We documented our experiences as comments in the document margins of transcribed interviews.

> Keeping focus on participant perspectives

> Bracketing used to control for researcher bias

Participants

Participants attended PWIs in midwestern (*n* = 7), south central (*n* = 2), and southeastern (*n* = 2) states of the United States. The 11 (eight female, three male) participants' ages ranged from 27 to 43 years (*M* = 31.5 years, *SD* = 4.8). Participants' enrollment status at the time of the interviews was reported as follows: two in the 1st year of their doctoral programs, one in the 2nd, six in the 3rd, and one in the 4th (one participant chose not to provide this information). Three participants reported grade point averages in the range 3.0–3.5 and eight in the range 3.6–4.0.

> Description of participants

Procedure

Purposeful sampling procedures were used to recruit participants (M. Q. Patton, 2002) through the CESNET and COUNSGRADS listservs. To be considered for inclusion in the study, participants had to identify as African American doctoral students currently enrolled in CE programs. Eleven students indicated their willingness to participate in the study and completed a demographic questionnaire and informed consent form, which were delivered and returned through standard mail. The first author then e-mailed each individual to make interview arrangements.

> Purposeful sampling

> Criteria used for selecting participants

The first round of data collection consisted of e-mailing structured interview questions and served two purposes: to confirm eligibility for participation in the study and to provide a foundation for the semistructured questions in the second semistructured interview. In the first structured e-mail interview, we asked participants to describe their experiences as African American students at their university, in their department, in their classroom, and with their advisor. Because all participants reported experiences described as challenging, participants were afforded the opportunity in the second interview to expand upon their responses to questions from initial interviews. It should be noted that students also reported some positive experiences, particularly in relation to self-perception of their ability to get their needs met with little assistance from others.

> Use of first structured interviews

> Second, semi-structured interview

(continued)

Figure 11.3 (Continued)

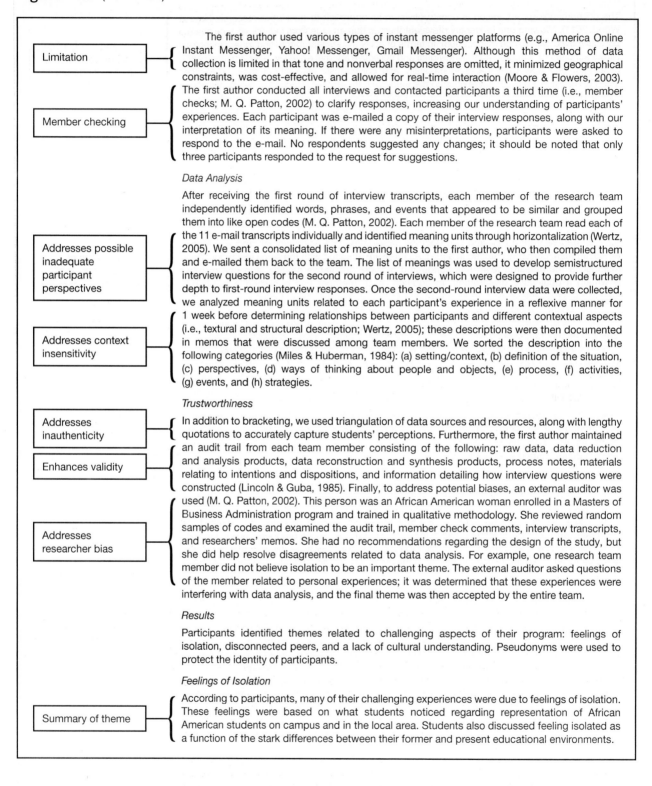

Limitation

The first author used various types of instant messenger platforms (e.g., America Online Instant Messenger, Yahoo! Messenger, Gmail Messenger). Although this method of data collection is limited in that tone and nonverbal responses are omitted, it minimized geographical constraints, was cost-effective, and allowed for real-time interaction (Moore & Flowers, 2003).

Member checking

The first author conducted all interviews and contacted participants a third time (i.e., member checks; M. Q. Patton, 2002) to clarify responses, increasing our understanding of participants' experiences. Each participant was e-mailed a copy of their interview responses, along with our interpretation of its meaning. If there were any misinterpretations, participants were asked to respond to the e-mail. No respondents suggested any changes; it should be noted that only three participants responded to the request for suggestions.

Data Analysis

After receiving the first round of interview transcripts, each member of the research team independently identified words, phrases, and events that appeared to be similar and grouped them into like open codes (M. Q. Patton, 2002). Each member of the research team read each of

Addresses possible inadequate participant perspectives

the 11 e-mail transcripts individually and identified meaning units through horizontalization (Wertz, 2005). We sent a consolidated list of meaning units to the first author, who then compiled them and e-mailed them back to the team. The list of meanings was used to develop semistructured interview questions for the second round of interviews, which were designed to provide further depth to first-round interview responses. Once the second-round interview data were collected, we analyzed meaning units related to each participant's experience in a reflexive manner for

Addresses context insensitivity

1 week before determining relationships between participants and different contextual aspects (i.e., textural and structural description; Wertz, 2005); these descriptions were then documented in memos that were discussed among team members. We sorted the description into the following categories (Miles & Huberman, 1984): (a) setting/context, (b) definition of the situation, (c) perspectives, (d) ways of thinking about people and objects, (e) process, (f) activities, (g) events, and (h) strategies.

Trustworthiness

Addresses inauthenticity

In addition to bracketing, we used triangulation of data sources and resources, along with lengthy quotations to accurately capture students' perceptions. Furthermore, the first author maintained

Enhances validity

an audit trail from each team member consisting of the following: raw data, data reduction and analysis products, data reconstruction and synthesis products, process notes, materials relating to intentions and dispositions, and information detailing how interview questions were constructed (Lincoln & Guba, 1985). Finally, to address potential biases, an external auditor was used (M. Q. Patton, 2002). This person was an African American woman enrolled in a Masters of Business Administration program and trained in qualitative methodology. She reviewed random samples of codes and examined the audit trail, member check comments, interview transcripts,

Addresses researcher bias

and researchers' memos. She had no recommendations regarding the design of the study, but she did help resolve disagreements related to data analysis. For example, one research team member did not believe isolation to be an important theme. The external auditor asked questions of the member related to personal experiences; it was determined that these experiences were interfering with data analysis, and the final theme was then accepted by the entire team.

Results

Participants identified themes related to challenging aspects of their program: feelings of isolation, disconnected peers, and a lack of cultural understanding. Pseudonyms were used to protect the identity of participants.

Feelings of Isolation

Summary of theme

According to participants, many of their challenging experiences were due to feelings of isolation. These feelings were based on what students noticed regarding representation of African American students on campus and in the local area. Students also discussed feeling isolated as a function of the stark differences between their former and present educational environments.

Underrepresentation. According to Danielle, being isolated from other African Americans on campus was intensified by not being embraced by other students: "Being a minority student has been difficult. I do not see people that look like me, and I am not accepted into the 'majority' group." This sentiment was echoed by Keisha, who referred to the lack of African Americans on campus as a "travesty." Students seemed to infer that the racial makeup of the area surrounding their university was also a salient factor in their feelings of isolation. For instance, Alecia, who attends school in a small rural area, stated that "the whole atmosphere of this little town feels like an old black and white movie from the 50s or 60s."

Illustrative of voices from participants

Previous educational experiences. One evident challenge related to isolation was students' previous educational experiences, which seemed to form the basis for students' expectations of their CE experience. For instance, whereas two students used such descriptors as "difficult" and a "travesty" to describe their experience, Dawson, in contrast, portrayed his experience as "ordinary," yet not "totally normal." For Dawson, the isolation was viewed as requisite to the experience of being an African American student at a PWI. For him, previous attendance at a PWI prepared him for the social isolation from other African American students. Dawson stated, "At the university level, the experience is not atypical considering the fact that the majority of my public interactions occur in a PWI" and "although this is ordinary, the experience does not ever feel totally normal," suggesting that although he was prepared for the experience, he was cognizant of the abnormality associated with the experience. Constance, having completed her undergraduate years at a historically Black college or university (HBCU), questioned her qualifications for entry into the doctoral program, resulting in uncertainty with regard to her CE program choice:

> I felt like an outsider and as if I was being questioned indirectly [by my peers] on how I was able to "get into" the institution. Being on a campus where the majority of the students did not look like me or have backgrounds similar to mine, I questioned my belonging… whether I made the right choice in accepting the offer to attend.

Participant of voices

In contrast, Jamila did not attend an HBCU before enrolling in her current program. However, she attended a PWI with numerous opportunities for African American students to socialize with one another. This atmosphere highlighted a sense of isolation in her current situation:

> It's just weird. At the place where I went to undergrad and did my master's, there were a lot of Black organizations on campus in addition to the fraternities and sororities. So, even though I wasn't a part of many of them, there was always that sense that I wasn't alone, and I could attend events where I would feel comfortable, and I could know that issues that mattered to me would be addressed.

Participant of voices

In addition to being comprised of members with similar racial backgrounds, these student organizations, in many cases, also have places where they can congregate. Although this participant said she did not participate in these organizations, it is interesting that she found comfort in knowing of their existence on campus. Perhaps her affinity for the groups was partially based on knowing that there was a place on campus she could go to receive support from same-race peers (Harper & Patton, 2007).

Explanation integrated with literature

Peer Disconnection

For various reasons, students did not experience a great deal of cohesion with particular students in their program in general and as a cohort in particular. The reason for this was a lack of connection between students. Specifically, they mentioned unfulfilling orientations and disrespectful classroom exchanges as fostering this feeling of disconnection.

Summary of theme

Quality of program orientations. Like African American students in many other graduate programs where they may be considered an ethnic minority, students in CE can feel very lonely for a variety of reasons. It is quite common, however, for program faculty to create new student orientations that are focused on passing along valuable, new information to incoming students. For eight students, including Taylor, however, orientations were viewed as insufficient because of their narrow focus. According to Taylor, "University orientations and even department orientations… focused primarily on introducing faculty and staff."

Some students stated that they participated in orientation programs that were more substantial. For instance, three students mentioned orientation programs that were designed to create a sense of community among all students. Despite such measures, nine students consistently portrayed relationships with peers that suggested poor cohesion. Danielle, for

Figure 11.3 (Continued)

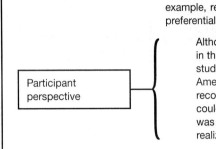

example, reported that close relationships with peers were damaged because faculty showed preferential treatment toward White students. Danielle stated,

> Although our cohort has been close, I still feel alienation at times from the others in the group. I remember a conversation we had where the other African American student and I were discussing with the group the lack of support for us [African American students] and the fact that we have to do more to receive the same recognition they [Caucasian students] do. The White students we were talking to could not understand what we were talking about and said they did not think there was a problem for minority students in the program. One person said she has never realized that we felt that way.

Classroom interactions. Tara did not enter her program with a cohort of peers; thus, she also felt a distance between herself and other students in the program. She felt this friction was a by-product of multiple classroom interactions that she deemed to be disrespectful:

> They [classmates] would always put me on the defensive with certain questions as if I didn't have a right to my opinion... made me feel as if I had to explain why I felt that way or that there was a right or wrong answer for me to give when an opinion was warranted. Then I would have people explain things to me in the classroom as if I were not competent enough to know what they were talking about or could not think for myself.

She also reported that faculty, in an attempt to get her to rely on her peers for assistance, sometimes referred her to her colleagues for particular answers to questions. However, "when it was time for them to help me, everyone would seem, all of a sudden, so busy. So, eventually, I just tried to figure things out on my own and sometimes suffered as a result."

The classroom was also an uncomfortable context for Alecia. According to her, this discomfort was due to other students' misperception of her as someone who did things to draw attention to herself:

> I love education. I mean it's just part of who I am. I like things to look good; I enjoy being professional, and clear, and whatever else comes with that. Because of this, whenever our faculty gives us an assignment to present, I use Powerpoint. To me that's just what a presentation means (sometimes). For the nature of what we are required to do, Powerpoint is definitely appropriate. So anyway, [students] in my cohort started getting mad at me for using Powerpoint (how silly is that?) and were not afraid to say it. Comments like "Oh, it's Alecia's turn to present; we know what we're in for" and "Where's your Powerpoint?; we know you made one." [Furthermore], when I submit papers, even if it's a small paper of thoughts and ideas etc., no matter what, it's APA style... that means a cover page, only to hear little snide remarks about that too.

On the other hand, Jamila's overall experience in her program is quite different from the experiences of some of the other students in this study because her cohort and Dawson's cohort were the only ones that were composed of predominantly African American students. In her program, a large contingent of African American students presents a unique set of circumstances, particularly in the classroom environment:

> The majority of my cohort is African American, and we usually have classes together, which means that we usually make up the entire class or the majority of the class. When we have White instructors, it seems as if they are very surprised that we are not as dumb as they thought we would be, or as militant.

Faculty Misunderstandings and Disrespect

Students reported numerous instances where professors' lack of cultural understanding was an overwhelming impediment to overall satisfaction with their program. In addition, they also described their relationship with some faculty members as distant rather than the close relationship that the students seemed to desire. Seven students reported feeling pressured to pretend to be someone they were not when in the program environment, or to code switch (Celious & Oyserman, 2001), in order to give the appearance to faculty that they have an affinity

Participant perspective

Demonstrates authenticity

Explanation for discrepant findings

Summary of theme

for their peers in particular and for the program as a whole. For example, according to Constance, there was an expectation among the faculty in her program that students became close with one another, without regard to the students' level of interest in one another:

> Some of the individuals within my college appear to have different values than me and focus on things that at times are of little interest. I find myself wearing many hats to just get through the day. I believe that racial and ethnic identity/background has a lot to do with it. I also believe that my experiences within my family and growing up make me different, as well. So at times I feel like I am playing a game to just fit in and get things done. Some days you just don't feel like smiling and having a 10-minute conversation about something of no interest. But oftentimes I feel I have to because of the environment. It is a close environment and you are expected to engage, but some days you don't really want to and I don't believe that [faculty] take into account the difference of some of the students.

Rebecca recalled labeling "my days as 'good race days' and 'bad race days'... depending on how I was treated from a professorial standpoint during my first semester here." As an example, she offered an incident with a professor who "discouraged me from researching Black females because 'everyone is doing research on Black females.'" She thought this was quite disturbing because issues related to African American females were important, and she felt it was wrong to be discouraged from pursuing a research area she was passionate about. This indicates that she and her needs were invisible to the faculty member.

Use of specific incident to illustrate theme

Taylor suggested that faculty in his program were somewhat uncomfortable around him as a function of his unique style of dress, which, according to him, was not representative of the cultural norms in his program:

> Most faculty and staff have been supportive, although there were some who left me with the impression that they are not as comfortable in my presence as opposed to other students within the program. (It should be noted that my nonprofessional dress can be stereotyped to a specific culture [hip-hop culture] and I believe this has unfairly led to prejudgment.)

Discussion

This study explored African American students' perceptions of challenges they experience as doctoral students in CE programs. Moreover, the study investigated structures and practices that contribute to students' challenges. Major themes emanating from the findings were, to some extent, consistent with previous findings associated with African American students' experiences.

Summary of study and findings

The first theme of feelings of isolation is in line with reported experiences of African American doctoral students at PWIs in general (Lewis et al., 2004). The participants in our study were fully aware of the small number of African American students on campus as a whole and in their programs particularly, which is not surprising because such awareness has been found to be quite common (Harper & Patton, 2007; Shealey, 2009). However, our study's findings suggest that students' level of stress and irritation with isolation may be related to the level of support they received in former academic settings. For instance, previous positive experiences at HBCUs seemed to create an expectation that CE programs would provide similar faculty and peer support. In particular, we found that students who previously attended HBCUs had grown accustomed to a certain level of comfort that was not replicated at their current PWIs. Those who attended PWIs before enrolling in their CE program acknowledged that the experience was somewhat abnormal, but were not surprised by the transition. This finding supports CRT, which recognizes that racism is engrained in the American education systems (Solorzano & Ornelas, 2002); racism and microaggressions perpetuated the marginalization of students of color in PWIs in our study. Interestingly, students also mentioned their frustration with the lack of African American representation off campus, which suggests that environments were also salient to the students' educational experiences.

Consistency with previous research

Explanation

Integration with conceptual framework

A second theme in the findings was peer disconnection, which, according to our findings, appeared to be related to the quality of program orientations and classroom interactions. Poor bonding with White peers is a consistent finding in the literature related to African American students attending PWIs at all levels of education (Harper & Patton, 2007; Henfield et al., 2011). Because of a lack of communication and positive interaction with peers, participants often struggled with feeling misunderstood and disrespected, failing to build positive working relationships. Previous research suggests that connections between doctoral students and

Connection to literature

(continued)

Figure 11.3 (Continued)

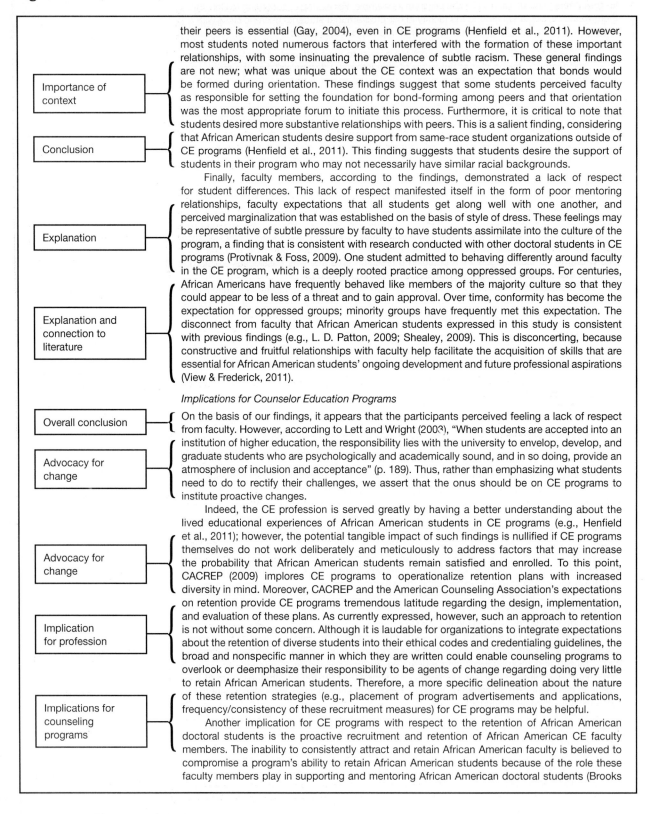

Importance of context	their peers is essential (Gay, 2004), even in CE programs (Henfield et al., 2011). However, most students noted numerous factors that interfered with the formation of these important relationships, with some insinuating the prevalence of subtle racism. These general findings are not new; what was unique about the CE context was an expectation that bonds would be formed during orientation. These findings suggest that some students perceived faculty as responsible for setting the foundation for bond-forming among peers and that orientation was the most appropriate forum to initiate this process. Furthermore, it is critical to note that students desired more substantive relationships with peers.
Conclusion	This is a salient finding, considering that African American students desire support from same-race student organizations outside of CE programs (Henfield et al., 2011). This finding suggests that students desire the support of students in their program who may not necessarily have similar racial backgrounds.
Explanation	Finally, faculty members, according to the findings, demonstrated a lack of respect for student differences. This lack of respect manifested itself in the form of poor mentoring relationships, faculty expectations that all students get along well with one another, and perceived marginalization that was established on the basis of style of dress. These feelings may be representative of subtle pressure by faculty to have students assimilate into the culture of the program, a finding that is consistent with research conducted with other doctoral students in CE programs (Protivnak & Foss, 2009). One student admitted to behaving differently around faculty in the CE program, which is a deeply rooted practice among oppressed groups. For centuries,
Explanation and connection to literature	African Americans have frequently behaved like members of the majority culture so that they could appear to be less of a threat and to gain approval. Over time, conformity has become the expectation for oppressed groups; minority groups have frequently met this expectation. The disconnect from faculty that African American students expressed in this study is consistent with previous findings (e.g., L. D. Patton, 2009; Shealey, 2009). This is disconcerting, because constructive and fruitful relationships with faculty help facilitate the acquisition of skills that are essential for African American students' ongoing development and future professional aspirations (View & Frederick, 2011).

Implications for Counselor Education Programs

Overall conclusion	On the basis of our findings, it appears that the participants perceived feeling a lack of respect from faculty. However, according to Lett and Wright (2003), "When students are accepted into an
Advocacy for change	institution of higher education, the responsibility lies with the university to envelop, develop, and graduate students who are psychologically and academically sound, and in so doing, provide an atmosphere of inclusion and acceptance" (p. 189). Thus, rather than emphasizing what students need to do to rectify their challenges, we assert that the onus should be on CE programs to institute proactive changes.
Advocacy for change	Indeed, the CE profession is served greatly by having a better understanding about the lived educational experiences of African American students in CE programs (e.g., Henfield et al., 2011); however, the potential tangible impact of such findings is nullified if CE programs themselves do not work deliberately and meticulously to address factors that may increase the probability that African American students remain satisfied and enrolled. To this point, CACREP (2009) implores CE programs to operationalize retention plans with increased diversity in mind. Moreover, CACREP and the American Counseling Association's expectations on retention provide CE programs tremendous latitude regarding the design, implementation, and evaluation of these plans. As currently expressed, however, such an approach to retention
Implication for profession	is not without some concern. Although it is laudable for organizations to integrate expectations about the retention of diverse students into their ethical codes and credentialing guidelines, the broad and nonspecific manner in which they are written could enable counseling programs to overlook or deemphasize their responsibility to be agents of change regarding doing very little to retain African American students. Therefore, a more specific delineation about the nature of these retention strategies (e.g., placement of program advertisements and applications, frequency/consistency of these recruitment measures) for CE programs may be helpful.
Implications for counseling programs	Another implication for CE programs with respect to the retention of African American doctoral students is the proactive recruitment and retention of African American CE faculty members. The inability to consistently attract and retain African American faculty is believed to compromise a program's ability to retain African American students because of the role these faculty members play in supporting and mentoring African American doctoral students (Brooks

& Steen, 2010; Henfield et al., 2011). This requires that CE and university personnel address the barriers—limited mentorship by senior faculty, for instance—found to be detrimental to recruitment and retention efforts aimed at African American CE applicants and faculty members (Bradley & Holcomb-McCoy, 2004; Brooks & Steen, 2010).

Although this is quite useful, specific strategies to recruit diverse students (e.g., scholarships, open houses, conference meetings) may be more easily understood than practices designed to retain students upon admittance. It can be argued that the small number of African American students on campuses and in counseling programs is a structural challenge that is difficult to change. However, the perception of a lack of support is a troubling product of a program's cultural practices that can be changed. For instance, many of the challenges that participants perceive are a function of unmet expectations. One way to address this concern is to adopt a culture of intentionality in which clarifying program expectations for students in the program is a practice that becomes common praxis very early on. Because many students in this study expected more from their orientation meetings, those meetings may serve as an ideal opportunity to address such topics and to establish strong bonds with their peers. The potential danger in this cultural shift is that students perceive the discussion as oppressive; it may be viewed as a practice designed to establish a hierarchical atmosphere. To avoid this, faculty may elect to suggest that students provide anonymous written feedback regarding their expectations of faculty members also. This practice may clarify students' perceptions in a manner that demonstrates the faculty's desire to develop a better understanding of the students' needs while maintaining respect for their need for privacy.

For this to be considered a healthy discussion, faculty cannot be afraid to discuss race openly and honestly. They should be willing and able to openly talk about common challenges associated with being a racial minority at a PWI and measures they plan to take to help ensure that incoming and currently enrolled students feel comfortable in the program. Some faculty members may be uncomfortable openly discussing the topic of race. Particularly, when the numbers of African American students enrolled in the program are considerably small, faculty, as well as students, may find such a discussion alienating to African American students and it may be counterproductive. In such instances, it may be more appropriate to set aside a time during the student orientation to discuss a diverse array of organizations students can join and include race-based on-campus (e.g., Black Greek student organizations, Black graduate student organizations) and off-campus (e.g., churches) organizations that African American students have been traditionally known to rely on for support (Johnson-Bailey et al., 2009; View & Frederick, 2011).

Last, given students' perceptions of faculty members as lacking respect for student differences, it is imperative that faculty members become more cognizant of how a history of oppression may influence students' perception of their behavior and nonbehavior. Faculty should create a culture of respect for differences by explicitly communicating the value they place on individuality. Along these lines, African American students in CE programs have been found to desire support from a mentor (Henfield et al., 2011). The lack of diversity among faculty may prove to be a structural challenge in that students desire mentors who are of the same racial background (Lewis et al., 2004). Nonetheless, students need to be paired with a faculty advisor who is warm and inviting, yet skilled and unafraid to discuss subjects associated with challenges that often accompany racial minority underrepresentation at PWIs in general and in CE programs specifically.

Limitations and Areas for Future Research

This study's findings have certain limitations. First, on-site observations of participants on their respective campuses could have yielded greater context and foundation for the findings; however, such observations were not feasible. Second, because of the decision to use e-mail and instant messenger for data collection, the researchers could not obtain additional information from students' nonverbal or verbal behavior. Third, although we ascribed some of African American students' expectations of CE faculty to their having attended HBCUs, this attribution may not necessarily be the case for a significant number of African American CE students. If such a question had been posed directly, perhaps students may have attributed their expectations to a different set of variables. Fourth, because of the structured nature of the first interview, it is possible there were other contexts that students perceived to be more salient that were not reported. Finally, we assessed the perceptions of African American students only. Including the perceptions of non-African American peers and CE faculty could have broadened the scope of this study.

Future research investigations could provide a more in-depth focus on specific structural and cultural challenges and longitudinal studies related to students' overall experiences.

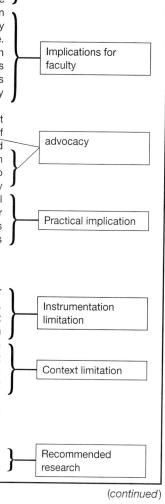

Advocacy for change

Practical implication

Advocacy

Implications for faculty

advocacy

Practical implication

Instrumentation limitation

Context limitation

Recommended research

(continued)

Figure 11.3 (Continued)

Recommended research

{ Scholars could also explore faculty members' perceptions of their roles as advisors to African American students, because this relationship appeared to be quite important to the students in the study. This study demonstrated that African American students experience a number of subtle-racist incidents inside and outside the classroom; thus, additional research could explore the prevalence and impact of race in CE programs as a whole and in classrooms in particular.

REFERENCES

Bradley, C., & Holcomb-McCoy, C. (2004). African American counselor educators: Their experiences, challenges, and recommendation. *Counselor Education and Supervision, 43,* 258–273.

Brooks, M., & Steen, S. (2010). "Brother where art thou?" African American male instructors' perceptions of the counselor education profession. *Journal of Multicultural Counseling and Development, 38,* 142–153.

Celious, A., & Oyserman, D. (2001). Race from the inside: An emerging heterogeneous race model. *Journal of Social Issues, 57,* 149–165.

Chavous, T., Rivas, D., Green, L., & Helaire, L. (2002). Role of student background, perceptions of ethnic fit, and racial identification in the academic adjustment of African American students at a predominantly White university. *Journal of Black Psychology, 28,* 234–260.

Council for Accreditation of Counseling and Related Educational Programs. (2009). *2009 standards.* Retrieved from http://www.cacrep.org/doc/2009%20Standards%20with%20 cover.pdf

Daniel, C. (2007). Outsider-within: Critical race theory, graduate education and barriers to professionalization. *Journal of Sociology and Social Welfare, 34,* 25–42.

Ellis, E. (2001). The impact of race and gender on graduate school socialization, satisfaction with doctoral study, and commitment to degree completion. *The Western Journal of Black Studies, 25,* 16.

Gasman, M., Hirschfeld, A., & Vultaggio, J. (2008). Difficult yet rewarding: The experiences of African American graduates in education at an Ivy League institution. *Journal of Diversity in Higher Education, 1,* 126–138.

Gay, G. (2004). Navigating marginality en route to the professoriate: Graduate students of color learning and living in academia. *International Journal of Qualitative Studies in Education, 17,* 265–288.

Gildersleeve, R. E., Croom, N., & Vasquez, P. (2011). "Am I going crazy?!": A critical race analysis of doctoral education. *Equity & Excellence in Education, 44,* 93–114.

Harper, S. R., & Patton, L. D. (Eds.). (2007). *Responding to the realities of race on campus.* New Directions for Student Services. San Francisco, CA: Jossey-Bass.

Hays, D. G., & Wood, C. (2011). Infusing qualitative traditions in counseling research designs. *Journal of Counseling & Development, 89,* 288–295.

Henfield, M. S., Owens, D., & Witherspoon, S. (2011). African American students in counselor education programs: Perceptions of their experiences. *Counselor Education & Supervision, 50,* 226–242.

Hill, N. R. (2003). Promoting and celebrating multicultural competence in counselor trainees. *Counselor Education & Supervision, 43,* 39–51.

Johnson, P. D., Bradley, C. R., Knight, D. E., & Bradshaw, E. S. (2007). Preparing African American counselor education students for the professorate. *College Student Journal, 41,* 886–890.

Johnson-Bailey, J., Valentine, T., Cervero, R. M., & Bowles, T. A. (2009). Rooted in the soil: The social experiences of Black graduate students at a Southern research university. *The Journal of Higher Education, 80,* 178–203.

Kline, W. B. (2008). Developing and submitting credible qualitative manuscripts. *Counselor Education & Supervision, 47,* 210–217.

Ladson-Billings, G., & Tate, W. F. (1995). Toward a critical race theory of education. *Teachers College Record, 97,* 47–68.

Lett, D. F., & Wright, J. V. (2003). Psychological barriers associated with matriculation of African American students in predominantly White institutions. *Journal of Instructional Psychology, 30,* 189–196.

Lewis, C. W., Ginsberg, R., Davies, T., & Smith, K. (2004). The experiences of African American Ph.D. students at a predominately White Carnegie I-research institution. *College Student Journal, 38,* 231–245.

Lincoln, Y., & Guba, E. (1985). *Naturalistic inquiry.* Thousand Oaks, CA: Sage.

Miles, M. B., & Huberman, A. M. (1984). *Qualitative data analysis: A source book of new methods.* Beverly Hills, CA: Sage.

Moore, J. L., III, & Flowers, L. A. (2003). Collecting qualitative data on the World Wide Web: A step-by-step guide for counselor educators and student affairs professionals. *Journal of Technology in Counseling, 3.* Retrieved from http://jtc.columbusstate.edu/vol3_1/Moore/Moore.htm

National Science Foundation, Division of Science Resources Statistics. (2010). *Doctorate recipients from U.S. universities: 2009.* Special Report NSF 11-306. Arlington, VA. Retrieved from http://www.nsf.gov/statistics/nsf11306/

Oseguera, L., & Rhee, B. S. (2009). The influence of institutional retention climates on student persistence to degree completion: A multilevel approach. *Research in Higher Education, 50,* 549–569.

Patton, L. D. (2009). My sister's keeper: A qualitative examination of mentoring relationship experiences among African American women in graduate and professional schools. *The Journal of Higher Education, 80,* 510–537.

Patton, M. Q. (2002). *Qualitative research and evaluation methods* (3rd ed.). Thousand Oaks, CA: Sage.

Protivnak, J. J., & Foss, L. (2009). An exploration of themes that impact the counselor education doctoral student experience. *Counselor Education and Supervision, 48,* 239–256.

Quezada, R. L., & Louque, A. (2004). The absence of diversity in the academy: Faculty of color in educational administration programs. *Education, 125,* 213–221.

Rendon, L. I., Jalomo, R. E., & Nora, A. (2000). Theoretical considerations in the study of minority student retention in higher education. In J. Braxton (Ed.), *Reworking the student departure puzzle* (pp. 127–156). Nashville, TN: Vanderbilt University Press.

Rodgers, K. A., & Summers, J. J. (2008). African American students at predominantly White institutions: A motivational and self-systems approach to understanding retention. *Educational Psychology Review, 20,* 171–190.

Shealey, M. W. (2009). Voices of African-American doctoral students in special education: Addressing the shortage in leadership preparation. *Race, Ethnicity and Education, 12,* 349–361.

Solorzano, D., Ceja, M., & Yosso, T. (2000). Critical race theory, racial microaggressions, and campus racial climate: The experiences of African American college students. *Journal of Negro Education, 69,* 60–73.

Solorzano, D. G., & Ornelas, A. (2002). A critical race analysis of advanced placement classes: A case of educational inequality. *Journal of Latinos and Education, 1,* 215–229.

View, J. L., & Frederick, R. (2011). Sneaking out of the big house? Perceptions of African American mentees in a graduate level teacher education program on a White campus. *The Journal of Negro Education, 80,* 134–148.

Wertz, F. J. (2005). Phenomenological research methods for counseling psychology. *Journal of Counseling Psychology, 52,* 167–177.

Yosso, T. J. (2005). Whose culture has capital? A critical race theory discussion of community cultural wealth. *Race, Ethnicity and Education, 8,* 69–91.

Key Terms

Case study
Credibility
Critical studies
Ethnographic
Fieldwork
Grounded theory
Narrative inquiry
Participant perspectives

Phenomenological
Positionality
Purposeful sampling
Reflexivity
Validity/Trustworthiness
  Confirmability
  Context insensitivity
  Inadequate participant perspectives

Inadequate transparency
Inauthenticity
Instrumentation
Reactivity
Researcher bias
Sampling

Discussion Questions

1. How does the main purpose of qualitative research differ from quantitative research, and what is the implication of this difference for the design of an empirical study?
2. Describe the difference between quantitative threats to validity and qualitative threats to validity/trustworthiness. What is the implication of the differences for how studies are interpreted to identify noise?
3. How is it possible for qualitative studies that investigate just a few individuals or cases to contribute to knowledge or improved practice?
4. What are unique challenges to using each of the qualitative approaches?

Application Exercise

1. Team up with one or two others and locate a recently published qualitative research article. Identify the approach(es) used and the extent to which each of the nine characteristics in Table 11.1 is included, and whether any of the nine threats to validity/trustworthiness seem plausible.

Check for Understanding Answers

1a. Take your pick and refer to Table 11.1: natural contextualized setting; direct data collection; rich narrative descriptions; process orientation; inductive-(deductive) data analysis; participant perspectives; socially constructed meaning; emergent research design; researcher reflexivity.

1b. Qualitative research seeks a deep understanding of phenomena pertaining to certain people and contexts; the purpose of quantitative research is to gather data to objectively answer predetermined research questions.

1c. Qualitative designs are emergent; quantitative predetermined and fixed. Emergent designs are needed to provide flexibility in what is needed to gain deep understanding.

2a. Validity/trustworthiness is extent to which the findings represent an accurate representation of reality. It is important for establishing principles that need to be addressed to understand the extent to which noise is interfering with the findings and distorting reality.

2b. Take your pick: context insensitivity; inadequate participant perspectives; researcher bias; inadequate transparency; inauthenticity; instrumentation; confirmability; sampling; reactivity.

3a. Ethnographic studies examine culture and utilize multiple sources of data with prolonged engagement in the field; narrative inquiry is focused on personal stories and relies on information from a few key individuals.

3b. Identify purpose (case); identify participants and settings; sample; schedule data collection; collect data; analyze data; interpret data and draw conclusions.

3c. Ethnography is more difficult because it requires extensive time in the field, with multiple sources of data, including prolonged observation as well as interviews.

Chapter 12
Qualitative Data Collection

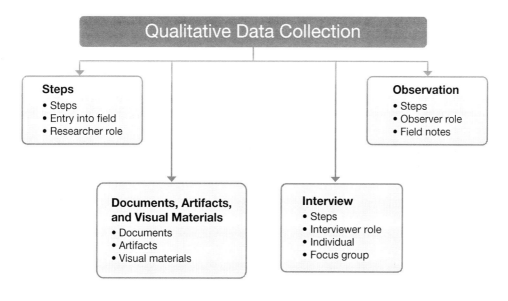

Qualitative Data Collection

Steps
- Steps
- Entry into field
- Researcher role

Observation
- Steps
- Observer role
- Field notes

Documents, Artifacts, and Visual Materials
- Documents
- Artifacts
- Visual materials

Interview
- Steps
- Interviewer role
- Individual
- Focus group

 # Learning Outcomes

12.1 Identify essential steps to take to gather qualitative data.

12.2 Know how to collect observational data.

12.3 Describe how interview data are collected.

12.4 Distinguish among document, artifact, and visual material data collection techniques.

Chapter Road Map

Now that you have identified the purpose and approach to your qualitative study, you are ready to proceed with data collection. Although data collection techniques are somewhat aligned with each approach, all four major types—observation, interviews, document analysis, and visual materials—are commonly used. We look at each of the techniques for gathering data in this chapter, then turn to data analysis strategies in Chapter 13.

Introduction to Collecting Qualitative Data

Learning Outcome 12.1 Identify essential steps to take to gather qualitative data.

Before examining the four major types of qualitative data collection, it is helpful to review the phases used more generally for gathering qualitative data. Once these phases are summarized briefly, major components used in the actual implementation of an investigation are discussed in more detail.

General Steps

As emphasized in Chapter 1, qualitative research is appropriate for exploring processes (e.g., how something occurs), understanding context (e.g., under what circumstances something occurs), or testing theory (e.g., how an established theory applies, or does not apply, to a particular stakeholder group). Once you have determined the appropriate methodology, the first phase (as outlined in Figure 12.1) involves identifying the nature of the site(s), participants, and/or types of documents and visuals that will best align with your purpose and overall approach. In this planning stage, ideal sources of data—whether people, documents and artifacts, or events—are identified to obtain needed depth of understanding. Purposeful sampling strategies were discussed in Chapter 5 (it would be helpful to review those, as they are integrated with data collection). For case studies and ethnographic studies, it is particularly important to identify the site or sites, the locations, settings, groups, agencies, or organizations that will provide the best data for understanding the investigated phenomenon. Part of the decision is being confident that you will be able to collect the data you need. For example, if you are studying life in "honors" college dormitories, you would want to plan for having access to as many aspects of dorm life as possible.

The nature of the approach taken in the study determines to a large extent what data collection techniques are needed. Both ethnographic and case study investigations rely on multiple forms of data collection, whereas phenomenological, narrative, and critical studies primarily use interviews.

The next phase is planning how to gain access to the field to determine specific sources of data (sites, participants, documents) and data collection techniques. Then, beginning with Phase 3, a series of recursive steps is implemented—recursive in the sense that qualitative studies use an emergent design. Qualitative research often evolves throughout the course of a study as the researcher engages in critical reflexivity and adapts to new, sometimes unanticipated components of the research. Note in Figure 12.1 how some phases loop back to inform changes in the design—this is the *recursive* aspect of data collection. What is collected depends, to some extent, on what has been found through previous data collection and analysis efforts. The recursive process is often facilitated with what is called researcher *memoing*, a procedure described in greater detail in the next section. Once data are collected and analyzed (Phases 5 and 6), the recursive process is triggered, sometimes leading to additional data collection.

Memoing

Before exploring the phases of data collection in more detail, it is important to emphasize the role *memoing* plays throughout a qualitative research study. As the primary instrument of qualitative data collection and analysis, researchers must remain mindful

Figure 12.1 Phases in Collecting Qualitative Data

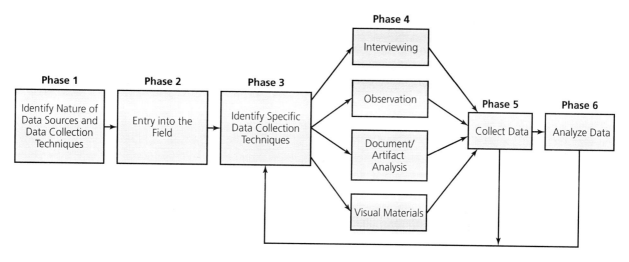

of their perceptions and biases that might influence their approach to the study at multiple stages. In this way, the researcher remains critically reflexive throughout the study. **Memoing** is a technique for bracketing possible perceptions to establish reflexivity. This begins with the selection of a research topic. Why was this important to the researcher? Are there any underlying assumptions that may have guided the selection of this topic that may potentially bias the approach? Next, what was the rationale for designing the methods of data collection? Are they most appropriate for addressing the research questions or were they perhaps selected for the sake of convenience or comfort level of the researcher? For example, did the researcher decide to conduct individual participant interviews rather than focus groups because of some discomfort with moderating a group discussion, even if focus groups might be most effective for generating rich data for the study? When collecting data, was the researcher able to effectively track the experiences of participants while remaining mindful of the focus of the study, or did he or she instead guide participant responses to align with anticipated findings?

When analyzing the data, did the researchers simply seek to confirm what was in the existing literature, or did they allow the data to offer a robust, nuanced picture of the phenomenon being studied? In the reporting of findings, what did the researcher decide to include or omit? How much do the emergent themes reflect the accounts of participants rather than simply any underlying assumptions of the researcher? By engaging in memoing throughout each of these steps in the process, researchers are able to remain mindful of their role in potentially influencing the outcomes of the study. While it is not possible to fully eliminate the potential for bias in a qualitative study (or perhaps most research studies), memoing is a critical method for helping to minimize and address this risk.

With memoing and reflexivity in mind, key phases (beginning with Phase 2) are now described in greater detail.

Entry into the Field

Whether the researcher actually goes into field settings, such as schools, for observation, or conducts interviews and collects documents and artifacts, it is important to identify an appropriate role, obtain permission, and establish a suitable rapport.

Table 12.1 Examples of Researcher Roles in Collecting Data

	Complete Insider	Partial Participant	Complete Outsider
Observation	Counselor observes students participating in small groups.	Researcher from outside the school helps counselors observe small groups.	Researcher from outside the school observes students in small groups.
Interview	Principal interviews teachers in his or her school.	Researcher from outside the school interviews teachers in their school.	Researcher from outside the school interviews teachers at a university.
Document and artifact review	Teacher reviews memoranda concerning formative assessment practices in his or her department.	Teacher from another department reviews memoranda.	Researchers from outside the school review memoranda.

The researcher role defines the position of the investigators and their relationships with others. At one extreme, the researcher is a **complete outsider**, totally detached from the naturally occurring behavior and activities of the participants. There is no involvement with what occurs in the setting. The researcher is detached—coming in, gathering data, and then leaving. A **complete insider**, on the other hand, is a researcher who has an established role in the setting in which data are collected, engaging in genuine and natural participation. Between these extremes, as illustrated below, the researcher may be labeled partial participant or *insider/outsider*.

Complete Outsider   Partial Participant   Complete Insider

Examples of different researcher roles are presented in Table 12.1 for the three major types of data collection.

Entry into the field often requires the establishment of a trusting relationship with individuals in the proposed site. For example, if a researcher wishes to collect data in a school it will be important to establish contacts at the site so that the principal and other leaders of the school are familiar with the intentions of the researcher and purposes of the project. This may also require going through a formal review process with the school district, which is often similar to an institutional review board (IRB) at a university. While establishing trusting relationships may contribute to the threat of reactivity, it also presents a clear benefit for ensuring that participants at the research site are comfortable, well-informed, and potentially ready and willing to contribute to the process (e.g., as gatekeepers for purposeful sampling).

It is not uncommon for researchers to change their roles as data are collected. The nature and duration of different roles are determined, in part, by the situation. As situations change, roles also change. When first entering a site, the researcher might take on primarily a complete outsider role. As the study progresses, more of an insider role could develop. In studies with a limited time frame, it is difficult for the researcher to be an insider, which is why in ethnographies extended time is needed to "walk in the shoes" of the participants.

Researcher roles will also vary depending on the type of qualitative study. In many ethnographies, case studies, and grounded theory approaches, the interactions are widespread but the researcher is relatively unobtrusive in collecting data. In phenomenological studies, the interaction is closer and more personal. This may include multiple interviews with the same participants to establish prolonged engagement and enhance the validity/trustworthiness of the findings. (Chapter 13 provides a discussion of validity/trustworthiness.)

In obtaining initial permission to collect data, it is best if there is an agreement that permits access to all potentially helpful sources of data. This is important because the gathering of data evolves from initial approaches as the researchers learn from current data (recursive). It is also important to be clear about how confidentiality and anonymity will be maintained, consistent with IRB approval (refer to Chapter 2). For example, a school participating in a research project may not be willing to provide secondary demographic or academic performance data for student participants for triangulation of qualitative findings, but may allow students to self-report this data. Protection of confidentiality or anonymity may require the use of pseudonyms (fake names) for participants. Focus group data collection may require a separate assurance of confidentiality by the group agreeing to not share what was discussed with anyone outside of the study.

Rapport with individuals at the research site is enhanced when the researcher takes time to understand others' perspectives and shows respect for different viewpoints and personalities. Appropriate rapport is first needed with those who have responsibility for allowing entry into the site (e.g., principal of a school). These individuals are essentially "gatekeepers." If a trusting, positive relationship is not established with these individuals, subsequent good relationships with others and access to information is mitigated. You want to come into the site as a known entity, not as a stranger without the support of the gatekeeper(s). For school sites, this often begins with establishing positive relationships with district personnel who are responsible for allowing research in their schools. In-person contact is needed to establish the desired relationship.

While interacting with members of the site, it is very important to use honest, authentic, and sincere communication. Rapport is also enhanced when the researcher is able to participate in daily activities, establish common interests, and relax and act naturally. Establishing a partial participant or complete insider role enhances relationships.

Finalize Specific Data Sources and Collection Techniques

Once access to the field is obtained, the specific data sources (e.g., sites, individual participants, documents) and data collection techniques that will be used are finalized. For instance, in an ethnographic case study, the selection of participants would be completed after identifying the site and entering the field to determine where the data will be collected, time frames, and events of interest. Consider planning observations for researching how students respond to a computer program to help them become better writers. There would be a need to use the most informative settings (e.g., within a classroom or computer lab), determine when observations should be made (e.g., morning, afternoon, beginning of the school year, days of the week), and decide what students would be doing during the selected times at the designated locations (e.g., actively writing with the software or revising based on feedback).

In case study research, it is critical to identify and sharply articulate what the "case" is, as well as what data sources will be necessary to more fully understand the experiences of the case. For example, a study exploring the experiences of multiple students as individual cases may primarily rely on interview data (similar to phenomenological studies), but it will likely also be necessary to include triangulating sources of information to offer a more robust understanding of those experiences (e.g., field notes, observations, interviews with other relevant stakeholders). If a school serves as a case, it will likely be necessary to collect interview, observation, and demographic data to offer a rich description of what it means to exist in that space.

An important consideration in selecting the group is the type of data collection that will be used. For observation—other factors being equal—the smaller the group, the greater the chance that the researcher's presence will change participants' behavior. For example, in a case study of teenage same-sex friendships in which the researcher interacts extensively with two or three pairs of participants, the researcher's involvement may affect the friendships. It is usually easier to remain unobtrusive and relatively anonymous with a large number of participants. Of course, a larger number of participants makes it more difficult to keep detailed records on everyone; depth is sacrificed for less intrusion. The main consideration is that the selection of sources of data must facilitate gaining sufficient depth of information.

Check for Understanding 1

1a. What are the steps taken to collect qualitative data?

1b. Why is the recursive aspect of collecting qualitative data important? How does memoing relate to the recursive nature of qualitative data collection?

1c. Explain the difference between a complete outsider role and the role of partial participant.

The next phase in collecting data is to implement appropriate ways to gather the information. In the next few sections, the major types of qualitative data collection techniques are reviewed in detail, starting with observation, a mainstay of qualitative research.

Observation

Learning Outcome 12.2 Know how to collect observational data.

By observing naturally occurring behavior over many hours or days, researchers hope to obtain a rich, deep understanding of the phenomenon being studied. Often, as in an ethnography, observation is *comprehensive* in that it is continuous, without constraints or boundaries. Other observations may be more targeted; this is typically the case when observations are used with interviews to triangulate data, and with approaches other than ethnography.

Steps for Collecting Observational Data

Qualitative observations are designed and implemented in a sequence of steps, illustrated in Figure 12.2. These procedural steps emphasize the relationship between the role of the researcher and type of site, as well as the recursive nature of the process.

Based on the central questions of the study, you would identify the needed characteristics of a site to be able to gather data that address the questions. A part of this process

---

Figure 12.2 Steps in Collecting Observational Data

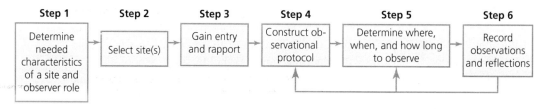

is identifying the observer role (more on that in the next section). Following site selection, access to the site and rapport are established. A protocol that consists of an outline of what will be observed is constructed, along with a plan for where, when, and how long initial observations will take place. Once data are recorded, the recursive nature of the design is implemented, as what was observed and reflected upon impact subsequent observations.

Observer Role

An important aspect of the observation is the nature of the role that is established (refer to Table 12.2). Very similar to what was described earlier, you can think of the degree of participation and involvement for observation as a continuum, in this case ranging from *passive* to *complete* participation. Passive participation occurs when the researcher is a **complete observer** totally detached from the behavior of the participants who are being studied. If the role of the researcher doing the observation is as a genuine participant in the activity being studied, yet identified to others in the setting as the researcher, the individual is called a **participant observer**. For example, to study the life of a college freshman, the participant observer would become a college freshman, directly experiencing everything other freshmen experience. This is essentially what an anthropologist would do in conducting ethnographic research on a culture. The anthropologist would virtually become a member of the group and live just as others in the group live, but would still be known as a researcher. If the researcher is a member of the group and not known as a researcher, the role would be known as a **complete participant**.

In educational research, it is rare for the observer to literally adopt the same status as the individuals who are being studied. There may be some participation in some of the activities, but it is usually limited. The researcher interacts with the participants to establish a rapport and a relationship but does not become a member of the group. When participation is limited, the researcher is called an *observer participant* or *participant observer.*

The extent of participation by an observer often changes during a study. In the beginning, the researcher may limit participation to become more accepted and establish a trusting relationship. As the group being studied becomes comfortable with the researcher, participation increases. Another variable that affects the extent of participation is the nature of the research question. If, for example, the study is focused on the perspectives of students, then it makes sense to participate more with the students than with the teacher. On the other hand, if teacher perceptions are the focus of the study, then the researcher should take on more of an observer role.

The more the researcher is actively involved with the participants, the greater the chance that this involvement may significantly alter what occurs. Any degree of participant involvement is likely to affect the interpretation of what is observed. As a consumer, you need to look for clues as to whether researcher participation may have been an important influence on the results (e.g., researcher relationships affecting

Table 12.2 Roles of the Qualitative Observer

Passive Participation	Moderate Participation	Active Participation	Complete Participation
Complete observer:	Observer participant:	Participant observer:	Complete participant:
Observes without becoming a part of the process in any way.	Identified as a researcher but does not take on the role of the participants.	Participates as a member of the group but is known as a researcher.	Participates as a member of the group and is not known as a researcher.

interactions with others). The researcher should indicate a sensitivity for this effect and should take precautions to ensure that their participation does not significantly distort the observations.

Ethics of Observation

It is important to note that in observational research it is possible (perhaps even likely) that the researcher is engaging in data collection with individuals who have not directly consented to being a participant in the research. For example, if a researcher conducts a study that involves interviewing consenting students in a school, there may also be a need to engage in some formal observations of classrooms or student interactions in the common spaces of the building (e.g., hallways or cafeteria) for added contextualized information. In this case, it may be true that the vast majority of students and faculty in the school are not formally involved in the study, even though they are contributing to the observational data of the researcher.

With this in mind, the researcher needs to establish clear boundaries regarding what data will be collected and from whom. It would be inappropriate, for example, to attempt to conduct formal interviews with individuals being observed who have not consented to participate in the study. While informal conversations with nonconsenting participants may contribute to a researcher's field notes (as discussed later in this chapter), bridging the gap between observation and direct interviewing would likely require a formal consent process. Additionally, it may be necessary for the researcher to provide some information about the study as well as the purpose and parameters of the observation session to the individuals who may be a part of it. In a school setting, this may take the form of an e-mail sent to the staff or an announcement made to students the day before the observation. By sharing this information prior to conducting the observation, stakeholders in the setting will be more aware of why the researcher is there (e.g., that they are not being evaluated in any way) and what to expect from his or her presence (e.g., that the researcher will simply be observing rather than asking any questions). While taking such steps could contribute to participants behaving differently around a researcher (thus compromising the credibility of the observational data), their behavior may be altered anyway by the presence of a researcher (as discussed in the following sections). Informing potential participants is a foundational component of ethical research that must not be overlooked when conducting observations.

Recording Observational Data

Observations are often recorded as brief notes while the researchers are observing. The recording is usually based on a protocol that lists general categories of settings or of what behaviors or occurrences are targeted. Regardless of the degree of structure, these brief notes are then expanded to become what are called *field notes*. **Field notes** are detailed written descriptions of what was observed, as well as the researcher's interpretations. They constitute the raw data that the researcher analyzes to address the research problem. An assumption of ethnographic research is that nothing is trivial, so whatever is seen, heard, or experienced is recorded and considered. Observation sessions will typically last 1 to 2 hours, although a researcher may choose to engage in a longer session if valuable to understanding the context of a study (e.g., observing an entire school stay at a research site). Good observation is hard work and requires excellent listening and seeing skills, so researchers should plan the length of an observation with this in mind. Longer sessions make it difficult to keep an in-depth recording of what is observed simply because there are too much data.

Field notes include two kinds of information. The first type is *descriptive.* The purpose of the description is to use pictures, words, drawings, maps, and diagrams that capture the details of what has occurred. The field notes usually include a description of the setting, what people looked like, what they said, and how they acted. The date, place, and time are recorded, as well as a description of the activities in which people were involved. Portraits of the participants—including their dress, mannerisms, and physical appearance—may be included. Often, a description of the researcher and their dress and actions is also included. As much detail as possible is recorded, including direct quotes or close approximations of what was said.

With descriptive field notes, interpretations are avoided. Thus, rather than using words such as *angry, motivated,* or *effective,* the researcher would describe the specific behaviors observed. The observation is usually fairly unstructured in the sense that there are no or few predetermined categories or checklists. Whatever is observed is recorded in a form that captures the perspectives of the individuals being studied. Note in Excerpt 12.1 how the researcher indicates the descriptive information that was observed and how these descriptions were recorded in the field notes.

EXCERPT 12.1

Descriptive Observations

In the field notes, I documented the student's behavioral engagement as indicated by her affect, work patterns, body language interactions with teachers and others, contributions to discussions and questions asked. I also noted behavioral patterns among other students to record peer environments, and I recorded the academic activities of each class, class-wide interactions, and comments made by the teacher—especially those signaling student competence. (p. 500)

SOURCE: Cooper, K. S. (2012). Safe, affirming, and productive spaces: Classroom engagement among Latina high school students. *Urban Education, 48*(4), 490–528.

The second kind of information in the field notes is *reflective.* These are researcher speculations, feelings, interpretations, ideas, hunches, and impressions—subjective notions related to the purpose of the research. Reflections include thoughts about emerging themes and patterns, thoughts about methodological problems or issues, considerations of ethical concerns, and introspective thoughts about researcher opinions, attitudes, and prejudices. It is important to keep these reflections separate from the descriptive information. In the field notes, they are often identified as *observer comments* or *memos.*

Most observations result in notes about *who, what, where, how,* and *why* something happened. Examples of how each of these dimensions is manifested in studies are presented in Table 12.3.

It is critical for the field notes to be accurate and extensive. You will be able to judge the level of detail provided by the excerpts the researcher uses to illustrate conclusions, and the overall amount of data analyzed.

The example of field notes in Excerpt 12.2 will give you some idea of the detail that may be recorded in an ethnographic study. These field notes were taken as a pilot for a study on understanding the culture of a high school What is reproduced here represents about half of the notes for an observation period of an hour and a half.

Table 12.3 Dimensions of Observation Foci

Observation	Description
Who is in the group?	How many students are present? What races or ethnicities are represented? What are the ages of the students? How long have they been in the school?
What is happening?	In what activities are the students involved? How long are the activities? How are students communicating? How long is the duration of their involvement? What topics are commonly discussed? Who talks and who listens? How do students behave with each other and with the teacher?
Where is the class located?	What are the physical dimensions of the setting? What technology is available? Where is the class located in the school?
When does the class meet?	How long and how often do students meet to engage in the activity? When during the day do students typically engage in the activity?
Why does the class engage in the activity?	Do students agree on why the activity is important? What reasons are given for the activity? What meanings do students give the activity?

EXCERPT 12.2

Field Notes

Field Notes—D. Naff. January 28, 2018. Bryant High School (pseudonym).
Time Frame: 8:30–10:00 am
Observation during 1st period – 9th grade World History

It was a cold but sunny day when I arrived at BHS (pseudonym). Upon entering the building, I checked in at the main office as a visitor. The building appeared to be somewhat older (perhaps built in the 1980s or 1990s) but well-maintained. There was evidence of a positive school climate in the front lobby, with the name of the school scrolled on a banner as well as a case displaying various academic and athletic trophies won by the school. Students were congregated in the cafeteria in the middle of the school as well as the hallways as I walked to my assigned teacher's classroom. The student body appeared to be fairly racially diverse, although the students appeared to primarily form groups of the same race in the common spaces. Upon arrival at the classroom, I introduced myself to my assigned teacher (who I emailed yesterday to remind of my pending visit) and she escorted me to a desk in the back of the room. She was White and appeared to be in her late 30s or early 40s. We talked briefly about what classes she had for the first two periods of the day, and she seemed distracted by the activity in the hallway. She explained that it was an expectation by the administration that teachers stand in the hallways outside of their classrooms before the bell rang to greet students and help usher them into the classroom. I offered to stand in the hallway with her so she could fulfill her duty and I could get a sense for how students interacted with each other. Students walked by her classroom, and some had headphones in their ears or were wearing hoods. She asked these students to remove their headphones or hoods by pretending to engage in those behaviors herself. Upon noticing this, some students obliged while others seemed to ignore the request. She explained to me that while it was written in the code of conduct for the students to not engage in these behaviors, most teachers did not find it reasonable to write referrals to administration when students did not follow them. The bell for the first period rang and she ushered a few remaining students into her classroom. She greeted each of them by name as they entered.

OR: I wonder about the purpose of having a rule against wearing headphones or hoods in the school when teachers find it difficult to enforce. Also, it appears that the majority of students wearing headphones or hoods are Black, potentially contributing to more opportunities for teachers to have punitive interactions with these students.

At the beginning of the period, the teacher announced to the class who I was and that I was there to conduct a classroom observation for a research study. She did not offer any additional details about the study. Most of the students turned back to look at me and some said "hello." I said "hello" back to them, and they quickly turned around again to face the teacher. The class seemed to be racially diverse, as approximately 15 students appeared to be White, approximately eight appeared to be Black, and approximately four appeared to be Latinx. This seemed to be roughly proportionate to the racial makeup of the school based on the enrollment data we used when selecting the school as one of our case study sites. The teacher began her lesson, which focused on ancient Greece, reminding students of what they had discussed in the last class before beginning to discuss new content. Most of the students appeared to be highly engaged in the lesson, and several had the same type of laptop computer. These appeared to be issued by the school or division, and while most were taking notes, some appeared to have other websites on their screens that were unrelated to the lesson. One Black male student had his head down on his desk, perhaps asleep. When the teacher asked students questions, several appeared eager to participate. While some raised their hands, others offered answers without being called on by the teacher. There appeared to be a good rapport established in the classroom as students did not seem to be frustrated by their peers answering without raising their hands, and the conversation with the teacher often felt lighthearted and informal.

OR: It struck me that the teacher decided to introduce me to the class but did not offer details about the purpose of the study. I was relieved that she did not indicate that its focus was about classroom discipline, as this might have altered the way students behaved. I also find it interesting that the students seemed to forget about my presence in the room shortly after my introduction, as no one looked at me again for the remainder of the period.

The teacher transitioned from a lecture to an activity where students worked in pairs to fill in a map. Throughout the activity, there was a lot of conversation between students as well as movement around the room. Conversations between students often appeared to be focused on the activity but sometimes seemed to veer into tangential topics, although students seemed to typically refocus on the task in these cases. During this activity, the student who had his head down on his desk got out of his seat and walked to the teacher's desk to ask her a question. She was answering a question from another student about the map worksheet at the time and did not seem to notice the other student at her desk. The student waited for approximately 20 seconds and then walked out of the classroom. He did not return for the remainder of the period. This occurred with approximately 20 minutes left in the class.

OR: I wonder if this is the typical format of the class – to begin with some review of the previous class, followed by lecture, and concluding with a class activity. Overall, the group appeared to be highly engaged in the class so it seems that this approach may have proven over time to be effective.

OR: While this teacher appeared to allow some flexibility in the class for conversations between students and movement around the room during the activity, allowing the student to leave without first asking permission or returning later in the period seems problematic. I made a note to ask the teacher about this during her interview later in the day.

Brief notes were made during the observation, and immediately after the visit time was taken, as soon as possible, to make both the descriptive and reflective notes. (OR stands for observer reflection.) This is important—you have to summarize in narrative fashion as soon as possible following the observation, even when you are able to take notes during the visit.

While some of the content of these field notes may have been tangential to the focus of the study (e.g., the weather on the day of data collection), they could prove helpful in reminding the researcher of the experiences that day when eventually analyzing the data. These notes are also a good illustration of the importance of writing "observer reflections" separate from the descriptions of what the researcher observed, as they help delineate observable evidence from impressions of it. The final observer reflection in these field notes included a prompt for asking this teacher about the student who left her room. The teacher later explained in her interview that this student had an Individualized Education Plan (IEP) that allowed him to leave class and go to a resource room in the school for additional support from a one-on-one teacher. She indicated that she knew he was going to this room and would follow up with him in the next class about any content that he missed. In this case, the observer reflection not only prompted a prolific discussion during interview data collection about the importance of understanding student background when managing classroom behavior, but also identified an assumption about how discipline should be handled that would not have been appropriate for this student. As a "complete observer" in this classroom, it was clear that there were established norms in this space that facilitated an understanding of the context that undergirded what was observed.

Not all observation notes and reflections are this extensive. Sometimes they may be presented as bullets or a short paragraph describing the visit, with a general summary of what occurred and what was observed.

A final excerpt that illustrates qualitative observation (Excerpt 12.3) is from a case study of low-income children and youth in a community school. The main purpose of these observations was to learn about the nature of a wide range of interactions. Note that the researchers identified themselves as nonparticipants.

EXCERPT 12.3
Qualitative Observations

Nonparticipant school observations were also conducted to supplement the interviews and gain a better sense of how students, teachers, parents, and community partners interacted without disrupting the regular school schedule. To capture a diverse range of interactions in different grade levels and subject areas, observations lasting between 15 and 30 minutes were conducted of kindergarten, ESOL, third-grade science, and physical education classes. Also, observations of after-school and summer program activities, breakfast and lunch periods, morning meetings, school-family council meetings, and the end-of-year spring festival were conducted. Handwritten notes were taken during these observations to (a) capture general impressions of the exchanges occurring and (b) document specific exchanges and events that reflected these impressions. (p. 148S)

SOURCE: Galindo, C., Sanders, M., & Abel, Y. (2017). Transforming educational experiences in low-income communities: A qualitative case study of social capital in a full-service community school. *American Educational Research Journal, 54*(1S), 140S–163S.

Check for Understanding 2

2a. What are the steps taken to collect observational data?

2b. What are complete participant and complete observer roles in qualitative research, and how do these roles likely impact the research?

2c. What are three important characteristics of taking what turn out to be good field notes?

The Hedgehog and Fox Consider Observation to Collect Data

Since the purest form of qualitative data is from observations, and I'm a good observer, I'll do them with the class over the next 6 weeks to see how engaged students are with their learning and how they react to feedback.

I need to be sure that observations are the best approach for learning about student engagement and reactions to feedback in this class. It may be better to do just a few observations to have time to do some interviews with students. The interviews might provide some insights from students that I can't pick up with observations.

Interviewing

Learning Outcome 12.3 Describe how interview data are collected.

Interviews, ranging in format from structured to unstructured, were described in Chapter 7 as a quantitative data collection technique. In qualitative research, interviews are perhaps the most widely used method of collecting data. This is because a well-conducted qualitative interview allows you to capture the thoughts and feelings of participants in their own language, using words, phrases, and meanings that reflect their perspectives. The interviews help you understand in rich detail participant experiences and events that you cannot observe directly. As a result, you are able to extend understandings beyond what you can directly experience. Interviewing is a mainstay of qualitative research because it is relatively economical in both time and resources (at least compared with observation) and has the flexibility to encourage emergent directions and probing that can effectively capture participants' views, beliefs, emotions, thoughts, and thinking.

Gathering qualitative interview data involves two stages: first designing the interview, then conducting it.

Designing Qualitative Interviews

The steps taken to design qualitative interviews are illustrated in Figure 12.3. The first step is to clearly identify the purpose of the interview. What is the nature of the information you are trying to obtain? Would some other type of data collection be more

Figure 12.3 Steps in Designing Qualitative Interviews

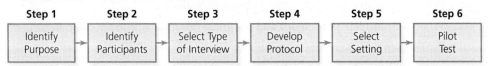

appropriate? Purpose will drive the more specific research questions, type of interviewing, and nature of the participants who need to be interviewed. For example, if the purpose is to capture lived experiences of individuals, the interviews may be extensive, more unstructured than semistructured, and conducted with participants who have clearly lived the experiences. Suppose you want to know what life is like for a teenager who struggles with depression. Lived experiences would mean that the teenage participants would have to have demonstrated a certain length and depth of depression.

The second step is to select the participants. This is based on making sure the interviewees can provide the needed information, as well as what is practical and feasible. One type of individual interview, the **key informant interview**, is used extensively in ethnographic studies. It is based on the assumption that in-depth interviews with a few "key" participants—individuals who are particularly knowledgeable and articulate—will provide insights and understandings about the problem. For example, with certain students, those with at least 2 months of part-time work, experience may be better able to provide information on the effect of part-time employment while participating in sports than with those working less than 2 months. Or, in a study of how a new curriculum has been integrated in a low-performing school, the assistant principal responsible for instruction would probably be a key informant.

However, the qualities that make key informants valuable also may result in an understanding that does not represent the full range of information. Thus, the researcher should carefully describe key informants and address the question of representativeness. Key informants should be selected after the researcher has become familiar with the setting, gained entry, and established trust to increase the likelihood that they will provide needed information truthfully. Selecting key informants to represent the diversity of perspectives present in the setting lessens the potential for bias.

The third step is to identify the type of interview that will be conducted. Here you have several options, based on whether they are done individually or in small groups, how structured the protocol needs to be, and the mode (in person, by telephone, or over the Internet). The most commonly used format is in person, individually or with small groups.

Types of Qualitative Interviews

The choice of interview structure is based on the following continuum of flexibility:

In an *unstructured* interview, the researcher begins with a general idea of what needs to be asked, but does not have a list of prespecified questions with precise wording. A general direction is established with the respondent and then specific questions are formulated based on what the respondent says. The respondent, not the interviewer, controls the interview and does most of the talking. The interviewer must be flexible and allow the respondent to control the flow of information but at the same time keep the overall focus on the research problem being investigated. This type of interview is most common with phenomenological studies.

One type of unstructured format is an **informal conversational interview**. Here, the questions emerge from the immediate context and are asked in the natural course of events spontaneously; there is no predetermination of questions, topics, or phrasing, and nothing is planned ahead. For example, a researcher may meet a student in the hallway and have a conversation from which data are generated. This occurs in many ethnographic field studies because the researcher typically has many unplanned, informal conversations.

With the *semistructured* interview, topics and some possible questions are selected in advance, but the researcher decides the sequence and wording of the questions during the interview and may use pre-established prompts and **probes**. This moderate level of structure is the most common in qualitative research, for both individual and small group interviews. It allows for important topics to be covered but also gives respondents freedom to emphasize other areas. One variation of the semistructured approach has a pre-established set of questions and prompts that are asked in order. Using this format, all participants get the same questions in the same order. This ensures extensive comments on each area, but may constrain and limit the naturalness and relevancy of the responses. This kind of interview tends to be less engaging and more formal, and reduces interviewer flexibility to probe in new and potentially important ways.

There are two types of probes: *clarifying* and *elaborating*. Clarifying probes provide an explanation, whereas elaborating probes seek more detail. For example, when asked about which types of tests made a student most nervous, the response could be "multiple-choice tests." That could be followed with probes such as the following:

"What are multiple-choice tests like?" (clarifying)
"Why do they make you nervous?" (elaborating)
"Can you tell me about a recent multiple-choice test that made you nervous?" (elaborating)

There are also structured qualitative interviews, though these are much less common. In the structured format, the questions are all predetermined and asked in the same order for all participants, with specific, predetermined prompts. This is similar to what is used in most quantitative interviews, except that the questions are all open ended and less targeted.

Note in Excerpt 12.4 how the researcher justifies the use of semistructured questions.

EXCERPT 12.4

Semistructured Individual Qualitative Interviews

The purpose of this study was to understand undergraduate students' attitudes about search data privacy in academic libraries and their preferences for how librarians should handle information about what students search for, borrow, and download.... Using a qualitative approach through the lens of interpretive description, I used the constant comparative method of data collection and analysis to conduct semi-structured interviews with 27 undergraduate students at a large, urban public research institution… This combination of structure and flexibility made the semi-structured approach ideal for ensuring consistency in the core set of questions asked in each interview so that data could be compared (Bogdan & Biklen, 2007; Guest et al., 2013), while also allowing flexibility so that each participant could contribute meaningfully to the study based on their individual attitudes, experiences, and background. (pp. 12, 87)

SOURCE: Gariepy, L. W. (2019). *Undergraduate students' attitudes about the collection, use, and privacy of search data in academic libraries: An interpretive description* [Unpublished doctoral dissertation]. Virginia Commonwealth University.

Author Reflection *Not to get too picky, but some will claim that written answers to open-ended questions constitute qualitative research, or a qualitative phase of a mixed methods investigation, primarily because the analysis is qualitative. In my mind, qualitative research is more than just the analysis, and answers from in-person interviews tell you much more than you can get from written answers. You are able to probe and observe nonverbal behavior to gauge comfort, honesty, confidence, and a host of other indicators that you can't get with written responses.*

Protocol and Setting

The fourth step in interviewing is to determine the protocol, or the set of questions and prompts. Even an unstructured interview has a protocol, although the few questions or areas are very broad and allow for great variation in responses. More typically, the protocol will contain 5 to 10 questions, written on paper with space between the questions for jotting down notes and observations.

The fifth step is to identify the setting in which the interviews will take place. Here, it is important to choose a setting that will enhance the comfort level of the participants, while at the same time allow for audio recording of the interview. Then the protocol is pilot tested, ideally in the selected setting or one very similar to it, and revised as needed. The pilot test is conducted with one or just a few individuals.

An example of part of a qualitative interview protocol is shown in Excerpt 12.5. I have included one of three major questions for the semistructured interview of teachers. Note the use of probes as needed to provide more detail and greater depth, and to assure that certain areas were addressed.

EXCERPT 12.5
Qualitative Interviews

2. I would also like to invite you to talk a little bit about the students in your classroom this year. I imagine that each class of students is unique. How would you describe this year's class as a whole?

- Now can you further describe some of the individual students in your current class, in whatever ways make most sense to you? No names or first names only.
- And now, specifically related to learning and academic achievement, how would you characterize the profiles or clusters of your students this year? -Children who "stand

out" in some particular way? -Children who you are concerned about? -Children who you are delighted to have in your class?

• Anything else you might wish to add about the particular children in your class this year? (p. 34)

SOURCE: Evans, M., Teasdale, R. M., Gannon-Slater, N., La Londe, P. G., Crenshaw, H. L., Greene, J. C., & Schwandt, T. A. (2019). How did that happen? Teachers' explanations for low test scores. *Teachers College Record, 121*(2).

Conducting Qualitative Interviews

Rubin and Rubin (2012) use a very apt subtitle of their book on qualitative interviewing: *The Art of Hearing Data*. Good qualitative interviewing is indeed an art, albeit a systematic one. Each interviewer is an artist in the sense that they will have their own style and approach, one that develops over time with practice. It is not a haphazard process, however; there are standards and a process that lead to gathering needed information and the credibility of what is learned. The goal is to conduct the interview as an engaged listener, trying hard to listen to what is being communicated, with a minimum of interviewer talk. Openness is needed for flexibility and acceptance of participant responses and for appropriate probing that leads to depth of understanding, to richness and complexity. In qualitative language, you need to obtain "thick" descriptions that provide detail and depth.

As with all interviews, the skill of the interviewer is critical to gathering valid data. As a general rule, skill is directly related to training and experience—the more training and experience, the greater the skill. This is readily apparent in the ability of the interviewer to first establish rapport and trust, then know how to ask additional follow-up questions and look for specific examples, details, or particulars that lead to greater insights. Being genuine, maintaining eye contact, dressing appropriately, and connecting with the respondent are important.

One way good to keep the interview going to obtain rich information is to *not* ask questions that can be answered dichotomously (e.g., yes or no). Notice in Table 12.4 how dichotomously answered questions can be rephrased to be more effective.

INDIVIDUAL INTERVIEWS Individual interviews are one on one. Your skill in adapting to each individual is critical to establishing trust and acceptance. Remember, you are the "expert" researcher (even if you don't feel that you are!). It's important, then, to be informal and at ease, to start with some casual conversation that is easy for the participant. Smile and relax; reveal something about yourself if the opportunity presents itself. Listen carefully for key words and note nonverbal indicators, such as

Table 12.4 Dichotomous Questions Revised to be Open-Ended

Dichotomous Questions	Open-Ended Questions
Did the teachers have difficulty in the seminar?	What did you expect teachers to have difficulties with during the seminar?
Did the teachers change?	How did the teachers change?
Did you learn anything from the workshop?	What did you learn about the teaching strategies presented in the workshop?
Were any problems identified at the committee meeting?	What problems were identified at the committee meeting?

body language and tone, to provide clues about the person's emotions and level of comfort. You need to connect, and connect quickly, in a way that encourages candid conversation that will be unique for each individual. Patience is a must—you don't want to dominate by asking too many questions.

Sometimes you will be conducting a one-on-one interview and the participant just does not say much, because they may be shy, introverted, or guarded, even intimidated. Doing one-on-one interviews with individuals who will not share much limits needed data! This means that when you select participants, you must consider their willingness and ability to communicate. In my recent study of middle school students' perspectives about assessment and grading, I asked teachers to nominate students who would be willing to engage in talking with me. Even so, in an individual interview you will need to be very skilled at establishing the right relationship.

Creswell and Poth (2018) discuss power asymmetry that may exist between the interviewer and interviewee. This is essentially an unequal power relationship, one in which the interviewer is perceived to have such strong influence in the interview that it becomes a mostly one-way conversation dominated by the researcher's agenda and control over the interviewee. Obviously, you will want to minimize such a dynamic.

One type of individual interview, the **life-history interview**, is structured toward learning about the participant's life. The data from life histories are helpful in obtaining a historical perspective or a broad perspective on how an individual has developed. Excerpt 12.6 is from a life-history study of first-generation female students of color in which individual interviews were used to gather data. Note the use of "retrospective accounts of their experiences."

EXCERPT 12.6

Life History Individual Qualitative Interviews

Individual interviews. We first conducted in-person interviews with each participant. The semi-structured interview protocol was influenced by standpoint theory and phenomenology: To elicit students' voices, the questions were open-ended rather than shaped by specific analytical frames (Maxwell, 2012; Merriam, 2001). With interviews lasting 60 to 90 minutes, we collected students' retrospective accounts of their experiences with K-12 schooling and accessing college. Prompts related to these domains included the following: (a) Please tell me about your K-12 educational experiences and (b) Now I'd like to hear about the process and experiences you went through leading up to applying to college. We also inquired about students' reasons for pursuing master's degrees and about their graduate school experiences, which we have explored separately (see Portnoi & Kwong, 2011). (p. 440)

SOURCE: Portnio, L. M., & Kwong, T. M. (2019). Employing resistance and resilience in pursuing K-12 schooling and higher education: Lived experiences of successful female first-generation students of color. *Urban Education, 54*(3), 430–458.

FOCUS GROUP INTERVIEWS   A small group interview technique that is used extensively in qualitative research is the **focus group interview**. A focus group is typically an interview of 6 to 12 individuals that lasts 45 minutes to an hour and a half. It is used to promote interaction among the individuals that leads to a rich understanding of whatever is being studied. That is, the goal of achieving a greater depth of understanding is achieved because of the interactions generated in the discussion. A moderator guides the discussion, based on a topic guide or protocol that has been prepared in advance, typically with five to seven open-ended questions. A semistructured format is used to assure coverage of important topics and allow for new topics to emerge. Mertens (2019) points out that "why" questions should be avoided since they can lead to a defensive reaction and an unequal power relationship. The focus group technique is most useful for encouraging participants, through their interaction with one another, to offer insights and opinions about a concept, idea, value, or other aspects of their lives about which they are knowledgeable.

Some so-called focus groups are little more than small group discussions or mostly individual interviews conducted in a group setting. To be effective, focus groups need to be conducted by someone with skill in redirecting questions. It is not a matter of simply going from one individual to another and asking a question. The goal is to generate and support interaction among all in the group.

The group should be homogeneous with respect to important participant characteristics. For example, in learning about a vision for a university school of education, it would be most effective to have untenured professors in one group and tenured professors in another group, alumni in a separate group, and students in yet another group. This ensures that the voice of each group is clear and well represented. If the group is mixed, one perspective may dominate, or the session may turn out to be a series of individual responses in a group setting. This means that when there is a single or very few numbers of focus groups, there is less generalizability. This is a common tradeoff with obtaining depth of understanding and insights. The exception to the "homogeneous rule" is when the goal of the discussion is to see how individuals representing different populations react to each others' perspectives. This can be valuable to gain insight into the level of concern or resolve one subgroup displays in reaction to other subgroups (e.g., when the goal is to ascertain whether different groups would agree with proposed recommendations for changes).

Typically, focus group sessions are audio recorded; notes may be taken by a second researcher (because it is difficult to conduct the interview and take notes at the same time!), and some sessions are videotaped. My experience in conducting both individual and group interviews is that the participants generally do not have a concern about tape recording, and having a verbatim record is very important for data analysis.

A description of a focus group is shown in Excerpt 12.7. Note the use of "warm-up" questions, a script with follow-up probes, and an assistant to take notes.

EXCERPT 12.7

Focus Group Interview

Consistent with focus group methodology ... broad topics ... were identified that would elicit the discussion of effective involvement strategies, [forming] the basis of the focus group script. Follow-up probes were used to make sure participants discussed strategies at home, at school, and other aspects of involvement ...[T]he focus group discussions began with warm up questions...Trained focus group facilitators led each group, along with an assistant who took notes. . . . All focus groups were audio recorded and recordings were transcribed. (p. 15)

SOURCE: Hill, N. E., Witherspoon, D. P., & Bartz, D. (2018). Parental involvement in education during middle school: Perspectives of ethnically diverse parents, teachers, and students. *The Journal of Educational Research, 111*(1), 12–27.

Check for Understanding 3

3a.   What are the steps taken to conduct qualitative interviews?

3b.   Why are most qualitative interviews semistructured rather than unstructured or structured?

3c.   What is the key advantage of using focus group rather than individual interviews?

Documents, Artifacts, and Visual Materials

Learning Outcome 12.4 Distinguish among document, artifact, and visual material data collection techniques.

The third primary method of collecting qualitative data is by reviewing *documents, artifacts,* and *visual materials.* **Documents** are written records. They can be virtually anything written or printed, such as yearbooks, e-mails, websites, school budgets, dropout rates, committee minutes, memos, letters, newspapers, diaries, test scores, and books. If the documents provide firsthand information, they are *primary* sources. In a primary source, the document is written in first person by someone who has had direct experience with the phenomenon, organization, or group being studied. *Secondary* sources are secondhand documents, such as descriptions of an event on the basis of what is heard from others or a summary of more extensive primary information.

Artifacts are archival sources that are different from documents. These would include comments in student files; records of testing results; statistical data; objects such as athletic letters, trophies, posters, and awarded plaques; bulletin boards; photographs and videos; art objects; film; physical trace evidence (e.g., wearing on the floor); e-mails; ritual objects; and sounds, smells, and tastes.

Visual materials are photographs, videotapes, drawings, paintings, movies, documentary films, graphics, social media, or other visual representations that go beyond a narrative description to provide important understandings and insights. Visual material includes what can be documented in such platforms as YouTube, Instagram, Facebook, and Twitter, as well as logs, bulletin boards, online communities, and websites (a new branch of ethnography that uses social media is called netnography).

The most common use of documents is to verify or support data obtained from interviews or observations. For example, teacher notes taken at the end of the school day that reflect on the successes and obstacles in using a new curriculum could be used to supplement researcher observations about implementing the new curriculum. Student essays could also be examined if written as part of the curriculum. The researcher usually finds existing documents and artifacts that have been produced, but occasionally, a researcher will ask participants to keep records or narratives as a way of producing documents. It should be clear, however, that a document is written or created as a natural outgrowth of the situation, and not in response to some kind of predetermined structure imposed by the researcher.

Excerpt 12.8 provides a description of how both documents and visual narratives were used to investigate the use of visual storytelling as a teaching and learning strategy for first-year university students. In this study students took photos, added text and music, and wrote a reflection paper about their learning. This is also an example of a life-history narrative.

The final excerpt in this chapter (Excerpt 12.9) illustrates the use of multiple sources of qualitative data, including the use of answers to open-ended survey questions.

EXCERPT 12.8

Documents and Visual Material

Data were generated from two sources: the visual narratives and the reflection papers. Qualitative analysis was used to identify emergent themes (Patton, 2002). Separate analysis documents were recreated for each data set...Students employed different formats to tell the story of the first-year experience through their eyes. Eleven groups used PowerPoint, one group used Prezi and one group used Windows Movie Maker. Many students organized their narratives temporally, starting their stories with images of moving in and welcome week activities... . In reflection papers, students provided thoughts about the visual narrative project and what they took away from the experience. (pp. 626, 628)

SOURCE: Everett, M. C. (2017). Fostering first-year students' engagement and well-being through visual narratives. *Studies in Higher Education, 42*(4), 623–635.

EXCERPT 12.9

Using Multiple Sources of Data

Yin (2003) suggested that a case study should involve collecting data from multiple sources. This study adopted seven data sources:

- Recorded instruction videos: During each learning unit, a digital camera recorded all learning scenarios. The researcher used these data to examine the instructional process of each learning unit.
- Teacher's teaching notes: The schoolteacher wrote a self-reflection in her teaching notes after the completion of each learning unit. From a teaching perspective, the notes presented what the teacher saw in the class.
- Learning materials: All learning materials presented on the IWB were collected. These data were used to ensure consistency between the instruction videos and teaching notes.
- Peer feedback: Two schoolteachers in other classes were invited to observe the learning units by providing written peer feedback. These data offer an objective viewpoint on students' learning process.
- Students' work sheets and homework: Students' in-class and assigned homework drawings were collected after the completion of the study. These drawings were compared with the students' drawings in the previous semester (without IWB intervention).

- Parent survey: After all learning units were finished, a questionnaire was sent to the students' parents. The survey consisted of five open-ended questions on the parents' perceptions of visual art learning.
- Interviews with parents and students: After each learning unit, the schoolteacher conducted an informal interview (no semi-structured guidelines) with several parents and students. The style of the informal interview was a conversation focusing on drawing practice between the schoolteacher and different parents (without children) and students (without parents), which created a low-pressure environment. The informal interview was conducted within 15 minutes. The teacher summarized the interview results in interview notes. (pp. 92–93)

SOURCE: Chou, P., Chang, C, & Chen, M. (2017). Let's draw: Utilizing interactive white board to support kindergarten children's visual art learning practice. *Educational Technology & Society, 20*(4), 89–101.

Check for Understanding 4

4a. What are some examples of documents, artifacts, and visual materials that could be used as qualitative data?

Table 12.5 summarizes the strengths and weaknesses of observations, interviews, and document and artifact analysis.

Table 12.5 Strengths and Weaknesses of Different Types of Qualitative Data Collection

Type	Strengths	Weaknesses
Observation	• Can observe behavior in natural settings. • Researcher is able to observe behavior firsthand as it occurs. • Enhances understanding of the context. • Useful for gauging engagement, interest, and attitudes. • Unintended behavior can be observed. • Allows an understanding of sensitive areas that individuals may not want to discuss.	• Observer can change the behavior of the participants. • Limited to when observations are made. • Observer bias or expectations may influence what is recorded and how it is interpreted. • Labor- and resource-intensive. • May be difficult to record important behavior that occurs quickly.
Interview	• Allows researcher to control the conversation and obtain the information needed. • Facilitates verbatim transcriptions as raw data. • Good backup if observations are not possible or are impractical. • Direct interaction allows recording of nonverbal behavior that accompanies answers to questions. • Participants are able to provide historical perspective.	• Information is indirect, not naturally occurring. • Skill, biases, and expectations of the interviewer may affect results. • It may be difficult to establish rapport to obtain in-depth and authentic responses. • Participants may be uncomfortable, inarticulate, or uncooperative. • Anonymity cannot be assured, which may affect the disclosure of sensitive information.
Documents, artifacts, and visual materials	• If unobtrusive, it will not be affected by participant awareness. • Audiovisual data provide creative sources of information. • Allows participants to share their perspectives in unique ways. • Provides data for which participants have had significant and thoughtful input. • Relatively inexpensive with fewer needed resources. • Provides alternative sources for triangulation. • Accessible when convenient for the researcher. • Provides detailed participant language and wording.	• Is not naturally occurring behavior. • Does not allow probing for additional information. • Sources may not be accurate or complete. • Data may be difficult to understand and code. • Medium may be disruptive and unnatural. • May provide incomplete or partial information.

Author Reflection *Heed this warning if you want to do qualitative research: Patience and extensive periods of time are needed for gathering, analyzing, synthesizing, and interpreting the data. The amount of time needed to do good qualitative research almost always surprises people. At first it seems relatively simple—just do some interviewing or observation—but if it remains simple, so will the results. I learned this lesson well in one of the first qualitative studies I directed, on the resilience of at-risk students. I continually miscalculated the amount of time needed to do the study, always thinking that it should take less time than it did! Plan accordingly when carrying out (or reading) qualitative studies so you won't be frustrated in this digital age of immediacy.*

Key Terms

Artifacts	Documents	Life-history interview
Complete insider	Field notes	Memoing
Complete observer	Focus group interview	Participant observer
Complete outsider	Informal conversational interview	Probes
Complete participant	Key informant interview	Visual materials

Discussion Questions

1. What are the advantages and disadvantages of researchers who establish each of three possible roles in the setting to collect data?
2. Suppose you want to do an observational study of what dorm life is like for student athletes. What type of observation role would be best justified?
3. What are the main, common limitations to doing qualitative observations and interviews?
4. What are unique challenges to using each of the qualitative approaches?

Application Exercise

1. Your task is to conduct two qualitative interviews with individuals who have completed a college education. The central question of the research is "What are the primary benefits of attending college?" Use semistructured questions to prepare a protocol, conduct, and tape record the interviews. Immediately after the interview record notes and observations about the strengths and limitations of the interviews. Also compare the interviews – how were they different, and why? Do you think the nature of your relationship with the individuals affects their responses?

Check For Understanding Answers

1a. The steps are first determining the nature of data sources and data collection techniques, followed by entry into the field and finalization of data sources and data collection techniques, then data collection and analysis.

1b. Because the researcher needs to use an emergent design that changes based on findings to result in a more complete understanding. Memoing provides a strategy for facilitating the recursive process.

1c. A complete outsider has no connection to the site or participants, the researcher who gathers data is external and maintains that role; a partial participant becomes familiar with participants before and during data collection, and internal role that does not go so far as having the same role as a participant.

2a. Determine site characteristics and observer role; select site(s); gain entry; construct protocol; determine when and where to observe; record observations and reflections.

2b. Complete participant is the observer taking the role of the participants, which could bias the observations; complete observer is an outsider who maintains distance, which could lead to uneasy feelings of participants.

2c. Taking brief notes when observing, separating descriptive notes from observer reflection and interpretations, and making detailed notes as soon as possible following the observation session.

3a. Determine purpose then participants; select the type of interview (individual or group); establish protocol; select setting; pilot test.

3b. An unstructured format provides assurance that important topics will be covered and also presents opportunities for participants to provide unplanned yet helpful information; unstructured may fail to provide adequate coverage; structured may not provide sufficient flexibility to allow for emergent themes.

3c. To generate interactions among the individuals that lead to insights, agreements, disagreement, and emergent ideas.

4a. Take your pick among many, e.g., newspaper articles, college yearbooks, teacher evaluations, social media, emails, posters, wall decorations.

Chapter 13
Qualitative Data Analysis, Validity/Trustworthiness, and Reporting

by David Naff and James McMillan

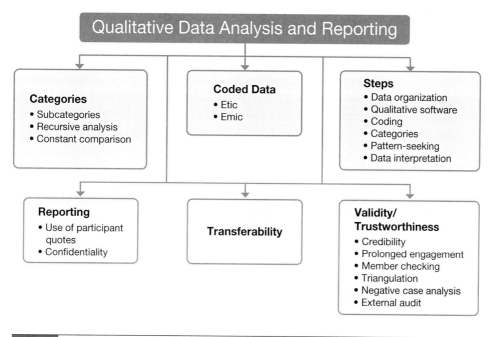

Learning Outcomes

13.1 Be able to organize and code qualitative data.

13.2 Know how to analyze and interpret qualitative data, to identify patterns and to develop themes.

13.3 Understand the processes of establishing validity/trustworthiness and transferability for qualitative studies.

13.4 Differentiate among different strategies for reporting qualitative findings, including how to establish an effective balance between participant quotes and narrative.

Chapter Road Map

Qualitative data have been collected. Now the really hard work begins: data analysis and interpretation. In this chapter we review commonly used approaches to analyzing qualitative data. We then review procedures for establishing validity/trustworthiness, and conclude with a discussion of how to report qualitative findings that enhance transferability.

Data Analysis and Interpretation

The overall goal of qualitative data analysis and interpretation is to discover patterns, ideas, insights, explanations, and understandings. A thorough analysis requires three steps (refer to Figure 13.1): organization of the data, use of codes to derive categories, and interpretation of the coded data to search for themes, patterns, and relationships.

Step 1: Data Organization and Coding

Learning Outcome 13.1 Be able to organize and code qualitative data.

The first step in data analysis is to organize the data, separating it into workable units or segments. With many pages of data, organizing can be quite a task. Initially, all the data must be transcribed into words, from audiotapes, video, documents, artifacts, or researcher notes and observations. The transcriptions should include differentiated participant and researcher dialog. If there are multiple participants in the recording (e.g., in a focus group), it is important to identify quotes to ensure an accurate representation of the conversation. This is where it can be helpful to have participant first names or pseudo names included in the transcript. Researcher questions and comments are needed to make sense of what the participants say (e.g., what interview question they are answering). Some transcriptions include descriptors of what happens (e.g., prolonged silence, interruptions, inaudible voice).

It is critical to capture the conversation as close to verbatim as possible to ensure accurate and complete data for analysis. Researcher transcribing of recorded interviews (e.g., typing from an audiotape), often facilitated by using software, can be a very tedious task. Many programs offer the ability to upload an audio or video file directly into the software with controls for playing, pausing, and slowing down the recording while manually transcribing. Other programs offer a machine transcription, and some of these are able to distinguish between speakers and separate the transcript content accordingly. With machine transcriptions, it is imperative that the researcher reviews the transcript for accuracy along with the recording as they often contain errors (although the technology continues to improve). Although you may opt to pay a person or professional service for transcription, it is typically very beneficial to do the transcription yourself, or least part of it. This takes additional time, but it also offers the opportunity to get "closer" to the data by listening to and processing the information for the first time since collecting it.

Researchers differ about whether to include "filler" words in a transcript (e.g., "um," "like," "you know," etc.). Some argue that leaving them out compromises the integrity of the transcript, while others contend that leaving them in makes the transcript more "noisy," reducing the signal of the participant's perspective. Whether or not to include these words is up to the researchers and their team.

Figure 13.1 Steps in Qualitative Data Analysis and Interpretation

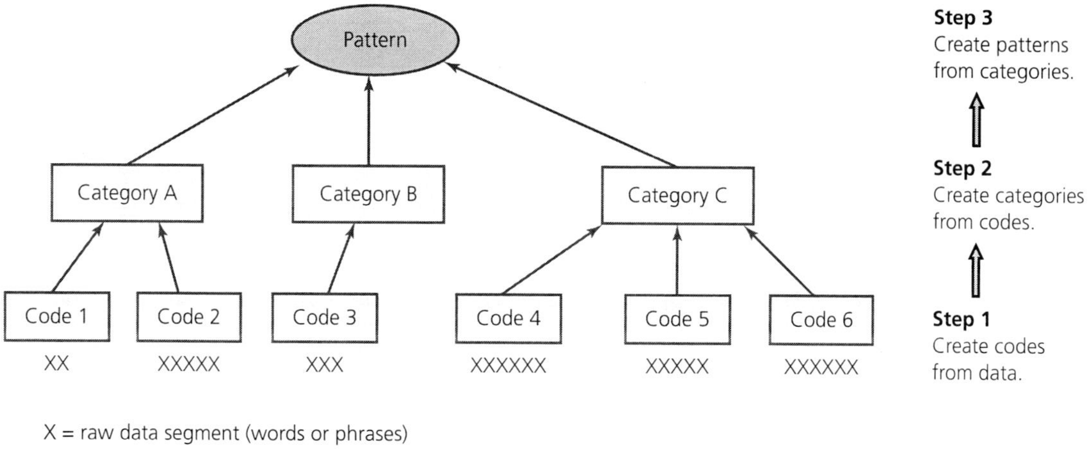

X = raw data segment (words or phrases)

Most studies organize the transcribed data according to their source. **Emic** data contain information provided by the participants, in their own words. By capturing language, actions, expressions, terms, and explanations, as voiced by the participants, the richness, depth, and authenticity of the findings can be addressed. **Etic** data are representations of emic data by the researcher. This is usually illustrated with themes or conclusions that explain trends and findings. For example, in a study of teachers' reasons for using particular grading practices, the participants might say something like "I use objective tests to show parents how grades were determined" and "I use tests that have the same type of items as the high-stakes test given at the end of the semester." These statements represent emic data. The researcher might synthesize these and call them "external pressures," which would be etic data.

The most common approach to organizing both emic and etic data is to read through the transcripts and look for words, phrases, or events that seem to stand out, and then create codes for these words and phrases. **Codes** are labels that are used to provide a common way of describing text. It is a decision-making process in which the researcher determines which text will receive the same label. In this way, separate segments of comments are "named" or identified according to specific codes. Codes may originate from the conceptual framework for a qualitative study, or may emerge during analysis in either the terms and phrases used by the participants (**in-vivo** coding) or those assigned by the researcher. "Families" of codes that can be applied to most studies often are related to setting and context, participants' definitions of a setting, participants' perspectives about other people and aspects of a setting, process changes over time, activities, events, techniques participants use to accomplish things, and relationships and social structures. The part of the text that is most central to the code may be bolded, bracketed or highlighted during analysis.

While the number of codes used will vary from one study to another, typically 30 to 50 codes will be used. Some may be *major* codes, which tend to be broad, whereas others may be *subcodes*, which are divisions among the major codes. For example, in an ethnographic study of the effect of a new testing program, major codes might be time of testing, effect on teacher, effect on student, effect on school climate, and effect on teacher relationships. Subcodes under "effect on students" could include motivational effects, effort, student preparation, student reactions after testing, and student reactions after receiving scores.

Because the formulation of codes, the key building block of qualitative findings, is up to each researcher, it is important to know about how the codes were created. Look for some kind of systematic process in the development of the codes, such as using general research questions that are stated prior to the research, questions that are generated during the study, language used in interview protocols, and emic data.

The most effective process for coming up with and using appropriate codes is to first read through the entire transcript. It is also good to take some pilot data, if possible, and generate some codes, have others do the same thing independently, then meet and discuss what makes best sense. When reading through the transcript again, identify initial codes, generating more codes than will be used as the final list, since some may only be used sparingly and are not critical to the study. Often, several individuals will code the same text to determine inter-coder agreement. This is usually done with a few transcriptions to make sure the coding is consistent.

The first sets of transcripts that are coded may be selected randomly or intentionally to be representative of different perspectives in the study (e.g., a student, teacher, and administrator). The coding of the remaining transcripts may be completed by different individuals. This is a good way to bring different perspectives to interpretation of the same data.

Note in Excerpt 13.1 how the researchers first read transcripts prior to actual coding, followed by inter-coder agreement to enhance validity/trustworthiness.

An example of a coded interview transcript, from a study Dr. Naff conducted on the decision-making processes of first-generation college students, is illustrated in Figure 13.2. Note that it is possible to have multiple codes for a single segment. You will also see that some of the codes were connected to categories like "COST," "CAPITAL," or "VALUE." The transcript also shows the value of using probes to elicit rich responses that provide greater depth and detail. The research team for this study coded this transcript with computer software that allowed for quick assigning of codes and adding of memos in the margins. The memos helped us talk through our coding decisions and detect emerging themes across participants.

EXCERPT 13.1

Coding Transcripts

Interviews were transcribed verbatim.... The first author read all transcripts in full repeatedly to get a sense of the whole (immersion in data), then re-read assigning key codes based on recurring concepts.... The codes were entered as free nodes ... and inductive thematic analysis was used to develop and interpret the themes. To increase the validity and interpretation of the data, the second author reviewed and coded each interview transcript to check for inter-code agreement. (p. 695)

SOURCE: Veitch, J., Arundell, L., Hume, C., & Ball, K. (2013). Children's perceptions of the factors helping them to be "resilient" to sedentary lifestyles. *Health Education Research, 28*, 692–703.

Check for Understanding 1

1a. What are the steps researchers use to analyze qualitative data?

1b. What are two sources for creating codes? Which of these is typically most valued, and why?

Figure 13.2 Example of Coded Interview Transcript

Tell me about what barriers you perceived when deciding to pursue college.

Well, we were obviously concerned about the financial cost. The grant money I received helped, but there was still a lot more we had to pay. –COST_FINANCIAL, CAPITAL_FINANCIAL

Memo: I wonder whether how first-generation students perceive financial cost is much different than continuing generation students?

What led you to decide to come to college, even though it was expensive?

It was just too important to me. It was too important to my family. For me to be the first to go, I couldn't give up that opportunity. Nothing was going to stand in my way. – VALUE_ATTAINMENT, CAPITAL_FAMILY

Memo: It looks like having a high sense of attainment value helped her push through the perceived cost.

It sounds like you received a lot of support from your family during this process?

They definitely wanted what was best for me. My parents didn't have much money to offer, but they gave me lots of moral support. They also didn't know much about how to navigate the college application or enrollment processes because they had never gone, so a lot of that I had to figure out on my own. – COST_EFFORT, CAPITAL_FAMILY, CAPITAL_FAMILY_LOW.

Memo: This is consistent with our other participants—having well-intentioned, supportive parents who are unable to offer much tangible support in the enrollment process.

Did knowing that you had to navigate your college applications on your own ever deter you from following through on your goal of going to college?

Not really. Don't get me wrong, it was very hard sometimes, but I also had a great school counselor who helped me along the way. I am not sure that I would be here without her. CAPITAL_SCHOOL, RESOURCEFULNESS

Memo: It is great that she had this resource (school capital), but she also had to be willing to take advantage of it (resourcefulness).

She showed you that you could do it.

Right. At first my confidence was really low, but once I submitted that first application, I knew that I could do it. I even started helping my friends with their applications. – SELF-EFFICACY_LOW, SELF-EFFICACY_HIGH, CAPITAL_PEERS

Memo: It sounds like her self-efficacy started low but increased. I wonder whether encountering this challenge made her even more confident than she otherwise would have been.

It sounds like your friends were also planning on going to college?

Yeah. Most of them were. – CAPITAL_PEERS

Memo: What a resource to have a friend group where most, if not all, are going to college.

How did they support you during this process?

We just gave each other a lot of moral support. I also think it helped to be a part of a friend group where it seemed like everyone was going to college. If any of us ended up not going, it would have been weird. It was like a good kind of pressure, you know? – CAPITAL_PEERS, COST_SOCIAL_LOW

Memo: While some students might have felt like they were giving up something else of value (e.g., time with friends) to pursue college, she experienced the opposite. Social/opportunity cost was low because of her peer capital.

Were any of them going to be the first in their family to go too?

I think I was the only one in our group. That actually gave me a sense of pride. It made me feel special.– VALUE_ATTAINMENT

Memo: Attainment value of college seems to be a consistent theme across participants. It seems to help them push through perceived barriers.

Step 2: Identify Categories

Learning Outcome 13.2 Know how to analyze and interpret qualitative data, to identify patterns and to develop themes.

In the second step, coded data are analyzed inductively to form a much smaller number of *categories*. This synthesis and reduction of data can be arduous. Before the wide usage of computers, often each segment of text would be sorted into piles according to different codes. Imagine a table with 30 piles of cards, each pile having 10 to 50 or more data elements! Fortunately, there are many qualitative data analysis software programs available that make this process intuitive and efficient. Table 13.1 describes features of four prominent software programs to give you a sense of what they can accomplish. While

Table 13.1. Qualitative Analysis Software Program Features

Program	Features
ATLAS.ti	• Upload documents, audio files, or video files • Codebook manager for creating and storing codes • Code data by right clicking on quote and selecting "add codes" • Comment box available for adding memos and notes to quotes • Available in online and desktop versions • Ability to collaborate with multiple researchers and calibrate coding • Automatic coding available
Dedoose	• Upload documents, audio files, or video files • Available online only • Visualize coding results • Ability to collaborate with multiple researchers and calibrate coding • Code data by selecting quote and then clicking on the code from a list • Automatic "upcoding" to categorize codes
MAXQDA	• Upload documents, audio files, or video files • Ability to create short summaries of texts ("paraphrases") while coding • Code by selecting quotes and clicking on codes in split screen • Visualize coding results • Split screen feature for comparing documents side by side • Ability to transcribe audio in the software • Automatic coding available
NVivo	• Upload documents, audio files, or video files • Create hierarchies of codes by organizing them into "nodes" (categories) • Code by selecting quote and clicking on "code" button or right clicking • Visualize coding results • Ability to collaborate with multiple researchers and calibrate coding • Available in desktop version • Automatic coding available

most qualitative software programs have a cost associated with using them, they may also be available for free through universities for students and faculty.

The researcher's job in summarizing is to examine all the entries that have related codes and organize and synthesize them to capture the essence of the information. In organizing codes look for superordinate and subordinate concepts. For example, in a study of first-generation college students, a code from an interview transcript segment "As a first-generation college student I was really concerned about expectations from the rest of my family" could be "family expectations." A comment such as "My parents told me I could do as well as other freshmen" could be a subordinate code "positive expectations" under "family expectations.

Codes are then examined to see whether they fall into more general groupings. These are typically called *categories* (or sometimes *themes*). A **category**, then, is formed from coded data as a more general and abstract idea that represents the meaning of similarly coded information. There are both major and subcategories in most studies, as illustrated in Excerpt 13.2.

EXCERPT 13.2

Categories and Subcategories

Categories and themes were identified and organized into tables and subcategories.... Each of these [two main] categories was broken down and refined into subcategories by deleting, conflating, and remaining as needed.... Based on the analysis of these categories and subcategories the overarching theme of the valuable and unessential was developed. (p. 270)

SOURCE: Sherwood, S. A. S., & Reifel, S. (2013). Valuable and unessential: The paradox of preservice teachers' beliefs about the role of play in learning. *Journal of Research in Childhood Education, 27,* 267–282.

EXCERPT 13.3

Recursive Analysis

Moreover, iterative methods were used to identify themes in the participant narratives. I fully transcribed each interview and read through the transcripts several times to pinpoint salient themes, patterns and relationships.... I coded the transcripts while reading them, and I repeatedly reevaluated my coding scheme. I looked for consistency and contradictions with and across the mother's narratives. Furthermore, I drafted three sets of memos that captured my preliminary analysis of the individual, school-based and cross-participant findings. Once I was confident of the trustworthiness and usefulness of my coding scheme, I clustered my data by code and did a final review. Inductive analytical methods were used to confirm or disconfirm the salience of my theoretical framework. (p. 498)

SOURCE: Cooper, C. W. (2008). School choice as "motherwork": Valuing African-American women's educational advocacy and resistance. *International Journal of Qualitative Studies in Education, 20*(5), 491–512.

When the researcher is engaged in forming categories, the very important **recursive** process occurs. The recursive process in this stage of the analysis is iterative. It involves the repeated application of a category to fit codes and data segments. This is sometimes called **constant comparison**, in which the researcher is continually searching for both supporting and contrary evidence about the meaning of the category. This reinforces the idea that qualitative research is an ongoing, active, and often cyclical process of analyzing and re-analyzing data. The recursive process is usually reported as part of data analysis, as illustrated in Excerpt 13.3.

Regular review of field notes to plan next steps keeps you close to the data and familiar with major themes. There is a need to write many observer memos as you are interviewing, observing, or reviewing documents, because these comments form the basis of important insights and categories. Sometimes playing with analogies and metaphors will provide an overview of organization of ideas.

Qualitative data are stored in many ways. Often data are kept on the software used for analysis, particularly if it allows for sharing and collaboration between researchers on a team. Data are also stored on a shared spreadsheet, such as in an online drive. The benefit of this approach is that it can be easier to collaborate as a research team with the data and store it for later use, particularly if the qualitative software is subscription

Authors' Reflection *With the variety of software now available for conducting qualitative analyses, it is possible you may have varied preferences on your team for what to use. Some software includes functionality that allow you to actively collaborate in the software by seeing the coding of your teammates. Other software is best used individually and then discussed later as a group. From our experience, it can be helpful to use the same software initially but then allow people to use their preferred programs for analysis of subsequent transcripts once the team agrees on a coding approach. Regardless of the software used, we strongly suggest the use of a common program for storing the data after analysis since it is important for team members to have ready access to it when writing up the findings.*

based. Whatever method you use for storing qualitative data, it needs to remain secure (just like quantitative data) according to IRB standards at your university or institution. This is critical if there is potentially identifiable information in the data such as names, demographics, or locations.

Step 3: Data Interpretation

In the third step, relationships among the categories and patterns are examined to suggest generalizations, models, and conclusions. At this point, you will interpret the findings inductively, synthesizing the information and drawing inferences about how categories may be sequenced, converged, subsumed, or otherwise connected or related. This is *pattern-seeking*. You essentially reveal what you have found and what it means by describing connectedness among the categories, giving due consideration to context and researcher positionality. This step is most closely related to what is used to answer the research questions.

The process of *pattern-seeking* begins with the researcher's informed hunches and ideas as data are being collected and interpreted. Once tentative patterns are identified, additional data are examined to determine whether they are consistent with that pattern. It is also common to have different researchers review data independently to see whether they come up with the same patterns. This is a more deductive process, one in which there is a search for negative or discrepant data that would not support the pattern (this is also a method for establishing trustworthiness). Discrepant data are used to modify the pattern. Pattern-seeking is also characterized by enlarging, combining, subsuming, and creating new categories that make sense logically.

Often, overarching visual models, in the form of a diagram or chart, are created to show the relationships among several themes and patterns. Figure 13.3 is a model Dr. Naff developed for his dissertation, which was a multiple case study of students attending a high-poverty urban high school who were aspiring to be the first in

Figure 13.3 Contextualized First-Generation Student Decision Making About Attending College

SOURCE: Naff, 2017, p. 69.

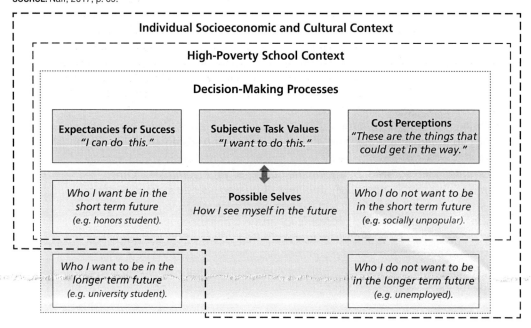

their families to go to college. The study explored how the students perceived themselves in the future ("possible" selves), how those perceptions informed their present decision-making processes about college (using an expectancy value theory framework), as well as how their sociocultural experiences contextualized those perceptions and decision-making processes. While elements of the study were informed by existing theory, their contextualized experiences required more inductive analysis. What resulted was a rich exploration of how they made decisions about pursuing 4-year college in an environment in which a college-going "possible self" was not often reinforced by relevant examples in their school and community where college attendance and completion was rare.

For each major finding and interpretation, actual quotes from participants, field notes, or documents are used to illustrate the points and enliven the results. The model also gives the reader an opportunity to see how the researcher has been thinking and the basis for conclusions. Because the analysis depends on the researcher, when reading qualitative studies, it is best to know the individual's perspectives, background, and theoretical orientation.

Excerpt 13.4 is from a case study of how school employees cope emotionally during changes in educational conditions. Note how participant quotes are used to illustrate points. Excerpt 13.5 is from an interview study with 16 female first-generation students of color as they pursued higher education. Quotes were used to support themes that converged to support three student profiles that illustrated how the students demonstrated resilience.

EXCERPTS 13.4 AND 13.5
Use of Participant Quotes

Participants employed various coping strategies. They resorted to a support network to cope with fear and anxiety: "We sought help from our colleagues to resolve negative feelings and deal with these changes. We spoke to each other, reflected on the changes, and compared our strategies" (T2). Also, participants described several personal characteristics that helped them cope, such as their motivation for learning: "I am naturally curious and like to keep learning for the benefit of our students and their learning. I do not get concerned or worried; I get excited to learn and improve" (T5). Another participant described how her motivation for learning helped her face challenges: "I never for a second hesitated to learn and explore new ideas and strategies. I am happy and comfortable learning and improving myself. These are part of my personal characteristics, which helped me face challenges of change" (T6). Another participant described how her motivation to learn helped her cope: "I attended all kinds of workshops, even if they were not mandatory, to cope with the demands of change. I am dedicated to improving myself and learning, and I get excited about new ideas and applying them." (p. 56)

SOURCE: Karami-Akkary, R., Mahfouz, J., & Mansour, S. (2018). Sustaining school-based improvement: Considering emotional responses to change. *Journal of Educational Administration, 57*(1), 50–67.

Even though some students had encountered challenging family influences, such as siblings or cousins who had stopped attending school, or others who were not fully supportive of their educational trajectories, virtually all students found strength in their families, echoing Goffen's (2009) findings. In fact, one of the most prevalent indicators in the data was the value most students' families placed on education—a clear facilitative factor. As Nina put it, "school was just important" in her family. Tara's father had perpetuated

> the value of education as part of their Filipino culture even with his limited formal schooling. Likewise, Alice stated, "We had a lot of pressure from our family. So, although they weren't there physically to tutor us or help us, academically they were constantly reinforcing us to do well." Alice's Korean parents could not assist her with English courses, presenting a potential situational factor; yet, they nevertheless instilled a desire for education. (p. 444)
>
> SOURCE: Portnoi, L. M., & Kwong, T. M. (2019). Employing resistance and resilience in pursuing K-12 schooling and higher education: Lived experiences of successful female first-generation students of color. *Urban Education, 54*(3), 430–458.

Check for Understanding 2

2a. Why is recursive analysis important in analyzing qualitative data?

2b. What is the relationship between codes, themes, and pattern-seeking?

Validity / Trustworthiness

Learning Outcome 13.3 Understand the processes of establishing validity/ trustworthiness and transferability for qualitative studies.

The validity/trustworthiness of qualitative research was introduced in Chapter 11, with nine "threats" that need to be considered: context insensitivity, inadequate participant perspectives, researcher bias, inadequate transparency, inauthenticity, instrumentation, confirmability, sampling, and reactivity. In this chapter, we focus on specific procedures and techniques to minimize these threats. **Validity/ trustworthiness** addresses whether the data collection strategies and analyses warrant the findings and claims. In good qualitative studies the procedures will assure readers that appropriate evidence has been gathered and analyzed in a way that justifies what is reported, interpreted, and concluded. A valid/trustworthy qualitative study has value; it has been carefully done so that the findings are close to the signal.

Here are some examples of questions researchers might ask to address validity/ trustworthiness:

- Are the themes and the patterns that emerge from the data reasonable?
- Are they accurate, consistent, and meaningful?
- Are they authentic to the participants represented in the study?
- How much confidence is there in the results and conclusions?
- Could a case be made that the findings could transfer to others?

Strategies for Establishing Validity / Trustworthiness

The validity/trustworthiness of a qualitative study is determined from a holistic perspective. As you will see, many of the nine following strategies (Creswell & Guetterman, 2019) relate directly to the threats. Validity, then, is strengthened by the extent to which these strategies are implemented.

1. *Prolonged engagement.* It is important for the researcher to be closely engaged with the participants and the setting to provide details for the narrative that presents the results. This suggests a need to have extensive experience and close involvement.

There must be sufficient engagement so additional time in the setting or with the participants would not change the results. Think of prolonged engagement resulting in *saturation*—after which additional observations or interviews or document review would not add new findings. Prolonged engagement assures adequate participant perspectives and authenticity.

2. *Member checking.* **Member checking** is completed when the researcher asks the participants to review transcripts, interpretations, and conclusions to confirm accuracy and authenticity. This could be accomplished by having participants review interviewer or observer conclusions about what was said or done if there is no recorded transcript. For example, an interviewer can summarize his or her notes at the end of the interview to see whether the notes accurately reflect the point of view of the participants. The researcher can also check with the participants about codes, categories, themes, patterns, and other findings to see whether these are viewed by the participants as fair, reasonable, accurate, and complete. This can be done by sharing drafts of final products, in writing or by interviews, and allowing participants opportunities to make comments. Qualitative research literature often refers to member checking as the most important method for establishing validity/trustworthiness because it reviews the data and findings directly with the participants who provided them. Member checking helps address confirmability, inadequate participant perspectives, and inauthenticity to improve trustworthiness. Two types of member checking (there are actually subcategories of member checking) are described in Excerpt 13.6 in a study that used interview data.

EXCERPT 13.6

Member Checking

Two member checks were conducted with participants. First, each participant received an electronic transcript of her interview and was invited to participate in a member-check session to verify the ideas expressed in her interview.... Students were asked... if anything in the transcript was in error or concerned them.... In addition... each preservice teacher received an electronic version of preliminary findings and was asked for their feedback. (pp. 270–271)

SOURCE: Sherwood, S. A. S., & Reifel, S. (2013). Valuable and unessential: The paradox of preservice teachers' beliefs about the role of play in learning. *Journal of Research in Childhood Education, 27,* 267–282.

---

3. *Triangulation.* **Triangulation** addresses confirmability. It is a technique that seeks convergence of findings, cross validation, among different sources and methods of data collection. That is, data are collected from different individuals at different times or in different places, or several sources of data are used to see whether the results are consistent. For example, if researchers are studying student engagement in a class, they could observe the students, interview the students, and ask the teacher for their opinion. Or, the effectiveness of staff development could be judged by observing workshops and interviewing the participating teachers. If the results from each source of data point to the same conclusion, then the researcher has *triangulated* the findings (this process does not need three or more sources of data; it can be done with two). Triangulation is a widely used technique for establishing trustworthy findings, especially in case study research. In Excerpts 13.7 and 13.8, the researchers used triangulation in their studies.

> ## EXCERPTS 13.7 AND 13.8
> # Triangulation
>
> Data sources included classroom observations, teacher interviews, and curriculum fidelity data. Although fidelity data provided some information about teacher responses to the PD, triangulating this data with teacher accounts of adapting the curriculum to their particular context enabled more nuanced understandings about how teachers adapt information from PD sessions to their particular teaching contexts. (p. 231)
>
> **SOURCE:** Baker, M. (2018). Early childhood teachers at the center: A qualitative case study of professional development in an urban district. *Early Childhood Education Journal, 46,* 231–240.
>
> ---
>
> Trustworthiness was established by first triangulating the data using multiple data sources, including teacher questionnaires, teacher interviews, and student interviews. Second, the teachers reviewed the transcribed interviews. This member-checking procedure (Creswell & Miller, 2000) permitted teachers to verify the content of the interviews and offer any clarification of points, if needed.... Finally, the data were examined by and discussed with a peer debriefer trained in qualitative research. (p. 190)
>
> **SOURCE:** Xiang, P., Solomon, M. A., & McBride, R. E. (2006). Teachers' and students' conceptions of ability in elementary physical education. *Research Quarterly for Exercise and Sport, 77*(2), 185–194.

4. *Negative case analysis.* Actively looking for findings that present discrepant information is needed to reflect the reality that not all data will provide the same information, and to change results when justified to establish confirmability. Presenting negative cases enhances the trustworthiness of the study because it shows that the researchers are examining the cases in detail. In other words, it is helpful for the researchers to present the extent to which information that contradicts themes, patterns, and overall results is contained in the data. This technique can also emphasize the conditions under which a theme or pattern may not hold, which can provide invaluable insights.

5. *Peer debriefing.* Peer debriefing is completed by asking a colleague or another person to review the study for credibility and determine whether the results seem to follow from the data. Someone who is knowledgeable about the topic and qualitative analyses, but sufficiently detached to provide a fresh perspective, is preferred. That person's own biases should be reflected in their evaluation, which gives feedback about the selection and meaning of categories, themes, patterns, and study conclusions. Peer debriefing is a common technique to address both researcher bias and confirmability.

6. *External audit.* An external audit is similar to peer debriefing. An external auditor, however, is unfamiliar with the project and provides a more objective review. Like a peer debriefer, the external auditor examines all aspects of the study to look for coherence, reasonableness, accuracy, data analysis, interpretation, and conclusions, and points out weaknesses or "threats" to validity/trustworthiness.

7. *Researcher reflection.* The researcher's self-reflection of possible biases, background, and values supports the credibility of the study. It is important to know that the researcher understands how their own perspectives and positionality—shaped by gender, socioeconomic status, or position (among other factors)—will influence their expectations, interpretations, and conclusions. Good researchers know that their subjectivity may influence results, and direct examination of this subjectivity, through reflection, adds to validity/trustworthiness by mitigating the threat

EXCERPT 13.9

Researcher Reflection

My social positionality as a Caucasian, able-bodied male may have detracted from the study because of my culturally- and socially-imposed blinders to the realities of other peoples' experiences different from my own—which may have been manifested in the classroom to an important extent without my even knowing it. Using the strategy of progressive subjectivity (Guba and Lincoln, 1989) to record my initial and on-going expectations of how I thought authority would be negotiated in the classroom, however, helped assure that I moved beyond my initial preconceptions and effectively derived the finds from the actual words and actions of participants. (p. 104)

SOURCE: Brubaker, N. D. (2009). Negotiating authority in an undergraduate teacher education course: A qualitative investigation. *Teacher Education Quarterly, 36*(4), 99–118.

of researcher bias. This is reflected in Excerpt 13.9. Note the use of "positionality" and "progressive subjectivity" as terms that address researcher preconceptions and expectations.

8. *Thick descriptions.* Credible qualitative studies use detailed, in-depth, thorough, and extensive descriptions—which are sometimes described as "thick" and/or "rich." That is, there is abundant use of detail. This enhances validity/trustworthiness because it indicates extensive engagement with the data and an appreciation of how all information is valuable. It enables the reader to understand the complexity and realism of the site and participants. For example, a rich, detailed description of a college student commons may be needed to understand the dynamics of students meeting there for discussions with faculty. Thick descriptions include presenting verbatim language from participants and detailed field notes. The research procedures should also be described in detail. Using thick descriptions addresses context insensitivity and inauthenticity threats to validity.

Note in Excerpt 13.10 how multiple strategies are employed to ensure validity/trustworthiness.

EXCERPT 13.10

Establishing Validity/Trustworthiness

The researchers implemented numerous strategies to enhance the integrity of this study.... First, they all practiced transparency (Creswell, 2013) to articulate biases that might influence data analyses. Triangulation (Creswell, 2013) was used (a) to design the interview questions through the literature and the focus group to create culturally respectful interview questions.... Member checking (Creswell, 2013) was done with a sample of five respondents. Searches for disconfirming evidence and negative cases (Creswell, 2013) were undertaken in three separate efforts: the analysis of the last five transcripts, the analysis of transcripts based on the interviewers' ethnicity, and the analysis of African American and non-African American transcripts to assess for substantive differences. (p. 58)

SOURCE: Collarhide, C. T., Bowen, N. V., Baker, C. A., Kassoy, F. R., Mayes, R. D., & Baughman, A. M. (2013). Exploring the work experiences of school counselors of color, *Professional School Counseling, 17*(1), 52–62. American School Counselor Association.

The Hedgehog and Fox Employ Different Strategies

It's pretty clear that after some interviews, several of the students are saying that their experience with sports, compared to other factors, has resulted in better grades. I'm ready to conclude that being in sports will likely enhance grades.

Some of the students indicate that being involved with sports has resulted in better grades. It would be good to check my conclusions with the students directly. It may also be helpful to see whether parents notice a connection between sports and grades. I'll also check carefully for discrepant cases—students who think being in sports has had a negative impact on their grades. In addition, I need to explore in greater depth why students feel the way they do about being in sports and what it is about being in sports that would help them with schoolwork.

Authors' Reflection *While reflection by the researcher at the completion of a study is an important step for establishing validity/trustworthiness in the findings of a qualitative study, this isn't the only time that this should occur. From the onset, the researcher needs to be critically reflexive of why they decided to pursue this study, the purpose behind what theories are included in the conceptual framework, how the research questions are worded, what data sources are selected, how interview protocols are worded and administered, and how the data are interpreted. As the primary instrument for data collection and analysis, the researcher can influence the direction and outcomes of a study at many stages. Consequently, it is important to remain critically reflexive, keeping notes along the way.*

Transferability

The principle of "generalizability" in qualitative studies is very different from what is used for quantitative studies. In qualitative studies, there is no planned intent to generalize to other participants, settings, instruments, interventions, or procedures. There is little or no emphasis on replications, except with some case study research. Researchers engaged in qualitative studies use the term *transferability,* rather than generalizability. **Transferability** refers to the appropriateness of applying the results to other contexts and settings. A transferable finding is one where the results may resonate with the reader in some way that will be useful in a similar context, with similar individuals. For example, the voices of students struggling with homelessness in a study may feel familiar to a school social worker, offering an empirical foundation for future work with students in a similar situation.

Transferability is enhanced by a thick description of the site, participants, and procedures used to collect data. This makes it easier for others to know whether or not there is a good fit between their situation and the context in which the data were collected. In qualitative research, the person who wants to use findings from one study in their context, rather than the researcher of the original study, is responsible for determining transferability, though the researcher often addresses it. If the contextual, participant, and procedural details match, the user has greater confidence that it is appropriate to "generalize" the findings.

While lack of generalizability is often considered a limitation of qualitative research, transferability can be a strength. A well-designed quantitative study may use survey or secondary data that has potentially generalizable implications, but the results may not be particularly relevant or actionable to the reader. A limitation of quantitative research is that we learn little about the experiences of the participants in a way that enhances our confidence that the results are applicable. When the goal of the qualitative research is to offer results that may be relationally valid and may inform future research or practice with people who have lived a particular phenomenon, transferability becomes an asset.

Check for Understanding 3

3a. How are triangulation and member checking used to enhance credibility of qualitative research?

3b. What is the difference between transferability in qualitative studies and external validity in quantitative studies?

Reporting Qualitative Findings

Learning Outcome 13.4 Differentiate among different strategies for reporting qualitative findings, including how to establish an effective balance between participant quotes and narrative.

In contrast with quantitative reporting of results, qualitative studies rely on a less standardized format in which the goal is to use selected data as evidence of derived categories, patterns, themes, and conclusions. In this section, we review several considerations for effective reporting of qualitative findings.

Selecting Quotes for Use in the Reporting Narrative

For Dr. Naff's dissertation, over 17 hours of audio interview data were collected. This resulted in hundreds of pages of interview transcripts to analyze, code, and interpret. However, for the sake of parsimony, the majority of the quotes from participants did not appear in the final manuscript (much to the relief of the dissertation committee!). It can be difficult to winnow participants' comments into a small number of exemplary quotes. You may feel compelled to honor the voices of the participants by including all of their perspectives. However, there are methods for ensuring that participant voices are appropriately incorporated without making the findings section excessively lengthy. Here are four important reminders and guidelines that will help:

1. *Participant perspectives can contribute to the theme, even if their quotes are not used.* After coding interview data, the researcher establishes themes based on patterns detected across participants' responses. This typically requires the incorporation

of multiple perspectives reflecting a similar sentiment. Thus, even if a participant is not quoted to illustrate a particular theme, there is still a good chance that the interview data contributed to the finding.

2. *Some participants illustrate particular themes better than others.* Similar to the previous point, you will likely find that some participant quotes illustrate a finding much better than others. These may be quotes that stand out to you throughout your analysis as being particularly exemplary of a particular theme. These quotes are good to incorporate into the narrative of your report. Others may not capture the finding as effectively, even if they supported its development by illustrating that multiple participants offered similar accounts.

3. *Not everything collected in an interview is worth including.* Think about the last in-depth conversation you had with someone. Was every piece of it worth sharing? Were there some things that you said that were more or less meaningful than others? Similarly, interviews are conversations between a researcher and participant. Not everything stated in the interview will be worth reporting, although it may help provide the researcher with helpful context during analysis.

4. *It is helpful to use quotes from several participants.* To the extent possible, it is best to use quotes from several participants when writing up qualitative findings. This provides a convincing rationale for commonality among the participants. Therefore, it is important to keep track of which quotes came from which participant during analysis and reporting. Otherwise, it is possible that the researcher may believe that a particular sentiment is well supported across several interviews when it is actually just a point of elaboration for one participant, which would be less indicative of a theme. How to attribute quotes to participants is also an important consideration, as discussed later in this section.

Balancing Narrative with Participant Quotes

There is no one right way to write a qualitative findings section. The researcher needs to thoughtfully balance the use of narrative describing the analysis of the data with the incorporation of quotes to provide supportive evidence. Heavy reliance on narrative without sufficient quotes may feel like conjecture to the reader, while heavy use of quotes without enough narrative can make the analysis feel disconnected and superficial. Striking this balance will likely require multiple drafts of a findings section, with feedback from other members of a research team or colleagues to make sure that the key points are clear and well supported. Take the following examples from a hypothetical study of student perceptions of career and technical education (CTE) courses. The first relies too heavily on narrative:

Example A (not enough quotes):

> Students discussed their hesitancy to participate in CTE courses. They perceived them as not being academically challenging and several were concerned that participation would potentially harm their grade point average as the classes were not at the honors level and therefore did not award quality points for the added rigor. Other students, however, felt that these courses were challenging but did not receive the recognition they deserved for the amount of rigor involved. This contrast in perspectives illustrated how some students may have been interested in CTE but hesitated to enroll due to their perception of rigor, which other students argued to be an inaccurate account of the CTE workload.

In the above example, the reader is left wondering about what students actually had to say about CTE courses. How did the researcher know that they were interested but unwilling to enroll? What statements did students make that suggested that they were concerned about the impact on their GPA if they took the courses? Did the students offering divergent perspectives on this topic base this on their experiences taking a CTE course or were they simply repeating something they heard? Not only is the incorporation of participant quotes foundational to the constructivist nature of most qualitative inquiry, it is also necessary for providing sufficient evidence to support the researcher's claims.

The following example incorporates quotes from multiple participants in the same hypothetical study, but lacks in narrative to pull them together.

Example B (not enough narrative):
Students discussed how they felt about CTE courses in their school. Said one student:

> My weighted GPA is already above a 4.0, so even if I got an A in a CTE class it would hurt me because it would bring down my overall average. I have worked hard in honors and AP classes to bring up my GPA.

Said another:

> I heard those classes are not that hard and aren't good for someone who wants to go to college.

Not every student agreed that CTE courses were not sufficiently rigorous. As one student indicated:

> I have taken culinary arts for the past 2 years, and it is one of my hardest classes. We have to learn things from a textbook and classroom lectures, but we also have to work in a kitchen to prepare food for other students. The grading is also really strict in that class, so I have to stay on top of everything to do well. It frustrates me when people say that classes like that aren't as hard and I don't know why we can't get honors credit for them.

The above example prioritizes student voice well, but without a synthesizing narrative it does little to elaborate on the importance of what they are saying. It is essentially a list of quotes, rather than any sort of empirical analysis. The reader is left wondering, "What is the nature of the connecting theme?"

The following example, from the same hypothetical study, more effectively balances the use of narrative and participant quotes.

Example C (balance of narrative and quotes):

> As students elaborated on their perceptions of CTE courses, they offered varying accounts of the level of rigor involved in the classes. This tended to largely be based on the additional quality GPA points assigned to honors and advanced placement classes that often did not apply to CTE, a point raised by more than half of the participants in the study. As one student reflected, this disincentivized enrollment in these classes, "My weighted GPA is already above a 4.0, so even if I got an A in a CTE class it would hurt me because it would bring down my overall average." Said another, "It might be useful to know how to do some of the things they teach in those courses, but I worry about how it would look on my transcript to have a non-honors class on my schedule." In addition to GPA implications, students sometimes based their perceptions of rigor in CTE on what they had heard from peers. As one student recalled, "I heard those classes are not that hard and aren't good for someone who wants to go to college." These perceptions reflected the implications of how students make decisions about the level of rigor in their classes and how this tends to be reinforced by not assigning honors level credit to CTE classes.

Conversely, about one third of students in the study indicated that they had taken these classes, and the majority of that subgroup argued that the perception of CTE being too easy was inaccurate. As one student advocated, the level of rigor in CTE could be robust.

I have taken culinary arts for the past 2 years, and it is one of my hardest classes. We have to learn things from a textbook and classroom lectures, but we also have to work in a kitchen to prepare food for other students. The grading is also really strict in that class, so I have to stay on top of everything to do well. It frustrates me when people say that classes like that aren't as hard and I don't know why we can't get honors credit for them.

In this example, the author incorporates quotes throughout the narrative to illustrate the analysis of how students make decisions about enrollment in CTE courses based on perceptions of rigor and GPA implications. Note that there is only one block quote used, while the other quotes are woven into the narrative. Using too many block quotes may pose concerns similar to example B where a findings section feels more like a list of quotes than analysis. Not using enough block quotes may lead to some of the signal of the findings getting lost in the narrative. There are often longer quotes from participants that are particularly exemplary of a theme and therefore merit being emphasized separate from the narrative. Again, the appropriate incorporation of block quotes may require feedback from other members of a research team or other colleagues who can indicate how effectively the writing conveys the meaning of the findings.

Confidentiality in Presenting Results

The protection of participant identities is particularly relevant to qualitative research because the foundational data included in a findings section typically includes quotes from individual participants. Researchers may use labels (e.g , participant 1, participant 2, etc.) when assigning quotes in a findings section. They may also use pseudonyms (fake names) to protect participant identities. The use of pseudonyms can be particularly helpful in case study research when individuals serve as the cases. The researcher might share the pseudonyms of participants along with some background information that could provide helpful context to understanding their responses, but here confidentiality needs to be protected. For example, this may include demographic variables like race/ethnicity, age, gender, year in school, or professional position. When attributing particular demographic variables to a pseudonym, it is important that it still not be possible to reasonably trace the responses back to any individual person. Protecting the identity of the site where the research was conducted can be helpful in this regard (e.g., using a pseudonym like "Rural Middle School."). However, it is possible (perhaps even likely) that someone in the site where the research was conducted will read the report and be aware that the study took place at that setting. Thus, it is imperative that the researcher keep the identity of participants anonymous when reporting their results. For example, if there was only one Asian American student in a school, the researcher might need to leave out the student's race/ethnicity or use a less identifiable descriptor in reporting (e.g., "racial minority").

When reporting qualitative findings, the researcher may choose to use participant numbers or pseudonyms when sharing quotes so the reader can keep track of who said what. This can be helpful in illustrating the breadth of perspectives included in a study or emphasizing how common a particular sentiment was (e.g., "Participants 1, 6, 7, and 11 each believed ..."). However, this can also become confusing or noisy to the reader, particularly if there are too many participants to keep track of in a report.

Instead, the researcher may consider using participant numbers as a way to keep track of responses internally, and instead report findings using terms like "the majority of participants indicated" or "about a third of participants expressed concerns about …" In the example from the hypothetical study of student perspectives of CTE courses, no participant numbers or pseudonyms were assigned, but the authors did share information about the frequency of responses. In a study with a small number of participants, it might be more appropriate to use pseudonyms to indicate which students said what, emphasizing to the reader the consistency of their responses. Regardless of whether the participants are identified in some way in the findings section, the researcher should consider offering contextual information to help the reader interpret the findings. For example, it was beneficial to know which students had previously taken a CTE course when understanding their perceptions of the level of rigor.

Check for Understanding 4

4a. What are three criteria for determining which participant quotes to include in summarizing the findings from qualitative research?

4b. Why is it important to achieve the right balance between participant quotes and the researcher's narrative?

Consumer (and Researcher) Tips
Criteria for Evaluating Qualitative Research

1. **The researcher's background, interests, and expectations should be clear.** Because a qualitative study is influenced greatly by the researcher's perspective, it is necessary to know the researcher's background and positionality—previous experiences, motivations for the research, and characteristics that may affect the recording or interpretation of data. Good researchers acknowledge how their expectations and preconceived ideas affect what they observe, interpret, and conclude.

2. **The conceptual and theoretical frameworks for the study should be clear.** The frameworks selected by the researcher guide the study and affect the results. You should look for an explanation of such frameworks early in the study, along with other thoughts and perceptions of the researcher.

3. **The method of selecting participants should be clear.** Qualitative studies often investigate a few persons in depth, rather than many participants more superficially. Consequently, the choice of participants is critical to the results of the study. The researcher should indicate how and why the participants were purposefully selected and the extent to which they are representative of others in the setting.

4. **Field notes should contain detailed descriptions of just about everything.** This goal may seem impossible, but it is one for which researchers strive. They should give detailed descriptions of behaviors and indicate the place, time, date, and physical setting of the observations. While it may not be possible to have entirely objective field notes, the descriptions should avoid using interpretive words such as *effective, positive attitude,* and *hostile.* Field notes that are not detailed suggest that the researcher may have missed important behaviors or may have biases that anticipated the results.

5. **Researchers should be trained to conduct data collection.** Because the researchers are directly involved in collecting data—either as observers, interviewers, or reviewers of documents and artifacts—they should be trained in the procedures

they use. Although adequate training is not easy to determine, you should look for some indication of previous experience that has been checked for adequacy. Untrained individuals are tempted to conduct qualitative research because it sounds so promising and interesting (and does not involve statistics). What often occurs, though, is that there is only a cursory level of involvement.

6. **Descriptions should be separate from interpretations.** In the core of a qualitative article, you will find descriptions of what was observed or recorded, along with interpretations of the data. The descriptions are the basis for the researcher's analyses and interpretations. If these descriptions are not clearly separate from the analyses and interpretations, it is difficult for you to judge the reasonableness and relative objectiveness of the researcher's claims (e.g., if there was selective presentation of data or if inductive processes seem reasonable on the basis of the data presented).

7. **The researcher should use multiple methods of data collection.** The quality of qualitative research is greatly enhanced by multiple methods of collecting data. If only one method is used, the findings may be significantly influenced by the limitations of the technique. Multiple methods allow for triangulation, which is the strongest type of evidence for the validity/trustworthiness of the findings. If the study is limited to one method, this limitation should be addressed.

8. **The study must include substantial amounts of time with participants.** Accurate and credible qualitative research requires the researcher to become intimately involved with what is being studied, to know it completely. It usually takes a long time to achieve this intense level of involvement. It cannot be done in interviews of 20 minutes or observations that last a few hours. You need to know how much time the researcher spent with the participants. Sufficient time will be reflected in the detailed data and in the researcher's depth of understanding.

9. **The validity/trustworthiness of the research should be addressed.** Researchers should summarize their procedures to enhance the validity/trustworthiness of the findings (e.g., triangulation, member checking, thick descriptions).

Authors' Reflection *Qualitative research often involves revisiting analysis and interpretation of findings with multiple steps taken to enhance validity/trustworthiness. We have found as well that it takes considerable time to do the recursive process thoughtfully and effectively. However, by making this investment in time and effort you will likely be rewarded with a depth of understanding that will have lasting and positive impacts.*

Key Terms

Category
Codes
   In-vivo
Constant comparison

Emic
Etic
Recursive
Transferability

Validity/Trustworthiness
   Member checking
   Triangulation

Discussion Questions

1. What are the advantages and disadvantages of using participant voices to create codes?
2. How are codes used to create categories?
3. What are some good strategies for creating categories and patterns?
4. What would be the *most efficient* ways to establish validity/trustworthiness?

5. What ways of establishing validity/trustworthiness have the greatest level of rigor?
6. Why is it important to illustrate major points with participant quotes?

Application Exercise

1. Identify someone who has recently conducted a qualitative study. Ask the individual about how they did the coding and how the codes were synthesized to result in categories and patterns. Ask about how the process unfolded, how much time it took, and what was most important in establishing validity/trustworthiness. Then compare their responses to suggestions in the text.

Check for Understanding Answers

1a. Create codes from data; create categories from coded data; create patterns from categories.

1b. From general research questions and interview protocols; from reading transcripts of participant voices or other text. Codes that arise from the participants' comments are most valued because they are more authentic and closer to participant understandings and representations.

2a. Because as new categories are formed, initial codes may need to be revised.

2b. Codes are combined to lead to themes; pattern-seeking shows how the themes are related.

3a. Triangulation verifies accuracy by showing the same findings from two or more sources; member checking strengthens accuracy by showing how participants verify transcripts, descriptive findings, and interpretations.

3b. Transferability is a more nuanced judgment about the applicability of findings to similar contexts and individuals, which generalizability is determined by specific attributes of participants, context, measures, and intervention.

4a. Identify the best or most exemplary example; use only selected quotes; include quotes from several individuals.

4b. Too many quotes or quotes that are too long tend to result in choppy presentation of "data" that are not sufficiently analyzed; too few quotes reduce confidence that the analysis is clearly based on participant voices.

Part IV
Mixed Methods and Action Research

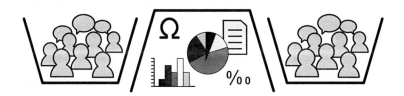

Three mixed methods designs are summarized in Chapter 14 to show how the strengths of both qualitative and quantitative data collection and analyses can be used to address research questions that either approach by itself is unable to answer. The designs show how variations in sequence, timing, and weighting of the qualitative and quantitative components are aligned with research questions. We also discuss mixed methods data analysis and how to report mixed methods findings.

The final type of study presented, action research, integrates principles of quantitative, qualitative, and mixed methods designs to investigate problems identified by practitioners. Chapter 15 explains the nature of action research, with an emphasis on the recursive action research cycle that is used to enhance the usefulness of the findings for the practitioner. By combining the strengths of the empirical process with actual issues and questions, individuals, groups, and schools will be able to immediately access results that lead to improvement in teaching, student learning, and other important practices.

Chapter 14
Mixed Methods Designs

By Sharon Zumbrunn and James McMillan

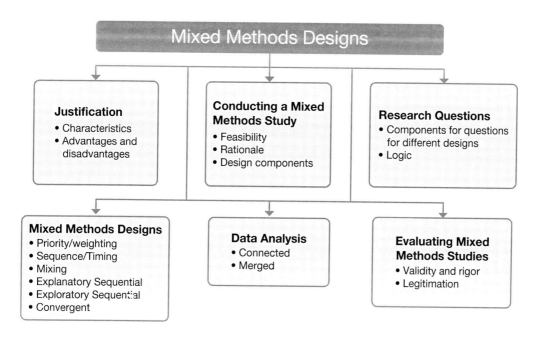

Mixed Methods Designs

Justification
- Characteristics
- Advantages and disadvantages

Conducting a Mixed Methods Study
- Feasibility
- Rationale
- Design components

Research Questions
- Components for questions for different designs
- Logic

Mixed Methods Designs
- Priority/weighting
- Sequence/Timing
- Mixing
- Explanatory Sequential
- Exploratory Sequential
- Convergent

Data Analysis
- Connected
- Merged

Evaluating Mixed Methods Studies
- Validity and rigor
- Legitimation

 ## Learning Outcomes

14.1 Identify the major characteristics, advantages, and disadvantages of mixed methods research.

14.2 Describe the steps in conducting mixed methods studies.

14.3 Classify, diagram, and know when to use different mixed methods designs.

14.4 Know the criteria for evaluating the quality of mixed methods research.

Chapter Road Map

Now we look in more detail at a relatively recent and increasingly popular approach to empirical research—mixed methods. Mixed methods designs are grounded in the idea that we can take the best of quantitative and qualitative designs and combine them in a single study to obtain knowledge and insights that are otherwise not attainable. In this chapter, we take a look at all aspects of crafting, conducting, reporting, and evaluating these intriguing designs.

Why Mixed Methods Studies?

Learning Outcome 14.1 Identify the major characteristics, advantages, and disadvantages of mixed methods research.

Quantitative approaches to educational research were dominant during the first seven decades of the 20th century, then qualitative became popular, beginning around 1980. Now there is a third approach: **mixed methods**. Why do we have this third approach to conducting research? Why is it needed, given the acceptance of both quantitative and qualitative methods? The answer rests, in part, on the limitations of each of these two traditions, and the realization that sometimes the best approach to answering important research questions is to use both qualitative and quantitative methods in the same study. This is especially the case when the goal or purpose of the research is to obtain an understanding of both outcomes (products) and explanations of outcomes (processes). For example, quantitative evidence gathered from teacher surveys might help a school administrator understand how teachers think and feel about the implementation of a new policy, and qualitative interviews with teachers might help explain the barriers or resistance teachers perceive that make it difficult for them to implement the new policy.

Mixed methods designs are also useful when the results of quantitative data collection and analysis do not adequately explain results, and additional data are needed to help interpret the findings. This is especially beneficial when the outcomes for individuals or a small group differ in significant ways from the pattern of results for the majority of the sample or from researcher expectations. Finally, researchers might choose to use mixed methods designs when they first need to identify key concepts and themes (through qualitative data collection) to then design quantitative techniques to investigate the problem further. In these situations, the qualitative data collection and analysis provide useful information to the researcher by highlighting the important factors and relevant questions that become the focus of subsequent quantitative investigations. In Excerpt 14.1, note how the authors delineate their justification for using a mixed methods study to investigate college students' service involvements.

EXCERPT 14.1

Justification for a Mixed Methods Design

In this study we use mixed methods to answer the following research questions:

1. How do the science teachers in the study describe the relevance of their course content and communicate these views in their daily interactions with students?

2. To what degree do the students in the study perceive their daily course content and the domain of science as useful?

3. To what extent is the way that teachers describe and communicate relevance related to students' beliefs about the utility of daily course content and the domain of science more generally?

As we endeavor to answer each of these questions, we will consider the role that perceptions of competence, interest, and gender, play with respect to teachers' relevance-related beliefs and behaviors, students' utility perceptions, and the relationship between the two.

The use of mixed methods is critical to addressing these questions. Qualitative methods enable us to gain a rich descriptive understanding of how a small number of teachers think about the relevance of their course content and how they communicate this relevance to their students during instruction. But these data alone cannot illuminate whether and how teachers' statements shape their students' perceptions. Quantitative methods allow us to gather data on the utility perceptions of a large number of students in these teachers' classrooms. The mixing of methods allows us to consider the relations between teachers' talk and students' perceptions, while also examining whether these associations vary systematically by student characteristics like prior interest, perceived competence, and gender. Mixing also facilitates triangulation, complementarity (Greene, Caracelli, & Graham, 1989) and completeness (Bryman, 2006) across multiple sources of data to provide a more comprehensive and coherent account of how teachers think about and enact relevance and how this influences students' perceptions of science utility. (p. 11)

SOURCE: Schmidt, J. A., Kafkas, S. S., Maier, K. S., Shumow, L., & Kackar-Cam, H. Z. (2018). Why are we learning this? Using mixed methods to understand teachers' relevance statements and how they shape middle school students' perceptions of science utility. *Contemporary Educational Psychology, 57*, 9–31.

Consider an investigation about the relationship between high-stakes testing results and the dropout rate. On the surface, this question lends itself nicely to a non-experimental, quantitative study in which characteristics of students, including scores on high-stakes tests, can be entered into a regression model to determine whether performance on the tests (once other variables have been "controlled") predicts dropping out. On a deeper level, though, it also would be helpful to understand *why* students did not perform better on the tests and *how* failure to pass high-stakes tests affects students' motivation to graduate. These issues could be studied more effectively with qualitative data gathered from student and teacher interviews. By combining the quantitative data with qualitative data, a more complete understanding of the relationship between the variables can be obtained, and incomplete, inconsistent, or unexplained findings can be clarified and resolved.

It is important, then, to clearly identify and explain your reasons for using both quantitative and qualitative methods in a single investigation. Readers should have enough information about why you have chosen a mixed methods design to be able to determine for themselves whether your methods are justified. Creswell and Plano Clark (2017) suggest that researchers devote a paragraph to describe the purpose for the study that includes four topics: (1) the overall intent of the study, (2) the type of design, (3) the types of quantitative and qualitative data to be collected, and (4) the insight that will be gained from integrating the data. By including these four elements, there will be a clear logic in the justification for using mixed methods.

Care must be taken when "mixing" methods, however. Effective integration depends on the thoughtful design of all components included in the work. At its heart, mixed methods studies use more than one method in a single study in an integrative fashion so the sum is greater than the parts.

Mixed methods research designs are used in a number of different fields, not just education; other terms are sometimes used, including *mixed, multiple methods, multi-methods, multitrait, combined, blended, hybrid,* and *integrative research,* although *mixed methods* (sometimes *mixed-methods*) is the term most frequently used. You also will find different ideas about what constitutes mixed methods, and that there is a trend toward using the term rather liberally to include any study that has some degree of both quantitative and qualitative methods. Our perspective is that an investigation is considered to be mixed methods when there is an *integrative approach* in which substantive quantitative and qualitative data are gathered, analyzed, "mixed," and reported. This is what makes mixed methods studies unique and results in enhancement, insight, clarification, and explanation that would not be possible if one method was used without the other.

Advantages and Disadvantages of Using Mixed Methods Designs

There are several advantages to using mixed methods designs when conducting research (refer to Table 14.1). The two most significant advantages are (1) the ability to provide a more thorough understanding of a research problem or issue because of the opportunity to examine multiple forms of data that are more comprehensive than data that might be collected via either quantitative or qualitative methods alone, and (2) the ability to answer complex research questions that cannot be addressed through the use of quantitative or qualitative methods alone. In addition, the use of mixed methods allows us to capitalize on what are viewed as the strengths of one method in a way that compensates for what have typically been viewed as the weaknesses of the other. These are particularly relevant given the nature and complexity of most educational settings. Focusing on an outcome (e.g., student achievement) does not necessarily help us understand how we "get there"; similarly, sometimes we focus so much on process that we lose sight of where we are going. Mixing methods allows us to investigate both, resulting in more useful findings.

Table 14.1 Advantages and Disadvantages of Mixed Methods Research

Advantages	Disadvantages
Provides more comprehensive data.	Researcher needs skills to conduct and interpret results from both quantitative and qualitative designs.
Includes multiple approaches to compensate for limitations with using a single method.	Often requires more extensive data collection.
Allows investigation of different types of questions within a single study.	Often requires more time and resources.
Allows examination of complex research questions.	Can be difficult to combine approaches when writing reports and forming conclusions.
Sometimes includes triangulation to enhance credibility of the findings.	

There also are some disadvantages to using mixed methods designs. First and foremost, the ability to successfully implement a mixed methods study will require a solid level of expertise and comfort with both quantitative and qualitative methods. A passing or rudimentary level of understanding of procedures and data analysis techniques of each is insufficient for conducting credible mixed methods studies. Gaining the required level of expertise requires study and practical application of each method. Second, mixed methods research typically involves data collection (and subsequent analysis) that is more extensive and labor intensive, takes additional time, and often requires more resources than might be required of a study employing either quantitative or qualitative methods alone. As a result, researchers who wish to use mixed methods may choose to collaborate in partnerships to which each person brings a different methodological expertise. Finally, the writing styles and formats used to report the results of quantitative and qualitative studies are often different. These differences can make it challenging to report the results of a mixed methods study in a way that balances the writing style and format of each individual method and at the same time integrates findings to present a coherent report, rather than reading as though two separate studies have been combined into a single report.

Authors' Reflection *We believe that the rich findings that can result from mixed methods studies are often well worth the extra time and effort it takes to conduct research of this kind. Also, in our experience, having a team of researchers is very important. We have found that a well-matched, collaborative team can make the research both more effective and more efficient.*

Check for Understanding 1

1a. What is the major reason for conducting a mixed methods study rather than either a quantitative or qualitative study?

1b. What are the major advantages and disadvantages of conducting mixed methods studies?

The Hedgehog and Fox Consider Using a Mixed Methods Design

Doing a mixed methods study sounds exciting! I'll be using the newest and best approach to research.

Let's think clearly about whether a mixed methods study is needed and whether I have the skills, time, and resources to conduct it. I need to have a clear rationale, and specific quantitative and qualitative methods in mind to be sure I'll be able to do the study. Do I really have the skills to be successful?

Steps in Conducting a Mixed Methods Study

Learning Outcome 14.2 Describe the steps in conducting mixed methods studies.

As illustrated in Figure 14.1, there are nine steps to conducting mixed methods studies, regardless of the specific design that is implemented. These steps are unique compared with studies that are solely quantitative or qualitative because of the implications of combining these approaches in a single study. Considerations such as feasibility, rationale, and design components are important in framing questions, carrying out data collection, and analyzing data. Moreover, since specific research questions need to be aligned with different methods, the general design of the study is often identified prior to establishing the questions. Specific actions needed to carry out the quantitative and qualitative parts are then delineated. The steps presented here, then, are appropriate for all types of mixed methods studies. More specific procedures, aligned to different designs, will be discussed later.

1. *Identify purpose.* This first is needed to provide the basis for step 2. Essentially, the general purpose of the research needs to include elements that are best investigated with mixed methods. This could be a general research problem statement or question, or explanation of the issue that needs investigation.
2. *Identify the rationale.* As previously discussed, it is essential to identify the reasons for conducting a mixed methods study prior to the development of other aspects of the study. If you are unable to identify clearly why you are conducting this type of study, then you are unlikely to be able to justify your purpose clearly to readers. Here, it is important to communicate why a mixed methods design is essential, rather than a design that is either quantitative or qualitative.
3. *Establish the feasibility of conducting a mixed methods study.* Feasibility is a function of the level of training and expertise of the researcher(s) or team, as well as the resources and time available for data collection and analysis. If any of these is less than adequate, successful implementation is unlikely. There may also be additional expenses.
4. *Determine mixed methods design.* In this step you will determine which specific mixed methods design will be employed. This depends on the purpose of the study and resources to complete both quantitative and qualitative phases.

Figure 14.1 Steps in Conducting Mixed Methods Studies[1]

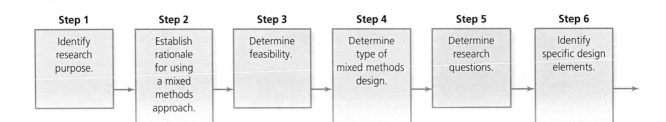

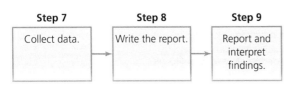

[1]Adapted from Creswell (2008)

5. *Establish specific research questions.* As with all good research, it is important that research questions align with the purposes and nature of the design. At this stage, questions should be refined to ensure that they clearly reflect the design and can be answered by the identified data collection methods. While typically design elements follow from questions, in mixed methods research the nature of the design (e.g., convergent, exploratory) determines the questions that need to be formulated. In the case of explanatory sequential designs, it may be difficult to define the qualitative questions prior to analysis of the quantitative data. Usually, researchers develop separate quantitative, qualitative, and mixed methods research questions to incorporate into a single study.

6. *Determine specific design elements.* Based on the research questions, the specific nature of the design can be established to ensure that the data will address each question. Determining the types of data, the priority and sequence of data collection, and the specific forms of information to be gathered is indispensable to planning the specific procedures to be followed. It also is useful at this point to map out the design. The mapping uses a special notation system, as you will see in a later section of the chapter.

7. *Collect the data.* The sequence of data collection should already be identified by the type of design that was chosen. In terms of the overall research process, this stage is likely to be lengthy and time consuming. It is important that conventional procedures for each type of data are followed to ensure the appropriateness of data collection.

8. *Analyze and interpret the data.* Quantitative and qualitative data will be analyzed separately and independently, although *when* each set of data is analyzed depends on the type of design. However, all mixed methods studies combine the quantitative and qualitative data collected, regardless of the chosen design. Interpretation depends in part on how the quantitative and qualitative data merge, support each other, or provide explanations or generalizations.

9. *Write the report.* As with many aspects of mixed methods studies, writing up the results of a study in a research report will depend on the type of design employed. Regardless of the design, though, the procedures employed in both the quantitative and qualitative components of the study need to be clearly explained in detail, and are usually reported separately within the methods section of the report. In explanatory and exploratory sequential designs, results for quantitative and qualitative analyses may be reported in a separate section for each phase of the study. In contrast, reports of convergent designs are most likely to integrate the quantitative and qualitative results structured around the research questions into a single results section of the report.

Check for Understanding 2

2a. How are the steps to conduct a mixed methods study different from steps used to conduct a quantitative or qualitative study?

2b. Why is it important to identify the type of mixed methods design prior to the specific research questions?

Research Questions for Mixed Methods Studies

With mixed methods research there are at least two types of research questions (quantitative and qualitative) as well as often one or more mixed methods research questions. The questions align to the major elements of the research design.

EXCERPT 14.2
Explanatory Sequential Design Research Questions

Our mixed-methods study addresses these gaps in the field's knowledge by examining these two questions:

1. What are the relative contributions of strategy expertise, English-language proficiency, content knowledge, and epistemic beliefs to monolingual and bilingual middle school students' comprehension of multiple expository science texts?
2. What disciplinary meaning-making features are evident in students' interactions with multiple texts on a scientific topic?

The first question was examined using correlation and regression analyses and the second question using verbal think-aloud data that reveal features of students' meaning-making processes that could not be captured using traditional quantitative measures. (p. 231)

SOURCE: Davis, D., Huang, B., & Yi, T. (2016). Making sense of science texts: A mixed-methods examination of predictors and processes of multiple-text comprehension. *Reading Research Quarterly, 52*(2), 1–26.

When one type of data is collected before the other, the design is generally categorized as *sequential* (refer to Table 14.2). There are two primary types of **sequential mixed methods designs**: *explanatory sequential* and *exploratory sequential*. In *explanatory sequential* designs, the purpose of the qualitative data is to follow up on or explain aspects of the quantitative data. Hence, specific quantitative questions are presented first, followed by qualitative questions. An example of research questions with this type of design is illustrated in Excerpt 14.2.

The mixed methods questions integrate the two approaches in a way that is consistent with the purpose. For instance, a researcher might ask, "How do classroom observational data explain why students report that class is boring?" Thus, mixed methods questions reflect the "mixing" nature of the data. While mixed methods research questions are rare (Creswell & Plano Clark, 2017), they are strongly recommended since they target the reason for doing a mixed methods study in the first place.

The sequence of questions is the opposite for what is called the *exploratory sequential* design. With this type of design, qualitative data are gathered before the collection of quantitative data. Now, the questions need to reflect the logic that qualitative results are used to inform the quantitative phase. For example, the qualitative question could be something like "What factors contributing to taking drugs are identified by high school students?" Often, this type of design is used to develop a survey, as shown in Excerpt 14.3.

If both quantitative and qualitative data are collected at about the same time, then the design may focus on convergence of the information resulting from each method, giving equal emphasis to each. This is typically called a *convergent* or *triangulation* type of study, with all questions stated together. Here, the researcher wants to know the extent to which the findings from both strands, the qualitative and quantitative, converge so that the findings from one approach reinforce the findings from the other approach. That is, do the qualitative and quantitative data show the same thing? For example, if you use both survey data and interview data to examine attitudes toward

EXCERPT 14.3

Exploratory Sequential Research Questions

The main purpose of this mixed methods study was to develop a relationship process model that defined the perceptions, interactions, and conditions that impacted attraction to, and use of, local community state college contract training services by Utah small to midsized business managers.

Research Questions:

1. What are the attributes and factors that Utah training decision makers perceive as important for attraction to, and utilization of, contract training providers?
2. How do Utah training decision makers perceive their local community/state colleges' contract training services, particularly on the attributes they consider important for attraction to, and utilization of, training providers?
3. What are the factors and processes that explain why Utah training decision makers do or do not use community/state college contract training services? (p. 40)

SOURCE: Bryant, D. (2014). Factors and processes that impact use of Utah community state college contract training: A mixed methods study. *Community College Journal of Research and Practice, 38*(1).

taking a research methods course, will the findings from each approach be the same (besides being on the positive side!)? Excerpt 14.4 offers an example of research questions for a study using a convergent design.

Further examples of these three major types of research questions are presented in Table 14.2.

EXCERPT 14.4

Convergent Design Research Questions

The purpose of this study was to investigate the sources of math and science self-efficacy among students in Grades 6–12 attending public schools in a rural community in Appalachia. A convergent mixed methods design was used in which quantitative and qualitative data were collected and analyzed separately before being integrated (Creswell & Plano Clark, 2017).... We first used quantitative analyses to examine the measurement of and structural relationships between the hypothesized sources (independent variables) and rural adolescents' self-efficacy (dependent variable). We then used qualitative analyses to investigate the content and patterns of students' responses to open-ended questions about what makes them feel more and less confident in math and science. In both types of analyses, we examined possible gender differences. In an integrative analysis phase, we then compared the results from the two methodological approaches. We discuss the insights revealed from this integrative approach and highlight findings that could not have been obtained by either quantitative or qualitative methodological approaches alone. Our guiding research questions were as follows:

1. What is the relationship between the four sources of self-efficacy hypothesized by Bandura (1997) and rural Appalachian students' self-efficacy in math and science six months later? (Quantitative)

2. How do rural Appalachian students describe the events that raise and lower their math and science self-efficacy? (Qualitative)
3. To what extent do qualitative and quantitative results converge? (Mixed methods) (pp. 34–35)

SOURCE: Usher, E. L., Ford, C. J., Li, C. R., & Weidner, B. L. (2019). Sources of math and science self-efficacy in rural Appalachia: A convergent mixed methods study. *Contemporary Educational Psychology, 57*, 32–53.

Table 14.2 Types of Mixed Methods Research Questions

Type	Definition	Method	Example Questions
Explanatory sequential	Findings from quantitative methods are followed by qualitative methods to provide explanations for the quantitative findings.	Teacher survey about grading practices is followed by teacher interviews to explain why zeroes are used extensively in grading students.	*Quantitative:* What are teachers' grading practices? *Qualitative:* Why do teachers use zeroes in grading students?
Exploratory sequential	Qualitative methods are used to generate information to be used in conducting the quantitative phase of the study.	Teacher interviews about grading practices are used to develop a survey that is given to a large sample of teachers.	*Qualitative:* How do teachers describe their grading practices? *Quantitative:* What is the predictive validity of the scores across teachers?
Convergent	Quantitative and qualitative data are collected at about the same time to allow for triangulation of the findings.	Concurrent interviews with and surveys of both teachers and students.	*Qualitative:* How do teachers describe their grading practices? How do students describe their teachers' grading practices? *Quantitative:* What is the relationship between teachers' grading practices and their beliefs about student ability? What is the relationship between teachers' grading practices and student motivation? *Mixed methods:* To what extent do the quantitative and qualitative results coincide?

Sampling in Mixed Methods Studies

Sampling for mixed methods research was discussed in Chapter 5. For the quantitative phase, the sample is selected using either probability or nonprobability procedures; for the qualitative phase, purposeful sampling is used. This results in a number of combinations of different kinds of sampling that can be found in a single study (e.g., stratified, convenience, cluster, systematic for the quantitative phase; snowball, extreme case, typical case, maximum variation for the qualitative phase). Usually, as with research questions, sampling follows the logic of the design. Whereas an explanatory sequential study may start with a probability or convenience sample to generate the quantitative findings, and purposeful sampling for the qualitative part of the study, an exploratory sequential study may begin with extreme case sampling and then use a probability sampling procedure for the quantitative part of the study. A convergent design uses sampling that will allow a synthesis of findings from each group of participants. For this design, the samples are typically very similar so that it makes sense to combine data from each phase.

What is unique for some mixed methods studies is that the sampling for each stage of the study is connected. For example, the participants who are interviewed in an explanatory sequential study may be identified by their responses to the survey. In studying grading practices, a survey could be given to a random sample of teachers, and, of the respondents, the teachers showing the most extreme practices could be selected for the interviews.

Although many mixed methods studies collect all data from the same pool of participants, samples also can be completely independent. An illustration of this type of sampling is given in Excerpt 14.5. This study focused on parents' family engagement conceptualizations. The qualitative data were obtained from one sample to develop a measure that was validated with a completely separate sample of caregivers.

EXCERPT 14.5

Independent Mixed Methods Sampling

The present mixed-methods investigation employed an emic approach to understand family engagement conceptualizations for a pan-Latino population. One hundred thirteen parents from 14 Head Start programs were identified and specific items were co-constructed to capture family engagement behaviors [qualitative data]. Then, 650 caregivers participated in a second study examining the construct validity of the resulting 65-item measure across two language versions: Parental Engagement of Families from Latino Backgrounds (PEFL-English) and Participación Educativa de Familias Latinas (PEFL-Spanish) [quantitative data]. (p. 593)

SOURCE: McWayne, C. M., Melzi, G., Schick, A. R., Kennedy, J. L., & Mundt, K. (2014). Defining family engagement among Latino Head Start parents: A mixed-methods measurement development study. *Early Childhood Research Quarterly, 28*(3), 593–607.

Types of Mixed Methods Designs

Learning Outcome 14.3 Classify, diagram, and know when to use different mixed methods designs.

Mixed methods designs can vary considerably, depending on the weight given to each approach and when each method is used. Although there are many different designs, the three designs introduced in Chapter 1 and presented here are the most commonly used: *explanatory sequential, exploratory sequential*, and *convergent*. (Creswell and Plano Clark [2017] explicate mixed methods experimental, mixed methods case study, and mixed methods participatory-social justice designs.)

Notation

To assist readers in identifying the type of design employed, Creswell & Plano Clark (2017) suggest incorporating the following notation system, in combination with visual diagrams, to illustrate the design for readers:

- Uppercase letters (e.g., *QUAN* or *QUAL*) to indicate the method given *priority* (primary method used) in the study

- Lowercase letters (e.g., *qual* or *quan*) to indicate a method was given a lower priority (less emphasis) in the study

- Arrows (→) to indicate that methods occur in a sequence

- Plus (+) to indicate that methods occur concurrently

- Parentheses ( ) to indicate that one method is embedded within an intervention (e.g., QUAN(qual))

- Brackets [ ] to indicate that a core mixed methods design is used within a series of studies (e.g., QUAL → QUAN → [QUAN → qual])

This notation allows for diagrams that show the logic of the design. The diagrams help clarify three important characteristics of the design:

- Which component of the design, if any, is dominant (all caps)? Or do the components have equal status?
- Are the components sequential—one following the other—or concurrent?
- In sequential designs, which component occurs first?

Priority/Weighting

Priority refers to the weight or emphasis the quantitative and qualitative methods receive within a study. Depending on the type of design and purpose for the study, there are three choices with respect to weighting: (1) quantitative and qualitative data can be given equal weight, (2) qualitative data can be weighted more heavily than quantitative data, or (3) quantitative data can be weighted more heavily than qualitative data. As previously indicated, in terms of notation, priority/weighting is depicted by uppercase or lowercase letters.

Choosing how to weight the quantitative and qualitative methods in a study depends primarily on the purpose of the study and which data collection and analysis methods are best suited to answering the research questions. Additional considerations, as noted earlier, include the availability of resources and time constraints, the relative expertise of the researcher(s) in implementing quantitative and qualitative methods, as well as the intended audience. Limitations in terms of time and resources may force the researcher to prioritize and focus more on one method than the other, especially if researchers are uncomfortable or lack the expertise to implement either quantitative or qualitative methods effectively. Finally, if the intended audience is more familiar with one method or expects a certain method to be employed, researchers might choose to emphasize that method.

Sequence/Timing

Sequence refers to both the timing of implementation of the quantitative and qualitative methods and the order in which data are gathered (Creswell & Plano Clark, 2017). As indicated earlier, sequential studies are those in which either the quantitative methods are implemented before the qualitative methods (i.e., explanatory sequential) or the qualitative methods are implemented before the quantitative methods (i.e., exploratory sequential). With respect to notation, sequence is indicated by (+) for concurrent designs or (→) for sequential designs. Concurrent studies are those in which both the quantitative and qualitative methods are implemented simultaneously (i.e., convergent designs).

Mixing

Mixing refers to the ways in which the quantitative and qualitative data are combined and the types of data that are mixed (Creswell & Plano Clark, 2017). Different strategies are used to mix data during the investigation. One option is to connect data by using the analysis of one type of data to inform the data collection of the other type. Explanatory and exploratory sequential designs employ this strategy. In explanatory

---

EXCERPT 14.6

Mixing Quantitative and Qualitative Data

The quantitative and qualitative components were selected and integrated purposefully (Creswell & Garrett, 2008; Creswell & Plano Clark, 2011; Mertens, 2007) for the purpose of revealing embedded meanings in the particular localized context of the Southeastern United States. While both forms of data are equally important, the qualitative data received interpretive priority by virtue of its capacity to showcase collective meaning, contextual complexity, and temporal depth (Bidart et al., 2014). Our parallel convergent design (Creswell & Plano Clark, 2011) best diagramed as: ([quan + quan] + QUAL)) (Morse & Niehaus, 2009) featured in Figure 1, involved two forms of quantitative descriptive data providing the cross-case legitimacy that the community of practice (i.e., campus administrators) sought, while the inclusion of two in-depth qualitative cases reinforced the locally salient contexts that manifest when colleges navigate undocumented students' issues. State-level measures described the sociopolitical climate and the emergent community order (Schneiberg & Soule, 2005) pertaining to the relative receptivity to undocumented immigrant college students' postsecondary access and opportunity. Campus-level data specified how routine, normative administrative practices in higher education functioned to constrain or enhance campuses' abilities to act. Extensive use of case-level newspaper data captured the nature of the public discourse and framing applied by capuses and other stakeholders to illuminate the driving forces for oppression (or change), or "the various levels of contexts, organizations, and individuals that give impulse to the process" (Bidart et al., 2014, p. 746) of how campuses navigated postsecondary access and opportunity for undocumented students. (pp. 420–421)

SOURCE: Barnhardt, C. L., Reyes, K., Vidal Rodriguez, A., & Ramos, M. (2018). A transformative mixed methods assessment of educational access and opportunity for undocumented college students in the Southeastern United States. *Journal of Mixed Methods Research, 12*(4), 413–436.

---

sequential designs, the quantitative data analyses influence the qualitative data collected; for exploratory sequential designs, the qualitative data analyses influence the quantitative data collected. Another option involves merging the two types of data into a single dataset, usually during the interpretation phase or discussion section. In this case, quantitative and qualitative data are analyzed and reported separately within the results section. We might also choose to merge datasets during analysis. Convergent designs typically employ this strategy and involve a single phase. Excerpt 14.6 outlines how researchers refer to mixing.

Regardless of the research questions and type of design chosen, it is important to emphasize again that all mixed methods studies should include an explicit rationale for the type of design chosen. The rationale should be aligned with quantitative and qualitative types of data, and include a discussion of priority/weighting, an indication of sequence/timing, and a summary of how data are mixed.

Explanatory Sequential Design

In an **explanatory sequential design** there are two phases or components, qualitative following quantitative, often with the primary emphasis on quantitative methods. Initially, quantitative data are collected and analyzed; in the second phase, qualitative data are collected and analyzed. The design is notated as follows:

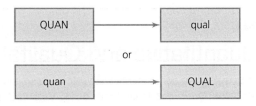

Explanatory sequential designs are used when the purpose of the study is to elucidate, elaborate on, or explain quantitative findings. Sometimes qualitative data are used to analyze outliers or other extreme cases.

A two-phase study by Zumbrunn, McKim, Buhs, & Hawley (2014) is a good example of an explanatory sequential design. In the first phase of this study, a large sample of college students ($N = 212$) was surveyed to examine how classroom contextual characteristics and student motivation, engagement, and feelings of classroom belonging related to academic achievement. A subsample of students from the quantitative phase was interviewed in the second, follow-up qualitative phase to explore students' classroom experiences that either fostered or impeded students' classroom belonging perceptions. Thus, the qualitative phase was used to augment the findings from the quantitative phase and provide explanations for student beliefs of belongingness. The steps taken in the study are illustrated in Figure 14.2.

This same approach was taken by a study that examined teachers' asset-based pedagogy (ABP - their instructional choices that affirm students' ethnicity and culture). As illustrated in Excerpt 14.7, the researchers first gathered survey data from teachers and achievement data for students, and then employed interviews of teacher participants.

In Excerpt 14.8, an explanatory sequential design was employed to study the process by which task instructions affect middle school students' topic beliefs and justifications.

Figure 14.2 Example of Steps in Conducting an Explanatory Sequential Study

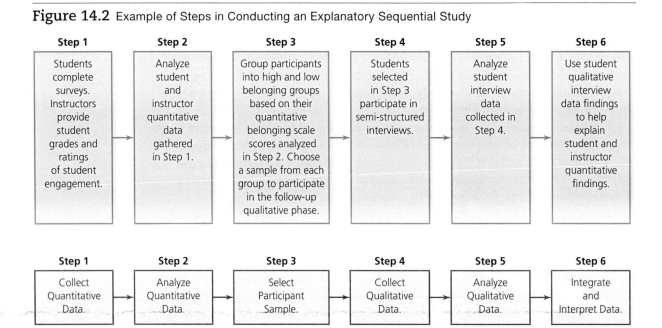

EXCERPT 14.7

Explanatory Sequential Design

This study used an explanatory sequential mixed method design. A mixed methods research design is a procedure for collecting and analyzing data produced through multiple methods, usually both quantitative and qualitative methods, where data is "mixed" or integrated at some stage of the research process for the purpose of gaining a better understanding of the research problem (Creswell, 2005). Explanatory sequential mixed methods designs usually consist of two distinct phases. The researcher first collects and analyzes quantitative data, which is followed by a qualitative data collection and analysis phase to help refine, explain, build on, or elaborate the initial quantitative results (Creswell, Plano Clark, Gutman, & Hanson, 2003). The quantitative phase of the current study examined whether teachers' expectations and critical awareness of their Latino students predicted their ABPs and students' subsequent mathematics achievement. Given the robust sample size of the quantitative data along with its purpose for establishing the predictive qualities of teacher beliefs and ABPs, it was given priority in this study's design (Creswell, 2003). The qualitative phase of this study sought to elaborate on the quantitative findings with interviews of select teachers who had the highest scores on teacher expectations and critical awareness; to discuss how they enacted ABPs in their classrooms. Integration (Ivankova, Creswell, & Stick, 2006) occurred at three points during the study: first, during the development of the qualitative interview protocol based on the quantitative survey items; second, during the selection of teachers for interviews; and third, during the interpretation phase of the findings (see Fig. 2). This mixed methods research was guided by a pragmatic perspective (Shannon-Baker, 2016), which underscores that knowledge can be both contextualized and generalizable, allowing for both subjectivity and objectivity (i.e., intersubjectivity) in our collection, analysis, and interpretation of the data. (pp. 75–76)

SOURCE: Matthews, J. S., & López, F. (2019). Speaking their language: The role of cultural content integration and heritage language for academic achievement among Latino children. *Contemporary Educational Psychology, 57*, 72–86.

EXCERPT 14.8

Explanatory Sequential Designs with Random Assignment

When using a sequential explanatory mixed methods design, a researcher uses qualitative data to follow-up or explain initial experimental findings (Creswell and Plano Clark, 2011 and Tashakkori and Teddlie, 1998). In the present study, we used qualitative data to further explain readers' topic belief changes. The purpose of the qualitative phase was to explain why some students' topic beliefs became weaker after they read, whereas other students' topic beliefs became stronger after they read. (p. 6)

SOURCE: McCrudden, M. T., & Sparks, P. C. (2014). Exploring the effect of task instructions on topic beliefs and topic belief justifications: A mixed methods study. *Contemporary Educational Psychology, 39*, 1–11.

Exploratory Sequential Design

An **exploratory sequential design** is another two-phase design, but in this case the qualitative data are gathered first, followed by a quantitative phase. In these designs, results from the qualitative data analysis are used to help determine the focus and type of data collection in the quantitative phase. The purpose of this design is typically to use the initial qualitative phase with a few individuals to identify themes, ideas, perspectives, and beliefs for the larger-scale quantitative part of the study. The premise is that exploration is needed because "(1) measures, instruments, or experimental activities are not available; (2) the variables are unknown; (3) there is no guiding framework or theory; or (4) there is a need to make an existing quantitative measure or instrument as specific to the participants or culture as possible" (Creswell & Plano Clark, 2017, p. 84–86).

Often, this kind of design is used to develop a survey. By first collecting qualitative data, we can use participants' ideas and language in the construction of a survey. This increases the validity of the survey scores because the data are well matched to the way the participants—rather than the researchers—think about, conceptualize, and respond to the phenomena being studied. It could be represented as follows:

For example, in a study by Bridwell-Mitchell (2013), the researcher conducted qualitative observations and interviews with teachers to develop and test an instrument to measure teacher practices and beliefs about school reform. Here, the major emphasis is the quantitative measure, and qualitative observations and interviews helped to form the survey. The steps taken in this study are illustrated in Figure 14.3.

If the quantitative portion of the study was used to confirm, determine, or expand on qualitative findings, then the qualitative part of the study will be emphasized:

An exploratory sequential design is illustrated in Excerpt 14.9. You will see that the authors make it clear that the quantitative component of the study followed the qualitative part.

Figure 14.3 Example of Steps in Conducting an Exploratory Sequential Study

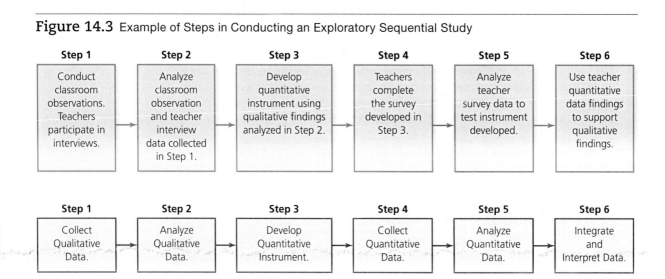

Step 1	Step 2	Step 3	Step 4	Step 5	Step 6
Conduct classroom observations. Teachers participate in interviews.	Analyze classroom observation and teacher interview data collected in Step 1.	Develop quantitative instrument using qualitative findings analyzed in Step 2.	Teachers complete the survey developed in Step 3.	Analyze teacher survey data to test instrument developed.	Use teacher quantitative data findings to support qualitative findings.

Step 1	Step 2	Step 3	Step 4	Step 5	Step 6
Collect Qualitative Data.	Analyze Qualitative Data.	Develop Quantitative Instrument.	Collect Quantitative Data.	Analyze Quantitative Data.	Integrate and Interpret Data.

EXCERPT 14.9

Exploratory Sequential Design

[The] purpose of the current study was to explore new faculty success and examine its predictors using an exploratory-sequential mixed methods design (QUAL → QUAN = instrument development, generalize findings; Creswell and Plano-Clark, 2010). In the first phase, focus groups were conducted to qualitatively explore the factors new faculty report as impacting their success; specifically, our analysis sought to identify any previously established factors from the literature and to allow for the emergence of any new factors. In the second phase, qualitative findings were used to create quantitative measurement scales. Online survey data were then used to test the reliability and validity of the factors quantitatively and to statistically compare the predictive utility of these factors on multiple indicators of success. (p. 373)

SOURCE: Stupnisky, R. H., Weaver-Hightower, M. B., & Kartoshkina, Y. (2014). Exploring and testing the predictors of new faculty success: A mixed methods study. *Studies in Higher Education, 40*(2), 368–390. https://doi.org/10.1080/03075079.2014.842220

Convergent Design

The **convergent design** simultaneously implements both quantitative and qualitative methods—collecting and analyzing data concurrently. For each segment of the research, the researcher would employ the most appropriate quantitative or qualitative techniques, merging results together to facilitate a single interpretation. Convergent designs typically are used when researchers are interested in validating and expanding on the quantitative findings through the use of qualitative methods. The purpose is to develop a more thorough understanding of a single phenomenon.

A special subtype of convergent designs, called *nested designs*, involves using different methods to gather information from individuals or groups at different levels within a system (Tashakkori & Teddlie, 1998). For example, you might use observations of students, interviews with teachers, surveys with administrators, and focus groups with parents. The general purpose is the same, but the interest is in gaining multiple perspectives from individuals or groups who have different roles within a system. This design could be represented in several ways, depending on the priority placed on either quantitative or qualitative methods:

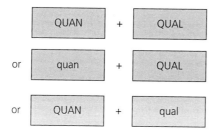

To illustrate a convergent design, consider a hypothetical study on school culture. A quantitative school culture survey could be used in conjunction with some focus groups of students, teachers, and administrators. To the extent that that survey's results match focus group results, the validity of the conclusion that a certain type of culture exists in the school is enhanced. The advantage of the survey is that a large

Figure 14.4 Example of Steps in Conducting a Convergent Study

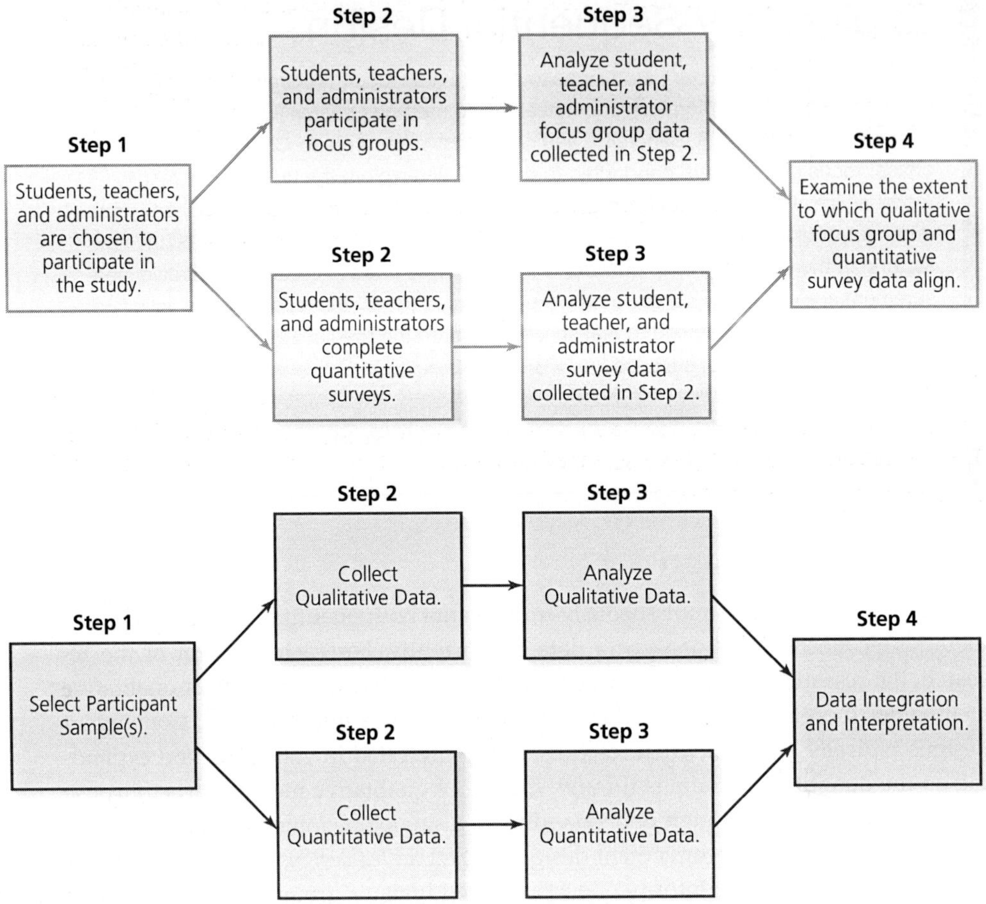

number of students, teachers, and administrators can be represented, while the focus group would provide descriptions in voices specific to each group. The steps taken in this study are illustrated in Figure 14.4.

In Excerpt 14.10, the researcher explains how both quantitative and qualitative data are obtained and integrated.

EXCERPT 14.10

Convergent Design

[W]e utilized qualitative methods to explore the perspectives of middle school parents, students, and teachers regarding their goals for parental involvement in education and what works in supporting achievement during middle school. We used qualitative methods, focus groups in particular, because they are an effective means to learn about a population's values, styles of thinking, and the language used to discuss constructs (Vogt, King, & King, 2004). In addition to the focus groups, participants also completed a short quantitative survey on parental involvement in education, satisfaction with school, and other characteristics. The quantitative assessments allowed us to characterize the sample based on levels of involvement and general relationships with the school. In addition, these quantitative data provided a context for understanding the qualitative findings…The current study integrates the voices of students, parents, and teachers to broaden and deepen our understanding of how families, students, and schools function together to support achievement during adolescence. (p. 14)

SOURCE: Hill, N. E., Witherspoon, D. P., & Bartz, D. (2018). Parental involvement in education during middle school: Perspectives of ethnically diverse parents, teachers, and students. *The Journal of Educational Research, 111*(1), 12–27.

The advantages and challenges of each of the three major mixed methods designs are presented in Table 14.3. Table 14.4 presents some examples of types of data collection procedures and their uses, broken down by each type of design, as well as the sequence of implementation.

Table 14.3 Advantages and Challenges of Different Mixed Methods Designs

Type of Design	Advantages	Challenges
Explanatory sequential	• The two-phase structure makes its implementation straightforward. • The two-phase structure makes writing the report straightforward because it can be completed in two phases. • The focus on quantitative methods in the first phase often appeals to researchers whose primary expertise is quantitative methods.	• The two-phase structure requires additional time for implementation and data collection. • Researchers need to decide whether to collect data from the same sample or separate samples from the same population in both phases. • Because the researcher cannot always identify how participants will be selected or specific qualitative research questions for the qualitative phase until after initial quantitative results have been examined, it can be more difficult to obtain IRB approval.
Exploratory sequential	• Separate phases make implementation and data collection straightforward. • The inclusion of the quantitative component in a design that generally emphasizes qualitative methods is likely to make this design attractive to researchers whose primary expertise is quantitative methods.	• The two-phase structure requires additional time for implementation and data collection. • Researchers need to decide whether the same individuals will serve as participants in both phases. • It is difficult to specify the quantitative procedures to be implemented until the qualitative phase is complete. • Prior analysis of qualitative data can create issues with obtaining IRB approval.
Convergent	• It is an efficient design in terms of time for implementation and data collection, as both types of data are collected and analyzed at the same time. • Because the quantitative and qualitative data can be collected and analyzed independently of one another, these designs are well suited to collaborations or research teams.	• Because of the concurrent nature of data collection, additional effort and expertise in each method are required if researchers are working alone on a study. • Researchers may encounter situations in which the results of the quantitative and qualitative data analyses diverge (i.e., do not agree or appear to tell different "stories"), which may require additional data collection to determine the nature of the inconsistencies.

Source: Based on McMillan & Schumacher (2010) and Creswell & Plano Clark (2017).

Table 14.4 Data Collection, Design, and Analytic Procedures in Mixed Methods Studies

Sequence of Data Collection	Design	Examples
Sequential	Explanatory (quantitative followed by qualitative)	• Following up on outliers or extreme cases: Gather quantitative data and identify outlier or residual cases. Collect qualitative data to explore the characteristics of these cases. • Explaining results: Conduct a quantitative survey to identify how two or more groups compare on a variable. Follow up with qualitative interviews to explore the reasons why these differences were found. • Using a typology: Conduct a quantitative survey and develop factors through a factor analysis. Use these factors as a typology to identify themes in qualitative data, such as observations or interviews.
	Exploratory (qualitative followed by quantitative)	• Locating an instrument: Collect qualitative data and identify themes. Use these themes as a basis for locating instruments that use parallel concepts to the qualitative themes. • Developing an instrument: Use responses from participants to support overarching themes identified in the qualitative data. During the next phase, use themes to create scale items in a questionnaire. Alternatively, look for existing instruments that can be modified to fit the themes found in the qualitative exploratory phase of the study. After developing the instrument, test it out with a sample of the population. • Using extreme qualitative cases: Quantitative surveys follow qualitative data cases that are extreme in a comparative analysis during the second phase.
Concurrent (quantitative and qualitative data collected simultaneously)	Convergent	• Comparing results: Directly compare the results from qualitative data collection to the results from quantitative data collection. Support statistical trends by qualitative themes or vice versa. • Consolidating data: Combine qualitative and quantitative data to form a more complete understanding of a phenomenon. Compare original quantitative variables to qualitative themes.

Source: Based on Creswell & Guetterman (2019).

Check for Understanding 3

3a. When is it best to use either an explanatory sequential, exploratory sequential, or convergent design?

3b. What is the primary difference between explanatory and exploratory sequential designs?

3c. What are the primary challenges of conducting a convergent mixed methods study?

Data Analysis

Data analysis in mixed methods studies obviously includes both quantitative and qualitative procedures, but additional considerations and techniques are determined by the nature of the design and key decision points that are made throughout the study. In both types of sequential designs, the analysis of data is fairly straightforward, but distinct approaches to data analysis are needed to provide the best transitions. One type of data needs to inform the next stage of the research. This is often described as *connected* or *iterative* data analysis. In an explanatory sequential design, the right kind of quantitative data analysis is needed to provide the best qualitative component. For example, you might use descriptive statistics of student test scores to group students into achievement-level groups (e.g., low, average, high), then use follow-up qualitative interviews with students from each group to explore typical study strategies students employ and whether strategies differ across achievement groups. Alternatively, in an exploratory sequential design, the right kind of qualitative data analysis is important to ensure effective data collection in the quantitative stage. Suppose you are using interviews to capture words used by graduate students to describe their professors to develop a survey to be given to a large sample of graduate students. The data from the interviews must be carefully coded, employing standard qualitative analysis strategies such as constant comparison, to result in the most effective questions for the survey.

In convergent designs, conventional qualitative and quantitative analyses are supplemented by *merged* data analysis. **Merged analysis** is a technique for showing how the various types of data compare. This can be accomplished with tables or other types of displays that show congruence of results, consistency, and discrepant evidence that may suggest contradictions. For convergent studies, key decisions for additional analysis are made both at the time individual data are examined and when merged data may suggest the need for further analyses.

Reporting Mixed Methods Results

As with any other investigation, clarity and transparency are critical attributes of effective reporting of study methods and findings. However, due to the complexity of mixed methods designs, there are more components to consider when reporting results compared to studies employing either a quantitative or qualitative methodological approach.

First, it is important to be mindful of the language you use throughout your mixed methods report. That is, be thoughtful that the words you use to describe the purpose, methodology, and findings align with each specific tradition. Table 14.5 shows examples of expressions often aligned with quantitative and qualitative traditions.

Next, a visual aid (often a diagram) that illustrates the specific components of your design is strongly recommended (e.g., Figures 14.2, 14.3, and 14.4). Then, adapting the organization and structure of your report to align with the specific mixed methods design is an excellent way to guide your reader. Often, the organization of topics to include reflect those depicted in the procedural diagram. Creswell and Plano Clark (2017) and DeCuir-Gunby & Schutz (2017) offer additional excellent guidance on writing a mixed methods graduate student dissertation or thesis, proposal for external funding, or empirical journal article.

Table 14.5 Example Expressions to Describe Quantitative and Qualitative Work

Quantitative	Qualitative
Examining	Exploring
Measure/measuring	Describe/describing
Results	Findings

Authors' Reflection *When reporting sequential explanatory studies, we have found that including the section "The Need for Follow-Up Qualitative Data" after the methods and results for the quantitative phase, and before the methods and findings for the qualitative phase, can help to explicitly bridge the two sections and orient the reader.*

Consumer (and Researcher) Tips
Criteria for Evaluating Mixed Methods Research

Learning Outcome 14.4 Know the criteria for evaluating the quality of mixed methods research.

As you now know, credibility and validity of findings from research vary considerably; this applies to mixed methods studies as well. In critically evaluating mixed methods research studies, several issues should be considered in addition to the criteria used to evaluate studies that are solely quantitative or qualitative. As noted earlier, what sets mixed methods studies apart from other research designs is the intentional and substantial collection of both quantitative and qualitative data. Focusing on this critical feature is the primary way to evaluate the validity and rigor of mixed methods designs. For example, collecting data via quantitative surveys employing Likert scales and including a few open-ended questions at the end of the survey as the qualitative component is less rigorous than including participant interviews as part of the design. For the most part, mixed methods studies should be able to "hold their own weight" with regard to standards of rigor and quality for both quantitative and qualitative methods.

Once it is clear that research design is substantial in both phases, other considerations become important. In sequential designs, unique validity concerns focus on the connection of the two phases, and whether one has appropriately built on the other (*sequential validity*). For explanatory designs, were the sampling and instrumentation adequate to identify participants for the qualitative component? Was evidence for psychometric properties appropriate? Was the qualitative phase conducted with sufficient detail to provide solid guidance for the quantitative component? Essentially, you are looking for issues or weaknesses that could invalidate the credibility and quality of the transition that occurs between the stages of the study.

For convergent designs, validity focuses on the merging of the data and whether there are weaknesses or limitations that would compromise the conclusions. It may be that the operational definitions used for the quantitative portion of the study do not match what is gathered in the qualitative part of the study. Often, the tables that are needed to show how data are merged are incomplete or insufficient. If contradictory findings are not explicitly searched for and addressed, bias could be introduced.

Mertens (2019, p. 314) presents questions that can be applied to the evaluation of mixed methods studies at this point:

1. What are the multiple purposes and questions that justify the use of a mixed methods design?
2. Has the researcher matched the purposes and questions to appropriate methods?
3. To what extent has the researcher adhered to the criteria that define quality for the quantitative portion of the study?
4. To what extent has the researcher adhered to the criteria that define quality for the qualitative portion of the study?

5. How has the researcher addressed the tension between potentially conflicting demands of paradigms in the design and implementation of the study?

6. Has the researcher appropriately acknowledged the limitations associated with data that were collected to supplement the main data collection of the study?

7. How has the researcher integrated the results from the mixed methods? If necessary, how has the researcher explained conflicting findings that resulted from different methods?

8. What evidence is there that the researcher developed the design to be responsive to the practical and cultural needs of specific subgroups on the basis of such dimensions as disability, culture, language, reading levels, gender, class, and race or ethnicity?

Leech, Dellinger, Brannagan, & Tanaka, (2010) and Creswell and Plano Clark (2017) provide additional considerations in evaluating mixed methods studies. Leech et al. describe a validation framework that can be used to evaluate the credibility of the research, and provide three examples from published studies. Creswell and Plano Clark summarize several efforts by mixed methods scholars to establish criteria for evaluating the quality and credibility of mixed methods studies. (Also refer to Collins, Onwuegbuzie, & Johnson (2012) for a discussion of validity criteria for mixed methods studies, what they call *legitimation*.)

Check for Understanding 4

4a. What are four criteria that should be used to evaluate the quality of a mixed methods study?

Anatomy of a Mixed Methods Article

The following article (Figure 14.5) is an example of the way a mixed methods study is designed and reported. This particular study used a convergent design.

Figure 14.5 Anatomy of a Mixed Methods Study

Majoring in STEM—What Accounts for Women's Career Decision Making? A Mixed Methods Study

Christine Bieri Buschor, Simone Berweger, Andrea Keck Frei, and
Christa Kappler Zurich University of Teacher Education

The aim of this longitudinal, mixed methods study was to gain an understanding of whether female academic high school students who intended to study science, technology, engineering, or mathematics (STEM) actually enrolled in such studies 2 years later, and how these women perceived this process retrospectively. The results revealed a high persistence of students' intentions to pursue a career in STEM areas. In comparison with students who entered the social sciences or humanities, STEM students demonstrated higher competencies in mathematics and placed more importance on pursuing investigative activities. Qualitative analysis revealed that learning experiences, parental support, and role models were decisive in terms of the female students' choice of studies. Since their childhood, these students have developed a sense of identity as scientists. The authors discuss the implications of their findings for teaching and learning in K–12 classrooms. The globalization of markets has led to a great world-wide demand for qualified employees in state-of-the-art technologies. This stands in contrast to the stagnating number of students entering science, technology, engineering, and mathematics (STEM) in various European

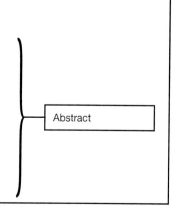

Abstract

(continued)

Figure 14.5 Continued

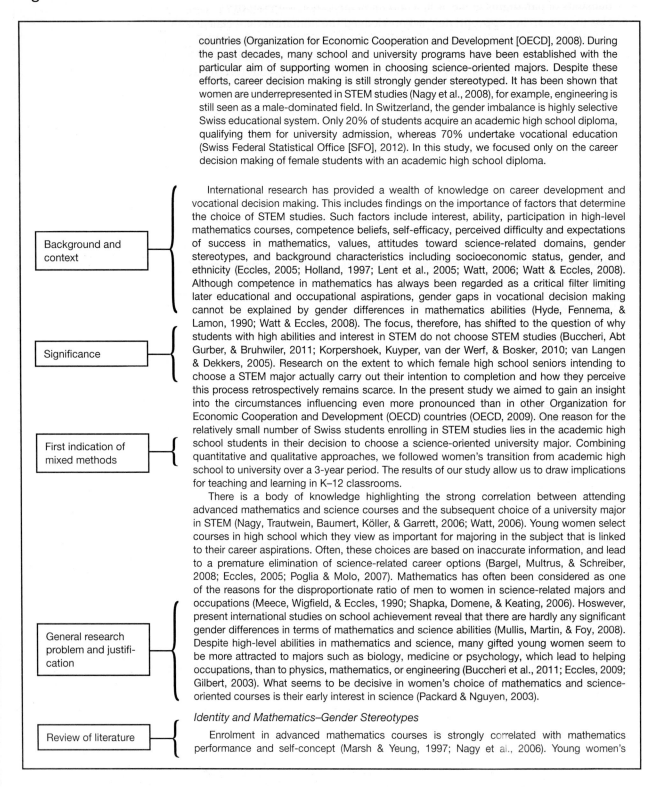

countries (Organization for Economic Cooperation and Development [OECD], 2008). During the past decades, many school and university programs have been established with the particular aim of supporting women in choosing science-oriented majors. Despite these efforts, career decision making is still strongly gender stereotyped. It has been shown that women are underrepresented in STEM studies (Nagy et al., 2008), for example, engineering is still seen as a male-dominated field. In Switzerland, the gender imbalance is highly selective Swiss educational system. Only 20% of students acquire an academic high school diploma, qualifying them for university admission, whereas 70% undertake vocational education (Swiss Federal Statistical Office [SFO], 2012). In this study, we focused only on the career decision making of female students with an academic high school diploma.

Background and context

International research has provided a wealth of knowledge on career development and vocational decision making. This includes findings on the importance of factors that determine the choice of STEM studies. Such factors include interest, ability, participation in high-level mathematics courses, competence beliefs, self-efficacy, perceived difficulty and expectations of success in mathematics, values, attitudes toward science-related domains, gender stereotypes, and background characteristics including socioeconomic status, gender, and ethnicity (Eccles, 2005; Holland, 1997; Lent et al., 2005; Watt, 2006; Watt & Eccles, 2008). Although competence in mathematics has always been regarded as a critical filter limiting later educational and occupational aspirations, gender gaps in vocational decision making cannot be explained by gender differences in mathematics abilities (Hyde, Fennema, & Lamon, 1990; Watt & Eccles, 2008). The focus, therefore, has shifted to the question of why

Significance

students with high abilities and interest in STEM do not choose STEM studies (Buccheri, Abt Gurber, & Bruhwiler, 2011; Korpershoek, Kuyper, van der Werf, & Bosker, 2010; van Langen & Dekkers, 2005). Research on the extent to which female high school seniors intending to choose a STEM major actually carry out their intention to completion and how they perceive this process retrospectively remains scarce. In the present study we aimed to gain an insight into the circumstances influencing even more pronounced than in other Organization for Economic Cooperation and Development (OECD) countries (OECD, 2009). One reason for the relatively small number of Swiss students enrolling in STEM studies lies in the academic high

First indication of mixed methods

school students in their decision to choose a science-oriented university major. Combining quantitative and qualitative approaches, we followed women's transition from academic high school to university over a 3-year period. The results of our study allow us to draw implications for teaching and learning in K–12 classrooms.

There is a body of knowledge highlighting the strong correlation between attending advanced mathematics and science courses and the subsequent choice of a university major in STEM (Nagy, Trautwein, Baumert, Köller, & Garrett, 2006; Watt, 2006). Young women select courses in high school which they view as important for majoring in the subject that is linked to their career aspirations. Often, these choices are based on inaccurate information, and lead to a premature elimination of science-related career options (Bargel, Multrus, & Schreiber, 2008; Eccles, 2005; Poglia & Molo, 2007). Mathematics has often been considered as one of the reasons for the disproportionate ratio of men to women in science-related majors and occupations (Meece, Wigfield, & Eccles, 1990; Shapka, Domene, & Keating, 2006). Hoswever, present international studies on school achievement reveal that there are hardly any significant

General research problem and justification

gender differences in terms of mathematics and science abilities (Mullis, Martin, & Foy, 2008). Despite high-level abilities in mathematics and science, many gifted young women seem to be more attracted to majors such as biology, medicine or psychology, which lead to helping occupations, than to physics, mathematics, or engineering (Buccheri et al., 2011; Eccles, 2009; Gilbert, 2003). What seems to be decisive in women's choice of mathematics and science-oriented courses is their early interest in science (Packard & Nguyen, 2003).

Identity and Mathematics–Gender Stereotypes

Review of literature

Enrolment in advanced mathematics courses is strongly correlated with mathematics performance and self-concept (Marsh & Yeung, 1997; Nagy et al., 2006). Young women's subject-specific self-concept seems to be mediated by self-image, which is also influenced by comparisons with a prototypical student who likes or dislikes this subject. The better the self-image corresponds to that of a prototypical student who likes the subject, the stronger the preference for this subject, and vice versa (Hannover & Kessels, 2004; Kessels, Hannover, & Rau, 2006). Moreover, young women often seem to perceive a stereotype threat and a conflict between their identity as a woman and their identity as a scientist (Settles, Jellison, & Pratt-Hyatt, 2009). Stereotype threat is linked to the idea that women underperform in mathematics tests due to a concern that their performance might confirm negative stereotypes about their group (Kiefer & Sekaquaptewa, 2007; Nosek, Banaji, & Greenwald, 2002; Schmader, 2002). Women seem to be more likely to engage in gender stereotype endorsement when they are exposed to a lower percentage of women in a specific context (e.g., a science program), which may trigger an identity conflict (Bonnot & Croizet, 2007; Delisle, Guay, Senécal, & Larose, 2009).

Study- and Job-Related Expectations

Career decision making is linked to occupational and private roles. Young women who describe themselves as being more family-oriented and less job-oriented show a more negative attitude toward jobs in the STEM field than women who place a high importance on a professional career (Hannover & Kessels, 2004). Studies reveal that women who decide to enter the field of STEM show a very strong expectation that they can make the world a better place (Lupart, Cannon, & Telfer, 2004). Similarly, some studies provide evidence that attaching a lower value to people-oriented job aspects, such as helping others, is one of the most important factors in predicting the choice of a major in physics or mathematics (Eccles, 2007; Poglia & Molo, 2007). In addition, factors such as career options, job security, engaging in investigative activities, having an applied course of studies, and the subsequent career, are relevant to young women's choice of a STEM major (Bargel et al., 2008).

Persistence in STEM and Parental Support

Longitudinal studies show a decreasing interest in both mathematics- and science-oriented careers for women from Grade 7 to 12. The persistence rate of women was found to be significantly lower than that of men (Larose et al., 2008; Seymour, 1995; Van Leuvan, 2004). Persisting in STEM studies can also be linked to parental support: Some studies illustrate that mathematics abilities can be negatively influenced by parents' gender-role attitudes. Parents' gender stereotypes seem to influence girls' self-perceptions and experiences, and can promote gender-typed occupational choices (Jacobs, Chhin, & Bleeker, 2006). In contrast, women with career aspirations in science often grew up in an academic environment and had parental role models in the STEM field (Packard & Nguyen, 2003). A Swiss study revealed that women studying STEM often had a father with a university degree in STEM (Gilbert, 2003).

> Review of literature

Method

The purpose of this mixed-methods study was to examine the career and vocational decision making of women during the transition from Swiss academic high school to higher education. Specifically, the study was designed to gain an understanding of whether female students who intended to study STEM ultimately enrolled in a science-oriented major 2 years later and how they perceived the process of choosing a major. Female students in the social sciences and humanities (SSH) served as a reference group because this provides a contrasting category to mathematics and science (Nosek et al., 2002). The study addresses the following research questions:

> Specific research problem statement

Research Question 1: To what extent are the female students who intend to choose STEM at the end of academic high school persistent in their choice 2 years later?

Research Question 2: What factors play a role in women's choice of a STEM major rather than one in social sciences or humanities?

Research Question 3: How did women studying STEM perceive the process of choosing a major retrospectively?

> Research questions

To address these questions, a mixed-methods approach incorporating triangulation was used. Triangulation is generally understood as a process of using different perspectives in order to provide a deeper understanding (Denzin & Lincoln, 2005). We conceptualized our study as a primarily quantitative, sequential design with a focus on triangulation in terms of seeking convergence, divergence, and complementarity (Erzberger & Kelle, 2003; Tashakkori & Teddlie, 2010).

> Description of specific mixed methods design

(continued)

Figure 14.5 Continued

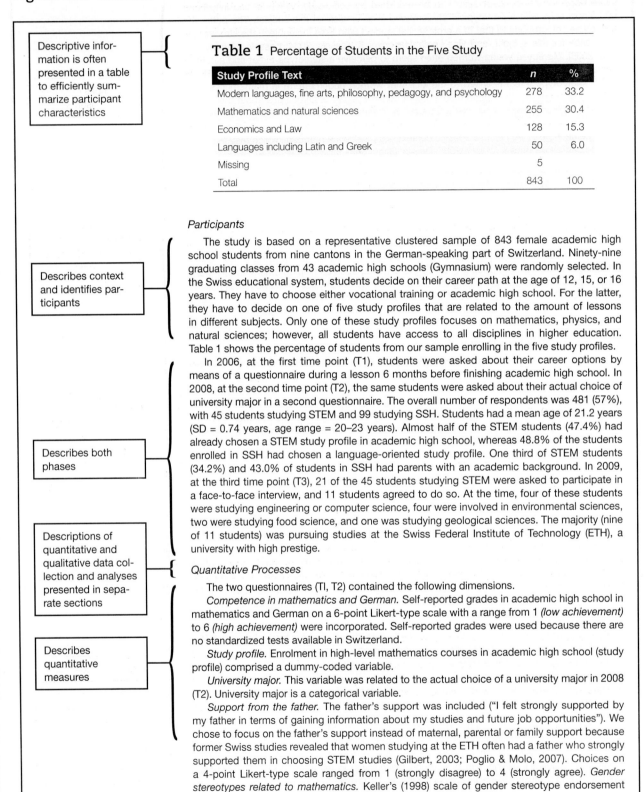

Descriptive information is often presented in a table to efficiently summarize participant characteristics

Table 1 Percentage of Students in the Five Study

Study Profile Text	n	%
Modern languages, fine arts, philosophy, pedagogy, and psychology	278	33.2
Mathematics and natural sciences	255	30.4
Economics and Law	128	15.3
Languages including Latin and Greek	50	6.0
Missing	5	
Total	843	100

Describes context and identifies participants

Participants

The study is based on a representative clustered sample of 843 female academic high school students from nine cantons in the German-speaking part of Switzerland. Ninety-nine graduating classes from 43 academic high schools (Gymnasium) were randomly selected. In the Swiss educational system, students decide on their career path at the age of 12, 15, or 16 years. They have to choose either vocational training or academic high school. For the latter, they have to decide on one of five study profiles that are related to the amount of lessons in different subjects. Only one of these study profiles focuses on mathematics, physics, and natural sciences; however, all students have access to all disciplines in higher education. Table 1 shows the percentage of students from our sample enrolling in the five study profiles.

Describes both phases

In 2006, at the first time point (T1), students were asked about their career options by means of a questionnaire during a lesson 6 months before finishing academic high school. In 2008, at the second time point (T2), the same students were asked about their actual choice of university major in a second questionnaire. The overall number of respondents was 481 (57%), with 45 students studying STEM and 99 studying SSH. Students had a mean age of 21.2 years (SD = 0.74 years, age range = 20–23 years). Almost half of the STEM students (47.4%) had already chosen a STEM study profile in academic high school, whereas 48.8% of the students enrolled in SSH had chosen a language-oriented study profile. One third of STEM students (34.2%) and 43.0% of students in SSH had parents with an academic background. In 2009, at the third time point (T3), 21 of the 45 students studying STEM were asked to participate in a face-to-face interview, and 11 students agreed to do so. At the time, four of these students were studying engineering or computer science, four were involved in environmental sciences, two were studying food science, and one was studying geological sciences. The majority (nine of 11 students) was pursuing studies at the Swiss Federal Institute of Technology (ETH), a university with high prestige.

Descriptions of quantitative and qualitative data collection and analyses presented in separate sections

Quantitative Processes

The two questionnaires (TI, T2) contained the following dimensions.

Competence in mathematics and German. Self-reported grades in academic high school in mathematics and German on a 6-point Likert-type scale with a range from 1 *(low achievement)* to 6 *(high achievement)* were incorporated. Self-reported grades were used because there are no standardized tests available in Switzerland.

Describes quantitative measures

Study profile. Enrolment in high-level mathematics courses in academic high school (study profile) comprised a dummy-coded variable.

University major. This variable was related to the actual choice of a university major in 2008 (T2). University major is a categorical variable.

Support from the father. The father's support was included ("I felt strongly supported by my father in terms of gaining information about my studies and future job opportunities"). We chose to focus on the father's support instead of maternal, parental or family support because former Swiss studies revealed that women studying at the ETH often had a father who strongly supported them in choosing STEM studies (Gilbert, 2003; Poglio & Molo, 2007). Choices on a 4-point Likert-type scale ranged from 1 (strongly disagree) to 4 (strongly agree). *Gender stereotypes related to mathematics.* Keller's (1998) scale of gender stereotype endorsement regarding achievement, abilities, interest and importance of mathematics was used. It contained four items (e.g., "Generally, boys achieve better in mathematics than girls"). A 4-point Likert-type response format with choices ranging from 1 (*strongly disagree*) to 4 (*strongly agree*) was employed. The internal consistency as measured by Cronbach's alpha was .74.

Study and job-related expectancies. In accordance with theories emphasizing a good fit between students' interest and career choice (Holland, 1997; Packard & Nguyen, 2003), we included the following variables: (a) fit between interests and a future occupation, (b) choice of a major mainly focusing on problem solving versus theoretical aspects, (c) choice of a future occupation offering possibilities for investigative activities, (d) choice of a future occupation with a strong focus on practical aspects, and (e) choice of future occupation providing a large amount of social contact. In response to each item, students described their preferences on a 4- point Likert-type scale ranging from 1 (*strongly disagree*) to 4 (*strongly agree*). In addition, occupational self-concept (von Rosenstiel & Nerdinger, 2000) was included (e.g., "I place great importance on work rather than on my private life"), based on a 5-point Likert-type scale with choices ranging from 1 (*strongly disagree*) to 5 (*strongly agree*).

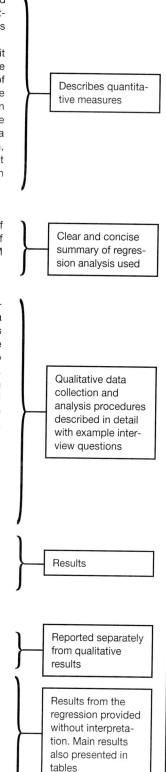

Describes quantitative measures

Quantitative Data Analysis

For our purposes, logistic regression was used to predict the discrete outcome choice of STEM versus SSH in college major. The impact of the predictors is related to the odds ratios. If the odds ratio (exp B*) exceeds 1, it means that there is a higher likelihood of choosing a STEM major than of choosing a major in the field of SSH (Tabachnick & Fidell, 2001).

Clear and concise summary of regression analysis used

Qualitative Processes

Narrative interviews were used in order to analyze STEM students' career decision-making process. In 2009, 11 students participated in an interview held at our university by a female interviewer. At the beginning of the interview, the following open-ended question was presented to the students: "How did it happen that you chose a STEM major?" As we were particularly interested in the students' perception of choosing a nontraditional career, we also asked about their experiences relating to gender if this aspect did not emerge in the narratives. The interviews were recorded and transcribed verbatim. As the interviews were conducted in Swiss German (mother tongue dialect), we had to transcribe them into High German (official written language). For the purpose of this article we had them translated into English. To analyze the data, we applied strategies from grounded theory, which has been defined as a comparative analysis for discovering theoretical concepts and themes from data rather than testing hypotheses (Corbin & Strauss, 2008; Glaser & Strauss, 1974). A collaborative research team conducted the systematic coding of the data through open, axial and selective coding. In a first step, we divided the data into small units, which we analyzed and compared in terms of differences and similarities. In this way, we were able to identify themes and concepts. In a second step, questions referring to why, how, and what happened (interactions), as well as strategies and consequences of these interactions, helped us to group concepts into categories on a more abstract level and to establish connections between categories in order to identify patterns. In a third step, categories were further analyzed to enable us to select a core category around which the major categories could be grouped. During this iterative process, concepts and themes were constantly redesigned and reintegrated. Table 2 contains the themes that emerged in the students' narratives. These themes will be further described in the Results section.

Qualitative data collection and analysis procedures described in detail with example interview questions

Results

Quantitative Results

The results from the longitudinal study indicate that 25 of 29 female students who intended to choose a STEM major were persistent in their choice 2 years later. Additionally, 12 students who intended to choose another major changed to a STEM major.

Reported separately from qualitative results

Predictors of choosing STEM. Logistic regression analysis (Method Enter) was undertaken to examine the impact of 12 predictors on the likelihood of choosing a STEM major rather than a major in social sciences or humanities. Table 3 provides an overview of the predictors used in the model. After deletion of missing cases, a sample of 115 women studying STEM (*n* = 34) and SSH (*n* = 81) was included in the analysis. The predictors, as a set, distinguished between the two groups. The prediction rate for an overall success rate was 92% even though the two groups were not equal in number (n = 34 in STEM, n = 81 in SSH). Table 4 encompasses regression coefficients, Wald statistics, odds ratios, and 95% confidence interval for odds ratios for each of the predictors. The odds ratio (exp B*) shows some change in the likelihood

Results from the regression provided without interpretation. Main results also presented in tables

(continued)

Figure 14.5 Continued

of choice of STEM rather than SSH on the basis of a one-unit change. According to the Wald criterion, the 12 variables predicted choice decision with 79% variance, Nagelkerke's R^2. The results show that six of 12 predictors were statistically significant. The following three predictors had a positive impact on choosing a STEM major: (a) value of a future occupation offering possibilities for investigative activities, (b) a major mainly focusing on problem solving, and (c) competence in mathematics. Three predictors showed a comparatively weak negative effect on choosing STEM: (d) value of a future occupation providing a large amount of social contact, (e) competence in German, and (f) a job primarily focusing on practical aspects. In contrast, the

Table 2 Themes that Emerged in the Students' Narratives

Theme	Definition
Early sense of identity as a future scientist	Students revealed that they felt an early passion for natural sciences or information technology, a curiosity about the world and a desire to understand things.
Emotional and learning support	Many parents were supportive and stimulated their children's love of learning by providing science materials.
Role models in the broader network	Parents' or siblings' friends or neighbors working in or studying science served as role models for the students.
Parental concern	Parents feared that studying science, technology, engineering, or mathematics (STEM) would overstrain their daughter.
Mathematics as a means to an end	Students perceived mathematics as a necessary condition to study natural sciences.
A sense of uniqueness Broad range of interest	Being a minority in STEM studies enhanced their pride and feeling of uniqueness. Students displayed interdisciplinary interests, ranging from philosophy to natural and technical sciences.
Minimizing risks and optimizing profit	Students aimed to choose a major relating to a clear job profile and providing broad career options and job security at a university with a strong reputation.

Themes are often summarized in a table to help the reader navigate through the qualitative results prior to introducing the results section

Table 3 Predictors of the Logistic Regression Model (Means and Standard Deviations for the Sample and Subsamples)

	STEM women			SSH women			Total		
	n	M	SD	n	M	SD	n	M	SD
Competence in mathematics	38	4.92	0.70	86	4.29	0.76	124	4.48	0.80
Competence in German	38	4.72	0.50	86	4.88	0.54	124	4.84	0.53
Study profile	38			86			124		
Support from the father	37	2.27	1.09	84	2.43	0.95	121	2.38	0.99
Gender stereotypes	38	3.46	0.34	86	3.59	0.42	124	3.55	0.40
Fit between interest and occupation	38	3.89	0.31	86	3.83	0.38	124	3.85	0.36
Major focusing on problem solving	38	2.95	0.84	86	2.71	0.82	124	2.78	0.83
Major focusing on theoretical aspects	38	1.76	0.59	85	1.98	0.77	123	1.91	0.72
Job with possibilities for investigative activities	38	3.05	0.99	86	1.95	0.68	124	2.29	0.94
Job with a strong focus on practical aspects	38	2.74	0.89	86	2.94	0.77	124	2.88	0.81
Job providing large amount of social contact	38	3.03	0.79	86	3.59	0.62	124	3.42	0.72
Occupational self-concept (career orientation)	38	4.18	0.87	85	3.91	1.05	123	3.99	1.00

Note. STEM = science, technology, engineering, or mathematics; SSH = social sciences and humanities, *a* Dummy variable.

Table 4 Logistic Regression Analysis of the Likelihood of Choosing a STEM Major Rather than a Major in Social Sciences or Humanities

Predictor	B	SE B	P	e^n (Odds Ratio)
Constant	1.91	4.59	.69	6.73
Competence in mathematics	1.26	0.61	.04	3.53
Competence in German	-2.11	1.00	.03	0.12
Study Profile (enrolment high level mathematics courses)	1.53	1.22	.21	4.64
Support from the father	-1.05	0.42	.30	0.65
Gender stereotypes related to mathematics	-0.27	0.51	.60	0.76
Study-related expectancies				
Fit between interest and study	0.47	0.43	.27	1.60
Major mainly focusing on problem solving	2.09	0.73	.00	8.05
Major mainly focusing on theoretical aspects	-0.32	0.60	.59	0.73
Job-related expectancies				
Possibilities for investigative activities	2.43	0.65	.00	11.37
A strong focus on practical aspects	-2.36	0.82	.00	0.21
A large amount of social contract	-1.57	0.56	.00	0.21
Occupational self-concept	-0.52	0.48	.28	0.59

Note. B = unstandardized beta; STEM = science, technology, engineering, and mathematics. $x^2(12, N = 115) = 93.148$; Nagelkerkes $R^2 = .79$, $p < .001$.

following six predictors were found not to be statistically significant: (a) study profile (enrollment in high-level mathematics courses), (b) gender stereotype endorsement regarding the belief that boys achieve better in mathematics and are more interested in mathematics than girls, (c) perceived support from the father, (d) a good fit between interests and a future occupation, (e) choice of a major mainly focusing on theoretical aspects, and (f) an occupational self-concept with a strong career orientation.

Qualitative Findings

⎫ Presented by earlier
⎭ introduced themes

Early sense of identity as a future scientist. The narratives shed light on the close link between early interest in science and family influence. Early science-related learning experiences and the students' keen interest in science in general played a crucial role in their decision-making process. Being a scientist seemed to be an important goal for students who chose STEM. However, most of these students concentrated on studying science but did not yet have specific career plans. Since early childhood, they had developed a passion for natural sciences and a drive to understand the world. As one student put it,

> [t]his [the choice of a major] is because I have always been interested in it [science]. And I can imagine working in one of these fields.... because I have always loved it.... and I have always wanted to know why things are the way they are. (Transcript H, lines 80–88)

Parental support by providing learning settings. Most parents had provided a stimulating learning setting, which seemed to instill in their children the intrinsic need to gain knowledge and explore phenomena in natural sciences and technology. Some students had experienced discussions on environmental topics, whereas others had received materials such as microscopes or science journals for children. Parents are described as emotionally supportive. Parental support was one of the reasons to which students referred when they explained why they ultimately chose a STEM major:

> They supported me in choosing science... because they had always supported me in doing whatever I wanted to do.... If I had wanted to study mathematics, I could have done it. (Transcript C, lines 265–269)

(*continued*)

Figure 14.5 Continued

Role models in the broader network. The students had important role models in their broader network rather than in their core family. This network mainly encompassed parents' friends, neighbors, and brothers' friends who either served as a source of information or supported the women during their decision-making process. Models from social media, such as female superintendents in crime thriller series, were also mentioned.

Parental concern. Some parents were concerned about their daughters' choice. In the following quote, a student talks about her father's attempt to convince her to enter a university of applied sciences with a more practically oriented curriculum rather than the ETH, which is well known for its high requirements:

> My father told me that I had to be aware of these aspects [moving out, high requirements in math]. I had always been working so much during high school and therefore he wondered if I was able to live up to my own expectations. He then suggested that I could rather study at a university of applied sciences.... I was strongly influenced by his advice and was finally convinced. (Transcript S, lines 50–63)

Mathematics as a means to an end. The students hardly ever mentioned their mathematics ability. Moreover, they presented their abilities in mathematics cautiously as "not bad" rather than "good." If mathematics played a role in the students' narratives, it was merely seen as a necessary evil to pass the examinations. Furthermore, students showed a pattern of external attribution when coping with failure in mathematics tests. Learning settings in high school, however, emerged in the women's narratives. Advanced science courses and teachers providing challenging learning opportunities were described as important contextual factors for their choice. As one student put it,

> I think if he [the teacher] had not provided interesting lessons, it [the choice of a major] would have taken another direction. (Transcript M, lines 212–214)

A sense of uniqueness. The analysis further revealed contextual conditions fostering or blocking the process of choosing a STEM major. Some students expressed their preference for collaborating with men rather than with women. The students reported that they felt widely accepted by male students and warmly welcomed by lecturers at the university. Comparisons with others and a sense of uniqueness emerged as topics when the women talked about choosing their major:

> I am going to study manufacturing systems engineering.... I am a little bit proud and tell myself that this is something special. I could also study chemistry but you could study it at any university. And then you get the feeling that somehow engineering is inherently special and you feel... it is not arrogance, but it means not studying something boring such as economics or law. (Transcript C, lines 76–84)

Broad range of interests. Due to the students' broad range of interests, varying from philosophy and psychology to specialized science majors (e.g., criminalistics), it was difficult for the students to choose a major. Only through a constant process of balancing different options and seeking information relating to the vast field of science did they finally decide on a major. Students described themselves as being curious, confident, and determined to achieve their goals. There was also evidence of a strong sense of seeking autonomy.

Minimizing risks and maximizing profit. Students also referred to strategies such as minimizing risk and maximizing profit. In particular, students who chose the field of engineering mentioned that they preferred a science-oriented and hands-on major that would offer a variety of career options in different fields of work. In the students' view, their choice of a STEM career (and studying at ETH) was closely linked to social prestige and high job security due to a worldwide shortage of experts in the field. Having a variety of career options was also associated with the possibility of balancing family and work obligations.

Discussion

Brief statement of purpose { The aim of this study was to gain an understanding of whether female students who intended to choose a STEM discipline before finishing academic high school did or did not ultimately choose a science-oriented major within a 2-year time span. To this aim, quantitative and qualitative results were combined. Overall, the students were persistent in their choice. This is in contrast to other studies showing that a high amount of women who had been interested in STEM studies at the end of high school ultimately changed their aspirations (Larose et al., 2008; Mau, 2003). In our study, STEM students showed a broad range of (science-related) interests and described their decision making as a complex process throughout their development from early childhood into adulthood. According to their narratives, they have always had a strong wish to be a scientist: These students already showed a clear sense of identity as scientists, whereas their vocational choice and career planning, including family planning, seemed to be vague. Furthermore, the importance of a future job offering possibilities for investigative activities had the strongest impact on predicting the choice of a STEM major rather than a major in SSH in the prediction model. Therefore, the fascination for the content of these disciplines and the identity as a (future) scientist seem to be most relevant to female students for choosing STEM. One explanation for being noncommittal about their vocational choice might be women's tendency not to plan a specific career in science because they are more concerned with their future family-planning as opposed to men (Frome, Alfeld, Eccles, & Barber, 2008). Results from both strands revealed the high correlation between the deep passion for science and the actual choice of a STEM major. As illustrated in the interviews, early fascination for science-related learning was one of the most important triggers for choosing a STEM major, which concurs with other studies (Nauta & Epperson, 2003; Seymour, 1995). It was shown that both a strong preference for studies emphasizing problem solving as well as a future job offering the possibility for investigative activities had a positive impact on choosing STEM. Qualitative findings concurred with these results: Students expected to contribute to problem solving in an applied field. This could be linked to their early learning experiences, which were often of an experimental nature. The finding may also be interpreted as a strong wish to work as a professional or leading expert in the field, who assumes responsibility rather than merely carrying out work. Moreover, these students seek a career that provides not only a wide range of career options but also security and the possibility to balance family and work obligations. These results are broadly in line with other studies revealing that women in STEM have a strong expectation to change the world. At the same time, they show a certain desire to conform, which can also increase the likelihood of leaving a STEM discipline due to a stereotype threat from society (Bargel et al., 2008; Kerr & Robinson Kurpius, 2004; Lupart et al., 2004).

The results from the quantitative findings further revealed that a preference for a job providing a large amount of social contact decreased the likelihood of choosing STEM. This result is consistent with the assumption that STEM students attach less value to people-oriented jobs than other students (Eccles, 2009). Furthermore, gender stereotypes were not a statistically significant predictor of choosing STEM versus SSH, nor did they emerge explicitly in the students' narratives. An explanation for this might be found in the interviewing situation where the women made an effort to portray themselves as equal to men by not bringing up gender differences. However, students' self-concept in mathematics, which was cautiously presented as low in the narratives, might be an indicator of implicit stereotypes, because linking the self with being female and mathematics with being male can lead to difficulties in associating mathematics with the self (Nosek et al., 2002). It is assumed that these stereotypes have an impact on career decision making. Not verbalizing gender in the narratives does not mean that this is not an issue. There might be subconscious mechanisms leading to the students' choice that cannot be detected in the narratives by analyzing them with strategies from grounded theory.

The study profile did not have an impact on the choice of STEM over SSH. Corresponding with other studies (Schaefers, Epperson, & Nauta, 1997), however, high abilities in mathematics were a significant predictor. Interestingly, this result diverged from the students' description of their mathematical skills as "not bad" rather than "good." Mathematics seemed to be a necessary evil to pass the examinations, which could be interpreted as an adaptive strategy to cope with possible failure in the upcoming examinations. This is comparable with Seymour's findings that women who were persistent in STEM studies expanded their adaptive coping strategies in order to survive in a male-dominated faculty (Seymour, 1995).

In the quantitative strand, support from the father in STEM was not found to be a predictor of choosing STEM. Other studies, however, stress the importance of the father as a role model, particularly for students of engineering (Eccles, 1994; Gilbert, 2003). Qualitative findings contributed to complementarity by illustrating the ambiguity of parental support. Parents seemed to be completely supportive during career decision making. Otherwise, they seemed deeply concerned with their daughters' needs and the high requirements of the rigorous ETH. We assume that parents' (particularly fathers') worries concerning study and job-related requirements can be a barrier for students considering a STEM career. Alternatively, as observed in the narratives, support from other role models and motivating teachers may compensate for parents' ambiguity.

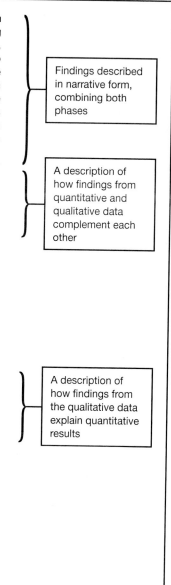

Findings described in narrative form, combining both phases

A description of how findings from quantitative and qualitative data complement each other

A description of how findings from the qualitative data explain quantitative results

(continued)

Figure 14.5 Continued

Limitations presented succinctly

Limitations

There were several limitations in this study. First, the small sample size, which is due to the generally small number of high school students in Switzerland, constitutes a major limitation. For the second time point, only 57% of the students reported the actual choice of their major, which led to restrictions in the regression model. The results may therefore not be reliable if generalized to other students, despite the fact that the proportion of women in the sample is an accurate representation of the proportion of female students in different subjects at Swiss universities (SFO, 2008). Second, there may be a bias in the sample of students who agreed to be interviewed. Third, this study did not contain interviews with students from the field of social sciences and humanities, which could be used for comparative purposes.

Conclusion and Implications for Education

Our results clearly indicate that the decrease in interest in a career in science does not occur during the transition from academic high school to university, but rather takes place prior to matriculation into universities. Consequently, encouraging girls and adolescents to choose STEM careers in K–12 classrooms seems to be highly important. We can conclude that it is crucial to enhance girls' early passion for science from the very beginning of their education. Teaching in science should, therefore, be focused on providing learning settings with a high level of cognitive activation such as challenging experiments. The goal is to enhance girls' competence and self-efficacy beliefs relating to mathematics and natural sciences in order to strengthen their early sense of identity as a (future) scientist. Concurrently, these early learning experiences should be more closely linked to the girls' (and boys') perceptions and preconceptions of occupational activities. Problem-solving tasks in a technical area, for instance, could be presented along with images of female role models in engineering or science. In this process, the focus is on the link between early science learning at school and future occupational activities including reflection on gender stereotypes rather than on early vocational decision making. This link may contribute to reducing gender stereotypes. In this context, teachers' awareness of their own gender stereotypes relating to mathematics and science is an important precondition. Furthermore, science teachers could enhance parents' preconceptions and gender stereotypes relating to mathematics by raising their awareness of these processes.

FUNDING

The research reported here is supported by a grant from the Swiss National Science Foundation and by the Gebert-Rüf Foundation.

REFERENCES

Bargel, T., Multrus, F., & Schreiber, N. (2008). *Studienqualität und Attraktivität der Ingenieurwissenschaften [The quality and attractiveness of majors in engineering sciences]*. Bonn, Germany: BMBF.

Bonnot, V. C., & Croizet, J. P. (2007). Stereotype internalization, math perceptions, and occupational choices of women with counter-stereotypical university majors. *Swiss Journal of Psychology*, 66, 169–178.

Buccheri, G., Abt Gürber, N., & Brühwiler, C. (2011). The impact of gender on interest in science topics and the choice of scientific and technical vocations. *International Journal of Science Education*, 33, 159–178.

Corbin, J., & Strauss, A. L. (2008). *Basics of qualitative research*. Los Angeles, CA: Sage.

Delisle, M.-N., Guay, F., Senécal, C., & Larose, S. (2009). Predicting stereotype endorsement and academic motivation in women in science programs: A longitudinal model. *Learning and Individual Differences, 468–475. Denzin, N. K., & Lincoln, Y. S. (2005). *The Sage handbook of qualitative research*. London, UK: Sage.

Eccles, J. S. (1994). Understanding women's educational and occupational choices: Applying the Eccles et al. model of achievement-related choices. *Psychology of Women Quarterly*, 18, 585–609.

Eccles, J. S. (2005). Subjective task value and the Eccles et al. model of achievement-related choices. In A. J. Elliot & C. S. Dweck (Eds.), *Handbook of competence and motivation* (pp. 105–121). London, UK: The Guilford Press.

Eccles, J. S. (2007). Where are all the women? Gender differences in participation in physical science and engineering. In S. J. Ceci & W. M. Williams (Eds.), *Why aren't more women in science?* (pp. 199–210). Washington, DC: American Psychological Association.

Eccles, J. S. (2009). Who am I and what am I going to do with my life? Personal and collective identities as motivators of action. *Educational Psychologist, 44,* 78–89.

Erzberger, C., & Kelle, U. (2003). Making inferences in mixed methods: The rules of integration. In C. Teddlie & A. Tashakkori (Eds.), *Handbook of mixed methods in social and behavioral sciences* (pp. 3–50). Thousand Oaks, CA: Sage.

references continued

Key Terms

Convergent design

Merged analysis

Mixed methods

Mixing

Priority

Sequence

Sequential mixed methods designs

Explanatory sequential design

Exploratory sequential design

Discussion Questions

1. What is mixed methods research, and how is it distinguished from quantitative and qualitative designs?
2. When are mixed methods designs useful?
3. How do explanatory sequential, exploratory sequential, and convergent designs differ in purpose and procedure?
4. What are the key advantages and disadvantages of each type of mixed methods design?
5. Why is it important for researchers to clearly explain their rationale for conducting a mixed methods study?
6. How do explanatory sequential, exploratory sequential, and convergent designs differ in *priority* and *sequence*?
7. What are some key considerations in evaluating mixed methods studies?

Application Exercise

1. Locate and review a mixed methods empirical article a journal in your field of study. What type of mixed methods design is used in the study? What are some strengths and weaknesses of the study? How could it be improved?

Check for Understanding Answers

1a. When both quantitative and qualitative data are needed to find the signal.

1b. The major advantages are merging the best features of quantitative and qualitative so findings are not limited by a single approach, allowing for more complex questions to be investigated, and promoting a stronger understanding of the phenomena being investigated; the main disadvantage is that it requires expertise in both approaches and takes more time and resources.

2a. Primarily in the addition of three unique steps, identifying feasibility, rationale, and design prior to research questions.

2b. To guide the nature of the research questions to be aligned with what can be investigated with the design.

3a. Explanatory sequential when the need is to explain quantitative findings and add insights and understanding; exploratory sequential when qualitative data are first gathered to inform quantitative design and procedures; convergent when both approaches are used simultaneously to triangulate findings.

3b. Explanatory uses qualitative second to explain quantitative results; exploratory uses qualitative first to frame quantitative step.

3c. Inconsistencies may require additional data collection; additional expertise and resources may be needed; difficulty of simultaneous data collection.

4a. Take your pick: appropriate justification for the design; questions clearly aligned with methods; quantitative standards met; qualitative standards met; demands of conflicting paradigms addressed; limitations acknowledged; findings integrate the qualitative and quantitative data; subgroup characteristics accounted for.

Chapter 15
Action Research

By Jesse Senechal and James McMillan

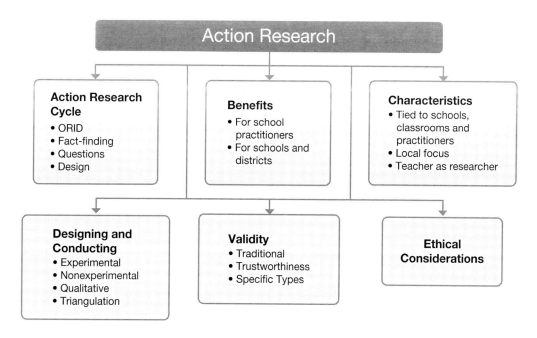

Learning Outcomes

15.1 Compare the characteristics, strengths, and limitations of action research to traditional types of empirical research.

15.2 Be able to identify and construct appropriate action research questions.

15.3 Be able to design experimental and nonexperimental action research.

15.4 Know and apply the criteria for evaluating the validity of action research.

Chapter Road Map

If you work in schools, or plan on doing so, you may think of educational research as something you read about in journals or review in professional development. However, teachers, counselors, administrators, and other building-level instructional staff can be more than just consumers of research; they can be the researchers, too. In this chapter we discuss school-based action research, a form of systematic investigation that is initiated, designed, and conducted by practitioners to improve teaching and learning, and to initiate change within schools.

What Is Action Research?

Learning Outcome 15.1 Compare the characteristics, strengths, and limitations of action research to traditional types of empirical research.

With the recent emphasis in schools on reflective practice, evidence-based practice, data-driven decision making, and continuous improvement, the field of school-based practitioner research and inquiry continues to grow. The focus of this chapter is on one form of practitioner inquiry—**action research**. Action research is exciting because it brings together the characteristics of systematic inquiry that have been reviewed through this book with workplace practice, making it highly relevant and useful.

The term *action research* was first used by Kurt Lewin, a social psychologist, in the 1940s (Bradbury, Mirvis, Neilsen, & Pasmore, 2008). As presented by Lewin, action research is a method of inquiry adopted in a wide range of social and organizational settings that involves a cyclical process of inquiry among practitioners that moves from identification of problems to planning, action and evaluation. Action research is often illustrated by a spiral, where problem posing leads to knowledge development, which leads to the identification of new problems and new cycles of inquiry (Pine, 2009). Figure 15.1 presents an example of the action research spiral. This figure will be discussed in more detail in a later section, in which we walk you through the steps involved in the action research process.

Action research within schools is called by a variety of terms, including *classroom research, teacher research, teacher action research,* and *classroom action research.* This reflects the fact that action research emerged from several parallel but distinct traditions. For example, in some cases, action research aligns closely with the theories and practice of organizational science, where the focus is on efficiency and continuous improvement. A contemporary iteration of this is the growing use of school-based inquiry teams that are part of a *networked improvement community* (Bryk, Gomez,

Figure 15.1 Ongoing Cycles of Action Research

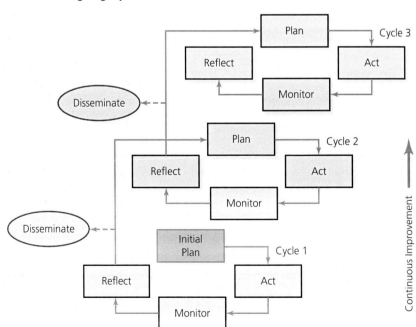

Grunow, LeMahieu, 2015). In other cases, the theories and practices of action research can reflect a more critical stance. For example, the tradition of **participatory action research** presents a method for critiquing and transforming social systems through a social justice lens (Freire, 1972). In this approach, action research in schools directly addresses issues of educational inequity by empowering key stakeholders at the ground-level (students, teachers, parents) to construct knowledge and speak back to the powers within the system.

Despite the differences in origins, however, these traditions reflect on common understandings of epistemology and method. In this chapter, we use the term *action research* to refer to the category broadly, and *school-based action research* to refer to action research in schools. The descriptor *school-based* is meant to emphasize the idea that action research is not just for teachers. Principals, counselors, librarians, school nurses, and even security staff can engage in the action research process. Below are three definitions that help us understand the unique characteristics of action research. The first definition applies to action research broadly, whereas the others are specific to school-based action research.

- Action research is a participatory process concerned with developing practical knowing in the pursuit of worthwhile human purposes. It seeks to bring together action and reflection, theory and practice, in participation with others, in the pursuit of practical solutions to issues of pressing concern to people, and more generally the flourishing of individual persons and their communities. (Reason & Bradbury, 2008, p. 4)

- Action research is a process of concurrently inquiring about problems and taking action to solve them. It is a sustained, intentional, recursive, and dynamic process of inquiry in which the teacher takes an action—purposefully and ethically in a specific classroom context—to improve teaching/learning. (Pine, 2009, p. 30)

- Collaborations among school-based teachers, and other educators, university-based colleagues, and sometimes parents and community activists. The efforts of action research center on altering curriculum, challenging common school practices, and working for social change by engaging in a continuous process of problem posing, data gathering, analysis, and action. (Cochran-Smith & Lytle, 2009, p. 40)

As you can tell from these definitions, action research has many similarities to traditional ideas of research. It involves posing questions, using theories, collecting and analyzing data, and coming to conclusions. As with traditional applied educational research, it is also focused on improving the practices of teaching and learning. However, there are several ways that action research is also a significant departure from traditional approaches to research. These differences include the following:

- *Action research presents new ideas about practitioner/researcher roles.* School-based action research changes the role of school practitioner from being a potential participant of research to central actor in the research process. While it is common for university-based researchers to play a supporting role as the facilitator of the action research process, the school practitioner is the primary investigator. The practitioner is the one who has final responsibility for identifying the problem, posing the question(s), developing the instruments, collecting and analyzing the data, and presenting the findings.

- *Action research aspires to local relevance, not generalizability.* The results of school-based action research are intended to inform practice in local settings. Action research could influence instructional decisions, curricular changes, or school policies, for example. As such, the sampling, data collection methods, analysis, and dissemination reflect this emphasis on practical and local problem solving.

The results of action research studies are not intended to be generalizable beyond the specific context where the study is conducted; however, much like case studies, the findings may be transferable and relevant to other classroom and school settings.

- *Action research presents new ideas about how research knowledge is created.* School-based action research challenges ideas about how research-based knowledge is created and used within schools. Under the traditional research model, knowledge about teaching and learning is developed by those outside schools and then disseminated through journals and reports to be consumed by practitioners and policy makers. Often, the effect of research knowledge on practice is unclear. With school-based action research, knowledge is created in the context of practice and in response to particular problems. Broader dissemination within an action research framework is a bottom-up rather than a top-down process.

- *Action research presents new ideas about the relationship between theory and practice.* Unlike traditional educational research, in which the processes of theory development and testing happen separately from the practices of teaching and learning, teacher action research rests on the idea of *praxis*. In school-based action research, theory directly informs practice, which, in turn, shapes theory.

Another important characteristic of action research is that it is often a collaborative process. Although an individual teacher or school staff member can conduct an action research study, generally action research occurs within and among supportive networks that include other school personnel and, in many cases, university researchers. In some cases, action research communities within schools can focus on common problems and work to solve them collaboratively. This community of research practice also provides action researchers with technical support—for example, with instrument development or data analysis—and critical peer feedback that tends to improve the quality of the research.

Table 15.1 outlines some of the differences between action research and traditional research. However, it should be noted that many forms of action research—and traditional research, for that matter—do not fit neatly into this framework.

Table 15.1 Characteristics of School-Based Action Research Versus Traditional Educational Research

Characteristic	School-Based Action Research	Traditional Educational Research
Goal	New knowledge that is relevant primarily to the local setting	New knowledge that is meant to generalize or transfer to other settings
Who determines the research question and carries out the study?	Practitioners: teachers, principals, counselors, other school personnel	Trained researchers: university professors, scholars, graduate students
Approach to context	Research is responsive to and highlights the unique qualities of local classroom and school context	Research attempts to control the confounding variables of context
Literature review	Brief, with a focus on secondary sources	Extensive, with an emphasis on primary sources
Instrumentation	Measures are often developed locally and are convenient and easy to administer and score	Measures are typically off-the-shelf and selected on the basis of technical adequacy
Sampling	Convenience, purposeful sampling of teachers and students in the targeted setting	Tends to be random or representative
Design	Tends to be nonexperimental or quasi-experimental; emergent through the action research cycles	Whatever design is needed; fidelity to initial design is important
Data analysis	Descriptive	Descriptive and inferential
Dissemination of results	Focus is primarily on local dissemination within school departments and schools and possibly moves to broader audiences	Focus is primarily on broad publication and presentation to the research community

Author Reflection *In my (Jesse's) experience as an action researcher and as a leader of action research groups, I find that it is always helpful to have a collaborative network of other practitioner researchers to support your work. One of the most important reasons for this is that it creates a motivation to keep going. The action research meetings create a form of peer accountability that pushes people to follow through with their plans.*

Check for Understanding 1

1a. What are the strengths of school-based action research when comparing it to traditional forms of research?

1b. What are the limitations of school-based action research when comparing it to traditional forms of research?

Benefits of Action Research

Ultimately, all research conducted within schools should be assessed in terms of its potential value to improve teaching, and also to enhance student outcomes. In this regard, action research has a unique set of benefits. This includes direct benefits to the school practitioner leading the study and the students in their class, to the schools and districts in which it occurs, and, potentially, for the broader field of educational research. Following are some reflections on these levels of benefit.

School Practitioners Involved in the Research

The primary benefit of school-based action research goes to the teachers and other school personnel leading the research, and the students with whom they directly work. Those who are involved in this form of reflective practice are likely to be more effective at meeting desired student outcomes, whether they are academic, behavioral, or social (Schön, 1983). In fact, many have framed school-based action research as an enhanced model of professional development (Pine, 2009; Zeichner, 2003)—one that changes the question from "How can we best train our teachers?" to "How can we promote ongoing professional learning among our teachers?" (Cochran-Smith, 2002). Along these lines, school-based action research promotes a culture of learning, self-assessment, and reflection that allows opportunities for professionalism and leadership. Often, this level of engagement with research helps practitioners understand the

Authors' Reflection *When I (Jesse) talk with teachers and other school practitioners about the benefits of action research, I often hear them share that it makes them feel like professionals. I believe that a large part of this has to do with the idea that action research encourages them to take action on identified problems, to think critically (using professional judgment), and to consider ways to share their professional knowledge. To me, these sentiments shared by the teacher action researchers suggest that schools and school districts should do more to support this form of professional development.*

benefits of existing research literature as well as evidence-based systematic inquiry. When practitioners start thinking and acting like researchers, learning about research becomes relevant and meaningful.

Schools and Districts Where Action Research Occurs

Despite the urgency of many of the problems that face our schools, the culture of schools and school districts often makes change a frustratingly slow process. It is also the case that change-oriented policies informed by traditional research are often perceived by practitioners as disconnected from their realities and are responded to with resistance or reluctant compliance, rather than full support (Fullan, 2007; Heibert, Gallimore, & Stigler, 2002). In many research studies, teachers either see findings that they believe are so obvious that they do not warrant investigation or are not relevant because they were conducted in other settings and therefore do not address the particular set of problems they face in their classrooms and schools. School-based action research is designed to change this dynamic. It positions teachers as the agents, rather than the subjects, of change within their classrooms and within schools (Cochran-Smith & Lytle, 2009). In this way, action research has the potential to shift the climate of a school to a more open atmosphere in which it is standard practice to openly ponder teaching methods, take risks, and depend on others to design studies and to understand the usefulness of results. When it is used regularly within schools, it creates a systemwide mindset for school improvement and a professional problem-solving ethos.

Benefits to the Field of Educational Research

A persistent problem in the field of education is the gap between research and practice (Eisner, 1985; Heibert et al., 2002). Although thousands of well-designed research studies are conducted each year on various dimensions of teaching and learning, it is rare for the knowledge created by those studies to reach the hands of those for whom the knowledge would be most useful—that is, teachers and other school-level staff. School-based action research has the potential to bridge this gap. Not only does it bring teachers into the culture of research and thus expand the community of researchers, but it also leads to a new type of research knowledge, grounded in everyday practice, that have the potential to contribute to the development of knowledge in the educational research community.

Conducting Action Research

Now that we have a working definition of school-based action research and understand some of the benefits of this approach, the next question is, "How is it done?" In this section we review the steps involved in conducting an action research study by walking through the process illustrated in the action research spiral (Figure 15.1). This begins with a discussion of how to select a topic and develop an initial plan. We then move on to discuss ways of taking professional action and collecting data to monitor results. Finally, we discuss reflecting on the results (data analysis) and disseminating the results. Excerpt 15.1 shows how the action research cycle is discussed within the context of a published study.

> EXCERPT 15.1
> # Cyclical Process in Action Research
>
> This study was conducted in three phases over a two-year period and involved students and staff from three faculties.... An action research process based on cycles of action and reflection... was used to develop peer assessment procedures that were responsive to the student and staff needs and concerns. This process was participatory, collaborative, and reflexive. (p. 427)
>
> SOURCE: Ballantyne, R., Highes, K., & Mylonas, A. (2002). Developing procedures for implementing peer assessment in large classes using an action research process. *Assessment and Evaluation in Higher Education, 27*(5), 427–441.

Identifying and Refining Your Research Focus

Learning Outcome 15.2 Be able to identify and construct appropriate action research questions.

With most research efforts, the first steps are often not only the most challenging, but also, in many ways, the most important. The demise of many research studies can be traced to a failure of the researcher to select and refine the topic, or to ask the right research questions. A research topic can be too broad or too narrow. Questions can be framed using the wrong variables or expressing the wrong relationship between them.

First steps are especially important for action research. When you begin an action research process, you want to make sure that you are heading down a path that will lead to learning and effect change in your local setting. However, it is also important to understand that within the action research process, the research focus and design are emergent. Questions change, as do approaches to answering them. This is an important point to remember when beginning an action research project. Although you will want to make sure that you put good work into the initial step of your process, it is best to understand that not everything has to be perfect before you begin. In fact, we have found that often school-based action researchers need to go through several research cycles before they find real clarity with their topic and question.

> **Author Reflection** *I (Jesse) have found that one of the biggest challenges in helping teachers and school practitioners become action researchers is that they have to overcome certain personal associations with the idea of research. When they hear the word research, many of them begin to think about experiments, statistics, and complicated analyses. What I try to show them is that the practices of research are really not that different from what they do every day as they design lessons and assessments. Action research is just about using the tools of research to make the practice of teaching or working in a school more systematic.*

SELECTING A RESEARCH TOPIC/PROBLEM Selecting a focus area is the initial step in any kind of research; for action research, this typically begins with school practitioners asking themselves: "What are the everyday problems I face in my professional practice?" Answering this question leads to a broad list of issues, including concerns that school practitioners have related to the academic, behavioral, or social outcomes of the students with whom they work; concerns about the professional and organizational culture of schools; and concerns about out-of-school contexts, including issues related to parental involvement or school/community relationships. The challenge for school practitioners is not in finding a problem to research—schools and classrooms are full of problems—but rather in settling on a problem that is researchable and, when answered, leads to improved practice. When advising school practitioners as they embark on an action research study, we usually provide the following three criteria to help them choose an appropriate topic.

- *The topic should be something that you would like to see change or improve.* Like all research, action research is about investigating a topic, but its major purpose is about solving, not just understanding, a particular problem of practice. For that reason, research topics should be selected because there is a real need for change in practice and improvement in outcomes.

- *The topic should be something that you can control.* There are many problems within schools and school systems that impact teachers and other school professionals. However, many of these are beyond an individual teacher's ability to influence. For teachers, action research often involves some aspect of classroom practice because this is where teachers have the most control and the greatest opportunity to take action and effect change. However, there are other actions that can be taken and researched in a school. For example, a school counselor could start a new advising program, a teacher could initiate a new professional development model with his or her department, or an administrator could develop a new policy for parental outreach. These could all be topics of action research projects. The important thing to remember is that you do not want to tackle a problem over which you *do not* have control.

- *The topic should be something you feel passionate about.* Action research is a very rewarding process, but it takes time and energy. In schools, time and energy are often scarce resources. For this reason, it is important that you pick a topic that you care about and that will continue to engage your interest as you move from cycle to cycle. If the topic is not of high interest to you when you begin, it is more likely that you will get pulled away from the research when your work gets busy.

INDIVIDUAL REFLECTION ON YOUR TOPIC Once a topic is identified, the practitioner researcher should spend time reflecting on the topic. This means putting forward what you already know—or what you think you know—about the topic. We have found it useful to use an **ORID** method of questioning in this reflection process (**O**bjective, **R**eflective, **I**nterpretive, **D**ecisional). With ORID questioning, the researcher thinks about the problem that underlies the selected topic by moving through a series of questions that fall into four categories:

- *Objective questions.* The first category of questions calls on the researcher to describe the problem as objectively as possible. One approach to this that we find useful is to focus on the sense perceptions about the problem. For example, how does the problem look in the classroom or in students' work? When the problem occurs, what do you hear being said? The point with this is to put forward objective information without making inferences about why the problem may be occurring. This helps establish some distance from the problem so that the researcher can begin seeing it with fresh eyes. It may also help in the development of measurements. How do objective observations change when this problem is not present?

- *Reflective questions.* The second category of questions calls on the researcher to give an open reflective response to the problem. This involves answering questions such as "How does this problem make you feel?" or "What experiences do you associate with this problem?" If you chose a topic because you are passionate about it, it's important to be honest about the roots of that passion. This is helpful because these passions often are the roots of the biases we bring to the research process. To write about them is to begin to account for their effect on the research process.

- *Interpretive questions.* The third step is for the researcher to attempt to analyze the problem with the goal of determining the causes. In this case, the questions could include "Why is this problem happening?" "What are the root causes?" and "What other explanations might there be?" Here it is important to brainstorm all the possible explanations. This could include those that you believe to be true, as well as some that do not seem to work. These causes are important to establishing the research question and the possible action that might be taken.

- *Decisional questions.* The final step is to decide what possible actions could be taken to resolve the problem. Here, questions include "What can I do differently?" "What are my next steps?" and "What actions are appropriate?" These questions are the basis of the "action" in action research.

We encourage action researchers to write up their responses to these questions at the start of an action research *journaling process*. Documenting your thinking at the beginning of an action research study allows you to come back and assess your learning. After conducting several action research cycles, you can return to your initial ORID reflection and think about how your perception of the problem and its causes has changed. The following example shows what a teacher's reflection on the problem of student engagement in cooperative learning activities might look like. The example is shorter than a typical ORID reflection, but it does give a sense of the process.

Problem
I am trying to incorporate more group work into my social studies class. However, students are not completing the assignments during cooperative group time. I have tried creating more structure within the groups by developing group roles and responsibilities (i.e., facilitator, recorder, reporter), but this hasn't fixed the situation.

O (Objective)
During group work time in my class, I see students within groups having off-topic side conversations. I see very little note taking or scribing of group process occurring. I hear students talking about off-topic subjects. The work that is turned in from groups is often incomplete.

R (Reflective)
I really believe that group work is important. It connects to my core philosophy of teaching. Students need to learn how to work collaboratively to solve problems. I also believe it creates opportunities for student leadership. However, I feel like the students are taking advantage of the situation. When groups are not working, it makes me want to revert to a teacher-centered lesson. This frustrates me.

I (Interpretive)
Maybe the failure of groups has to do with group composition. Certain combinations of students might be more likely to go off-topic than others.
Maybe the failure of the groups has to do with unclear expectations of the product.
Maybe the problem is related to my failure to hold students accountable for group work.

Maybe the failure of group work has to do with students' lack of understanding of the role responsibilities.

D (Decisional)

I could experiment with different group configurations in my class. I could try mixing students randomly or according to ability level, rather than having self-selected groups.

I could establish clear expectations of product and hold the group accountable for meeting the expectations.

I could lead a discussion with the students about the role responsibilities of the different group members (facilitator, recorder, reporter).

In addition, we also encourage action researchers to spend time talking with others about their project ideas. Not only will your own thoughts be clarified by articulating them to others, but through the discussions you will also get different perspectives, ideas, and suggestions about the nature of interventions, measurement of variables, and data analysis. Involving others helps establish a team mentality and keeps individual perspectives in context. Actually, it's a good idea to require this kind of interaction.

FACT-FINDING ABOUT YOUR TOPIC Although individual reflection on your topic—as with the ORID process—is an important first step, many action researchers also find it useful to spend time collecting new information about their topic before they settle on their initial question or plan their first action. We generally think about initial fact-finding in terms of two distinct activities: (1) reviewing the literature and (2) preliminary data collection.

It is always helpful to do some reading on the topic. Chances are very good that other practitioners and researchers have written and thought about the same topic. Academic journals, professional journals, and the websites of professional organizations have many good ideas and resources. We have found that reading on a topic often gives action researchers a useful vocabulary for discussing the nature of the problem they are addressing, as well as the key variables. These articles will serve to develop your practice-based theories of the factors leading to the problems you are addressing. They may also challenge your assumptions. The important part of doing a literature review for action research is to *stay focused* and *keep it brief*. There is so much out there that it is easy to keep reading, and this may send you into tangentially related topics. Action research is primarily intended to inform specific practices, so the literature must be reviewed with that purpose in mind. Practitioners have limited time, which is why secondary sources are excellent. Trying to understand primary studies may simply take too long for this type of research.

Another fact-finding step that many action researchers take is to collect some preliminary data. This phase of data collection is exploratory. Although there may be a question that underlies this phase of the investigation, it is generally open-ended. The real goal is to use this exploratory phase to develop the topic, refine the question, and plan the first "action." One way of thinking about this is to consider the idea that the action research spiral (Figure 15.1) could start with a phase of monitoring and reflection, before the research gets to the planning and first action. In some cases, preliminary data collected can also serve as a type of baseline. From our experience working with action researchers, this preliminary data collection may involve analyzing student work, reviewing existing documents, or conducting informal interviews with students or colleagues. As an example, consider the ORID reflection above related to group work. For this, preliminary data collection could include a short survey of students to understand their experiences of and perspectives on group work.

DEVELOPING YOUR INITIAL RESEARCH QUESTION   Once topics are identified, researchable questions need to be formulated. Research questions define the focus and the scope of your project. A research question for an action research study specifies the independent and dependent variables for a quantitative or mixed methods study, as well as the action (intervention) being taken. The central phenomenon needs to be identified for a qualitative study. The question should not be too broad or too narrow. Generally, research questions go through many drafts before they are settled. But again, with action research it is important to remember that questions can evolve and change from cycle to cycle. For this reason, action researchers should not feel pressure to come up with the perfect question.

Excerpt 15.2 describes an elementary science resource teacher's investigation of the effectiveness of an instructional unit on student learning. Note how the description of the study, in first person, follows from the question, and includes the selection and use of several different data collection methods. Note, too, how the researcher gathered data, then made changes to assess the impact of the new instructional procedures. This is what action researchers do—test what they learn.

EXCERPT 15.2
Action Research Questions and Process

I wanted to answer a question directly related to my own classroom, make changes, and then explore if these changes were effective or not…. My research question was "What are the students' conceptions of the specific life science topics and how are they influenced by the teaching of a unit on crayfish adaptations?"… My data sources included clinical interviews… before, during, and after the unit; observations of lessons; and students' work, including concept maps, questionnaires, drawings, and journals. (p. 35)

SOURCE: Endreny, A. (2006). Children's ideas about animal adaptations: An action research project. *Journal of Elementary Science Education, 18*(1), 33–42. Copyright © by Western Illinois University (WIU).

Check for Understanding 2

2a.   What are important considerations when selecting a topic for action research?

2b.   When designing an action research project, what are some preliminary steps the researcher can make to help inform the research question and method?

Once the research question for the action research study has been determined, the next step is to develop a plan for answering the question—the research design. Developing a research plan involves considering questions about the types of data collected, the participants or elements from which the data will be collected, and how the data will be analyzed. In this section, we discuss the most commonly used experimental and nonexperimental designs used for action research studies. The focus here is on how they are adapted to a school-based action research context. This section will also include a short discussion of how the validity of action research studies is assessed.

Designing and Conducting Experimental Studies

Learning Outcome 15.3 Be able to design experimental and nonexperimental action research.

With the emphasis on application and effecting change in the local school setting, it is often best to think about experimental designs when conducting an action research study. For a teacher, this may mean trying to isolate the effect of a classroom intervention on student achievement or attitudes; for an administrator, it may mean assessing the impact of a new policy on attendance or discipline referrals. The challenge with conducting an experimental action research study is the same as the challenge faced by traditional researchers: It is difficult to control all the contextual variables and isolate the relationship between the independent and dependent variables. With these experiments, it is generally not feasible to have a true control or comparison group into which students or staff are randomly assigned, which is a hallmark of experimental studies. However, there are still approaches that allow school-based action researchers to establish some claim to causality.

- *Pretest–posttest designs.* Often, action researchers use a simple pretest–posttest design in which the participants (e.g., students/staff) complete a pretest, experience an intervention, and then take the posttest. Here, the most significant threat to internal validity is history, but that can usually be addressed because the teacher is intimately involved in the situation and will know what other influences may have occurred. In some ways it is as though the school practitioner is an anthropologist, from a qualitative perspective, in knowing very well what has transpired during the experiment. This is a great supplement to an experiment.

- *Quasi-experimental designs.* Although it might be unrealistic to use random assignment within an action research study, in many cases it is feasible to establish some type of comparison group. For a teacher, this might mean implementing the intervention with only one section of a class or only one group within a class. When using a comparison group, it is important to try to establish the equivalency of the groups. For example, comparing an honors section of a class with a non-honors section would not make sense. Comparison groups may also raise ethical issues. Delivering what you believe to be a better instructional model to certain students, and not others, may be a violation of professional ethics.

- *Single-subject and time series designs.* A common design used in school-based action research that does not require a comparison group is the single-subject or abbreviated time series design. Within a school setting, the participants could be one or just a few students, a small group, or a class. Causality is established by monitoring a baseline of an outcome measure and then introducing an intervention to assess the impact on the outcome. Using this approach, a teacher might use a regular weekly assessment for several weeks and then consider the effect of a new teaching approach on the scores.

SAMPLING Sampling for school-based action research studies is to some extent a given—whoever is in the class or school being studied will comprise the sample. However, there are some choices to be made. Sometimes it is best to use all students in a class, especially when the inquiry has clear implications for all of them, and sometimes it is better to select a sample from a larger group, as when investigating certain types of students or when conducting a small-scale experiment in which there is a control or comparison group. When particular classes or smaller groups are selected to participate in a study, it is typical for the practitioner researcher to use some form of purposeful sampling. Depending on the research question, participants might be chosen because they represent a particular group (e.g., reluctant readers), or the sampling might look for maximum variation.

DATA COLLECTION   Choosing the right approach to data collection is a challenge. Not only are there qualitative and quantitative approaches, but also within each of those broad categories there is a wide range of types of data and data collection tools that can be used. Figure 15.2 presents a general framework that illustrates the primary forms of data collection for action research.

Quantitative measures can be divided into two broad categories: (1) cognitive measures, such as tests, quizzes, papers, and projects designed to assess knowledge and understanding, and (2) noncognitive measures, such as questionnaires that gauge attitudes, values, and beliefs. Qualitative data collection also has a range of forms. Mills (2014) suggests that it is helpful to think about qualitative data collection techniques in one of three categories: experiencing, enquiring, or examining. These categories are especially relevant to the nature of action research. *Experiencing* refers to the use of direct observation of participants. Teachers constantly observe, so it is relatively easy and convenient for them to formalize their observations to be more systematic and rigorous. *Enquiring* in qualitative approaches means interviewing students, teachers, parents, or whoever would be most appropriate, to obtain information. It is best to have a semistructured format so that, as in observing, there is some degree of focus. A completely unstructured interview is simply too broad and has less probability of eliciting important information. *Examining* refers to the use of existing documents, records, and other artifacts that are already available or will become available. Examples include student work, minutes of meetings, archival data, attendance, discipline referrals, test scores, and student participation in co-curricular activities. Student journals and responses to open-ended questions and prompts can also be used. This overview of potential data sources reinforces the idea that in school-based action research, access to data is not generally a problem, and classrooms are full of noise that gets in the way of finding what you want to know. For this reason, the school-based action researcher needs to turn down the volume (reduce the amount of data) before starting to tune in the signal.

Figure 15.2 Data Collection for Action Research

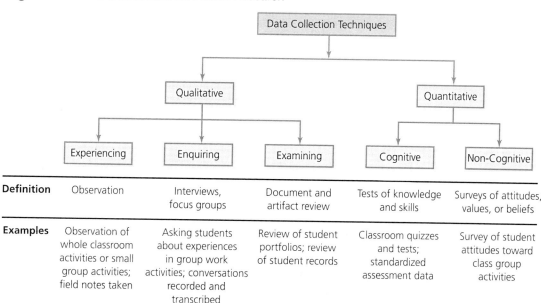

	Experiencing	Enquiring	Examining	Cognitive	Non-Cognitive
Definition	Observation	Interviews, focus groups	Document and artifact review	Tests of knowledge and skills	Surveys of attitudes, values, or beliefs
Examples	Observation of whole classroom activities or small group activities; field notes taken	Asking students about experiences in group work activities; conversations recorded and transcribed	Review of student portfolios; review of student records	Classroom quizzes and tests; standardized assessment data	Survey of student attitudes toward class group activities

With action research experiments—in which you are attempting to assess the effect of interventions on individuals and groups—it is most common to focus on quantitative measures. Although standardized measurements can be used, often the measures used for action research are locally developed and targeted to the class, the school, or the specific intervention (e.g., classroom practice). There are advantages and disadvantages to both approaches. Standardized assessments are likely to have been tested for validity and reliability; however, it is often hard to find ones that match the particular content knowledge, attitudes, or behaviors your research is targeting. If your assessment is not appropriately aligned to the dependent variables identified by your research question, it is less likely that you will be able to show an effect. For example, if a science teacher conducts a study that involves a classroom lesson designed to develop students' "knowledge of ecosystems," it would not make sense to use the end-of-year state assessment as a measure of the intervention's impact. Although state assessments are well-designed tests, from a psychometric standpoint, there may only be a handful of questions about ecosystems. Even if the intervention was successful, it is likely that overall scores would not show an effect. With locally developed assessments, though, you can tailor the questions to the nature of your intervention. However, in this case, the quality of the measure needs to be established. School-based researchers need to have others review intended measures for clarity and credibility, making sure that researcher bias is minimized. These external reviews of the instrument will provide validity evidence to support the accuracy of the evaluations.

Authors' Reflection *In terms of data collection, school-based action research offers both opportunities and challenges. On the one hand, schools are great places to conduct research, because data and potential data are everywhere—piles of student work could be reviewed; field notes could be written every day on classroom observations; memos and grade books could be analyzed. However, this creates a potential problem of data overload. The challenge is to sift through everything that is available and find that which is most relevant to your research question. This is a case when the saying "less is more" definitely applies.*

DATA ANALYSIS When quantitative measures are used, the best kind of summary and interpretation is descriptive, using calculations such as mean, range, and standard deviation for quantitative and mixed methods studies. The data need to be cleaned to remove any outliers or any obviously inaccurate numbers. A descriptive summary presents what you found; the interpretation focuses on what the summary means. Graphs of results, including bar graphs and histograms, are commonly used. Descriptive statistics should be interpreted on the basis of practical, not statistical, significance. With the small number of participants used in action research, it is very difficult to obtain statistical significance. What is most important is a descriptive summary that best informs the practice of education within the specific context.

Designing and Conducting Nonexperimental Studies

Although experimental methods are a common approach for action research studies, many action researchers choose to conduct nonexperimental designs. The goal with these studies is not to establish a direct causal connection, but rather to use a range of data collection techniques to describe and build understanding about the school setting as it changes as a result of an action research study. Often, these nonexperimental studies are framed as case studies. The research questions for case studies are more general and exploratory than experimental studies. Rather than asking questions about particular relationships between predefined variables, the research questions for case studies leave room for new ideas and unexpected findings to emerge.

DATA COLLECTION   Case studies may use data collected from any of the techniques specified in Figure 15.2; however, it is more typical for them to employ mixed methods data collection techniques, with the greatest emphasis on interviewing and observation. One of the hallmarks of a case study is to collect data about the topic from multiple sources and use triangulation to enhance the depth and scope of the findings. Table 15.2 illustrates the concept of triangulation in action research. As shown, there are multiple data sources for the research question. Note that the data collection methods include both quantitative and qualitative approaches. Each data source on its own could provide an answer to the question; however, each also seems to have its limits. For example, observing student group work and listening to the qualities of the conversation in mixed-ability groups might give the teacher a real sense of the effect of the group. However, a quantitative benchmark assessment might show something different. Each data source gives a part of the picture of what is happening. This information might all point to one answer—for example, that mixed-ability groups have a strong positive effect—or they might point in different directions—for instance, the observations suggest one effect, the tests something else. In either case, triangulation has allowed you to discover something interesting.

Table 15.2 Triangulation in Action Research

Research Question	How does using mixed-ability group configurations in a social studies class affect a student's ability to conduct an analysis of primary documents?	
Data Source	**Data Type**	
Source 1	Qualitative	Teacher observations of group activities with field notes completed after each class
Source 2	Qualitative	Interviews with sample of students of varying ability levels
Source 3	Quantitative	Student standardized benchmark assessments
Source 4	Quantitative	Locally developed rubric-graded student writing assessments
Source 5	Quantitative	Student survey self-reported knowledge growth

One final point about triangulation is that you want to be careful to not overload yourself with data. Even though there may be multiple data sources that could help develop an answer to your question, you will want to pick just some of the possibilities. In this way, Table 15.2 might be seen as an example of a brainstorm for possible data sources rather than a realistic plan.

DATA ANALYSIS   The data analysis for action research case studies depends on the type of data collected, but generally involves basic descriptive techniques (for quantitative) and thematic analysis (for qualitative). The strength of the findings in a case study do not stand on the interpretation of any one set of data, but rather are built through cumulative meaning developed through triangulating multiple sources.

Regardless of the initial approach of the research, it is often necessary to change methods during the action research spiral. For example, an initial cycle might involve an exploratory case study approach, which might be followed by a second cycle that uses a more focused experimental design. As with all research, action research methods should be determined in relation to the research question, which also could evolve.

To see whether my action research study on small groups was successful, I am going to examine the achievement data from end-of-year exams.

If I am going to try to understand how my small group approach is working to improve student achievement, I need to collect data from multiple sources that will give me timely information about student mastery of content, as well as their experience of the group work model.

Check for Understanding 3

3a.   What are the steps for conducting action research?

3b.   What is the primary difference between experimental and nonexperimental action research designs?

Validity in Action Research

Learning Outcome 15.4 Know and apply the criteria for evaluating the validity of action research.

Making a determination about the validity or validity/trustworthiness of the conclusions drawn from action research, as with all empirical investigations, depends heavily on the research design and data collection methods that were employed. As such, action researchers should use the recommendations for ensuring the validity of interpretations of results that have been discussed in previous chapters of this book. Because action research involves a range of approaches that include both quantitative and qualitative methods, action researchers—depending on the nature of their study—may draw on the traditional positivist notions of validity and generalizability (Shadish, Cook, & Campbell, 2002) or interpretivist/constructivist ideas about trustworthiness and authenticity (Guba & Lincoln, 1989). However, in addition to these recommendations, some have suggested that action research requires an additional set of criteria for judging integrity or quality (Pine, 2009). One example is a framework put forward by Anderson, Herr, and Nihlen (2007), who offered five forms of validity specific to action research:

- *Outcome validity.* Because action research is an approach used to resolve particular problems of practice, outcome validity is an assessment of the successful resolution of the particular problem. An action research study has outcome validity when the problem is solved.

- *Process validity.* Similar to the idea of internal validity for quantitative studies, process validity is concerned with the way in which the action research study was conducted.

An action research study that pays attention to the idea of process validity demonstrates an attention to how the cycles of action research are deliberately and thoughtfully planned in ways that are effective for answering the question guiding the study, as well as ensuring the ongoing learning of individuals within the system.

- *Democratic validity.* Because action research is about effecting change in local settings, it is important that the perspectives of stakeholders are addressed. Democratic validity is concerned with representation of the stakeholders in either the process of conducting the action research or as data sources. For example, in an effort to ensure democratic validity, a researcher would want to gather multiple perspectives on an issue from the relevant groups that have a stake in the problem, such as students, other teachers, parents, and administrators.

- *Catalytic validity.* This concept of validity addresses the extent to which participants and researchers within action research studies are inspired to change not only their practices, but also their ways of thinking about the realities of their school setting.

- *Dialogic validity.* Traditional research is often assessed through a process of peer review. With action research, dialogic validity refers to the extent to which the research has inspired conversation and learning among peer practitioners.

Reflection, Dissemination, and Continuation of the Action Research Cycle

In action research, each cycle concludes with a phase of reflection and planning for future research. This is a time when the effectiveness of the action is evaluated, learning is assessed, and questions for future action research cycles are developed. It is also a time when an action researcher may consider opportunities for dissemination.

Reflection and Planning

Action research rarely has a clear end point. As illustrated in Figure 15.1, the action research process is typically ongoing. Once an action has been taken and the data collected and analyzed, the next step is to reflect on the effects of the research cycle and plan the next cycle. The period of reflection requires researchers not only to assess the degree to which the particular research question was answered, but also to consider how the context has changed as a result of the research. As a result of the actions taken by the researcher, students may be learning differently, or teachers may be collaborating or communicating in new ways. There is also the possibility that the action had no effect or an unintended effect—that is a finding as well. Either way, the action researcher now has the opportunity to reflect on the findings from the research cycle and the new context, and then pose a new question. In some cases, the new question might be a slight adjustment to the previous cycle's question; in others, the question moves the research study in a dramatically different direction.

Dissemination

Whereas most traditional educational research is focused on generating knowledge that can be generalized to other settings and contribute to a body of knowledge in a field of study, the primary purpose of school-based action research is to effect change in local settings. For this reason, action research is not usually published nor widely disseminated. Unlike traditional research, the central goals of action research are met without sharing the findings with a wider audience. Nonetheless, there clearly is significant value in communicating with others what is learned in action research studies. The type of knowledge generated by action researchers is likely to be relevant and valuable to other practitioners, especially ones who work in similar school contexts. The knowledge could also potentially inform understandings of the phenomenon among the broader educational research community.

When thinking about the dissemination of action research, there are a number of possibilities. Typically, during the initial phases of the study in which initial ideas and questions are formulated, there is little discussion outside close professional contacts. Once a clear focus and possible design is identified, and certainly after findings are obtained, there are a number of ways in which others can learn from the research. Here we identify three common dissemination practices.

- *Professional conversations.* Although it is far from a formal presentation of findings, the simple act of talking about action research studies with colleagues at school and through professional networks is a legitimate form of dissemination. In these conversations, practitioner researchers often explain and justify their research by summarizing the problem, question, methods, and findings. These conversations are a great first step toward more formal methods of dissemination. In fact, most action research is conducted in the context of a supportive action research community where these conversations occur on a regular basis.

- *Professional presentations.* Another common way to disseminate school-based action research is to present it within the school (for example, at department meetings); within school district professional development sessions; or at state, regional or national conferences. Presentations are valuable in that they encourage the practitioner researcher to organize his or her methods and findings into a coherent narrative. They also are opportunities for encouraging dialogue and getting feedback from peers.

- *Publications.* The most ambitious form of dissemination for action researchers is to write up and publish the research. These written reports of research could be published locally through school or school district publications, on websites, or in professional journals. Although it takes a significant amount to time to write up the method and findings of an action research study, it is a very valuable and rewarding exercise. We have found that the process of writing encourages deeper reflection among action researchers and leads to more meaningful learning. Publications are also a way for the school-based action researcher to build his or her professional credentials. At the end of this chapter, there is an example of a written report from an action research study. There are journals dedicated to publishing action research.

The preceding outlets obviously overlap and build on each other. Informal conversations, for example, might lead to more formal presentations within schools and at conferences that might eventually lead to written publication. Also, when action researchers consider dissemination, especially in more formal venues, it is important that they attend to the ethical dimensions of research. That is, before they present data collected in classrooms and schools, the school-based action researcher needs to be certain that the benefits of sharing the research findings outweigh the risks to participants and/or parents and families. This is a point that will be developed in more detail in the next section.

Ethical Considerations and Human Subjects Protection

Guidance for ethical research practice can be found within the research policies of school districts and university research departments. Essentially, these policies revolve around the three core principles established in the 1979 Belmont report as discussed in Chapter 2: (1) respect for persons, (2) beneficence, and (3) justice. Action researchers are expected to abide by the same principles, but because action research is different in many ways from traditional research, ethics and human subject protections are addressed in a slightly different form as well (Brydon-Miller, 2008). School-based action research is also complicated by the fact that it occurs within schools and often involves the collection of data from students—a group that is generally considered a "vulnerable population" by institutional research review policies. The following scenarios illustrate some of the complicated ethical dynamics of school-based action research. Each scenario is followed by questions that lead us to consider the nature of the ethical dilemma and possible solutions.

Scenario 1: A seventh-grade English teacher is conducting an action research study related to student engagement in reading activities. In one of his research cycles, he wants to consider the effect of having students work with a new set of high-interest young adult graphic novels he just received as part of a grant. The grant is also paying for a local artist to come into class and help students write and illustrate their own graphic novels. His research plan is to have half the class participate in the graphic novel unit during independent reading and the other half spend the time reading the standard passages from the textbook. To measure engagement, he will give the students weekly surveys that include a reading engagement scale.

- Is it ethical to allow only half of the class to participate in the grant-funded reading activities?
- How might the teacher design the study to make the process more fair?

Scenario 2: A member of the counseling department at a large high school is concerned about differences between certain racial and ethnic groups in the number of students applying to college. Through her research, she has learned that some of her counselors are doing a better job getting students representing racial and ethnic minority groups to apply to postsecondary options. For one of her action research cycles, she wants to interview all the counselors to get their perspectives on the department's strengths and weaknesses, and to get ideas about how the department could do a better job overall.

- What risk does this study pose to the counselors involved?
- How could the counselor running this study minimize this risk?

Scenario 3: An elementary school principal is conducting an action research study on improving teachers' parental outreach in her school. For one of her action research cycles, she wants to recruit a group of teachers to engage in intensive parent outreach activities after school and then keep a field journal of parent interactions. At the faculty meeting she asks for teachers to volunteer.

- Are teachers being coerced into participation in the study?
- How could the principal solve this problem?

With each of these scenarios, more information would be needed to develop solid answers to the questions posed. However, we hope that these cases hint at some of the ethical challenges that a school-based action researcher might face. When beginning an action research cycle, it is important to reflect on the ethical dimensions of the work. We strongly recommend that you do this in conversation with peers. Often it takes the perspective of someone outside of a study to see the potential ethical problems. This is another reason to conduct your action research projects in the context of a research group in which continuous peer review is part of the process. Once problems are identified, solutions can be developed. This might involve changing an intervention, a sampling strategy, or a plan for dissemination. Although it is rarely the case that you would be able to eliminate all risk from a study, it is your obligation as a researcher to do your best to minimize risk.

When there is an expectation that the results of a school-based action research cycle will be disseminated, it is also important to ensure that there is approval from the school and school district levels and that proper research policies and procedures are followed. In some cases, this might mean obtaining permission from parents (i.e., parental consent) to conduct research with their children, and quite possibly obtaining permission from the students (i.e., student assent). This permission process allows parents and students to carefully consider the risks and benefits of participation in the study. Sometimes this type of active consent process results in a smaller sample than anticipated, so you will need to be careful about bias in the sample. Regardless, priority should be placed on clearly communicating to parents and students what participation in the study involves and allowing for voluntary participation.

Check for Understanding 4

4a. Why is triangulation a valuable design approach when conducting action research?

4b. What are some criteria for assessing the validity or credibility of an action research study?

Consumer (and Researcher) Tips
Criteria for Evaluating School-Based Action Research

1. **Determine the motivation and involvement of the researcher.** Good action research is conducted by individuals who have a vested interest in the study. At the same time, this motivation should not result in researcher bias. The more the researcher is involved in doing an intervention and obtaining information, the greater the opportunity for bias. Look for the ways in which the researcher addresses this potential issue.

2. **Look for consistency between the research question and the methodology.** Action research uses whatever methodology is most appropriate, so the determining factor is the nature of the question. Much action research has some kind of qualitative component. That approach is best when the emphasis is on deeper understanding of a practice or how interventions affect learning in particular classrooms or school contexts.

3. **Look for whether multiple methods of data collection have been used.** There are many advantages to using multiple methods of data collection, especially in action research, in which there may not be sophisticated psychometric properties of the measures. Triangulation of data sources will strengthen the credibility of the findings.

4. **Confirm that there has been an emergent, cyclical process of research–action–reflection.** It is essential to institute the cyclical nature of action research to provide space for critical reflection. It is not simply a matter of doing a single study; there needs to be a continual research spiral where ideas turn into practices that are then reflected on to consider future actions.

5. **Determine whether there is any external peer review or feedback.** In the best of circumstances, school practitioners who are conducting action research receive some kind of "external" review of their methodology, results, and reflection. As mentioned throughout this chapter, this can be accomplished by another professional in the school or district. It is an important step to maintain quality control and give feedback that will facilitate further good research, which provides credible information that can be used to change practice.

Anatomy of an Action Research Report

The following article (Figure 15.3) is an example of how school-based action research is conducted and reported.

Figure 15.3 Anatomy of an Action Research Study

Can Using Daily *Number Talks* Help First Graders Internalize Numbers?

Maria DiSanto, *Elizabeth Scott Elementary, Chesterfield County Public Schools, Virginia*

This action research project investigates strategies for improving students' number sense in a first grade classroom. The action element of this project involved integrating number talks (Parrish 2010) into formative assessment activities designed to gauge student knowledge of number combinations up to ten. With number talks, the teacher works in whole group, small group, and individually with students as they talk through their reasoning process in answering mathematical questions. The participants in this study consisted of five elementary school students selected along a range of variables including gender, academic ability and ESL status. The teacher researcher recorded each student multiple times as they participated in both individual and group number talks around the Hiding Assessment, a number sense activity. The results of the study suggest that students have very different ways to process mathematical equations and that number talks, especially in group settings, are very effective in building students' number sense.

Abstract

INTRODUCTION

Number sense is an important component of my school's math curriculum for first grade. One component of number sense is the understanding of number combinations up to ten. Children in first grade are expected to know all eleven combinations of ten (5 + 5, 9 + 1, 7 + 3, 2 + 8, and so forth). One crucial way student performance with number sense is measured is through the use of the *Hiding Assessment*. With the Hiding Assessment, the teacher sits with a student—or group of students—and puts up to ten manipulatives on a table. She then hides a portion of the items and asks, "how many did I take?" One glaring problem with the *Hiding Assessment* is that it doesn't have an area to record a child's reasoning (thinking). The assessment only looks at right or wrong answers. Based on the diversity of my school/classroom, I find it imperative to model and discuss thinking. My research question developed out of limitations of the assessment and my belief that learning can be enhanced by asking students to communicate their thoughts about how they approach mathematical questions (explain their "thinking"). By listening, I believed I could discover and understand where the challenges are for my students.

Research problem focused on instructional strategy

(continued)

Figure 15.3 Continued

<table>
<tr>
<td>

Brief review of
literature

</td>
<td>

BACKGROUND

Many studies have demonstrated the value of having elementary students share their internal mathematical thinking. For example, Richardson (1999) argues that students should practice math orally by describing the parts of a number (thinking of different ways in which a number can be broken up into parts) as well as determining missing parts of a number (develop relationships needed to know how to work with addition/subtraction facts). Providing justification for this approach, Van de Wall and Lovin (2005) state that children construct their own knowledge and that we cannot teach students by telling. They suggest that teachers must help students construct their ideas about numbers using the ideas they already know. They propose three factors that influence learning: student reflective thinking, social interaction with others in the classroom, and use of models or tools for learning. Sherry Parrish (2010) builds on this tradition, suggesting that students must have the opportunity to share and discuss computation strategies so they can clarify their own thinking, consider/test other strategies to see f they are mathematically logical, investigate/apply mathematical relationships, build a repertoire of efficient strategies, and make decisions about choosing efficient strategies for specific problems.

</td>
</tr>
<tr>
<td>

Informal style:
first person

</td>
<td>

To better understand student reasoning and the barriers that my students face, I became interested in an instructional method called *Number Talks* (Parrish, 2010). With *Number Talks*, the teacher works in whole group, small group, and individually with students as they talk through their reasoning process in answering mathematical questions. *Number Talks* consist of the teacher posing a mathematical question (e.g., "Look at the tens charts; what number do you see?"). Students then offer to answer the question. Instead of stating that the students were correct or incorrect, the teacher asks questions about how they came up with their particular answers. For example:

</td>
</tr>
<tr>
<td>

Literature provides
idea for intervention

</td>
<td>

1. How did you figure that out?
2. Can you show me how you solved that problem?
3. Do you know a different way how to solve it?
4. How many ways can you come up with to solve the problem?
5. Did anyone solve it in a different way?

Through this tool, I saw the potential to help my students develop their critical thinking and comprehension of numbers.

</td>
</tr>
<tr>
<td>

Suggests multiple
cycles

</td>
<td>

From idea to Action

For one cycle of my action research, I decided to incorporate the *Number Talk* method with students as they complete the *Hiding Assessment.* The results and limitations of the initial *Hiding Assessment* were the catalyst for my research question: What are the ways that first

</td>
</tr>
<tr>
<td>

Research question

</td>
<td>

grade students in a multi-ability class communicate their thoughts about how they determine the missing part of a number? The goal of my research is to investigate systematically what first grade students think as they work with the number combinations and then use this information to adapt and improve instruction for a range of learning styles.

</td>
</tr>
<tr>
<td>

Qualitative data
collection

</td>
<td>

Method

To answer my research question, I decided to record and analyze the thinking of my students as we used the *Number Talk* method with the *Hiding Assessment.* While all of my students participated in the *Number Talk* activities, I chose five students for my research; these

</td>
</tr>
<tr>
<td>

Sampling strategy

</td>
<td>

students varied in ethnicity, ability level, and learning styles. In a 3-week span, I recorded the five participants four times individually and twice in small group *Number Talks.* While all non-pullout students, as part of the standard curriculum, participated in the number sense activities and the

</td>
</tr>
<tr>
<td>

Ethical
considerations
addressed

</td>
<td>

Hiding Assessment with *Number Talks*, data was only collected and analyzed for this study from the five participants. Student assent and parental consent were both secured before beginning the study.

</td>
</tr>
<tr>
<td>

Data analysis
strategy

</td>
<td>

After collecting the data, I transcribed each recording including every comment made in the discussion. I coded my responses and my students' responses. In the presentation of findings, I refer to my students using pseudonyms in order to protect their identity.

</td>
</tr>
<tr>
<td>

Additional ethical
considerations

</td>
<td></td>
</tr>
</table>

Figure 15.3 Continued

Analysis of Number Talk Sessions

Through analysis of the *Number Talk* audio recordings and observations during the actual interviews, I was able to identify some general strategies that all of the participants used to answer the question "How many did I take?" This included counting on, counting back, manipulating the blocks, counting on fingers and whisper counting. I have classified the participants' responses in their individual interviews into several categories: (1) correct answer with equation as the "thinking," (2) correct answer with explanation of as the "thinking," and (3) wrong answer with explanation as the "thinking."

> Overview of findings

Correct Answer with Equation as the "Thinking"

Many students responded to the question, "How do you know?" with a number equation. So the answer was supported with the number equation as the student's "thinking." In this excerpt working with nine blocks, Amy answers the question with an equation but she couldn't explain her thinking.

> Me: How many blocks did I take?
> *Amy: 5*
> Me: How do you know?
> *Amy: Because 4 + 5 = 9*
> Me: Is there another way to think of this?
> *Amy: No*

> Direct presentation of data to support points

Amy answers quickly with an addition equation. However, she couldn't give me the turn-around fact, a related subtraction fact, or any other way of thinking.

At times, when a student would respond with a number equation, I would further question him/her to elicit more thinking. Often, I would get a different equation that would have the same total (the number that we started with). By answering this way, the students show that they know different ways to make the number. Chris demonstrates this when he explains his thinking in this excerpt as we work with 9 blocks.

> Me: How many did I take away?
> *Chris: Um, 4*
> Me: How do you know?
> *Chris: Because 4 + 5 + 9 and 5 + 4 = 9*
> Me: Any other way you can think of it?
> *Chris: 1 + 8*

Chris answers correctly by stating two addition equations. When asked if he can think of a different way, he gives me a different equation for 9. The equation still equals 9; however it doesn't use the numbers 4 and 5. His answer does show me that he knows different ways to make 9.

Correct Answer with Explanation as the "Thinking"

Some students answered the questions, "How do you know?" or "Is there a different way to look at it?" with really coherent and thoughtful reasoning. Karly exhibited her thinking in this manner as the following excerpt shows while working with eight blocks.

> Me: Close your eyes. How many do I have now?
> *Karly: 7*
> Me: How do you know?
> *Karly: We started off with 8 and I minused 1 and there was 7. And then I saw one.*
> Me: You started off with 8, you saw 1, you minused 1, and it gives you…
> *Karly: And it gives me the answer 7.*

Karly answers correctly and she explains her thinking process. I restated her statement for clarification. Then Karly finished her thinking.w

(continued)

Figure 15.3 Continued

Wrong Answer with Explanation as the "Thinking"

Many times, my students tried to explain their thinking but they came up with an incorrect conclusion. I am still pleased to hear their reasoning; I can learn from this information. Here is an example from an interview with Alex as we work with nine blocks.

> Me: Now, how do you know I have 6 now?
>
> *Alex: Because you just told me it was 4 and then you taked away 4 and then you have how many like I had.*
>
> Me: All right, how many did we start with?
>
> *Alex: We started with 9.*
>
> Me: We started with 9.
>
> *Alex: And then, we tooked away, but...*
>
> Me: What do you have in front of you?
>
> *Alex: We tooked away the three and spread it out from the 6.*

Alex attempts to explain his thinking but I can't understand him. I restated his statement for clarification/redirection. He then tells me that we started with 9. He continues his explanation but then gets stuck. I try to question him about what he already knows. He states the correct numbers but in an incorrect manner. I didn't take 3 away from 6. I took 3 away from 9.

Analysis of Group Number Talk Sessions

Dialogue was more in-depth during the group *Number Talks*. It was helpful for my students to hear others' thinking. It provided a model for some of the students to follow. The group discussions helped the students feel comfortable to try and solve the problem in different ways. Here is a sample of group *Number Talks* while we work with the number ten.

> Me: All right, now let's look at Amy. Amy, how many do you have in your hand?
>
> *Amy: I have 4 because 6 + 4 = 10 and you take away 4 of them and it equals the 6.*
>
> Me: All right, so you have 6 in front of you. Anyone else have a different way of looking at it?
>
> *Chris: Um, she took away 4.*
>
> Me: How do you know she took away 4?
>
> *Chris: Because 10 – 4 = 6.*
>
> Me: Karly?
>
> *Karly: You would have 10 and you minus 5 and then add 1.*
>
> Me: One more way? Alex?
>
> *Alex: If you had 10 and you subtract 4 and then you get 6.*

Amy closed her eyes and drew blocks from the ten in front of her. She had to figure out how many she had in her hand by looking at what was left in front of her. She answered correctly and explains her thinking. Then Chris answers correctly; he states the correct subtraction equation. Karly explains a different way to get to ten. And finally Alex explains his thinking. The children were able to feed off of each other and try different approaches. While Karly's thinking and explanations in all of the group talks were consistent with her explanations in the individual talks, Alex and Amy were more coherent in their explanations while participating in the group than they were in their individual interviews. Neither Carl nor Chris explained their thinking in the group talks. This is consistent with Chris' individual interviews. However, Carl did share his thinking in his individual interviews.

Pretest Versus Posttest

Use of quantitative data; provides triangulation

The *Hiding Assessment* pretest was administered to all of my students at the beginning of the school year. No documentation about thinking and reasoning was taken at that time. The *Hiding Assessment* posttest was administered in the final weeks of school. Below is a table that shows the number each child proficiently knew for all the combinations for at an application level.

Figure 15.3 Continued

Student Name	Pretest (before *Number Talks*)	Posttest (after *Number Talks* throughout the whole year)
Alex	6	10
Amy	5	10
Carl	5	10
Chris	4	9
Karly	4	10

It is hard to say that the students made growth solely based on the daily *Number Talks*. The students may have made the same amount of progress without the use of the daily practice of "thinking aloud." However, I did notice a significant improvement in each child's communication skills and ability to explain their thinking throughout this action research process.

> Caution about causal claims from study

DISCUSSION

Number Talks are very effective in building students' number sense. I saw growth and true understanding of numbers develop within my participants. Each child showed me different ways of thinking. This opened my eyes to how all children think very differently and why they all need differentiation. There are three important discoveries I obtained from my action research data.

> Direct benefit to teacher-researcher

The first is that children can actually think critically about mathematical equations regardless of the amount of training they have had in the past. Secondly, children have different ways to process mathematical equations. Some explain the process in steps; some simply provide an answer or an equation. It may take some students more practice with "thinking out loud." That is the ultimate goal for me as a teacher; to facilitate students' critical thinking processes about math. This action research project has shown me that I am capable of helping my first graders become critical thinkers. The third glaring discovery for me was the power of group *Number Talks*. Group discussions helped my students clarify their thoughts and share them in a safe learning environment. The children seemed to feed off of each other's ideas. This environment took the spotlight off of the individual and freed the students to share when they felt comfortable. I could also restate my students' responses so that everyone was able to understand the concept and possibly think of another way to approach the problem.

> Reflection on key learnings

For action research cycles, I have several ideas for future actions related to instruction around student number sense. It will be important to conduct *Number Talks* in a different manner. I already conduct whole group *Number Talks* daily; however, it is hard for first graders to focus and participate in such a large group. I think breaking my students into groups of five would be more conducive to their ability to "share their thinking." When giving the initial *Hiding Assessment,* I will ask my students to explain their thinking. I will record that conversation as well as a few more individual conversations about combinations of numbers (9 + 1, 5 + 5, 7 + 3, etc.). I will also record several group talks with the participants. Then, I will introduce *Number Talks* into my daily math routine. After a month, I will conduct individual mini-*Hiding Assessment* with the participants. I will touch base every two months to record their thinking on similar *Hiding Assessment* checks. Every month, I will record a group *Number Talk* with the participants. I will space out my interviews throughout the year so I can collect data over a period of time. At the end of the school year, I will administer the final *Hiding Assessment* and I will record the thinking of my participants. I hope to find out how much group talks impact each child's overall thinking. Also, I hope to see data on their progress throughout the entire year.

> Ideas for future action research cycles

> Planning stage for next cycle

Key Terms

Action research
ORID
Participatory action research

Discussion Questions

1. What makes action research more relevant to practitioners than other types of research?
2. What is the "cyclical" nature of action research, and why is it important?
3. What is the ORID process?
4. Why does action research often use both qualitative and quantitative methods?
5. How does triangulation strengthen the design of an action research study?
6. How does the concept of validity differ in action research compared with other forms of educational research?
7. How is the credibility of action research determined?

Application Exercises

1. Identify a problem of practice from a work setting or organization that you know well. Use the ORID method of reflection to describe and better understand the problem.
2. Based on the work from the exercise above, design an action research cycle and write up the research plan. The plan should include (a) a description of the problem, (b) the research question(s), and (c) the data collection and analysis approach. Remember to consider best practices in actions research design (triangulation, local measurement, etc.).

Check for Understanding Answers

1a. A common problem of traditional research on schools, is that it is often perceived as out-of-touch with the realities of classroom practice. With school-based action research, the topics, questions, methods, and findings emerge directly from practice, making it inherently relevant.

1b. Because action research, in its design, is so embedded in practice, it makes it very difficult to generalize from the findings to other settings and populations.

2a. Topics selected for action research projects should be focused on solving a problem, within the researchers' locus of control, and of high interest to the researcher.

2b. Prior to posing the research question, the action researcher should engage in reflective writing that shares experiences of and ideas about the topic. If time permits, the researcher should also explore literature that provides insights into the topic.

3a. Select topic, reflection, fact-finding, initial question, design, data collection, data analysis, conclusion.

3b. Experimental studies are more tightly designed and targeted; nonexperimental studies tend to be more open, evolving case studies.

4a. Triangulation is the practice of collecting data from multiple sources about a single phenomenon or construct. Because action research uses more context-specific (rather than standardized) forms of measurement, triangulation allows the researcher to build the validity of the findings through convergence of sources.

4b. While traditional notions of quantitative and qualitative validity can apply to action research, its quality can also be judged through alternative criteria that consider the quality of process and outcomes of the work.

Part V
Communicating Research Results

Both consumers and researchers communicate their work to others. This may well be in the form of a research proposal for a class, a thesis or dissertation, or manuscript that is used to propose a presentation or publication. This final chapter describes the academic/scholarly voice and tone you will need to use, along with appropriate writing style, steps to complete the writing, and formatting. There is also considerable attention to writing the discussion and conclusion sections of research reports.

Chapter 16
Writing Research Proposals, Reports, and Articles

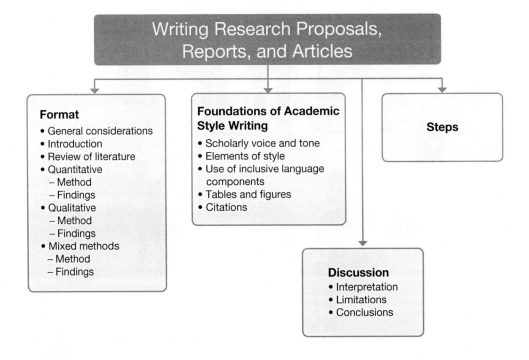

Writing Research Proposals, Reports, and Articles

Format
- General considerations
- Introduction
- Review of literature
- Quantitative
  - Method
  - Findings
- Qualitative
  - Method
  - Findings
- Mixed methods
  - Method
  - Findings

Foundations of Academic Style Writing
- Scholarly voice and tone
- Elements of style
- Use of inclusive language components
- Tables and figures
- Citations

Steps

Discussion
- Interpretation
- Limitations
- Conclusions

 ## Learning Outcomes

16.1 Identify key elements of effective scholarly/academic writing.

16.2 Know the sections and subsections used to format quantitative, qualitative, and mixed methods studies.

16.3 Apply the guidelines for writing effective discussion/conclusion sections.

16.4 Describe the steps used to write research proposals, reports, and manuscripts to submit to journals, and the importance of audience in determining what is presented.

Chapter Road Map

Research that contributes to a better understanding of the signal is clearly and concisely communicated. Whether you are a consumer of research or are tasked with writing about and/or presenting research, the clarity of how all aspects of the investigation are described is critical. With empirical research, there are unique conventions, writing styles, and punctuation that guide effective communication. While some of these are consistent with communication in other arenas (e.g., English, historical, persuasive), many are unique to what is needed for empirical research. In this chapter you will learn how to write in a scholarly/academic style and organize proposals, reports, and articles.

Foundations of Scholarly / Academic Style Writing

Learning Outcome 16.1 Identify key elements of effective scholarly/academic writing.

Whether a proposal, report, or article, there are some general guidelines about scholarly/academic writing and format that are important. One way to think about the writing is to conceptualize it as a unique form of communication to others. This perspective is helpful in making decisions about format and style because effective writing is based more on how others understand your ideas and rationale than on a simple reporting of what you have found. In this section, three critical foundational areas are examined that undergird effective communication of research.

For those who have little experience with reporting empirical studies, the first essential step in being successful is recognizing the elements contained in scholarly/academic *voice* and *style*. The hallmark of scholarly/academic communication is to be clear and to the point, precise, and logical. It is all about presenting a compelling case, arguing based on evidence that something has meaning. Ambiguity is avoided, misunderstandings minimized; logical arguments are presented with smoothness and flow.

It is very likely that scholarly/academic voice and style are quite different from writing you have done in the past. Most of us have experienced what could be called a literary style, one in which the emphasis may be on creative or artistic prose. Often meaning is not immediately clear, and there is much use of adjectives and complex sentences with metaphors and other techniques to grab attention and sensationalize. This doesn't suggest, however, that scholarly/academic writing should be boring, staid, or dreary. The challenge is to communicate so that essential clear meaning is conveyed in a manner that is engaging and interesting, even compelling.

Another way of thinking about scholarly voice and style is that language and conventions are formalized. In contrast, much communication is informal and casual, replete with colloquialisms and jargon. The goal with scholarly/academic communication is not to impress with the writing or speaking, it is to clearly and convincingly present a logical argument based on evidence, using language that immediately makes sense to the audience. In other words, you want the audience to be able to understand and appreciate your work. This is done most effectively with short sentences, words with clear, universal meaning, simple descriptions, and other specific elements of grammar and structure.

Scholarly Voice and Tone

One of the most challenging aspects for students in learning how to write research documents is to use appropriate "scholarly voice." Voice is your style, perspective, and approach to communication, something that is based on your purpose or intended goal. Some examples of voice that are *not* scholarly could be reflective, humorous, conversational, casual, poetic, and persuasive. **Scholarly voice** is *formal* and *academic* because of the intended audience and purpose—to write to others in a way that systematically, clearly, and objectively presents information, as well as to add interpretation, analysis, limitations, and conclusions. Scholarly voice is "academic" in the sense that the communication adheres to conventions of academia—what is expected of those engaged in intellectual, often scientific, deliberations.

Much of what constitutes scholarly voice in writing (**scholarly tone**) is contained in format, words, language, and specific conventions that are utilized. For example, with scholarly writing there is an expectation that assertions and opinions are supported; that offensive, casual, hyperbolic, and colloquial language are avoided; and that citations are used to demonstrate an understanding of related literature.

Sometimes academic writing voice is described as antiseptic, dull, tedious, and boring, with complex sentences and "intelligent"-sounding words. These are not characteristics of good academic voice. Yes, the writing needs to be direct, clear, and well-organized. But that doesn't mean it needs to be so formal that it is uninteresting and disengages the reader. It should not be viewed as presenting "just the facts." This point is effectively emphasized in the APA *Publication Manual* (APA, 2020):

> Although scientific writing differs in form and from creative or literary writing, it need not lack style or be dull... when describing your research, present the ideas and findings in a direct, straightforward manner, while also aiming for an interesting and compelling style (p. 115).

Author Reflection *Over the years I have seen students struggle with scholarly writing because they are used to creative writing, and from writing term papers or "researching" a topic (what they thought was scholarly). The absolute best way to learn how to use scholarly voice is to read it, over and over again, and then notice examples of how non-scholarly writing can be edited to be more scholarly. I've done this kind of editing "live" with students and it can be very helpful.*

Elements of Style

You are probably well aware of four major writing styles: expository, descriptive, narrative, and persuasive. Scholarly/academic research writing style comes closest to expository, but as I've noted, it is not a simple reporting of findings—researcher interpretation is critical. Overall, style is using conventions, word choice, sentence structure, and other elements that convey effective communication relative to purpose and audience.

There are many style elements that, together, comprise good academic writing. Scholarly/academic writing style is a package of many things to avoid because they could make communication less clear and concise, and things to include so that the writing is engaging, logical, and professional.

Here is what to *avoid*:

- Ambiguity
- Shifting of topic or tense in a paragraph
- Grouped synonyms (e.g., "There is consensus and agreement among administrators that..." rather than "Administrators agree..."
- Expletive constructions (e.g., 'There are..." or "It is...")
- Wordiness and redundancy (e.g., "at the present moment" would be better written as simply "now")
- Advocacy language
- Bias
- Contractions (e.g., use "do not" rather than "don't")
- Casual language (e.g., colloquialisms, slang, jargon, metaphors, clichés, platitudes, hyperbolic language, pejoratives; alliterations)
- Long, compound, and run-on sentences
- Use of the word "must"
- Use of "he or she"
- Long or many quotes
- Overuse of short sentences that results in choppy narrative.
- Word usage that may signify multiple possible meanings (e.g., "significant")

Here is what you want *to do*:

- Use simple, concise, clear sentences
- Use logical consistency (continuity and smooth sequencing of words and sentences [flow])
- Vary sentence structure and length (e.g., alternate length and type; vary citations to at the beginning of some sentences, others in the middle or end)
- Vary subject and word choice (e.g., alternate "studied," "investigated," "examined," "researched," and "explored")
- Strive for objectivity
- Support statements with citations when needed
- Use active voice with first person in describing your work (generally)
- Use passive tense (but not too much)
- Use transitions (e.g., accordingly, in addition, also, similarly, for example, hence, in conclusion, consequently, as a result, therefore, thus, notably, then, in contrast, however, that is, to illustrate, specifically, moreover, furthermore, although)
- Use inclusive language (e.g., to not exclude or single out people)
- Proper use of pronouns (e.g., "that" for restrictive clauses; "which" for nonrestrictive clauses)

Academic writing takes practice, patience, and time. Three writing strategies, in particular, will help: (1) reading research reports to learn by example; (2) setting drafts aside for days or even weeks before rewriting; and (3) asking colleagues to review a revised draft to provide feedback. Of course, meticulous checks for grammatical errors, spelling mistakes, typos, spacing issues, and format are needed. Careful, correct writing gives readers confidence that the researchers have been scholarly toward substantive aspects of the investigation (e.g., research questions, methodology, findings). Conversely, reading a research report or article that is not carefully written in an appropriate scholarly style not only leads to ambiguity, it also suggests that the author(s) may not have applied scholarly tenets more broadly.

Using Inclusive Language

It is important to use language that avoids inaccurate attribution to groups of individuals, offensiveness, and biased assumptions of persons of specific characteristics or groupings, such as age, gender, racial or ethnic identify, sexual orientation, religion, disability, or other characteristics. The goal is to write in a way that is affirmative and inclusive. This avoids bias in both the accuracy of the findings and interpretations, as well as whether readers are offended by assumptions or interpretations. Using the word "man" to describe both women and men, for example, is not inclusive; it would be more accurate and less offensive to use "people" or "individuals."

Some suggestions for enhancing inclusivity are summarized, with examples, in Table 16.1. The guidelines are intended to enhance accuracy, to focus only on relevant characteristics, and to use language that is appropriately specific (e.g., citing exact ages rather than a general description; using names of disability condition, not "people with disabilities"; avoiding generalized origins of peoples such as "Asian American"; and

Table 16.1 Inclusive Language for Different Topics[1]

Topic	Description	Example
Age	Provide specific information about ages; avoid generic terms; use appropriate terms for different age groups.	An older adult population was identified, including those age 65 and higher. Millennials, those born between 1980 and 1995, were compared to Gen Z students those born between 1996 and 2010 in this cross-sectional study.
Disability	Use subgroup preferences for how to describe participants; use language that maintains the dignity of individuals and groups; use person-first language; avoid terms that suggest limitations or restrictions.	Each participant was identified as having an intellectual disability. Parents of students with learning disabilities were invited to participate in the intervention.
Gender and sex	Use as a description of a social group with cultural attributes that align with biological sex; "sex" refers to biological sex; gender identity is a person's psychological sense of gender; use terms individuals use to describe themselves; use "their" if gender is unclear or unknown; avoid "his or her," or "opposite sex"; use "male" or "female" as adjectives when appropriate.	Approximately 20% of the participants in the control group identified as transgender; six individuals identified as gender-nonbinary. A greater percentage of male participants in the group of experienced teachers (80%) indicated that test score data should be used in determining teacher effectiveness.
Racial and ethnic identity	Use "race" to describe physical differences with social implications; use "ethnicity" when referring to individuals with shared cultural characteristics; use terms appropriate for specific racial and ethnic groups; use terms participants use to describe themselves; avoid using "minorities" and "Afro-American."	Both Asian and Asian American students were surveyed. European American and European New Zealand students' mathematics scores showed a significant difference. The sample contained 65 Black students, 15 Haitian students, and 72 White students.
Sexual orientation	Sexual orientation refers to who someone is sexually, romantically, and emotionally attracted to; use appropriate terms to specify sexual orientation (e.g., bisexual, queer, asexual, straight, heterosexual, lesbian); define acronyms such as LGBTQIA; avoid the term "homosexual."	This study investigated campus engagement of individuals who were self-identified as lesbian. A total of 18 students (70%) identified as heterosexual; the remaining students identified as asexual, bisexual, or gay.
Socioeconomic status (SES)	Use to describe participants; use precise terms and definitions to minimize bias; include information on income, education, occupation, and race and/or ethnicity; avoid pejorative terms such as "low income," "inner city," and "welfare mothers."	A proxy for socioeconomic status, percentage of students eligible for free and reduced-price lunch, was used to adjust for differences in income and education. Socioeconomic status, as measured by a combination of family income, mother's level of education, and father's occupation status, was used as a covariate in the analysis.

[1]Adapted from the *Publication Manual of the American Psychological Association* (2020).

describing specific criteria for socioeconomic status, such as college graduate, rather than a general term such as "low" or "high"). Operational definitions of groups with specific characteristics are preferred to general descriptions. Like other aspects of writing, it is best to have others review your text to focus on whether or not the language is inclusive.

Check for Understanding 1

1a. How is scholarly/academic writing different from literary writing?

1b. What is the difference between scholarly/academic voice and scholarly/academic tone?

1c. What are four do's and four don'ts in effective scholarly/academic writing?

Tables and Figures

Tables and figures that display data are indispensible tools in reporting research. They provide concise presentations of large amounts of information, and if properly designed, aid readers in understanding the results. Figures, maps, drawings, charts, and other visual displays can be used to illustrate in attractive and engaging ways theories, models, demographics, correlations, and other aspects of both planning research and reporting results. Tables are essential with large numbers of variables and statistical tests.

It is beyond the scope of what can be presented in this chapter to summarize all the elements of appropriate design and use of tables and figures. Details are available online or through books such as the APA *Publication Manual*. I would emphasize, however, that there are important guidelines for producing effective tables and figures, and it is well worth your time to know about and use these guidelines. The following lists contains some basic principles:

- Confirm that each table or figure is needed
- Label all elements in tables and figures (e.g., all columns in tables)
- Place labels near the targeted element
- Use sufficiently large text size
- Keep titles brief but complete
- Include sufficient information so the table or figure stands on its own, without the need to refer to the text
- Keep them simple and straightforward, without glitz
- Use tables and figure only for large numbers of variables or analyses
- Call out each table and figure in the text (e.g., "As shown in Table 1...)
- Avoid redundancy with text or within the table or figure (e.g., redundant correlations in a correlation matrix)
- Include only essential information (e.g., not all the statistical information from an SPSS or SAS output)
- For tables, limit the number of lines and borders, as well as shading
- For figures, use clear images, sharp and smooth lines
- Avoid the use of color in manuscripts

Citations in Text

An important element in scholarly writing is to appropriately cite others' work, including ideas and theories, as well as specific research. Generally, cite work you have read. Using mostly primary sources, cite others whose work has influenced your research and is incorporated into your rationale, design, and interpretation. All claims about "facts" and "knowledge" that are not generally known and agreed-on need citations. For example, a phrase like "first-generation college students are more likely to struggle academically in their first semester" needs one or more citations to empirical work that has demonstrated this finding. Use an appropriate number of citations—not too many but not too few. Given the significant increase in academic journals, reports, and articles, there are often many more studies and authors researching a topic than can be cited. Overcitation (e.g., more than a few citations for a statement; repeating the same citations sentence after sentence) is distracting and unnecessary. Too few citations may lead to plagiarism, which obviously needs to be avoided (citations are needed when others' ideas are paraphrased; direct quotes; data; tables and figures from other work; long text passages).

The APA *Publication Manual* (2020) includes a comprehensive summary of how to incorporate citations in text, including how to handle such issues as number of authors to include, when to omit year of publication in repeated citations, when to include page numbers, multiple works by the same author in the same year, and a number of other specific conditions. Overall, the author–date citation system is used, and, of course, each author–date citation needs complete information in the reference section.

Citations are best presented by varying when they are made in the sentence, and whether the citation includes both author(s) and date(s) or just the date(s). For example, the following four formats are often used at different points within the text to provide varied sentences:

> Torrance (2018) found that adolescents' motivation to attend college is influenced significantly by peers.
> A recent study by Torrance (2018) found that adolescents' motivation to attend college is influenced significantly by peers.
> A recent study (Torrance, 2018) found that adolescents' motivation to attend college is influenced significantly by peers.
> A recent study found that adolescents' motivation to attend college is influenced significantly by peers (Torrance, 2018).

Reference Lists

The APA *Publication Manual* also includes comprehensive illustrations of what to include about each source in the references section, and the specific formats and punctuation used for different types of sources (e.g., articles, reports, books, book chapters, online work). All references include author(s), date, title, and source. Since there are so many variations in what is published, the guidelines for format and punctuation are extensive. Fortunately, there are quickly and easily accessed resources to know what is needed for each type of source, including online resources on the APA website. Some software programs are designed to take source information and put it in APA or some other format, but you still need to check each reference entry for accuracy. Like grammar, punctuation, and typos, references need to be exactly correct.

Formats for Proposals, Reports, and Articles

Learning Outcome 16.2 Know the sections and subsections used to format quantitative, qualitative, and mixed methods studies.

Different formats for quantitative and qualitative articles were introduced in Chapter 1, and throughout Chapters 3, 4, and 5 differences were noted between quantitative, qualitative, and mixed methods research questions, literature reviews, and sampling.

In this section, further information is provided to help you organize your writing, depending on the nature of the document (proposal, report, article) and type of research (quantitative, qualitative, mixed methods). We will begin with some general considerations, then explore needed elements for empirical investigations.

General Considerations

There are a few important general format considerations, regardless of the type of research or document. Overall, the format of the document needs to enhance organization and clarity. This is best accomplished with the following:

- A separate title page containing the title, author(s), affiliation, and date
- Page numbering in the upper right-hand corner (the title page is page 1)
- Use of widely available 11- or 12-point font (e.g., 11-point Calibri; 12-point Times New Roman)
- Use of running heads for manuscripts submitted for publication
- With the exception of tables and footnotes, double-spaced lines
- 1-inch margins
- Left-justified margins, with right margin uneven
- First line of each paragraph indented
- Use of clearly identified headings (e.g., bolded, italic) to identify the content of each section (generally no need for an "Introduction" heading or more than three headings; center level-1 headings)
- Reference section that begins on a new page

The goal is to have a document that is easily read and understood. Depending on the audience and organization or journal that receives the document, there may well be unique formatting requirements. For manuscripts submitted to journals, the journal guidelines need to be followed. All APA journals, for instance, use the formatting described in the APA *Publication Manual*.

Abstract

Most research reports and articles will include an abstract (proposals often do not have an abstract). The abstract is a short summary of the main elements of the manuscript (100–150 words). It typically includes the problem that was investigated and a brief description of participants, research design (measures, procedures), findings, and/or conclusions.

Introduction

As described in Chapter 1, the introduction is usually a few paragraphs in which the study and problem is put into context. Hopefully, the first sentence will be at least somewhat compelling. Often, it begins with historical antecedents that frame the

---

EXCERPT 16.1

Introductory Paragraph

Community colleges serve a vital role in the education of science, technology, engineering, and mathematics (STEM) majors in the United States. Almost half of all students who completed a STEM degree (bachelor's, master's, or doctoral) during the years 2008–13 received at least part of their education at community colleges; between 2000 and 2015, the amount of STEM-related associates degrees awarded increased 135% to over 90,000 per year (National Science Board [NSB], 2018). Community colleges also serve as an important entry point into higher education for traditionally underrepresented populations in STEM, thereby promoting more equitable STEM participation (American Association of Community Colleges [AACC], 2016; Bailey, Jenkins, & Leinbach, 2005; Hagedorn & Purnamasari, 2012). Several recent policy documents have highlighted the importance of community colleges in the preparation of students for the STEM workforce... However, most research to date on STEM pipeline persistence from academia to the workforce has focused on four-year colleges, which limits understanding of the potential of two-year pathways in diversifying STEM participation (Wang, 2016). (p. 280)

SOURCE: Cohen, R., & Kelly, A. M. (2020). Mathematics as a factor in community college STEM performance, persistence, and degree attainment. *Journal of Research in Science Teaching, 57*, 279–307.

---

context and scope of the general problem or issue. As illustrated in Excerpt 16.1, the purpose is to place the subsequent more specific problem into a larger context (in this case community colleges, and underrepresented populations in STEM). This is the first step of making an argument that the research will make a contribution (note the last sentence in this excerpt). Ultimately, there needs to be a logical argument why the topic needs to be investigated and why the methodology is appropriate to provide credible findings (this is sometimes called the *conceptual framework*) (Ravitch & Riggan, 2016). For mixed methods studies, this includes a rationale for why both quantitative and qualitative approaches are needed.

For quantitative and mixed methods studies, the specific research questions or hypotheses may be stated at the end of the introduction. For qualitative investigations, there will usually only be a general research purpose or question. Qualitative study introductions may also state the general nature of the approach to the research (e.g., case study, phenomenological), with an explanation of why this approach is best for the study, and researcher positionality.

Beins (2012) suggests the following starting points for the introduction:

- Cite an actual event
- State an important issue
- Create a fictional scenario
- Summarize previous research
- Present a statistic
- Use a quotation
- Describe a common occurrence

Author Reflection *I have often struggled, as have my students, to come up with a "compelling" first sentence in the introduction. For me, the best approach is to let it bubble up. While writing other parts of the introduction and review of literature, an engaging, interesting sentence often reveals itself.*

Review of Literature

The review of literature section for empirical reports and articles was examined extensively in Chapter 4. This included recommendations for writing this section of the document. Essentially, the review of literature places the current or proposed study within existing research, showing the relation to previous investigations and theories. It is best to indicate how the research differs from what has been done. This is accomplished with a brief summary of previous research, a critique of the studies, and an indication of how the proposed or conducted research is informed by or fits within the existing research.

Writing the review of literature begins with a thorough search and vetting of which previously completed studies should be included. The literature matrix of these studies, as shown in Chapter 4, and conceptual maps showing how the studies are related, will help to show which studies should be considered together and the sequence of what is presented. Try not to write a paragraph on each study; it is more effective to write about topics or methodologies and use individual studies as illustration. Write very explicit statements about how the literature relates to your study (e.g., say directly, "The implication of this study for the current investigation is that…"). It is also helpful to include an overall summary of the review. This is often followed by the specific purpose, question, or, in the case of quantitative and mixed methods studies, research hypotheses.

Methodology

The purpose of the method part of the document is to describe in detail the design of the study, how participants were selected (or, in the case of a proposal, will be selected), the nature of the measures and procedures for gathering data, and, for experimental studies, the nature of the intervention. A complete description is needed to allow others to evaluate the credibility of the investigation and, if desired, to replicate the study. Beyond these general purposes, though, writing the method section can vary greatly by whether the study is quantitative, qualitative, or mixed methods.

QUANTITATIVE METHOD SECTION ELEMENTS   There are four common elements of the method section in quantitative studies: design, participants/data sources, measures, and procedures. The challenge in writing these subsections is to be both precise and sufficiently detailed. In my experience, this balance is best achieved by being concise yet complete, and writing in a very straightforward manner. You are not trying to convince anyone of anything; simply report what you did. Actually, since the four subsections are pretty much universal; it makes the writing comparatively easy by focusing on one subsection at a time.

Table 16.2 shows what needs to be addressed in each of the four subsections for quantitative reports and articles. Not all studies will include each element, and some reports, depending on the audience, will not provide as much detail as found

Table 16.2 Quantitative Document Methodology Subsections and Elements[1]

Subsection	Elements
Design	• Indicate whether it is an experimental or nonexperimental design, followed by a more specific description (e.g., descriptive, quasi-experimental, longitudinal, secondary data). • Describe procedures to enhance internal validity. • Describe independent and dependent variables operationally. • Indicate time frame of the study, including when data were collected. • Indicate planned data analyses, including how to handle missing data and outliers. • Describe settings in which data are gathered and interventions implemented, as well as time frame.
Participants/Data sources	• Indicate important characteristics of participants (e.g., age, gender, race, ethnicity, grade level). • Describe how the participants were selected, identified, or recruited (e.g., random, nonrandom, volunteer). • Describe how participants were assigned to groups. • Describe IRB procedures, including use of incentives. • Describe sample size, power, and how sample size was determined. • Address criteria for inclusion, exclusion, and attrition. • Describe nature of secondary data.
Measures	• Describe measures or instruments used with participants for data collection. • Summarize evidence of validity and reliability (both from previous research and the present study) for each score reported and used in the analyses. • Provide examples of survey items, response scales, interview protocols, and observation schedules.
Procedures	• Describe the nature of the intervention, if present, and procedures to ensure intervention fidelity. • Describe the unit of intervention assignment and unit of analysis. • Describe procedures for administering measures. • Describe planned statistical analyses for each research question.

[1]Adapted from APA Journal Article Reporting Standards (https://apastyle.apa.org/jars) and Cooper (2020).

with manuscripts submitted for journal publication. The most significant factor that impacts the method section is whether or not there is an intervention that is described as part of the procedures. A proposal to conduct a study will have the same elements, but, of course, will use future tense, and there may need to be an explanation of why certain measures or procedures were selected.

QUALITATIVE METHOD SECTION ELEMENTS For qualitative studies, the method section is written in a less structured manner, with the need for an additional element: researcher description (refer to Table 16.3). This is because researcher positionality, identity, and background is so important to the study. This is often addressed after a general description of the design, if it has not been summarized in the introduction section. Another important factor with qualitative design is that it is iterative. That is, it often evolves, requiring additional narrative to describe and present a rationale for the changes. This is different from the linear logic of a quantitative design.

MIXED METHODS DOCUMENT METHOD SECTION ELEMENTS Writing the method section for a mixed methods study requires an integration of quantitative and qualitative subsection elements, along with a few new elements. What is most important is that the methodology described is consistent with the nature of the mixed methods design. Thus, in the introduction section, it is important to justify why a mixed methods study is needed, and to include a rationale for the relative contribution of the quantitative and qualitative parts (e.g., emphasis and sequence). As pointed out in Chapter 14, design often precedes the research question, so it needs some explanation in the introduction.

Beyond the elements needed for the quantitative and qualitative parts of the study, the design section also needs to specify the precise nature of the mixed methods aspect of the study (Creswell & Creswell, 2018). This includes repeating the nature of the design (e.g., explanatory sequential, exploratory sequential, convergent), along

Table 16.3 Qualitative Document Methodology Subsections and Elements[1]

Subsection	Elements
Researcher description	• Describe the background and perspectives of the researcher(s), including prior understandings of the phenomena investigated, and advocacy roles with the phenomena (e.g., demographic, cultural, value, prior training). • Describe prior researcher-participant relationships, roles, and interactions, and any related ethical issues.
Design	• Indicate the nature of the design, data collection, and analysis, including philosophical or paradigmatic approaches. • Provide a rationale for the design and how it was more appropriate than other approaches. • Note design weaknesses and procedures to address weaknesses. • Describe any changes in design, with appropriate rationale. • Indicate researcher role in the study (e.g., participant, observer). • Describe the context in which the data were gathered.
Participants/Data sources	• Indicate important characteristics of participants (e.g., age, gender, race, ethnicity, grade level). • Describe other sources of data (e.g., documents, observation, Internet). • Describe how and why the participants and/or other data sources were selected, identified, or recruited (e.g., purposeful, snowball, availability), including inclusion/exclusion criteria. • Describe IRB procedures, including use of incentives. • Justify how both initial and final sample size was determined. • Indicate participant attrition.
Measures	• Describe all methods and measures used to collect data (e.g., interviews, observation, documents). • Describe data recording methods and duration (e.g., audio-recording, length of interviews). • Describe data collection protocols and provide examples of questions in interviews and criteria for observations.
Procedures	• Describe entry to the field and the context in which data were gathered and nature of engagement (e.g., duration). • Describe the use of reflexivity. • Describe changes in design as data were collected. • Describe procedures for conducting interviews and observations, including how data were recorded and transcribed. • Describe planned data storage and coding/thematic analysis.

[1]Adapted from APA Journal Article Reporting Standards (https://apastyle.apa.org/jars) and Levitt (2019).

with clear descriptions of the emphasis of each phase. This is typically shown with a diagram, as illustrated in Chapter 14, with details about the quantitative and qualitative phases. This is followed by a description of the planned mixed methods analyses and an explanation of how the data from each phase will be used or merged.

Findings Section

Like the methods section, writing the findings section differs considerably for qualitative, quantitative, and mixed methods studies. In this section we will consider the major components of each. In a proposal there are no findings, though it is expected that the intended statistical or qualitative analyses procedures that will be used are identified. Sometimes proposals will include a section that shows how the results will be presented.

QUANTITATIVE FINDINGS SECTION   For quantitative studies, the findings (or results) section includes a summary of data and statistical analyses in sufficient detail to allow others to judge the adequacy and appropriateness of the analyses, and conclusions. This includes a complete summary of all descriptive data (e.g., frequencies, means, standard deviations, correlations), as well as results of inferential statistical analyses. Elements that are often used as headings in the report include the following:

• Participant recruitment, flow through all stages of the study, and attrition
• How missing data and outliers were addressed

- Descriptive data (number of participants, mean, standard deviation) for the total sample and separate units of analysis
- Summary of whether assumptions of statistical tests were met
- Inferential statistical test results, including exact p values, degrees of freedom, descriptive data, and confidence intervals for all analyses (whether or not statistically significant)
- Effect size analyses, including confidence intervals.
- Model details for complex statistical analyses (e.g., structural equation modeling)
- Tables and figures to show results for many variables and interactions
- Data analysis software

Keep in mind that the findings section should be written in an objective style, without interpretation or statements of the value of the specific findings. Here "just the facts, and all the facts" is needed, presented clearly and succinctly.

QUALITATIVE FINDINGS SECTION ELEMENTS   In contrast to what is typically a fairly "dry" presentation of quantitative results, qualitative findings are written in a more expressive and engaging fashion, often with expressions of surprise, insight, reflection, and interpretation. This is due in part to the emerging nature of the design and also to the need for analyses that are narrative and descriptive. Context, researcher interpretations, and participant voices are integrated in ways that lead to justifiable patterns, themes, and conclusions. Levitt (2019) describes this section as a combination of writing a novel and presenting empirical data.

It is significant to note that qualitative researchers present their findings in varied ways. Both the types of headings and subsections, and sequence in which they are found, can be different from one study to another. Typically, the results are presented in concert with the design, and often the discussion is combined in the same section as findings. That said, as an adjunct to what was discussed in Chapter 13, presenting qualitative results typically includes the following sections and elements:

- Use an orienting paragraph to describe how the findings will be presented.
- Describe coding used, including an indication of the number of codes and number of quotes or excerpts for each code.
- Describe themes, patterns, and other syntheses of data, including quotes or excerpts as illustrations of participant or data source voices, and summarize findings to illustrate thick analyses.
- Use diagrams, charts, and other visual aids to explain models and illustrate findings.
- Present quantitative descriptive data sparingly, as appropriate.
- Organize findings in a manner that is consistent with the design (e.g., grounded theory, case study).

MIXED METHODS FINDINGS SECTION ELEMENTS   With mixed methods findings there are three major subsections: one for qualitative; one for quantitative; and one for mixed results. The findings are typically reported in a sequence that is consistent with the design (whether quantitative or qualitative was first), with greatest attention to what is most emphasized. Elements previously discussed for quantitative and qualitative sections are needed, followed by a description of the "mixed" findings. This is often done by referring to the mixed methods question(s), then showing the results that address that question. Similar to qualitative findings, there is a fair amount of variability in how mixed methods results are presented. In some reports you will find that results of each phase are reported separately, while others will focus mostly on the data that integrate both phases. It is helpful to examine models of mixed methods studies in your field to know about the nature of the findings section, especially the extent to which findings are integrated with discussion.

Check for Understanding 2

2a. What are the four subsections that make up the method section of quantitative articles?

2b. What are two important differences between quantitative and qualitative methods sections?

Discussion and Conclusions

Learning Outcome 16.3 Apply the guidelines for writing effective discussion/conclusion sections.

For reports and articles, once results are presented, there is a discussion of what was found, with interpretations and conclusions. All findings are subject to interpretation, and conclusions follow from interpretations. As you might expect, the quality of interpretation varies considerably—we'll start with the discussion section.

Discussion

The purpose of the discussion is threefold: (1) to present an interpretation of the results; (2) to state the conclusions; and (3) to indicate recommendations for further study, professional practice, and/or policy. Use the discussion to explain the meaning of the results and to speculate about their implications. The discussion is more than a restatement of the results; it is a general summary of findings and an evaluation of the methodology and results to help readers understand what the results suggest and how they can be used. It is essentially a synthesis of the study reflecting your professional judgment. The synthesis integrates the research problem and review of literature with the results, and explains *why* the results were obtained and what the results *mean*. Professional judgment is reflected in the nature of the synthesis and the implications suggested in the form of conclusions and recommendations, framed by the significance of the study.

You will find that discussion sections are the least structured parts of an article and that authors differ about content and organization. Some authors begin the discussion with conclusions and then analyze the conclusions, whereas others will explain why they obtained the results, describe the limitations of the study, and then present the conclusions. Some may even combine results with discussion and conclusions. We consider each of the major aspects of the discussion section, even though the order in which these are found in articles will vary.

The most common way to begin the discussion is by summarizing the most important findings. This is often contained in a single paragraph, which typically has a sentence that describes the major research question or purpose. Note in Excerpt 16.2 how the findings are succinctly and clearly identified.

EXCERPT 16.2

Summary of Findings

The present study compared the academic self-concept of equally able students in different school tracks to examine the presence of the BFLPE [Big-Fish-Little-Pond Effect] in the Taiwanese education system. The overall-school analysis revealed a negative correlation between the school-average ability and academic self-concept of students, which supported the BFLPE and replicated previous research findings. The results of adjacent-school comparisons showed that academic self-concept was lower for students at the bottom of the first-ranked school than for their counterparts at the top of the second-ranked school, which supported the BFLPE. However, the academic self-concept did not differ between the bottom of the second-ranked school and the top of the third-ranked school, supporting the absence of the BFLPE. (p. 228)

SOURCE: Sung, Y., Huang, L., Tseng, F., & Chang, K. (2014). The aspects and ability groups in which little fish perform worse than big fish: Examining the big-fish-little-pond effect in the context of school tracking. *Contemporary Educational Psychology, 39*(3), 220–232.

Interpretation of Results

Once the study is summarized, the emphasis turns to a thorough interpretation of the results. This is essentially an analysis of the results, which consists of reasoned speculation to answer the following kinds of questions:

> Why did the results turn out as they did?
> What may have affected the results?
> Are there any limitations that should be noted?
> To what extent were hypotheses supported?
> What is the meaning of the findings?
> How do the results relate to previous research findings?

Interpretation of the results may be related to the research problem and/or hypothesis, theory, statistical procedures, the methodology of the study, and previous research on the problem.

INTERPRETATION RELATED TO THE PROBLEM AND/OR HYPOTHESIS Discussion sections often begin with a restatement of the problem or hypothesis, followed by some indication of the answer to the problem or degree of support for the hypothesis. There may be an evaluation that the findings provided a strong or clear answer or that the hypothesis was strongly or marginally supported. Unexpected findings may be summarized as surprising. In this type of interpretation, the authors indicate their professional opinion about how well the data answer the questions. When reading these interpretations, it is important to think about how researcher bias may have influenced the opinions that are expressed. Your judgment about the relationship between the questions and the findings may be quite different from that of the researcher. Sometimes researchers will focus only on findings that support their expectations, although this is not what is expected of ethical researchers.

INTERPRETATION BASED ON THEORY When research has a clear theoretical basis, it is helpful to interpret results in light of that theory. Sometimes competing theories are examined, which would also result in a discussion of how the results are related to the

---

EXCERPT 16.3

Interpretation Based on Theory

On the theoretical level, these findings suggest that the act of teaching (i.e., explaining material to others) may promote generative processing necessary for long-term meaningful learning. According to the cognitive theory of multimedia learning (Mayer, 2005, Mayer, 2009 and Mayer, 2011), generative processing involves actively constructing a coherent representation of the material that fits with learners' prior knowledge, by engaging in the cognitive processes of organizing and integrating. (p. 81)

SOURCE: Fiorella, L., & Mayer, R. E. (2014). Role of expectations and explanations in learning by teaching. *Contemporary Educational Psychology, 39*(2), 75–85.

---

contradictory theories and the extent to which the study contributed to a resolution. Note in Excerpt 16.3 how the authors address theoretical implications of their findings.

INTERPRETATION RELATED TO METHODOLOGY   As stressed throughout this book, methodology is very important in understanding and analyzing results. This includes selecting participants and the nature of samples, instrumentation, interventions, and other procedures. Often, methods are used as a reason for obtaining certain results and also suggest specific limitations. Consequently, when researchers interpret the results, they refer to specific aspects of the methodology. Even if the researchers do not do this, you should! You may find significant weaknesses that are not addressed by the researcher in explaining the results.

For quantitative studies, interpretations related to methodology focus on whether the methods affect internal validity. For experiments, the results are examined to see whether there are any methodological factors that could constitute plausible rival hypotheses. For nonexperimental quantitative studies, the focus is on measurement and participant selection. Limitations based on methodology in quantitative investigations are emphasized more with results that fail to show statistical significance.

In qualitative studies, interpretations based on methodology emphasize the researcher's role in gathering and analyzing the data. There is less emphasis on the "limitations" of the methods and more emphasis on the meaning of the results as influenced by methodology.

For mixed methods studies, there is a need to address methodologies in both the quantitative and qualitative phases. In particular, it is necessary to reflect on how well the different methods align with the purpose of the study and whether different methods may have altered the findings.

INTERPRETATION RELATED TO SELECTION OR NATURE OF PARTICIPANTS
One aspect of the methodology that may affect interpretation of the results is the selection of participants. As noted in Chapter 5, volunteer and available samples may give unique and limited results. Often there is a tendency to ignore the effects of specially selected participants.

In studies that include participant characteristics as variables, the discussion often examines whether these characteristics are helpful in explaining the results, such as when there are interactions with interventions. In Excerpt 16.4, the authors discuss how an intervention was stronger for some types of participants than for others.

EXCERPT 16.4

Interpretation Based on Participant Characteristics

Finally, it is important to note that, after synthesizing results from the previous study, the intervention effect was stronger for low-achieving students than for average-achieving students, and, although not statistically significant, students with LD also showed a positive growth rate difference compared with their average-achieving peers. Research suggests that in contrast to reading, where children with lower initial scores tend to make faster progress over time than children with higher initial scores, in math, children with both low- and high-initial scores seem to progress at the same rate, thus maintaining the discrepancy apparent early in school into elementary, middle, and high school (Montague, Enders, & Castro, 2006; Montague, Enders, Cavendish, & Castro, 2011; Morgan, 2009). That is, children with higher initial scores maintain higher performance, whereas those with lower scores maintain low scores across time. Interestingly, the present study only partially follows that pattern. In our sample, the lowest performing students (particularly the low-achieving students) in the treatment group closed the performance gap between themselves and their average-achieving peers, who also improved, but at a slower rate of growth. (p. 479)

SOURCE: Montague, M., Krawec, J., Enders, C., & Dietz, S. (2014). The effects of cognitive strategy instruction on math problem solving of middle-school students of varying ability. *Journal of Educational Psychology, 106*(2), 469–481.

FOR QUANTITATIVE AND MIXED METHODS STUDIES: INTERPRETATION RELATED TO MEASUREMENT OF VARIABLES A second type of interpretation is to examine how the measurement of variables may affect the results. Many of the points in Chapters 6 and 7 are relevant:

- Instruments should show evidence of validity and reliability.
- Instruments should be sufficiently sensitive to discern relationships.
- Procedures for administering an instrument can be important.
- Possible effects of observers and interviewers must be documented.
- There is the possibility of response set and faking in noncognitive measurement.
- Norms may not be appropriate.

Excerpt 16.5 is an excellent example of explanation of results related to the generic nature of the dependent variable, essentially an insensitive measure that leads to nonsignificant findings. Note, too, that the excerpt goes on to point out that even these statistically nonsignificant results have some practical implications.

EXCERPT 16.5

Discussion Based on the Nature of the Dependent Variable

The FCAT math test reports are global in the sense that they produce a composite score; that is, they do not break out scale scores that would provide insight into performance on various strands of math skills, concepts, and applications tested (e.g., computation, applied problem solving, measurement, geometry). Thus, it is not surprising that the intervention, which addressed only one of the several components of the FCAT, did not effect significant change in performance. The statistically nonsignificant improvement, however, still translates into practically important gains in performance on a test that determines grade promotion, eligibility for certain courses, and even graduation (Florida Department of Education, 2012). (p. 479)

SOURCE: Montague, M., Krawec, J., Enders, C., & Dietz, S. (2014). The effects of cognitive strategy instruction on math problem solving of middle-school students of varying ability. *Journal of Educational Psychology, 106*(2), 469–481.

FOR EXPERIMENTAL STUDIES, INTERPRETATION RELATED TO THE INTERVENTION A third category of factors in interpreting results concerns experimental interventions. The specific nature of some aspect of an intervention, or the manner in which treatments are administered, may influence the results (refer to Excerpt 16.6).

EXCERPT 16.6

Interpretation Based on the Nature of the Intervention

An unexpected finding was that students in the comparison condition received lower scores on their posttest measures of quality and on the development of their claims than they did at pretest. The most plausible reason for this finding appears to be based on the limitation in the study, noted by the American history professor and high school history teacher, that the posttest materials were slightly harder than those presented at pretest. We believe that students in the experimental group were better equipped to deal with these more difficult materials, after learning the historical reasoning and writing strategies, and their performance was not negatively impacted. In contrast, students in the comparison group had engaged in group discussions that emphasized understanding of specific historical content rather than strategic processes that could be transferred to new learning situations (i.e., different source materials). Hence, their performance suffered when asked to read more difficult materials, and to respond in writing to an historical essay prompt at posttest. (p. 189)

SOURCE: De La Paz, S., & Felton, M. K. (2010). Reading and writing from multiple source documents in history: Effects of strategy instruction with low to average high school writers. *Contemporary Educational Psychology, 35*, 174–192.

INTERPRETATION BASED ON PROCEDURES FOR ANALYZING DATA For quantitative and mixed methods studies, an important factor in the discussion concerns the statistical procedures used in the study. One issue is whether assumptions for statistical procedures have been violated. In studies in which violation of the assumptions could have important implications, there should be an indication of whether the assumptions have been met or a discussion on the potential impact of not meeting the assumptions.

Some researchers assume that the failure to find a statistically significant difference should be interpreted to mean that there is, in reality, no difference. As noted in Chapter 10, there are many reasons that researchers fail to find a significant difference or relationship, only one of which is that there really exists no difference or relationship. With the increasing use of effect size statistics, researchers often include a discussion of this measure in the interpretation part of the article. The most complete treatment of effect size will place the results within the context of what has been found in other studies. For example, if an effect size estimate for a particular study is stronger than what has been previously reported, it would be useful to point that out. It may also be helpful to know about whether the samples used in different studies could have an impact on effect size. For proposals, it is best to indicate how effect size will be addressed.

In qualitative research, the approaches used to code, categorize, and develop themes are critically important in synthesizing the data. There may not be specific statistical methods, but the data are still analyzed! The manner in which codes were identified and applied can affect the results. For example, if a researcher has not checked preliminary coding or engaged in constant comparison of categories as data are collected, this may result in significant limitations related to analysis. Different qualitative software programs may use different criteria for coding and categorizing, which could affect the results. There may be something about the manner in which qualitative researchers assess their role in a study that affects the results. If documents were analyzed, how, specifically, was that accomplished? Would a different approach to document review provide different results?

Excerpt 16.7 describes how researchers went about data analysis for their qualitative study. They use "bracketing" and "data extraction" and identify "essential structures," but how, specifically, were these processes completed? Did each researcher do this independently? Could different approaches result in different findings?

EXCERPT 16.7
Qualitative Data Analysis

We bracketed the transcribed teachers' stories. Through this process, we were able to dissect the stories in searching for essential structures. Data were extracted from the teachers' stories about their experiences in the alternative teacher preparation program and the realities of their urban classrooms.... The characteristics of a high-quality mathematics teacher were also extracted from their stories. (p. 149)

SOURCE: Junor Clarke, P. A., & Thomas, C. D. (2009). Teachers' perceptions of connections and disconnects between their alternative preparation and teaching in urban classrooms. *Urban Education*, 44(2), pp. 144–159.

INTERPRETATION RELATED TO PREVIOUS RESEARCH   The purpose of a review of previous research is to place the study in the context of other investigations. Once the study is completed, the results should be discussed in light of the reviewed literature to help explain the reasons for the results and the meaningfulness of the study. Although the style of relating results to previous studies will vary, there is usually an indication of whether the current findings are consistent or inconsistent with previous research. When the results are inconsistent or contradictory, the authors should provide explanations.

In Excerpt 16.8, the authors discuss how their study was different from previous investigations of the same intervention, extending and expanding the significance of the results.

Interpretation as related to previous studies and other literature is the most common feature of discussion sections. Such an interpretation is important because it places the results more directly and explicitly in the context of other research, thereby

EXCERPT 16.8

Interpretation Based on Previous Research

Like other studies focused on teaching students comprehensive sets of strategies (e.g., Brown et al., 1996; Dole, Brown, & Trathen, 1996; Palinscar & Brown, 1984; Paris et al., 1984; Paris & Jacobs, 1984; Paris & Oka, 1986) and those conducted specifically on the LSC (e.g., Clark et al., 1984; Lenz & Hughes, 1990; Woodruff et al., 2002), these findings suggest that the strategies instruction had an effect on comprehension and use of metacognitive strategies, particularly for sixth graders. However, findings from the present study differ from the aforementioned studies in several important ways. First, like Anderson's (1992) study of transactional strategies instruction and Westra and Moore's (1995) study of reciprocal teaching, the present study yielded significant findings with sixth-grade adolescent struggling readers. Second, this study was conducted with a much larger sample across a much longer period of time than previous studies of strategies instruction, suggesting that sixth-grade struggling readers were beginning to internalize the strategic processing routines that would enable transfer to occur. Finally, findings from this study were examined using a randomized controlled field trial and analyzed using multilevel modeling techniques that heretofore had not been used in studies of the impact of strategies instruction on long-term comprehension and strategy use. In light of Slavin et al.'s (2008) synthesis of research on reading programs in middle and high schools and their plea for more rigorous studies, these findings are particularly critical. (p. 270)

SOURCE: Cantrell, S. C., Almasi, J. F., Carter, J. C., Rintamaa, M., & Madden, A. (2010). The impact of a strategy-based intervention on the comprehension and strategy use of struggling adolescent readers. *Journal of Educational Psychology, 102*(2), 257–280.

enhancing the contribution of the new research to a recognized body of knowledge. It also demonstrates that the authors have a good understanding of the literature, which increases their credibility.

Excerpt 16.9 is an example of how results are interpreted by relating them to other studies or literature.

EXCERPT 16.9

Interpretations Related to Other Studies and Literature

Taken together, our results are in line with the conclusions of other studies that a short version (Marsh, Ellis, Parada, Richards, & Heubeck, 2005) or even a single-item measure of an original long scale may provide suitable alternatives (e.g., Robins et al., 2001). In particular, single-item self reports may be adequate when a construct is concrete, highly schematized for most individuals, unidimensional in content, and when it primarily reflects subjective experience (Robins et al., 2001). (p. 200)

SOURCE: Gogol, K., Brunner, M., Goetz, T., Martin, R., Ugen, S., Keller, U., ... & Preckel, F. (2014). "My questionnaire is too long!" The assessments of motivational-affective constructs with three-item and single-item measures. *Contemporary Educational Psychology, 39*(3), 188–205.

Conclusions

One of the final parts of a research report or article is a statement of the conclusions. Conclusions are nontechnical summary statements of the results as they pertain to the research problem, often presented as answers to the questions, hypotheses, or purposes of the research. Sometimes conclusions simply repeat a technical, statistical presentation of the results in short summary sentences in nontechnical language. In other studies, the conclusions will be based on the interpretation of the results, reflecting the professional judgment of the investigators. Usually, the major or most significant findings are summarized as conclusions.

Conclusions may be stated at the beginning or at the end of the discussion section and may precede or follow interpretations of the results. If there are several major findings, one may be presented and discussed, followed by another. The term *conclusion* may or may not be used. By beginning the discussion with conclusions, the author provides a succinct overview of the most important findings, which helps to orient the reader to the discussion that follows. Often, conclusions are stated succinctly in the abstract of an article.

It is best to indicate *why* the conclusions are supported. Excerpts 16.10 and 16.11 provide examples of conclusion statements that do not contain statistical terms or answers to specific research questions.

EXCERPTS 16.10 AND 16.11

Conclusion Statements

Like much of the recent research on the topic, our findings suggest that the benefits of living on-campus are not extensive. While there are positive effects for some measures of engagement (i.e., collaborative learning, discussions with diverse others, and student-faculty interaction) particularly when comparing on-campus students to those living farther than walking distance, this was not the case for other forms of engagement, nor for students' perceived gains in learning and growth in cocurricular areas. (p. 265)

SOURCE: Graham, P. A., Socorro Hurtado, S., & Gonyea, R. M. (2018). The benefits of living on campus: Do residence halls provide distinctive environments of engagement? *Journal of Student Affairs Research and Practice, 55*(3), 255–269.

In summary, this study indicates that the cause/effect structure can be taught successfully to second graders at risk for academic failure. Students at the second-grade level have not all mastered word recognition and are not fluent readers, and they may not have a completely mature understanding of cause/effect. However, they can gain from explicit instruction in reading comprehension and should not be deprived of the opportunity to receive instruction that would provide a strong foundation for later learning. (p. 13)

SOURCE: Williams, J. P., Pollini, S., Nubla-Kung, A. M., Snyder, A. E., Garcia, A., Ordynans, J. G., & Atkins, J. G. (2014). An intervention to improve comprehension of cause/effect through expository text structure instruction. *Journal of Educational Psychology, 106*(1), 1–17.

Limitations

An important aspect of the discussion is to indicate any limitations to the conclusions. It is also important for proposals to indicate potential limitations. There is often reference to how results or conclusions are limited to individuals with certain characteristics, to features of the design, or to particular settings. This is essentially a way to address the generalizability, translatability, or comparability of the findings. Beyond the particulars of a research setting, you need to consider whether it is reasonable to expect the results to represent a general pattern that would occur again and again. This consideration can be directly addressed from the researcher's perspective in a report or article, but it is also necessary for you to judge the extent to which the conclusions are useful in different contexts. For this reason, it is helpful for you to think about the following factors that may limit the results.

LIMITATIONS RELATED TO PARTICIPANT CHARACTERISTICS The participants in a study have certain characteristics, such as age, race, ability, and socioeconomic status. Strictly speaking, results and conclusions are limited to other individuals who have the same, or at least very similar, characteristics. In research jargon, this factor is referred to as **population external validity**.

There are two ways in which limitations related to participant characteristics affect the use of the results. The first concerns generalizing from a sample, or the individuals used in a study, to a larger population or to other people. For example, if a study of fourth-grade students shows that cooperative learning strategies are better than individualized approaches, the results are limited to other fourth-graders with similar characteristics. Similarly, research conducted with high school students is limited to other high school students; research done with males should not be generalized to females; what may be true for one type of student may not be true for other types of students; and so forth.

One key to understanding the extent to which results should be limited to participant characteristics is to know the characteristics. That may seem rather obvious, but you will find in some studies that the participants are not adequately described. An important aspect of a quantitative study is whether probability sampling was used. If representative sampling was used, then the limitations apply to the population rather than to the sample. If available samples were used, you need to examine the procedures to see whether limitations are suggested—for example, as with paid or volunteer samples.

A second limitation is to be careful not to generalize what is true for a group to individuals or subgroups. For example, if you determine that teachers' expectations of students seem to be affected by reviewing test scores from the previous year, the overall finding is true for the group as a whole and may not be true for any individual teacher or for certain groups of teachers. In other words, expectations may be influenced in some types of teachers but not in other types of teachers, even though when all types of teachers are analyzed together, there are significant results. It is similar to saying that although in the entire group of twelfth-grade students there is a positive relationship between attendance and achievement, the relationship may be more or less positive for particular groups of twelfth-graders.

Excerpts 16.12 through 16.14 show how results may be limited because of the way participants were selected.

EXCERPTS 16.12–16.14
Limitations Based on Participant Selection

Classrooms and participants were selected from a typical disciplinary alternative school in southeastern United States. Therefore, results do not necessarily generalize to other populations from other disciplinary alternative schools in other school districts. (p. 323)

SOURCE: Pane, D. M., Rocco, T. S., Miller, L. D., & Salmon, A. K. (2014). How teachers use power in the classroom to avoid or support exclusionary school discipline practices. *Urban Education, 49*(3), 297–328.

We designed this study to test relations among improvements in reading rate and other aspects of reading. Because all of our students were slow readers for their grade level, we cannot expect the relations found for these poor readers in Grades 2 and 4 to generalize to average-reader populations. (p. 16)

SOURCE: O'Connor, R. E., Swanson, H. L., & Geraghty, C. (2010). Improvement in reading rate under independent and difficult text levels: Influences on work and comprehension skills. *Journal of Educational Psychology, 102*(1), 1–19.

The present results may not be generalized to all teachers working in multicultural classrooms in the Netherlands due to the possibility of a sample selection bias. Participation in the present study was voluntary, and many teachers refused to participate, mostly due to time constraints. Those teachers who were willing to participate may therefore not be fully comparable to those teachers who refused to participate, which makes our sample less than completely representative of the population of elementary school teachers working in multicultural classrooms in the Netherlands. (p. 522)

SOURCE: Van den Bergh, L., Denessen, E., Hornstra, L., Voeten, M., & Holland, R. W. (2010). The implicit prejudiced attitudes of teachers: Relations to teacher expectations and the ethnic achievement gap. *American Educational Research Journal, 47*(2), 497–527.

LIMITATIONS RELATED TO CONTEXTUAL CHARACTERISTICS   Contextual characteristics are specifics of the setting and context in which the study is conducted. They include the place of the study—whether in a classroom, laboratory, playground, home, and so on—and what is present in this setting—for example, the type of equipment in a playground or the objects in a classroom. If research on prosocial behavior is studied in a day-care center, for example, the results may not be generalizable to unstructured play in a neighborhood. What may occur in one school may not occur in another because of differences in their structure and specific features. Limitations because of settings are part of the conditions of conducting the research. (Other conditions are considered later.) Together, they may be referred to as factors affecting the **ecological external validity** of the research. Ecological external validity is strong when the results can be generalized to different settings. This is obviously a limitation in studies that occur in a single classroom or school. As with participant characteristics, your judgment of generalizability will depend on how well the setting is described. If your situation is similar in most respects, the findings may be useful. On the other hand, if your situation is quite different—for example, an inner-city school compared with a suburban school—the results may not be useful.

Note in Excerpt 16.15 that the authors are careful to point out that their results pertain only to writing self-efficacy in a particular context.

EXCERPT 16.15
Contextual Limitations

Second, this study does not address issues of genre or other contextual factors tied to writing self-efficacy. It seems highly probable that, for most writers, self-efficacy differs substantially by type of writing and writing contexts. For instance, there obviously are many genres (e.g., poetry, narrative, exposition) and categories of content to write about (science, history, sports) for which writers' self-efficacy would vary widely. (p. 36)

SOURCE: Bruning, R., Dempsey, M., Kauffman, D. F., McKim, C., & Zumbrunn, S. (2012). Examining dimensions of self-efficacy for writing. *Journal of Educational Psychology, 105*(1), 25–38.

LIMITATIONS RELATED TO METHODOLOGY One of the most common limitations is related to the nature of the methodology that was used. Often nonexperimental studies that examine relationships will indicate that causal conclusions should not be reached. Similarly, caution is often suggested in making causal conclusions for quasi-experiments or for studies in which internal validity is weak. Notice in Excerpt 16.16 how the researcher suggests that other methods of collecting data could provide additional insights. In Excerpt 16.17, the researchers remind the reader about the limitations of using a cross-sectional design.

EXCERPTS 16.16 AND 16.17
Limitation Based on Methodology

Third, more rigorous qualitative methods should be considered. As Vanderburg and Stephens (2010) observe, little is known about what coaches do and how coaches assist teacher development. Careful analysis of video or audiotaped coaching conversations would contribute greatly to understanding the phenomenon of instructional coaching as a lived experience, revealing what happens in the interactional space between coach and teacher. (p. 600)

SOURCE: Teemant, A. (2014). A mixed-methods investigation of instructional coaching for teachers of diverse learners, *Urban Education, 49*(5), 574–604.

The present study is of course not without limitations. Principal among these is the fact that it employed a retrospective, cross-sectional design. With this type of design, the participants' pretransition recollections could have been influenced either by their post-transition experiences or by forgetting given that they were surveyed in October, approximately two months after the students had entered their new school. (p. 218)

SOURCE: Akos, P., & Galassi, J. P. (2004). Middle and high school transitions as viewed by students, parents, and teachers. *Professional School Counseling, 7*(4), 212–221.

LIMITATIONS RELATED TO WHEN THE RESEARCH IS CONDUCTED Time is related to limitations in several ways. The first is that interventions may be effective at one time but not at another. What may work in the morning may not work in the afternoon, for instance, and what may be effective in the fall may be ineffective in the winter. Responses of participants to interventions and measures also vary according to time. Students' responses may be much more accurate in the morning than in late afternoon. Measures of self-concept will be affected by when the students respond, as will attitudinal measures. From a broader perspective, the socio-historical context in which the research is carried out may limit the findings. That is, how students respond will be affected by the cultural values at the time the research is conducted. In the case of Excerpt 16.18, the researchers point out that data collected right after the intervention are limited and should not necessarily be generalized to outcomes at a later time.

EXCERPT 16.18

Limitations Based on When Research Is Conducted

An additional limitation in terms of the research design is that we report assessments of outcomes relatively close to the implementation of the intervention. Intervention activities ceased in March; data collection to assess the effect on students began for student and teacher surveys 6 to 8 weeks following the last intervention activity. Follow-up data that include longer-term assessments of intervention effects, specifically, beyond the year of intervention and once students no longer have the intervention teacher, are currently being collected. (p. 371)

SOURCE: Hamm, J. V., Farmer, T. W., Robertson, D., Dadisman, K. A., Murray, A., & Meece, J. L. (2010). Effects of a developmentally based intervention with teachers on native American and white early adolescents' schooling adjustment in rural settings. *The Journal of Experimental Education, 78,* 343–377.

LIMITATIONS RELATED TO INTERVENTIONS   In experimental research, generalizability is limited by the nature of the intervention. It is necessary to know how an intervention is defined and carried out to know whether it will be useful to you in your situation. For example, there has been a great amount of research recently on what is termed "project-based teaching," but its definition may vary from study to study. The same would be true for such practices as cooperative learning, homogeneous and heterogeneous grouping, individualization, praise, and reinforcement. You need to look at what is sometimes the fine print in the methodology section to know precisely how an intervention is defined and implemented. Results and conclusions are, of course, limited to this operational definition and the procedures for implementing the treatment.

LIMITATIONS RELATED TO MEASURES   Quantitative research is limited by the manner in which the variables are measured. For example, an independent variable may be "on-task behavior" and the dependent variable "attitudes toward learning." Both of these variables can be measured in several ways. Results of research are generalized to other situations in which the variables are measured, or at least conceptualized, in the same manner. Thus, it is necessary to understand in some detail how the variables are defined and measured, as illustrated in Excerpts 16.19 and 16.20.

EXCERPTS 16.19 AND 16.20

Limitations Related to Measures

Evaluating the effects of these STEM-focused schools by using the TerraNova assessments as the yardstick has obvious limitations. Achievement in the three traditional content areas of mathematics, language arts, and reading were examined, but not examined were domains in which the STEM-focused schools may quite possibly be having tremendous effect. These might include areas of critical thinking, scientific reasoning, ability to design experiments, computational thinking, and interest and awareness related to STEM careers. Just as it would not be reasonable to evaluate a specialty school that focuses on the fine arts solely on its ability to advance students' understanding in the traditional content areas, the same argument can be made for STEM-focused schools. (p. 264)

SOURCE: Judson, E. (2014). Effects of transferring to STEM-focused charter and magnet schools on student achievement. *The Journal of Educational Research, 107*(4), 255–266.

The present study had several limitations. First, the operationalization of student engagement in the present study is limited. Behavioral engagement was defined as effort and perseverance in learning and emotional engagement was defined as having a sense of belonging. Operationalization corresponded to these definitions. Student engagement has been conceptualized and operationalized in various ways (Fredricks et al., 2004). For example, behavioral engagement can be defined as attending class, avoiding disruptive behaviors, concentrating, making an effort, finishing work, or participating in extracurricular activities. Thus, findings of the present study may not be directly comparable to findings of studies using different measures of student engagement. (p. 183)

SOURCE: Lee, J. (2014). The relationship between student engagement and academic performance: Is it a myth or reality? *The Journal of Educational Research, 107*(3), 177–185.

BEING REASONABLE ABOUT LIMITATIONS   There is a tendency to be too strict in analyzing the limitations of research. If we are overly strict, the results of studies would be useful only in a few situations and to other individuals who are just like participants in the study. It is better to use our best, reasonable, professional judgment about limitations. The situation may be somewhat different, as may be the measures or participants, but the differences may not be great enough to affect the usefulness of the findings. For example, suppose you read a study that examines the effect of advance organizers on a lesson. (Advance organizers are broad conceptual frameworks to structure and organize the material.) The study is conducted with a biology unit, using seventh-graders as participants, and finds that students who use advance organizers show better learning and retention. If you need to teach a social studies unit to your class of sixth-graders, should you simply dismiss the implications of the study because your situation is not exactly the same? In a case such as this, the limitations of the study may suggest some caution in using advance organizers in your class, but overall there is sufficient overlap to conclude that what worked in the study would probably work for your social studies unit as well.

The Hedgehog and Fox Consider Limitations of Findings

Wow, there are so many limitations to this study. I don't think that it can be of much use.

While there are some limitations to this study the overall credibility is good. It makes sense to carefully examine each limitation to determine how much it might affect what other settings and types of individuals the results generalize to. There are certainly some methodological issues that can be addressed in future research.

Recommendations and Implications

Toward the end of the discussion section, you will often find statements that suggest future research or practice as a result of the study. These statements are called *recommendations* and *implications*. In journals primarily intended for other researchers, the recommendations tend to be oriented toward changes in specific methods in the study, such as instruments, sampling, or procedures. Recommendations and implications in journals that consumers are likely to read tend to be related to practice. It is important to be specific with recommendations and implications. It is not very helpful to say, simply, "Further research is needed in this area." What is needed is an indication of what types of research are necessary. For proposals, it is effective to reiterate how the research will lead to potential recommendations and implications.

Excerpts 16.21, 16.22, and 16.23 are examples of recommendations and implications that have adequate specificity. Excerpts 16.24 and 16.25 show recommendations for practice.

EXCERPTS 16.21–16.23

Recommendations for Further Research

Findings from the regression analyses highlight several directions for future research. First, children's pretest vocabulary scores and English language proficiency at the end of fourth grade explained over 50% of the variance in reading posttest scores. These results suggest that future intervention studies might couple efforts to improve vocabulary instruction and English language proficiency in an effort to prevent summer reading loss among low-income Latino children from language minority families. (p. 29)

SOURCE: Kim, J. S., & Guryan, J. (2010). The efficacy of a voluntary summer book reading intervention for low-income Latino children from language minority families. *Journal of Educational Psychology, 102*(1), 20–31.

Future research should also consider the perspectives of other institutional members, such as faculty and administrators. Listening to student voices is a critical first step that now needs to be incorporated with other institutional agents if change is possible. Exploring how administrators and faculty contribute to the current culture of an institution, as it relates to how graduate students are guided and supported in their career pursuits, is an important next step. Using critical race theory as a lens for assessing the institutional environment and addressing system issues that hinder academic careers of students of color would build on the current research and provide deeper recommendations for administrative practice. (p. 116)

SOURCE: Haley, K. J., Jaeger, A. J., & Levin, J. S. (2014). The influence of cultural social identity on graduate student career choice. *Journal of College Student Development, 55*(2), 101–119.

Future studies should also include an in-depth analysis of the current status of middle level teacher preparation programs through the lens of the Framework for Effective Middle Level Practices for effective middle level practices. The analysis should include a review of current program requirement, courses, and field and clinical experiences to determine the level to which programs infuse the constructs of the framework. (p. 19)

SOURCE: Howell, P. B., Cook, C., & Faulkner, S. A. (2014). Effective middle level teaching: Perceptions on the preparedness of newly hired teachers. *Middle Grades Research Journal, 8*(3), 1–22.

EXCERPTS 16.24 AND 16.25

Implications for Practice

The findings suggest that student affairs programs and courses on racial issues should not only focus on teaching race as a social construction, but should contemplate the possibility that students may hold multiple conceptions of race, and that a more fluid level of racial thinking may be a better goal for students than a static social or biological conception of race. Thus, educators should provide multiple opportunities to diversify students' tool kits of racial conceptions. (p. 240)

SOURCE: Johnston, M. P. (2014). The concept of race on campus: Exploring the nature of college students' racial conceptions. *Journal of College Student Development, 55*(3), 225–242.

Our results indicate that policy designations of economic risk should include parent education information, at a minimum, and that cutting educational funding may block low-income mothers with the most at-risk children from a pathway of action that likely has the most payoff. (p. 283)

SOURCE: Crosnoe, R., & Cooper, C. E. (2010). Economically disadvantaged children's transitions into elementary school: Linking family processes, school contexts, and educational policy. *American Educational Research Journal, 47*(2), 258–291.

Check for Understanding 3

3a. What information is integrated with findings in the discussion section?

3b. What two major sources of limitations are often addressed?

Consumer (and Researcher) Tips

Criteria for Evaluating Discussion and Conclusion Sections

1. **The results should be interpreted.** It is important to do more than repeat the major findings of the study. The discussion should include interpretations of the research problem, methodology, and previous research. It should include a detailed analysis of how imperfections in the design and extraneous variables may have affected the results and how the results are integrated with other literature on the topic. All major findings should be addressed in the discussion, including those that are unexpected, surprising, and conflicting. There should not be an analysis of every specific result, but important findings should not be ignored or overlooked.

2. **Conclusions should answer research problems.** Each problem or research question should be clearly answered by the conclusions. The answers should accurately reflect the results and interpretations of the data.

3. **Conclusions should be limited by participant characteristics.** The discussion should include an analysis of how the characteristics of the participants, such as age, gender, and socioeconomic status, limit the generalizability of the conclusions. Overgeneralization, either in terms of these characteristics, or by suggesting that what may be true for the group as a whole is true for individuals or subgroups, should be avoided.

4. **Conclusions should be limited by the nature of interventions and measures.** Indicate how specific aspects of interventions and measures should be considered in interpreting conclusions. Point out, when appropriate, how different operational definitions of treatments and measures might lead to different conclusions.

5. **Statistical significance should not be confused with practical significance.** Be careful not to interpret statistically significant results to mean that they have practical value or importance. Statistical significance does not necessarily mean that the results will have important practical implications.

6. **Failure to show statistical significance does not necessarily mean that there is no relationship or difference.** Be careful in interpreting results that fail to show statistical significance. Most studies do not provide an adequate test of whether the statistical insignificance reflects no relationship, nor whether weaknesses in the design account for the findings.

7. **Limitations of findings should be reasonable.** Find a middle ground between being overly strict or too confining and completely ignoring obviously important limitations. There are shortcomings to all research, but there is no need to dwell on every possible specific limitation. Important limitations should be mentioned even though the results support a hypothesis.

8. **Recommendations and implications should be specific.** Recommendations and implications for future research should be included in the discussion and should specifically describe the changes in methodology that would be desirable in subsequent studies. Recommendations and implications for practice should be made only when the data and design support such inferences.

> **Author Reflection** *Now that you have (presumably) read some research articles, have you noticed how many qualifiers are used to limit, restrict, or otherwise provide a basis for caution? Although it seems like such language simply allows the researchers to avoid stating in clear terms what was found, it also is very much needed to help you draw accurate conclusions so that possible influences on practice are not overgeneralized. In my experience, in fact, many authors do not give sufficient attention to limitations and often reach untenable conclusions. Also, when you write up a study, you will find that the interpretation section is quite challenging because of the need to incorporate previous studies when explaining why the results were obtained. Although there is a need for analysis of the results, in light of different kinds of limitations, it is also important to bring in other studies to shed light on the interpretations, conclusions, and implications and recommendations.*

Steps in Writing Research Proposals, Reports, and Articles

Learning Outcome 16.4 Describe the steps used to write research proposals, reports, and manuscripts to submit to journals, and the importance of audience in determining what is presented.

My experience is that if you break down writing of research proposals, reports, and manuscripts that are submitted for publication as articles into a sequence of steps it simplifies the process and results in a stronger product. No matter which section of the document you are writing, there are six sequential steps, as illustrated in Figure 16.1.

Figure 16.1 Steps in Writing Research Proposals, Reports, and Articles

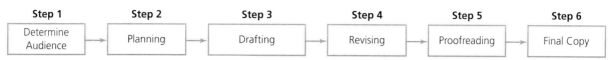

Step 1	Step 2	Step 3	Step 4	Step 5	Step 6
Determine Audience	Planning	Drafting	Revising	Proofreading	Final Copy

Audience

It is critical to consider the audience to whom you are communicating your work. This requires identification of those who will hear and/or read your work. Key distinctions among different audiences and implications for writing are shown in Table 16.4. Primarily, you need to know about the level of technical expertise of the audience. A report written for school administrators and teachers, those with some albeit limited technical knowledge, should look very different from a manuscript written for publication in a research journal. At the same time, with open-access publication (e.g., Elsevier, AERA, Sage Open), research is increasingly viewed by many different audiences. This suggests a need to take multiple audiences into account.

Knowing the interests and professional roles of the audience is helpful in providing examples they will find engaging and relevant. Using terms the audience will understand is a vital component of effective communication. For example, reporting results of sophisticated statistical tests to a lay audience or politicians, using unfamiliar terms, will disengage the audience from even trying to understand. Comprehension is much easier when the terminology is familiar and friendly. For lay audiences, keep the focus on descriptive results.

The audience for manuscripts written to be submitted for publication is peer reviewers and editors *of the specific journal*. This suggests that an excellent strategy for writing style, format, length, citation requirements, and other aspects of the document is to become familiar with recently published articles from that journal. You will learn, for example, about the level of detail expected in a review of literature, typical major headings, and use of tables and figures, as well as more general style and presentation. On a more general level, there are discipline-specific guidelines and expectations. Even fields within the larger discipline of education (e.g., English education, math education, educational leadership) will have unique conventions and styles.

Table 16.4 Writing Implications Based on Nature of Document and Primary Audience

Nature of the Document	Primary Audience	Implications
Research proposal	Reviewers and editors	Use appropriate technical language; assume knowledge of research terms and procedures; follow submission requirements carefully; review other successful proposals.
Research report	Lay public	Avoid technical language; focus on purpose, general findings, and conclusions; include executive summary; suggest implications for practice.
	Policy makers	Avoid technical language; explain terms; focus on purpose, general findings, and conclusions; include executive summary; suggest policy implications.
	Peer professionals	Use appropriate technical language; assume knowledge of research terms and procedures; follow submissions requirements carefully; review previously published reports.
	Practitioners	Avoid technical language; explain terms; focus on purpose, findings, conclusions, and implications for practice and application.
Research article	Peer professionals	Use appropriate technical language; assume knowledge of research terms and procedures; follow submission requirements carefully; review journal standards and required style; review published articles in the journal.

Author Reflection *I have found that scholarly/academic writing for empirical research is tough—you need to plan sufficient time and have reasonable expectations. Most important, just write something, anything, since that will lead to more. And when you get in a groove, stay with it until you drop... those grooves don't come along all that often.*

Check for Understanding 4

4a. What is the sequence of steps to use in writing empirical research proposals and reports?

4b. What is the main difference between writing for a lay audience compared to writing for peer professionals?

Key Terms

Ecological external validity
Population external validity

Scholarly tone
Scholarly voice

Discussion Questions

1. What is the purpose of a discussion section in an article?
2. What are the major components of a discussion section?
3. Why is it important to relate findings to previous research?
4. What aspects of the methodology of a study may have implications in interpreting the results?
5. How is the purpose of the conclusions different from the purpose of the interpretation of results?
6. What is the difference between limitations based on generalizing to other people and generalizing to individual participants?
7. In what ways should conclusions be limited to the timing of the research and to the nature of interventions, measures, and data analysis?
8. What is wrong with the simple recommendation "further studies need to be done"?
9. How do quantitative and qualitative discussion sections differ?

Application Exercise

1. Identify a recent article in your area and evaluate it for writing quality. Use the points for effective scholarly/academic writing and appropriate formatting in your evaluation. Examine the discussion section to determine the quality of the interpretation and nature of limitations. What would be two or three changes that would result in an improved article?

Check for Understanding Answers

1a. Scholarly/academic writing is formal, precise, logical, and clear, with simple sentence structure; literary writing is creative, artistic, complex, and nuanced.

1b. Scholarly/academic voice is a formal and established style, perspective, and approach; scholarly/academic tone is more specific formats, word choice, language, and conventions.

1c. For effective scholarly/academic writing take your pick: *use* appropriate inclusive language, correct pronouns, simple clear sentences and smooth continuity, sentence and word variation, subject and word choice, transitions, objective terms, both active and passive voice; *avoid* ambiguity, shifting tense, grouped synonyms, wordiness and redundancy, bias, contractions, casual language, overuse of short sentences, long compound sentences, use of "must."

2a. Design, participants, measures, procedures.

2b. The inclusion of a researcher description section and an emphasis on the evolving nature of the design and data analyses.

3a. Previous literature; weaknesses and limitations in the sample, procedures, and data analyses; threats to validity.

3b. Population and ecological external validity.

4a. Determining audience, planning drafting, revising, proofreading.

4b. Writing for a lay audience stresses descriptive data in nontechnical language; for peers the writing is scholarly/academic with appropriate technical language and description to allow replication and judgment of quality of the research.

APPENDIX A

The *Intelligent* Consumer and Researcher: Putting It All Together

My aim in this text has been to present and explain fundamental principles of educational research that you will be able to use in evaluating and conducting research. As a consumer of educational research, you need to be able to locate, read, critically analyze, and then use the results of research, when appropriate, to enhance teaching and learning. As a researcher, you need to know principles for how studies are designed and implemented, and how data are analyzed, to find what is closest to the signal by reducing noise. I have emphasized how knowledge derived from research can enhance your role as a professional who will constantly make decisions and judgments. Hopefully, you have adopted a fox-like disposition in your thinking about research.

Research on educational problems can provide information that will improve your judgments, but the quality of published research varies greatly. In fact, there is evidence that a substantial percentage of published studies have serious flaws, and only relatively small percentages of studies are replicated. Thus, it is essential that you have the knowledge and skills to evaluate critically the research you read. A consumer of educational research may use the information provided in studies, but you must be an *intelligent* consumer. Intelligent consumers can make their own judgments about the credibility and usefulness of research. By being able to understand the researcher's intent, the type of design used, the deficiencies in sampling and measuring, the results, and the conclusions, the intelligent consumer can judge the quality and usefulness of the study. As a researcher, you need to know what constitutes high-quality research design, data analysis, and data interpretation.

Throughout the text, key points for analyzing and evaluating different aspects of research reports have been summarized as *Consumer (and Researcher) Tips*. In this appendix, these tips have been rephrased as questions that you will want to ask yourself when reading, designing, or conducting a study. The intent is to gather, in one place, the most important questions that should guide your evaluation. If you remember that every study will contain some deficiencies, the answers to these questions, when considered as a whole, will provide an overall impression of the credibility and usefulness of the findings. You may also find what could be called "fatal flaws"—deficiencies that are so serious that they render the results useless.

QUESTIONS FOR QUANTITATIVE STUDIES

1.0 Research Problem
    1.1 Is the problem researchable?
    1.2 Is the problem significant? Will the results have practical or theoretical importance, or will there be a contribution to existing knowledge?
    1.3 Is the problem stated clearly and succinctly?

1.4 Does the problem communicate whether the study is descriptive, experimental, or nonexperimental?

1.5 Does the problem indicate the variables and population studied?

2.0 Review of the Literature

2.1 Does the review of literature seem comprehensive? Are all important previous studies included?

2.2 Are primary sources emphasized?

2.3 Is the review up to date?

2.4 Have the studies been critically reviewed and flaws noted, and have the results been summarized?

2.5 Does the review explicitly relate previous studies to the problem?

2.6 If appropriate, does the review establish a basis for research hypotheses?

2.7 Does the review establish a theoretical framework for the significance of the study?

2.8 Is the review well organized?

3.0 Research Hypothesis

3.1 Is the hypothesis stated in declarative form?

3.2 Does the hypothesis follow from the literature?

3.3 Does the hypothesis state expected relationships or differences?

3.4 Is the hypothesis testable?

3.5 Is the hypothesis clear and concise?

4.0 Selection of Participants

4.1 Are the participants clearly described?

4.2 Is the population clearly defined?

4.3 Is the method of sampling clearly described?

4.4 Is random sampling used? If so, what type?

4.5 What is the return rate in a survey study?

4.6 Were volunteers used?

4.7 Was there an adequate number of participants?

5.0 Instrumentation

5.1 Is evidence for validity and reliability clearly stated and adequate? Is the instrument appropriate for the participants and sufficiently sensitive to measure the variables?

5.2 Are the instruments clearly described? If an instrument is designed for a study by the researchers, is there a description of its development?

5.3 Are the procedures for gathering data described clearly?

5.4 Do the scores distort the reality of the findings?

5.5 Does response set or faking influence the results?

5.6 Are observers and interviewers adequately trained?

5.7 Are there observer or interviewer effects?

6.0 Design

6.1 Nonexperimental

6.1a If descriptive, are relationships inferred?

6.1b If comparative, are criteria for identifying different groups clear?

6.1c Are causal conclusions reached from correlational or comparative findings?

6.1d Is the correlation affected by restriction in the range and reliability of the instruments?

6.1e If causal–comparative, how comparable are the individuals in the groups being compared?

6.? Experimental

6.2a Is there direct researcher control of an intervention?

6.2b Are the design and procedure described clearly?

6.2c Is there random assignment of participants?

6.2d What extraneous/confounding variables are not controlled in the design?

6.2e Is each replication of the intervention independent of other replications? Is the number of participants equal to the number of intervention replications?

6.3 Single-Subject

6.3a Is the measurement of the target behavior reliable?

6.3b Is the target behavior defined clearly?

6.3c Are there enough measures of the behavior to establish stability?

6.3d Are procedures, participants, and settings described in detail?

6.3e Is there a single intervention?

6.3f Are there experimenter or observer effects?

7.0 Results and Analysis

7.1 Is there an appropriate descriptive statistical summary?

7.2 Is statistical significance confused with practical significance?

7.3 Is statistical significance confused with internal or external validity?

7.4 Are appropriate statistical tests used?

7.5 Are levels of significance interpreted correctly?

7.6 How clearly are the results presented?

7.7 Are data clearly and accurately presented in graphs and tables?

8.0 Discussion and Conclusions

8.1 Is interpretation of the results separate from reporting of the results?

8.2 Are the results discussed in relation to previous research, methodology, and the research problem?

8.3 Do the conclusions follow from the interpretation of the results?

8.4 Are the conclusions appropriately limited by the nature of the participants, interventions, and measures?

8.5 Is lack of statistical significance properly interpreted?

8.6 Are the limitations of the findings reasonable?

8.7 Are the recommendations and implications specific?

QUESTIONS FOR QUALITATIVE STUDIES

1.0 Introduction and Problem

1.1 Are the researcher's background, interests, and potential biases clear from the outset?

1.2 Does the researcher have the skill and training needed to conduct the study?

1.3 Is the problem feasible?

1.4 Is the problem significant?

1.5 Is there a clear conceptual and theoretical framework for the problem?

    1.6 Does the introduction include an overview of the design of the study?

    1.7 Is the purpose of the study clearly stated?

2.0 Review of the Literature

    2.1 Is the review preliminary? Does it indicate that the researcher is knowledgeable about previous work in the area?

    2.2 Is the review up to date?

    2.3 Does the review establish an adequate background and theoretical framework for the study?

    2.4 Is the review well organized?

    2.5 Is the literature analyzed as well as summarized?

3.0 Methodology

    3.1 Is the method of selecting participants clear?

    3.2 Is the selection of participants biased?

    3.3 Will the participants selected provide a credible answer to the research question?

    3.4 How involved is the researcher in the setting? Will the researcher's involvement affect the findings?

    3.5 Are data collectors trained?

    3.6 Are multiple methods of data collection used?

4.0 Results and Analysis

    4.1 Is there adequate detail in presenting results?

    4.2 Are there direct quotes from participants?

    4.3 Is there adequate immersion in the field to develop a deep understanding of what is being studied?

    4.4 Is there an analysis of triangulation?

    4.5 Is there consideration of researcher bias or perspective in interpreting the results?

    4.6 Is validity/trustworthiness addressed in a thoughtful and comprehensive manner?

    4.7 Are the analyses recursive with evidence of researcher reflection?

    4.8 Are patterns and themes clearly based on coded data?

5.0 Discussion and Conclusions

    5.1 Are descriptions clearly separate from interpretations and researchers' opinions?

    5.2 Is the adequacy of the findings addressed in terms of validity and/or trustworthiness?

    5.3 Are the results discussed in relation to previous research?

    5.4 Do the conclusions follow from the interpretation of the results? Are the conclusions consistent with what is known from previous research?

    5.5 Are appropriate limitations indicated?

    5.6 Are appropriate recommendations and implications indicated?

QUESTIONS FOR MIXED METHODS STUDIES

1.0 Introduction and Problem

    1.1 Is the problem feasible and researchable?

    1.2 Is the problem significant? Will it have practical and/or theoretical importance?

1.3 Is the problem stated clearly and succinctly?

1.4 Are separate research questions asked for the quantitative and qualitative aspects of the study, as well as mixed methods questions?

1.5 Is there a clear rationale for using mixed methods?

1.6 Does the quantitative research question indicate the variables, population, and logic of the design?

2.0 Review of the Literature

2.1 Is the review primarily preliminary or comprehensive?

2.2 Are primary sources emphasized?

2.3 Is the review up to date?

2.4 Are studies analyzed as well as summarized, and are they related to the research questions?

2.5 Does the review establish an adequate background and theoretical framework for the study?

2.6 Is the review well organized?

3.0 Selection of Participants

3.1 Is the selection process for the participants clear?

3.2 Are the participants well described?

3.3 Is it likely that the participants will provide credible data?

3.4 Are the participants likely to be biased?

3.5 If sampling was used, what was the return rate? Is it adequate?

4.0 Instrumentation

4.1 Is there adequate evidence of reliability and validity?

4.2 Are instruments clearly described?

4.3 Are procedures for data collection clearly described and adequate?

4.4 Are interviewers and/or observers adequately trained?

4.5 Is there likely to be bias from participants, interviewers, and/or observers?

4.6 Are multiple methods of data collection used?

5.0 Design

5.1 Is it clear whether the design is explanatory sequential, exploratory sequential, or convergent?

5.2 Is it clear whether one phase is emphasized more than the other?

5.3 If nonexperimental quantitative, is the study descriptive, comparative, causal–comparative, ex post facto, or correlational?

5.4 If experimental, is the intervention clearly described?

5.5 If experimental, are possible extraneous/confounding variables accounted for?

5.6 Is it clear how the researcher gained entry into the field, and is the role of the researcher in data collection clear?

5.7 Are there multiple settings and contexts from which data are gathered?

5.8 Is the design likely to provide credible information to answer the research questions?

6.0 Results and Analysis

6.1 Are data clearly and adequately described, including the use of tables and figures?

6.2 Is there adequate discussion of practical significance? Is it distinguished from statistical significance?

    6.3 Are field notes and interviewer notes adequately detailed?

    6.4 Are verbatim transcriptions and quotations used?

    6.5 Is there triangulation?

    6.6 Are codes and categories adequately described?

    6.7 Are results clearly separate from researcher opinion?

7.0 Discussion and Conclusions

    7.1 Are the results discussed in terms of previous research, methodology, and research questions?

    7.2 Is the credibility of the results addressed in terms of reliability, internal validity, and trustworthiness?

    7.3 Do conclusions follow logically from the results and interpretation?

    7.4 Are appropriate recommendations and limitations indicated?

QUESTIONS FOR ACTION RESEARCH STUDIES

1.0 Introduction and Problem

    1.1 Is the topic of the research something that the practitioner is motivated to study?

    1.2 Is the problem feasible and researchable?

    1.3 Is the study likely to lead to results that will have practical implications to improve the practice of the researcher?

    1.4 Is the problem clear and succinct?

    1.5 Is the research question aligned with the appropriate methodology?

2.0 Review of Literature and Preliminary Data

    2.1 Is there an adequate sense of other studies that have researched the same area?

    2.2 Do existing studies help inform the methodology?

    2.3 Do preliminary empirical data support the need for the study?

3.0 Methodology

    3.1 Is it clear whether the study is quantitative, qualitative, or mixed methods?

    3.2 Are the participants clearly identified?

    3.3 Are the instrumentation and other methods of gathering data described clearly?

    3.4 Are the procedures clearly summarized?

    3.5 If there is an intervention, was it clearly described and implemented as planned?

    3.6 Have multiple methods of data collection been used and appropriately triangulated?

    3.7 Has there been an emergent, cyclical process employed in which there is research–action–reflection?

    3.8 Is the researcher capable of carrying out the design and analysis?

4.0 Interpretation and Conclusions

    4.1 Has there been adequate external peer review and/or feedback?

    4.2 Has there been an appropriate emphasis on descriptive data?

    4.3 Has there been researcher reflection about the impact on practice?

Glossary

A–B design Single subject design in which there is a baseline and intervention condition.

A–B–A withdrawal design Single subject design in which there is a baseline, intervention, and baseline condition.

Action research Research aimed at solving a specific problem or issue.

Agreement Type of evidence for reliability based on the extent to which different individuals agree on the value of what is measured.

Alpha level See *level of significance*.

Alternative hypothesis The hypothesis used in hypothesis testing which is opposite the null hypothesis.

Analysis of covariance An inferential statistical procedure in which two or more means, as adjusted by one or more covariates, are compared.

Analysis of variance An inferential statistical procedure in which two or more means are compared.

Anonymous Unknown or unnamed sources of information.

Applied research Research used to test theories and ideas in real life settings.

Artifacts Documents and materials used with text for qualitative research.

Attenuation Underestimation of the true relationship.

Bar chart Graph of frequency of scores from unordered categories.

Baseline Initial recording of behavior prior to an intervention in single subject research.

Basic research Research used to understand and explain fundamental phenomena to develop theories.

Beneficence Ethical principal to ensure that participants are not harmed and that positive benefits outweigh risks.

Bivariate correlation Correlation between two variables.

Blind review Manuscript review process in which the reviewers do not know author names or affiliations.

Case study An in-depth investigation of one or more entities (individuals or bounded systems) in their natural context.

Categorical variable Variable that has qualitatively different levels or attributes.

Category In qualitative research, groupings of data into units used to establish patterns.

Causal-comparative A type of nonexperimental design in which non-controlled interventions are tested.

Central phenomenon Main issue or focus of investigation in a qualitative study.

Checklist A type of question format in which the respondent selects one or more options from a list.

Child assent A procedure to ensure children understand the nature of their participation in a study and agree to participate.

Chi-square test of independence An inferential statistical procedure that uses frequencies to determine whether there is a significant relationship between two categorical variables.

Cluster sampling A type of selection in which groups of individuals are selected randomly from a larger number of groups and all members of each selected group are used as data.

Codes In qualitative research, a label that is attached to text used to build categories and understand results.

Coefficient of determination The proportion of variance among variables that is shared, often calculated as the square of a correlation coefficient expressed as percentage.

Coefficient of multiple correlation Indice that shows the relationship of a set of variables together to the dependent variable.

Comparative designs A nonexperimental design in which two or more groups are compared on the dependent variable.

Complete insider Observer who is part of the group that is being observed.

Complete observer In qualitative research, an observer who is completely uninvolved with the context and participant behavior.

Complete outsider Observer who is outside of the group that is being observed.

Complete participant Observer who has the same role as a participant.

Conceptual definition Description of a variable using words and concepts (non-numerical).

Concurrent criterion-related evidence A type of evidence for validity in which measures of the same trait are positively correlated.

Confidence interval A range of values that describes a specified probability of containing the true value of the population.

Confidentiality Procedure to ensure participants' responses are not individually identifiable.

Confirmability A threat to the validity of qualitative research in which there is a lack of adequate verification of findings.

Confounding variable Variable that has different levels systematically aligned to levels of the independent variable.

Constant comparison A method of analyzing data, used extensively in grounded theory qualitative research.

Constructed response A type of item in which the respondent generates an original answer to a question.

Contamination An observational influence that provides biased results based on researcher knowledge of the study.

Context insensitivity A threat to the validity of qualitative research in which there is inadequate attention to the context of the phenomena that are being studied.

Continuous variable   Variable with an increasing number of values within a range of possible values.

Convenience sample   A nonrandom type of sampling of accessible or available individuals.

Convergent design   A mixed methods design in which both quantitative and qualitative data gathering and analyses are completed simultaneously.

Correlation   A statistic that indicates the extent to which two or more variables are related.

Correlation coefficient   A number between −1 and +1 that shows the direction and strength of the relationship between two variables.

Correlational design   A nonexperimental design that uses simple or complex correlational statistical procedures.

Credibility   In qualitative research, the extent to which results accurately portray views and meanings of participants.

Criterion-referenced/standards-based   Type of test score that is based on how an individual performed in relation to established criteria or standards.

Critical studies   A type of qualitative research that focuses on advocacy for marginalized individuals and groups.

Cross-sectional   A type of longitudinal survey design in which different groups are compared at the same time.

Cumulative frequency distribution   A type of frequency distribution in which the total number or percentage of scores at or below a specific score or interval of scores is indicated.

Debriefing   A process of informing participants of the nature of study after it is complete, explaining deception, and allowing participant questions.

Deception   Procedure to mask from participants the true intent of the study.

Degrees of freedom   Number of observations used for inferential statistical calculation less restrictions.

Dependent samples *t*-test   Inferential statistical test of the difference between two groups that are matched or contain the same participants.

Dependent variable   The outcome, result, or what is predicted by the independent variable.

Descriptive statistics   Procedures for summarizing data about or from a sample.

Diffusion of intervention   A threat to internal validity that occurs when the intervention and/or outcomes of one group disseminate to other groups.

Disciplined inquiry   A systematic, logical way of accumulating knowledge based on professional standards.

Disproportional stratified sampling   A type of stratified sampling in which individuals are selected from subgroups that results in disproportional representation of each subgroup in the population.

Documents   Written materials used as data in qualitative research.

Dosage   The amount or intensity of the intervention; also a threat to internal validity.

Ecological external validity   Generalizability of findings to other similar settings, procedures, and measures.

Educational research   Systematic, disciplined empirical inquiry of information in the field of education.

Effect size   A standardized measure of the practical significance of findings.

Emic   A method of description in qualitative research that focuses on participant perspectives and what is inherent to the culture.

Empirical research   A first-hand, systematic gathering, analysis, and reporting of information.

Epistemology   Philosophy of and justification for how knowledge is accumulated.

Equivalence   A type of evidence of reliability based on consistency of results from alternate or different measures of the same trait given at about the same time.

Equivalence and stability   A type of evidence of reliability based on consistency of results from alternate or different measures of the same trait given at different times.

ERIC   United States Department of Education electronic database in education.

Ethics   Standards and principles for determining what behavior is right or best.

Etic   A method of description in qualitative research that focuses on interpretations of the investigator.

Ethnographic   Qualitative research that focuses on the study of culture of a group.

Evaluation research   Research aimed toward making decisions about program effectiveness.

Evidence based on content   A type of evidence for validity that supports the inference that the score is representative of a larger domain of scores or construct.

Evidence based on convergent/discriminant evidence   A type of evidence for validity in which items measuring the same or similar traits are correlated more positively than items measuring different traits.

Evidence based on internal structure   A type of evidence for validity in which items are clustered consistent with theory or subgroups.

Exempt   IRB review category for research involving very minimal if any risk to participants.

Expedited   IRB review category used for studies with minimal risk.

Experimental research   Research that establishes cause and effect relationships through control of an intervention.

Experimenter effects   Threat to internal validity in which the experimenter impacts results independent of the intervention.

Explanatory sequential design   Mixed methods design in which the qualitative phase follows the quantitative phase to provide explanations for the results.

Exploratory sequential design   Mixed methods design in which the qualitative phase is completed first to inform the quantitative phase.

Ex post facto   A nonexperimental design in which interventions have occurred in the past.

External validity   The extent to which results can be generalized to other individuals, groups, and conditions.

Extraneous variable Uncontrolled condition, event, or occurrence that influences results.

Factorial analysis of variance Analysis of variance procedure in which there are two or more categorical independent variables.

Factorial designs Designs in which there are more than two independent or moderator categorical variables.

Faking Error that occurs when participants deliberately provide false or inaccurate responses.

Field notes Researcher notes during or after observation of participants in the field.

Fieldwork Collection of data in naturally occurring settings.

Focus group interview Small group interview of systematically selected participants to generate perceptions toward an issue or other phenomena.

Frequency distribution An organization of ungrouped data that indicates the frequency of each score.

Frequency polygon Line graph of a frequency distribution.

Full board IRB review for studies that involve greater than minimal risk to participants.

Google Scholar Electronic database of articles, reports, and books in most fields.

Grade equivalent Score based on grade-level year and month in relation to the norm group.

Grounded theory A type of qualitative research in which the focus is on the generation of theory from real-world data.

Grouped frequency distribution Procedure in which the frequency of scores of mutually exclusive groups of scores is indicated.

Halo effect Observer effect that occurs when initial impressions or early ratings effect subsequent ratings.

High-inference A type of observation in which the observer makes inferences from observed behavior.

Histogram Two-dimensional graph that shows the score or score interval frequencies.

History Threat to internal validity in which events that are confounded with interventions impact the results.

Inadequate participant perspectives A threat to the validity of qualitative research in which participant voices are not adequately understood and included.

Inadequate transparency A threat to the validity of qualitative research in which there is a lack of information and data that lessens detail and depth of understanding.

Inauthenticity A threat to the validity of qualitative research in which the procedures fail to capture actual participant voices and experiences.

Independent samples *t*-test Inferential statistical test of the difference between two groups that contain different participants.

Independent variable The antecedent or intervention factor that influences or is related to the outcome.

Inferential statistics Procedures used to estimate values of the population from descriptive statistics based on a sample.

Informal conversational interview Field-based, unstructured interviews used in qualitative research.

Information sheet Information that provides participants with a description of the study for making an informed decision about whether or not to participate in the research.

Informed consent Procedure that ensures participants understand the study and what participation would involve, and allows for voluntary participation.

Institutional review board (IRB) Group of individuals with expertise in ethics that reviews and approves research with human subjects.

Instrumentation Threat to internal validity in which unreliability or measurement procedures impact the results.

Interactions In factorial designs, the extent to which differences between levels of one variable are consistent across levels of the other variable.

Internal consistency A type of evidence for reliability based on the correlation of items measuring the same trait at one time.

Internal validity The extent to which alternative hypotheses are ruled out as factors that impact causal relationships.

Interpretive/constructivist Research paradigm that emphasizes socially constructed knowledge, context, and individual meaning.

Interval scale A type of measurement scale in which category or score intervals are equal.

Intervention fidelity The extent to which an intervention occurs as planned.

Intervention replication Threat to internal validity in which the number of independent replications of the intervention is smaller than the number of individuals in the study.

Interview A type of data collection involving verbal responses to questions.

In-vivo In qualitative research, codes that use language of the participants.

Justice Ethical principle that assures fairness for all participants.

Key informant interview Interview of individuals with first-hand, well-informed perspectives of the phenomena under investigation.

Leading questions A type of question that prompts a specific, desired response.

Level of significance Preset value of what the *p*-value needs to be to reject the null hypothesis.

Life-history interview Interviews that focus on past and present lived experiences.

Likert scale A type of self-report response scale that shows agreement/disagreement.

Literature database Electronically available, organized, and indexed publications and reports.

Literature map Diagram that shows how several studies on the same topic are related.

Literature matrix Table that summarizes key aspects of several studies on the same topic.

Logistic regression Regression analysis in which a set of variables predicts categorical group membership.

Longitudinal A type of survey in which the same sample or population is measured over time.

Low-inference   A type of observation in which the observer objectively records specific behaviors.

Margin of error   A range of scores generated from a sample that indicates the probability of likely values for the population.

Maturation   A threat to internal validity in which changes to participants over time affect the results.

MAXMINCON   Acronym for designing experiments that includes maximizing (within reason) differences in interventions, minimizing error, and controlling extraneous/confounding variables.

Mean   Arithmetic average of all scores in a distribution.

Measurement   Assignment of numbers to indicate different values of a variable.

Measurement reliability   The extent to which measures are free from error by showing predicted consistency.

Measurement scales   Type of measurement property based on the nature of the variable.

Measurement validity   An overall judgment of the appropriateness of inferences drawn from the measurement of a variable.

Measures   Techniques used to generate numbers or values used in measurement.

Measures of central tendency   Statistics that show the average, middle, or most frequently occurring scores.

Measures of variability   Statistics that show the dispersion or spread of scores in a distribution.

Median   The mid-point in a distribution that divides the scores into two equal halves based on score frequency.

Mediating variable   Unmeasured factor identified as the mechanism of influence on the dependent variable or, in structural equation modeling, a factor that explains the effect of one variable on another.

Member checking   A trustworthiness procedure in which participants check accuracy of findings.

Memoing   Method of recording reflective notes about categories, themes, and patterns.

Merged analysis   Used with mixed methods studies as a technique to compare data.

Meta-analysis   Statistical summary that systematically combines results of many studies on the same topic.

Metasearch engine   Combines several search engines to identify sources.

Mixed methods   An approach to research that combines quantitative and qualitative methods.

Mixing   In mixed methods research, an indication of how different types of data are combined.

Mode   The most frequently occurring score in a distribution.

Moderating variable   Variable that shows how different levels of this additional variable impact the relationship of the independent variable to the dependent variable.

Multiple-baseline design   Single subject design that includes more than one individual or condition.

Multiple comparison procedures   Inferential tests of significance between two means when comparing more than two means.

Multiple regression   A type of multiple correlation analysis is which a set of variables is related to a continuous dependent variable.

Multivariate   Inferential statistics used for analyses of two or more related dependent variables.

Narrative inquiry   A type of qualitative research that focuses on human stories as data to investigate phenomena.

Negative correlation   A measure of correlation in which increases in the value of one variable are accompanied by decreases in the other variable.

Negatively skewed   Distribution of scores in which the mean is lower than the median.

Nominal scale   A type of measurement scale in which the variable has unordered, mutually exclusive categories.

Nonequivalent-groups posttest-only design   Experimental design in which nonrandomized groups are compared on posttest scores.

Nonequivalent-groups pretest–posttest design   A quasi-experimental design in which groups are not randomized and receive both a pretest and a posttest.

Nonexperimental research   Establishes quantitative descriptions and relationships without an intervention.

Nonparametric statistics   A group of statistical analyses for data unable to meet assumptions needed for parametric statistics, or for analyzing frequencies.

Nonrandom sampling   A type of sampling in which individuals are not selected randomly from a larger group.

Nonrefereed   Process in which peer review is not used to evaluate manuscripts submitted for publication.

Nonresponse bias   Effect that occurs when individuals who choose not to respond result in error in reporting results for the population.

Normal curve   Symmetrical, bell-shaped frequency polygon of scores with standard characteristics.

Norm-referenced   Type of test score that is interpreted by how an individual compares with the performance of a norm group.

Null hypothesis   A statement of no statistical relationship or difference.

Observation   A type of data collection involving researcher observations of participant behavior.

Observer bias   Tendency for observers to record what they expect or want.

Open access   Resources available without charge or permission.

Operational definition   How a variable is measured or manipulated.

Ordinal scale   Type of measurement scale in which variable categories are ordered.

ORID   Method of questioning used for reflection in action research.

Outlier scores   Scores that are extremely high or low in comparison to the overall distribution.

Parametric statistics   A set of statistical analyses of population parameters when assumptions of normality are met.

Participant   Person from whom data are or were collected.

Participant attrition   Threat to internal validity that refers to the systematic loss of participants over the course of a study.

Participant effects   Threat to internal validity in which unplanned participant reactions to study conditions impact the results.

Participant observer   Observer who takes on a participant role but is known as a researcher.

Participant perspectives   Voices, ideas, beliefs, points of view, and behaviors of participants.

Participatory action research   A method of action research that addresses social justice and inequity.

Peer review   Process in which experts evaluate manuscripts submitted for publication.

Percentile rank   A statistic that indicates a known percentage of scores in a distribution that are the same or below a particular score.

Phenomenological   A type of qualitative research in which participant interviews are used to examine an identified phenomenon of interest in depth based on participant lived experience, self-awareness, and consciousness.

Pie chart   Circular depiction of scores that shows relative proportions.

Population   Larger group of individuals to which results apply from data gathered from the sample.

Population external validity   Generalizability of findings to other individuals and groups similar to those in a study.

Positionality   In qualitative research, the researcher's understanding of how their background and perspectives may inform or affect data gathering, interpretations, and conclusions.

Positive correlation   A measure of correlation in which increases in the value of one variable is accompanied by increases in the other variable (and decreases are accompanied by decreases).

Positively skewed   Distribution of scores in which the mean is higher than the median.

Positivism   Research paradigm based on the scientific method that establishes cause and effect relationships.

Postpositivism   Research paradigm that posits uncertainty in the nature of causality.

Pragmatic   Research paradigm emphasizing the application of research to real-world settings.

Prediction study design   A nonexperimental study in which a set of variables is used to predict a trait or behavior that occurs in the future.

Predictive criterion-related evidence   A type of evidence for validity in which scores are positively related to future scores of a predicted variable.

Pretesting   Threat to internal validity in which taking the pretest impacts the results.

Primary source   Original article or report with direct, first-hand researcher involvement.

Priority   The relative weight of quantitative and qualitative data in mixed methods studies.

Probes   Prompts used in interviewing to elicit further responses.

Proportional stratified sampling   A type of stratified sampling in which individuals are selected from subgroups in the same proportion to their representation in the population.

PsycINFO   American Psychological Association electronic database of sources in psychology and related fields.

Purposeful sampling   A nonrandom type of sampling in which individuals are selected according to specific characteristics or criteria of interest.

Qualitative   An approach to conducting research that derives meaning inductively from non-numerical data.

Quantitative   Approach to conducting research that emphasizes objectivity and statistical representations of information.

Quasi-experimental design   Experiment in which there is no random assignment of participants to different groups.

Questionnaire   Instrument with written prompts or questions to provide self-reported answers.

Quota sampling   A nonrandom type of sample in which individuals are selected from identified groups to be reasonably representative of the population.

Random assignment   A procedure used in experiments in which each participant has an equal chance of being allocated to each group.

Random sampling   A type of sampling from a population in which there is a known probability of selecting each individual.

Randomized-to-groups posttest-only design   True experimental design that includes randomization of participants and a posttest.

Randomized-to-groups pretest–posttest design   True experimental design that includes randomization of participants, a pretest, and a posttest.

Range   The difference between the lowest and highest score in a distribution.

Rank-ordered   A type of response format in which answers are ordered sequentially.

Ratio scale   A type of measurement scale in which there is a true value of zero for the variable and differences can be expressed as ratios.

Reactivity   A threat to the validity of qualitative research in which the presence of the researcher impacts participant voices and behavior.

Recursive   An iterative method of analysis in qualitative research in which categories are repeated applied to determine fit with data.

Refereed   Process of using peer review to evaluate manuscripts submitted for publication.

Reflexivity   In qualitative research, ongoing critical reflection of analyses to reconceptualize or revise findings.

Relationship   Shows how differences among values of one variable vary systematically with values of a second variable.

Reliability   See *measurement reliability*.

Reliability coefficient   Correlation statistic that indicates the degree to which scores are free from certain sources of error.

Research design   The plan for carrying out an empirical investigation.

Research hypothesis   Anticipated or predicted outcome in a quantitative study.

Research paradigm   A belief system and set of philosophical and theoretical approaches to research.

Research problem   Issue or concern that describes the need for research.

Research synthesis   A nonstatistical systematic narrative summary of studies on the same topic.

Researcher bias   A threat to validity in which researcher preconceptions and actions influence the results.

Response set   Tendency of a participant to respond the same way to all questions, regardless of content.

Restriction in range   Truncated set of scores showing a small range.

Retrieval algorithms   Algorithm that determines retrievals and order of sources from a search.

Sample   Group of individuals from whom data are or were collected.

Sampling   A threat to the validity of qualitative research in which the nature of the participants selected biases the results or leads to inaccurate findings.

Sampling bias   Sampling that is controlled by the researcher that results in misleading findings.

Scale   A way of showing gradations or different amounts of a variable.

Scatterplot   Graph of two variables that shows the nature of the correlation.

Scholarly tone   Format, words, language, and conventions used in scholarly voice.

Scholarly voice   A style of academic writing that is clear, systematic, and objective, adhering to academic conventions of communication.

Scientific   A systematic approach to research that emphasizes objectivity, precision, order, and control.

Search engine   Automated process for identifying sources based on topic and use of web pages.

Secondary data analysis   Analysis of data that have been gathered in the past.

Secondary source   A summary or review of others' research or writing based on primary or other secondary searches.

Selected response   A type of item in which the respondent selects one or more provided answers.

Selection   Threat to internal validity in which characteristics of participants in different groups are not the same and differentially impact the results.

Semantic differential   Scale that uses opposite adjective pairs for recording responses.

Semistructured questions   A type of interview question in which the respondent provides brief answers to targeted questions.

Sensitivity   The capability of a sample or measure to obtain varied responses from participants to show relationships or change over time.

Sequence   In mixed methods designs, an indication of which approach, quantitative or qualitative, follows the other.

Sequential mixed methods designs   Designs in which the quantitative phase is implemented prior to the qualitative phase, or vice versa.

Simple analysis of variance   Analysis of variance in which there is a single independent variable.

Simple frequency distribution   Procedure for showing the frequency of each score in a distribution.

Simple random sampling   A method of probability sampling in which each individual in the sampling frame has the same probability of being selected for the sample.

Single-group posttest-only design   Experimental design in which one group has an intervention and posttest.

Single-group pretest–posttest design   Experimental design in which one group has an intervention and both a pretest and posttest.

Single-subject designs   Experimental study of one or a few individuals.

Social desirability   Tendency for participants to respond in a socially acceptable or expected way.

Stability   Estimate of reliability based on consistency of scores from the same group on different occasions.

Standard deviation   A statistic that describes a standard percentage of scores in intervals formed by equal distances from the mean in a normal distribution.

Standard error of the mean   Estimate of the standard deviation of sample means.

Standard score   Transformed score that indicates percentile rank based on a normal distribution.

Standardized achievement test   Large-scale, commercially prepared test of knowledge in selected content domains.

Standardized aptitude test   Large-scale, commercially prepared test of knowledge, ability, or skills.

Standardized test   A type of test, typically a large-scale test, that has standard procedures for administration and scoring.

Standards-based tests   A type of test in which performance is based on achievement of different levels of proficiency.

Statistical regression   Threat to internal validity in which groups of extremely high and low participants, as groups, score closer to the mean on subsequent measures of the same variable.

Statistics   Numerical procedures for summarizing and analyzing data.

Stratified random sampling   A type of probability sampling in which individuals in the population are divided into groups and individuals are randomly selected from each group.

Structural equation modeling   A type of correlational technique that shows trends in correlations to suggest causal links among variables.

Structured questions   A type of interview question in which participants choose provided options as answers.

Subject directories   Terms to allow searching of databases by topic.

Survey population   Larger group of individuals from which a sample is selected.

Survey research   A quantitative nonexperimental investigation in which answers to electronic or paper-based questions are summarized and analyzed.

Systematic random sampling A type of probability sampling in which a list of individuals is used to create intervals from which each nth individual is selected for the sample.

Target population Larger group of individuals to which results from a sample generalize.

Test Formal set of uniform questions of knowledge or abilities.

Theory Propositions that explain how phenomena are related.

Thesaurus Listing of terms with definitions and descriptions of use.

Transferability In qualitative research, the extent to which results can be applied to other participants and contexts.

Transformative Research paradigm that focuses on social justice for marginalized, disenfranchised peoples.

Triangulation A procedure in which data from different sources and methods converge to establish trustworthiness.

True experimental designs Experiments in which there is random assignment of participants to two or more groups.

t-Test Inferential statistical test of the probability that two means are different.

Type I error Rejecting a true null hypothesis.

Type II error Failing to reject a null hypothesis that is not true.

Univariate Statistical analyses with a single dependent variable.

Unstructured questions A type of interview question that is broad, providing open-ended answers.

Validity See *measurement validity*.

Validity/trustworthiness An indication of the validity of qualitative research in portraying reality.

Variability Spread or distribution of a set of scores.

Variable Concept or factor that can be described as having different values.

Visual materials Photographic and other visual aids used as data in qualitative research.

z-score Standard score with a mean of 0 and a standard deviation of 1.

References

American Educational Research Association (AERA). (2008). *AERA offers definition of scientifically based research. Alternate definition of scientifically based research (SBR), supported by AERA Council, July 11, 2008*. Retrieved from https://www.aera.net/Research-Policy-Advocacy/Research-Policy-Advocacy-News/Definition-of-Scientifically-based-Research

American Educational Research Association (AERA). (2011). Code of ethics. Retrieved from http://www.aera.net/Portals/38/docs/About_AERA/CodeOfEthics%281%29.pdf

American Psychological Association (APA). (2020). *Publication manual of the American Psychological Association* (7th ed.). Washington, DC: American Psychological Association.

Anderson, G., Herr, K., & Nihlen, A. (2007). *Studying your own school: An educator's guide to qualitative practitioner research*. Thousand Oaks, CA: Corwin Press.

Beins, B. C. (2012). *APA style simplified: Writing in psychology, education, nursing, and sociology*. West Sussex, UK: Wiley-Blackwell.

Berger, R. (2015). Now I see it, now I don't: Researcher's position and reflexivity in qualitative research. *Qualitative Research, 15*(2), 219–234.

Bogdan, R. C., & Biklen, S. K. (2007). *Qualitative research in education: An introduction to theory and methods* (5th ed.). Boston, MA: Allyn & Bacon.

Bradbury, H., Mirvis, P., Neilsen, E., & Pasmore, W. (2008). Action research at work: Creating the future following the path from Lewin. In P. Reason & H. Bradbury (Eds.), *The SAGE handbook of action research: Participative inquiry and practice* (pp. 77–92). Thousand Oaks, CA: Sage Publications, Inc.

Bridwell-Mitchell, E. N. (2013). The rationalizing logics of public school reform: How cultural institutions matter for classroom instruction. *Journal of Mixed Methods Research, 7*(2), 173–196.

Brydon-Miller, M. (2008). Ethics and action research: Deepening our commitment to principles of social justice and redefining systems of democratic practice. In P. Reason & H. Bradbury (Eds.), *The SAGE handbook of action research: Participative inquiry and practice* (pp. 199–210). Thousand Oaks, CA: Sage Publications, Inc.

Bryk, A. S., Gomez, L. M., Grunow, A., & LeMahieu, P. G. (2015). *Learning to improve: How America's schools can get better at getting better*. Cambridge, MA: Harvard Education Press.

Campbell, D. T., & Stanley, J. C. (1963). Experimental and quasi-experimental designs for research on teaching. In N. L. Gage (Ed.), *Handbook of research on teaching* (pp. 171–246). Chicago, IL: Rand-McNally.

Chambers, C. (2017). *The 7 deadly sins of psychology: A manifesto for reforming the culture of scientific practice*. Princeton, NJ: Princeton University Press.

Cochran-Smith, M. (2002). What a difference a definition makes: Highly qualified teachers, scientific research, and teacher education. *Journal of Teacher Education, 53*(3), 187–189.

Cochran-Smith, M., & Lytle, S. L. (2009). *Inquiry as stance: Practitioner research for the next generation*. New York, NY: Teachers College Press.

Collins, K. M. T., Onwuegbuzie, A. J., & Johnson, R. B. (2012). Securing a place at the table: A review and extension of legitimation criteria for the conduct of mixed research. *American Behavioral Scientist, 56*(6), 849–865.

Cooper, H. (2020). *Reporting quantitative research in psychology: How to meet APA style journal article reporting standards* (2nd ed., revised). Washington, DC: American Psychological Association.

Creswell, J. W. (2008). *Educational research: Planning, conducting, and evaluating quantitative and qualitative research* (3rd ed.). Upper Saddle River, NJ: Prentice Hall.

Creswell, J. W., & Creswell, J. D. (2018). *Research design: Qualitative, quantitative, and mixed methods approaches* (5th ed.). Thousand Oaks, CA: Sage Publications, Inc.

Creswell, J. W., & Guetterman, T. C. (2019). *Educational research: Planning, conducting, and evaluating quantitative and qualitative research* (6th ed.). New York, NY: Pearson Education, Inc.

Creswell, J. W., & Plano Clark, V. L. (2017). *Designing and conducting mixed methods research* (3rd ed.). Thousand Oaks, CA: Sage Publications, Inc.

Creswell, J. W., & Poth, C. N. (2018). *Qualitative inquiry & research design: Choosing among five approaches* (4th ed.). Thousand Oaks, CA: Sage Publications, Inc.

DeCuir-Gunby, J. T., & Schutz, P. A. (2017). *Developing a mixed methods proposal: A practical guide for beginning researchers*. Thousand Oaks, CA: Sage Publications, Inc.

Dillman, D. A., Smyth, J. D., & Christian, L. M. (2014). *Mail and Internet surveys: The tailored design method* (4th ed.). New York, NY: John Wiley & Sons.

Eisner, E. (Ed.). (1985). *Learning and teaching the ways of knowing*. Chicago, IL: University of Chicago Press.

Fabiano, E. (1989). *Index to tests used in educational dissertations*. Phoenix, AZ: Oryx Press.

Fanning, A. J. (2005). Mixed methods research: A research paradigm whose time has come. *Educational Researcher, 33*(7), 14–26.

Freire, P. (1972). *Cultural action for freedom*. New York, NY: Penguin Press.

Flavell, J. H. (1976). Metacognitive aspects of problem solving. In L. B. Resnick (Ed.), *The nature of intelligence* (pp. 231–235)

Fullan, M. (2007). *The new meaning of educational change*. New York, NY: Routledge.

Gariepy, L. (2019). *Undergraduate students' attitudes about the collection, use, and privacy of search data in academic libraries: An interpretive description* (Unpublished doctoral dissertation). Virginia Commonwealth University, Richmond, VA.

Goldman, B., & Mitchell, D. (2008). *Directory of unpublished experimental mental measures* (Vol. 9). Washington, DC: American Psychological Association.

Goodwin, W. L., & Driscoll, L. (1980). *Handbook for measurement and evaluation in early childhood education: Issues, measures, and methods*. San Francisco, CA: Jossey-Bass.

Guba, E. G., & Lincoln, Y. S. (1989). *Fourth generation evaluation*. Thousand Oaks, CA: Sage Publications, Inc.

Hiebert, J., Gallimore, R., & Stigler, J. W. (2002). A knowledge base for the teaching profession: What would it look like and how can we get one? *Educational Researcher, 31*(5), 3–15.

Keyser, D. J., & Sweetland, R. C. (Eds.). (1984, 1994). *Test critiques* (Vols. 1–10). Kansas City, MO: Test Corporation of America.

Leech, N. L., Dellinger, A. B., Brannagan, K. B., & Tanaka, H. (2010). Evaluating mixed research studies: A mixed methods approach. *Journal of Mixed Methods Research, 4*(1), 17–31.

Levitt, H. M. (2019). *Reporting qualitative research in psychology: How to meet APA style journal article reporting standards.* Washington, DC: American Psychological Association.

Levitt, H. M., Creswell, J. W., Josselson, R., Bamberg, M., Frost, D. M., & Suárez-Orozco, C. (2018). Journal article reporting standards for qualitative primary, qualitative meta-analytic, and mixed methods research in psychology: The APA publications and communications board task force report. *American Psychologist, 73*(1), 26–46.

Lincoln, Y. S. (2010). "What a long, strange trip it's been ...": Twenty-five years of qualitative and new paradigm research. *Qualitative Inquiry, 16*(1), 3–9.

Loeb, S., Dynarski, S., McFarland, D., Morris, P., Reardon, S., & Reber, S. (2017). *Descriptive analysis in education: A guide for researchers* (NCEE2017-4023). Washington, DC: U. S. Department of Education, Institute of Education Sciences, National Center for Educational Evaluation and Regional Assistance.

Maddox, T. (2008). *Tests: A comprehensive reference for assessments in psychology, education, and business* (6th ed.). Kansas City, MO: Test Corporation of America.

Maxwell, J. A. (2013). *Qualitative research design: An interactive approach* (3rd ed.). Thousand Oaks, CA: Sage Publications, Inc.

McMillan, J. H., & Schumacher, S. (2010). *Research in education: A conceptual introduction* (7th ed.). Boston, MA: Allyn & Bacon.

Mertens, D. M. (2019). *Research and evaluation in education and psychology: Integrating diversity with quantitative, qualitative, and mixed methods* (4th ed.). Thousand Oaks, CA: Sage Publications, Inc.

Miller, D. C., & Salkind, N. J. (2002). *Handbook of research design and social measurement* (6th ed.). Thousand Oaks, CA: Sage Publications, Inc.

Miller, M. D., Linn, R. L., & Gronlund, N. (2013). *Measurement and assessment in teaching* (11th ed.). Upper Saddle River, NJ: Merrill Education/Prentice-Hall.

Mills, G. E. (2014). *Action research: A guide for the teacher researcher* (5th ed.). Boston, MA: Pearson.

Naff, D. (2017). *One in eight: Deciding to pursue a college-going self in a high-poverty high school* (Unpublished doctoral dissertation). Virginia Commonwealth University, Richmond, VA.

Pine, G. J. (2009). *Teacher action research: Building knowledge democracies.* Thousand Oaks, CA: Sage Publications, Inc.

Powell, M. A., McArthur, M., Chalmers, J., Graham, A., Moore, T., Spriggs, M., & Taplin, S. (2018). Sensitive topics in social research involving children. *International Journal of Social Research Methodology, 21*(6), 647–660.

Ravitch, S. M., & Riggan, M. (2016). *Reason & rigor: How conceptual frameworks guide research* (2nd ed.). Thousand Oaks, CA: Sage Publications, Inc.

Reason, P., & Bradbury, H. (Eds.). (2008). *The SAGE handbook of action research: participative inquiry and practice.* Thousand Oaks, CA: Sage Publications, Inc.

Rogers, R., Labadie, M. & Pole, K. (2016). Balancing voice and protection in literacy studies with young children.

Journal of Early Childhood Literacy, 16(1), 34–59.

Rubin, H. J., & Rubin, I. S. (2012). *Qualitative interviewing: The art of hearing data* (3rd ed.). Thousand Oaks, CA: Sage Publications, Inc.

Schön, D. A. (1983). *The reflective practitioner: How professionals think in action.* New York, NY: Basic Books.

Shadish, W. R., Cook, T. D., & Campbell, D. T. (2002). *Experimental and quasi-experimental designs for generalized causal inference.* Boston, MA: Wadsworth Cengage Learning.

Shavelson, R. J., & Towne, L. (Eds.). (2002). *Scientific research in education.* Washington, DC: National Academy Press.

Shulman, L. S. (2005). Seek simplicity ... and distrust it. *Education Week, 24*(39), 36, 48.

Silver, N. (2012). *The signal and the noise: Why so many predictions fail – but some don't.* New York, NY: Penguin Press.

Sweeney, L. (2000). Simple demographics often identify people uniquely. *Data Privacy Working Paper 3*, 1–34.

Tashakkori, A., & Teddlie, C. (1998). *Mixed methodology: Combining qualitative and quantitative approaches.* Thousand Oaks, CA: Sage Publications, Inc.

Tetlock, P. E., & Gardner, D. (2015). *Superforecasting: The art and science of prediction.* New York, NY: Crown Publishers.

Touliatos, J., Perlmutter, B. F., Straus, M. A., & Holden, G. W. (2001). *Handbook of family measurement techniques.* Thousand Oaks, CA: Sage Publications.

Zeichner, K. M. (2003). Teacher research as professional development for P–12 educators in the USA. *Educational Action Research, 11*(2), 301–326.

Zumbrunn, S., McKim, C., Buhs, E., & Hawley, L. (2014). Support, belonging, motivation, and engagement in the college classroom: A mixed method study. *Instructional Science, 42*(5), 661–684.

Index

This page intentionally left blank

This page intentionally left blank

This page intentionally left blank